HARVARD HISTORICAL STUDIES • 181

Published under the auspices
of the Department of History
from the income of the
Paul Revere Frothingham Bequest
Robert Louis Stroock Fund
Henry Warren Torrey Fund

MAKING TOLERATION

The Repealers and the Glorious Revolution

———⊰◆⊱———

SCOTT SOWERBY

HARVARD UNIVERSITY PRESS
Cambridge, Massachusetts
London, England
2013

Library of Congress Cataloging-in-Publication Data

Sowerby, Scott, 1973–
Making toleration : the repealers and the Glorious Revolution / Scott Sowerby.
p. cm.
Includes bibliographical references (p.   ) and index.
ISBN 978-0-674-07309-8
1. Religious tolerance—England—History—17th century. 2. James II, King
of England, 1633–1701. 3. Great Britain—History—James II, 1685–1688.
4. Religion and state—England—History—17th century. 5. Great
Britain—History—Revolution of 1688. 6. Great Britain—Politics
and government—1660–1714. 7. Religion and politics—
Great Britain—History—17th century. I. Title.
BR757.S65 2013
274.107—dc23   2012034734

Contents

Note to Readers

In this text, the original spelling, capitalization, and punctuation have been preserved in quotations, except that standard abbreviations have been silently expanded. Dates follow the "old style" Julian calendar used in Britain until 1752, which was ten days behind the "new style" Gregorian calendar of continental Western Europe. The start of the year has, however, been taken as 1 January rather than the 25 March of the Julian calendar. In those cases where a source was dated by its author in the new style, the old style date has been added. Thus a letter dated 24 April 1688, new style, will be dated in the text as 14/24 April 1688.

When the author, date, or place of publication of a seventeenth-century work is not specified in the work itself but can reasonably be surmised, these bibliographic details have been added to the notes using square brackets. For books and pamphlets, the place of publication is London unless otherwise stated. To assist readers who wish to consult the sources on which this study is based, reference numbers from *Early English Books Online* (based on the first and second editions of Donald Wing's *Short-Title Catalogue*) have been added to citations of works printed in the later seventeenth century. A full bibliography of manuscript sources is available at the end of this book. Readers who wish to consult a bibliography of printed sources may download a copy at the author's website at http://www.scottsowerby.net.

MAKING TOLERATION

Introduction

Why do revolutions happen? Theories of revolution are as various as the sociologists, historians, political scientists, and philosophers who produce them. Most of these theories revolve around the idea of popular grievances, whether those grievances are seen as fundamentally social, economic, religious, or political in nature. When governments respond unsympathetically to grievances, it is often said that a feedback loop develops as the people are inflamed to a greater extent. This loop forms the basis of a model that can be described as the "thermodynamic" model of revolutions. The "thermal" part of the model stems from the observation that grievances can feed on themselves. The "dynamic" part of the model consists of a push and pull between the people and the state, as governments respond or fail to respond to grievances, either tamping down revolt or allowing it to erupt.

The influence of the thermodynamic model can be seen in the fiery metaphors commonly used to describe the course of a revolution. Grievances fuel discontent. Revolutionary leaders pour forth inflammatory rhetoric. The people are a tinderbox ready to ignite. The moments when government confronts the people are described as flashpoints. Repression often backfires upon the government that attempts it, while a government that backs down from a confrontation is given credit for defusing the situation. The thermodynamic model suggests that the making of a revolution is like the operation of a steam engine; if popular grievances are not relieved, the pressure will build up until it explodes into revolution.

Another set of metaphors about revolution involves not fire, but water. An unpopular government is beset by a rising flood of popular grievances. Government repression is like a dam thrown across a stream; it may hold for a period of time, but it will be overwhelmed before long. A leader who seeks to stem the flow of popular discontent without giving way before it is like King Canute, who stood on the English seashore in the eleventh century and commanded the tide not to come in. A more farsighted ruler, like Louis XV of France, might be inclined to mutter, *après moi, le déluge.*[1]

These metaphors for revolution, whether thermodynamic or hydraulic in nature, rely on the similar idea of an irresistible buildup of pressure that must eventually find an outlet. The thermodynamic model might be traced back to Sigmund Freud's ideas of repression, sublimation, and transference were it not for the fact that these metaphors long precede him.[2] The metaphors draw an implicit parallel between the laws of physics and the operations of politics. And yet, though many features of our world operate on thermodynamic principles, the phenomenon of revolution is not one of them.

Repression by the state does not always lead to revolution. Despite their deep unpopularity many oppressive regimes continue in power and encounter only token resistance. To observe this phenomenon is not to justify tyranny but merely to note its lamentable tendency toward effectiveness. Repression is not always counterproductive; often it works. It does not always give way before the flood; sometimes the dam holds firm. Repression alone is not sufficient to cause a revolution; it must be coupled with opportunity. Such opportunities may be created by the regime itself, either through a split between two ruling factions or through a foreign policy misadventure that leads to a humiliating defeat. In the absence of such opportunities, a regime that is determined to repress its people can often maintain its grip.

Governments create their own oppositions by providing them with opportunities to flourish. This interplay of government and opposition can lead to results that seem counterintuitive. Under the thermodynamic model of revolutions, a decrease in repressive activity by the state should provide a safety valve that releases pressure on the system, thereby diminishing the likelihood of revolution. But, in fact, such a decrease often creates new political opportunities for an opposition to exploit, thereby placing more pressure on the system, not less. A revolution can be caused by a relaxation of repression. Thus Mikhail Gorbachev, in giving way to the demands of protesters at the end of the Soviet era, only served to inflate those demands. As was observed by Alexis de Tocqueville, "the social order overthrown by a revolution is almost always better than the one immediately preceding it, and experience teaches us that, generally speaking, the most perilous moment for a bad government is one when it seeks to mend its ways. Only consummate statecraft can enable a King to save his throne when after a long spell of oppressive rule he sets to improving the lot of his subjects."[3] The contention of this book is that just such a situation occurred in England in the late seventeenth century. The reforms of King James II enabled the Revolution of 1688–1689.

Reform can be dangerous for rulers because it requires openness to the role of the people in facilitating change. Once the public sphere is expanded in this manner, it can be difficult for even an imperious ruler to restrict it again. James II was not lacking in imperiousness, but he was also a reformer. The first and last Roman Catholic to assume the English throne after the sixteenth century, he saw an opportunity to transform the English nation and to liberate his co-religionists by leading a public campaign for liberty of conscience. His campaign helped to open up new venues for discussion and debate. He could not later close them down without wrecking his chances of securing a pro-toleration parliament.

James is generally seen as deaf to public opinion because his opponents depicted him as such while justifying his overthrow in the event that has become known, with less than scrupulous neutrality, as the "Glorious Revolution." But James did not fill the jails of London over the course of his reign; he emptied them, with two successive general pardons in March 1686 and September 1688. He extended individual pardons to many of the dissidents who had fled to exile in the Netherlands at the end of his brother's reign. He sought to persuade his opponents to join his campaign for repeal of the laws and Test Acts that penalized religious nonconformity. He funded the printing of pamphlets advocating repeal and conducted a public progress through several English counties to rally support for the cause. He did not do all these things because he was an agreeable man constitutionally inclined to conciliation; on the contrary, he had permitted a brutal response by Judge Jeffreys to the rebellion led by the duke of Monmouth in 1685.

About 250 of the rebels were executed and many of their remains were drawn, quartered, and put on display. Jeffreys's depredations have gone down in history as the "Bloody Assizes." The English county militias were disarmed at the time of the Monmouth rebellion, much to their resentment, and the confiscation of their arms reduced the ability of local groups to support any kind of armed revolt. But these were not acts that James repeated. Beginning in 1686, he settled on a political strategy that privileged reform above repression.

James's image was tarnished nevertheless by two divisive and controversial acts he undertook in the waning years of his reign, the ejection of the fellows of Magdalen College, Oxford, and the imprisonment of seven refractory bishops. Historians have highlighted these episodes in crafting their accounts of the period. Repression led to agitation and agitation led to revolution: thus the events of James's reign took on the form predicted by the thermodynamic model. But the model has been made to work by redefining the king's actions to make them fit the thermodynamic narrative. Accordingly, the week-long imprisonment of seven bishops in the Tower of London, where they dined on venison and were visited by the cream of London society, has been recast as an impetuous crackdown by an imperious monarch on rebellious forces in the Church of England.

Although the king's actions were highly controversial, it is not clear that they were highly repressive. If political repression is defined, following the sociologist Charles Tilly, as any government action that hinders the ability of an opposition to mobilize, then James II's English policy in 1687 and 1688 does not seem to meet this test very effectively.[4] Neither the dismissal of a group of Oxford fellows nor the confinement of seven high-ranking ecclesiastics for a period of seven days did much to hinder the ability of an English opposition to mobilize. If James had been intent on neutralizing his opposition, he ought to have imprisoned the bishop of London, who was doing far more to mobilize a revolt than either the cautious archbishop of Canterbury or the other incarcerated bishops. He ought to have imprisoned Lord Lovelace, who stated in public that a warrant signed by a Catholic justice of the peace was null and void and, when brought before the king and privy council to give an account of his behavior, simply refused to answer the charges. But Compton and Lovelace remained at large.[5] They kept their freedom because the king, in the latter half of his reign, was pursuing a policy of reform.

If James had been pursuing a conservative policy in 1687 and 1688, as he did at the beginning of his reign, he would not have needed to appease his enemies—he could have harassed and imprisoned them. But he hoped to gain his enemies' support or, at the very least, to secure their neutrality in the upcoming election campaign. Though many English tories were removed from office in 1688 after they refused to support the king's toleration campaign, they were not disarmed, imprisoned, or transported to the colonies as many radical whigs and Monmouth rebels had been in 1685. Removing the tories from office incited their sense of grievance without preventing them from acting on those grievances. At the end of his reign James faced an alarming set of enemies, but he did not behave with anything like the steel shown when he faced down rebellions in England and Scotland at the outset of his reign. He was more eager to co-opt than to coerce. He did not even want the seven bishops to go to the Tower. He wished to bring them to trial, but the charges drawn up on his instructions were punishable with a stiff fine, not a prison term. The seven were committed to the Tower for a week to await their trial because they stood on their privileges as peers and refused to give a recognizance when charged with a misdemeanor, even after the king asked them directly to do so. James could have chosen to release them without a recognizance, but by the rules of the court their trial would then have been delayed four months until the next term began. An October trial would have overshadowed his plans to hold parliamentary elections that fall. The imprisonment was a legal tactic, and it did not harm the bishops; instead, it vastly enhanced their credit with the public.

This story of royal permissiveness is not the story that the revolutionaries themselves told. The opponents of the king were building a movement; in order to build it, they needed to develop a sense of grievance that would underpin their mobilization. Thus every twitch of repression and every twinge of royal pique became part of a narrative of victimization in which the freedoms of Protestant England were about to be subverted by militant Catholicism. The perfect conditions for a revolution were the ones that arrived in England in 1687 and 1688: a widespread feeling of being repressed by the state, combined with a relative absence of actual repression by the state.

Only occasionally did the English revolutionaries of 1688 admit that their courage in opposing their king was enhanced by the fact that he had tied his own hands. One such moment of *realpolitik* is seen in the invitation of the so-called "Immortal Seven" to William of Orange in June 1688. These seven English notables, including the bishop of London, urged William to invade immediately because the king and his supporters had chosen for the time being to carry out their policies in "a parliamentary way." They warned that if the king's parliamentary policy failed, "other measures will be put in execution by more violent means."[6] The seven rebels were well aware that the king had relaxed the state's machinery of repression while he was pursuing a parliamentary act of toleration and that this relaxation offered them a window of opportunity to mount a military coup. James may not have been a lenient man by nature, but his political strategy in England was forcing him to be so.

The Glorious Revolution, then, was in large part a response to the enhanced political opportunities provided by the king's reform policies. Successful mobilization of a popular movement requires not only a widespread sense of grievance, but also political opportunity, and opportunity is hard to find when the state is devoting all its energies to violently repressing its subjects. The opposition movement that emerged late in 1687 and grew throughout the following year was not a spontaneous movement; it was a reaction to the king's endeavors. Many of its great triumphs were simply rejections of the king's efforts to gain the support of his people. In April 1687, James issued his *Declaration for Liberty of Conscience*, which decreed that the religious worship of Catholics and Protestant nonconformists should not be disturbed. He instructed the bishops of the Church of England to organize addresses from the clergy thanking him for his edict. The clergy of the diocese of Oxford refused to sign such an address, creating a public scandal, which was magnified when the reasons for their refusal were printed in a widely circulated pamphlet.[7] Later that year, James instructed his officials to conduct a survey of political opinion more extensive than any previous survey of its kind. The results proved disquieting as a majority of the king's justices of the peace and deputy lieutenants refused to support the repeal of the penal laws and Test Acts. These refusals were brandished by the opposition as emblems of heroic defiance by local notables rejecting the king's policies. Yet these flashes of defiance would not have happened if the king had not asked for their support. This disastrous outcome led many to argue at the time that the king would have been wiser not to have conducted his survey at all.

King James was opening up new venues for political action that he could not readily control. His tenuous grip was loosened by the clergy's widespread refusal to follow orders and read the *Declaration for Liberty of Conscience*. Seven bishops led this movement of refusal, petitioning the king to be excused from obeying the royal command. James retaliated by charging them with publishing a seditious libel, which led to their brief imprisonment followed by a trial at which they were, surprisingly, acquitted. By the standards of the time, the trial was scrupulously fair; even though the jury was selected in large part by the king's agent, the clerk of the crown, James did not attempt to empanel a jury of Catholics as many of his opponents had feared he would. After the acquittal, the king still had the option of citing the bishops to the Ecclesiastical Commission, but he chose not to exercise it. He may have been cowed by the large public demonstrations in London in favor of the bishops, but he also, presumably, wanted to minimize the damage that the episode had done to his campaign for a pro-repeal parliament.

The great majority of the English clergy followed the lead of the seven bishops in refusing to read the king's *Declaration* during divine service. This swelling of opposition occurred as clergy seized on the political opportunity that had come to them because the king had reached out for their support. Their action was reactive. They did not proceed to the next obvious step of open opposition, which was to cease to pray for the prince of Wales, who had been born shortly before the bishops' trial.

Many English men and women whispered in the summer of 1688 that the newborn prince was supposititious. Some repeated the allegation that Jesuits at court had arranged for the queen to fake her pregnancy in order to disinherit James's eldest daughter, Princess Mary, who was married to Prince William of Orange, stadholder of the Dutch Republic. The English clergy, had they so wished, could have refused to read the prince of Wales's name during the public prayers for the royal family that were part of the weekly service. If they had done so *en masse,* the king would have found it difficult to penalize them all. But the only cleric who is known to have taken this step before October 1688 was Princess Mary's own chaplain serving abroad in The Hague. The clergy largely waited until after the invasion of the prince of Orange in November 1688 to drop the prince of Wales's name from their public prayers.[8] The secular opponents of the king, meanwhile, proved unwilling to take the sorts of measures that might have crippled James's government. They did not attempt to organize a tax strike. Only a very few joined Lord Lovelace in refusing to recognize orders signed by Catholic justices of the peace. Most of the king's officials continued to enforce writs that many did not believe to be legal. Despite widespread discontent, administrative breakdown did not occur.[9] This tacit compliance continued until William landed at Torbay.

The opposition, then, did not so much create its own political opportunities as it seized on the ones the king presented to them. The opposition movement was in fact a countermovement. It took root in 1687, and not earlier, because James began to organize his movement for toleration at that time. It took root in England, and not initially elsewhere, because political opportunities were expanding in England while they were contracting in Scotland, Ireland, and the American colonies. There was resistance to James's policies in Scotland and Ireland before 1688, but it lacked the broad and unifying phases of collective action that were characteristic of the opposition movement in England. Before the end of 1688, there was no event in Scotland or Ireland to compare with the astonishing refusal of most English clergy to read James's *Declaration for Liberty of Conscience*.

James stirred up trouble for himself in England by appealing to the nation to support his new agenda of reform. Those appeals empowered his opposition by providing occasions for resistance. The king's Scottish, Irish, and American policies, by contrast, did not rely on winning over the people. James appointed powerful proconsuls to enforce royal policies in these realms. Lord Perth, Lord Tyrconnell, and Sir Edmund Andros had no interest in courting their opponents or in legitimizing new venues for discussion and deliberation. Though the king's policies provoked much discontent, they did not provoke any widespread and organized countermovement in Scotland, Ireland, or America before the end of 1688, by which time the king had lost control of the English army and navy. Rather than act themselves, most Americans, Scotsmen, and Irishmen remained fixated on the news from England, where the king's policies had opened up new opportunities for resistance.[10]

Thus it is no surprise that the Glorious Revolution began in England.

Tyrconnell in Ireland, for example, had a degree of latitude to repress his enemies that James did not grant to himself in England.[11] The underlying political temperaments of Tyrconnell and James might have been quite similar, but their style of government was not. England did not revolt first because it was somehow more politically sophisticated than the king's other realms; it revolted because it was being governed according to a different set of policies.

One might argue, of course, that had Prince William of Orange chosen to land in Scotland on 5 November 1688, the revolution would have begun there. But historians do not usually date the beginning of the revolt to the landing of William's forces. England had already been experiencing political convulsions for the previous six months as a result of the campaign by the clergy to oppose the reading of the king's *Declaration*. The historian Mark Goldie has dubbed this earlier phase the "Anglican Revolution."[12] Although the clergy who led this revolution had aims that differed from William's, they helped to soften political support for the king and made it easier for the prince to overthrow him when he landed. At the time of the "Anglican Revolution," the king's other territories in Scotland, Ireland, and America were still relatively quiet without any outpourings of opposition on the scale of those seen in England.

Despite the "Anglican Revolution," James's policies might have had some chance of success if William had not invaded. The king's campaign for a tolerationist parliament was neither stillborn nor fruitless. He attracted substantial support, especially from Quakers, Baptists, Congregationalists, and Catholics, but also from some Presbyterians and Anglicans. William Penn was the most famous of these supporters, but he was not alone. The king's political survey found that about 23 percent of former members of parliament supported his proposals for toleration, while 61 percent opposed them outright, 8 percent opposed them in part, and another 8 percent gave evasive or incomplete replies. These numbers, while discouraging, did provide a base of former members of the House of Commons on which to build. The king believed that he could win the public debate and gain a tolerationist parliament, and he called for elections to be held in October 1688, though he later cancelled the elections upon news of William's imminent invasion. He saw an opportunity for a lasting religious settlement and attempted to seize it.

The long-term effects of James's policies were profound. Among the most significant was the legislative enactment of religious toleration for Protestant nonconformists in England in May 1689, six months after James's departure from England and three months after the enthronement of William and Mary. This shift should not be attributed to John Locke's writings on toleration, which first appeared in print that same year. Although Locke's *Epistola de Tolerantia* was published at Gouda a few weeks before the passing of the Toleration Act, it was not translated into English until several months afterward and had no demonstrable effect on the parliamentary debate.[13] Rather, it was James II's toleration campaign that forced the hand of the almost entirely Anglican parliament and led it to grant a set of concessions to nonconformists.

The parliament that overthrew the king in 1689 dared not ostracize the nonconformists; if it did so, it risked losing them to the Jacobite cause. Unlike the vengeful Cavalier Parliament of 1661, the Parliament of 1689 adopted a religious settlement that sought to incorporate Protestant minorities into the nation. The Act of Toleration extended religious liberty not only to the moderate Presbyterians and partial conformists who had largely avoided the king's movement for repeal, but also to the Baptists, Quakers, and Congregationalists who had frequently joined it. The settlement of 1689 was not a winner-take-all settlement; instead, the losers, James II's supporters, were treated leniently. This newly established pragmatism about religious difference helped to bring together the eighteenth-century British Empire under a Protestant banner, as New England Congregationalists and Presbyterians joined Anglicans in opposition to Catholic influences.[14] The compromises struck in 1689 created the unique polity that rose to global influence in the eighteenth century.

In 1685, at the outset of King James II's reign, few could have predicted that three years later the Scottish Presbyterians and Irish Protestants would be relatively quiescent, while the clergy of the Church of England would launch a movement of defiance. The Anglican bishops and clergy had long preached against resistance theory, while Scotland had a more substantial and more recent tradition of resistance to authority, especially among the Presbyterian Covenanters. Anti-popish rhetoric was just as strong, if not stronger, in Dublin and Edinburgh as in London. Jonathan Scott has argued that the late seventeenth century in Britain was in many ways a recapitulation of the early seventeenth century.[15] But if history was repeating itself in 1688, it was doing so in reverse. The British troubles of the late 1630s and 1640s had begun in Scotland and swept through Ireland before spreading to England. In 1688, England was exporting unrest rather than importing it. The reason for this reversal, as so often in a composite monarchy, is found in the different policies applied by the ruler to different territories. England revolted first in 1688, not because it was being treated worse than the other kingdoms, but because it was being treated better.

Political Movements in Post-Reformation England

James II's reign in England was short-lived, lasting only three years and ten months. The story of those years has generally been told as a crescendo of rising opposition to royal policies. It can be encapsulated in a few paragraphs. James came to the throne in February 1685 and called an English parliament almost immediately. Because of the loyalist reaction at the end of his brother's reign, the parliament was stocked with tories, eager to demonstrate their loyalty to the king. The parliament voted the king an ample financial settlement worth about two million pounds a year. That summer, while parliament was still in session, Charles II's illegitimate son, the duke of Monmouth, launched an invasion from the Netherlands. The duke landed in Dorset with a few of his followers, gathered a large army of mostly untrained peasants who flocked to his banner, and was easily defeated by James's trained forces. At the same time, the earl of Argyll launched an invasion along the western coast of Scotland, which met a similar fate. In the autumn, parliament returned for a second session and expressed displeasure at the king's decision to employ Catholics as officers in his army, which was forbidden under the provisions of the 1673 Test Act. The king, arguing that these officers were his loyal servants, refused to dismiss them.[16] He then prorogued parliament, putting a stop to the debate. Although the parliament was kept in being for another year and a half through a series of prorogations, it never met again.

James moved to secure a judgment from the high courts approving his use of the royal dispensing power to relieve individual subjects from having to follow the provisions of the Test Act. In preparation for the case, he dismissed six of the twelve high court justices and replaced them with judges whom he expected to rule in his favor. The case, *Godden*

Catholic threat

Scotland

v. Hales, was decided in June 1686. Eleven of the twelve judges ruled that James could indeed dispense with the Test in individual cases.[17] This ruling was taken by many as an affront to parliament's authority to make laws, especially since the king had manipulated the membership of the bench in advance.

James called his Scottish Parliament together in April 1686 in an effort to gain liberty of conscience for Catholics in that country, but his proposals were stonewalled, even though the Scottish Parliament was usually more pliant than the English one. The king then decided in February 1687 to alter his proposed toleration to include some Protestant nonconformists as well as the Catholics and proclaimed the new policy by royal fiat without securing parliamentary support. These policies created unrest in Scotland, though the worst episode of anti-Catholic rioting in this period happened early in 1686 after the opening of Catholic chapels in Edinburgh and so was a precursor to rather than a consequence of the later disputes in parliament.[18]

Having failed in Scotland, James tried to gain the support of tories in England for a parliamentary act of toleration that would include both Catholics and Protestant nonconformists. He hoped that the loyalty of the English tories might lead them to accept his proposals. But most of the tories were opposed to toleration, especially toleration of the more extreme nonconformists, and the king's entreaties largely fell on deaf ears. In January 1687, James dismissed his brothers-in-law Laurence and Henry Hyde, the earls of Rochester and Clarendon, from their positions of lord treasurer of England and lord lieutenant of Ireland. Rochester was replaced by a treasury commission made up of two Catholics and three Anglicans, while Clarendon was replaced as head of the Irish administration by the Catholic earl of Tyrconnell.[19] These dismissals appeared to some to represent a shift of alliances in which James was discarding the Anglican tories in favor of the Protestant nonconformists. This transition had been in the works for some time: James had been dismissing tories such as the bishop of London from government office since December 1685, and he had provided a limited toleration for some English nonconformists as early as March 1686.[20] In April 1687, he took a further step and announced a new policy of complete toleration for Protestant nonconformists as well as Catholics in England, which he proclaimed in his *Declaration for Liberty of Conscience.* The *Declaration* suspended entirely the operation of the laws and Test Acts that penalized religious dissent. James hoped that his 1685 Parliament, which was still technically in being, might be persuaded to support his new toleration policy, and he interviewed many members of parliament individually to discover their views. He eventually became persuaded of the fruitlessness of this approach and dissolved the parliament in July 1687.

The king then launched a pro-toleration campaign designed to prepare the country for a parliament that might repeal the penal laws and Test Acts, thereby lending parliamentary sanction to his *Declaration for Liberty of Conscience*. Beginning in November 1687, he began to "regulate" the parliamentary constituencies, using his powers of dismissal to purge the parliamentary boroughs of Anglicans and recommending as their replacements a mixture of Catholics, nonconformists, and some Anglicans.[21] These maneuvers caused unease among many of his English subjects who believed with good reason that the independence of parliament was being threatened. James also exerted his authority over the universities, sending royal mandates requiring the appointment of Catholics to fellowships and even to the headships of colleges in Oxford and Cambridge. When Magdalen College, Oxford, defied the king by refusing to make a Catholic their president, the Ecclesiastical Commission set up by James ejected most of the fellows in November 1687, causing a public uproar.[22]

In the spring of 1688, James issued a new and longer version of his *Declaration for Liberty of Conscience* and required the Anglican clergy to read it from their pulpits on two successive Sundays. His elder brother had used this method in the past to broadcast his proclamations, but James's order was not welcomed; instead, most of the Anglican clergy defied him, led by seven bishops who petitioned the king against reading the document. James decided to treat the bishops' petition as a seditious libel and had them prosecuted in the Court of King's Bench. The trial attracted enormous attention and, when the jury voted at the end of June to acquit the bishops, most Anglicans and even many nonconformists celebrated.

The king also had a reason to celebrate; three weeks before the trial, his young queen, Mary of Modena, had given birth to a son. This caused more public unease. Under the English laws of succession, his two daughters by a previous marriage were supplanted as the king's heirs by the new prince of Wales. Both of the king's daughters were staunch Anglicans, but the new child would certainly be raised Catholic, which raised the prospect of a Catholic dynasty in England. Some claimed at the time that the birth had been faked, that the queen had never been pregnant and that an imposter or "supposititious" infant had been smuggled into the birthing chamber, even though more than seventy witnesses had been present at the event. Shortly after the birth of the new prince and the acquittal of the seven bishops, seven leading notables of England signed a letter to Prince William of Orange inviting him to invade England with an army of his native Dutchmen.[23]

William, the consort of James's elder daughter Mary, had already been contemplating an invasion before he received the invitation from the seven notables, though his preparations accelerated in July.[24] He assembled an army composed of Dutch troops, soldiers on loan from Brandenburg, and mercenaries from Switzerland and Scandinavia, along with the six battalions of the Anglo-Dutch Brigade and volunteers from the English and Scottish émigré communities in the Netherlands.[25] When James became convinced in late September that William was planning to invade, he began a program of concessions designed to recapture the support of the Anglicans. He abolished the Ecclesiastical Commission, reversed the manipulation of the parliamentary constituencies, and reinstalled the former fellows of Magdalen College. These concessions were greeted with much skepticism as they were clearly provoked by the threat of a foreign invasion. William set sail from the Netherlands on 1 November and landed with his army at Torbay on the southwest coast of England on 5 November, having evaded James's fleet due to favorable winds.[26] James assembled a large force of English, Scottish, and Irish troops to await the landing. The two armies met on Salisbury Plain, but no major battle was fought, largely because some of James's leading commanders defected to William's side. At the same time, a considerable proportion of the English population, including the county militias of the West Country and much of the nobility, appeared to acquiesce in the invasion and did little to hinder the prince's advance.

James retreated back to London, followed days later by the Dutch prince who seized control of the capital. The English king then fled for France, as did his queen and his infant son. James was caught by some fishermen on his first attempt at escape when he fled in disguise with a few servants, but his second attempt, on 23 December, proved successful.

The resulting power vacuum presented an opening to the prince of Orange, who called a national "Convention" in the form of a parliament, which voted, after much wrangling, that James had abdicated the government and that the throne was thereby vacant. The assembly then offered the English crown jointly to William and Mary, with William having sole control over the royal administration. At the same time, the Convention passed a Declaration of Rights, later enacted as the Bill of Rights, which specified the limits on the prerogative powers of the king that were said to be embodied in existing law. William and Mary accepted the offer of the throne after hearing the Declaration of Rights read aloud. The new government then took England into a costly but ultimately successful war with Louis XIV's France, thereby propelling England's rise as a world power.

This story of James's reign, which dominates conventional historiography, is one of a gradual alienation of a people initially loyal to their king. As many historians have observed, contained within this narrative of rising discontent is an account of the growth and development of an oppositional movement. The alienation of the tories from the king, combined with the increasing alarm of the whigs, led to the formation of a broad-based movement of opposition. The king bowed to the power of this movement by fleeing the kingdom without putting up much of a fight.[27] This story, though compelling in some respects, fits uncomfortably with how we expect a typical revolution to operate. In the classic thermodynamic model of revolutions, an opposition movement organizes peacefully, the government responds with violence, and the insurgents respond with counterviolence targeted against the machinery of the state. In the case of the Glorious Revolution, however, it is difficult to view the government as having turned to violence first. It was William who first turned to arms. In order to justify the prince's resort to violence, a narrative of grievances was constructed whereby the English government had been trampling on the people's liberties to such an extent that an armed response was justified. As one of the Dutch colonels put it in justifying the invasion, "force must be opposed by force," and it was James who had "raised the first force" in seeking to destroy the "Religion Lawes Liberties and Lives" of his subjects.[28]

Another odd feature of the Glorious Revolution is the nature of the movements that created it. Revolutions are frequently caused by

movements of reform that are stymied by repressive governments.
When an oppositional movement forms against a government, a loyalist countermovement typically rises up to defend the government.
The contest between these two movements can be highly destabilizing.
This was the experience of England a generation before 1688, in the
Civil Wars of the 1640s, when an insurgent movement of parliamentarians, spearheaded by many Puritans, was opposed by a royalist movement intent on defending the king's prerogatives. In the case of 1688,
there were also two movements, and those movements proved to be
destabilizing. But the first movement to emerge was not, in fact, the
oppositional movement that overthrew the king. It was, instead, a
movement for reform sponsored by the king. This reform movement
brought together Catholics and some Protestant nonconformists and
Anglicans under the banner of religious toleration for all Christian
groups. An opposition movement then emerged to counter this movement for reform.

The whigs and tories who joined the Revolution of 1688–1689 were
alienated not just by the king's high-handed policies, but also by the
existence of a broad-based movement for a religious toleration that
would include radical nonconformists and Catholics. Many whigs and
tories believed that this movement could enable a Catholic takeover of
England as the Catholics, after their liberation from the Test Act, would
be able to take seats in parliament and might then work alongside their
Catholic king to overthrow the Elizabethan religious settlement. Many
participants in the countermovement agreed with the sentiments of the
whig clergyman and opposition pamphleteer, Samuel Johnson, who
wrote in the late summer of 1688 that the repeal of the penal laws and
Test Acts would constitute "so Great and so Fatal a Revolution" that the
Protestant religion would be left in danger of being "Swallowed up."
The appropriate response to the great revolution being pushed by the
king, Johnson asserted, should be to declare *"Nolumus Leges Angliae
mutari;* We will not have the Laws of England Altered."[29]

Statements of this kind have led several historians to describe the
Glorious Revolution as a conservative or conservationist revolution.[30] It
is certainly true that the Glorious Revolution sought to prevent the
sweeping changes desired by James II. But even a countermovement
ends up advocating some kind of change; the act of trying to preserve
the past always involves defending a more coherent and specific version

of the past than ever truly existed. In the case of the Glorious Revolution, the oppositional countermovement championed religious toleration for Protestant nonconformists, though not for Catholics, as a way of siphoning off nonconformist support from James's toleration campaign. This led in 1689 to a signal change in the English polity, the Act of Toleration, which hardly represented a conservative policy. Similarly, the Declaration of Rights of 1689 claimed merely to be a statement of existing law, but by codifying the law it changed it. It is never possible to return to the past.

The curious fact about the Glorious Revolution is that the movement of reform that emerged in 1687 was sponsored by the state, while the countermovement was aligned against it. This situation was quite different from that of the Civil War of the 1640s, when the Puritans had rallied against the king while the royalists had rallied in defense of the king. The Civil War was more typical of the usual dynamic between a movement, a countermovement, and a government. The way this dynamic usually works is that the insurgents argue for new policies of reform, which provokes the government into sponsoring a loyalist countermovement. The friction between the two movements leads to further strife. But the situation in James's reign differed in that the government sponsored the insurgent movement. This might have led to a less vigorous countermovement, since the countermovement in this case lacked government support, were it not for the fact that a majority of the bishops of the Church of England stepped in to provide a focus for the opposition. Meanwhile the king, crucially, allowed the countermovement to expand without exerting himself to repress it as fully as he could have. He did this because he still had hopes of winning over the Anglicans to his reform agenda.

Where the Glorious Revolution is similar to other revolutions is in its conflict between two movements. Modern revolutions have often been caused by the conflict between two programs. The two conflicting programs typically, though not invariably, inspire two opposing popular movements. The movements that create a revolution do not need to have a particular ideological orientation; what matters is the depth of commitment of the two sides to their competing claims, the willingness of at least one side to rally around an alternative locus of sovereignty, and the inability of the state to suppress the claims of those opposed to the government. Many different kinds of ideologies can cause revolutions: they can be backward-looking or forward-looking, centralizing or fissiparous. They do not have to be modernizing.[31]

Occasionally, only one movement is enough to cause a revolution. Sometimes a government, when faced with an insurgent movement, fails to rally any popular countermovement at all behind its policies and simply folds. A modern example would be the Tunisian Revolution of 2010–2011, when a protest movement drove a long-standing leader with a powerful army into exile in less than a month. But a revolutionary dynamic often includes one movement struggling against another, each advancing competing claims about the proper locus of sovereignty. Thus, in the American Revolution, the loyalists faced off against the revolutionaries. In the French Revolution, the monarchists faced off against the Jacobins. In the Russian Revolution, the White Army of the monarchists and liberals fought the Red Army of the socialists. In the Chinese Revolution, the People's Liberation Army under Mao Zedong fought the Kuomintang under Chiang Kai-shek. In the Nicaraguan Revolution, the Sandinistas were at first successful but were eventually opposed by the Contras, whose very name indicated their counter-revolutionary fervor.

It would be surprising if the Glorious Revolution had not been characterized by a similar conflict between two movements, given that the dynamic of opposition between a movement and a countermovement had been a recurrent feature of English history long before 1688. This conflict can be traced back to the English Reformation in the early sixteenth century. In the reigns of Henry VIII and Edward VI, the emergent evangelical movement was opposed by traditionalist movements such as the Pilgrimage of Grace and the Prayer Book Rebellion.[32] A century later, in the early years of the reign of Charles I, the Puritan movement was opposed by the Arminian or Laudian movement. The Puritans argued for Calvinist theology and a simplified liturgy, while the Laudians opposed absolute predestination and preferred a more elaborate liturgy.[33] Some scholars have argued that the Laudian movement is better seen not as a conservative countermovement that was designed to stop the Puritans, but rather as an insurgent movement initiating change and unsettling a Calvinist consensus that had prevailed in the reign of James I.[34] Either way, the Puritans and Laudians helped to divide England in the years before the Civil War and, when war came in the 1640s, the former Puritans tended to support the parliamentarians while the Laudians tended to support the royalist movement.[35] The contest between parliamentarians and royalists spilled over into the Restoration period, as the royalists, now known as cavaliers, championed policies of religious persecution against the nonconformist groups that had developed out of the Puritan movement over the course of the Civil War and Interregnum. When political parties emerged in the late 1670s and early 1680s, the whig party, arguing for the toleration of Protestant nonconformists, formed first and was followed by the loyalist tory party, which saw itself as the heir of the cavalier and royalist tradition.[36] Division begat division in a manner that was almost biblical.

This contentious dynamic of movements facing off against countermovements was ultimately a consequence of the English Reformation, which broke the fundamental religious unity of the nation and led to recurrent concerns among large segments of the population that the established church either did not embody their preferred mode of worship or might not embody that mode in future. The partisan dynamic was reinforced by print, which had emerged in England a half-century before the Reformation. Print culture made it easier for minority groups to mobilize and to make claims on the majority. The growth of the print-based public sphere and increasing public involvement in politics strengthened the reach of popular movements.[37] This shift led at times to instability, since a movement did not have to comprise a majority of the nation to succeed, so long as it was able to command the resources of the state. A popular movement, moreover, was difficult to oppose effectively without forming a popular countermovement. The post-Reformation growth of political conflicts between movements and countermovements also occurred in other European societies with religious divisions, such as the Netherlands and France.[38]

Struggles between movements and countermovements are one of the defining features of the modern age. This contentious dynamic first emerged in Europe with the print revolution and the Reformation; it was not, as some sociologists would have it, a product of the late eighteenth or nineteenth centuries.[39] There had been popular movements in medieval Europe, such as the Lollards in England, the Hussites in central Europe, and the crusaders throughout Western Europe, but these movements tended not to attract countermovements from within their own national communities. In most cases, they either faded away over time or were suppressed by governments in a top-down fashion rather than being contested by a popular countermovement. Because of the lack of destabilizing contests between movements and counter-movements, the medieval period was not an age of revolutions in the way that the early modern and modern periods came to be.

Movements and Monarchs

The emergence of these political contests had a signal impact on the early modern English monarchy. Medieval monarchs had been faced with a different set of problems than those that plagued their early modern heirs. They had governed in ways that later monarchs might have preferred to follow but found difficult to recapture. In medieval England, it had been easier for the king to remain above the fray, serving as a balancer of court factions, leaning to one side or the other with the shifting political winds. Political problems, when they emerged, could be blamed on "evil counselors" whose services were then dispensed with. The advantage of this method of governance was that the king never got his hands dirty. It was relatively easy for the king to avoid picking sides because the conflicts in this system were not as rigidly ideological as they later became. The number of influential players remained small, and appeals to the populace at large were discouraged. Some of these methods of government survived into the early modern period, but they were increasingly challenged by movement politics, which required a different governing response.

In periods of relative calm, such as the decade and a half between the accession of James Stewart as king of England in 1603 and the out-break of the Thirty Years War in 1618, the English monarch could hope to rule in ways reminiscent of the older style of faction balancing. The system of government employed by King James I early in his reign, sometimes described as "consensus politics," combined intense factional infighting with a considerable degree of unity among the governing elite on questions of ideology.[40] The king was able to play the consensus builder, bringing together factions or suppressing them as necessary, while never becoming overly identified in the public mind with any one faction.[41] But the unity of the English elite came under intense pressure during the first decade of the Thirty Years War and then fell apart com-pletely during the Civil Wars of the 1640s. James's son, Charles, faced a different set of political problems. In order to have a fighting chance against the parliamentarians, King Charles I found that he had to become popular, issuing public statements and rallying a royalist movement.[42] After war broke out, religious divisions widened and political participation expanded, as thousands of ordinary men and women were given the opportunity to pick a side in the conflict.

Charles's two sons, the future kings Charles II and James II, were born in the early 1630s and came of age in an era of division. They learned its lessons well. The revolutionary and post-revolutionary English polity, with its bitterly divided public culture and expanding set of political actors, could not always be governed by the balancing of factions. Monarchs would, at times, have to intervene forcefully in the public sphere or risk irrelevance. Even Charles II, a habitual Machiavellian, became a movement builder in the final years of his reign. He took a clear stand against the newly formed whig party with his *Declaration to all his Loving Subjects* of 1681, a declaration that was designed to bolster the fortunes of the fledgling loyalist movement known as the "tories."[43] In the last years of his reign, he sponsored a tory surge that was designed to annihilate the whig party.

Neither Charles II nor his father, Charles I, had been natural movement builders. They would have preferred to govern by balancing factions and by letting their ministers take the political risks for them. But the effectiveness of this sort of politics depended on an ideological consensus that no longer existed. As a result, Charles I had to build a royalist movement in the 1640s if he wanted to defeat the parliamentarians, while Charles II had to build a tory movement in the 1680s if he wanted to block the whig exclusionists. James II eagerly seized upon the hard-won lessons of his father and brother. He did not attempt to remain above the fray of political debate; instead, he embraced the role of controversialist. Unlike his two predecessors, who built political movements because they had to, James built political movements because he wanted to. As duke of York, he criticized his sibling's approach to political conflict, which he characterized as insufficiently forceful. The younger brother expressed his frustration with the elder in 1679, declaring that "his Majesty ought not apprehend, but that he is strong enough, to deal with and punish his Enemys, if he will but be resolute, and stick to himself, and countenance his friends."[44] This sort of statement is usually interpreted as a sign of James's incipient authoritarianism. But James was also attending to the new imperatives of English politics. If the king took a clear stand, then it would be easier for his supporters to rally around him. By leading from the front, the king became more vulnerable, as any public reaction against his proposals was more likely to target him personally. At the same time, taking a stand meant that the king could harness popular energies on behalf of his policies. The royal charisma could be used to fortify a political movement.

As it happens, James was an anomaly. The phase of English history in which monarchs became movement builders was not a lasting one. Only a few generations after this new political world came into being, monarchs lost their ability to intervene decisively in it. It was safer for monarchs in the eighteenth and nineteenth centuries to remain veiled in majesty, above the tumult of ordinary politics, calling prime ministers to office and then dismissing them when their policies proved unable to command support. Better to risk irrelevance than revolution, many monarchs concluded. The example of James II proved to be a cautionary tale. But if the shifts in monarchical behavior seen in the later Stuart period tended to head in the other direction in the modern age, with monarchs becoming faction balancers once more, it was because monarchs were becoming less powerful, not because the political system was becoming less populist. Queen Victoria was able to rule in ways that seem reminiscent of Queen Elizabeth because the real political action was now going on elsewhere. It was the prime ministers who directed the scene, staking their prestige on shaping public opinion and falling when their political parties lost their majorities in the House of Commons.

To many historians, King James II has seemed an aberration. He was something other than the typical English monarch in the Elizabethan mode, shrewd and cautious. He did not seek to be beloved by all. Instead, he picked fights, made enemies, and backed causes. He sealed his own doom by tying his fate too closely to that of the causes he espoused. His transformational politics did not succeed, but they are worth exploring for what they tell us about the possibilities of political life in England on the verge of the Enlightenment.

1

Forming a Movement

James and the Repealers

King James II has not generally been seen as a populist. In most histories of his reign, he is depicted either as defying English opinion or as being oblivious to it. Historians have often suggested that James failed to understand that the English government was weak and that it depended on the support of local elites. As a consequence he foolishly thought he could rule in a top-down fashion. The king's high-handedness, according to this argument, alienated the English nation, especially the gentry. James's policies never had much chance of success, in this view, because he failed to appreciate the true underpinnings of his power. England was effectively a monarchical republic, whether the king liked it or not, and he could not survive without the support of the county elites who staffed local government.[1]

A different account of the king's fall better fits the known facts. In this account, James did not misunderstand the nature of English governance, and he did not seek to impose an absolutist system of authoritarian government in England.[2] Rather, he recognized that English government was weak and that it depended on the consent of local agents. As a result, he sponsored a popular movement to provide him with the extensive network of volunteers he needed to enact social and political change. In appealing to the public for support, James provided occasions for public resistance, thereby enabling the formation of a powerful countermovement to his policies. A foreign invasion then provided a focal point around which that countermovement could rally, becoming the occasion for a widespread rebellion. The victors in that rebellion inscribed in the historical record the view that they had successfully faced down a despot.

This is not to deny that James deployed at times the coercive and bureaucratic tools that he had at his disposal. He would have been foolish not to do so. But the tools at his disposal were limited, and he did not rely exclusively on them. He knew that it was not enough for an English monarch to command assent to innovations without also inspiring support. He was aware that he needed to engage local agents who would join his side voluntarily. At times he made considerable efforts to reach out to the English public. He may have done so because he surrounded himself with men who had experience in political organizing, such as the Quaker William Penn, his close friend and ally, and Sir William Williams, his solicitor general and the former speaker of the House of Commons. Together, the king and his allies sought to rally a popular movement for religious toleration. The formation of this movement began when James made it clear, in the spring of 1687, that he was throwing the resources of the state behind a broad-based campaign for toleration. The movement that subsequently emerged was a curious mixture of top-down state sponsorship and bottom-up popular organizing.

The sophistication of James II's campaign for religious toleration suggests the depth of his engagement with the public sphere. Yet the king's printed statements have often been dismissed as ham-handed or duplicitous. Many historians have treated with skepticism the king's *Declaration for Liberty of Conscience* of April 1687, in which he proclaimed his belief in liberty of conscience and suspended the execution of the laws and Test Acts that penalized religious nonconformity. Almost as soon as James issued his *Declaration*, contemporaries questioned his sincerity in issuing it, and historians have expressed similar doubts.

Many of the king's contemporaries contended that James was engaged in a duplicitous design to divide and conquer his enemies by detaching the Protestant dissenters from the Anglicans and using their support to destroy the Church of England, after which the dissenters themselves would be destroyed. As the marquess of Halifax memorably put it in his warning to the dissenters, "You are therefore to be hugged now, only that you may be the better squeezed at another time."[3] Historians have alleged that James's priority was to obtain toleration only for his fellow Catholics, which is why he spent the first year of his reign seeking the support of Anglicans for the toleration of Catholics. According to this argument, once the king saw that the Anglicans would not support his policy, he switched his appeals to the Protestant nonconformists and became willing to offer them toleration in an effort to secure their support for Catholic toleration.[4]

James's defenders, both in his own time and subsequently, noted that he had proclaimed his opposition to religious persecution long before his accession, and thus his *Declaration* could be said to have stemmed from long-held principle. James told Gilbert Burnet in 1673 that he was "against all violent methods, and all persecution for conscience sake." In the same year, he met William Penn, who asked him to help to secure the release from prison of the Quaker leader George Fox. James agreed to help, telling Penn that he was "against all Persecution for the sake of Religion."[5] Despite this expansive rhetoric, James's actions as duke of York suggest that he did not yet conceive of liberty of conscience as an indefeasible natural right. He often treated it as a grant that could be given to those who were deemed worthy and withheld from those deemed unworthy. When asked to obtain royal pardons for nonconformists, he frequently agreed to help particular individuals. But he was reluctant to obtain pardons for wider groups. He agreed to help the Scottish Quaker Robert Barclay secure the release of his father from prison in 1677, but he refused to write a letter to free all of the Quakers imprisoned in Aberdeen at the time.[6]

After James's accession to the throne, he continued to treat toleration as a royal grant to be extended only to those found worthy of it. During Monmouth's Rebellion in 1685, when many Quakers were imprisoned on suspicion of aiding the rebels, he wrote a letter on behalf of Robert Barclay, indicating that he considered the Scotsman to be exceptional among Quakers for his loyalty: "I have not great re[a]son to be well satisfyd with the Quakers in generall, yet I look on this bearer, Robert Barkley, to be well affected to me."[7] Certain favored nonconformists would be granted toleration, but only if their loyalty had been tested and they had been found deserving. The link between toleration and good behavior was made explicit in the king's grant of protection to the Jews of London in November 1685. He ordered that these men and women, who were being harassed by informers, should not be prosecuted on account of their religion, "but [may] quietly enjoy the free Exercize of their Religion, whilst they behave themselves dutifully and obediently towards his Government."[8] The grant of liberty of conscience was made conditional on good behavior and was depicted as a gift, not as a right.

The first year of James's reign proved to be a bitter disappointment for the Quakers and other nonconformist friends of the new king. The king had floated the idea of a general toleration, or at least a general pardon, to coincide with his coronation, but he withdrew these proposals after opposition from some of his councillors.[9] Yet even as Quakers and Baptists languished in jail, James took steps, both in England and in Scotland, to free Catholics from their legal disabilities right from the outset of his reign.[10] Some contemporary evidence indicates that the king told the archbishop of Canterbury at the time of his accession that he would never grant toleration to Protestant nonconformists. The king was especially suspicious of the loyalties of nonconformists in the wake of Monmouth's Rebellion in the summer of 1685, which had attracted the support of some of the English dissenters. Many English nonconformists, including about 1,400 Quakers, remained in prison during the first year of James's reign.[11] James later claimed that he had waited to grant toleration to English nonconformists because of the importunities of some of his advisors who belonged to the Church of England.[12] But surely some of his hesitation stemmed from his own sense that nonconformists were politically suspect. The king's reluctance to liberate potentially rebellious nonconformists was even more evident in Scotland, where he never offered a complete toleration to the Presbyterian field conventiclers at any point in his reign, instead seeing their activities as a threat to his rule.

The nonconformists imprisoned in England were eventually freed about a year after the king's accession by the general pardon of March 1686. In the same month, James ordered that all prosecutions of Quakers for recusancy, or absence from Church of England services, should cease.[13] The king's general pardon erased all previous prosecutions for religious nonconformity. But it did not protect nonconformists from being penalized again in the future, with the exception of the Quakers, whom the king specifically shielded from future prosecution. A further policy launched in June 1686 helped to correct this flaw. Certain nonconformists who were deemed to be loyal were encouraged to take out a royal patent dispensing them from having to comply with any of the laws against nonconformity. If cited before a court, they

could produce their patent and plead immunity under the royal dispensing power. The issuing of these patents was supervised by the Catholic lawyer Robert Brent, who later became a key player in the king's
regulation of the parliamentary boroughs. Many Baptists, in particular,
took out patents.[14] This policy endured until the king proclaimed his
Declaration for Liberty of Conscience in April of the following year, which
suspended entirely the execution of laws against nonconformity. The
king made this bold move even though it was unclear whether the high
court ruling in *Godden v. Hales,* which had affirmed the king's more limited power to dispense from the laws in individual cases, could legitimately be stretched to justify a royal suspending power.[15]

The king's ambivalent attitude toward Protestant nonconformity in
the early years of his reign can also be detected in his response to Louis
XIV's revocation of the Edict of Nantes in October 1685. The French
king's actions caused an uproar among Protestants in England. James
was unhappy with the methods taken by Louis, but he was also worried
about the political principles of the Huguenots. He told Sir William
Trumbull on 30 October 1685 that "though he did not like the Huguenots (for he thought they were of Anti-Monarchicall Principles) yet he
thought the Persecution of them was Unchristian, and not to be equalled
in any Historie since [the birth of] Christianity: That they might be no
good men, Yet might be us[e]d worse than they deserv[e]d, and it was a
proceeding he could not approve of."[16] The king's ambivalence resulted
in a curious set of actions. He ordered the public burning of copies of
Jean Claude's *Account of the Persecutions and Oppressions of the Protestants of
France,* though he told the French ambassador that he did this because
the work had insulted the French king, and kings, in his view, should
stick up for each other.[17] At the same time, he permitted the French
Protestants to migrate to England to escape persecution, and he issued
a brief for moneys to be collected to assist them. Yet the brief included
an uncharitable clause requiring any Huguenot who wished to receive
assistance to conform to the liturgy of the Church of England. Some
Huguenots were willing to do this, but others were not. The addition of
this clause can perhaps be explained by the king's suspicion that the
Huguenots, like other nonconformists, might prove disloyal.[18]

A sympathetic account of James's evolving position would say that
he had changed his ideas on religious toleration over time, as he came
to see liberty of conscience less as a royal grant and more as a natural

right. Like other granters of liberty before him, James may have found that liberties had an expansive power: once he developed a rationale for the granting of liberty to some, he saw that the rationale could be extended to others as well. A less sympathetic account would say that James had altered his position for political convenience. Alternatively, James could have been engaging in motivated reasoning, as he came to believe sincerely in the position that was most helpful to his political interests.

Yet even if the king was being insincere, and it is debatable whether he was or not, the movement for toleration that he created had its own impetus and influence. The king's inner thoughts are important, but so too are the ways in which his pronouncements were interpreted, acted upon, and reacted to. While many people at the time thought the king was being insincere in advocating toleration, many others thought he was sincere, and even those who doubted the king had to reckon with his followers.

The King's Tolerationists

Historians have described James II's tolerationist supporters as atomized individuals responding to incentives from the king. They have emphasized the supposed avarice of these men and the inducements used by the king to promote their compliance. The men and women who participated in the king's campaign for religious toleration have usually been described as the king's "collaborators" and have often been portrayed in an unflattering light. The contempt was spread particularly thick by J. R. Western, who characterized the king's whig supporters as "venal turncoats" who abandoned their principles for money. J. P. Kenyon, with a lighter touch, wrote that "none of them [were] knights in shining armour." John Miller dismissed them as a "small and motley collection of opportunists, extremists, and men over whom he [the king] had a hold." These men have generally been described, following a seminal article published by J. R. Jones in 1960, as James II's "whig collaborators."[19]

In this framework, each individual tolerationist was deemed to be responding to a certain set of selective incentives from the king; the cultural links between one tolerationist and another were rarely examined. This interpretation of James II's toleration campaign relied on a reductive model of patron-client relations, where anyone who received money or favors from a higher authority was considered to be devoid of any authentic ideological commitments to the cause he or she was espousing. Thus the king's allies were seen to be doing his bidding rather than following their own inclinations, and they were described as part of a top-down exercise in absolutism rather than a bottom-up exercise in popular politics. The very nomenclature of "collaboration" meant that the ideological affiliations between one collaborator and another were unlikely to be explored, since collaborators do not necessarily possess a shared ideology.

Although the king's allies have generally been treated as isolated individuals in the historical literature, the assiduous research techniques of twentieth-century historians did mean that the fairly large number of "collaborators" eventually had to be acknowledged. This trend reached its apogee in 1983 with that exercise in prosopography *par excellence,* the History of Parliament, which identified dozens of "whig collaborators" during James II's reign.[20] This avalanche of identifications created an opening for Mark Goldie to ask, in an important set of articles, whether the men so identified should be described as a small group of "collaborators" since there were so many of them. As an alternative, he suggested that they be described as "James II's whigs."[21] W. A. Speck, following Goldie, noted that the term "collaborator" is pejorative in that it has "echoes of Europe under the Nazi occupation."[22] But Goldie's proposed alternative has not caught on; instead, the term "whig collaborator" has continued to be employed, though more hesitantly: it is now generally placed within quotation marks, whereas before it was baldly stated without any qualification.[23] This can hardly be deemed a suitable compromise. If "collaborator," with its echoes of Vichy France, is a pejorative term, then placing it within quotation marks does not make it substantially less so.

Given the large number of tolerationist allies of the king, it seems fair to ask whether they might better be described as a movement. The tolerationist movement under James II might profitably be compared to earlier political and religious movements, such as the Puritan and Laudian movements in England before the Civil Wars. Like those earlier movements, the tolerationist movement was unified by a sense of common purpose and propelled by a sense of agency that enabled its participants to believe their efforts might have success. The participants

in the tolerationist movement were also unified by a sense of antago-
nism against a common enemy. In their case, their enemies were the
"persecutors" who had harassed them over the previous quarter century.[24] The tolerationist movement was unlike the earlier Puritan movement in that it had royal sponsorship and did not take an oppositional
stance against the government. It was thus more like the Laudian movement of the 1630s or the tory movement of the early 1680s, both of
which operated with royal sponsorship.

It would be preferable to describe the king's tolerationist supporters
using a name that they gave themselves. But we cannot do so, because
they did not choose a name. The men and women who rallied together
for religious toleration in England in 1687 and 1688 saw no need for a
collective name. They presented themselves as a large group of concerned citizens. Their common cause was to enact a new "Magna Carta
for liberty of conscience" that would include the repeal of the laws and
Test Acts that penalized both Protestant nonconformity and Roman
Catholicism.[25] They were visionaries. They claimed that their program
had universal benefits and was not designed to aid a mere clique or
party. They thought of themselves as those who were "zealous for liberty of conscience" and who "had appeared forward for the Establishment of Liberty of Conscience."[26] These were descriptions, but they
were not names.

Since the pro-repeal movement did not name itself, in order to
investigate it a label must be found. The term "repealer" is an apt description for a group that sought to rescind the penal laws. Until recently, the
Oxford English Dictionary dated the first emergence of the word to 1765,
with a reference from Blackstone's *Commentaries* to "the makers,
repealers, and interpreters of the English laws." But the term did in fact
appear nearly a century earlier, in 1687, although it did not pass into
general use and disappeared shortly after the Revolution of 1688–1689.
It was applied to the repeal movement by a handful of hostile observers.
It was not in itself particularly disparaging, but it was occasionally
modified to give it a pejorative sense, as in the phrase "as rank a Repealer
as any is in England."[27] It served as a convenient anchor to ground
those terms of abuse.

The word "repealer" was coined by the marquess of Halifax in his
Letter to a Dissenter, published in September 1687. Halifax wrote, in reference to the addresses thanking the king for liberty of conscience, that

it should not be supposed "that all the Thankers will be Repealers of the TEST, when ever a Parliament shall Meet."[28] In Halifax's usage, a repealer was a person who took a certain action: one became a repealer in the moment in which one voted for repeal of the Test Acts in parliament. There were not yet any repealers in England, according to this usage, because no one had secured the opportunity to vote for repeal in parliament. One could promise to be a repealer, but one did not become a repealer by the act of promising to be one.

Samuel Johnson extended the meaning of the word "repealer" in his 1688 opposition tract, *A Letter from a Freeholder.* He charged that "the Counties of England have been practised upon, to be made Repealers, both within doors and without: They have been Catechised, whether, if they were Parliament-Men, they would Repeal the Penal Laws and Tests; or, if they were not Chosen themselves, whether they would Chuse such as would."[29] In this usage, one could become a repealer either within the doors of parliament, by taking the action of voting for repeal of the penal laws and Test Acts, or outside the doors of parliament, by taking the action of voting for a pro-repeal candidate in a parliamentary election. Johnson's usage was similar to Halifax's in that a repealer was someone who took a certain action, not someone who belonged to a certain group.

Other writers used the word in a different sense, applying it to a group and not just to an individual who undertook a certain activity. This different usage appeared in a newsletter of March 1688. Its author wrote, "Sir Thomas Meers [Meres] is displaced from being a commissioner of the Foreign Plantations and one of the Commissioners of the peace, for refusing to be one of the Repealers."[30] In this usage, "the Repealers" was a group that Meres could have joined, presumably by pledging that he would vote for pro-repeal candidates in the upcoming elections. Such pledges were demanded of many royal officeholders at this time. By refusing to take the pledge, Meres held himself clear from any affiliation with the group of "Repealers."

The notion of repealers as a group was also advanced in a dialogue by the dramatist Thomas Brown. Brown's short satirical piece, published in 1688, imagined a conversation between three characters: the pro-repeal journalist Henry Care, the Tory journalist Sir Roger L'Estrange, and an unnamed "Honest Dissenter." In the drama, Care and L'Estrange were talking when L'Estrange, spotting the approach of the "Honest

Dissenter," remarked to his fellow journalist that the man looked "as if he had a spite to the Tests and Penal Laws." Care replied that he would talk to the dissenter, boasting that "if I do not make him as rank a Repealer as any is in England, I'll forfeit all the gain of my *Occurrences*."[31] The claim that Care was profiting financially from his occupation as editor of the weekly *Publick Occurrences* was a common jibe at the time. The remainder of the dialogue consisted of an argument between Care and the "Honest Dissenter," in which it rapidly became clear that the dissenter was not a proponent of repeal. The "Honest Dissenter" thus became the hero of this anti-repeal piece.

In Brown's dialogue, the word "repealer" was used as an identifying label for a group. The defining feature of that group was that its members had pledged to support the cause of repeal by giving affirmative answers to questions such as the one that Care posed to the dissenter in the dialogue: "Will you, whenever there is a Parliament call'd, endeavour to choose such men as will take off the Tests and Penal Laws?"[32] Before asking his question of the dissenter, Care described it as a "Catechism," noting that "no man must expect his Reward, before he can say his Catechism."[33] The author of the dialogue thus parodied Care's recruiting campaign as a sort of religious instruction. In this parody, the repealers themselves were by implication a quasi-religious group, with initiates being instructed by their superiors. By writing of the repealers as though they were a religious body, Thomas Brown came close to describing them as a group with a collective identity and a common purpose, what we might now term a "movement."

The Repealer Movement

Over the course of eighteen months from April 1687 to October 1688, the repealers pressed for a broad-based religious toleration that would include both Protestant nonconformists and Roman Catholics and would establish their rights to political participation as well as freedom of worship. They sought the legislative repeal of various laws including the Test Act of 1673, which required all national officeholders to take the sacrament in the Church of England; the Test Act of 1678, which barred Catholics from sitting in Parliament; the Elizabethan and Jacobean recusancy statutes that required all adults to attend Church of

England services every Sunday; and the statute of Charles II that levied a fine on anyone who attended a nonconformist conventicle.[34] The repealers also argued for a new law that would declare religious freedom to be inviolable. In pressing for these actions, they decisively changed the politics of the royal court by encouraging King James II to dissolve his first parliament in July 1687 and to mount an electoral campaign for a new, pro-toleration parliament.

The repealers drew from every Christian group in England, including the Quakers, Baptists, Familists, Congregationalists, Presbyterians, Anglicans, and Catholics. They attracted participants from each end of the political spectrum. Many of the people who have been called "whig collaborators" became repealers, but so too did many tories, especially those who were Catholics or who had Catholic relations. This broad coalition was held together by the king, who provided much of the organizational framework for the repealer movement, including funding and publicity.

With the benefit of the king's patronage, at least twenty-seven town councils came to be controlled by repealers, including important centers such as Cambridge, Gloucester, Reading, Bedford, Exeter, and Nottingham. Assisted by financial support from the king, the repealers propagated their message in print. About eighty pro-repeal tracts were published in 1687 and 1688. These printed works, and the many hostile responses to them, set the public agenda of England for much of the latter half of James II's reign. As one observer put it, "Many Pamphlets [are] published to show what absolute necessity there is for all people to give their Consent for the Repealing of the Test Acts . . . this truly imploys at this time most peoples Tongues Pro and Contra as well [as] all the Press."[35] Alongside the repeal pamphlets, a pro-repeal newspaper was published by Henry Care and continued under the editorship of Elkanah Settle after Care's death in August 1688. This paper, *Publick Occurrences Truly Stated,* ran to thirty-four issues before the repealer movement came to a halt in October 1688. In addition, approximately sixty addresses pledging support for the repeal campaign were sent to the king from various English counties, towns, churches, and constituencies. Repeal was a widespread, active, and successful movement.

The repeal movement was not confined to an elite of writers and courtiers but included considerable numbers of ordinary citizens. It was not limited to London but extended the length and breadth of the country, from Canterbury to Carlisle and from East Anglia to the West Country. It conducted an impressive publishing campaign. Yet the activities of the repealers have never been analyzed as a whole. Historians have conceded that some individuals, notably William Penn and Henry Care, were genuinely committed to the cause of repeal. To these two are usually added the Congregationalist Stephen Lobb and the Presbyterian Vincent Alsop. These four, however, have been seen as outliers even in the denominations of which they were a part. Most Quakers, Congregationalists, and Presbyterians have been characterized as discomfited by the pro-repeal lobbying of these men.[36] Indeed, historians have minimized the examples of Penn, Lobb, and Alsop by identifying other members of their respective denominations who dissented from their views. That the repeal campaign could not command the support of all Quakers, Baptists, or Presbyterians has been taken to mean that it was not popular.[37] Such a test of unanimity would surely depopulate Stuart England of all its political affiliations.

If the repealers are written back into history, then much of the narrative of later Stuart politics can be reconstructed around them. Their significance is seen most clearly in interpretations of James II, the Glorious Revolution, and the Act of Toleration. If the repealers are left out of the narrative, then James appears to be a misguided monarch with little popular support, while the Revolution seems a predictable reaction to the king's delusions, and the post-revolutionary Toleration Act becomes a beneficent gift to nonconformists as a reward for their good behavior under the previous regime. This entire history takes on a different shape when the repealers are brought back in. James might then be seen as an audacious monarch, trying to make the impossible possible by relying on repeler support, the Glorious Revolution seems like a conservative counter-revolution designed to maintain Anglican privilege in the face of repealer demands, and the Toleration Act appears to be a strategic concession by a harried majority designed to prevent the exiled king from continuing to garner support from nonconformist activists. If the repealer movement did not in fact occur, then the former is the correct story, and the familiar narrative of the Glorious Revolution remains as it has often been told. But given how readily the narrative can be retold, it seems worthwhile to reconsider the evidence for a popular pro-repeal movement.

Repealer Addresses and Publications

Soon after James issued his *Declaration for Liberty of Conscience*, groups of tolerationists gathered to sign public addresses thanking him for doing so. The first address, from Baptists in London, was presented to the king within a fortnight; an address from Presbyterians followed two weeks later. These addresses were published on the front page of the government-controlled *London Gazette*, giving them a mass readership. More than two hundred addresses from various groups and regions were sent to the king over the next year and a half, thanking him for his *Declaration*. About sixty of the addresses offered specific pledges of support for the repeal campaign. This was not the first addressing campaign in English history, as the technique had been employed frequently since the early Stuart period. Nor was it the largest in recent memory: the tory addressing campaign of 1683 in abhorrence of the Rye House Plot had resulted in many more petitions, 323 in all, while the 361 addresses sent to James II celebrating his accession in 1685 were even more numerous. But the addresses sent in 1687 and 1688 were frequent enough to indicate considerable popular enthusiasm for the king's *Declaration*.[38]

Some historians have dismissed the addresses thanking the king for his *Declaration* as manufactured or engineered through pressure from the king's servants.[39] That is a fair description of the missives sent by the Anglican clergy. Those addresses were all virtually identical, which suggests that they were following a set form handed down from above. Several loyalist bishops exerted pressure on the clergy to produce addresses. Meanwhile, several groups of clergy resisted the pressures from above and refused to address, most notably in the dioceses of Oxford, London, Bristol, and York.[40] But the addresses from the clergy of the Church of England accounted for only six out of more than two hundred published in the *Gazette*. It is less likely that the government engineered many of the other addresses, such as the address sent by the Congregationalists of Cockermouth in Westmorland. It seems unlikely that either the central or the county administration would have felt a need to engineer a public endorsement from such a remote and obscure congregation. The address appears to have been inspired by the congregation itself. According to the church minute book, at a meeting in August 1687, "a collection was made of about three pounds, for the presenting of an address to the King, which was well accepted by him.

The Lord continue our liberty." The missive, which was published in the *Gazette,* thanked the king for proclaiming "That Conscience ought not to be constrained."[41]

Three pounds was a considerable sum for a congregation in a small town. As this example suggests, presenting an address to the crown was costly. The usual practice was to delegate a group of emissaries to present it, which would require a long journey for those who resided far from London. Upon arrival at court, the king's household officers typically demanded gratuities in return for access to the presence chamber.[42] Even a repealer might blanch at these expenses. One Catholic lord lieutenant, known for his support of repeal, nevertheless discouraged the burgesses of Bury St Edmunds from sending a formal address of thanks for the king's *Declaration.* A formal address, he noted, would be "troublesom[e]" to them. He instead advised them simply to write a letter of thanks, which he would show to the king informally, with no expenses required.[43] The fact that many groups and congregations managed to send formal addresses despite the cost suggests a degree of local support for the king's *Declaration.*

The addressing campaign was accompanied by a publishing operation of considerable magnitude. At its center were the only newspapers permitted to publish in England in the last year of James II's reign: the government-controlled *London Gazette,* which appeared twice a week, and Henry Care's *Publick Occurrences Truly Stated,* which appeared once a week. The *London Gazette* performed a linking function for local repealer groups by publishing all of the addresses of thanks for the king's *Declaration,* thus enabling each group to read the addresses sent by other groups. It also performed a propaganda function by indicating, through its publication of addresses, the wide spread of pro-repeal sentiments across the country. The *Publick Occurrences* similarly combined a linking function with a propaganda function. Henry Care, a nonconformist who had been a prominent whig polemicist in the reign of Charles II, edited the newspaper for six months, from February 1688 until his death in August of that year. The paper then continued for ten more weeks under the editorship of the playwright Elkanah Settle. Care was a leading repealer author who wrote fervent editorials in each issue defending the cause of repeal. He drew upon a network of correspondents from local repealer groups who sent him tales of altercations between repealers and Anglicans, which he then published.[44]

With only the official *Gazette* as competition, Henry Care's paper attracted a considerable nonrepealer readership, who complained about the amount of repealer editorializing they had to wade through in order to read the week's news. Some Anglicans charged Care with seeking to undermine the Church of England. His paper was accused of being a "Jesuites Pisse pot thrown by Henry Care in the church of England men's faces."[45] In almost every issue, Care told at least one story of persecution suffered by nonconformists. In one number, he reported that a new dissenting meeting house in Reigate had been broken into by some "violent Church [of England]-Men," who "tore to pieces the Pulpit and Sounding-Board, [and] cut the Pulpit-Cloth, Cushion, and Cloth of the Communion-Table, all to Shreds."[46]

Stories of persecution like those told in the *Occurrences* were an essential part of movement formation for the repealers: retelling old stories of persecution and sharing new stories helped to provide them with a sense of animus against their collective enemies. As Care wrote, in defense of his own reporting: "We shew the mischievous Effects of the Penal Laws, That with a just detestation they may be Repealed, and the like may ever be prevented for the future." Care aimed to convince his readers that many Anglicans still harbored a desire to return to persecution. But he insisted that he did not intend to criticize all Anglicans, only those who supported the penal laws; he wrote favorably of the "Sober Moderate and (God be thanked) numerous Party of the Church-of-England, and amongst the Clergy too, who are in earnest, Enemies to Persecution."[47]

Care's newspaper was joined briefly by another serial, probably written by the nonconformist minister Charles Nicholets, called *The Weekly Test Paper*. This paper came out only four times and did not attempt to report on the news, instead confining itself to editorializing for repeal.[48] In addition to these two serials, the repealers published a large number of individual works advocating repeal. At least seventy-seven repealer pamphlets and three repealer broadsides were published in 1687 and 1688.[49] Most of these works, seventy in all, were published anonymously or with the author's initials only, and the authorship of only twenty-one of these can be reliably traced. This leaves over half of the total without attribution, a not unusual proportion in an age of anonymous pamphleteering. The thirty-one tracts with known authors were penned by a surprisingly wide array of figures, including an Anglican bishop, a Congregationalist minister, a Quaker woman, a Catholic controversialist, a whig journalist, and a member of the tiny nonconformist group the Family of Love.

At least fifteen different printers, publishers, and booksellers had a hand in the publication and distribution of these pamphlets. Some, such as Nathaniel and Mary Thompson, were tory publishers, while others, such as Francis Smith and Jacob Tonson, were whigs. Of the eighty repealer tracts, fifty-four can be readily traced to a publisher. Fourteen repealer tracts were published by the Quaker Andrew Sowle, ten by the Baptist George Larkin, eight by the tory Randal Taylor, five by the whig Richard Janeway, four by the Catholic Henry Hills, and three by the Catholic Matthew Turner.[50] The publishers of the repealer pamphlets were remarkably diverse in their religious and political backgrounds. This diversity was appropriate for a movement that drew its support from a variety of groups. It was also a reflection of the amount of money that the king was pouring into the campaign, which presumably attracted some publishers who might have had little genuine fervor for repeal.

Many of the repeal pamphlets were funded directly or indirectly by the king, in part through a committee that sent agents throughout the kingdom to proselytize on behalf of repeal and regulate the parliamentary constituencies. Most of these agents were Baptist ministers.[51] The agents, also known as the regulators, were given instructions that authorized them to set up networks of correspondents. They were charged to seek out men in each town who would agree to receive books and pamphlets in the post and distribute them in "coffee-houses, and houses of publick entertainment, for the information of the country."[52] These networks would then be used to funnel repeal pamphlets into the countryside. The regulators were advanced at least £1,066 from the secret service moneys for "buying of books and pamphletts," a sum sufficient to purchase about two hundred thousand pamphlets, or one pamphlet for every twenty-five people in England. They distributed one hundred thousand pamphlets in the month of May 1688 alone, according to one contemporary estimate.[53] By pushing repeal propaganda through those networks, the regulators helped to build a movement that could respond to direction from the center.

The king occasionally commissioned a particular work to smooth the path toward repeal. In April 1687, he placed the author Nathaniel

Johnston on a retainer of four hundred pounds a year. According to Johnston, the king asked him to demonstrate through his work that the "Abb[e]y Lands are so secured that none neede feare any resumption." The "abbey lands" were those lands taken from the Catholic Church when King Henry VIII dissolved the English monasteries. Some of the king's critics had claimed that repeal could unsettle the title of Protestants to those lands, allowing the Catholic Church to reclaim them. Johnston's book, *The Assurance of Abb[e]y and other Church-Lands,* sought to counter such fears. The king closely supervised the production of this work, which was completed within a year and published by the king's printer, Henry Hills.[54]

Other repealer authors and printers attracted the king's patronage without being subjected to such intensive supervision. George Larkin, the Baptist publisher of Care's *Publick Occurrences,* received a grant from the secret service money, as did Thomas Milbourne and William Penn's printer Andrew Sowle. The three printers together secured over two hundred pounds in royal grants.[55] Both Larkin and Sowle were responsible for ten or more repealer pamphlets each. Although Milbourne's name does not appear on any of the repealer pamphlets, he was printing at the time for the publisher Richard Janeway, who published five repealer pamphlets.[56] Some tracts were distributed by Sowle through the Quaker network of meetings, including one hundred copies of the anonymous repealer pamphlet *Vox Cleri Pro Rege* and twenty-five copies of *Old Popery as Good as New.*[57] Many more were distributed through the coffeehouse network established by the Baptist regulators.

The king's patronage laid repealer authors open to charges of insincerity. One anonymous pamphleteer charged Henry Care with having written lies in exchange for his "Bread." The journalist indignantly refuted such charges, referring to them as the "stale Witticism, That H[enry] C[are] Writes for Bread." He contended that his writing for money was no different from an Anglican minister preaching for a living.[58] Although Care did not specify the source of the "bread" he was receiving, it appears to have been a combination of royalties from the sale of his newspaper and direct funding from the king. Upon his death, his widow received a payment of one hundred pounds from the secret service money.[59]

The repealers also attracted an international audience. Pamphlets by Henry Care and William Penn were translated into Dutch, and John

Northleigh's work appeared in French. Nine repealer pamphlets in all were reprinted in Dutch translations and four in French.[60] Penn's *Good Advice to the Church of England* was translated into Dutch by the Amsterdam Quaker Willem Sewel, a prolific translator who later went on to publish a history of the Quaker movement. Its printer was Abigael Swart, an Amsterdam bookseller descended from English nonconformists who had fled to the Netherlands earlier in the century. It seems unlikely that Swart agreed with the contents of Penn's pamphlet given that she was also a leading publisher of Williamite propaganda in 1688.[61] The circulation in Dutch of repealer pamphlets should not be taken as a sign of widespread sympathy for James II's repeal policy in Amsterdam or The Hague. But it does suggest that the arguments of the repealers were being taken seriously.

King James and the English Public Sphere

James II intervened in the public sphere by subsidizing repealer publications. He also sought to intervene more personally, without the use of intermediaries. Most notably, he conducted a public tour with his friend and ally William Penn in the summer of 1687, several months after he issued his *Declaration for Liberty of Conscience.* At towns along the route the king spoke with small groups urging them to support his toleration campaign. The royal progress was a common event in early modern England, but usually the monarch's presence was itself the message; there was little precedent for a king to make a journey urging his subjects to vote a certain way in parliamentary elections. Meanwhile, Penn spoke to larger crowds, attracting a popular audience with his calls for religious toleration.

William Penn was an intellectual architect of James II's toleration project. A Quaker, he had long been a champion of constitutional reform, both in his frame of government for his colony of Pennsylvania and in his political writings. As he wrote in 1675, "England's Circumstances are greatly changed, and they require new Expedients."[62] The key reform would be religious toleration, which would secure the property rights of nonconformists, thereby increasing the nation's industriousness while reducing the anger that fueled opposition movements.[63] Penn had argued that the confiscation of goods and money from dissenters constituted a violation of their rights to private property as guaranteed by the Magna Carta.[64] From this claim it was a short step to his contention that the laws of England should guarantee liberty of conscience as well as property rights. As early as 1679 he had described a proposed new law securing religious liberty as a kind of "Magna Charta."[65]

This phrase was picked up again in 1687 by Penn and his friend the king.[66] The Quaker drew large crowds to his speeches that year, in part because he was seen as a public spokesman for the repeal movement. He defended the king's *Declaration for Liberty of Conscience* before an audience of three thousand in Bristol, a sizeable crowd in comparison to the city's population of no more than twenty-five thousand.[67] He spoke to large, religiously diverse crowds on a tour across England in the summer of 1687. At Devizes in Wiltshire, he spoke in the market house to an audience said to be composed of "many thousands." The crowd was religiously mixed, with people of "all sortes" present. At Marlborough in Wiltshire, he spoke to an audience of hundreds. He stood in the penthouse of a local Quaker residence and addressed the assembled audience on the streets. According to one contemporary, he used his "publick discourses" to praise the king's *Declaration* and "to defame the Test."[68] Later in the summer, he accompanied James on his public progress through the West Midlands and gave speeches along the route. He was willing to speak uninvited in marketplaces even when that attracted hostile attention, as at Shrewsbury where the townsmen cried him down. At Chester he held forth in a local theatre where "above a thousand people" came to hear him defend liberty of conscience.[69] Although attendance at a meeting does not necessarily entail support for a political agenda, the large crowds drawn by the Quaker leader show that the king's tolerationist policies were attracting a great deal of public attention in the summer of 1687.

The king, like the Quaker, used the royal progress as an opportunity for political mobilization. When he had the opportunity, he entered into conversation with groups of local leaders, delivering short speeches urging them to support his toleration campaign. One of the most noteworthy of these speeches was delivered by the king to a group of whig gentlemen in Chester. In his remarks, the king informed them that

> he hoped we would join with him in endeavouring to set aside all animosities, and distinctions of parties and names, which would be done

by removing the occasions, which were the Penall Laws and tests, and when he should think fit to call a Parliament, he hoped we would send him such men as would join with him in taking them away, that we might all agree and be easie. . . . the King sayd he had as soon as he could graunted a toleration, and hoped we would join with him in making a magna Charta for Conscience as well as properties and other liberties, he was sure no man should be debarr[e]d of either while he lived, suppose said he there should be a law made that all black men should be imprisoned, twould be unreasonable and we had as little reason to quarell with other men for being of different opinions as for being of different Complexions, desired we should shew our selfs Englishmen, and he was sure no Englishman could desire to see others persecuted for differences of opinion, and therefore again told us, the way to reconcile all differences was to take of[f] those Lawes which made men uneasie under them and deprived them of theyr Rights.[70]

The hinge of King James II's argument at Chester was the notion that religious opinion and skin complexion were comparable characteristics. The nature of the comparison, though not stated explicitly in the speech, can be inferred from the substance of the argument. The basis of the analogy would appear to be that both religious opinion and complexion were involuntary. Neither of these characteristics was chosen, so the individuals who possessed them could not reasonably be punished or stigmatized for them, either through imprisonment by law or through "quarreling" by individuals.

Perhaps what is most noteworthy about the king's analogy between religious belief and complexion is its novelty. Although Sir William Temple had made a parallel analogy in 1673 between religious opinion and the color of one's eyes, and John Locke was to draw a similar analogy about hair color in his *Letter Concerning Toleration,* published in 1689, James was unique in this period in drawing an analogy between religious opinions and skin color.[71] It is unclear whether he developed this analogy himself or whether he picked it up in conversation with Penn, but the Quaker did not use it in his own published writings. The novel analogy suggests that James had developed a sophisticated rationale for an expansive liberty of conscience.

The king dispensed with the idea of toleration as a privilege or a royal grant in his speech at Chester; instead, he elevated it to the status of an indefeasible right. The king described the penal laws as a burden that made his subjects "uneasie"; his toleration project would ease that burden by taking off the statutes that "deprived" his people of their "rights." The king's use of the term "rights" was a statement of the concept that Isaiah Berlin was later to term "negative" liberty: the notion of a freedom from the coercive power of other human beings.[72] By calling for a "magna Charta for Conscience as well as properties and other liberties," the king was suggesting that toleration should be accorded a status in law similar to that accorded to the great charter. His rhetorical strategy was to elevate liberty of conscience to the status of a right that ought to be guaranteed in the same way as private property. English subjects could then appeal to liberty of conscience as a transcendent guarantee against which temporal laws could be tested and found legitimate or illegitimate.

The proposed Magna Carta for liberty of conscience was a touchstone of James's rhetoric in 1687 and 1688. He spoke of it on at least eleven separate occasions. During his summer progress, he called for a new "Magna Charta" when meeting with groups of nonconformists at Gloucester, Whitchurch, and Chester, as well as with the whig gentlemen at Chester referred to above. The king's first known use of the expression came in April 1687, four months before his remarks at Chester, when he informed a group of Presbyterians that he "heartily wished there was A Magna Charta for Liberty of Conscience as well as for their Properties."[73] Earlier in that same month, a similar expression had appeared in a published tract: a call for "another Great Charter, to bury all our Prejudices, and Establish a lasting Civil union among the Inhabitants of this Ancient and Famous Kingdom." This tract was written by William Penn.[74] It is possible that the king picked up his new expression in conversation with the Quaker leader. When asked once why he spent time with Penn, he replied that the Quaker "talk'd Ingeniously" and that he "heard him willingly."[75]

By the end of 1687, Penn's concept of a new Magna Carta for liberty of conscience had been widely popularized.[76] In the eyes of many, the new charter would be a new form of collective belonging. Pamphlets published by the king's followers developed the contractual logic inherent in the idea. One author proposed the institution of a "new test" whereby every adult male in the kingdom would swear annually to "observe and keep Unviolable" the "new Magna Charta" for liberty of conscience. These oaths would be sworn on the king's birthday. In a nod to Penn, the author made an exception for Quakers and others who were unable to swear an oath; they would be permitted to make an affirmation instead.[77] Henry Care wrote in September 1687 that liberty of conscience was everyone's concern, not just the concern of a few: "For if it be not General, it cannot be Effectual; But by a General Security equally including All Parties, the Fears and Jealousies of Each must vanish." To institute this general security, Care added, the king and parliament should enact a new law declaring that "Liberty of Conscience is part of the Constitution of this Kingdom" and that anyone who endeavored "to undermine or subvert such [a] Settlement, shall be adjudg'd Criminal, and liable to such Penalties as shall be thought fit."[78] The new Magna Carta would effectively become a new social contract, and anyone who refused to subscribe to the new contract would be treated as a criminal.

With his speeches and policies, King James II carved out a new rhetoric on toleration in 1687. His newly expansive rhetoric went far beyond any statement that he is known to have made before that year. Over the course of two years, from 1685 to 1687, he had shifted from making grants of liberty of conscience to individuals and groups of whom he approved, to issuing a general pardon that freed dissenters in large numbers indiscriminately, to making a universal grant of toleration for all English people, which he sought to make irrevocable by an act of parliament. In his speech at Chester, James described the underpinnings of his new line of argument, declaring liberty of conscience to be a fundamental right of all English subjects.

The King's Army

The king's public interventions on behalf of liberty of conscience were extensive and painstaking. But it has been debated to what extent these interventions constituted his governing philosophy in the latter half of his reign. The king's fundamental agenda, many historians have averred, is seen not in his campaign for religious toleration, but rather in his promotion of Catholics to public office and his development of a large standing army. With a Catholicized administration and army, the king put himself in a position to establish absolutist rule in England, once the campaign for toleration had succeeded in dividing the Protestants into quarreling factions. Historians have argued, moreover, that

this covert agenda was obvious to contemporaries, who as a consequence were largely unwilling to support his toleration campaign.[79]

Historians have often asserted that James would have liked to fill
the offices of state with Catholics, that under this king, as J. P. Kenyon
put it, "Catholicism was an instant recommendation to the highest
offices."[80] The king did at times take religion into account when
assigning offices. In one of the ugliest episodes of his reign, he pressed
his lord treasurer, the earl of Rochester, to convert to Catholicism and
then dismissed him from office for refusing to do so, stating that "no
man must be at the head of his affairs that was not of his own opinion."[81]
This was a religious test for office that, if broadly applied, would have
Catholicized the upper reaches of the English government. And yet the
head of the army remained Protestant throughout James's reign, as did
a majority of his leading officers in both civil and military affairs. James
never came close to Catholicizing his administration.

This is not to say that James's appointments to office of his co-
religionists, however few in number they may have been, were uncon-
troversial. The Test Act of 1673 had banned Catholics from public offices,
and James exercised the royal dispensing power in a disconcertingly
sweeping fashion, dispensing each of his Catholic appointees from
having to comply with the law. But, although the king's appointments
stirred controversy, their cumulative effect was not to exclude Protestants from public service. In the army, James appointed over twelve
hundred new Protestant officers and about two hundred new Catholic
officers, with the percentage of Catholics in the officer corps rising from
no more than 5 percent at the start of the reign to about 10 percent by
the end of 1685 and about 11 percent in October 1688. The initial rise
was indeed sharp, but the rate of growth dropped considerably after the
first year of the king's reign. The number of Catholics in the officer
corps would remain below 15 percent in perpetuity so long as James
continued to appoint six Protestant officers for every new Catholic
officer. In the navy, the king appointed no more than sixteen Catholic
officers. For service in the royal household, the king appointed at least
thirty known Catholics, about 4 percent of the total number of officers,
and it is possible that another fifteen of his household appointees were
Catholic. In the privy council, by the summer of 1688, thirteen of the
forty-three councillors were Catholic.[82]

The central administration was not swamped by Catholics. Many Protestant holdovers from Charles II's administration were retained, and James continued to appoint Protestants as well as Catholics to high positions at court. Instead, it was in the county administrations that Catholics replaced large numbers of ejected Protestants. The growth in Catholic numbers was especially noticeable with respect to the unsalaried offices of justice of the peace, deputy lieutenant, and sheriff. By 1688, James had appointed approximately 238 Catholic justices of the peace and 172 Catholic deputy lieutenants, or about 23.9 percent of the total number of J.P.s and deputy lieutenants in England and Wales. Meanwhile, in 1688, Catholics became sheriffs in fifteen of the fifty-two English and Welsh counties, taking on an onerous and unremunerative task that many Anglicans sought to avoid.[83] In an unexpected twist, Catholics were more likely to hold offices where the financial rewards were the least.

Historians have long been aware that this Catholic king, who supposedly was intent on appointing as many Catholics to office as possible, did not in fact appoint large numbers of his co-religionists to his central administration. To resolve this conundrum, historians have typically asserted that James appointed few Catholics because so few of his co-religionists were available and qualified.[84] It is doubtless the case that most Catholics had less administrative experience than many of their Anglican competitors, since they had been excluded from office for over a decade under the provisions of the Test Act of 1673. It is not clear, however, that all available and qualified Catholics were appointed to public office under James. William Blundell, the head of a well-known Lancashire Catholic family, spent three fruitless years seeking an office at court, from November 1685 to August 1688. He was unable to make any progress, even after scheduling interviews with John Warner, the king's Catholic confessor, who assured him that he would "not forget my Cause," and with Edward Petre, the well-connected Jesuit courtier, who encouraged him in his efforts. The results were similar for Francis Radcliffe, a younger son of the Catholic earl of Derwentwater, who sought an office at court in 1688. He was frustrated in his aim, although he eventually raised a troop of cavalry on his own initiative that was then incorporated into one of James's regiments during the invasion emergency in the fall of 1688.[85]

Catholic dissatisfaction with their lack of success in gaining lucrative offices grew over the course of the reign. In 1688 an anonymous Catholic penned a complaint on behalf of all "Catholic Gentlemen who pretend to the Honour of the Kings Service." The author averred that there were "a great many honest Catholick Gentlemen" who were eager to "serve our Royall Master in our Severall Capacityes." According to this brief, many Catholics had spent "money and Time in following the Court in Order to get Employments: But having lived long on the hopes of Blessings to come we have eat[en] up our own bread expecting when the Royall Manna should fall." In short, they had found that it was "impossible we should ever get into any Employments." Although some Protestant courtiers had claimed that Catholics lacked enough experience to serve, the petitioner rebutted this "specious Argument," citing the loyalty of Catholics as well as their intelligence and education. The complainant hoped that the king would appoint a committee to "receive our Applications" for positions and to discover "what every one" of the Catholic gentlemen in question had "done to deserve his favour and in what each one is most capable to serve him."[86]

This anonymous petition suggests that the cases of William Blundell and Francis Radcliffe were not anomalous. A considerable number of Catholics seem to have pursued an office at court without success. Nor were the complaints of these unemployed Catholics poorly publicized. The English Catholic bishops alluded to them in their pastoral letter of 1688, when they urged those Catholics who were "not yet in public Employment, to bear their Lots with Modesty and Patience, without Murmuring or Envy."[87] The question of experience would have been moot for many of these Catholics, since they were often pursuing positions for which little or no experience was required. William Blundell was seeking a position with a good salary and mentioned the customs administration as a goal. A salaried position in the customs might not require any experience, as the officeholder typically hired a deputy to perform the actual duties of the post. The head searcher for Gravesend in the customs administration, for instance, earned four hundred pounds a year and hired a deputy for one hundred pounds to perform his duties for him.[88] It is difficult to know exactly what was keeping these Catholics out of public office, but it was not likely a lack of experience. It may have been a lack of money. One well-informed observer warned Francis Radcliffe that he was unlikely to get a salaried office since he had failed to grease his path with bribes, and those "that pay

nothing" were sure to lose out in the hunt for patronage to those that
offered "round sumes" to the king's favorites.[89]

James's appointments policy may have been designed to balance
the interests of various groups rather than to elevate one group above
the others. One courtier wrote early in 1687 that the king had said that
"he will dispense his favours equally between his Church of England
subjects and his Romish." A newsletter writer noted at about the same
time that the king had declared that "he will dispense his favours
equally according to Meritt and not with respect to the religion of either
person." These statements suggest a desire on the king's part to appear
even-handed.[90]

James expressed his thinking on appointments more fully in his
advice to his son, written three years after the Revolution. The exiled
king's advice was based on the optimistic assumption that his son would
eventually succeed to the throne of England. He suggested that his heir
should consider adopting a quota system wherein one of the two secretaries of state would be Catholic and the other would be Protestant,
while the secretary of war would be Catholic and the secretary for the
navy, Protestant. The treasury commission would consist of five men:
three Anglicans, one Catholic, and one dissenter. Although James urged
his son to appoint "As many Catholicks as can be in the Army, [along
with] some Ch[urch] of Eng[land] and Dissenters," this could be a
reflection of the fact that a largely Anglican army had failed him in
1688. Evidence dating from three years after the Revolution is too late
to serve as a definitive guide to James's policy as king, but it does suggest the ease with which he could slip into thinking in terms of quotas.
James had, in fact, appointed a confessionally divided commission of
the treasury in 1687 after he dismissed the earl of Rochester. The commission was composed of three Anglicans and two Catholics, in a fairly
close approximation of the advice he would later give to his son.[91]

The king's appointments policy was not based on principles of pro-
portional representation. By 1688, Catholics represented a tiny percentage
of the English population, although they tended to be concentrated in
the gentry and peerage, the groups from which crown officeholders
were typically drawn. The king knew the results of the 1676 Compton
census, which showed Catholics at one-half of 1 percent of the English
population, dissenters at barely above 4 percent, and Anglicans at 95
percent. He must have been aware that he was appointing Catholics to

office out of proportion to their numbers in the population at large.[92] But in James's eyes, English Catholics were more politically weighty than their numbers suggested. He repeatedly praised the loyalty of Catholics, who had supported the Stuart monarchy through the Civil Wars and Interregnum.[93] James's appointments policy looked to many like favoritism toward his co-religionists, and it caused great discontent among many Anglicans. Yet the king's evident favor toward Catholics did not necessarily mean that he was abandoning his favor toward either Anglicans or Protestant nonconformists, who also secured lucrative appointments in his administration. Nevertheless, to his critics, the king's appointment of several hundred Catholics to office looked like a sign of worse things to come.

These fears were heightened by the king's maintenance of a large standing army. This too has been taken by historians to be a sign of James's aggressive intentions. James inherited from his brother an English army of 8,865 men, which he expanded to about 20,000 during Monmouth's Rebellion of 1685 and its immediate aftermath. The army remained at that level until March 1688, when James added another 2,100 men. Then, in September 1688, he expanded the English army in response to the imminent Dutch invasion, with the force amounting to roughly 31,000 men by late November. Although the king's peacetime English army of roughly 20,000 troops was a modest force compared to those fielded by continental rulers at the time, it was not customary for an English ruler to keep such a large force at hand during peacetime. James justified his sizable army by referring to Monmouth's Rebellion, arguing that, since the nonprofessional county militias had proved ineffective, he needed to have a professional force on hand to put down rebellions or repel invading forces.[94] Many wondered at the time whether this military buildup was a prelude to authoritarian rule after the manner of Louis XIV's France.

Though James's military buildup was facilitated by the invasions of 1685 and 1688, it was also, in important ways, limited by his fiscal policy. The tory Parliament of 1685 granted James an ample revenue that proved sufficient for him to expand the military, up to a point. Crown revenue from all sources averaged about £2.0 million to £2.1 million per year during James's reign. Of this he devoted roughly £1,100,000 to military spending, including somewhat more than £600,000 per year for the army, just over £400,000 for the navy, and a bit less than £100,000 for military ordinance or munitions. Of the remaining revenue, approximately £600,000 was devoted to civil government and the royal household and about £300,000 to interest payments and the retiring of debts from Charles II's reign.[95] Of these expenditures, perhaps the most surprising was the king's decision to spend so much on servicing his brother's debts, given that his brother's creditors were not in a position to insist on repayment.

Over the course of his reign, James made significant progress on retiring Charles's debts. The exact total of the debt outstanding on James's accession is not known, but it appears to have been in the neighborhood of £3 or 3.5 million. Of this, some £1.5 million was composed of debts stemming from the Stop of the Exchequer in 1671. The principal on those debts was never fully honored by any English government, and during the reign of King William the debts went through a restructuring in which parliament agreed to repay the principal at half of its original value. James did little to honor the Stop debts, apart from paying approximately £45,000 in interest. But he made significant inroads on the remainder of his brother's liabilities. As the leading historian of later Stuart crown finance, C. D. Chandaman, has indicated, James appears to have devoted close to one million pounds to honoring his brother's commitments. His creditors included many of Charles II's former servants, whose salaries had not been fully paid by the former king and who were in no position to demand payment from a new king, as the money owed to them was considered to attach to the deceased king's person, not his regality. James chose nevertheless to repay much of the arrears, to the tune of about £260,000.[96]

The considerable sums that James devoted to paying down debt are particularly surprising in view of the fact that his overall revenues, while healthy, remained relatively modest. In James's reign, the percentage of national income extracted by the crown, including trade duties, hovered around 4 percent, while during the 1690s, this figure increased to an average of about 6 percent. James's income was larger than that received by his brother at the end of his reign, but it was not as large as the income received by Charles when parliament voted additional supplies for war with the Dutch in 1671–1672 and 1673–1674 (see Table 1.1). Neither was English crown income particularly large in comparison with the revenues of other leading western European states. Comparable data is not available for most other European powers, but scattered data for the province of Holland in the Netherlands suggests that the burden of state taxes was heavier there than it was in England. In the 1670s, between 10 and 12 percent of Holland's national income was taken as state taxes, though this had fallen to 9.7 percent by 1700.[97]

Only the most general estimates of the burden of state taxation on the overall economy can be provided for France, due to a lack of certainty about the size of its national economy in the seventeenth century. One historian has suggested that the French king's income in the 1680s represented as much as 15 percent of the national income.[98] Using the raw data provided by this and other scholars, a range of estimates of the overall burden of royal taxes can be ascertained for the years 1685 to 1688. Louis XIV possessed an income of 124 million livres in 1685 (approximately 9.4 million pounds sterling). This increased slightly in the following year before dropping in the two years after that, producing an average income for the years from 1685 to 1688 of 121 million livres (approximately 9.1 million pounds sterling). The French king's income, then, was more than four times that of the English king, which averaged about 2.0 to 2.1 million pounds sterling in this period. Meanwhile, the overall size of the French economy, according to the best available estimates, lay somewhere in the broad range between 900 and 1,500 million livres in 1690.[99] Those estimates are imprecise, but they can still be useful. Dividing one set of figures by the other generates the following range of estimates for royal taxation as a proportion of the national income: at the lower end, the French king may have extracted 8.1 percent of the French national income in the years 1685–1688; at the upper end, he may have extracted as much as 13.5 percent. Although the difference between the two figures is sizable, a meaningful comparison with the English case can still be made. The lower figure, 8.1 percent, is about double what James II received as a proportion of the English national income, while the higher figure, 13.5 percent, is more than three times as much. In either case, it is evident that England was contributing a much smaller share of its wealth to its king's treasury than was France. This raises questions about the extent to which King James could have imitated in England the methods of rule employed in France, even if this is truly what he wanted to do.[100]

James was aware that he was not commanding a large share of his people's income. The political economist Sir William Petty calculated that the king's revenue represented only one-thirtieth of the yearly expenses of his subjects from across his territories. Petty believed that it would be possible to raise that proportion from 3.3 percent to 5 percent without placing an "Intollerable burden" on the king's subjects. He met with the king in 1686 and appears to have shared his proposals with him. But the king told Petty that he would not "raise his Revenue but as the Wealth of his subjects encreased."[101] This conversation suggests that James was content with the proportion of the national revenue he was receiving, although he had no objection to gaining more money as the overall economy grew in size.

The king, then, had a healthy income but not a massive one, especially in comparison to other European powers. His effective power,

Table 1.1 English Crown Income and Expenditure, 1670–1700

Fiscal Year	GDP	Income Total	as % of GDP	Expenditure Total	as % of GDP
1670–1671	54,400,000	1,328,591	2.44%	1,790,661	3.29%
1671–1672	49,285,000	2,298,679	4.66%	2,512,271	5.10%
1672–1673	51,975,000	1,925,216	3.70%	2,340,409	4.50%
1673–1674	58,950,000	2,268,141	3.85%	2,565,134	4.35%
1674–1675	57,160,000	1,609,509	2.82%	1,848,501	3.23%
1675–1676	50,960,000	1,439,539	2.82%	1,268,533	2.49%
1676–1677	50,810,000	1,503,279	2.96%	1,832,649	3.61%
1677–1678	59,380,000	1,981,092	3.34%	2,714,122	4.57%
1678–1679	56,910,000	1,727,684	3.04%	2,366,681	4.16%
1679–1680	56,485,000	1,750,272	3.10%	2,112,222	3.74%
1680–1681	55,990,000	1,386,686	2.48%	1,520,283	2.72%
1681–1682	54,805,000	1,384,269	2.53%	1,157,108	2.11%
1682–1683	58,410,000	1,366,701	2.34%	1,311,778	2.25%
1683–1684	56,530,000	1,398,248	2.47%	1,436,899	2.54%
1684–1685	62,675,000	1,500,940	2.39%	1,388,057	2.21%
1685–1686	50,410,000	2,113,644	4.19%	1,971,394	3.91%
1686–1687	55,330,000	2,132,271	3.85%	2,220,040	4.01%
1687–1688	50,800,000	1,954,877	3.85%	2,160,862	4.25%
1688–1689	48,960,000	2,871,064	5.86%	5,478,914	11.19%
1689–1690	52,125,000	2,871,064	5.51%	5,478,914	10.51%
1690–1691	50,760,000	2,871,064	5.66%	5,478,914	10.79%
1691–1692	62,900,000	4,111,089	6.54%	7,061,550	11.23%
1692–1693	67,170,000	3,782,615	5.63%	8,954,142	13.33%
1693–1694	70,170,000	4,003,798	5.71%	9,175,120	13.08%
1694–1695	63,685,000	4,134,168	6.49%	10,064,927	15.80%

moreover, was limited by his reluctance or inability to go further into debt. A comparison of James's reign with that of his successor, William, is instructive in this regard. The crown debt increased to roughly £14 million by the end of William's reign, as the Financial Revolution, parliamentary support for the war with France, and the foundation of the Bank of England in 1694 enabled William to borrow increasing sums. As a result, William was able to support much higher levels of expenditure than his Stuart predecessors had (see Table 1.1). James abhorred debt because it might make him dependent on parliament, while William was willing to make concessions to parliament in exchange for increasing taxes and loans to support the war with France. As James wrote in his

Fiscal Year	GDP	Income		Expenditure	
		Total	as % of GDP	Total	as % of GDP
1695–1696	69,520,000	4,823,452	6.94%	9,676,052	13.92%
1696–1697	69,830,000	3,298,441	4.72%	10,484,434	15.01%
1697–1698	74,165,000	4,578,102	6.17%	7,892,370	10.64%
1698–1699	71,575,000	5,163,812	7.21%	7,887,139	11.02%
1699–1700	65,075,000	4,343,787	6.68%	5,561,536	8.55%

Note: All figures are in pounds. Income figures are based on the fiscal year beginning on Michaelmas (Sept. 30) and do not include income from government borrowing, except for some short-term, highly secured debt in the period before 1688 that cannot easily be separated from the income tallies. Expenditure figures, which are also based on the fiscal year, include interest payments and repayment of principal on loans. Figures for GDP are based on calendar years. Since the GDP figures are preliminary estimates, and the fiscal and calendar years do not match exactly, the figures for income and expenditure as a percentage of GDP should be treated as indicators of trends, not as precise calculations.
Sources: Data for crown income and expenditure for 1670–1688 is from C. D. Chandaman, *The English Public Revenue, 1660–1688* (Oxford, 1975), 333, 354–363. Data for crown income and expenditure for 1689–1700 is from H. W. Chisholm, ed., Parliamentary Papers, 1868–9, vol. 35, *Public Income and Expenditure,* 4–23. For the period from 5 Nov. 1688 to 29 Sept. 1691 the data is available only as a lump sum of all income and expenditures; I have followed the example of other historians by dividing that lump sum by three and distributing it equally among the three years. Income and expenditure for the five weeks between 30 Sept. and 4 Nov. 1688 is thus not included in these tallies, and the figures for 1688–1689 should be taken as representing William's first year of rule, not James's final year of rule. Data for GDP is from Stephen Broadberry et al., "English Gross Domestic Product, 1300–1700: Some Preliminary Estimates," draft working paper (2008), 44, with an average taken of the two estimates of GDP provided there.

advice to his son after the Revolution, "a King of England ought to be carefull to live within his Reveneu, and not to lett himself be carryd away to exceede his income, by flatterers or ill Ministers, who designedly would run one in debt to betray him to a Parliament."[102] James could have raised his debt load modestly without needing parliament's support, but, over the long term, only parliamentary guarantees of debt and the promise of elevated levels of future taxation could sustain a significantly larger debt burden.

James's military-fiscal policy suggests a defensive mindset, a king who feared being undermined either by a future parliament or by a foreign invasion. He worried about revolts, which was not surprising given that his reign had begun with twin invasions of England and Scotland. He told the French envoy Bonrepaus in 1687 that he was fortifying the landward defenses of Portsmouth so that he would be able to "retreat there and be there in security in case of any civil war in his kingdom."[103] He devoted significant sums to the English navy, the first line of defense against an assault from abroad. He worked fairly carefully within the constraints of the resources available to him. Indeed, he did not exhaust those resources; he paid down debt rather than building it up. This is not to say that he gained much public credit for his budgetary prudence. His military buildup was seen at the time as excessive. But it is important not to overstate the scope of his initiatives, despite the public disquiet that greeted them.

Because the reign of this king was so brief, interpretations of his policies have tended to be influenced by predictions of what his future policies might have been had a revolution not intervened. Many English Protestants were alarmed by the growing number of Catholics in public office. This rapid growth might be portrayed as the first stage in a steep upward curve of Catholicization. Alternatively, it could be seen as a measured increase that did not result in Catholic majorities among officeholders and that had already plateaued in some respects by the time of William's intervention. Similarly, James's military buildup might be seen as either defensive-minded or aggressive, depending on one's perspective about his ultimate intentions.

Some of the king's contemporaries believed that if the Test Acts were repealed at some future date, then the administration would be flooded with Catholics. Others held the opposite belief, that if the king "had the penal Lawes & Test taken of[f] fewer Catholiques would be imployed then ever."[104] Predictions about James's ultimate intentions were used both by his contemporaries and by later historians to frame his policy initiatives. The king's opponents saw his appointments of Catholics to office as the thin edge of a very large wedge aimed directly at English Protestantism. The repealers, for their part, thought that the king's policies in late 1687 and early 1688 could serve as the foundation for a lasting truce between the various religious groups in England. The royal policies, in their view, were a harbinger of future prosperity, not of imminent destruction.

The king's policies did not spring fully formed from his own mind: they were a product of the interplay between his intentions, the views of his courtiers, and opinions expressed by the broader populace. For a full view of royal policy-making it is necessary to explore not only the monarch's intentions but also the ways in which the public responded to royal initiatives. The relationship between King James II and the majority of his subjects has long been portrayed as an antagonistic one, and James can certainly be criticized for not doing enough to assuage the legitimate concerns of many of his Protestant subjects about the direction of his policies. But he also deserves credit for helping to build a popular movement in favor of religious toleration. The conflict between the king's supporters and his skeptics is both a fascinating story in its own right and a powerful explanation for the revolution that toppled him after only three years and ten months of rule. The overthrow of King James was a consequence not merely of his own shortcomings, but also of broader rhythms of English public life that he never fully controlled.

2

Writing a New Magna Carta

The Ideology of Repeal

John Locke's *Letter Concerning Toleration,* though celebrated by posterity, narrowly missed its moment. It was published at Gouda in late April 1689 by Locke's friend Philippus van Limborch. Gouda, a Dutch city, was far enough from London that Locke's book could have had little influence on the debate on toleration in the House of Commons on 17 May. Locke himself, who was in London at the time, received a copy of the book only in early June; by then, the Act of Toleration had received royal assent. The *Letter* was republished in English in the autumn, with a preface contributed by the repealer William Popple, who translated the work from the Latin original. But the debates in parliament had long since moved on to other matters.[1]

Locke has received the lion's share of scholarly attention on tolerationist thought in later Stuart England, despite the fact that he had less influence on the pivotal toleration debates in early 1689 than another set of thinkers who had been publishing works in the years before the Toleration Act, including Giles Shute, Ann Docwra, Charles Nicholets, and Elizabeth Rone. These thinkers, along with the better-known authors William Penn and Henry Care, can be grouped into a repealer school of thought on toleration.[2] The repealers argued for toleration as a natural right, as did Locke. They also made a pragmatic, *politique* case for toleration as an advance that would stabilize the kingdom, strengthen the state, and build a more powerful national community based on a renewed sense of national unity. Unlike many other thinkers of their day, they were willing to endorse a strengthened monarchy charged with protecting the rights of minorities even if that meant overriding the powers of the legislative assembly; they were reluctant to defend the powers of the legislature because they had seen over the previous quarter century how an Anglican majority could capture that body and use it to build a persecuting state. As a result, they endorsed James II's *Declaration for Liberty of Conscience* and his assertion of a controversial power to suspend the penal laws and Test Acts.

The repealers, like many Enlightenment thinkers, believed that contemporary life required a new and better mode of behavior and that old disagreements could be settled through devising new constitutional arrangements. Their arguments typically emphasized the benefits of innovation rather than the veneration of tradition. They were suspicious of majority rule and sought an enlightened monarch to institute reforms and bring about constitutional change. They were cosmopolitan rather than xenophobic, irenic rather than doctrinaire, and wedded to notions of mercantile competition in which toleration would advance English trade at the expense of other nations' prosperity. They argued for a set of constitutional, cultural, and intellectual changes, including a new form of sociability. Repeal was a movement for both political reform and social change.

The thought of the repealers was attractive to King James in part because he himself was a member of a persecuted religious minority. He stated that, for him, toleration was a reciprocal act: "as he Expected the Free Liberty of his owne [Conscience] soe he Desired not to Abridge that of anothers."[3] But James was not solely interested in toleration because it would enhance the status of Catholics such as himself. He also saw it as a reform that would strengthen the monarchy. He was the first Catholic to take the English throne since Mary Tudor, but he was not the first Stuart monarch to embrace toleration. His elder brother, Charles, had pressed for toleration despite being a member of the Anglican majority (though he converted to Roman Catholicism on his deathbed). Charles had promised religious toleration in his Declaration of Breda before his restoration to the throne, a promise that he sought to fulfill in 1662 and again in 1672, although he was forced each time to retreat by largely Anglican parliaments. In sponsoring toleration, James was following a path that his brother had laid out.

A royal proclamation of toleration appealed to James in part because it enhanced his power. It enabled an alliance between the crown and the Protestant nonconformists. It reduced instability and disorder. It put a stop to divisive and tumultuous practices, such as the roving gangs of informers who hunted down nonconformists at worship and took their cut of the consequent fines. The informers were seen by many as "legal thieves" preying on upstanding citizens and robbing them by force of law.[4] Putting a halt to these prosecutions might lead to economic growth. Under the umbrella of toleration, wealthy nonconformists would feel more secure and hence would be more willing to invest their capital in trading enterprises, while persecuted émigrés from the Continent would settle in England, bringing their manufacturing skills with them. As repealers were quick to note, greater economic growth would lead to higher tax receipts, which in turn would enable England to project more power overseas. All this would enhance the king's influence along with the national wealth and would strengthen his ability to govern.[5] Alienating some of the more intransigent Anglicans might seem a small price to pay.

Many of the repealers were urban merchants and manufacturers, so the language of trade and commerce was a natural fit for the movement. Dissenters had long congregated in the towns, where they could more easily practice the skilled trades and commercial enterprises from which many of them earned their living. There they might also find safety in numbers. They gained a degree of shelter from persecution in boroughs where the local authorities, recognizing their economic clout, extended them some protections.[6] England's towns had been growing in size and wealth since the Restoration of Charles II, in part because of the skilled labor of nonconformists. An "urban renaissance" was reflected in the development of new institutions such as the coffeehouse, which became a nexus for news and sociability. Support for repeal of the penal laws was particularly strong in the towns, "For what part of the Kingdom has felt the Smart of them [the penal laws] more, and at all times, and on all occasions represented their mischeif to the Trade, Peace, Plenty and Wealth of the Kingdom, so freely as the Town has always done?"[7] The experience of life under the penal laws had led many nonconformists to conclude that they had common interests in banding together against persecution.[8] It was easy for them to imagine a reconstituted England that would leave them better off than the country in which they were living.

The typical repeal pamphlet was an offer of advice, often presented in epistolary form. Of the eighty repeal tracts, all of which were published in 1687 or 1688, six had titles beginning with the words

"Advice," "Good Advice," or "Seasonable Advice"; three were titled an "Address"; and a further twenty-four were titled a "Letter" or "Letters" or an "Answer" to a letter. The tracts were often ostensibly addressed to a nonaligned reader, someone who was doubtful about repeal and needed reassurance. That reader could be an Anglican, a Catholic, or a Protestant nonconformist. Occasionally a pamphlet would seek to appeal to all three groups in turn, as in William Penn's *Good Advice to the Church of England, Roman Catholick and Protestant Dissenter*. Seven of the pamphlets included the word "interest" in their title, as in the *Advice to Protestant Dissenters Shewing 'tis their Interest to Repeal the Test*. The goal of the repealer authors was to inform their readers what their "interests" were in the current political situation.[9]

Those "interests" were presented in a framework that was reciprocal and transactional, with an emphasis on recognizing the legitimate interests of others so that they, in turn, would recognize one's own interests.[10] Repealers frequently cited Christ's commandment: "Do unto others as you would have them do unto you."[11] The repealer movement was a consciousness-raising movement. The repeal tracts were designed to "open the Eyes of all that are willing to see wherein the True Interest of the Nation lies, with respect to the Penal Laws and Tests."[12] The consciousness being raised was of collective, national interests, not merely of sectarian or class interests. Consciousness of the national good would be raised through empathy as repealer authors asked their readers to imagine not only what was in their own interests but also what was in the interest of their unborn children and future generations of English men and women.[13] The calculation of interest was depicted not as an emotional act, but rather as a rational act that any man or woman, when presented with accurate information, could take.

Repealers were dismissive of opinions that were not in conformity with their own reading of the national interest, and their pamphlets occasionally took on an elitist tone. "Prejudiced" opinions and "slavish" fears might lead men and women—perhaps even a majority of English men and women—to act against the common good. In such circumstances, it would be necessary for an enlightened vanguard to override the whims of the "prejudic'd Mobile" and forge a solution that benefited the collective interest.[14] Once the repeal of the penal laws and Tests was achieved, the scales would fall off the eyes of the unenlightened masses, the repealers predicted.[15] As one repealer put it, drawing an analogy that elaborated on the metaphor of the ship of state: "this unhappy

Nation; which like a Ship at Sea, has been long a sinking: The Captain indeed labours to save her, having found out her leaks, and calls to his men for assistance; but they like madmen, every one endeavour to secure something of her Cargoe, not considering that when the Ship is gone, all is gone; and instead of assisting, do unreasonably oppose him: So that he must save them against their wills, or they will inevitably perish."[16] It was on such grounds as these that repealers justified the king's use of his power to suspend the penal laws and Tests; as the "captain" of the ship of state, he was overriding the will of parliament in order to ensure the ultimate preservation of the nation.

The repealers often cited King James as their model of a self-interested, yet collective-minded, rational calculator. He was someone who had recognized that his own true interest lay in recognizing the interests of all other English men and women. The king had enacted liberty of conscience, for it "allays Animosities, secures his own Peace, encreases People, augments Trade, advances his Royal Revenue."[17] He could be trusted not to change course in future. He would not overrule liberty of conscience and impose Catholicism on the nation because it was not in his interest to do so. A promise might be broken, but interest "will not Lye."[18]

Any English man or woman could make the same calculations as the king and arrive at the same result, for everyone in the nation, from the monarch at Whitehall to a milliner in Whitechapel, would benefit from the growth in national wealth that liberty would bring. The "Encrease of Trade" would "enrich the whole Kingdom."[19] The imposition of arbitrary religious persecution, repealers argued, had been like putting the nation into a "state of force." In such a state, private property was always at risk of seizure and confiscation. This depressed commercial activity, for "Who will Trade where his gettings are none of his own?"[20] Liberty of conscience, by contrast, "incourages the Inhabitants of any Countrey, to be more Industrious, and more freely to venture their Stocks in Trade, being freed from Vexatious Prosecutions."[21] Security of property rights, underpinned by religious toleration, would lead to increased economic activity.

In a persecuting state, productive labor was wasted by the jailing of able workers whose only crime was that they happened to be noncon-formists.[22] Furthermore, the incidence of persecution and toleration in various nations helped to dictate the movement of peoples, and the nation that could capture the largest number of skilled migrants would prosper.[23] James himself made this point in his *Declaration for Liberty of Conscience*. Religious persecution, he contended, hurts "the Interest of Government, which it destroys by Spoiling Trade, Depopulating Countries, and Discouraging Strangers."[24] England was well positioned to benefit from inward migration, repealers claimed, because it was underpopulated and was not achieving its full economic potential.[25] The population of England had reached a peak of around 5.3 million in the mid-1650s and then declined to 4.9 million by the mid-1680s, a downward trend that was apparent to contemporaries.[26] Toleration could help to counteract these demographic trends. If England could not grow through natural increase, it might grow through increased immigration.

The economic benefits of toleration would redound not only to wealthy traders but also to the nation as a whole. Common laborers would benefit because trade "sets thousands of hands at work, and imploys the poor of the Land." Producers of goods would benefit, as the arrival in England of persecuted groups from abroad would lead to increases in "the Prices of all sorts of Provisions." Even the landed gentry would benefit, for rising national income from trade "advanceth the price of Land, that the Nobles and Gentry have so great a part of."[27] In making these arguments, repealers ignored the effects of inflation in whittling away the value of fixed incomes. They implied that an inflationary tide would lift all boats. It was easy for the repealers to overlook the detrimental effects of inflation because there had been little or no price inflation in England over the previous quarter century; the reign of Charles II had seen stagnation and even deflation in English prices.[28]

In a widely reported speech of October 1687 to the lord mayor and aldermen of London, King James endorsed a growth-based political economy, calling for the upcoming parliament to pass not only liberty of conscience, but also a bill mandating a public registry of lands and a bill for a general naturalization of all foreign immigrants in England, including Jews.[29] According to the earl of Ailesbury, the importance of trade was the king's common theme: "Trade he had much at heart, and his topic was, liberty of conscience and many hands at work in trade." Speaking to his privy council in March 1687, James elevated the importance of trade-based wealth above that of land-based wealth: "nothing can more Conduce to the Peace, and Quiet of this Kingdom, and the Increase of the Number as well as of the Trade of His Subjects (wherein the greatness of a Prince does more Consist then in the Extent of His

Territories) then an intire Liberty of Conscience."[30] The king noted in the 1688 edition of his *Declaration for Liberty of Conscience* that religious toleration would increase the wealth of England and would help the country to compete economically with neighboring states, meaning the Netherlands: "It would perhaps prejudice some of our Neighbours who might lose part of those vast Advantages they now enjoy, if Liberty of Conscience were settled in these Kingdoms, which are above all others most capable of Improvements, and of commanding the Trade of the World."[31] James was committed to encouraging immigration to England, thereby increasing the nation's labor supply and expanding its export industries.

The king's measures were applauded by one repealer, who predicted that the Huguenot refugees fleeing persecution in France would be encouraged by the prospect of naturalization to settle in England. A public registry of lands would also be a boon, increasing the circulation of credit by enabling farmers to borrow against the security of their property. The credit markets had been constrained by the excessive prudence of lenders who, lacking a registry to consult, were wary of the possibility of forged deeds and thus were reluctant to accept land titles as collateral for loans. James's proposed legislation might thaw out these frozen credit markets, this repealer suggested.[32]

The repeal pamphlets promised growth on many fronts: growth of wealth, of population, of credit, of trade, of production, and of demand. Liberty of conscience would serve the collective interests of the English nation; it would not take from the haves to give to the have-nots but would distribute increased benefits to all. This cooperative paradise would, however, end at the water's edge. In discussing international relations, repealers emphasized rivalry above cooperation, championing the selfish interests of the English nation. Repealers presented liberty of conscience as a tactical weapon in a cutthroat competition wherein nations labored to capture trade flows and manufacturing workers from each other. "[The] Nation that giveth Liberty [of conscience], is thereby Inriched," one repealer argued, "for by that means they become a Drein unto those Kingdoms or Nations that do persecute." Repealers claimed that the Dutch had benefited economically from their practice of religious toleration even as other nations, such as the Spanish, had declined by practicing religious persecution.[33]

If the English could succeed in neutralizing the Dutch advantage in matters of religious liberty, repealers argued, they would leapfrog the

Netherlands in economic growth, for England was ten times larger in geographic area and could sustain a larger population. As a pro-repeal poet rhymed, with the stilted diction characteristic of bad political verse, King James's program of liberty of conscience meant that "Holland no longer shall Our People drain; / No more our Wealthy Manufactures gain."[34] The Dutch had long prospered on the backs of other European nations in distress, repealer authors suggested. In the mid-sixteenth century, waves of persecution in France, England, and the Spanish Netherlands had pushed Protestant manufacturers and skilled laborers from France and England to Antwerp and then to Amsterdam. In recent years, one repealer noted, a group of persecuted nonconformists had fled from England to the Netherlands, where they had offered to divulge to their new hosts the secrets of English textile manufacturing. According to the repealers, the Dutch were seeking to maintain their strategic advantage by fomenting opposition to James II's tolerationist proposals, printing anti-repeal pamphlets in Amsterdam and exporting them to England, hoping thereby to prevent the English parliament from enacting toleration.[35]

These naked appeals to economic patriotism and national aggrandizement found little favor with the opponents of repeal. Many Anglicans believed that they would be the losers by liberty of conscience. They worried that gains made by Catholics and dissenters would come at their own expense. Catholics would take away their churches and universities, and nonconformists of all kinds would take away their salaried government offices. Furthermore, their own interests, as they understood them, were cultural and symbolic as well as economic in nature. Many Anglicans wished to live in a nation that was defined by its Protestant character, not by its willingness to tolerate all varieties of faiths, including Catholicism.[36] Anglican disaffection was displayed in the publication of a satirical broadside purporting to be an address from the imaginary "Sect of the Epicureans" to the king. The "Epicureans" sardonically praised the king for teaching "Men to conclude, That there is nothing Sacred or Divine but Trade and Empire, and nothing of such eternal Moment as secular Interest."[37]

The "Good Advice" of the repealers was perhaps more likely to find a receptive audience in the cities, where people of different religions were accustomed to rubbing shoulders with each other in the market, sharing conversations at the coffeehouses and feasting together at the civic guilds.

City dwellers were more likely to depend on someone from another religious group for their livelihood and thus might prove receptive to an appeal to cooperate rather than compete with other religious groups. One anonymous repealer author deployed an urban metaphor in defense of the repeal campaign, comparing the ideal commonwealth envisioned in the king's declaration of indulgence to a maritime port: "Surely in a populous maritime City, we wonder not; nor is it thought inconvenient, that Turks, and Jews, Chinesses, Abyssines, Japanners, or Persions, Italians, French, or Spaniards, or any other remote Nations, frequent the Exchange, and exercise their several Religions, provided they enrich it by Traffick." According to this author, the cosmopolitan values of a bustling *entrepôt* could serve as a model for all of England. Cosmopolitanism would enable members of diverse churches to thrive and prosper as they were assessed not on the contents of their creeds but rather on their commercial abilities, "For in the Kings Indulgence the Subjects are not considered, as conforming to Canons and Constitutions of Churches, but as obedient, grateful, or useful and industrious."[38] In a diverse world, the author suggested, the way to achieve prosperity was to accept cultural differences rather than to ostracize foreigners and thereby destroy the benefits of trade and exchange. Just as a maritime *entrepôt* was enriched by its willingness to grant access to traders from the most remote nations, England would be enriched by accepting its own internal diversity. Religious toleration was not only right in itself; it was also profitable.

The Culture of Repeal

The campaign for liberty of conscience, as the repealers envisioned it, was more than a campaign for legal change; it was an effort to create a more tolerant culture. The repealers believed not only in making toleration but also in making tolerance. The pursuit of liberty of conscience would establish "Concord and Amicable Conversations, in Families, Neighbourhoods, Cities, Common-Wealths and Kingdoms."[39] The new culture of tolerance would require new habits of thought. This would entail the exercise of mental discipline: "Let us apply therefore our Minds to the Promoting [of] this Union . . . Let us all search our Inclinations, and examine our Hearts; if any one discovers there any Sowerness [sourness] or Aversion to Peace . . . Let him purge and discharge it."[40] The new ethos was already emerging in England's capital city, according to one author: "there seems to me to be the beginning of a General happy Settlement, while I see Men of different perswasions in Religion, that before stood at a distance each from the other now, amicably to intermix and unite in their Trade, Correspondencies, and Business; yea, and in the publick Government both of the City and the Kingdom."[41] Another author, employing a civic metaphor, looked forward to the day when "to go under several different [religious] Denominations, shall be no more a Reproach to them, than it is for Citizens to be free of several Companies." King James promoted this culture of civility and tolerance in his speech at Chester when he called on his audience to "shew our selfs Englishmen, and he was sure no Englishman could desire to see others persecuted for differences of opinion."[42] The repealers were attempting to instill habits of sociable behavior.

This cultural shift would involve a rejection of "all Snarling, Quarrelling, Unneighbourly Tempers" and their replacement by new standards of address and composure. The new form of sociability was described as a "Spirit of Wisdom and Moderation," a "true and lasting Brotherly Affection and Harmony," and "the happiest civil Union, that any King and Kingdom were ever blest with."[43] It was depicted metaphorically as a victory of light over darkness. It was rhapsodized as a triumph of clear thinking over superstition: "Too long, too long, has the Noble and Brave Spirits of the English Youth been Oppressed and kept Under. Too long have they been shackled by Religious Mistakes and Superstitious Vanities! Methinks I see the Glorious Sun Arising o'er their Heads, which will Dispel all the Mists of Error, the Clouds of Oppression and Persecution, and will Clear all the Thick and dark Foggs, and let them see their way to Honour." A new age was dawning: "Your Fathers have been long in the Wilderness; but you are the Children of Promise, that must enter the Land of Canaan."[44] A more humane form of social interaction would eclipse religious persecution, which was condemned as "Brutish" and "Irrational."[45] The new Magna Carta for liberty of conscience would inaugurate a new enlightened culture.

Repealer authors did not shy away from describing this culture as a novel one. In place of the customary English veneration of tradition, they offered a forthright rejection of it: "there is too much reverence paid to Antiquity by some; and they are apt to draw very weak Conclusions; and say, Such a Father said such a thing, *ergo*, 'tis true." Repealer thinkers urged their readers to use their powers of reasoning to sift the good from the bad in English tradition. Antiquity ought not always to be followed, especially when opportunities for improvement beckoned, such as "this new Experiment of Liberty." It was not "Presumption" for modern men and women to claim "to be wiser then our fore Fathers." Modern men and women, in seeking to overturn the "unjust, unchristian Laws" that had issued out from the "misguided Zeal" of "our Mistaken or wilful Ancestors," should disregard any arguments from "Antiquity, Custom, and other such weaker Pleas." It was of little moment that the opponents of repeal could claim, "We have the Laws of our side," for the laws in question were "Essentially sinful," being "of such a Nature, as the Devil himself, if he had any shame in him, would even blush, and be ashamed of them." The campaign to repeal the penal laws was hailed as King James's "great revolution."[46] The repealers were revolutionaries.

The Quaker polemicist Ann Docwra exalted James's power to suspend the penal laws, arguing that "It is no new thing for Kings to Suspend superficial Laws." She urged Englishmen and women not to place "the Bond of their Community in the wrong things" such as "Church Traditions." Religious uniformity should not be the basis of citizenship. Instead, a collective willingness to tolerate the faith of others should become the bond of the community. All men and women, Docwra wrote, should be "true to their Principle," should act according to the "inward sense of the love of God in their hearts," and should allow others the liberty to do the same. Liberty of conscience would thus underpin a new and improved form of national community in which "all peaceable people may have rest."[47]

Repealer Constitutionalism

If repeal was a revolution, it was a polite revolution. Persecution was bad for business, it was bad for government, it was disruptive, and it was uncouth. Ann Docwra, William Penn, Henry Care, and other repealer authors sought to institute a new, more civil code of conduct in which people would be friendlier to those of other persuasions. That civility would lead to increased economic activity and social stability. The repealer revolution would reinforce rights of private property rather than disturb them, and it would enhance the king's prestige and power. A newly unified England would assert itself more forcefully in foreign affairs and increase its share of world trade.[48]

Religious toleration, as the repealer authors saw it, was a civilizing process that aimed to minimize social disruption. It was not the liberty to do as one pleased. It was, instead, the liberty to participate in public life on an equal basis with the members of other established Christian groups and the liberty to follow one's conscience, where conscience was defined as a set of practices that was not infinitely variable.[49] Blasphemy would continue to be punished under civil law, for that offense was "criminal in all Religions . . . as being contrary to good manners" and those who committed it "cannot be thought to be men of Conscience." No one could "pretend that it is his Religion to Blaspheme," for the "Light of Nature" was sufficient to show "all Rational Men" that it was wrong.[50]

The repealers proposed a toleration with limits. Those limits were not justified by any clear principle beyond a weak appeal to supposedly universal norms of decency. Most repealers did not address the question of where precisely the limit of toleration should be placed. They failed to specify which religious groups, apart from the major Christian denominations of Stuart England, might be included. Only one repealer, Henry Care, indicated that he supported the right of Jews "to live quietly amongst us," and even he felt compelled to add disparagingly that he would tolerate them "notwithstanding they are open Denyers of our ever blessed Saviour."[51]

Repealers mixed a rhetoric of liberty that seems profoundly whiggish with a rhetoric of obedience to monarchical authority that seems profoundly tory. They have often been misrepresented as men and women with no coherent political ideology beyond sheer opportunism. They were both tactical absolutists and committed constitutionalists. They argued that James should be permitted to use his prerogative powers to suspend the penal laws and Test Acts. But their long-term aim was to put limits on the royal dispensing power in religious matters. The new Magna Carta for liberty of conscience would bind the king just as much as it would bind his people. Their goal was not to elevate parliament above the monarch, or the monarch above parliament; it was to elevate their proposed constitution above both the monarch and the assembly. The logic of their position is similar to the reasoning that led some Enlightenment *philosophes* a century later to align themselves with Frederick the Great of Prussia.[52] The monarch had both the power and the will to push through the reforms that they desired.

The complicated position of the repealers produced some incongruous rhetorical effects. In 1688 a member of the Family of Love, a tiny heterodox group, published a broadside that deployed the language of ultratoryism. This Familist, Elizabeth Rone, used her work to castigate the Anglican ministers who had refused to read the king's *Declaration for Liberty of Conscience* during divine service as commanded. In her view, those ministers had made themselves "Rebels," and they should expect "severe Rebukes" from the king, including the loss of their benefices. Rone left the distinct impression that she would savor those rebukes, like a Hebrew prophet savoring the imminent vengeance of Yahweh. Her work can best be seen as a jeremiad: she condemned the ministers for being "disobedient" to their monarch, "For where his Word is, there should be true Power."[53]

The repealer rhetoric of obedience to the king was vehement, but it was also conditional. Rone qualified her emphasis on obedience by arguing that subjects should obey a monarch's decrees, "Especially when they are Just and Good." A monarch's unjust and bad decrees might not merit the same deference. Most of the repealers, with the exception of a few tories among them, were not aiming to exalt the power of English monarchs in general; they were interested, rather, in exalting the power of one particular monarch at one particular point in time. Future monarchs might prove to be less enlightened than James had been in 1687, and so their powers in matters of religion would need to be constrained. One repealer proposed a clause for the new Magna Carta for liberty of conscience in which James would agree to limit the royal dispensing power by renouncing his power to pardon anyone who committed an act of religious persecution.[54] James later affirmed that he supported liberty of conscience in order to "put it out of the Power of our Successors to Invade" the people's liberties, though this offer was made after he had lost the English throne and had become more willing to surrender royal prerogatives in order to regain it.[55]

The repealers were revolutionaries first and populists a distant second. Rather than rallying behind the *vox populi*, or voice of the people, they emphasized the *salus populi*, or welfare of the people, and they suggested that the people might require some assistance in determining their own true interests.[56] A few went so far as to denigrate the will of the people. One repealer, the scion of a prominent nonconformist family in Bedford, wrote that it was "the misery of this Kingdom, that so much Democrasie is mixed in the Government, that thereby the exercise of the Souvraign power should be in any manner limited by the suffrages of the common people, whose humours are allwayes fluctuating, and the most part of them guided, not by reason, but deliberation like mere animals." The partially democratic nature of English government had served to preserve the nation in earlier times of trial, this writer went on to argue, but its days of usefulness were over, as those same democratic elements were now threatening to destroy the nation.[57]

Other repealers, writing in a more populist vein, preferred to adopt the convenient fiction that the Anglicans were a minority of the English population and that all dissenting groups added together made up a majority.[58] Thus the Anglican parliaments of the 1660s and 1670s, by opposing toleration, had countermanded the will of the people. Some repealers also implied that the parliaments of the 1660s and the 1670s could not be considered truly representative of the nation because they had excluded nonconformists. The repealers were not willing to abide by the votes of parliaments composed largely of what they believed to be intolerant Anglicans. As Henry Care put it, "What better Hopes can Dissenters conceive of another Parliament of Bigotted Churchmen than of the Last?"[59]

When faced with a choice between liberty and democracy, repealers chose liberty. Their aim was to use all means necessary to elect one "honest, able, sober, grave [and] sage" parliament and then to have that ideal parliament pass an act that would forever remove liberty of conscience from the realm of electoral politics. They linked their campaign not to a program for expanded democratic rights—that would merely enshrine the tyranny of the majority—but to an explicit program of limiting the rights of the assembly. The proposed Magna Carta was designed to trump any future legislative act. No mechanism for constitutional amendment was proposed because the repealers did not wish to enable the new law to be amended. The new Magna Carta would be like the "Laws of the Medes and Persian[s]" from biblical times, which were "esteemed unalterable."[60] Such an arrangement would be unprecedented in the English legal tradition, for no parliament had ever bound the proceedings of its successors in such a fashion.

Such measures would hold only as long as future parliaments agreed to enforce them. But the inability to modify or annul the new Magna Carta might well prove troubling to future parliaments. As anyone who had read the biblical book of Daniel would have known, the problem with the irrevocable laws of the Medes and the Persians was that they could have disastrous, unintended consequences. It was just such a law, enacted thoughtlessly by Darius the Persian, that sent the prophet Daniel to the lion's den.

Repealer Cosmopolitanism and the Enlightenment

The repealer emphasis on creating a tolerant culture suggests parallels between their movement and the wider, trans-European movement that became known as the Enlightenment. Repealers deployed many of the themes that were to become part of Enlightenment culture, including tolerance, sociability, civility, the celebration of progress, a lack of deference to arguments from tradition, an attachment to "enlightened" rulers, the adoption of natural rights theory, and metaphors of light triumphing over darkness. Instead of relying on tradition or even on law to dictate the proper functioning of the state, repealers felt free to rely on rational method—"this new Experiment of Liberty."[61] The repealers can be considered one of the bridges between the English "common law mind" of the sixteenth and seventeenth centuries, with its emphasis on stability, permanence, and tradition, and the Enlightenment of the eighteenth century, with its emphasis on perpetual improvement through rational methods. Their new Magna Carta was Janus-faced: it looked both backward and forward, evoking a familiar medieval form and yet offering radical modern implications. They envisioned a brief period of sharp change followed by a long period of stability. Once the revolutionary moment had passed, England's prosperity would come through steady incremental growth, not radical change. Their metaphor of a journey to Canaan was apt, for once they reached the promised land no further journeys would be necessary. The repealer revolution would end, as Docwra put it, in "rest."[62]

Repealers, despite their emphasis on the role of rational argument, rarely cited Continental philosophers of toleration, with the exception of two references to Grotius.[63] Samuel Pufendorf and Pierre Bayle went unacknowledged. The great majority of the repealers' citations were to the Bible and to works of history, with occasional glancing references to Jeremy Taylor's writings on toleration from the 1640s.[64]

This is not to say that repealers were insular in their thinking. While philosophical texts by foreign authors appeared rarely in their pamphlets, examples of foreign practices appeared regularly. Their chosen examples ranged from across the globe and across time. Repealers aimed to demonstrate that many nations and empires had permitted religious diversity without suffering ill effects. The success of the Ottoman Empire was attributed by one author to toleration: "even among the Mahumetans, all over Turk[e]y, no man is compell'd to embrace the Mahumetan Superstition, but that all People, unless the Professors of Heathenish Idolatry, are left to the exercise of their own Religion. And this, as several Authors observe, was at first the chiefest means by which the Turks enlarged their Empire over the Christian World. For that many People rather chose to live under the Turk, permitting them the Liberty of their Consciences, then under the Exorbitant Tyranny of the Spanish Inquisition."[65] Previous English authors had occasionally referred to the tolerance of Muslims for Christians and Jews living in their midst, but rarely in as admiring a fashion as this.[66] English authors typically depicted the Ottoman sultans as tyrants and their peoples as enslaved. Not so in this case.

Instead of the customary appeal to English xenophobia, this repealer author sought to use a foreign empire as a positive example. The Orientalist binary was here reversed, with the "other" being preferred to the "self." The Turks were not villains to be anathematized but models to be followed. This example worked in part by evoking one form of English xenophobia, the fear of the "Exorbitant Tyranny of the Spanish Inquisition," in order to depict another feared group, the Turks, as tolerant by comparison. The same author even noted that the Turks had provided sanctuary to a persecuted population from Spain, the Moriscos, who had been driven from their homes by King Philip III: "nothing has rendered the Turk more powerful then the King of Spain's Expulsion of all the Moors and Turks out of his Territories, in the Year 1609, at what time above a Hundred and twenty Thousand of those Exiles retir'd into Africa and other parts of the Turkish Dominions, to the great benefit of the Turks, who learnt from them to Combat the Europeans with their own Weapons, and their own Arts of War."[67] This was an overstatement of the military impact of the expulsion of the Moriscos, and it is unclear from what sources the repealer author drew these conclusions. Although a few of the Morisco exiles did join privateering efforts against the Spanish, most settled peacefully in Turkey and North Africa, if they were able to find new homes at all.[68] The pseudohistorical example of the Moriscos' purported transference of Spanish military technology to the Ottomans served to sustain the author's larger argument that empires grow stronger when they practice openness to outsiders but weaken when they insist on unity of religious belief. This admiration of the Ottomans was conceivable in 1687, at a time when England was not in a position of global dominance and could more readily look to foreign examples for models of how to thrive. The Ottomans had reached the apex of their power in Europe only four years earlier, challenging the Holy Roman Emperor at the gates of Vienna. With success came respect.

Another repealer, the London tobacconist Giles Shute, made a similarly admiring observation of an overseas empire: "A few hours since, an Acquaintance of mine who came lately from the East Indies, told me, That there are 88 several Cast[e]s of persons, under the Government of the Great Mogull; that is, 88 several Sects or Opinions: And yet notwithstanding, they do all agree together very well, as to that point, and they do not Persecute, or Molest, or meddle one with the others Perswasion or Opinion in that way and manner: But are all subject to the higher Powers, and the Government takes no notice of their several Opinions or Cast[e]s, one more then another. But the powers are equally extended alike to all, for their Safety and Protection."[69] The London tobacconist's understanding of the caste system in India was highly imperfect and based more on anecdote than serious study. But he correctly noted the remarkable religious diversity of the Mughal Empire, choosing the arbitrary figure of "88" to denote the number of religions that thrived under Mughal rule. Religious diversity was no hindrance to social cohesion, provided that all religious groups practiced tolerance, agreeing not to stigmatize members of other groups. This was the case, Shute argued, in the Mughal Empire of the late seventeenth century. The emperor at the time, Aurangzeb, was in fact less tolerant of religious diversity than some of his predecessors had been. But in Shute's retelling of his friend's story, the emperor held together his composite empire through toleration, acting as a neutral arbiter and taking "no notice" of the religious opinions of his subjects. The point here was not to describe Aurangzeb's policies accurately but rather to shift the needle of English opinion by profiting from the credibility that merchants possessed in discussing foreign customs.

The Ottoman sultans and Mughal emperors governed composite empires, administering a diversity of peoples and using toleration to unify disparate groups.[70] The repealers wished to imitate their success.

They searched ~~cross-cul~~turally for available models of how to cope with religious diversity. Shute claimed to have received his information from a friend who had recently returned from the East Indies. This claim placed his story in a context of imperial encounter. As a tobacconist, retailing a product that had traveled across an ocean, he was connected to international networks of trade and communication. His shop, which was located in London's Limehouse ward, would have been filled with advertisements and trade cards alluding to the imperial origins of his goods. The community of Limehouse was centered around the docks and wharves on the Thames at the eastern edge of London, and his customers would have included many sailors. His cosmopolitanism was suggested by his eagerness to offer the Mughals as a positive model to be emulated. Shute and other tolerationists were seeking to emulate cultural practices that had proved to be workable in other societies. Although Shute is not known to have traveled abroad, other repealers had: Charles Nicholets voyaged to India and William Penn sailed to America.[71]

The anonymous repealer author who had praised the Ottomans also referred to Safavid Iran as a positive example, noting the willingness of the Persians to tolerate religious minorities in their midst, including Jews, Armenian Christians, Nestorian Christians, Melkite Christians, and "the Dissenting Sects in their own Religion," presumably meaning the Ismailis and Sufis.[72] Other repealers looked to emperors of the ancient world as exemplars. Henry Care praised the fourth-century emperor Valentinian I for permitting religious freedom in the Roman Empire.[73] Another favorite example was Cyrus of Persia, who founded the Achaemenid Empire in the ancient Near East. Cyrus held together his composite empire by granting freedom of religion to his subject peoples, including the Jews, whom he allowed to return to Judea from their exile in Babylon. The repealers frequently referred to King James as a new Cyrus.[74] This analogy was highly flattering to James, for it elevated him to imperial status, suggested that he deserved immortal fame, and depicted him as the indispensable centripetal force holding disparate groups together.

Repealers proposed a trans-historical vision of toleration as a method of governance that could stabilize any nation at any time. Within an English context this social form was innovatory, but elsewhere it was commonplace. In addition to the Safavids, Ottomans, and Mughals, repealers cited Switzerland, Poland, the Netherlands, and several German states where Catholics and Protestants practiced toleration and in some cases shared civic offices.[75] Repealer thinking was based on a universalized view of how human societies could thrive. Toleration, repealers argued, was a pragmatic response to diversity. It had powered the rise of the Ottoman Empire to greatness, and it could also power the rise of the English to greatness, so that the king of England might "hold again the Ballance of Europe" as his medieval ancestors had done.[76] Any nation or empire could use religious toleration to succeed.

The opponents of repeal, by contrast, used foreign examples primarily to instill fear, not envy. They circulated reports of the recent persecutions of Protestants in France and the Piedmont and warned that this could happen in England. They contended that the repealer project was ultimately a foreign Catholic plot to overthrow the Church of England, engineered by Jesuits who were disguising themselves as nonconformists and whispering in the king's ear. They drew on the potent themes of English anti-popery, where the popish "other" was anathematized.[77]

The repealers were animated by a different process of self-creation. Their writings emphasized the theme of adaptation, especially adaptation to diversity. Adaptation was a repealer trope in part because it was a nonconformist imperative. English nonconformists, whether Protestant dissenters or Catholics, needed to be aware not only of their own religious traditions, but also of the dominant religious tradition in their society so that they could find ways to mediate between the two. Some developed strategies for "passing" as Anglicans to avoid giving offense. These were the partial conformists and church papists, who occasionally attended Church of England services to qualify for public office or to evade recusancy fines. Others, such as the Quakers, refused to adopt such strategies, but they too needed to know the dominant religious tradition in order to calculate precisely when they wanted to give offense.

For nonconformists, adaptation to the "other" was a way of life. This was reflected in repealer writings. Henry Care, who seems to have been a Presbyterian but occasionally "passed" as an Anglican, argued that Englishmen had much to learn from some foreigners.[78] He referred to the example of Saga za Ab, an Ethiopian Christian whose account of his beliefs had been published by the Portuguese humanist Damiao de Góis. Za Ab was an ambassador from King Lebna Dengel of Ethiopia to the Portuguese court in the early sixteenth century. The ambassador had reproved Europeans for their religious discord, arguing that "there is no reason to Dispute so sharply touching Ceremonies, but rather that every one should observe and keep his own, without hating or troubling others." Care quoted this statement approvingly and went on to describe the Ethiopian's attitude as an example for all Englishmen and women: "Will not this Discourse from a Moor, make us European Christians Blush? Behold! a Man come from the utmost parts of the Earth, to teach us that Moderation and Mutual Forbearance, the practice whereof too many of us do not only Neglect, but wilfully Oppose."[79] Care's statement drew on the rhetorical tradition of the "quanto maius" trope favored by early Renaissance thinkers, in which a pagan virtue was used to condemn a Christian vice.[80] The repealer author made little effort to examine who Saga za Ab spoke for or how his church functioned. Instead, he simply pointed to him as the ultimate "other," noting that za Ab was African and suggesting hyperbolically that he came from the "utmost parts of the Earth." The rhetorical force of Care's example stemmed from his opposition of the words "Moore" and "European" and his suggestion that Africans should not be permitted to trump Europeans in matters of enlightenment and justice. The "other," in this example, became a stick with which to beat the English into mending their ways.

The Irish Example

Repealers looked east rather than west. They had relatively little to say about patterns of toleration in England's Atlantic empire. This was a curious lacuna given that one of the leading repealers was also the founder and namesake of a colony in America.[81] Repealers may have avoided mentioning the Atlantic colonies so as not to draw attention to the oldest of those colonies, which threatened to refute their case for the economic benefits of toleration. Even the most ingenious of the repealers could not depict Irish politics as a potential win-win situation. In the 1650s, under Oliver Cromwell, most of the lands of the Irish Catholic majority had been seized and dispersed to Protestants. The Catholics, understandably, wanted these lands back, and the Protestants, understandably, did not wish to return them. A bare toleration of Roman Catholic worship might not upend the Protestant ascendancy, but the admission of Catholics into political life and public offices threatened to do so, for they would prevail in any political battle by sheer force of numbers. Catholic emancipation might lead to economic growth in the long term, but it would cause massive capital flight immediately. And indeed, Irish Protestants began to send their capital abroad early in James's reign, when he began to appoint Catholics to Irish military and civil offices, although the Irish trade held up longer than many observers expected.[82]

In England, by contrast, the repealers could claim plausibly that James's *Declaration for Liberty of Conscience* had helped to bring economic growth. The economy remained buoyant throughout James II's reign. Customs receipts increased by about 10 percent from 1683–1684 to 1687–1688, while the yield from the excise and hearth taxes increased by a third from 1683–1684 to 1687–1688. Foreign trade peaked in 1686–1688 and did not attain those heights again for at least another decade. More tons of coal were shipped from Newcastle in the fiscal year 1687–1688 than at any other point in the seventeenth century. The economic boom of the later 1680s coincided with favorable weather conditions that brought the best run of harvests in living memory. The harvests in 1685 and 1686 were good, and those in 1687 and 1688 were especially abundant.[83] Repealers were quick to crow about this bounty. The natural philosopher Richard Burthogge rejoiced that, since the king's declaration of toleration, "Trade, which, before, lay ev'n gasping for Life . . . is Recover'd to a wonder, and grown Brisk and Quick."[84] Henry Care noted that "since his Majesties late Indulgence, Trade is visibly encreased."[85] James was not unaware of the propaganda benefits of the expanding economy. He instructed his circuit court judges in the summer of 1688 to trumpet the increase in trade and to attribute it to the effects of his *Declaration for Liberty of Conscience*.[86]

The opponents of the repealers did not attempt to refute these claims. Whether or not England had recently experienced incremental gains in its prosperity was immaterial, for those gains would be more than wiped out by the sudden and catastrophic decline they prophesied should the penal laws and Test Acts be repealed.[87] Opponents of repeal warned the dissenters that supporting repeal would mean purchasing a temporary toleration for themselves at the expense of sacrificing the future well-being of Protestant England. They warned the Anglicans that the king's measures would strip them of their property rights. The lands once owned by the medieval Catholic abbeys before their dissolution under Henry VIII would be confiscated from their present owners

and returned to the Catholic Church. The ejection of the Magdalen College fellows was but a foretaste, they alleged, of the coming ejection of
Anglicans from sinecures and public offices across the country.[88] The
risks, they contended, were too grave to permit any experimentation.
The forces of Counter-Reformation Catholicism were gathering strength.
James's "new Experiment of Liberty" would mean England's unilateral
disarmament in the face of this threat. Against the repealer hope of
gradual increases in prosperity, they offered a prediction of sudden and
utter calamity.

Both the repealers and their opponents were forward-looking,
attempting to extrapolate from current trends and to predict whether
royal policies would bring riches or ruin. It has recently been suggested
that growth-oriented whigs would have found little to entice them in
James II's vision of political economy.[89] But it is important to note that
not all reform-minded whigs were on the side of the opposition in 1688;
many endorsed the king's program.[90] These reformers were attracted by
James's political economy, rather than repelled by it. They anticipated
economic benefits not only from a parliamentary toleration but also
from the king's proposals for a public registry of lands and a general
naturalization of all foreign immigrants in England. They saw little to
fear in these proposals and much to hope for. The future, for them, was
bright.[91]

The opposition saw storms ahead. Their fears of a looming catas-
trophe were evident in the metaphors they chose to describe England's
potential future. These metaphors were often aquatic. Many Anglicans
thought of the penal laws and Tests as a "bulwark" against a rising
"tide" of popery. The Test Acts must not be abandoned, one Anglican
wrote in 1685, "for had we suffered such a breach in the Mounds of
o[u]r Church, a spring-tyde of popery wo[u]ld have raged." The king's
design, some feared, was to "make a breach to lett in popery as a mighty
torrent among us."[92] In modern times, aquatic language has tended to
be deployed as a metaphor for revolutions, with popular uprisings
depicted as a wave of protests overcoming the entrenched bulwarks of
tyranny. But the opponents of repeal did not adopt aquatic metaphors
to describe their own movement. The wave, in this case, was not on the
side of the Anglicans; instead, it was on the side of the king. At least
some of the king's opponents in 1688 saw themselves as repelling an
upheaval rather than creating one.

3

Fearing the Unknown

Anti-Popery and Its Limits

"My imagination grew stronger as the glass went about faster." It was an autumn evening in the year 1678, and John Potenger, an Anglican gentleman, had been invited to the home of a Catholic family, the Tichbornes, for dinner. He had a bit too much to drink, and the alcohol heightened his suspicions that something about his dinner companions was not quite right. Only a few days before, the Anglican justice of the peace Sir Edmund Berry Godfrey had gone missing in London. He was later found in a ditch with a sword protruding through his back, his death a mystery that was never solved. Shortly before he went missing, the justice had heard the testimony of the informer Titus Oates regarding the existence of a vast popish conspiracy to overturn the Protestant faith in England. As word of the justice's disappearance spread, many English Protestants jumped to the conclusion that he had been snatched by Catholics before he could alert the nation to the plot. This alarming news from London was very much on Potenger's mind as he sat at dinner with the Tichbornes. He began to wonder whether his hosts had something to do with the disappearance of the Protestant justice. Something about the way in which they discussed the rumors of a Catholic plot gave him a sneaking suspicion. He abruptly took his leave of the assembled company and summoned his footman, who proved even less sober. The two mounted their horses, but the footman, no better able to hold his seat than his liquor, fell off. A Catholic gentleman kindly offered to take Potenger home in his coach, but he insisted on leaving alone. He dismounted, took the reins of the two horses in hand and hurried off into the darkness, abandoning his footman.

As Potenger later described it, "In the open air, the Plot and the wine began to work, and I thought myself in as great danger as Dr. Oat[e]s said the nation was." He drew his sword and walked down the road in the pale light. He passed by a house, where he saw a young maid, who was "frighted to see me with my sword in one, and my horses in the other, hand." To stop her from raising an alarm, he moved toward the front of the house to block her exit. But she went out the back and cried for help. A group of local villagers gathered, eager to hunt down any Catholic plotters. Potenger heard them coming and took off, jumping over a fence and abandoning his horses. He hid in a ditch as the mob passed. He then moved away from the road and came to a house in the woods where he decided to seek help. The residents of the house were "very full of questions, believing me to be a conspirator, who came from Tichbourne house." He assured them he was not a Catholic, and they decided to send for a local gentleman, who helped to get him back home. A day or so later, Potenger was able to retrieve his horses from the local parishioners, though their leader told him that if they had caught him that night, they would have "certainly killed" him, as they took him "for a plotter."[1]

John Potenger's midnight ramble was not an isolated event; it represented a pattern of suspicious thinking that seized many English Protestants at the time of the supposed "Popish Plot" in 1678 and threatened to do so again in James II's reign. Many English Protestants in the late seventeenth century were convinced that their faith was being threatened by a plot to reestablish Catholicism as the authorized religion in England to the exclusion of all other faiths. They believed that this plot might lead to the execution of Protestant martyrs as in Queen Mary Tudor's days. They worried that the plot extended to the highest authorities, even to the king's closest advisors, and that, as a result, the monarch could not necessarily be trusted to rescue the nation from the plot.

These were the sorts of excessive fears the repealers were worried about. They were well aware of what might be termed the "paranoid style" of English politics, and they knew that these fears could be used to rally opposition to their proposals. Their ultimate goal was to set up a new framework of governance that would channel human energies away from conspiratorial thinking. They argued for a cultural shift in which individuals would attempt to master their passions, quiet their fears, and adopt an attitude of mutual trust. They sought to set up a legal structure—the new Magna Carta for liberty of conscience—that would help to restrain the nation's tendency to indulge in fears and rumors. They wanted Protestants like John Potenger to stop getting drunk on their suspicions, to control their impulses, and to behave more abstemiously.

King James was aware of his subjects' "fears and jealousies", and believed that these passions constituted a threat to the stability of his realm. As duke of York, James had urged his friends not to focus on "the imaginary dangers of Popery."[2] He was concerned about anti-popish fears in part because they had nearly deprived him of his crown before he had been able to assume it. The Popish Plot crisis of 1678–1681 had been provoked by the unsolved murder of Sir Edmund Berry Godfrey. As an atmosphere of crisis took hold, the nascent whig party formed and engaged in a failed effort to pass a bill through parliament excluding James from the succession on the grounds of his Catholicism. Many of the whigs argued that there was a Catholic plot to place James on the throne by having his older brother, Charles, assassinated. There was in fact no such plot, but the fears and rumors coursing through London helped to destabilize Charles's government and lent urgency to the cause of exclusion. The exclusionists were beaten back in part by Charles's savvy use of his prerogative powers to call and dismiss parliaments and in part by a broad-based loyalist reaction against what was seen as whig overreaching.

Historians often contend that by the time of James's accession in 1685 the political crisis surrounding the Popish Plot had largely passed and that any resumption of the crisis thereafter was primarily the king's fault.[3] It is true that James's accession was widely celebrated in England, even though the new king was a Catholic. But "fears and jealousies" of popery had not dissipated by 1685. Soon after the accession, anonymous letters were sent to the mayors of many of the parliamentary boroughs noting that the new king was a "papist," bidding them to "stand to their guard," and warning that the nation might soon be "overwhelm'd with popery." Early in that year, the bishop of Carlisle urged the Westmorland gentleman Sir Daniel Fleming to seek election to parliament, exhorting him privately that "all true sons of the Church of England were bound in Conscience to help now to defend her, when she was very likely to be in great danger."[4] Many English Protestants remained wary about the new king's intentions. Anti-popish fears had not been laid to rest by the peaceful accession of a Catholic king.

James dreaded a resumption of the anti-popish furor of 1678. He proceeded to take steps that he thought might settle the fears of his subjects. The rhetoric he deployed to counter the fears of popery could be described as a kind of anti-anti-popery. James instructed the high court judges sent out on circuit to "remove as much as may be all Fears and Jealousies that are endeavour'd to be insinuated by Persons ill affected to the Government." He gave similar instructions to his electoral agents in Wales, who were told to "remove as much as may be all feares and jealousies out of the peoples minds by telling them his Majestie only designes the universall happinesse of his people." The king's charm offensive was strengthened by his suspension of the laws against religious nonconformity. In his *Declaration for Liberty of Conscience,* published in 1687, he expressed his hope that "the Freedom and Assurance We have hereby given in relation to Religion and Property, might be sufficient to remove from the Minds of Our Loving Subjects all Fears and Jealousies in relation to either."[5] James's attention was fixed on his subjects' "fears and jealousies," and he worked to dispel them. The repealer movement was, in part, an effort to counter anti-popish anxieties. But those fears were not so easily dispelled. John Potenger, for one, was not easily persuaded; like many of his anti-popish compatriots, he opposed the repeal campaign in 1687 and 1688.[6]

Fears and Jealousies of Popery

The phrase "fears and jealousies," so often employed by the king over the course of his reign, was not a new coinage. It appeared regularly in pre-Civil War polemic and gained greater currency in the early 1670s when it was commonly applied to fears about popery. In 1672 Samuel Parker, the future bishop of Oxford, issued a work titled *A Preface Shewing what Grounds there are of Fears and Jealousies of Popery* in which he argued that grounds for those fears were lacking. This provoked a furious debate with Andrew Marvell, who responded in the same year with his *Rehearsal Transpros'd.* Parker and Marvell continued the debate with further salvos, thereby bringing greater attention to the "fears and jealousies" of popery.[7] Over the course of the 1670s and 1680s, "fears and jealousies" became a common meme: a quick handle by which an author could refer to the concept of "anti-popery" in an era when the term itself was not in common use. Even the journalist Roger L'Estrange, who was unusual in employing the term "anti-popery" at least once, in

1679, tended to rely instead on the phrase "fears and jealousies," presumably because of its greater currency.[8]

By employing the phrase "fears and jealousies," a writer or speaker could reframe the issues surrounding anti-popery. In this new diagnosis, the problem to be solved was no longer popery but rather fears of popery. As one critic of anti-popery wrote in 1688, striking a theme that would recur in modern history, "We have now nothing to Fear, but the Dismal Effects of Popular Fears."[9] Mitigating those fears might involve countering popular anxieties rather than restricting the political activities of Catholics. The repealer journalist Henry Care took this line of argument in April 1688: "Who cries out POPERY and ARBITRARY GOVERN-MENT, now, Gentlemen? . . . Who are they that repine and mutter, and would be clapping Dutch Spectacles on People's Noses, (tinctur'd with Fears and Jealousies,) to represent all Actions of the Government in false Colours, and frightful Shapes?"[10] In this metaphor, anti-popery was depicted as a pair of tinted spectacles that colored the perceptions of those who wore them. Care's description of these spectacles as "Dutch" in design was a reference to the pamphlets, many with anti-popish themes, printed in Holland and smuggled into England in 1688. The Dutch agenda, according to Care, was to alienate the English from their government by deploying anti-popish "Fears and Jealousies."[11]

In Care's understanding of contemporary political discourse, anti-popery acted like a lens that influenced people's interpretations of events. If the lens were to be removed, he hoped, then people would cease to see the "Actions of the Government" in "frightful Shapes" but instead would see them as they really were. His goal was to counter popular fears by encouraging his readers to support a general liberty of conscience, which would diminish any worries that one religion could dominate all the others. Misperceptions of Catholics would vanish. As he put it in another tract, a general liberty of conscience would eliminate the "Fears and Jealousies" of "All Parties."[12]

Tory and Whig Critiques of Anti-Popery

Early modern Englishmen and Englishwomen were not blind to the power of anti-popery in their society. Some sought to harness that power for their own ends, while others sought to oppose it. Protestant opposition to anti-popery during James II's reign can be reduced to two main types: one that was articulated by Anglican tories who supported the king's policies because they believed it was their duty to do so, and another that was articulated by dissenters and whigs who supported those policies because they believed it was in their interest to do so. The first type was a new variant on an older genre of opposition to anti-popery, expressed with greater intensity now that the king himself was leading the attacks. The second type was more innovative; it represented an abandonment by certain whig authors of their prior positions.

The two types of rhetoric, tory and whig, used similar methods for different ends. Both used the phrase "fears and jealousies" to refer to anti-popery. Both were torn by competing impulses: the desire to extinguish "fears and jealousies" altogether, thereby ensuring peace and prosperity for the kingdom, and the desire to retarget the "fears and jealousies" of the populace onto their enemies. The tory instinct was often to reorient public fears away from the king and Catholicism and toward rebellion and nonconformity. The whig writers who opposed anti-popery often sought to vilify the Anglican "persecutors" who were said to be fomenting these fears.

Some tory Anglicans supported James II in his critique of anti-popery because they had never been inclined to give any credit to anti-popish rhetoric and arguments. For them, anti-popery was alarmingly reminiscent of the Puritan rhetoric of the early seventeenth century. The tory dean of Durham, Denis Granville, wrote near the end of James II's reign that he had long been horrified by "Caballs to encrease Fears, and Jealousyes." These cabals had encouraged English subjects to rebel against their lawful lord. Granville believed that "a great number of Roman Catholicks in England have been highly loyall to their King," unlike the dissenters, "whose principles are Antimonarchicall, and destructive of Kingly Government." As a consequence, he averred, "my Fears and Jealousyes, runne quite a contrary way to most Men's with whom I converse, i.e, I am more affraid of the Subjects running into Rebellion, then I am of my Princes Exercising Tyranny, and more Jealous, that People, who call themselves sons of the Ch[urch] of England, will, rather than their King, destroy their Religion."[13] Granville denounced the widespread rumors that the Catholic King James would destroy the Church of England, but he did not condemn fear itself, which could have its place. For him, the proper object of "fears and jealousies" was not Catholicism, but rebellion.

The dean of Durham criticized anti-popery on prudential grounds as a source of instability, faction, and caballing. As he warned the clergy of Durham in a speech shortly after the invasion of William of Orange, there was a type of person who had "suck'd in sedition with his milk, [and who] is Antimonarchicall (whiles hee pretends to be Antipapisticall) in his nature." Three months earlier he had expressed his forebodings that the government and the Church of England might suffer ill consequences from anti-popish fears: with people "now agitated more than ever by an intemperate zeale against Popery," many were caught up in "an excessive fear that Popery will come in."[14] For Granville, William's invasion was the culmination of those intemperate fears. Shortly after preaching against the invasion and decrying the influence of the "Anti-papisticall" republicans, the dean departed England and joined his exiled king at Saint-Germain-en-Laye.

Opposition to anti-popery of the sort expressed by Granville was a rhetorical strategy with a long heritage. It had been a staple of antiexclusionist rhetoric during the crisis of 1678–1681 and of antinonconformist rhetoric before then. The centerpiece of this argument was historical in nature, relying for its persuasive power on an analogy between currently existing forms of anti-popery and the forms of antipopery that had been common in England on the eve of the Civil War. According to this line of reasoning, anti-popish rhetoric had in the past led to rebellion, disloyalty, faction, strife, and even the killing of the king; if permitted to propagate itself, it might do the same again.[15] To be a certain kind of high tory was to oppose exclusion, rebellion, and revolution and to reject explicitly the anti-popish tropes that underpinned these political maneuvers. This form of critique helps to explain the continuity of high tory, or ultra-loyalist, support for James II, from the successful efforts by loyalists to defeat any attempts to exclude the duke of York from the throne, to the willingness of many ultra-loyalists in the Parliament of 1685 to accept the king's employment of Catholic officers, to their taking up arms in defense of James during the Revolution of 1688–1689, to their tendency to become nonjurors and Jacobites in the 1690s.[16]

Such a man was Thomas Cartwright, dean of Ripon and later bishop of Chester. In the 1670s and early 1680s, he published a series of monarchist sermons that brought him to the attention of the court and led to his elevation to the episcopate by James II in 1686. He supported the religious policies of the king who elevated him, including the suspension of the penal laws against nonconformity and of the Test Acts that barred Catholics from serving in public office. He was friendly with Catholics but hostile to many dissenters. Upon the Revolution, he fled to France and then followed James to Ireland, where he contracted dysentery and died in 1689. There was some expectation that he would convert to Catholicism on his deathbed, but he defied these expectations by remaining an Anglican.[17] In his published writings during the reign of James II, he excoriated anti-popery as both impolitic and disloyal: "Railing therefore against Popery cannot produce any good Effect, and at this time it may easily produce many bad ones; among which none can be worse, than the Contempt which it will throw upon the King himself, on whom all Ill Language against his Religion, does ultimately redound to the debasing of him in the esteem of his Subjects."[18] Cartwright contended that "A Papist may be a Friend to Liberty, and a known Enemy to Persecution," pointing to the king as a prominent example of this. Anti-popery, he argued, "tends not so much to arm the Hearers against Popery, as to possess them with an hatred of their Sovereign for professing it" and was a form of "Sedition under the disguise of Zeal." The ill effect of "the groundless Jealousies of Popery's coming in" was that it "alarums the Rabble." Attacks on Catholics might be expected from "Anabaptists or Presbyterians" but should not be heard from "any True Son of the Church of England," who must not forget that Roman Catholics "are Englishmen and good Christians." As he told the fellows of Magdalen College in 1687, "Our Nation is in greater danger of being destroyed by Prophanness [profaneness], then Popery."[19]

These proudly loyalist arguments were echoed by Edmund Elys, another tory cleric who, like Cartwright, refused to endorse the Glorious Revolution and refused the oaths to William and Mary. Elys's career lacked the meteoric arc of Cartwright's; he remained the rector of East Allington in Devon until his deprivation after the Revolution. In a pair of pamphlets published in 1687, he advocated the repeal of the laws penalizing Catholics on the grounds that they were "Persons very Ingenious, very Well bred," who had proved their loyalty to the king by helping to suppress Monmouth's Rebellion. He exhorted his readers not to "be Affrighted by the Pharisaicall Multitude from Acknowledging All the Truth we find Profest, and all the Virtue we find Practiced by

Papists." He maintained that the Church of Rome was "a True Church" and that all Christians must, therefore, "exercise towards Persons of that Communion, not only Common Charity, but Brotherly Love." For these reasons Elys urged the Church of England to support the king's campaign against the penal laws.[20]

In opposing anti-popery, the ultra-loyalists were following King James's lead. In March 1686, James issued directions to the preachers of the Church of England commanding them to steer clear of controversial matters, meaning the theological differences between Catholicism and Protestantism. He also commanded his own Catholic priests not to "meddle with controversies." In a letter to the English archbishops, he provided a rationale for his instructions: he was concerned that some "men of unquiet and Factious Spirits" might preach in such a manner as would stir up "Fears and Jealousies" in their parishioners.[21] When John Sharp, dean of Norwich and rector of St. Giles-in-the-Fields, preached an anti-popish sermon in defiance of the new orders, the king ordered the bishop of London to ban him from preaching on the grounds that Sharp had insinuated "Fears and Jealousies to dispose them [his audience] to Discontent."[22] The bishop refused to comply and was called before the newly formed Ecclesiastical Commission, which eventually suspended him. The king's strategy might have worked if the anti-popish preachers really had been a few "men of unquiet and Factious Spirits," as he alleged, but they were in truth a considerable group of the most talented preachers in the Church of England. They had substantial support among the episcopate and were not easily marginalized. Heavy-handed efforts to restrict their preaching only incensed their supporters. The king persisted, nevertheless, in his campaign to restrict anti-popish preaching, telling the Scottish privy council to take "care that there be no Preachers or others suffered to insenuate into the people any feares or jealousies."[23]

Some tories followed the king's lead into the repealer movement. Thomas Cartwright became a repealer author, publishing anonymously the pamphlets *A Letter from a Clergy-Man* and *A Modest Censure of the Immodest Letter to a Dissenter.* He argued for the repeal of the penal laws and Test Acts on the classic loyalist grounds that, since the king had requested it, his people should accommodate him.[24] Cartwright, who had long been a proponent of the persecution of dissenters, reversed his stance in 1687, arguing that since the government no longer thought that dissenters were dangerous, the penal laws were no longer necessary. This abrupt reversal reflected an Erastian submissiveness to civil government that was a hallmark of Cartwright's politics.[25] Denis Granville accepted the new toleration policy much more grudgingly, noting with evident dismay that King James "Hath thought Expedient (in his Wisdome and Good pleasure) to take downe some part of our Fence, by Granting a generall Liberty, to the numerous Pretenders to Religion and sincerity, quietly to enjoy each their several way of w[orshi]p." The "Pretenders" to religion had found favor with the king, and the Church of England must therefore yield to the ruler's wishes, even if it meant losing part of their "Fence" against nonconformity. Like many tories, Granville associated the nonconformists with insubordination to royal authority. He went on to state that it was his obligation as a loyal subject to "submit to his Majesties Good Pleasure, (God blesse him) even in this, the most unintelligible act of his kindnesse."[26] But Granville never became an active participant in the repealer movement; his obedience went only so far. This was a common position among ultra-loyalist Anglicans: they were willing to do what James asked them to do, but not always with great enthusiasm, especially when they believed that the king was acting against his own best interests.

The whig supporters of James's toleration campaign attacked anti-popery from a different angle. When they took up the repealer cause, many found themselves reversing a lifetime of arguments about the dangers of popery. Henry Care had been one of the most emphatic exponents of anti-popery during the Popish Plot crisis, editing the stridently anti-popish serials, the *Popish Courant* and the *Weekly Pacquet of Advice from Rome*. Less than a decade later, the former tribune of anti-popery was editing a newspaper that criticized anti-popery, *Publick Occurrences Truly Stated*. In this political *volte-face* he was accompanied by the dramatist Elkanah Settle, who had penned some of the most vicious anti-popish satires and pamphlets published in Charles II's reign, but then succeeded Care as editor of *Publick Occurrences* after the latter's death in August 1688.[27]

Whig critiques of anti-popery, like their tory counterparts, alleged that anti-popery was a mask used to disguise a malevolent agenda. But where James II's tory supporters saw anti-popery as a cover for rebellion, his whig supporters saw it as a cover for self-interest. Care alleged that anti-popish authors were motivated by antipathy to toleration, not

antipathy to popery. Their dislike of toleration stemmed from their self-
interested desire to monopolize political power by pushing dissenters
out of lucrative public offices. It was for this reason that they opposed
James II's toleration campaign. As Care wrote in number fifteen of his
Publick Occurrences: "Nor indeed is this their Apprehension of Popery,
more real than their concern for the Illegality of the Declaration [for
Liberty of Conscience], yet both conveniently serve the Ends designed:
For tho[ugh] it would be much more honest, yet it would not be so
decent nor so politick, to say bluntly, 'We have got a jolly number of
Laws on our sides, whereby we have Engrossed to our own Party, all the
Preferments of the Nation, with Power to Crush all other [religious]
Perswasions . . . We have found the sweets hereof for many years, and
made the Dissenters of all sorts tremble before us.'" By "a jolly number
of Laws," Care was alluding to the discriminatory acts, including the
Corporation Act of 1661 and the Test Act of 1673, that he had enumer-
ated in *Draconica*, a published compendium of the penal laws then in
force. Those laws, he alleged, had been designed to bar non-Anglicans
from public office, so that Anglicans might reserve the "Preferments of
the Nation" for themselves.[28] Anti-popish attacks on King James's *Declaration for Liberty of Conscience* were, in Care's view, nothing more than
a cover for selfish ambition.

Settle had made a similar argument in 1683 when he had issued a
dramatic recantation of his prior views on anti-popery. In his recantation, he had argued that anti-popery was a ladder for ambitious politicians: "tho' Religion and Property are the pretended Quarrel against
the great Pilots above, their real Greivance is that their own hands are
not at the Rudder." His own anti-popish writings, he now averred, had
been motivated more by his "Malevolent spirit of Revenge" than by any
true belief in the Popish Plot. The crisis surrounding the supposed plot
had been a "False Fear" whipped up by the leading whigs to gratify
"their own Revenge or sinister Interests." If they had really believed the
anti-popish tales they were spinning, they would have abandoned their
houses in the vulnerable parishes of the metropole and fled to safety in
the American colonies.[29]

These spectacular reversals provoked much jaundiced commentary. In the eyes of skeptical observers, these propagandists had found
better patronage and adjusted their principles accordingly. Thus Anthony
Wood charged Henry Care with being "drawn over so far by the Roman

Catholic party for bread and money sake, and nothing else."[30] Similar aspersions were cast upon Settle.[31] But Care was unwilling to grant that he had changed in any fundamental way. He depicted his political maneuvers in 1688 as new tactics designed to reach a consistent goal: "Whatever I have heretofore written . . . was mainly design'd against the Spirit of Persecution, which where-ever it appears, I take for a Badge of Antichristianism."[32]

At the end of his career, Care continued to see a Manichaean world divided between the persecutors and the tolerant. His earlier anti-popish arguments had been based on the assumption that Catholics were persecutors. Once he was persuaded that this assumption was not always correct, he refocused his critiques purely on persecution. He became willing to admit that "there are many worthy Gentlemen and Lords, that are Roman Catholics in the Land; and as they are English Subjects, they have English Hearts."[33] His new goal was not to exclude Catholics from public life, but rather to reach an accommodation whereby "all Parties may be secured from Fears and Jealousies." The way to accomplish this was, in his view, for parliament to enact a law declaring "that Liberty of Conscience is part of the Constitution of this Kingdom; The natural Birth-right of every English Man." Passage of this act would remove from any group the power to persecute any other, and hence persecution would wither away as tolerance replaced the "persecuting principle." Since the king also wished to pass such a law, Care was his ally.[34]

Opposition to persecution could serve as a solvent of anti-popery among nonconformists, as many of them came to embrace King James as their ally against the "persecutors." The Quaker William Shewen drew a clear distinction between the king, who was tolerant, and other Catholics who might not be tolerant, contending that the king, though he practiced the Catholic "manner of worship," had rejected "the worst parts" of Catholicism, which were "force, violence and persecution." William Penn argued that fears of popery before the king's accession had been based on misguided apprehensions "that they [the Papists] strove for all at our Cost," but that the king's offer of a permanent religious toleration had "secur'd [us] against such Jealousies."[35]

William Popple, a friend of Penn and the eventual translator of Locke's *Letter Concerning Toleration*, agreed that the "tru[e] Ground of the Matter" was not popery, but persecution. Popple neatly deployed an anti-persecution frame of reference to counter an anti-popish frame of reference, arguing that laws should be erected that would prevent "Persecuting Papists," along with all persecuting Protestants, from holding public office in England, while those Catholics and Protestants who had "a Spirit of Moderation and Charity" should be permitted to enter the government.[36] This sort of reframing was a key maneuver in critiques of anti-popery. If persecution was the main problem with popery, and not all Catholics were persecutors, then it was the persecutors rather than the Catholics who should be sanctioned.

Opposition to anti-popery was not limited to a few tory and whig thinkers and politicians; it reached a wide popular audience in the 1680s. Numerous critiques of anti-popery were published in that decade. Many announced their opposition to anti-popery in their titles, as if this theme was considered a way of attracting readers.[37] Some went through multiple editions.[38] The number and variety of these pamphlets suggest a market for these writings. Not all of the tracts critical of anti-popery were lengthy treatises; some were briefer works that would have been suitable for coffeehouse reading. One example of this genre is a brief dramatic dialogue between two Anglicans, one named William and the other Francis. In this pamphlet, William takes the anti-popish position and Francis critiques it. Over the course of the dialogue, Francis gradually persuades William to reject anti-popery and to abandon his misguided, hasty "Fears and Jealousies."[39] This short, pithy, anonymous pamphlet with its undisguised agenda seems to have been intended as propaganda for a popular audience. Printed propaganda could potentially reach a wide audience in this period given increasing levels of literacy, especially in London, and the practice of reading pamphlets aloud in coffeehouses.[40] Opposition to anti-popery was also proclaimed from pulpits in Cambridgeshire, Worcestershire, and Yorkshire.[41] The political and theological debates regarding anti-popery were not conducted solely within the elite; they were also directed at a wider audience.

The wide penetration of anti-anti-popish rhetoric can be seen in the addresses sent to James II. Several addresses sent to the king in 1687 and 1688 thanking him for his *Declaration for Liberty of Conscience* referred to it as the edict that took all "fears and jealousies" away. Residents of Northamptonshire wrote that the king's declaration left no "room . . . for fears and jealousies in any [persons]." A group of dissenting merchants and tradesmen of London wrote that James's edict of toleration had banished "all Fears and Jealousies" from the "Hearts" of his subjects. The Painter-Stainers' Company of London informed the king that the "long Experience of your Majesties Justice and Goodness hath been a sufficient security against the least Jealousie." The corporation of Portsmouth advised the king that his declaration of toleration had "dispersed all the Fears and Apprehensions of Fire and Fagot, under Your Majesties Reign, which the wicked Enemies of Your Sacred Person and Religion, had maliciously distilled into the Minds of too many of Your credulous Subjects."[42] The corporation of Portsmouth, unlike many other English corporations at this time, had not been regulated or reformed by the king, and the authors of this statement were its usual borough officials. The evidence of these addresses suggests that critiques of anti-popery had reached a wide audience by 1687 and had modified the rhetorical practices of at least some segments of the populace.

Anti-Popish Reactions to Repeal

The repealers preached peace, quiet, and orderliness, but what they brought was disruption, tumult, and disorder. This was a direct result of their head-on collision with anti-popery. Many Anglicans and some nonconformists saw the repeal agenda as a Trojan horse designed to import Catholicism back to England. It was a "snake in the grass," they charged, lurking in the shadows and poised to strike.[43] Once the Test Acts were revoked, Catholics would flood into the government without hindrance and would advance their nefarious schemes to reimpose their faith in England. Many of the anti-popish Anglicans were convinced that the leading repealers were Jesuits in disguise and that the king's campaign for repeal of the penal laws and Test Acts was designed to tear down the legislative defenses of the Church of England so that Catholicism could be restored.[44]

The king's toleration campaign was seen, from this perspective, as a step toward Catholicization and arbitrary government. Many Protestants worried that, if the Test Acts were repealed and Catholics were eligible to sit in parliament, a Catholic king would appoint his co-religionists as sheriffs and instruct them to return Catholic members of parliament without allowing any real voting to be held in the shires, while Catholic mayors would do the same in the parliamentary boroughs. The king could also appoint enough new Catholic peers to form a majority in the House of Lords. A parliament so composed, some predicted, would vote to repeal the Acts of Supremacy and Uniformity and return England to Rome.[45]

The repealers attempted to counter this conspiracy theory. William Penn argued that fears of a Catholic takeover were unreasonable because the Catholics were too few in number, at less than 1 percent of the English population, to accomplish the designs being imputed to them.[46] The repealers also contended that the best defense against the ascendance of any one religious group in English society was to require all groups to pledge their support for religious toleration. Once these pledges were made and secured by the new Magna Carta, it would be in the interests of everyone to maintain the new settlement so that no one would be subject to the powers of any other group. To many Anglicans, however, this looked like surrender: Catholics would be allowed back into the government, where they could advance their plots, and in return all they would have to do is take an oath swearing that they would not persecute those of other faiths. They feared that Catholic priests would offer dispensations enabling their congregants to break such an oath when the time was right.[47]

It was unclear, moreover, whether all the revenues of the Church of England would continue to be devoted exclusively to Anglican uses under the new tolerationist polity, since some ministers who had left the Church had been permitted to retain the revenues of their cures. In 1686 Edward Sclater, the minister of Putney, converted to Catholicism, and James permitted him to continue to receive his salary of £160, so long as he hired an Anglican curate to perform his duties for him.[48] This was not the same thing as a Catholic takeover, in that Sclater was not permitted to continue to hold services himself at Putney. Repealers noted that James had no intention of repealing the Acts of Uniformity that banned the Catholic mass from any parish church or cathedral.[49] But by allowing Sclater to retain the revenues of his cure, James was effectively impoverishing the Church of England. When confronted by the bishop of Ely in September 1688 about the Sclater case and a few similar examples, James could only reply weakly that "there shall never be more such instances, but I would not be importuned to undo what I have done of this kind already."[50]

James had also threatened the prerogatives of the church when he ejected the fellows of Magdalen College and filled the vacancies with new fellows. Those new fellows were mostly Catholics, in part because few Anglicans were willing to endure the ignominy of accepting one of the vacated places.[51] Compounding his error, the king had allowed the Catholic fellows to use the college chapel for worship, even though this looked, as the bishop of Chester put it, "like [they were] turning the Protestants out of it."[52] The affair of Magdalen College had concentrated the minds of Anglicans: an institution that they had considered to be their own and that trained candidates for the ministry had been taken over by Catholics. Unsubstantiated and unreliable rumors spread that the vacant archbishopric of York might soon be filled by a Catholic.[53] Many Anglicans feared that, if the king got his way in parliament, the intrusions on their church's prerogatives would multiply further.

Countering Conspiratorial Narratives

James and the repealers faced a difficult challenge: how to deal with an opposition so wedded to a conspiratorial narrative that any attempt to counter the narrative was taken as further evidence of a conspiracy.[54] One option in this situation would have been to accommodate the conspiratorial thinking of their opponents by abandoning the most controversial parts of their agenda. James could have given up on the repeal of the Test Acts, for instance, and settled for repeal of the penal laws. This compromise had the potential to satisfy most of the repealers' demands for liberty of conscience while maintaining peace with Anglicans by allowing them to retain their monopolies of law-making, the administration of justice, and government officeholding. James eventually agreed to pursue this option in part, conceding in September 1688 that Catholics would not be permitted to sit in the House of Commons.[55] A similar compromise was proposed by James's *de facto* heir William of Orange, who in 1687 had his ally Gaspar Fagel write a letter noting that Prince William and Princess Mary supported the repeal of most of the penal laws but not of the Test Acts. The Fagel letter was published in January 1688 and widely circulated.[56]

The Fagel compromise was not, however, in keeping with the repeal campaign's systematic critique of the persecutory apparatus of the English state. Repealers worried that, if the Test Acts were retained, then the Anglicans would monopolize public offices and with their monopoly of that public power they would be able to bring back the penal laws at some future date.[57] Many dissenters, even some who were not committed to James's repeal campaign, were unhappy about the proposed compromise under which the Test would be preserved. As one of William's spies in England put it, "the great thing that the Papists buzze into the Dissenters ears is that they are eternally excluded by Fagels letter from all hopes of having any share in the governement."[58] Fagel's letter did not specify whether Protestant nonconformists should be permitted to enter public offices. The letter argued for retaining the Test and failed to distinguish between the doctrinal Test, which affected only Catholics, and the sacramental Test, which penalized both Catholics and those Protestant nonconformists who were unwilling to take communion in the Church of England. The question of the sacramental Test may have been left deliberately vague to avoid offending those Anglicans who were opposed to the holding of public office by Protestant nonconformists. After he took the throne in 1689, William did propose abolishing the sacramental Test, though his proposal was beaten back by Anglicans in parliament.[59]

The repealers insisted that any peace secured on the ground of a compromise that retained the Test would be a fragile and unstable one. They preferred a different plan for stabilizing the kingdom. They contended that, once the Magna Carta for liberty of conscience was passed, the concerns of Anglicans would dissolve on their own, as they came to see that they had nothing to fear from nonconformists or Catholics.[60] The repealers were not attempting to pursue the most pragmatic or least disruptive course of action. Their goal was to draw the sting of anti-popery all at once, by setting up a new legal structure that would render "fears and jealousies" unnecessary. This effort might increase disruption in the short term, but in the long term, they hoped, it would lead to greater social comity, as both Protestants and Catholics internalized the new codes of civility.

If the repealers had a Sisyphean task, at least many hands were pushing the boulder up the hill. The repealer tracts, numbering about eighty in all, advanced a critique of anti-popery as well as a positive vision for England's future. While many of the pamphlets were anonymous, those authors that are known came from a number of different religious groups—Catholic, Anglican, Presbyterian, Congregationalist, Quaker, Baptist, and Familist.[61] Although many of the authors were whigs, some were tories.[62] The diversity of these authors was representative of the movement writ large, which drew from all of the major religious groups in England and from both ends of the political spectrum.

Given the diversity of the repealers, it is perhaps understandable that their opponents tended to see them as Catholics in disguise. It was difficult to make sense of a movement with such a disparate membership, and much simpler just to assimilate them all into the category of popery. In arguing against anti-popery, moreover, the repealers made it more likely that they themselves would be seen as popish. Their critique of anti-popery had the unintended effect of increasing anti-popish fears in some quarters, by making it appear to some as though the influence of Catholics was growing. After all, denying the existence of a Catholic plot was exactly the sort of thing that Catholics in disguise would do.

The repealers were aware that they had taken on a difficult task in choosing to challenge anti-popery rather than accommodate it. They knew that there was only so much that a pamphlet or a dialogue could do to undermine a conspiracy theory that had a hundred years of history behind it. They put their faith in the future; even if they were unable to persuade their opponents to change immediately, they hoped that anti-popery would wither away over time, once the new Magna Carta for liberty of conscience was in force. But they were not unaware that they had an uphill climb. As one repealer ruefully put it, "Mens heads are much easilier laden with, then unladen of suspicions."[63]

4

⟨⟩

Taking Sides

The Three Questions Survey

The repealer movement had no membership rolls, no bureaucratic structure, no formal meetings, and no elected leadership. Its political ideology can be discerned from its published tracts and its newspapers, but these sources tell us little about the size and geographic range of the movement. Although these writings were numerous and the range of authors producing them was diverse, the audiences they attracted might in theory have been minimal. To place the repealer movement more fully in its social context, we must delve into a wider range of sources.

One of the most valuable of these sources is the political survey conducted at the king's behest near the end of 1687 and into the spring and summer of 1688. James wished to ascertain whether the leaders of local communities were willing to support his toleration campaign. To collect this information, he instructed the lord lieutenants of each county to gather together the deputy lieutenants and justices of the peace of that county and ask them three questions: first, if elected to parliament, would they vote for the repeal of the penal laws and Test Acts; second, would they vote in parliamentary elections for men who were committed to repealing the penal laws and Test Acts; and third, would they live on friendly terms with those of all religious persuasions, "as subjects of the same Prince, and good Christians ought to do."[1] These were the so-called "Three Questions," and they were asked of well over two thousand English and Welsh officeholders.[2] The answers were compiled and returned to London, where they served as the basis for a round of purges of the local judiciary and as a fount of intelligence underpinning decisions about electoral strategy. This was the most extensive survey of political opinion ever conducted up to that point in British history.

The third of the "Three Questions" was in keeping with the king's desire to promote peace and good order in his realm through religious tolerance. Nearly every respondent answered it affirmatively. The first and second questions were more controversial. The returns to these questions have survived for most counties and, as many historians have noted, a sizeable majority of the replies were negative or doubtful.[3] It is difficult, however, to assess the political import of these replies, since the sample from which they were drawn, the deputy lieutenants and justices of the peace, was hardly a representative one. Many of the whigs had been purged from the local judiciary during the tory reaction at the end of Charles II's reign, and James II had appointed many Catholics to the bench in the early years of his reign before the Three Questions began to be asked in November 1687. The sample pool for these questions was, therefore, skewed towards tories and Catholics. This bias is especially significant because the Catholics appear to have invariably given positive answers.

Historians have attempted to correct for this bias by removing from the sample the Catholics, most of whom are readily identifiable by their surnames and by the fact that they were often grouped together in the reported results.[4] This leaves a sample of Protestants. But even this more limited sample remains difficult to assess because so many of the Protestants had been appointed only recently to local office. It is possible that some of these men were leaders of their communities, but it is also possible that they were obscure men elevated upon the whim of the king. A better way to filter these results would be to look at the responses given by men who were known to have some standing in their local communities: men who had been previously elected as members of parliament. Filtering out the non-parliamentarians produces a much smaller sample, but it does ensure that the remaining returns can be taken as a proxy for a certain segment of local opinion. It also has the side benefit of enabling analysis of the results by age differences, something that can be done with former members of parliament but that would be difficult to accomplish with a larger group of relatively anonymous men.

Among the respondents whose answers survive, a total of 278 former members of parliament elected from 1660 to 1685 either gave answers or had their answers supplied by the lord lieutenant based on his knowledge of what they had said to the king in private interviews. This number represents slightly more than a quarter of all members from those parliaments who were still alive in 1688. Of the 278 former members, 65, or 23.4 percent, consented to give all the undertakings that the king demanded. These 65 respondents included 10 men who gave their assent only on the condition that the Church of England or the Protestant religion would be preserved and secured. This answer was in line with royal policy and was interpreted at the time as a positive answer: in most cases James subsequently retained or promoted in local office the men who answered in this way.[5]

A further 169 men, 60.8 percent of the total, refused to give undertakings to vote for repeal in parliament or to elect members who would vote for repeal. Ninety-two of these men simply said no, while the other 77 said that they could not answer the questions until they had heard the debates in parliament. Deferring an answer until the meeting of parliament was in keeping with early modern theories of representation. Seventeenth-century parliamentarians typically emphasized the importance of free debate in parliament and the expectation that members would approach that debate with open minds. This sort of answer was effectively a refusal, in the sense that the respondent was refusing to give an undertaking, and it seems likely that many of those who gave this answer did so because they disapproved of the king's religious policy but did not wish to oppose him outright. Although the answer might appear to be evasive, the respondent who refused to commit himself was providing the king with important information: he was stating that he could not be relied upon to undertake in advance to support the repeal of the penal laws and Tests.

The remaining forty-four men, or 15.8 percent of the total, gave partial undertakings, evasive replies, or incomplete responses. Of these, twenty-two gave an undertaking to repeal or revise the penal laws but refused to repeal the Tests. A further twenty men gave evasive replies, for instance by promising to serve the king in general but failing to answer the specific questions. Another two gave answers that do not seem to be a deliberate evasion but are so garbled or incomplete as to be impossible to classify.

The king's supporters tended to be men who had been elected for boroughs rather than the more prestigious counties, which as a general rule possessed larger electorates and were usually regarded as better barometers of public opinion. Across the country, James could command the support of only three men who had most recently been elected for a county, while thirty-one former county members gave a flat no, and nineteen former county members insisted on waiting for the debates before providing their answers. County members might fear the loss of their electoral interest, and with it their seats, if they backed James's controversial repeal campaign. As Sir Daniel Fleming warned his friend Sir John Lowther of Whitehaven, who had served as Cumberland's representative in every parliament since 1665: "I should not be just unto you, if I did not acquaint you with a Report that I have mett with (from more hands than one) of your haveing been closeted, and of your being an Affirmative-man. What influence this may have in Cumberland, in case of an Election, you can judge better than I."[6]

James's supporters were not necessarily political has-beens, but they were older on average than his opponents. This age difference becomes apparent when one divides the respondents into two groups as of 1 January 1688; those aged 50 or more and those aged 49 or less.[7] Among respondents in the 20–49 age group, James attracted positive undertakings from only 14.9 percent. Support for repeal was more than double among respondents aged 50 or more, with the king gaining positive undertakings from 31.8 percent of this age group. The younger group was composed of men who were unlikely to have had personal memories of the Civil War, the oldest members of this cohort having been four years of age when Charles raised his standard at Nottingham. These men had largely been spared any direct experience of the bloody consequences of political division that their fathers had faced. They might be less wary about risking a replay of the 1640s.

The very youngest members were especially unlikely to give positive undertakings. At the end of the year 1687, there were approximately seventy-three former members of parliament below the age of thirty. The responses of twenty-two of these men to the Three Questions have survived and, of these, only two gave positive undertakings for repeal. None of these younger men had gained a seat in parliament before 1679, and thus none had participated in a parliament in which Catholics were included. For them, the repeal of the Test Acts would be an innovation that would change parliament into an institution unlike any they had personally known, with the Catholic lords readmitted to the upper house and perhaps even the occasional Catholic elected to the lower house. Their fathers, with longer memories, could more easily recall a time when Catholics had been tacitly permitted to serve in parliament. For many members of the older generation, it was the Test Acts themselves that were innovatory.

The average supporter of James's repeal campaign among former members of parliament was fifty-four years of age on 1 January 1688, at a time when King James himself, coincidentally, was fifty-four years of age. Among those who refused to support James's repeal campaign, the average age was only forty.[8] The king's failure to attract more support among the young represented a serious blow to his electoral prospects. Moreover, the demographics of his supporters suggested that, over time, support for repeal might decay. The longer James waited to call a parliament that would vote on repeal, the less support he would have. In January 1688 there were 1,015 men living who had been elected to parliament between 1660 and 1685.[9] In 1688 alone 47 of these men died. Of the 47 men, 11 are known to have given replies to the Three Questions. Six of those 11 replies were positive undertakings. At 55 percent, this rate of positive responses was more than double the rate among former members of parliament as a whole. Among these members, repeal was literally a dying cause.

If James was an "old man in a hurry," as several historians have described him, he had good reason to be.[10] There was a narrow window within which the Test Acts could be repealed before they might become set in stone. The critical number, for James, was 259: the number of members required for a majority in a full House of Commons. But the survey demonstrated that the king was unlikely to find 259 former members of parliament who were willing to support his campaign. If he had simply recalled the Parliament of 1685, he would have been doomed to failure. He had recognized as much when he had dissolved that parliament in July 1687 rather than calling it to meet again. The House of Commons in that parliament had voted in November 1685 not to grant the king any additional taxes before addressing the question of why he had granted dispensations from the Test Act to enable Catholics to serve as army officers.[11] In 1687–1688, of the 191 members of the Parliament of 1685 who were asked the Three Questions and whose answers survive in the returns, James received positive undertakings for repeal from only 20.9 percent. This was 2.5 percent less than his overall success rate of 23.4 percent. The heavily loyalist Parliament of 1685, where tories held nearly 90 percent of the seats in the Commons, was, therefore, less likely to back his campaign than the parliamentary class as a whole.[12] This interesting result illustrates the widespread doubts about the king's religious policies among the tories, especially the younger tories who had served in the most recent parliament.

The king could have attempted to engineer a new parliament that would have included fewer of his opponents from the Parliament of 1685 and more of his supporters from the parliaments held before 1685. But there were limits to this strategy as well. The surviving returns gave him the support of 23.4 percent of all former members of parliament, and there were 1,015 former members alive in January 1688. Multiplying these two figures suggests that 238 former members of parliament might in theory have supported him. A majority was 259. Thus, even if every one of these former members succeeded in gaining election to the upcoming parliament, something that was highly unlikely to happen, James would still fall nineteen votes short. The old members, then, were insufficient for his purposes. The king was compelled to head into new territory and to attempt to bring into parliament a new class of men who had never served before.

Beyond the bare answers conveyed back to the king, the Three Questions provoked many other social and political effects. The questions disturbed local allegiances and alliances, as those who usually stood together in local politics were forced apart by their varying responses to the king's demands. Meanwhile, new alliances formed as men who had been suspicious of each other's motives agreed to give identical or nearly identical answers to the questions. These were ideal conditions for enlarging the scope of political activity in a community, as the local political leadership often broke apart in a very public fashion and men and women felt free to comment on the varying stances adopted by their community's leaders. Because the questions were often put to local officials at group gatherings, the king created a new set of venues for discussion and debate in towns across the kingdom. These venues could be hijacked and manipulated for purposes that he had not foreseen.

Because of their informality, these temporary venues of political interaction were not fully documented and many have been lost to history. In most cases, only the answers to the Three Questions survive to hint at the debates that took place. An unusually diverse range of sources survives, however, for one particular town in northern Lancashire. These sources reveal the manifold effects of the king's survey, as the shockwaves rippled outward from a local political earthquake.

Catholics and Country Fellows

The ground had shifted. Everyone knew this after the asking of the Three Questions in Lancaster in November 1687, but Roger Sawrey knew it better than most. He had participated in many of the great English events of the previous half-century and could see that the wheel was turning again. He had served as a lieutenant colonel under Oliver Cromwell and was posted in 1653 to Ayrshire in Scotland where he commanded a regiment. Upon the death of the Lord Protector in 1658, he was sent to Richard Cromwell's parliament at Westminster by the voters of Ayr and Renfrewshire. Around the same time Sawrey was promoted to the rank of colonel. Shortly thereafter he signed the invitation to General Monck, head of the Cromwellian army in Scotland, calling on him to intervene in English affairs, an intervention which brought about the Restoration of Charles II. Sawrey had profited from his political and military commands and just before the Restoration had purchased the manor of Broughton-in-Furness in the far north of Lancashire. He retired there to raise his family. He helped to establish a nonconformist church at Tottlebank, a few miles east of his home, in 1669, although he was already a member of a nonconformist church in London and did not transfer his membership to Tottlebank until 1695. As a Baptist, he was accustomed to being in the minority and holding to his principles. His nickname was "praying Sawrey," an allusion to his piety. To most he was known as Colonel Sawrey.[13]

Like other gentry in north Lancashire, Sawrey received a notice from the petty constable of his bailiwick in November 1687 informing him that all men possessing a freehold estate worth at least twenty pounds per year must appear at Lancaster on the twenty-first to meet with Lord Viscount Molyneux, lord lieutenant of the county. A Roman Catholic justice of the peace, Robert Dalton, had issued the order, presumably upon instructions from the lord lieutenant. The order was highly irregular, and some questioned its legality. Unlike the lord lieutenants of other counties in the kingdom, who asked the Three

Questions only of their deputies and of the justices of the peace, the lord lieutenant of Lancashire conducted a much wider survey, gathering responses from everyone of weight in the county, even those like Sawrey who held no local office.[14]

The colonel was present in Lancaster as instructed on the twenty-first. The old Cromwellian Baptist, unlike many of the local Catholic gentry, was not invited to dine with Lord Molyneux in his chambers at Stoop Hall, a hostelry on St. Mary's Street in the town. This was almost certainly Molyneux's first visit to Lancaster as the county's lord lieutenant; he had been appointed to the office only three months before, replacing the earl of Derby, a tory Anglican who was not thought to be amenable to the king's repeal campaign.[15] Molyneux, a peer, was the most socially elevated Catholic in Lancashire. The county was unusually well stocked with Catholic gentlemen, who mainly resided near the border with Cheshire in a band stretching across the flat plains of the River Mersey from Liverpool to Manchester. Molyneux's own estate was at Croxteth near Liverpool. His visit to Lancaster took him far from his home territory. The fact that he was reduced to dining in a hotel suggests that his welcome there had not been warm.

Lancaster was the final stop on Molyneux's journey across the county, from Liverpool in the south to Preston in the middle to Lancaster in the north. At Liverpool, he had given a speech condemning those who would doubt the king's promises to protect the religion and property of Anglicans, stating that to question the king's word in these points was tantamount to "defamation of the Government." Unlike some other lord lieutenants, who asked the Three Questions in a neutral fashion, Molyneux put himself on record as a supporter of repeal.[16] At table with the Catholic gentry, he may have rehearsed his arguments for repeal or, given his favorable audience, he may have discussed strategies with them for the public contest to follow.

The Protestant gentry held a competing banquet at the house of a local doctor, John Tarleton. They, too, may have discussed strategies for the upcoming meeting, although the events that followed suggested they were unable to come to any unanimous agreement. After both lunches had already begun, Molyneux, somewhat belatedly, invited the Protestants William Kirkby and Thomas Preston, who were already dining at Tarleton's, to join him at Stoop Hall for the meal. When they arrived, they found there was no room for them. Preston went back to Tarleton's, but Kirkby stayed, presumably finding a spot to stand awkwardly and wait for a space to open up at the table. The county community was already divided before the asking of the Three Questions had begun.

Roger Sawrey received word to attend the Lord Molyneux at two o'clock in his chambers at Stoop Hall. There he found an assembly unlike any other that had been held in Lancaster over the previous generation. A Quaker had come down from Furness, wearing the somber clothing of that society and refusing to remove his hat as a token of his unwillingness to pay outward signs of respect to anyone other than God. At least seven Catholic gentlemen were seated at the table, along with at least fourteen Anglicans. Representatives of the town's Presbyterian community had made an appearance. Along with old "praying Sawrey," the gathering of these men made for an unusually diverse public meeting. Among the major religious groups, only the Congregationalists were not represented.

All those assembled knew that the words they used on that day would be the most scrutinized words they would utter that year, if not in their lives. Outside the hall a crowd gathered, eager to hear news of the events taking place inside. The chamber was so full that the men in attendance strained at times to hear what was being said. They came together around a long table, with a clerk prepared to take down the replies as they were given. Molyneux read a short note announcing that the king required them to answer three questions. He then called on John Girlington, a local tory gentleman, to answer the questions first.

Being asked to stand up in public and state one's position was an unnerving experience. Perhaps this explains the force with which Girlington gave his reply. His opinion of the penal laws and Test Acts was that "he would have those Laws damned with the Contrivers of theme [them]."[17] By the "Contrivers" of the penal laws and Tests, Girlington most likely had in mind the whigs and their former chief, the deceased earl of Shaftesbury, who in the late 1670s had sought to exclude the duke of York from the succession. Many tories had come to see the Test Acts of 1673 and 1678 as measures designed to persecute the future king and to drive him out of his employments.[18] By damning the contrivers of the Test Acts, Girlington aligned himself with the king's tory supporters. This alignment was hardly a surprise given that he had close affiliations with local Catholics; his own family had been Catholic in the previous generation.[19]

If Molyneux had wished to set a confrontational mood by choosing Girlington to go first, he had chosen well. Thomas Preston of Holker was called on next.[20] He may have been seen as a waverer, a man who would break under the pressure of being called to follow the forceful Girlington. He had been invited to have dinner with the lord lieutenant, though he had failed to find a seat at the table. The eyes of his Anglican allies were upon him now, as were the expectant looks of the Catholics with whom he had failed to dine. He sought to give a moderate answer, stating that the sanguinary laws, those that prescribed death as a penalty for religious nonconformity, should be repealed. The other penal laws and the Tests, in his view, should be retained. He asked the clerk to set down his answer as "dubious." Molyneux intervened, informing him that "His Maiesties positive Orders were that every One should consent or denye." This was a misinterpretation; the king's orders had, in fact, allowed for "doubtfull" answers to be recorded.[21] Deprived by his lord lieutenant of the opportunity to equivocate, Preston had his answer placed in the negative column.

Next came Christopher Carus, a justice of the peace for Lancashire. He was an Anglican, but his wife was Catholic. He stated forcefully his opinion of the penal laws and Test Acts: he "was for haveing them burnt as the scotch Covenant was."[22] Carus was referring to the Solemn League and Covenant signed between the Scots and the English parliament in 1643, a document that had long been considered treasonous in England. Carus was reaching for the most vehement language in his vocabulary to denounce the Test. He was also being fairly original. Not even Henry Care, with all his Grub Street vehemence, had gone so far as to suggest that the Test Acts should be burned by the common hangman.

William Kirkby was among the next to speak. He was the Protestant who had been invited to dine with Molyneux and had stayed even though there was no room at the table. He was not in royal favor at that moment, having been removed as a justice of the peace in July 1687. In his prior service as a justice, he had been known for his zealous prosecution of nonconformists. On a single day in October 1683, he and his nephew Roger Kirkby had fined sixty-one people for absence from Church of England services. He had once complained that two of his fellow justices, William Knipe and Curwen Rawlinson, who were also present at Molyneux's table, had been lax in prosecuting nonconformists. His temper was well known to the one Quaker who was in attendance at the meeting at Stoop Hall, Thomas Lower, who had once complained that the Kirkbys had "an Invetterate enmity" to Quakers in general "and to mee In particular."[23]

Kirkby's voice, then, would seem likely to be raised against the king's proposals for religious toleration. But, according to two different witnesses, Kirkby gave his consent. Of all the answers given that day, this was the most surprising. His nephew, Roger, had given his consent as well, at Preston a day or two earlier.[24] It would seem that the loyalism of the Kirkbys had trumped their antipathy to dissent. William Kirkby had been a fervent tory in the elections of 1685, working against the electoral interest of the whig Lord Brandon and expressing hopes that this would "be a service Perticularlie acceptable to his Majestie."[25] He was offering his services to his king once again.

Eventually the questions came around to Roger Sawrey. All eyes in the room fell on the old Cromwellian. He began, rather tentatively, by saying that he was "against all those Laws that would hinder the true worship of god for Consions [conscience's] sake." This answer rings true as the authentic voice of old dissent, which appealed to the individual's conscience as the only true guide to worship. Molyneux retorted that "he must Answare in whole and not in part." Sawrey then gave a bolder and more direct answer: "Cutt them all of[f]."[26] He was placed in the assenting column. His shift in tone suggests the ways in which giving an answer in public could be a radicalizing experience. Under the pressure placed on him by the lord lieutenant, the heightened scrutiny of the occasion, and the influence of Carus and Girlington, who had already given strident answers, Sawrey came out with an answer that was strikingly combative. The old warrior was raising his sword again.

The difference between Sawrey's first answer and his second illustrates the gulf between two types of rhetoric within the nonconformist community. When asked the Three Questions, at first the colonel preferred to answer in the sort of irenic language that was common among many moderate nonconformists, a language that attacked no one directly while claiming a freedom that would extend to everyone. The lord lieutenant pressed him, saying that this was not adequate and that he must explain precisely what he meant. Sawrey then dropped his previous language and adopted a more radical tone. His new rhetoric was the language of the repealers: confrontational, all-encompassing, attacking the entirety of a corrupt system rather than the singularity of an egregious law. With his desire to "cut them all off," Sawrey appealed to an urgent sense of grievance that was not easily encompassed within a moderate language of patience and charity.

The remaining answers brought few surprises. The Quaker, Thomas Lower, supported the repeal of the penal laws and Test Acts. A physician by training, he was a member of Quakerism's first family, the Fells of Swarthmore Hall. He had met George Fox in 1656, became a Quaker soon afterwards, and married one of the Fell daughters in 1668, shortly before Fox himself married the matriarch Margaret Fell. Lower spent a year in Worcester jail with Fox in the early 1670s, at which time the Quaker leader began dictating to him the first draft of his *Journal,* the spiritual classic of the Society of Friends. In giving affirmative answers to the Three Questions, Lower may have been following the advice of his co-religionist William Penn, who had published four pamphlets advocating repeal over the previous six months.

The Presbyterians in attendance also gave affirmative answers. None of the surviving accounts bothered to mention the responses of the Catholics, which must mean that they were affirmative, since anything else would have defied expectations and provoked comment. The Anglicans were split, with a few giving positive replies but most giving negative replies or refusing to make a commitment. Answering in the affirmative were Gabriel Crofts, William Kirkby, Christopher Carus, and John Girlington. Answering in the negative were nine Protestant gentlemen, including Roger Sawrey's great-nephew, John Sawrey of Plumpton, who was said to have lost "a bot[t]le of wine for not Answareing as his unckle Collonel [Sawrey]" did. Thomas Parker, holder of the baronies of Morley and Monteagle, who resided at Hornby Castle several miles up the River Lune from Lancaster, was also present at the meeting. As a peer he was not obliged to give a response in public. His answer is not known, but presumably it was negative, since he was removed as a justice of the peace a few months later.[27]

As the hour wore on, the pattern of question and reply broke down, and some men spoke out of turn. Molyneux's clerk made an insolent remark after the deputy lieutenant Curwen Rawlinson's negative answer: as he wrote down the reply he spoke aloud, "Curwen Rawlinson esquire, lately a deputy lieutenant." This was a startling breach of protocol, but presumably the clerk, who was almost certainly a Catholic, felt empowered by the presence of Molyneux and the other Catholics in the room.

As the clerk predicted, Rawlinson did not last long in local office: he was removed from the commission of the peace a few months later and presumably lost his deputy lieutenancy around the same time.[28]

Meanwhile Thomas Brathwaite, a Catholic, felt free to interject a comment after the answer of Edward Wilson, a Protestant. Wilson contended that since he was a "private person" he was not obliged to give a candid answer to the Three Questions. He had been a justice of the peace until July of that year but had been removed from that office and so, he suggested, was not accountable to the lord lieutenant in the same manner as he had been before. Wilson said, in reference to the upcoming parliament, that "when the King shall please to call one [I] shall doe my endeavour to chuse a Loyall man," thereby sidestepping the question. Thomas Brathwaite was to write later that Wilson's answer had been "much taken notice of, ill resented, and looked upon as very bould by most present."[29] The portion of his reply that rankled was presumably his challenge to the lord lieutenant's authority to interrogate him. Brathwaite was said to have commented aloud on Wilson's answer, presumably disparagingly, though the exact words that he used were not recorded.

The fractious mood strained the nerves of all present. Lord Morley found himself so shaken that, after the gentlemen were dismissed, he "went to bedd in the afternoon," displaying a countenance that was "very much troubled." News of the event began to ripple outwards. As the gentlemen proceeded out of Stoop Hall, having given their answers, a crowd was waiting on the doorstep to hear what they had said. As one contemporary observed, "The Countrie fellows did inquire of each as they came from my L[ord Molyneux] how they voited if for the Negative, then they prayed for them if oth[e]rwise they had no good words for them."[30] Thus when Preston or Rawlinson emerged to say that he had refused to comply with the king, the crowd prayed for him, perhaps by crying out "God bless you, sir!" But when Kirkby or Girlington emerged to say that he had agreed to comply with the king, the crowd remained silent. The political debate in Lancaster had expanded to include not only the men in the lord lieutenant's chambers but also the people in the streets, who had not been asked for their opinions but who wished to voice them nonetheless.

Over the following week, three separate accounts of the gathering at Stoop Hall were posted to Sir Daniel Fleming, a former member of parliament in Westmorland: one from his son-in-law, another from his brother, and a third from an old friend. The letter from Fleming's old friend, Thomas Brathwaite, amounted to an attack on Edward Wilson, Fleming's son-in-law, for his "bold" answer; the letter from Fleming's son-in-law amounted to a defense against these charges. Wilson pleaded that he had only sought to give an answer that would offend neither the king nor the laws of the kingdom.[31] Sir Daniel considered the event significant enough to write it up at length in his diary, even though he had not himself been present.[32]

As word spread that William Kirkby had assented to the Three Questions, the county was said to be "very full of the[i]re talke against old Justis [Justice] (W[illiam] K[irkby]) . . . for being of Mr Sawreys and the Dr [Lower's] side."[33] By affiliating himself with the Baptist colonel and the Quaker physician, Kirkby had brought his own reputation into question. The public expectation seems to have been that the Anglican gentry would stick together in refusing the king; the shock was not that so many Anglicans had refused but, rather, that Kirkby had complied. It is interesting to note that Kirkby was reproved for allying himself with the Baptist and the Quaker, not for aligning himself with the Catholics, even though he did both. This suggests that anti-nonconformist sentiment remained strong among some segments of northern society.

Politics made for strange bedfellows. The old prosecutor of dissent found himself taking the side of his erstwhile victims. The movement for repeal brought together tories who were prepared to support the king's wishes simply because he expressed them and dissenters who were prepared to support the king's wishes because they wanted liberty of conscience. Opposition to repeal, meanwhile, separated former allies, as some of the more whiggish Anglicans proved unwilling to relinquish the anti-Catholic laws, while some whiggish Presbyterians were eager to see the entire machinery of persecution wound down, including the Test Acts. Repeal was the pivot around which Lancastrian politics revolved in 1688.

The king reinforced these newfound alliances through his control of local officeholding. John Girlington was added to the Lancashire commission of the peace, while Curwen Rawlinson and Lord Morley were removed. The king's agents recommended that Roger Sawrey be added to the bench as well, although it is not clear whether this was done.[34] A group of local Presbyterians were added to the Lancaster town council. Their takeover of the government was registered in symbolic form when the new mayor, John Greenwood, ordered that the town mace, which previously had been carried in procession every Sunday to the parish church, would be carried henceforth to the Presbyterian meeting. His order was only partially carried out, for the two bailiffs, both of them members of the Church of England, refused to enter the Presbyterian place of worship with the mayor, leaving him at the door and returning at the end of the service to meet him outside.[35]

When parliamentary elections were announced in the late summer of 1688, two pairs faced off for the two Lancaster borough seats: Thomas Preston and Curwen Rawlinson against repeal versus Fitton Gerard and Roger Kirkby in favor of it. Gerard was the younger brother of Lord Brandon, a leading whig who had embraced James II's proposals for reform. Preston and Rawlinson had been allies of Brandon in the parliamentary elections of 1685, but, now that he had swung over to the repeal side, they switched to opposing his electoral interest. Kirkby was the former tory member for Lancaster in 1685; like his uncle, he had given affirmative responses to the Three Questions, and in the fall of 1688 he received the king's nomination for the Lancaster borough seat. The new pro-repeal alliance of the Kirkbys and the dissenters served to pull together both ends of the spectrum, high tory and radical nonconformist, against the moderate whigs. As Thomas Preston noted with considerable understatement, "We are att present somewhat devided." According to Preston, the Quaker Thomas Lower and the Baptist Roger Sawrey had engaged, along with the two Kirkbys, to support the electoral interest of Brandon's brother, Fitton Gerard.[36] Thus the Quaker and the Baptist had come together with two high tories to support the brother of a leading whig. This unusual alliance was not immediately tested, as the elections were called off due to the imminent invasion of William of Orange. When new elections were held in January for the Convention Parliament after James II's flight from England, the whigs Preston and Rawlinson soundly trounced Roger Kirkby.

To the public eye in 1687, William Kirkby looked like a turncoat: a man who had first prosecuted the Quakers and Baptists and then, along with his nephew Roger, took up common cause with them. In the final year of Charles II's reign he had written that he had put "the laws in execution against all absentees from our Church" because it was "our duty, and in obedience to the King's commands."[37] In 1687 he agreed to comply with the new king's desire to repeal those same laws. It may be that Kirkby had never held strong opinions regarding the penal laws but had put them into execution because King Charles II had commanded it. Or it may be that Kirkby's undertaking in 1687 to support repeal went against his privately held opinions. He appears to have been a man whose sense of loyalty impelled him to vote the way his king desired him to.

Like Kirby, many of the men who assented to James's Three Questions were not necessarily repealers themselves. Some were tories who agreed to comply with the king's request simply because their monarch was asking them to do so. Though they may have been appalled by the prospect of tolerating nonconformists, they held to a set of political beliefs that required them to comply with their sovereign in all requests that were not illegal or immoral. These men can be classified as allies of the repealer movement, but they should not be classified as repealers because they did not adopt the collective identity of the movement.

Other gentlemen were less responsive to the king's wishes. Such men were willing to suffer dismissal from the commission of the peace and the deputy lieutenancy in order to maintain their standing as defenders of the Church of England. These men seized upon the opportunity afforded by the Three Questions to reaffirm their commitment to their religion and to their friends. Giving a negative response to the Three Questions was a social act, as Sir John Lowther of Lowther noted in his memoirs: "the Multitude of Opposers created an Assurance in Manie that were otherways Wavering to be of that Number." Lowther went on to argue that the social pressure to oppose repeal was so strong that some who gave negative answers did so while hiding their own inward approval of the king's policies: "Manie who approved the thing were yett of the Number of thos[e] that Denied Compliance, that they might not Dissent from their friends And tis Most Certain that a Great manie Chose to loos [lose] their Places which were Beneficiall, Rather than submitt themselves to the Censure of their Countries By whom they had been trusted in former Parliaments, which Verie Men had they Been Lett alone would Once for all have Given their Consent [to repeal] In Parliament."[38] Various peer-group influences might conspire to cause a man to oppose the king's request, including the desire not to alienate his countrymen or his friends. It was the publicity of the answers, combined with the underlying political opinions of some of the gentry, that created a movement of resistance.

Inspection and Publicity

The very act of inspection helped to alter men's positions. King James II was an early discoverer of the observer effect: he could not inspect his subjects without changing them. The asking of the Three Questions represented a new kind of public arena. Many local gentlemen were not certain how to react. Their reputations were implicated in their replies, but custom and routine did not provide any safe response. This new arena could disrupt existing patterns of self-representation. Tories, for example, could no longer take their accustomed pose of "loyal subjects," where loyalty meant both fealty to the king and fidelity to the Church of England. They had to develop new formulas to represent their political opinions.

Some gentlemen were eager to perform, using this new public arena to make bold and confrontational statements of opinion. But many proved more reluctant. It was not in their interest to make bold pronouncements. The controversy at Lancaster was painful for a man like Edward Wilson. In trying to avoid giving an answer, he gave what he hoped was an innocuous one, but it was taken badly and became a source of comment because he was deemed to have disputed the authority of the lord lieutenant to ask him a question. It was not just that Wilson was afraid of retribution from the king; he was also seeking to avoid any detailed inspection of his behavior by his peers and the "country fellows" who would comment on whatever he did. After he gave what was later taken to have been a bold, defiant response, he did not revel in the glory of his moment of resistance. Instead, he wrote to his uncle to let him know that he had not meant to challenge the king's authority. He had, to his dismay, lost control of his public image. His response to the Three Questions was now being discussed and critiqued publicly. His letter to his uncle was an exercise in damage control.

In many counties, collective behaviors developed almost immediately in response to this unnerving situation. New groups formed, developing new formulas. Lancaster was unusual in that so many different responses were given by different gentlemen. A few miles north,

at Penrith, the lord lieutenant was met with a unanimous statement
from many of the leading Protestant gentlemen of Westmorland. Before
the meeting of the gentry, two of the local leaders, the Anglicans Sir
Daniel Fleming and Sir John Lowther of Lowther, met to "agree upon
their Answers." Then, at the meeting with Lord Preston, Sir Daniel
requested leave for the gentlemen to withdraw for an hour to consider their answers, after which each would give their answer individually in writing. Lord Preston permitted this, and the Protestants
withdrew into one room and the Catholics into another. Fourteen of
the Protestant gentlemen then submitted identical written answers,
promising to choose "Loyal" men for Parliament and refusing to commit
themselves in advance to repealing the penal laws and Tests until they
had heard "the Reasons that shall rise from the Debate of the House [of
Commons]."[39] These Protestant gentlemen preferred to avoid unscripted,
individualized responses. Performance for these men was not instinc-
tive; the role they wished to fill was a scripted one that would maintain
their dignity by allowing them to retreat within the relative anonymity
of a group. The goal of this group was not to start a revolution but rather
to protect its members as much as possible from insinuations of having
betrayed either the king or the Church of England.

    To be sure, there were activists on both sides, repealers and their
opponents, who took advantage of the new public spaces on offer to
make provocative statements in defense of their respective causes. Some
men, initially reluctant, could be coaxed to perform, as Roger Sawrey
did at Lancaster, when he warmed up into his role. But many others
simply wanted to reduce their exposure. A local society built on reputations gained by years of service was being pushed into a public sphere
governed by principles of inspection and self-marketing. Some took to
this new world, but others did not. Many wanted to avoid standing out.
The content of their replies, then, could be governed as much by the
social context in which the questions were asked as by their own individual principles. There was safety in numbers—not necessarily safety
from royal punishment, which would be meted out for any negative or
evasive answer—but safety from shame. In Norfolk, the whig justice Sir
John Holland was unable to attend the meeting of the gentry due to ill
health, so he sent a letter with his answer to the questions: he "could
not (as my judgement at present is) be for taking away all the penal
lawes and Tests." When he later learned that his friends at the meeting

had given more straightforwardly negative answers, he rued the fact that his own answer differed from theirs. The difference was minor, amounting merely to his addition of the parenthetical phrase "as my judgement at present is." Yet he regretted nonetheless that he now stood alone in his response, "by myself." Even his slight hedge made him feel exposed. He decided to ask the lord lieutenant for permission to change his answer and "joyn with" that of his friends by dropping the parenthetical phrase. This permission was not granted.[40]

Most newsletter writers and intelligence gatherers in London reported the outcome of the Three Questions as one of widespread resistance to the king. And in a sense, those reports were accurate. The majority of gentlemen had not given the king the responses he wanted. But the movement of resistance was less forceful than it might appear to have been, based on the replies alone. The collective aversion to public exposure helps to explain why men who said no to the Three Questions did not then go on to rally opposition to the king in the spring of 1688. They did not organize a tax strike against the king or protest the employment of Catholics as justices of the peace. New public spaces were opening up in the late months of 1687 and the early months of 1688, and new forms of opposition were emerging, but they did not yet have the impetus of a revolutionary movement. A very large proportion of the English gentry—a majority, even—did not wish to place their heads above the parapet.

5

Seizing Control

The Repealers in the Towns

From November 1687 to September 1688, King James II directed a series of purges that ejected a substantial number of officeholders, 2,342 in all, from English borough councils. He mandated the appointment of some two thousand new officials as their replacements.[1] These sweeping purges went considerably beyond any previous attempts to control the boroughs, many of which sent members to parliament. The king and his agents regulated over half of the English parliamentary boroughs; these 107 boroughs had the right to elect 212 members of parliament, or just over 41 percent of the total membership of the House of Commons.[2] By ordering the regulation of these borough councils, or "corporations" as they were called at the time, James aimed to secure the election of a pro-repeal parliament once elections were held in the autumn of 1688. In its time, this was the most extensive effort of electoral management ever undertaken by the English state.[3]

These extensive preparations were made for a parliament that never sat. Most of James's appointees were themselves ejected in October 1688, shortly before the invasion of William of Orange. The planned parliamentary elections were cancelled as the king rushed to prepare England's defenses against the invaders. James decided to invest no further political capital in the regulation of the corporations and, as a concession to his opponents, reversed the changes he had made in them. The brief tenure of the king's appointees, who served in most cases for under a year, has made it difficult for historians to assess their intentions. The appointees may have been willing agents of the crown, or they may have been reluctant allies or even covert opponents biding their time to strike. If most of the appointees were repealers, then the king's plans for an upcoming parliament had some chance of success. If they were tories who were willing to do whatever the king asked of them, then his plans also had a chance of success. But if they were opponents of his proposals, then his electoral strategy almost certainly would have failed, even if William had not invaded.

Some historians have suggested that the king's appointees were largely whigs or, more precisely, that they were the whigs who had been ejected from their local offices in the early 1680s as part of the so-called "tory reaction," when Charles II recalled town charters and destroyed the whig ascendancy in the boroughs through the legal device of *quo warranto* proceedings.[4] It might have made sense for James to turn to these whigs for assistance. They possessed the local clout and electoral experience to steer their preferred candidates to seats in parliament. After they were ejected from office, their tory replacements had often governed with far less popular support. If it were indeed the case that James was merely restoring to office these local power brokers, then his policy can be seen as a conservative one, for he was returning the corporations to their original state. Such a conservative policy might, however, prove fatal to his radical measures. These experienced power brokers might choose to defend local prerogatives against central interference rather than join the king's campaign.

This account, though it has a certain plausibility, falls apart under scrutiny. The borough councils, or corporations, regulated by James during his repeal campaign were not always the same as the ones regulated under the tory reaction. There was considerable overlap, with ninety-nine corporations regulated during both the tory reaction and the repeal campaign, but thirty-six corporations were regulated in the former campaign but not the latter, while seventeen corporations were regulated in the latter campaign but not the former.[5] Moreover, even in the corporations regulated in both campaigns, the regulations in 1687 and 1688 were in most cases far more intensive than those done before. Many corporations saw virtually their entire membership replaced in 1687 and 1688, whereas the earlier purges had been more limited.[6] The two campaigns were so different in scope that it is mathematically impossible for one to be the inverse of the other.

In the city of Oxford, for example, Charles II removed 8 men in his regulation of the corporation, while James II removed 134. Charles targeted the whig ringleaders, while his brother targeted everyone who might disagree with his policy. Thus James in his regulation cannot be said to have been restoring the *status quo ante,* even if he had reappointed all 8 of the men removed by his elder brother (in fact, he restored only 2 of them).[7] Charles removed specific members whom he suspected of disloyalty, while James removed all of the members before reappointing those whom he believed to be loyal. His campaign in 1687 and 1688 was not simply a reversal of what had been done before.[8]

An alternative view, endorsed by many historians, is that James's program of regulation was a shambles and that many or most of the new members were not vetted at all. In this view, the fact that a man was added to a borough corporation in 1688 tells us little or nothing about his beliefs or attitudes. One historian cited the marquess of Halifax's jibe of April 1688 that regulation constituted "rapid motion without advancing a step."[9] Historians have also noted that some of the new appointees refused even to accept the offices to which the king had appointed them.[10] These lapses suggest that the vetting process employed by the king's agents was less than perfect. But the number of refusers appears to have been in the dozens rather than in the hundreds, and the great majority of the two-thousand-odd appointees did take up their offices.

Historians have also observed that many of the corporations were regulated more than once, with successive regulations sometimes only days apart. This pattern has been taken to mean that the men added to the corporation in the first round of regulation had refused to endorse the king's policies and so new men had to be found to replace them. Some corporations were regulated three, four, or even five times. One borough, Maldon in Essex, was regulated six times. These multiple regulations have led historians to allege that regulation was a perfunctory, error-strewn process.[11]

This misunderstanding of the regulators' methods stemmed from a misreading of one key source, the removal orders contained in the privy council registers. The misinterpretation came about because historians have typically read only the removal orders sent out by the privy council and not the letters of nomination sent out by the king's secretary of state, due to the one-sided nature of the sources available in the central repositories in London. On the pages of the privy council registers, one purge succeeds another, and historians have assumed that each purge of a given town was designed to correct errors made previously.[12]

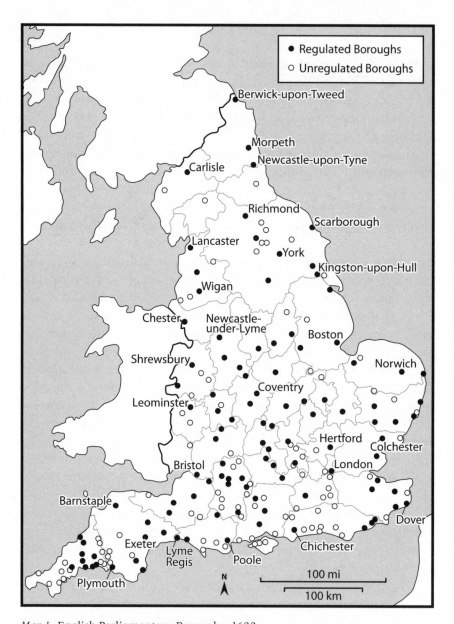

Map 1. English Parliamentary Boroughs, 1688.

The 205 English parliamentary boroughs in the reign of James II were distributed unevenly, with some counties possessing only a single borough, while Cornwall, in the southwest, had twenty-one. Of the 205 boroughs, 107 were regulated by James in the period from November 1687 to September 1688, either by order of the privy council, through the issuing of a new charter, or, in the case of London, by letters patent.

The town minute books held in the county and municipal record offices include both removals and replacements, thus providing a more complete picture. A survey of the surviving corporation records for thirty-six towns, representing over half of the corporations that received multiple orders from the privy council, shows that only 6 percent of the men removed in a second regulation had been added in the first regulation; the other 94 percent were men who had already been serving on the town councils before the first regulation.[13] The main purpose of the second regulations was not, therefore, to fix earlier mistakes by removing men who had been added in error. It was, rather, to continue regulations that had been half-started. J. R. Jones, whose early work on the regulations has been a point of contention in the later scholarship, was correct in suggesting that the second regulations were planned from the start, although he did not offer an explanation as to why the regulators would choose to proceed in such a time-consuming way.[14]

The multistage regulations were dictated by the legal structure of the borough charters. To perform an effective regulation, the regulators could not remove an entire council at once; such an order would dissolve the corporation by emptying the council and leaving no members behind to achieve a quorum. This would force the king to go through the expensive and time-consuming process of rechartering the corporation. Instead, the regulators needed to remove less than half of the corporation in the first stage, so that a quorum might remain to implement the king's mandate appointing new members to fill the empty places. Once these vacancies were filled, a second round of regulation could then sweep away many of the remaining old members and thereby obtain a majority of new men. An ideal regulation would be done in three stages, thus allowing a margin of safety and ensuring that the number of vacant seats remained well below 50 percent at all times. The need to maintain a quorum was a nuisance for the regulators. To avoid having to follow such cumbersome procedures in future, royal officials began inserting a novel clause in new town charters issued in 1688 stipulating that the ordinary rules of quorum would not apply when corporations were being regulated by the king.[15]

In describing the king's regulations, historians have been driven to making unfounded conjectures because it is genuinely difficult to summarize the behavior and attitudes of two thousand men, especially in the face of fragmentary evidence that is scattered across more than seventy county and municipal archives in England and Wales. Historians have also tended to begin with the assumption that James's policies were not well implemented and that popular support for his toleration campaign was weak. Thus the idea that the king could have found two thousand local supporters of his policies and then engineered their appointments to town councils has seemed too farfetched to be credited. Even if such supporters existed, it has seemed unlikely that the rudimentary central administration at James's disposal could have implemented such an ambitious agenda.

The picture looks different if a widespread movement for repeal can be shown to have existed. With such a movement to draw from, the agents employed by James would have been spared much of the work of organization and recruitment at the grassroots level. Local groups of repealers might have done this labor for them. Their assistance would not necessarily have ensured the success of James's policies—even the repealers might not have given the king everything he wanted. But with the repealers as his allies, the king's campaign was not hopeless. The surest way to assess the likely success of his policies is to look at what the new councillors actually did when they were in office, rather than to attempt to assess their intentions based on the mechanics of how often a town was regulated. The best-documented towns, such as Exeter and Derby, offer valuable insights into the mindsets of the new councillors, thereby allowing us to make projections about how the campaign was likely to fare in the country as a whole.

Fashioning a Regulation

Exeter was a one-industry town, and that industry was cloth. The women of Exeter worked as spinners and burlers, while its men worked as combers and weavers. Many of these spinners and weavers were dissenters. The population of Exeter in the later years of the seventeenth century has been variously estimated at between 13,000 and 17,700, placing it fourth or fifth among English cities, behind London, Bristol, Norwich, and possibly York. Of that population, some 3,000 were said in 1715 to have been dissenters. Most of these worshipped at one of the three Presbyterian churches, which together accounted for 2,250 of the dissenters. The remaining nonconformists were Congregationalists or Baptists, with a few French Protestants and a handful of Quakers. By 1676 the Presbyterians had gained control of the city's cloth trade, with members of that group responsible for over half of the serge exported by the city's largest traders in that year.[16]

In 1687 the cloth trade had been buoyant for over a decade. The customs revenue collected in Exeter increased in every year from 1684 to 1686, and in 1687 revenues hit an all-time high. One man who benefited from the boom was Thomas Jefford. He was renowned for his skill as a dyer and, according to one account, was thirsty in his ambition, "aspiring after Honour." He had earned a fortune in his trade, and now he wished to have influence in the government of his city. He had succeeded in acquiring a royal mandate in 1686 nominating him to the position of alderman but was rejected by the corporation as "disloyall and seditious," a man who had petitioned for the summoning of a parliament in the last years of Charles II's reign, who had celebrated the duke of Monmouth's progress in 1680, and who had received a copy of Monmouth's treasonous *Declaration* in 1685. In short, he was a whig. The tale spun by the council led the king to withdraw Jefford's nomination. A year later, in the changed climate of 1687, Jefford saw an opening. He underwent "large expences journeys and paynes" to obtain a regulation of the corporation. The regulation came down in two stages, in November and December 1687, and sheared away twenty-eight members of the old corporation.[17]

The king's mandate brought in at least seventeen new men, with Jefford himself as mayor. The royal appointees included nine dissenters, seven of whom can be identified as Presbyterians. Among these Presbyterians were several leaders of the city's cloth industry, including three men who between them had exported 79,067 pounds of serge in 1676. Over the next few months another three Presbyterians were added to the council, including Thomas Crispin, a prominent manufacturer who served as master of the company of weavers, fullers, and shearmen in 1687–1688.[18] These leading clothiers had been hemmed in by the penal laws for a generation.[19] Now they had their revenge.

With the keys to the city in their hands, the new council set about to avenge ostentatiously their years of exclusion from government. They unwound swiftly the previous council's patronage appointments. The master of the Exeter Grammar School, an Anglican minister, was dismissed and replaced with a nonconformist minister. Other dismissals included the master of the public workhouse, the holder of the Bodley lectureship, the porters of the East and West Gates, the city's attorney at law, and the five London lawyers appointed as the city's counselors. One of their new counselors was to be none other than Robert Brent, the Catholic head of the board of agents charged by the king with regulating the corporations. The corporation was to pay him an annual salary of three pounds, six shillings, and eight pence. In addition, the corporation voted to "gratify" him with an unspecified sum for his "great paynes taken in an[d] about the affairs of this City." They also voted to compensate their new mayor, Thomas Jefford, for the funds he had expended to obtain the regulation that had brought them to power.[20]

In a calculated statement of the dissenters' newfound dominance of Exeter politics, the council ordered that the sword of the city should no longer be carried in state every Sunday to Exeter Cathedral but instead would proceed to the Presbyterian meetinghouse. Two of the new corporation officials also helped to administer a commission of enquiry in Devon investigating the fines levied against religious nonconformists over the previous decade, with a view to exposing corrupt proceedings by those who had prosecuted the cases.[21] The new council, moreover, petitioned for a new city charter without consulting the bishop of Exeter, which left him anxious that the charter would override the established rights of the cathedral chapter. When the new charter arrived in Exeter, it was received, according to the pro-government *London Gazette*, with a public celebration, presumably composed largely of the allies of the nonconformist councillors.[22]

On that occasion the cathedral elected not to join in the celebration, and the great bells of St. Peters were not rung. The new charter extended the jurisdiction of the council to all places within the city, thus overriding the cathedral authorities, who had long claimed jurisdiction over the Close. The Anglican response to the new councillors was one of cold fury. The earl of Bath denounced them as "a packed chamber of Dissenters" who "domineered over" the city. John Cruwys, an Anglican cloth merchant from Devon, wrote that the replacement of the old members in borough councils with new members who had agreed to "subscribe a paper" in support of repeal was an act that "mightily incensed the people."[23]

The anger of the Anglican populace led to a riot that broke out in the city in July 1688 after news of the acquittal of the seven bishops had spread to Devon. Anglican crowds gathered to light bonfires and celebrate the news. The new civic authorities of Exeter, displeased, ordered the crowds to disperse. Violence ensued. One man attempted to stab the mayor with a knife, a second punched the high sheriff, and a third cried out, "you popish rogues." When the allies of the council brought out the city's fire engine to douse the bonfires, rioters threw sticks at them from the windows of a nearby house. Several of the rioters were committed to prison, though one of them was heard to predict boldly that the dean of the cathedral would be sure to "fetch them out agayne."[24]

These intercommunal tensions found their way into print. One Anglican from Exeter penned a ballad that accused the new council of being in league with the pope. The ballad reported that "To our once Loyal Town, is lately come down, / Such a Hodge-podge of Benchers, as never wore Gown." The new benchers, or councillors, had "Pawn'd th' Old Religion, to Purchase New Charters." The aim of these new councillors was to reverse the Protestant Reformation and advance the Catholic cause or, as the balladeer put it indelicately, to "Bugger Geneva, to Fructifie Trent." The poet was torn between blaming the devil for the new Exeter council or blaming the pope and came up with the inspired choice of blaming them both, in an act of interwoven devilry: "When Satan was squeamish, and long'd for a Dainty, / The Pope Fricasseed him this new Four-and-twenty" (four and twenty being roughly the size of the new council).[25]

The Exeter ballad extended to eight verses in which members of the new council were lampooned in turn, from Thomas Jefford to the Presbyterian alderman Edmond Starr, or "Lean Jeff[ord]" and "Fat St[arr]," respectively. The common thread running through these verses was the theme of popish treachery. The fact that none of the new councillors was, in fact, a Catholic was irrelevant. Their purported Protestantism was merely a disguise. The Exeter balladeer insinuated that anyone who aided James II's regulation of the boroughs must be aiming to overthrow English Protestantism.

The council's political agenda was set out in an address that they sent to the king. They praised James's policies and with good repealer logic asserted that his *Declaration for Liberty of Conscience* had been the main cause of the recent boom in the cloth trade. They pledged their support for his campaign to secure a parliament that would bring about a lasting liberty of conscience. Meanwhile, the Presbyterians of Exeter, in an indication of their pleasure with the direction of royal policy, had named their newly opened meeting house "James's Meeting."[26]

Thomas Jefford delivered the council's address to the king with his own hands and returned to London later in the spring to meet with him a second time. During these meetings, the mayor discussed the upcoming parliamentary elections, assuring the king that the electoral interest of the dissenters in Exeter was stronger than that of the city's Anglicans, presumably because they dominated the cloth industry, the leading source of employment in the city. At the second audience, the king, delighted with what he had heard, knighted Jefford. The newly knighted mayor also met with the Catholic head of the board of regulators, Robert Brent, bearing gifts from the Exeter council: fifty guineas for Brent and ten for his secretary.[27] Back in Exeter, the councillors worked to sew up the results of the imminent parliamentary election. During the year 1687, only three men had been granted the status of freeman in Exeter, which brought with it the parliamentary franchise. But from February 1688 many more freemen were created, starting with the son of the Presbyterian councillor John Pym. Seven were added to the freeman's roll between March and May. In August, as word of a new parliament began to spread, the additions gathered pace. No fewer than 169 new freemen were shuttled onto the rolls on the twenty-seventh of that month, and another 49 were added on 3 September.[28] The council had refashioned the electorate in a little over a week.

The king's electoral agents were pleased with the results of the regulation of Exeter and wrote that their allies in the city "propose to choose [as members of parliament] Mr Thomas Jefford, the present Mayor, and Sir Barth. Shore, who are both right, and will undoubtedly carry itt [the election]." Sir Bartholomew Shower was a lawyer born in Exeter who went on to demonstrate his support for the king's policies by assisting in the prosecution of the seven bishops.[29] The election to parliament of Jefford and Shower would provide two reliable votes for repeal in the upcoming parliamentary session. The regulation of this cloth town was seamless.

Thwarting a Regulation

The successful regulation of Exeter had as much to do with the efforts of the city's economically influential Presbyterians as it had to do with any organization by Robert Brent and the king's regulators. It reflected local issues as much as it did national ones. The Presbyterians in effect organized themselves to reverse the Anglican ascendancy on their council, to obtain a new charter, and to ensure that the freemen of the city would elect two repealer candidates as members of parliament. Between Jefford's thirst for honor and the Presbyterians' thirst for revenge, the repeal cause in Exeter took care of itself. Elsewhere the repeal movement was not as strong. In some towns and cities, men were put into office against their will and proved to be ineffective. Other men accepted the offices offered to them but showed little zeal for repeal. In such places, a regulation was likely to fail unless the king's regulators worked long and hard at turning over the unfruitful soil.

The regulators signally failed to do this deep tilling in the Midlands town of Derby. The town lacked the mercantile clout of Exeter and had a smaller population, estimated at four thousand in 1715.[30] Its leading industry was malting with a sideline in brewing. In 1693 the town possessed 76 malthouses and 120 ale houses. Derby's malt was exported throughout Staffordshire and Cheshire, and its ale was exported as far afield as London. The malting trade was particularly profitable in times of dearth, when maltsters who had stored up large volumes of grain could sell their stores at a high profit on the open market. With the bumper crop of 1687 driving down the price of grain, Derby was likely not prospering to the same extent as Exeter was with its buoyant cloth trade.[31]

As in most towns of its size, the narrow streets of Derby sheltered a sizable number of Protestant nonconformists, about four hundred according to one estimate. These dissenters met together in a single Presbyterian congregation.[32] Although all of the dissenters in Derby belonged to the one meeting, they were not united in their religious practices. Many of them, perhaps most, were partial conformists. The dissenters of Derby held to the once-common but now-fading Presbyterian custom of refraining from holding worship services on Sunday mornings. This practice allowed some of them to worship at the Church of England on Sunday morning and then again at the Presbyterian meeting in the afternoon.[33] Other members of the meeting, however, chose not to take part in Church of England services. As one Anglican observer described the split in 1688, some of the Presbyterians were "church presbiterians" while the others were more "vigorouse dissenters."[34]

The observer who noted this split was George Vernon, a whig gentleman who had served as member of parliament for Derby in 1679 and 1681. He championed the cause of repeal and became the king's nominee in 1688 for one of the two Derby parliamentary seats. He worked tirelessly, as he put it, "to convince my countrymen, how greate a blessinge, grace, and favour, his Majestie givinge ease and libertye to all his subiects was to this Nation."[35] At Derby in 1688, the Presbyterians divided into two camps, each with its own preferred candidates for members of parliament. According to Vernon, some of the more "vigorouse dissenters" preferred John Spateman or Thomas Woolhouse, while many of the "church presbiterians" were for Robert Wilmot or John Coke. Spateman, a Presbyterian, and Woolhouse, a Congregationalist, had both indicated their willingness to repeal the penal laws and Test Acts. Spateman had accepted a position as justice of the peace in Derbyshire and was said to be "ambitious" to serve in the parliament that the king was planning to call.[36]

Robert Wilmot and John Coke, by contrast, seem unlikely to have been supporters of repeal. Wilmot had refused to commit himself when the earl of Huntingdon had asked him the king's Three Questions regarding repeal. He stated that, if elected to parliament, he would listen to the debates of the House with an open mind and would not go to parliament with "any prejudging or obstinate humor or temper." He went on to serve as the sheriff of Derbyshire in 1688–1689 and as a member of parliament for Derby in 1690, which suggests his prominence in the local community.[37] Coke had served as one of Derby's representatives in the Parliament of 1685. In the November session of that parliament, he had shown his true colors by opposing the king's plan to retain Catholic officers in the army. After the king had made a speech reprimanding the House of Commons for its behavior, Coke had responded in the House that "we were all Englishmen, and he hoped we should not be frighted from our dutys by a few high words." For this act of defiance he had been sent to the Tower by the tory House and subsequently lost his commission in the army.[38] Thus the "church presbiterians" preferred parliamentary candidates who were unlikely to support repeal, while the "vigorouse dissenters" mentioned by Vernon appeared ready to elect two repealers to parliament.

The Presbyterians of Derby had split into two factions: one that remained aloof from the repealer movement and attended Church of England services, and another that remained aloof from the Church of England and supported the cause of repeal. Faced with such a situation, the decision of the king's regulators ought to have been an easy one.

They should have put into civic office the more "vigorouse," pro-repeal Presbyterians and kept out of office the "church" Presbyterians or partial conformists. Instead, they botched the regulation. Twenty-one members were removed from the thirty-eight-member council, with replacements nominated by the king. A sizable block of partial conformists was added to the new council, but it is unclear whether any of the more "vigorouse" dissenters were added. George Vernon described this regulation as a "Randome puttinge out some who would have complyd in every thinge; and puttinge in some that will complye in nothinge."[39]

Rather than reaping the fruits of the regulation, the repealer cause in Derby withered on the vine. According to Vernon, the new dissenting councillors wished to choose members of parliament "of theire owne faction to give themselves ease; butt are ielouse [jealous] of any body that will give ease to the catholiques." A desire to continue the penal laws and the doctrinal Test against Catholics, while granting toleration and perhaps access to public office to Protestant nonconformists, was characteristic of the moderate Anglicans and partial conformists who were often among the king's most zealous opponents. Their opposition to the king's proposals was fueled by their anti-popery. With such leadership in place in Derby, it fell to Vernon himself, who was not a member of the council, to organize an address from the town congratulating the king on the birth of the prince of Wales. He was able to get the townspeople to agree to this address only on the explicit condition that there would be nothing mentioned in it apart from an expression of joy at the birth of the prince. The new councillors of Derby did not even send an address to James thanking him for his *Declaration for Liberty of Conscience*, and they certainly did not send an address pledging to assist in his repeal campaign.[40]

At least one of the new dissenters on the council, moreover, seems to have worked in secret to ensure that no repealer candidate would be elected to parliament for the town. John Gisbourne Jr. wrote in August to Sir John Gell, a local Presbyterian gentleman and a former member of parliament for Derbyshire, to propose "a compr[o]mise of the Election betweene the Churchmen and dissenters." One of the compromise candidates, it had already been agreed, would be John Coke, the Derbyshire man who had spoken up against the king in the Parliament of 1685. The other, Gisbourne suggested, could be Gell's son Philip, his son-in-law William Eyre, or Robert Wilmot. This combination was necessary to stop the repealer Vernon, who "hath made more interest already here then was foreseene hee could."[41]

The John Gisbourne who wrote this letter was almost certainly the John Gisbourne whom the king had nominated as an alderman of Derby in January.[42] If they were indeed one and the same, then the man who was covertly organizing the opposition to repeal in Derby was one of the men whom the king had nominated to the town council a few months before. It would appear that Vernon had been correct when he alleged that the regulation was being undermined from within. Vernon blamed Robert Brent, the Catholic head of the board of regulators, for this debacle, referring bitterly to Brent's supposed "interest" with the dissenters in Derby. Brent's contacts in Derby, whoever they were, had been giving him counterproductive advice. As a result, Vernon was stymied.[43] Trouble was brewing for the repeal campaign in this malting town.

Repealer Irenicism

The councils of both Exeter and Derby were taken over by Presbyterians and their allies, but with opposite political effects. Exeter sent an address to the king pledging to support the repeal of the penal laws and Test Acts, while Derby refused to send such an address. Exeter's council proposed two men for the upcoming parliament who almost certainly would have voted for repeal, while Derby's council appears to have favored two candidates who would have opposed it. Presbyterians in different towns had different attitudes.

It was not just the Presbyterians who were split in their response to repeal. Some Anglicans participated in the movement, while most did not. Some Quakers participated, while others steered clear of involvement.[44] Even the Catholics, who generally supported repeal, occasionally preferred not to become too involved in the campaign themselves, out of a fear that they might alienate their neighbors. The repealer movement split every major religious group in England, though to varying degrees, with some groups largely unenthusiastic about repeal and other groups largely supportive.[45]

The key variable influencing an individual's decision to participate in the repealer movement was affinity to the Church of England. Thus the more "vigorouse dissenters" in Derby were more likely to support repeal than the "church presbiterians," who practiced partial conformity. Among the other religious groups, the Catholics, perhaps not surprisingly, were the most likely to support repeal. Over two hundred Catholic gentlemen across England and Wales gave affirmative responses to the king's Three Questions, and no Catholic is known to have given a negative or doubtful response. This widespread support for the king's religious policy was predictable enough given the evident lack of affinity of Catholics for the Church of England and their obvious willingness to oppose anti-popery. Although some Catholics expressed private concerns about James's policies, out of a fear that Anglicans might seek vengeance in a future reign, the widespread enthusiasm of Catholics in the nation as a whole for the king's policies should not be discounted.[46] James's co-religionists often went out of their way to support his repeal campaign by serving energetically in local offices and by attempting to convince their Protestant friends and neighbors to support repeal.[47]

Other nonconformist groups were also likely to support repeal. Among the Protestant nonconformists, the Quakers and Baptists could expect little favor from the Church of England and, after decades of persecution, often felt little goodwill toward it. These men and women were frequently willing to participate in the repealer movement, though some of them preferred to steer clear of it to avoid antagonizing their Anglican friends and neighbors. The more moderate nonconformists, however, such as the Congregationalists and Presbyterians, might hope to receive favor from the Church of England, including some measure of either tacit tolerance or legalized toleration, and often refused to take any actions that might aggravate the Anglicans. But even within these groups attitudes varied, with some "vigorous" Presbyterians and Congregationalists actively hostile to the Church of England while other "church" Presbyterians sought to maintain close ties with their Anglican friends.

The Anglicans were by definition attached to the Church of England, and one might assume on this basis that all Anglicans were opposed to repeal. Yet the attachment of Anglicans to their church varied from one individual to another. Elkanah Settle, the propagandist and playwright, was an Anglican, but he took over the editorship of the repealer newspaper *Publick Occurrences* after Henry Care's death. Whatever sort of Anglican he was, he was certainly not a dogmatic one, as he himself affirmed: "How Troublesome to the World has it been, Mens valuing themselves so extreamly for being of this or that perswasion?"[48] He may also have written the repealer pamphlet *An Expedient for Peace*, which used some of the same phrases and expressions as his writings in *Publick Occurrences*. The author of *An Expedient for Peace* argued that all Christian denominations were essentially the same: "We see all Rivers, little and great, at last discharge themselves into the Ocean; and all Divisions and Sects of Christians have the same End and Tendency, and Terminate in the same Center, viz. in indeavouring to Please, to Glorifie and honour their Maker." Thus a man, rather than calling himself by the name of his particular denomination, such as a "Catholick, Church-of-England-man, Presbyterian, Independant, etc," should simply call himself a "Christian."[49]

The *Expedient for Peace* argued against being excessively proud of one's own religious beliefs since these beliefs were based largely on custom. Every man was "of the Religion he was bred to, whether Turk, Jew, or Pagan; and thinks that always the best." People should strive to avoid the mindless conformity that was often a consequence of religious denominations: "when a man is linked to a Party, there is no unchaining of him; he delights in his Slavery and Chains, and reckons him an Enemy that would free him." The pamphleteer toyed with the idea of making it a "Felony or Treason" to call oneself by "any other Name, than that of Christian." Men and women should be free to worship as they pleased, but should not be permitted to use those differences in liturgy to seek preferential treatment by the state.[50] In similar fashion, Settle wrote in *Publick Occurrences* that he hoped the day would come "when the Malignity of distinguishing Christians by Nick-names shall be at an end." This sentiment was echoed in another anonymous repealer pamphlet *Some Free Reflections*, which expressed the hope that all Christians should "own no other Name or Profession but that of Christianity."[51]

This appeal to a simplified, ethical Christianity, reminiscent of that of Erasmus and Grotius, was taken up in a number of repealer tracts. Denominational labels caused religious strife, repealers argued, and abandoning these labels in favor of a unifying Christianity could help to put that strife to rest. One repealer author, who claimed to be an Anglican, contended that "The Sincere Conscientious Man, that is Pious to his God, and Honest and Just to his Neighbour," whether that man happened to be an Anglican, a nonconformist, or a Roman Catholic, should be considered "a good Christian."[52] Repealers alluded to a verse from the first epistle to the Corinthians where St. Paul wrote, "Now this is what I mean: each of you says, I am of Paul, or I am of Apollos, or I am of Cephas, or I am of Christ. Has Christ been divided up?"[53] Another anonymous repealer, who claimed to be a minister of the Church of England, expressed the hope that "all invidious and distinctive Titles may be abandon'd" and "the Divine Name of Christian describe all the Members of the Body of Christ, as once it did at Antioch," alluding to the unity of the first-century Christians in the Levant.[54]

The Anglican minister Daniel Kenrick, in a pro-repeal sermon delivered in the spring of 1688, suggested that some Anglicans had become too caught up in "Confessorian Boldness." He argued that a greater degree of modesty was more in keeping with the widespread distribution of religious truth, since "every one of us," whether Anglican or nonconformist, "aims at one eternal End." As he put it, "we all own one God and one Lord Jesus Christ." The "Crown of Heaven," meaning salvation, could be obtained by the "round-about Runner" as well as by the person who took the more straightforward path; different men could attain the same end, "tho' in the use of different Ways."[55]

Confessional divisions had initially entered into the early church, one repealer contended, when "Religion became twisted with secular Interest, and the Profession of Divinity became a Trade."[56] Bishops and their clergy, in this view, had found that they had rich benefices to defend and had learned that denouncing their opponents as heretics was a ready and easy way to defend their property. This strand of repealer thought took on an anticlerical tone in ascribing the process of confessionalization to the greed of clerics. Irenicism could reverse this process, some repealers argued, if men and women were willing to loosen their denominational ties.

Anglican irenicism of this sort might at first glance appear to be equivalent to Latitudinarianism, but it was hardly the same thing. The goal of the Latitudinarians was to expand the Church of England to encompass some of the Presbyterians and Congregationalists, while keeping the Catholics and Quakers out. Latitudinarians in James II's reign were generally hostile to the repealer movement, which they saw as excessively pro-Catholic and pro-Quaker. Gilbert Burnet, the Latitudinarian divine and future bishop of Salisbury, wrote several pamphlets against the repealers. Stillingfleet, Tillotson, and Tenison were no more favorable to the repealer design.[57]

The customary division of the later Stuart Church of England into "Low Church" and "High Church" cannot account for the diversity of Anglican responses to the repealer movement. Some of the Anglican repealers, to be sure, were High Churchmen whose ultra-tory zeal led them to follow the king even though they expressed distaste for Protestant nonconformity. The bishop of Chester, Thomas Cartwright, was just such a man. But other Anglican repealers such as Elkanah Settle and Daniel Kenrick cannot easily be classified as either High or Low Churchmen. Settle and Kenrick might, perhaps, be described as nominal Anglicans, but it would be more accurate to describe them as antinominal Anglicans. Rather than being Anglicans in name only, they were Anglicans who rejected denominational names and preferred to be described only as "Christians." They sought to reverse the process of confessionalization by rejecting "Confessorian Boldness" and by promoting Christian unity. Settle was not a Low-Church Anglican or a High-Church Anglican: he was an Anglican by default, having been born into the Church of England and never having decided to join any other faith.

Overheated rhetoric in opposition pamphlets about the perils facing the Church of England had little impact on these Anglican repealers. Some Anglicans, like Settle, were not as invested in the future fate of the Church as one might have expected. They had developed an aversion to the kind of exclusive, party-line rhetoric that they felt diminished Christianity by making religion into a tool that enabled one group to assert its dominance over others. They displayed an inveterate dislike of party labels and an individualistic preference for freethinking. They had no desire to leave the Church of England and join a nonconformist group, presumably because they saw in the nonconformist congregations many of the dogmatic features they disliked in the Church of England. But, at the same time, they felt no great need to defend the peculiar prerogatives of the Church of England.

It is difficult to know how large this group was. Certainly there were many nominal Anglicans who rarely went to Sunday services. But it is unclear how many of these sporadic churchgoers possessed the sorts of relativistic ideas articulated by Kenrick and Settle, including the idea that there were many ways to attain salvation. These more skeptical Anglicans, however many there were, should be considered a potential pool of supporters for the repealer movement.

The reaction of the Anglican establishment to the Anglican repealers was predictably hostile. The Anglican minister Daniel Kenrick, who preached a repealer sermon with irenicist themes in Worcester, was depicted as a traitor to his church. The bishop of Worcester, a stalwart opponent of the repeal campaign, was livid after Kenrick's sermon, which was delivered in Worcester cathedral at the assizes upon the invitation of the Roman Catholic sheriff Sir Walter Blount. The bishop said that Kenrick had "libelled the church of England" with his "Scurrilous invective." (Kenrick had compared the Anglican persecutions of non-conformists with Louis XIV's persecution of the Huguenots.) According to the bishop of Worcester, the clergyman had "excited the general indignation" of his largely Anglican audience, thereby rendering himself "odious to all sorts excepting the Bigot Romanists." The bishop also claimed that Kenrick, apart from his offensive sermon, was also guilty of acts of "incest, perjury, and other vices." He dared not prosecute him for these offenses, however, because "it would look like revenge" for the sermon. Kenrick was, nevertheless, cited to the spiritual courts for incest a few months later.[58]

Daniel Kenrick had a wide-ranging career; in addition to being a cleric, he was a physician and a poet. A friend of Aphra Behn, his poetry was published in *The Grove*. As a poet he was praised for his "Fire and Sprightliness of Thinking," and his freethinking was also evident in his willingness to offend his bishop. The bishop's charge of incest arose from the fact that he, upon the death of his wife Beatrice, had married his wife's sister, Victoria. Two months after his controversial sermon at the assizes, he was one of the few Anglican ministers to read the *Declaration for Liberty of Conscience* in church as the king had stipulated.[59] He was the rare clergyman who did not much care what the Anglican establishment thought of him.

Disaffection with Anglicanism and sympathy for repeal tended to go hand in hand. This is not to say, however, that all repealers were irenicists in the mold of Kenrick and Elkanah Settle. Many of the Catholics, Baptists, and Congregationalists who joined the repeal campaign did so because they believed that their own group needed to be protected from persecution, not because they believed that all denominational labels should be abandoned. But among the Anglicans, at least, the adoption of an irenical stance by some helps to explain why they might join a movement that seemed to many to be aimed against their own church.

The Regulators

In their responses to the repealer movement, Anglicans differed from Anglicans, Presbyterians from Presbyterians, and Quakers from Quakers. The task of sorting out all these differences fell to a handful of royal officials. King James sent agents across the country to identify sympathetic men who could be appointed to leading positions in the parliamentary boroughs. The king's agents, who were known as the "regulators," have often been depicted as bureaucrats who were paid to implement a top-down agenda of heavy-handed coercion.[60] But a closer look at their backgrounds reveals that they can hardly be seen as typical bureaucrats, for a majority of them were Baptist ministers from London.[61] Their occupations suggest that the regulating campaign may have had a popular base.

The regulators were probably fewer than fifteen in number. Thirteen are certainly known and of these at least ten were Baptists. Nine were pastors of Baptist churches, all but one in the capital. Their congregations met across a swathe of London and its suburbs: Nehemiah Cox and William Collins at Petty France in Westminster; Richard Adams, William Marner, and James Jones in Southwark; Thomas Plant at the Barbican; Benjamin Dennis at Stratford; and John Jones at Pinners' Hall near Liverpool Street. The size of their congregations gives some indication of their influence. Plant spoke to two thousand worshippers at the Barbican, representing the largest and wealthiest Baptist congregation in London, while Cox and Collins preached to well over five hundred at Petty France, the unofficial head church of the Particular Baptists. Richard Adams gathered a congregation of at least three hundred, and James Jones, at least two hundred. In addition to being Baptist preachers, many of them were artisans and small tradesmen in London. The group included a cabinet-maker, a milliner, a shoemaker, a tobacconist, a theologian, a doctor, and a tailor. With the exceptions of Nathaniel Wade and John Jones, who both joined Monmouth's Rebellion, few had anything other than casual involvement in whig politics before 1687, and only Wade, the lone Congregationalist in the group, had any prior experience in electoral management.[62]

The king funded handsomely the activities of the regulators.[63] But this pecuniary reward was unlikely to have been enough to attract them to the repeal cause, since by their activities they risked exposing their reputations to public censure. As nonconformist ministers dependent on the freewill offerings of their followers, their reputations underpinned their long-term livelihoods. It seems more likely that they, having experienced religious persecution themselves or having seen its effects on their congregations, wished to see the king prevail in his campaign for liberty of conscience. As two of them wrote in the spring of 1688, "since his Gracious Majesty, by the goodness of God, hath published His Royal Declaration, for Liberty of Conscience . . . We confess we most willingly fall in with his Majesty's gracious Designs, and shall, to our utmost, endeavour to carry them on . . . and pray he may live to see the Top-stone of this glorious Fabrick of Liberty of Conscience laid." The "Top-stone" they hoped to see laid was the "Perfection by Law" of the king's declaration in a pro-repeal parliament. A royal proclamation might prove temporary, but a parliamentary act of toleration would outlast the king's own life and thereby "for ever deliver this Nation from the Convulsions and Evils it has labour'd under in former Years."[64] The ideological aims of the regulators suggest that they should be described as repealers.

The brief of the regulators was to make contact with nonconformists in the localities, to gather names of men to be removed from councils and those to be appointed in their stead, and to send those names to Robert Brent, the Catholic head of the board of regulators.[65] Either Brent himself or another go-between, Henry Trinder, would forward the names to a subcommittee of the privy council headed by the earl of Sunderland, lord president of the council, which met regularly in the earl's Whitehall office.[66] That committee would then draft privy council orders for the removal of men from the corporations through the exercise of their legitimate power. But while the right of removal had been reserved by the crown, the right of election remained in the localities. Here the king could only issue mandates of appointment that were not enforceable at common law, although most councils chose to submit rather than incur the king's displeasure. Royal mandates had been employed previously to recommend officeholders for vacant places in the towns, but never as extensively as in 1688.

The idea of hiring Baptists as regulators may have come from Brent, given that he had prior connections with Baptists in his role as supervisor of the patents issued in 1686 and 1687 dispensing nonconformists from penalties assessed under the penal laws.[67] The Baptist ministers agreed to serve on the board of regulators even though they knew they would be working under the immediate supervision of a Catholic. This provided a practical demonstration of James II's project to unite both ends of the religious continuum in a tolerationist alliance.

The regulators described themselves, in a letter to one corporation, as men who had the "honour of Inspecting under the Lords Commissioners appointed p[er] his Majestie the Regulacon now on foote, of severall Corporacons."[68] As their powers of "Inspecting" were entirely unofficial, they had no authority to compel town councillors to meet with them or to follow their instructions. The regulators could not order; they could only advise. But their influence was decisive because the privy council generally rubber-stamped their recommendations.[69] Their inspections were often greeted with hostility in the localities, for their actions threatened local rights and prerogatives. In some quarters they were called "The Booted Apostles," a name previously applied to the French dragoons who had terrorized the Huguenots into abjuring Protestantism.[70] Their influence irked the lord lieutenants of some of the counties, who attempted to intervene on behalf of favored clients only to be rebuffed by Sunderland.[71] Under this state of affairs, a Baptist shoemaker could have more influence in the regulation of a town than the lord lieutenant of that county. From Bedfordshire, the earl of Ailesbury decried the influence exercised by the Baptist regulator Edward Roberts, whom he dismissed contemptuously as a "broken fanatic shoemaker." The earl threatened to resign his position on the grounds that he had become a mere cipher, "very insignificant in the Counties where I was Lord Lieutenant."[72]

Each pair of regulators had a caseload of approximately sixteen boroughs, which suggests some of the difficulties they faced. In the early stages of regulation, they were so overwhelmed that they appear to have relied mainly on gathering intelligence by letter rather than in person. Only gradually were they able to visit more of the boroughs themselves. In the first phase of regulations, which lasted from November 1687 to April 1688, they surveyed only twelve counties in person. Regulations were performed in this first phase, however, not only in the twelve counties visited by the regulators, but also in a further twenty-two counties, leaving only Cornwall, Herefordshire, Monmouthshire, Cheshire, and Westmorland untouched.[73] Winter travel was inconvenient and the roads were poor. After April the regulators began to travel more widely, sending back a second round of reports from eighteen counties, including eight that had not been visited in the first round.[74]

The practice of gathering intelligence via letters was easier on the regulators, but it left vast discretion in the hands of local correspondents. The regulators habitually sent out form letters instructing their informants on what to write. Each letter urged the recipient to give "the first and second names of other fit persons . . . [who] are for taking away the Penal lawes for Conscience, and the Tests: in which no regard is to be had to their perswasions or opinions in Religion." Local informants were asked to draw up a list of suitable names for town councillors according to the following model: "E G a Dissenter . . . G E moderate [Anglican] . . . E B Roman Catholick." Pro-toleration or "moderate" Anglicans could be permitted to remain on councils while anti-toleration or "violent" Anglicans were to be targeted for removal.[75]

The drafters of the form letters were aware that they were handing over enormous powers of discretion to the recipients of the letters, and they seem to have been at ease with the prospect. The letter stipulated that, if the local correspondent was "not Sure" which men in his community supported the repeal of the penal laws and Test Acts, then he should "Pitch on the most fit and lik[e]liest that will answer the End propos[e]d." A regulation could in theory proceed as follows. The local correspondent would write a letter recording either his hunches or his informed opinions about the attitudes of his fellow townsmen. These hunches would be redrafted by the board of regulators as a slate of recommendations to the privy council. This slate of recommendations would be embodied in a privy council order and a mandate under the sign manual. The set of official orders would be passed to Robert Brent, who either would send it back to the local informant for him to present in person to the relevant town council or would have a royal messenger deliver it to the town, a service for which the town councillors would pay a fee of approximately two to six pounds upon receipt.[76] The entire edifice of regulation—from opinion to recommendation to order—was in many cases based on the discretion of a single individual. Town officials had good reason to be uneasy.

That single individual was not always a person who commanded the respect of his fellow townsmen. The only copy of the form letter that survives is a letter that William Penn sent to a fellow Quaker in Huntingdon, most likely Richard Jobson. The town of Huntingdon was subsequently regulated three times in 1688, stripping it of its mayor and nine of its twelve aldermen. Jobson had in the past been harassed for his faith by the inhabitants of the town.[77] The letter asked the Quaker correspondent to identify some of his neighbors as "violent," or opposed to toleration, but did not clarify what criteria he ought to use in determining whom to place in that category. This request would seem to have been an open invitation for him to propose the removal of men who had once persecuted him. A Quaker, moving in different social circles than the Anglicans on the council, might not have been in a position to distinguish between those loyalist Anglicans who were willing to comply with the king's requests and those Anglicans who were not.

Thus a man who had once persecuted a Quaker neighbor but was now willing to submit to the king's wishes with regards to the penal laws and Tests could find his position on a local council in danger. This arrangement presented a problem for the more loyalist tories, who may have been willing to support the royal agenda for repeal but who often lacked good relations with dissenters. As a result, some loyalist Anglicans who were willing to support the king's toleration policy were removed from civic office. Edward Mainwaring of Staffordshire had given a positive reply to the Three Questions when asked as a deputy lieutenant whether he would comply with the repeal campaign. But his answer was not sent up to London until February 1688, too late to save his mayoralty of Newcastle-under-Lyme. In another case, John Fitzherbert was removed as a burgess of Malmesbury in December 1687, even though he agreed to support repeal when asked for his opinion as a justice of the peace around the same time.[78]

The only surefire way for town councillors to preserve their local positions was to cultivate a relationship with their regulator or the regulator's informant. This step often was not possible, for the local informant was under no obligation to reveal himself. Tory councillors could not gain much leverage by appealing to their usual patrons, since their patrons were often kept at arm's length by the board of regulators led by Brent. Town councillors, moreover, could not insure themselves by giving the correct answer to the Three Questions because in many cases they were not even asked a question. As the earl of Bath indignantly wrote in reference to his ejected friends from the corporation of Exeter, "You may easily imagine it to be a great mortification to them [the citizens of Exeter] to see the most substantial, rich, loyal citizens turned out of the government for no offence and never so much as asked any questions by the regulators." Sir John Bramston recorded in his memoirs that he was removed as high steward of Maldon "without askeing me any of the questions."[79]

In the unusual cases where the Three Questions were asked of town councillors, they were asked on an *ad hoc* basis by the regulators' local informants, not as part of a systematic campaign.[80] The king had made it clear that he did not wish to extend the asking of the Three Questions beyond the deputy lieutenants and justices of the peace to the mayors, aldermen, and councillors.[81] This was a tactical error on his part, for it deprived him of useful information about many tory councillors who may not have been friendly toward nonconformists but who would have been willing to do whatever the king asked of them. A better planned and more cautious regulation might have achieved better results, but James was in a hurry and his nonconformist allies had scores to settle with local Anglicans.

Without a formal, visible, and official process for deciding who would be removed from a local council and who would remain, many councillors felt adrift. Burgesses who appealed to their lord lieutenant for help in resisting a regulation found that the old lines of communication had been cut. During Charles II's reign, the privy council and the secretaries of state had controlled borough policy. They had received letters from lord lieutenants and had often acted on their advice. But in late 1687 the business of regulation had largely been transferred from the privy council itself to a subcommittee of the council, which in turn had become a forum for rubber-stamping nominations from the board of regulators. In this new environment, launching an appeal to a lord lieutenant, who would then appeal to a secretary of state or to the privy council, was frequently ineffective.[82] The most effective way of getting or keeping an office, many found, was to travel to London and to secure an in-person interview with the board of regulators. But for most this was not feasible. Many local officers were unwilling to travel all the way to London to retain an unsalaried local office like an aldermanship; and many were unwilling to make the sorts of political pledges that would have warmed the heart of a regulator. When the councillors of Hull attempted to intervene with Robert Brent through an intermediary, he responded curtly that their charter would be reissued, thereby implying that they might be thrown out of office in the new charter.[83]

Others were more successful with Brent either because of their ideology or because of their pocketbooks. When the Nottingham alderman Charles Harvey traveled to London to present a tolerationist address to the king from the new corporation, he gave ten shillings to Robert Brent's servant but only five shillings to the earl of Sunderland's servant, indicating the relative importance of the two in the regulating scheme.[84] The council of Exeter gave fifty guineas to Brent and ten guineas to his secretary. The council of Lyme Regis made a payment of five pounds, seven shillings, and six pence to Brent's assistant, the Baptist regulator Edward Roberts, for delivering a pro-repeal address to the king.[85] The council of Newcastle-under-Lyme paid thirty pounds for the regulation that brought them to power at the end of 1687; much of this money, presumably, was for fees to Brent and his servants. The council of Nottingham paid a charge of thirty pounds to unnamed "Cl[er]kes Agents and Sollicitors" for their "paines" in arranging the regulation of the borough.[86] The fact that some councils and councillors were paying for their orders of regulation suggests a partially bottom-up process driven by a degree of local initiative in the towns. One enterprising man, Thomas Launder, procured a letter from the regulators appointing himself as town clerk of Coventry, a salaried position. When he was refused the office by the Coventry council on the grounds that it was not then vacant, he left the council chambers "in a greate passion and immediatelye took post up towards London." The council, well aware of where the power in the realm now lay, sent a letter immediately to "Robert Brent Esq one of the honnourable Comissioners of Regulacons" explaining why they had been unable to comply with the king's order.[87] Old links of patron-client relations had shifted abruptly, and Robert Brent was now at the center of the web.

Religious Diversity in the Regulated Towns

The system of patronage that sprang up in 1688 was guided by Brent and the board of regulators, who in turn established a network of local informants in towns throughout England and Wales. Those local agents came from a variety of political and religious persuasions: Quakers in

Huntingdon and Preston; Catholics in Carlisle, Hull, and Berwick-upon-Tweed; Congregationalists in Nottingham; a Baptist in Leicester; and Anglicans in Lancaster, Barnstaple, Rye, and York.[88] They were directed by a board of regulators that was largely Baptist, who in turn were serving under the direction of a Catholic. The religious diversity of the agents suggests that religion was not the primary criterion by which Brent and the regulators chose their local informants.

This lack of denominational favoritism was also apparent in the selection of officeholders for the towns. One might expect the regulators and their informants to have selected appointees who were drawn from their own religious groups. Thus a Baptist regulator might be expected to choose Baptist appointees, while a Catholic informant might have chosen Catholics. This pattern did not occur in most cases. In Bury St Edmunds, a Baptist regulator oversaw the appointment of a diverse council that featured a Presbyterian, a Quaker, four Congregationalists, and five Catholics.[89] In Nottingham, two Congregationalist informants supervised a regulation that produced a council composed of Presbyterians and Anglicans as well as Congregationalists.[90] These outcomes were in keeping with the instructions sent out by the regulators, which urged local informants to nominate men committed to repeal without regard to "their perswasions or opinions in Religion."[91]

The work of the regulators led to entirely new patterns of officeholding in the localities, not a return to older patterns. Baptists were appointed as mayors of Maidstone and Marlborough and as councilmen and officers in Oxford, Abingdon, and Wilton.[92] Quakers were appointed as aldermen and councilmen in Tiverton, Devizes, Salisbury, Calne, Banbury, Hertford, Guildford, Leicester, Hull, King's Lynn, Norwich, and Bury St Edmunds.[93] Congregationalists were appointed in Bedford, Hull, Nottingham, Bridport, and Great Yarmouth. Presbyterians were appointed in Hull, Lancaster, Nottingham, and Canterbury, as well as Exeter and Derby.[94] Catholics were appointed in Doncaster, Scarborough, Newcastle, Carlisle, Wigan, Stafford, Evesham, Warwick, Cambridge, Totnes, and Tiverton, among other places.[95] Despite the eye-catching appointments of religious minorities, the majority of the new town councillors were Anglicans and Presbyterians. It could hardly be otherwise since the Presbyterians were the largest by far of the nonconformist groups and the Anglicans were so numerous that some parliamentary boroughs contained few nonconformists.[96]

Some councils appear to have made adjustments to accommodate the religious scruples of the more extreme nonconformists, particularly the Quakers. The newly regulated council of Chichester in Sussex passed a resolution that henceforward "all the members of this Common Councell may keepe on their hats," presumably as a concession to one or more councillors who had refused, on religious grounds, to remove theirs.[97] At Bury St Edmunds, a regulation in March 1688 brought in a Catholic as mayor. A month later, when the king nominated a Quaker, Edward Deekes, as an alderman, the new Catholic mayor admitted him to the council without tendering him the customary oath of office. Since the Quakers also refused on conscientious grounds to use the word "saint," contending that all Christians were saints in Christ Jesus, the new alderman of Bury St Edmunds was governing a town whose name he could not say.[98]

The service of even a few Quakers on local councils was an extraordinary step for a group that has often been deemed to have abandoned politics and become "quietist" after the Restoration of Charles II dashed their hopes of instituting a new Jerusalem in England.[99] Not all Quakers, however, were enthusiastic participants in the repealer movement. When the Society of Friends debated at their Yearly Meeting in London in June 1688 whether it was advisable for them to take up public offices, the meeting was split, with Stephen Crisp arguing that the way was not yet "made open," perhaps alluding to the conscientious objection of Quakers to taking the oath of office. William Penn argued for the establishment of an advisory committee that might offer counsel to individual Quakers deciding whether to take up public office. Such a committee could easily have become an arm of the regulators, forwarding to them the names of Quakers who were interested in serving. But Penn was overruled by George Fox, who insisted that it was "not safe to conclude such things in a Yearly Meeting." By contrast, the Yorkshire Quarterly Meeting, the subsidiary body of Quakers in Yorkshire, had fewer inhibitions: they purchased fifty copies of William Popple's repeal tract, *Three Letters,* and put together a guide to voting in the upcoming parliamentary elections that was then distributed to local meetings in Yorkshire.[100]

Some Baptists had, like the Quakers, a conscientious objection to oath taking, and this could cause problems for the king's regulators. In London, the wealthy Baptist merchant William Kiffin initially refused the office of alderman, citing his reluctance to swear an oath or wear a formal gown. Though he eventually took his office two months later and swore the requisite oath, he later suggested that he had done so out of concern for "the good of the orphans" under the City's supervision.[101] At Malmesbury six of the king's appointees, who were probably Baptists, refused to take the oath of office, one of them saying that "they were willing to serve his said Majestie and the Corporacon but would not sweare."[102] The king's regulators had to pay attention not only to the political opinions held by individual men and women, but also to the particular cultures of nonconformist groups and their willingness to adapt to a civic culture that was in many respects alien to their own. Some of the more intransigent Baptists and Quakers might be willing to endorse repeal and yet be unwilling to serve in an office that required them to bend their principles in any way.

The opponents of repeal highlighted the religious diversity of some of the councils as a way of suggesting their disreputableness. The new council of Nottingham was described after the Revolution as "a Crew of independents presbiterians Anabaptists and familly of love." The new mayor of Tewkesbury was said to be a Jew. Whether he was in fact Jewish, or whether the council of Nottingham actually included members of the notorious but tiny Family of Love, was beside the point.[103] The goal here was to discredit rather than to describe. Other accounts focused on the low social status of some of the new councillors rather than their religious beliefs. The royally appointed mayor of Cambridge, who was an Anglican, was depicted as a "thoro-pac'd knave" who had made new freemen from "the very dreggs and most infamous rougues about this Towne."[104] The new councillors were portrayed as inverters of the social order, rising beyond their stations to take places from the sober citizens who deserved to govern. The social and religious heterogeneity of these new men could be used against them. As the Exeter balladeer put it, they were "Such a Hodge-podge of Benchers as never wore Gown."[105]

Conflict in the Regulated Towns

These "Hodge-podges" often worked surprisingly well together, organizing addresses to send to King James and pledging to elect members of parliament committed to repeal. But, in some cases, they clashed. The

most prominent example of such infighting occurred in Newcastle-upon-
Tyne, where the king appointed twelve Catholics and twelve dissenters
to the corporation. The two groups proceeded to engage in a protracted
feud, with the new Catholic mayor complaining to the king that the dissenters were "all knaves and Rebells."[106] Ethnic differences compounded
these religious divisions, as the mayor was of Irish descent.[107] The king
was forced to deputize the lord lieutenant of the North Riding of Yorkshire, a Catholic peer, to compose the differences between the newly
appointed members. The lord lieutenant's solution was to recommend
the appointment of an additional twelve members to the corporation, all
of them Anglicans, who would then hold the balance of power between
the dissenters and the Catholics.[108] It is unclear why the lord lieutenant
thought that introducing a third faction would bring peace. The infighting
resumed at the mayoral election of September 1688. The Catholic faction
on the council nominated one of their members to serve as mayor, while
a nonconformist alderman, Ambrose Barnes, backed a fellow dissenter.
With the support of the town's Anglicans, the nonconformist candidate
defeated the Catholic.[109] In Newcastle, at least, bonds of shared Protestantism outweighed any bonds of shared attachment to the king or to his
toleration campaign.

The regulators, faced with factional strife like that in Newcastle,
were instructed to patch things up as best they could. Their directions
from the king in June 1688 were as follows: "whereas his Majesty is
informed that in some places there are some differences between such
of the Catholicks, Church of England men and Dissenters, as do even
concurr in promoting his Majestys measures in generall, You must
make it your principall care to endeavour to compose all such differences, by perswading all people to lay aside and forget all former feuds
and disagreements." This they proved unable to accomplish in Newcastle. With the new council in disarray almost from the moment of its
installation, no address was sent to the king from the city pledging to
elect pro-repeal members of parliament. The Catholic mayor, Sir William Creagh, along with a group of Catholic aldermen and some of the
dissenting magistrates, had attempted in January 1688 to pass an
address, but the common council had blocked it.[110]

Several other local councils also voted not to send addresses to
the king, even after they had been thoroughly regulated. The newly
regulated council of Leicester voted by a large margin not to send an

address along the lines of a form sent to them by the earl of Huntingdon, with only three of the fifty-two members voting for it.[111] The new council of Chichester voted against their mayor's proposal of sending an address thanking the king "for his declaracon for tolleracon."[112] The new council of Bristol also voted against sending an address, a decision that was particularly galling for repealers both because of Bristol's status as the second city of the kingdom and because of the large number of nonconformists in the city. The proposed address pledged to support the king's "gratious intentions of liberty to all your subjects" and to promote "the repeal of all laws contrary thereunto." The regulator Nathaniel Wade, who was also the town clerk of Bristol, personally attended the council meeting and insisted on casting a vote, even though as clerk he was not eligible to vote.[113] The address failed to pass the council by a vote of sixteen to eleven, with two votes unclear in the records. Among those who voted against the address was the new mayor, Thomas Day, who had been appointed to office by the king three months before, and six other men who had also been appointed to office in the recent regulation.[114] In Bristol, the regulation was turning on itself.

Elsewhere the votes on addresses were more propitious for the king. Twenty-seven parliamentary boroughs sent addresses to James in 1688 pledging their support for his repeal campaign. These addresses were published in the *London Gazette* and provoked comment at the time. As one newsletter writer noted, many of the regulated councils had, "as a proofe of their devotion to his Majesties servise," sent addresses pledging to choose members of parliament that "shall take away the Tests and penall Laws."[115] Most of the pro-repeal addresses were sent from a council that had recently been regulated. Only four of the twenty-seven towns did not have royally appointed mayors when they sent their addresses. These were Berwick, Droitwich, Lyme Regis, and Thetford. Berwick was a garrison town under the influence of its Catholic governor, Sir Thomas Haggerston. Droitwich's address was said to have been written by the high court judge Sir Thomas Street, who had a substantial property interest in the town.[116] Lyme Regis was regulated before its address in 1688 was sent, but the old mayor, who presumably saw the wisdom of complying with the king's campaign, had been left in place by the regulation.[117] Thetford's mayor, a dominant player in local politics, appears to have calculated that the best way to maintain his influence was to organize a pro-repeal address from his town.[118]

The common denominator among the twenty-seven addresses is that they proceeded from councils with activist mayors who were not afraid of courting controversy. At Canterbury, the Presbyterian mayor appointed by James descended into a squabble with his sergeant at mace, who refused to accompany him when he delivered the pro-repeal address to the king. The sergeant was dismissed for his defiance.[119] In the far west of England, at Dartmouth, the mayor appointed by James was so disliked by his successors that, when his accounts were audited after the Revolution of 1688–1689, his expenses were sifted with a fine-toothed comb. The auditors refused, in particular, to pay a bill of six pounds and thirteen shillings the former mayor had incurred for "treating," or hosting, Sir John Southcote, a Catholic justice of the peace for Devon in 1688.[120] In the far north of England, at Scarborough, the royally appointed mayor managed to get into a physical altercation with the local minister when the latter failed to read the king's *Declaration for Liberty of Conscience* during divine service. He pulled the minister out of the pulpit and then, according to one account, "pounded the Parson." The garrison commander at Scarborough Castle, displeased by the mayor's antics, had him tossed in a blanket by five of the garrison's officers.[121] The mayors of all three of these towns, Canterbury, Dartmouth, and Scarborough, organized their councils to send repealer addresses to the king.[122]

Other activist mayors used the votes on the addresses as a test of loyalty. At Carlisle, the mayor was a Protestant, Joseph Reed, who had previously served as mayor in 1681 and 1682. He worked closely with the three Catholic aldermen on the new council to secure a repealer address from the city. In the process, they took careful note of who participated and who did not. When some of the new common councilmen who had been added by the king refused to sign the address, they were marked down as refusers. Shortly thereafter an order of the privy council ejected the councilmen from office.[123]

The pro-repeal addresses from regulated councils were beacons of hope for the repealers, suggesting that their movement was succeeding in various places. Despite these successes, the regulators must surely have been uneasy about the many boroughs that had declined to send addresses. But even the failures could be useful in showing the regulators where they had work still to do.

Delegitimizing the Addresses

The repealer addresses were inconvenient for anyone who opposed James II's tolerationist campaign. The addresses suggested that the campaign might have popular support, at least in some places. In response, many Anglicans sought to delegitimize the addresses by suggesting that they had been produced through manipulation from above. Soon after the first addresses were published in the *London Gazette* in April and May 1687, opponents of repeal spread rumours that the king had paid £8,000 to various nonconformists in exchange for their signatures. John Tillotson, the dean of Canterbury and future archbishop, was said to have started the rumours and to have alleged that £2,000 of the total sum had been given to Henry Hurst and the London Presbyterians as a reward for their address. The allegations made their way through the coffeehouses. Both men and women participated in the whisper campaign, with Roger Morrice hearing the rumours from a widow named Clarkson and passing them along himself. Henry Hurst, who "followed the Lye from place to place," was understandably upset, blaming the dean of Canterbury for "this great Slander" on his name.[124]

The marquess of Halifax, a moderate Anglican who had moved into opposition early in the king's reign, advanced a similar line of attack in his widely read *Letter to a Dissenter.* He warned his readers that the court was employing men who in the past may have "sprinkled Money amongst the Dissenting Ministers" and who now had been given "the same Authority" to practice "the same Methods, and Disburse, where they cannot otherwise perswade." Some nonconformist ministers, he alleged, had fallen into "Temptations of this kinde" by accepting bribes and were now obliged to echo the court's arguments. They preached sermons of "Anger and Vengeance against the Church of England" because they were worried that "their Wages" from the court "would be retrenched" if they moderated their tone. Moreover, threats had been issued against those dissenters who were reluctant to sign pro-Catholic addresses ghostwritten by "Priests" acting as "Secretaries to the Protestant Religion." True sincerity, however, could not be coerced: "No man was ever Thankful because he was bid to be so."[125] Halifax's pamphlet sought to delegitimize the repealer movement. The addresses that were its most visible sign were, from this perspective, the work of only a few collaborators and some Catholics. If any people at all had signed them, they were temporizers, mercenaries, or criminals; that is, they were unfit for political participation.

In the face of this delegitimizing of the repealer addresses, Henry Care sought to relegitimize them. He laid out a challenge for the opponents of repeal, offering a reward of fifty pounds to anyone who could prove that the earliest addressers had copied their texts from a draft that had been given them. He was confident that his reward would not be claimed because the first addressers, meaning the London Presbyterians, Congregationalists, and Baptists, had been so "scrupulous" as to not "impart their Intentions to any but those of their own Communion." He indignantly rebutted Halifax's "false" and "scandalous" insinuations that some men had "sprinkled Money among the Dissenting Ministers." He offered the same reward of fifty pounds to anyone who could demonstrate that any money was "Given, Promised, or Propounded to any of the Persons that did first Address."[126]

Halifax had, however, made another observation about the addresses that Care did not attempt to rebut. The marquess expressed doubt that "all the Thankers will be Repealers of the TEST, when ever a Parliament shall Meet."[127] Thanking the king for his *Declaration*, with its promises of liberty of conscience for nonconformists, was not the same as promising to repeal the Test Acts, which would liberate the Catholics and enable them, along with Protestant nonconformists, to take public offices. Some of the addresses did make a specific pledge to vote for pro-repeal members of parliament, but many of the addresses made no such pledge. It was possible, moreover, that the pro-repeal addressers would change their minds before the parliament met; indeed, it was one of the aims of Halifax's pamphlet to persuade them to do so.

It was not only the opponents of repeal who were skeptical about the addressers. George Vernon, the leading repealer in Derby, expressed a similar concern to his patron, the earl of Huntingdon: "I wish his Majestie may not yett call a parliament; he will find [he] has [been] mistaken in many of these addressers; they who have promist such high thinges are neither able toe performe itt; and I am well assur[e]d some of them never disigne itt; farther then toe please for the present." An informant of the prince of Orange who went by the name "James Rivers" put it even more succinctly: "now the people are in one sense become Courtiers, they break their word to the Governement as much as the Governement used to break their word to them." In another letter, Rivers elaborated on this thought: "The presbiterians and Independents are coming off from the fondnes[s] they had at first for the toleration and the Court begins to suspect it." He claimed that these nonconformists "only Juggle for in many places to my certain knowledge such of them as declare themselves for taking off the Test etc. have promised their voices to men who have told them that they will never consent to it." An even stronger claim was made by an anonymous informant of the prince of Orange, who contended that the dissenters were only pretending to support the toleration campaign in order to lull King James into a false sense of security.[128] It was, of course, difficult for the regulators to verify whether dissenters were signing the addresses while at the same time planning secretly to vote against repeal. Nor was it possible to verify in advance whether a man who supported repeal in April would still support it in October. This was a serious problem for the regulators, but no more so than it is for any electoral campaign that depends on the energies of a popular movement.

There was no guarantee that someone who had signed a repealer address in the spring of 1688 would go on six months later to vote for a repealer member of parliament. Potential repealers might be demoralized by looking at the strength of the opposition arrayed against them. They might be swayed by the opposition, who were offering strategic concessions, including a more limited form of toleration that might be enough to appease them. Or they might decide not to show up at the polls because they had other things that they needed to do on the day of the election. Halifax was appropriately skeptical in doubting that all of the "Thankers" for the king's *Declaration* would prove to be "Repealers" when the elections were held.

The responses of whigs and nonconformists to the repeal campaign were not always predictable. The king's proposals triggered a range of responses from different groups across the country, with some of these reactions shifting over time and others remaining more stable. The repeal campaign offered to nonconformists a whole menu of degrees of commitment. They could subscribe an address thanking the king for liberty of conscience and, at the same time, think to themselves that by this subscription they meant no endorsement of the dispensing power. They could accept an office in a town in one of James's regulations and protest to their friends that they were doing so only to help poor orphans. They could speak quietly to one of the regulators and point out the persecuting Anglicans in the town so that these men would be removed from public office. They could publish on behalf of toleration or against the repeal of the Test Acts, or relay stories about persecution to Henry Care who would publish them in his *Occurrences*. They could take office in a town or on a judicial bench and then press for an address promising to support pro-repeal candidates in the parliamentary elections. Or they could take office in a town or on a judicial bench and then work covertly to stifle such addresses.

It is possible to point to numerous dissenters who fell into each of these groups. With such a range of commitments available to them and so many opportunities to appease both sides of the conflict, it would be misleading to characterize nonconformists as falling simply into two camps: those who supported repeal of the penal laws and Test Acts, and those who supported repeal of the penal laws but not of the Test Acts. Nor is it clear that an individual necessarily chose one position or one degree of commitment and then stayed in that position for the duration of the conflict. The struggle for the dissenters' allegiances offered so many opportunities to settle scores, to move up politically, and to advance an agenda that many found themselves uncertain in their own minds about which side deserved their support. That uncertainty would not be resolved until the moment they were required to make a choice between one candidate or another in the elections for parliament.

6

———⇒◆⇐———

Countering a Movement

The Seven Bishops Trial

Popular movements often provoke countermovements, and the repealer movement was no exception. Countermovements are typically the work of vested interests opposing change. But they need not be entirely reactionary; often, in the service of stopping radical change, they offer palliative concessions.[1] This was the case with the repealers and their opponents. The Anglicans who opposed repeal indicated that they were prepared to offer concessions under which many nonconformists would gain some form of toleration, although the precise terms of that toleration remained to be negotiated. If Anglicans could succeed in persuading nonconformists that they had turned over a new leaf on persecution, one of the central grievances driving the repealer movement would be removed.

For this strategy to work, the Anglican opponents of repeal would have to tread cautiously in their relations with nonconformists. Printed pamphlets attacking nonconformity, which had poured from the presses since the Restoration of Charles II in 1660, would now be impolitic. In the year 1687, according to Gilbert Burnet, the Anglican clergy decided "by a general agreement" not to reply to the "virulent books" being published by a "few of the hotter of the dissenters."[2] The clergy were aware that the repealers, who were eager to drive a wedge between the Church of England and the nonconformists, could use their own words against them. It would be unwise to offend the nonconformists at a time when James and the Catholics were courting them.

Despite these strategic imperatives, a few Anglicans did take up their pens to attack nonconformity in the latter years of James II's reign.

They soon found that they were unable to get those writings published. A spy for the Dutch at the English court who went by the name "James Rivers" wrote in February 1688 that "there are written papers (but nothing yet printed) going about against the repeal of the penal Lawes, which if they cannot be got suppressed (care is taken to doe it) will doe a great d[e]ale of hurt among the Dissenters."[3] Rivers did not specify who in particular was taking "care" to suppress such pamphlets or who was writing them, but he may have been referring in part to a sermon that John Prince, vicar of Berry Pomeroy in Devon, had preached in September 1687. According to Anthony Wood, the sermon "was sent to London with a design that it should be printed, but some, into whose hands it came, fearing it might somewhat offend the temporizing dissenters, advised a forbearance of the publication of it at that time." Prince had previously published a bitter attack on the nonconformists in the 1670s, but times had now changed. The content of his sermon in 1687 is not known, though the text was said to be from Mark 4:24, "Take heed what you hear."[4] This was a text often used by clergymen who wished to argue that nonconformists could properly be punished for listening to incorrect beliefs, just as they could legitimately be coerced into attending church to hear orthodoxy. In this line of reasoning, nonconformists were responsible for their beliefs and should "take heed" not to hear false doctrine by attending conventicles.[5] In the new climate of 1687–1688, such arguments were indeed impolitic.

This new strategy of self-censorship among Anglicans failed to sway repealers such as Henry Care, who remained adamant that a "persecuting spirit" still animated much of the Church of England. Care argued that the continued existence of this "persecuting spirit" was evident in the acts of vandalism committed against some dissenting chapels and in the anonymous threats that he and his printer had received because of their work on behalf of repeal. He also alleged that some Anglican ministers continued to preach against the toleration of dissenters, although none of these sermons appeared in print. Both he and the Congregationalist minister Stephen Lobb asserted that if the penal laws and Tests Acts were not repealed then persecution might return to England.[6]

The Anglican strategy of forbearance and self-censorship was placed in jeopardy when James II commanded the bishops and clergy of England and Wales to read his *Declaration for Liberty of Conscience* aloud in their churches during Sunday services in May and June 1688.[7] Given the objections that many Anglicans had to the king's *Declaration*, both because of the toleration it offered dissenters and the powers it asserted for the monarch to suspend laws passed by parliament, it was almost a certainty that some of the clergy would refuse to obey the royal order. Those refusals would likely be broadly publicized and would be seized upon by Care and others as evidence of the continued "persecuting spirit" among Anglicans. To avoid this outcome would require a careful balancing act. The bishops would need to lead a movement against reading the *Declaration* to assuage the hard-liners in their own church. At the same time, they would need to reassure the dissenters that their decision not to read the *Declaration* had been made purely on legal and constitutional grounds as a defence of the rights of parliament, rather than as an attack on the principles of toleration embodied in the document. By taking control of the movement of refusal, the bishops could draw public attention to themselves and away from any damaging statements of anti-nonconformist animus that might emanate from the hard-liners within their own church.

This balancing act was rendered even more difficult by the need to maintain sufficient ambiguity to assuage both sides. If the bishops pledged to support toleration in terms that were too explicit, then their own hard-liners might go into open revolt. But if their promises were too vague, then the dissenters would fail to be mollified. The ultimate success of this complicated maneuver was a tribute to the political skills of the archbishop of Canterbury, William Sancroft. It required adroit signalling from Anglican leaders, who simultaneously sent anti-toleration cues to their own parish clergy and pro-toleration cues to nonconformist ministers. The result was a triumph for the archbishop and a defeat for the repealers.

There were, nevertheless, many difficult moments along the way to this unexpected result. The nerves of many of the key players were strained nearly to the breaking point. The more politically savvy and well-connected actors sailed through these difficulties, but the less able or less fortunate found themselves foundering on the rocks. One particularly harrowing set of choices was faced by a minister on the outskirts of London named Sydrach Simpson. His dilemma reveals the hazards threatening the parish clergy in the spring of 1688.

The Ordeal of Sydrach Simpson

Whether to read or not to read? That was the question on Sydrach Simpson's mind on a Friday in May 1688. The king had commanded him, along with all other ministers residing within ten miles of London, to read aloud to his congregation the *Declaration for Liberty of Conscience* that Sunday. Soon he would be conducting the service at the parish church of Stoke Newington, to the north of London. He had dithered for days, and now only forty-eight hours remained. If he read the *Declaration* and the other London clergy did not, he would attract the opprobrium of his peers and be mocked as a timeserver. If he did not read the *Declaration* and the other clergy did, he would attract the attention of the king and risk suspension by the Ecclesiastical Commission. He told a fellow minister that he would give an "angel," a ten shilling coin, to know what the clergy of London would do at eleven o'clock on Sunday morning.[8]

The king's order had been transmitted to Simpson at the May visitation. It had been legally delivered, following the usual precedents in such matters. To defy such an order would, the cleric averred, break his "Canonicall oath" to follow orders transmitted through the church hierarchy.[9] But if defiance was illegal, so might be compliance. Many of the clergy believed that the *Declaration* was itself a violation of the law in that it implicitly assumed a power to suspend the laws against religious dissent. The king's power to suspend ecclesiastical laws was more than controversial, as the House of Commons had argued that it did not exist. Some clergymen interpreted the *Declaration* as an attack on the Church of England, for it established an unlimited toleration that would hobble the Church as it attempted to perform its age-old task of holding heresy at bay. Such a document would not be fit to read in church, even if the king and a bishop commanded it. Many clergymen found themselves in a dilemma: they could break the law as they conceived it by reading the *Declaration,* or they could break the law by not reading the *Declaration.*

The ministers of London and the countryside ten miles around London were instructed to read the *Declaration* on Sunday, 20 May 1688 and again on Sunday, 27 May. Then, on the first and second Sundays of June, the *Declaration* was to be read by the clergy in the rest of England. Presumably this extra time was provided because of potential delays in distributing the *Declaration* across the entire country. The result was that the provincial clergy had the luxury of waiting to see what the London clergy had done. The rector of Stoke Newington had no such luxury. He would be among the first to read the *Declaration* or among the first to defy the king. He had to choose, without knowing where his choice would take him.

It was this dilemma that occupied Simpson's mind on the Friday before the fateful Sunday. He had not yet received enough information to assuage his fears. He seems to have been unaware of the meeting of some of the clergy that had already taken place the previous Sunday, at which the bishops of Ely and Peterborough and fifteen London clergy had decided that they would not read the *Declaration*. Nor is it clear whether Simpson knew that the clergy of London had been canvassed that week. By Thursday night, nearly seventy London ministers had pledged not to read the *Declaration*, out of about one hundred in the City.[10]

But Simpson was not a resident of the City of London. Stoke Newington, his parish, was four miles northeast of St. Paul's, outside the city gates.[11] As a minister from outside the walls, he was at a disadvantage. He was not privy to the discussions taking place among clergymen in the City, yet he was required to read the *Declaration* on the same day, at the same time, as those who were at the center of affairs. He would gladly follow the other clergymen, if only they would give the lead.

He was, as he put it himself, "exceedingly troubled." His misgivings deepened when he heard that Dr. Thomas Turner, "whose person and judgment I exceedingly reverence," was in favor of reading the *Declaration*. Nor was he put at ease by two conversations that he had on the Friday, one with Henry Hesketh, minister of St. Helens in London, and the other with a man whom Simpson described only as "a person that came from Holburne." The latter must have been one of the servants of the bishop of Ely, Simpson's patron, who lived at Ely House in Holborn. Both Hesketh and the messenger from the bishop showed him a copy of a document called the "two particulars." This was presumably the document drafted by the bishops of Ely and Peterborough and fifteen clergy in their meeting on the previous Sunday. It argued that the clergy should not read the *Declaration* because to do so would be to endorse the king's power to dispense with, or set aside, "all Lawes Ecclesiasticall and civill." This refusal to read the *Declaration*, the document noted, was not due to any "want of due tendernesse towards Dissenters, in relation to whome We shall be willing to come to such a Temper as shall be thought fit when that matter comes to be considered and settled in Parliament and Convocation."[12] The offer of some form of parliamentary toleration or comprehension was designed to prevent the dissenters from taking offense at the failure of the clergy to read the *Declaration*.

Apart from showing the "two particulars" to Simpson, the emissary from Holborn provided little advice but stated only that "the Lord Byshopps had taken the affaire upon themselfes." The rector of Stoke Newington later complained that the bishop's servant had asked "me what I intended to doe . . . but [gave] not a word of what I sho[u]ld doe." He told the man that he would spend the next day waiting upon "some eminent ministers in London" to "Knowe their thoughts" and that he was resolved to do nothing that might hurt the Church of England. This equivocal answer left open the possibility that he might still read the *Declaration,* if he was advised to do so by the ministers he intended to meet on the following day.

That evening the bishop of Ely and six other bishops, including the archbishop of Canterbury, signed a petition to the king. Six of the bishops delivered the petition in person to the king at ten o'clock the same evening. Their appeal echoed the language of the "two particulars," asking the king not to require them to distribute the *Declaration* because the king's edict was founded on "such a Dispensing Power as has been often declared Illegal in Parliament." The petition also echoed the "two particulars" in affirming that the bishops were not lacking in "due tenderness to Dissenters."[13] As the emissary from Holborn had said, the bishops had indeed "taken the affaire upon themselfes." This action should have resolved Simpson's dilemma and provided him with a clear lead to follow. News of the bishops' petition spread throughout the City on Saturday, but somehow the news failed to reach Simpson.

On that Saturday, the rector of Stoke Newington spent a frantic day crisscrossing London and its suburbs, trying to find someone who could provide him with information of the clergy's intentions. He stopped first at the home of Dr. Nicholas Stratford, dean of St. Asaph and vicar of St. Mary Aldermanbury in London. The dean was not in. He traveled next to Dr. Edward Fowler, vicar of St. Giles Cripplegate. The vicar was not at home. He waited unsuccessfully on Dr. John Scott, rector of St. Peter-le-Poer. Presumably, all the ministers of London were also out gathering intelligence. In desperation, Simpson went to the house of Henry Hesketh, whom he had spoken to the day before, only to find that he was away in the country. Finally he met with Dr. William Beveridge, minister of St. Peter Cornhill in the City. The doctor had been present at the clergy's meeting on the previous Sunday when the resolution was taken not to read the *Declaration*.[14] He expressed his belief that most of the ministers of London would not read it. But Simpson was still doubtful. He told Beveridge that he trusted him, but that he wished he could have more certain knowledge of what the ministers would do. It was Beveridge who provoked Simpson's remark that he would give an angel to know what the clergy of London would do at the following day's service. Neither of the two appears to have known at this point that the bishops had petitioned the king the previous evening.

Exhausted by his journeying, Simpson retreated to a coffeehouse where he had arranged to meet his friend Dr. Timothy Puller, minister of St. Mary-le-Bow in London. There he found a conclave of clerics. Edward Gee, rector of St. Benet's and famous for his writings against popery, was present, as was Dr. John Meriton, rector of St. Michael Cornhill. Simpson had never liked Meriton—as he put it, he had "never fanzied [him] for his judgment in other things." Meriton now argued in favor of reading the *Declaration* while Simpson contributed to the conversation by speaking "against tolleration."

In speaking openly against toleration at a coffeehouse, the rector of Stoke Newington was stirring up trouble. He might have been overheard by a dissenter or a partisan of the king, who could blacken his name by accusing him of being a persecutor. Simpson's own father had been a well-known Congregationalist minister and master of Pembroke College, Cambridge, under the Commonwealth and Protectorate. The son of dissent had repudiated his heritage by becoming an Anglican minister. He may have felt obliged to speak against toleration in order to dispel any lingering doubts in the minds of his hearers that he retained any dissenting sympathies.

After Meriton took his leave of the gathering, the rector from Stoke Newington turned to the others again, pressing them to say whether the *Declaration* ought to be read. But they, fearing perhaps that they would be overheard, or perhaps distrusting Simpson's motives, "would not tell me any thing thereof." Their silence may have caused Simpson to doubt Dr. Beveridge's confident assertion from earlier in the day that most of the London ministers had already committed themselves not to read the *Declaration*. The mood in the coffeehouse was dark. It was difficult for any consensus to form: everyone wanted to know the other's opinion before divulging his own.

The rector left the coffeehouse and encountered some other persons, unnamed in his account, who "did exceedingly press me [not to fail to read the *Declaration*] from the severity of the punishment that wo[u]ld ensue." Back at Stoke Newington, he met with "the best church men in my parish." These laymen told him "that they could not tell how to direct me." This diffident response was typical of their usual attitude. The rector had not had collegial relations with his parishioners for years. They had accused him fifteen years earlier of failing to maintain the church fabric and had asserted a few years later their right to choose both of the churchwardens of the parish, beating back the rector's claims.[15] Now, in 1688, the parishioners of Stoke Newington made it clear that whatever their minister did, he would stand or fall alone.

Simpson must have slept poorly that night. The climactic moment surely arrived sooner than he would have liked. It was eleven o'clock on the morning of the twentieth, and he stood before his congregation, a copy of the *Declaration* in hand. No doubt he scanned the faces of his parishioners, looking for any sign of sympathy in their expressions. Unlike some other ministers looking for a way out, Simpson did not absent himself from the service that morning, nor did he pretend that he had lost his copy of the *Declaration*.[16] At the appointed time, he read the king's edict aloud. It must have seemed the safest choice. He might be criticized in some quarters for his action, but he would weather the criticism in the certain knowledge that his critics, unlike the king's ecclesiastical commissioners, had no power to eject him from his parish. Simpson did not anticipate that nearly every clergyman in London would fail to read the *Declaration* at the time appointed. But he soon learned of it.

The rector of Stoke Newington found himself completely wrong-footed. He had jumped one way, and almost all of his fellow clergy had jumped the other. Far from taking the safer path, he had exposed himself to ridicule. The king would not punish him, but his reputation among his fellow clergymen would suffer, and the bishops might not take kindly to his behavior. The next Sunday, reversing himself, he disobeyed the king's order and omitted the reading of the *Declaration* at Stoke Newington.[17] He knew that there was safety in numbers and that the king was unlikely to target him for particular sanction when so many others had disobeyed the order as well. But the rector's defiance came too late to buy him any glory. His sense of humiliation was acute. The rebellion of the London clergy was already being hailed as an epochal moment of courage that would be remembered throughout the ages. Simpson must have felt that he was on the wrong side of history.

Three weeks later he sat down to pen an apology to the bishop of Ely, his patron and one of the seven who had petitioned the king against reading the *Declaration*. Simpson wrote that he was "heartily sorry for my offence to God and the church, and to you in particular." He was particularly sorry to have offended the bishop because of "the interest I have heretofore had in your love." Almost as soon as he had read the *Declaration* in his church he had been "immediately" sensible of his "error." He had lost sleep over his actions. Ever since that morning he had been troubled "both day and night" with remorse. His error had come about, he explained, not because he approved of the king's *Declaration*, but because he "was overtaken by small arguments." He had sought advice from many different ministers, but the advice he had received had been mixed. For want of good counsel, a man's reputation had been lost.

The Anglican Uprising

The news that made Simpson's heart sink was soon relayed around the country. The *Declaration* had been read in only six of the ninety-seven parish churches within the city walls.[18] The names of the London ministers who had read the decree were publicized widely, to shame them for their compliance with the king. They were "much slighted and ridiculed and accounted but as time servers." Francis Thompson at St. Matthew in Friday Street, Timothy Hall at All Hallows Staining, and Adam Elliott at St. James Duke Place had read the royal edict; others had read it at St. Gregory by St. Paul's, St. Mary Magdalen Old Fish Street, and a church in Wood Street, presumably St. Alban Wood Street. It had also been read at two chapels in the City, Serjeants Inn in Fleet Street and the Rolls Chapel in Chancery Lane.[19] In addition, it had been read at a few places in Westminster and the liberties, including the Abbey, Holy Trinity Minories, and the king's chapel in Whitehall, where a member of the choir had to be enlisted to read it.[20] Fortunately for Sydrach

Simpson, the scrutiny placed on the London ministers did not extend to the extramural parishes, and his own name was not placed on these inventories of infamy.

The failure of so many ministers to read the *Declaration* was widely interpreted at the time as a tale of resistance to royal power. But Sydrach Simpson's story suggests that there was more to it. His behavior was not marked by a reluctance to take a side as much as it was marked by his desire to be on the same side as everyone else. His calculations were based on what he anticipated that other people would do. There was safety in numbers—not just safety from royal punishment, but also safety from popular abuse and the loss of the respect of one's peers. Simpson's hesitation was produced by a lack of knowledge about the intentions of others, an information deficit that resulted from the reluctance of many of the London ministers to be the first to come out publicly against reading the *Declaration*. No one wanted to act alone, and the bishops, by making their joint petition to the king late on Friday night, moved just too slowly to assist someone like Simpson who was a bit too far out of the loop to hear the news by Sunday morning.

Two years later, looking back on the events of 1688, Dr. John Meriton made a striking claim. This was the same Dr. Meriton who had met Simpson in the coffeehouse and argued in favor of reading the *Declaration*. His retrospective claim was that, if the bishops had not petitioned the king against reading the *Declaration*, "2 parts in three, of the clergy of England, would have read it."[21] This claim was not entirely implausible. Under different political circumstances, many of the clergy might have consented to read a royal edict that they disliked. Before the seven bishops had made their petition, few would have predicted such a widespread movement of refusal as the one that appeared. Prominent peers were asked for their advice at the time. The earl of Rochester, who had been lord treasurer until his dismissal in 1687, advised the clergy to comply with the king. The marquess of Halifax, trimmer *par excellence*, who had been dismissed as lord privy seal in 1685, refused to give any advice at all. The earl of Nottingham, who had opposed the king's measures early in the reign, offered this advice: "he was utterly against their refusall [to read the *Declaration*], unlesse they were unanimous therein."[22] This was not a catalogue of bravery. And why should not the clergy read it? They could always claim, as some later did, that they had not intended to give their approbation to the contents of the *Declaration* by reading it aloud but were merely following orders.[23]

The seven bishops made their bold move only after canvasses of the London clergy had indicated that most of the clergy would follow them. In a sense they were like Sydrach Simpson, wanting to know what others would do before they made their move, but they had the luxury of being able to insist on clear commitments and subscriptions from the clergy before they took action.[24] It might be assumed that, once the seven bishops and the London clergy had moved against reading the *Declaration*, the result in the rest of the country was a foregone conclusion. But it was not entirely so. Ministers in the countryside also wanted to be certain that everyone else in their dioceses would do as they did. If they were going to disobey the king's command, as many of them did, they wanted to do so in the safety of a local group. London was far away from many dioceses, and the archbishop of Canterbury might not be able to protect them if they defied the king while most of the clergy in their diocese agreed to read the petition, especially if their own bishop was in favor of reading. The ministers of many dioceses chose to canvass each other to ascertain their collective intentions. The impulse toward consensus was a powerful one. Only a minority of the clergy were bold enough to defy that impulse and make their decisions independently.

News of the petition of the seven bishops spread throughout the kingdom within a matter of days. The bishops' action was not reported in the officially licensed newspapers, the *London Gazette* and *Publick Occurrences*, but news of it passed by letter and by word of mouth. The day after the petition was delivered, the government halted the post in an attempt to prevent the news from spreading into the provinces, but this was not effective; by Monday evening, three days after the petition had been delivered, word had traveled as far afield as the village of Eyton on Severn, Shropshire, more than a hundred miles from London.[25] The government had little more success in preventing the text of the petition itself from being released. One printer published a hasty broadside that claimed to be the bishop's petition but was in fact the London clergy's "two particulars." This publication was at least partially accurate in that the petition was itself based largely on the "two particulars" and quoted extensively from them. But the printer got the names of the seven bishops wrong, incorrectly substituting the bishop of Norwich for the bishop of Chichester. This broadside was presumably the copy of the petition that was distributed around town a "day or two after" the bishops met with the king.[26] The government subsequently launched a prosecution of its publisher, which likely had a chilling effect on publications of this kind.[27]

Copies of the actual petition, as opposed to publications offering fabricated versions of it, were scarce in London for a few days. The French ambassador wrote to his royal master on Monday 21 May, three days after the delivery of the petition, to say that "at this point they have not given out any copies."[28] Initially, there were only two copies: the king had one and the archbishop of Canterbury had the other.[29] But two days after the delivery of the petition, the king had permitted one of the clerks of the privy council to make another copy for the use of the solicitor general.[30] The king had by then consulted with the judges, seeking to determine whether a successful prosecution could be launched against the bishops for their disobedience. Once the petition began to circulate at court, it was only a matter of time before it would fall into the hands of the ambassadors and would filter into the City. On the Tuesday after the delivery of the petition, the Dutch ambassador sent a copy of it to The Hague. On Thursday the French ambassador sent one to Versailles. The petition circulated widely in manuscript, but an accurate printed version of it did not appear for some time.[31] When it did appear, it was not as a separate publication but as part of a pamphlet by Henry Care designed to refute the bishops' petition. Care's publication went into two editions, attesting to the public's thirst for any copy of the bishops' petition, even one bound into a pamphlet designed to refute it.[32]

The provincial clergy were scheduled to read the *Declaration* on 3 June, two weeks and two days after the bishops had delivered their petition to the king. Over the course of this fortnight, the most closely watched men in England and Wales were the seventeen other bishops. If these men distributed the king's edict and thereby repudiated their primate's petition, the king could hope to escape from the crisis with some credibility intact. He could claim that the seven bishops were only a minority of the bench and that their divisive behavior was the work of an unrepresentative faction. If, however, the seventeen bishops failed to distribute the *Declaration*, then James would have less room to maneuver in the ensuing crisis, and any action he took against the bishops would likely be seen as an attack on the Church as a whole.

To the king's misfortune, the remaining bishops split evenly and, as a result, the *Declaration* was distributed in only a minority of dioceses. Of the twenty-four bishops of English and Welsh sees in 1688,

eight more joined with the original seven bishops to indicate their sup-
port for the petition. The new refractory bishops were the bishops of
Norwich (Lloyd), Salisbury (Ward), Gloucester (Frampton), Winchester
(Mews), Worcester (Thomas), Carlisle (Smith), and Llandaff (Beaw).
The bishop of London (Compton), who was under suspension, also supported the petition.[33] Another seven bishops parted from their brethren
by distributing the *Declaration*. The loyalist seven included the bishops of
Chester (Cartwright), Durham (Crewe), St. David's (Watson), Hereford
(Croft), Lichfield (Wood), Lincoln (Barlow), and Rochester (Sprat).[34] In
a classic bit of trimming, the bishop of Exeter, Thomas Lamplugh, did
both: he indicated his support for the petition of the seven bishops by
signing it after it was delivered, but he also distributed the *Declaration* in
his diocese as the king commanded.[35] The *Declaration* was also distributed in the vacant see of Oxford and appears to have been distributed
in the vacant see of York. The only bishop whose position on the *Declaration* is unknown is the bishop of Bangor, who most likely took no
position at all, given that he was seventy-seven years old, almost blind,
and no longer able to perform all of the duties of his see.[36]

The king could take some consolation from the fact that the *Declaration* had been distributed in some of the largest dioceses in England,
such as Lincoln and Chester, and that he had attracted the support of
some of the more senior members of the episcopate, such as the bishops
of Durham and Hereford, who had held their sees for fourteen and
twenty-six years, respectively. In contrast, the seven petitioning bishops,
with the exception of the archbishop, were some of the least experienced on the bench. Their average term of service as bishops in June
1688 was less than five years, and this average would have been even
lower were it not for the inclusion of the archbishop, who had served
since 1678. Most of the seven had been appointed to their sees during
the tory reaction, at a time when some leading churchmen had been
developing theological positions that emphasized the independence of
the Church from royal control.[37] King James himself had elevated or
promoted, in the first year of his reign, three of the seven men who
were later to defy him publicly.[38]

The seven loyalist bishops who distributed the king's *Declaration*,
not including the trimming bishop of Exeter, had an average term of
service of just over a decade each. Only two of these bishops, Chester
and St. David's, had been elevated by James. The age of the bishops who

supported James was turned to the king's disadvantage in contemporary polemics, where some of them were portrayed unfairly as verging on senility.[39] Their experience, however, did not match that of the eight who did not initially sign the petition but later indicated their support for it: these bishops had an average term of service of 11.8 years.

The *Declaration* was distributed in approximately eleven of the twenty-six English and Welsh dioceses, including the two vacant sees. It was also distributed in at least part of the diocese of London.[40] For the parish clergy in the remaining dioceses, reading the king's edict would have meant defying both the guidance of the archbishop of Canterbury, as expressed in the petition of the seven bishops, and the guidance of their local diocesan who had chosen not distribute the *Declaration*. If these clergy had wanted to read the *Declaration*, they would have had to obtain their own copy from the *London Gazette*. It was highly unlikely that clergy serving under the refractory bishops would ever be prosecuted successfully by the king, since they could plead that the *Declaration* had not been forwarded to them by their bishop as required under canon law. But the position was different for the clergy in those dioceses where the king's edict had been distributed.

The archbishopric of York was vacant, but the dean of York appears to have distributed the *Declaration*, although he did not give his own opinion as to whether it ought to be read or not. As a consequence, many clergy from the diocese came to York seeking advice, and a meeting was held at the home of Thomas Comber who, as the precentor, was a member of the governing chapter. As in London, the clergy wished to know what others were planning on doing before they acted themselves. The sense of the meeting was that the *Declaration* should not be read, and this verdict was reinforced by the coincidence that during the meeting a messenger arrived with five hundred copies of a pamphlet containing "reasons against read the declaration," one of which was read aloud at the meeting.[41]

This pamphlet was almost certainly *A Letter from a Clergy-man in the City, to his Friend in the Country, Containing his Reasons for not Reading the Declaration*.[42] The *Letter from a Clergy-man* set off a storm of controversy as soon as it was published, four days after the bishops had delivered their petition. It was distributed anonymously all over the country and numerous replies to it appeared in print.[43] The bishop of Norwich ensured that two thousand copies were sent to his diocese so that every one of his clergy would have at least one copy. Copies were also "spread amongst the clergy" in Derbyshire and distributed widely in Worcestershire.[44] Many clergymen, when making the decision not to read the *Declaration*, might not yet have read a copy of the bishops' petition, but they would have read this pamphlet.

The "letter" urged the parish clergy not to read the *Declaration* on the grounds that it was designed to boost the fortunes of Catholics and Protestant nonconformists at the expense of the Church of England. The author of the letter wrote that he could not read the *Declaration*, for to do so would be "to teach my People, that they need never come to Church more, but have my free leave, as they have the King's, to go to a Conventicle, or to Mass." The king's edict was wrong because it proclaimed "an unlimited and universal Toleration"; such a toleration was both illegal and immoral and had been "condemned by the Christian Church in all Ages." The letter acknowledged that it might be necessary to offer the dissenters some form of ease and that in the future, "when there is opportunity of shewing our inclinations without danger, they [the dissenters] may find that we are not such Persecutors as we are represented."[45] But the letter writer left undefined the terms of that ease: he offered this concession in such tentative terms that it was unclear whether a parliamentary act of toleration was in view or merely a more lenient enforcement of some of the existing laws. The letter thus reflected the new Anglican rhetoric about toleration. It did not attack all forms of toleration; instead, it attacked the idea of "unlimited" toleration, while leaving open the possibility of a more limited indulgence of some nonconformist groups. Critics of the letter dismissed its author's hints of some future concessions to dissenters as "very Faint," "obscure," and lacking a "Positive Promise" for dissenters.[46]

Most of the clergy in the counties followed the example of the London clergy and the advice of the *Letter from a Clergy-man*: they refrained from reading the king's edict. This was especially the case in those dioceses where the *Declaration* had not been distributed by the local bishop. In the diocese of Norwich, with its 1,200 parishes, only four or five ministers read the king's edict, and they were obliged to read it directly out of the *London Gazette*, since no other copy had been sent to them. In the diocese of Carlisle, where the bishop opposed the reading of the *Declaration*, none of the clergy did so.[47] Even in dioceses where the royal edict was distributed, few ministers complied with the king. None of the clergy of the city of Oxford read the edict, which had been distributed to them by the registrar of the vacant see. In the diocese of Oxford as a whole, it was read by only six ministers.[48] In the diocese of York it was read by "few"; in Gloucester it was read by "very few"; in Hereford it was read by four or five; in Lichfield by four or five; in Chester by three.[49] In the county of Hertfordshire it was read by three; in Shropshire, Leicestershire, and Buckinghamshire by two per county; and in Bedfordshire and Northamptonshire by only one in each county. In the city of Newcastle-upon-Tyne it was not read by any minister.[50]

These tallies were reported with relish by men who were opposed to the king's religious policies and thus had an incentive to understate the number of readers of the *Declaration*. But the tallies reported by the king's supporters were not much higher. The Catholic Lord Aston conceded that few clergy in the county of Stafford had read the *Declaration*. In Durham the powerful palatine bishop and his influential dean were united in wanting to see the *Declaration* read, yet the dean himself admitted that the edict had been read in only twenty of the sixty-five churches in the county palatine.[51] The loyalist bishop of St. David's, angered by the resistance to the royal edict in his diocese in Wales, suspended several clergy and ordained twenty new ministers who promised to comply with the king's wishes.[52] Taking into account all these reports, it seems unlikely that the edict was read in more than a few hundred of the nine thousand parishes of England.[53]

Those few clergy who read the king's edict often shared a similar cast of mind. Many were ultra-loyalist clergy who were so wedded to the notion of obedience to the commands of lawful authorities that they were willing to read a document that they disliked. Several clergymen in Cheshire read the *Declaration* even though they disagreed with its contents. They later trumpeted their loyalism in an address to the king, noting that "if the Matter of the Declaration were not according to our Wishes, yet the Publishing of it is according to our Duty, since it is issued out from the express Prerogative of Your Supremacy over us." The bishop of Lincoln told one of his clergy that he had distributed the king's edict as ordered but that he would not advise him whether or not to read it, leaving that for him to decide.[54] This was hardly a ringing endorsement of the *Declaration*. Daniel Kenrick, the minister of Eckington of Worcestershire, who read the *Declaration* because he approved of its contents, was surely an anomaly.[55]

The bishop of Hereford read the *Declaration* because, as he noted in a letter to the king, "A true Ch[urch] of England-Man can never rebell or bee disloyal in the least, his Religion commanding him absolutely to obey either by acting or by suffering and to lay himself as a Worm under your Majestys feet." Despite his obedience to the king, the bishop assured his friends that he did not approve of the contents of the royal edict.[56] Indeed, as he wrote in a pamphlet, he did not believe that his having read the *Declaration* aloud in his church necessarily implied that he approved of its contents: "should I read a Paper in the Church declaring the Kings Toleration of Sectaries, doth it in any way declare my Consent unto it? No certainly." By reading the edict, the bishop of Hereford was simply stating a fact (that the king had enacted toleration), not venturing an opinion (that the king was right to do so). The king's command to read the edict must be obeyed because a royal command could be defied only if the monarch commanded something that was against the word of God. In the bishop's view, this was not such a case.[57]

Clerical and Popular Opposition to Toleration

There is ample evidence that many of the provincial clergy disliked the king's *Declaration* and, by not reading it, were indulging their own inclinations as well as following the lead from London. Even those clergy who supported the idea of making limited concessions to Protestant nonconformists could still disapprove of the *Declaration* because it arrogated to the king a power that they believed belonged properly to parliament. While sharing these concerns about the legality of the edict, many provincial ministers also considered the *Declaration* to be dangerous and immoral because it licensed toleration for a variety of groups that they deemed to be heretical and schismatic. These clergymen were opposed to the ends of the *Declaration* as well as to its means. If their principled opposition to toleration became widely known, the Protestant nonconformists might well surmise that the Church of England had not truly had a change of heart about religious persecution. Anglican opposition to toleration might then serve to push wavering nonconformists back into the arms of the repealers.

Anti-tolerationist views were widespread among the English clergy in 1688, even if it was not always politic to express them in public.

Typically they were reserved for private letters and conversations. One clergyman from Kent revealed his opinions in a letter to his patron: "I cannot consent to the toleracon of those heresyes and doctrines which are contrary to Scripture and condemn'd by the Generall Councells, and yet are tolerated by that generall liberty, and there is not the least doubt, but that my publishing it [the *Declaration*], would bee construed a consent."[58] This minister condemned the idea of a "generall liberty" that would allow freedom of worship without any limits on heretical doctrines. Another minister from Buckinghamshire went further and condemned any form of toleration, whether limited or not. Referring to the king's *Declaration*, he wrote in a letter of explanation to his patron: "I think it a very unfitting thing for us to publish that to the people which we are bound in Conscience and Duty to dissuade them from. For all separation from the established Church is both illegal and Schismatical, and though the King may do his pleasure, we cannot concurr with him, or concern ourselves in it, or be instrumentall in promoting a thing which we do not approve."[59] The ministers of the Church of England had been fighting dissent in their parishes for their entire careers. Many of them believed that if a man or woman left the Church of England to attend a conventicle—whether it was a Quaker, a Baptist, or a Presbyterian one—that soul was in danger of the fires of hell. As one London clergyman put it in arguing against the reading of the *Declaration*, "we are abundantly satisfied that an unlimitted Tolleration is pernitious to Religion and the Soules of men."[60] To read the *Declaration*, then, was to abdicate God's calling. None of these clerics went so far as to argue that the penal laws should be strictly and ruthlessly enforced. But neither could they condone an unlimited toleration.

The dean of Worcester had argued the year before, in a letter to a friend, that members of the Church of England needed to join together "to convince their neighbours, friends, relations and acquaintances of the sinfull nature, and direfull effects of such a liberty [of conscience], and for my own part, I believe it to be so offensive to God to let loose all heresies, schismes, and blasphemies." Isaac Archer, a clergyman in Suffolk, wrote in his diary for March 1687 of his concerns for "the preservation of religion, now toleration is let loose."[61] One of William's spies at the English court noted ruefully that many of the Anglican clergy could not be persuaded to support the repeal of any of the penal laws, for "in the Church of England, as in all the churches in the world, there are a sort of bigots who . . . are incapable of reason."[62] As another of William's informants noted, "the truth is some people (churchmen) are for penal lawes and there is noe reasoning with such as pretend to speak in Gods name."[63] Then there was Sydrach Simpson, who spoke "against tolleration" at the coffeehouse and made a point of mentioning this fact in his letter to his patron, the bishop of Ely, evidently expecting him to approve.

Some of this opposition stemmed from the sweeping, unqualified language and the lack of any explicit confessional limits placed on liberty of conscience in James's *Declaration*. The *Declaration* simply proclaimed that all penal laws "for not coming to Church, or not Receiving the Sacrament, or for any other Non-conformity to the Religion Established, or for, or by Reason of the Exercise of Religion in any manner whatsoever, be immediately Suspended." The only limits specified were that religious meetings should be peaceable, should be open to the public, and should not be used to inspire sedition against the state.[64] One Anglican pamphleteer seized on the phrase "or for any other Non-conformity to the Religion Established" and observed that it licensed a toleration without limit: people were "left at liberty to be of any Religion or none at all," even if that meant they wished to "become Jews or Mahometans, or Pagan Idolaters, as well as to be Papists or Dissenters." Another opposition pamphleteer asserted that the repeal campaign was designed to offer freedom of worship not only to "Christians, and perhaps Jews," but also to "the Indians, who worship the Devil."[65] When the seven bishops were put on trial for their defiance of the king, some of their defense counsel criticized the king's *Declaration* on similar grounds, arguing that "the Declaration did evacuate the laws for Sabbath-breaking, Fornication, etc. and let loose the reins to the most extravagant sects and licentious practices." One of the bishops' lawyers, Sir Francis Pemberton, elaborated on this sentiment, specifying exactly which sects were the most outrageous ones: "If this Declaration should take effect, what would be the End of it? All Religions are let in, let them be what they will; Ranters, Quakers, and the like."[66] This allusion to the Ranters was perhaps surprising given that the antinomian sect known for its sexual license had not been heard of for several decades and had no more than a handful of members even in its heyday.[67] The fear being expressed by the bishop's defense counsel was that toleration would lead to sexual license and Ranterism because even antinomian religions would be permitted under the new dispensation.

The anti-tolerationist sentiments found among the Anglican clergy and gentry had a popular basis as well. One tory ballad that appears to have been composed in the summer of 1688 included the lines "From Freedom of Conscience, and Whig-Toleration . . . good Heaven deliver me."[68] Similar sentiments were expressed by the butchers of Clare Market, a marketplace near Covent Garden just outside the walls of the City of London, during a gathering in the summer of 1688 that became a public demonstration. One newsletter writer described their activities as follows: "The Butchers of Clare Markett at 12 or one at Night gott together to a great Number with their Cle[a]vers Chopping knives and steeles making therewith a most hideous Noise breaking the Windows of Diverse houses particularly the Earl of Castlemains and a great house above Covent Garden Cryeing out No Declaration No Toleration No Baxter No Pen No Lob."[69] This was a vivid demonstration of both anti-tolerationist and anti-repeal sentiment, fused together by anti-popery. The earl of Castlemaine was a Catholic peer who had spent part of the previous year in Rome on an embassy to the pope from James II. His residence was an obvious target for an anti-popish demonstration. "Baxter" was Richard Baxter the Presbyterian; "Pen" was William Penn the Quaker; "Lob" was Stephen Lobb the Congregationalist. The latter two were known allies of the king and leading figures in the repealer movement, while Baxter was perhaps the most well-known of all the Presbyterian ministers, though he had steered clear of the repealer movement. The slogans called out by the butchers expressed their desire to defeat the repealers, as they were symbolized by Penn, Lobb, and the king's *Declaration for Liberty of Conscience*. The butchers did not propose as an alternative a limited toleration for some nonconformists; instead, with vehement language, they opposed any toleration at all.[70]

Popular opposition to toleration was not the same thing as advocacy of persecution. Many of the clerical and lay opponents of toleration would most likely have been willing to acquiesce in a compromise in which the penal laws would be left on the statute books but would be enforced only against the more extreme dissenters. But the dissenters, having suffered through years of vigorous enforcement of those same laws, could be forgiven for not attending to these gradations of opinion. Only five years earlier they had been hounded out of their meeting houses in some of the most brutal episodes of religious persecution in English history.[71] Faced with demonstrations like the raucous meeting of the butchers of Clare Market, they might easily assume that the opponents of repeal were aiming at their destruction. The louder the protests against repeal became, the more the repealers themselves might benefit, if those protests served to convince the wavering nonconformists that the king's *Declaration* was all that stood between their families and a renewed bout of persecution.

Making Concessions

The movement of opposition to the king's toleration campaign was largely a reactive one. The butchers of Clare Market shouted no, not yes. The countermovement against repeal aimed to turn back the king's religious policies, especially his assertion of a royal suspending power over the penal laws and Test Acts. But the countermovement was not purely negative; it had some positive content as well. The archbishop, the six other bishops, and the clergy of London had expressed a willingness to offer "due tenderness" to dissenters in an upcoming parliament and convocation. This was a strategic concession designed to weaken the appeal of the repealer movement to nonconformists. Thus even the positive content of the anti-repeal movement was a means of forestalling wider changes, by offering a limited concession to prevent what they saw as a potential Catholic takeover. One of William's agents in England referred to "the Clergy of the church of England who (those that are wise among them) are at present so frightened and so sensible that only the Dissenters can ruin them, that they will bear with many things (which they would not doe at another time) to take the dissenters off."[72] This prescient statement was made three months before the bishops' offer of "due tenderness." It reflected the growing sense among the more politically savvy Anglicans in the spring of 1688 that some sort of concession to the nonconformists was needed in order to prevent them from "ruining" the Church of England by aligning with the Catholics.

Although the bishops' offer of "due tenderness" was a strategic concession to dissenters, it appears to have been genuine. The precise contents of the offer, however, remained to be defined. Talks were begun on the terms, and news of those talks was widely circulated as a means of reassuring nonconformists that the bishops were in earnest. Though little evidence has survived about the contents of these deliberations, the evidence that does survive indicates that Archbishop Sancroft was

seeking to find a formula for the comprehension of moderate nonconformists within the Church of England. According to the later testimony
of William Wake, Sancroft himself led one group of clergy in drawing
up recommendations for changes to the liturgy, while Simon Patrick,
dean of Peterborough, led another. The function of these committees
was to determine which elements of the liturgy could safely be altered
in order to satisfy the conscientious objections of nonconformists.[73] In
July of 1688, Sancroft and some London clerics met with certain nonconformist ministers, who were not named in the extant reports, to
consider these matters. The specter of future concessions raised the ire
of one of the seven bishops, the bishop of Ely, who groused that some
Anglican clergy seemed to be prepared "to Offer all our Ceremonys in
Sacrifice to the Dissenters, Kneeling at the Sacrament and All."[74]

Apart from opening negotiations on comprehension, leading Anglicans also claimed that they had never supported the persecution of
nonconformists in the first place. When the Quaker Richard Davies visited the bishop of St. Asaph in the Tower of London, the bishop told
him "they were put on to do those things which they had done against
Dissenters." This was either a deliberate misstatement or the bishop
was reinterpreting his past actions with unusual vigor. In 1683 he had
urged his chancellor in St. Asaph to pursue legal process against "every
Protestant dissenter (as those bloody wretches are pleased to call themselves)."[75] But times had changed, and wretches were now esteemed
friends. In print and in private, various Anglicans blamed Charles II's
counsellors for having promoted the persecution of the nonconformists
and claimed that the great majority of churchmen had only reluctantly
acquiesced in it.[76] This mode of argument attracted the ire of the repealer
Stephen Lobb, who retorted that Charles II had been renowned "for his
Clemency" and that it was "the men of the Church of England" who
had been responsible for persecution during that king's reign.[77]

Pamphlets defending the Anglicans from charges of being persecutors were printed in great numbers in Holland for export into England.
The English ambassador to The Hague intercepted ten thousand copies of
two tracts that he described as "the vindication of the Church of England
from persecution, and the Archbishup of Canterburys letter to the Clergie
of England how to behave themselves." The former appears to have been
a defense of the Church of England written by Gilbert Burnet. The latter
was a pastoral letter from the archbishop of Canterbury counseling his

bishops to visit nonconformists. In this letter, Sancroft urged his fellow bishops to persuade the nonconformists to rejoin the Church of England but, if that was not possible, at a minimum to join with them in praying for a "Universal Blessed Union of all Reformed Churches, both at Home and Abroad, against our common Enemies."[78]

These appeals for an alliance of Anglicans and moderate dissenters bore considerable fruit. Ten nonconformist ministers visited the seven bishops when they were imprisoned in the Tower of London by the king. This visit appears to have been intended as a show of solidarity with the Church of England.[79] Other nonconformists who may have once contemplated joining the repeal campaign now set themselves firmly against doing so. John Howe, the eminent Presbyterian minister, had been wavering, according to intelligence gathered by John Hampden and an anonymous Williamite agent in the early months of 1688. These two informants were alarmed that Howe had agreed to meet secretly with King James on several occasions, being conveyed to the king's study on at least one of those occasions by William Penn. Hampden remonstrated with Howe for the manner in which he was conducting himself and urged him to behave more cautiously in future. Meanwhile, the other Williamite informant wrote in February that he knew "not what to make" of Howe's behavior, suggesting that the Presbyterian minister might be temporizing: "he is neither in nor out." But by June, Howe's disposition had changed entirely. Around the time of the imprisonment of the seven bishops, the Presbyterian minister resolved finally to cut his ties with King James, and William's agent was able to relay to his masters the welcome news that "Hampden has brought of[f] Mr How[e] at last."[80]

The repealers, perhaps panicking at the shifting position of some of the Presbyterians, attempted to pour cold water on the promise of "due tenderness" made by the seven bishops. One repealer described the Anglican stance as merely "a Pretence of Love, and Peaceful Inclinations towards Dissenters" which was designed to prevent the dissenters from "using their Interest for abrogating the Penal Laws, and establish Liberty of Conscience." As the repealer journalist Henry Care put it, the promise of "due Tenderness" was a "Trick." Once the current propitious moment for toleration had passed, many of the Anglicans would return to their persecuting ways.[81]

What was at issue, then, was not just the credibility of the king, but also the credibility of the bishops. Even if the seven bishops themselves were genuinely committed to "due tenderness," they might not be able to deliver a majority for toleration in either parliament or convocation.[82] It was unclear, moreover, whether the offers being made by the bishops would extend to providing ease for the more radical nonconformists, such as the Quakers or Baptists. As long as the idea of "due tenderness" remained vaguely defined, a large gulf would remain between the proposals of the repealers and the concessions being offered by their Anglican opponents. The repealers still had a strong hand to play with the more radical nonconformists, even if their hand was weakening with many of the Presbyterians.

The King and the Bishops

The seven bishops, in their petition to the king, made an implicit offer to the nonconformists while keeping the contents of that offer vague enough to mollify the hard-liners on their own side. This balancing act enabled the Church to weather the crisis of the spring of 1688 with its unity largely intact. The same could not be said for the court. The prosecution of the seven bishops proved controversial even among the king's leading servants. The trial itself was a shambles, as the high court justices disagreed among themselves and then delivered varying and contradictory summations to the jury. The loss of nerve by some of the king's servants led to the disarray that made the acquittal of the bishops possible.

The king's decision to require his *Declaration for Liberty of Conscience* to be read in churches stemmed from his frustration with the ministers of the Church of England, who had been encouraged to send addresses of thanks for his *Declaration,* but had largely failed to do so.[83] Now the clergy would not be given the option of freely sending their thanks to the king; they would instead be required to read aloud the king's proposals. The initial impetus to require the Anglican clergy to read the king's edict appears to have come from the Congregationalist minister and leading repealer Stephen Lobb. He shared his idea with Sir Nicholas Butler, a recent Catholic convert and member of the privy council, who then proposed it in a council meeting.[84] The king's leading minister, the earl of Sunderland, who had not heard of the proposal before the meeting, was left wrong-footed when the king and council seized eagerly upon it.[85] The council's order to read the *Declaration* was soon published. The Dutch and Austrian ambassadors saw in this order a Machiavellian design to mortify the Church of England by forcing them to disobey the king, thereby seeming to be against toleration and consequently driving the dissenters into the arms of the court.[86] There is no direct evidence, however, that the king expected anything other than a full compliance from the Anglican clergy, whom he continually praised for their "loyalty." The king appears to have been genuinely taken aback when the bishops presented their petition against the *Declaration*. The bishop of Chester had informed him that the address would be "only a petition of submission," but what he received from the bishops was anything but submissive.[87]

The king had been blindsided by the seven bishops, but he had not yet been outmaneuvered. He still had a choice of whether or not to prosecute the bishops and, if the latter, what forum to use in making his case. One faction at the court pleaded for clemency. The earl of Sunderland and the Jesuit courtier Edward Petre argued for letting the bishops off with only a verbal warning.[88] The Catholic lords Arundell, Dover, Powis, and Belasyse also urged caution, although some of them may have wavered in this.[89] A heaven-sent opportunity for the king to retrieve his position was presented on 10 June, when his son was born. Many at court, including William Penn, urged the king to proclaim a general pardon that would conveniently encompass the bishops' infraction.[90] But the king's ire had been raised. He decided to go ahead with a prosecution, in part because a rumor had spread in the City that he dared not do so.[91] He felt that, if he did not prosecute the bishops, he would find opposition rising in other quarters as well. In this he was seconded by the solicitor general, Sir William Williams, who offered the corporeal metaphor that the bishops' defiance was like an ulcer that needed to be lanced before it festered and poisoned the state.[92]

With the decision taken to prosecute the bishops, the nervous courtiers turned their energies from averting the prosecution to shifting the blame for it away from themselves. The members of the Ecclesiastical Commission were particularly desperate to prevent the king from referring the matter to them. The Commission was the obvious venue for a prosecution of the seven bishops; it had proven its effectiveness by suspending the bishop of London in 1686 and ejecting the Magdalen College fellows in 1687 despite the widespread unpopularity of both decisions. But the lord chancellor, who was a member of the Commission, gave his opinion to the king that the bishops' cause was "onely tryable in Westminster Hall."[93] He had considerable ammunition to rely on in making this argument, including the act of 1641 abolishing the court of Star Chamber, which barred any future prerogative court from holding any jurisdiction over matters of common law, such as libel. The chancellor might also have argued that the bishops, if brought before the Commission, would challenge its legality and that this would bring the affair into Westminster Hall regardless.[94] Furthermore, the archbishop of Canterbury was himself a member of the Commission, though he had never attended its proceedings, and to call him before it for punishment might render that body ridiculous.

If Westminster Hall were to be the venue for the prosecution, the opinions of the high court justices would be paramount. They had already been summoned before the king to give their advice. On the morning after the bishops delivered the petition, the justices were called to Whitehall and asked whether the seven bishops had "incurred a Praemunire" by their petition. If found guilty of a praemunire, the bishops would forfeit all their lands and goods to the king and could be imprisoned at the king's pleasure. All of the justices with the exception of the Catholic justice, Sir Richard Allibone, said that the bishops had not incurred a praemunire.[95] The king's legal case in this regard was weak, in part because his officers had not followed the correct legal procedures when sending the order to the bishops. The bishops could not be prosecuted for disobeying an order that was "neither sealed nor sign'd in forme." The bishops' offense, according to the justices, could only be tried as a misdemeanor, which would be punishable by a fine levied on their lands and goods.[96]

The justices were then asked whether the king possessed a power to dispense with the laws, a power that the bishops had explicitly challenged in their petition. The judges had decreed in the case of *Godden v. Hales* in 1686 that the king did possess a power to dispense with particular statutes. But now, at least some of the justices informed the king that their decision in that case "did not mean that his Majesty had a power to dispense with laws in general but only to pardon the forfeitures of particular persons." In other words, the king possessed a dispensing power but not a suspending power. He could issue dispensations to particular persons for particular reasons but not suspend the operation of laws for all persons, as his *Declaration for Liberty of Con-*

science had done. The king was said to have been "displeased" at this interpretation of their previous decision and responded to the judges with "hard words."[97]

Boxed in by the advice of the justices and the lord chancellor, the king decided that the prosecution of the bishops would take place in the Court of King's Bench, not the Ecclesiastical Commission, and that the bishops would be charged with a misdemeanor, not a praemunire. The courtiers who were averse to the prosecution had succeeded in tamping it down, but not in extinguishing it entirely. The discontent among the king's courtiers with the course of events was suggested by the lord chancellor, who told the earl of Clarendon privately that he was convinced that the prosecution would be of "very ill consequence to the King."[98] The chancellor's dissatisfaction was a sign of larger problems at the court. While the Church was uniting, the court was fracturing. Whereas the archbishop of Canterbury had brought together most of his fellow churchmen by shrewdly anticipating the direction in which the majority wished to be led, the king had provoked disunity at court by leading his servants in a direction in which many of them did not want to go.

Delaying Tactics

The prosecution of the bishops began with an order summoning them to attend the privy council on 8 June to answer a charge of misdemeanor. Calling the bishops before the privy council was a legal tactic designed to speed up their prosecution. The high courts would not be in session until 15 June, the first day of Trinity term. If the bishops had merely been subpoenaed to attend the King's Bench on the fifteenth, they would not have been required to give an immediate answer to the charges. Instead, they would have been given time to consider how they would plead and would not have been called back to court until the Michaelmas term, which began on 23 October.[99] An autumn trial would have been inconvenient for the king, who was planning a parliament for November. He needed swift justice to be delivered against the bishops in order to buttress his authority before he took his campaign for liberty of conscience to the electorate.

A subpoena was not, however, the only way to begin a trial. If the bishops were charged with a crime by the privy council and then bound over to the first day of term, either on their own recognizance or through a commitment to prison, their legal position would be altered. They would come into the court "in custodia," an umbrella term which encompassed anyone who came to court either from a prison or under bail. When they reached the high court on the fifteenth, they would be required to give in their plea immediately, since they had already been given notice of the charge against them. In the legal terminology of the day, they would be "forced to plead instanter." This would permit the judges to set a trial date within the coming law term, which was to end in the middle of July.[100] The case would be off the court's docket within a month, and the king would be free to make his preparations for the autumn parliament.

The bishops were not ignorant of these tactics; they had consulted with some of the finest legal minds in England before attending the privy council. They wished to delay the trial. An October trial date would allow them more time to prepare, and the closer the date of the trial was to the planned parliament, the more the justices might be swayed by a desire to appease the members of that parliament, who would have the power to impeach them. The advice the bishops were given was that, if they refused to give a recognizance before the privy council, "their Proceedings with Us must be by Subpena out of the Kings Bench, and then we may Imparle [delay pleading] til[l] the Term after."[101] As grounds for refusing to give a recognizance, the bishops were advised to plead their privilege as peers. This was a bold strategy that was bound to irritate the king, but it would enable them to delay the date of their trial.

When the bishops were called before the privy council and asked to give bail, they refused, saying that as peers they were not required to give bail in such circumstances. This was not in fact the case, as the lord chancellor pointed out. Lord Lovelace had given bail in 1685, and the duke of Buckingham had given bail not long before that. The bishops said that they did not know these cases and would have to rely on what their counsel had advised them. They offered to give the king their word "as honest men, and Christians" that they would appear at the King's Bench when subpoenaed.[102] Within this offer lay a trap, as the king was well aware. The bishops knew that, if they were called to the court by a subpoena, they could push the trial date into the autumn. Such an outcome was exactly what James wanted to avoid. But the bishops would not yield, and so the king took the matter out of their hands, instructing the council to sign a warrant committing the bishops to the Tower of London on a charge of making and publishing a seditious libel. This commitment would jump-start the prosecution because the Court of King's Bench would later be able to assume that the prisoners knew "the Crimes they were to answer to."[103]

The bishops were taken from Whitehall to the Tower by water, carried on a barge to avoid any tumult in the streets of the City. As they passed down the Thames, the watermen in their boats cried out, "God bless the Bishops." They landed at the Tower wharf and passed by "infinite crowds of people on their knees, beg[g]ing their blessing and praying for them." The bishops carried themselves as martyrs, the archbishop telling the crowd that "it was the truth they suffer for" and the bishop of Bath and Wells bidding them to "be steadfast in their religion."[104]

The king was distressed by the outcome of the privy council meeting. A member of the council told Sir John Reresby the day after that, "if the King had known how farr this matter would have gone, he would not have enjoined the reading of the declaration in churches."[105] The king would have preferred that the bishops had been bound over on their own recognizances, rather than being sent to the Tower to await trial. The bishops would have preferred to give their word that they would attend the court when subpoenaed so that they could stand trial in October. But neither side would give way, and so the king was forced into a situation he did not desire. It is undoubtedly the case that the bishops profited more than the king from what happened next. Adulating throngs led them to the Tower; a constant parade of gentry visited them there; and a frenzy of public anxiety built around their cause. The lieutenant of the Tower, Sir Edward Hales, complained that "there is a greater concourses of coaches and people to see them [the bishops], then there is at Whitehall or St James's." Large crowds attended the chapel services in the Tower for a glimpse of the bishops when they came to worship. False rumors spread about the City, one claiming that two of the bishops, like so many previous occupants of the Tower, had already died there under mysterious circumstances. The day of their entry into the Tower became known as "black Friday."[106]

The week-long imprisonment of the bishops became a potent symbol of the clash between king and Church. The bishops themselves were never in any danger: they resided in comfortable apartments and dined on venison at the lieutenant's table. They had complete freedom of movement within the Tower. They had the sympathy of the Anglican guards, who kneeled before them and drank to their healths. They took the sacrament together in the Tower chapel on Sunday. The imprisonment was not designed to make them suffer; it was a legal strategy designed to speed up the trial. Although the bishops were not mistreated, they nevertheless presented themselves as martyrs for the cause of the Church of England. The bishop of St. Asaph wrote a mournful letter from the Tower in which he asked for the recipient's "prayers for the Church, in whose cause we suffer imprisonment, and are to expect as much more as it shall please God to permit our adversaries to bring upon us."[107]

The damage to the king's public image was incalculable. This one episode, more than any other, was later used by the revolutionaries to portray James as a despot. But the king's decision to send the bishops to prison was not inspired by arbitrary malice. James wanted an early trial, and the only way he could get it, short of overriding the law, was to persuade the bishops to enter into recognizances or to commit them to prison.

Striking the Jury

A week after the bishops were imprisoned, the law term began, and the crown acted swiftly to start the prosecution. As soon as the judges of King's Bench assembled, the attorney general moved for a *habeas corpus* to bring the bishops before the bar. At about quarter past eleven on the morning of the first day of term, the lieutenant of the Tower brought the bishops to Westminster Hall. The court was crowded with spectators, including eighteen members of the peerage, who exercised their privilege to sit on the bench, next to the judges. As the prelates entered the hall, spectators kneeled around them and asked to receive their blessings.[108]

In the pretrial hearing, the bishops' lawyers argued that the imprisonment of the bishops had been illegal because no peer ought to be committed for a misdemeanor. Their goal in challenging the legality of the commitment was to buy time for the bishops. If the imprisonment had not been legal, then the bishops could not be required to plead immediately since the judges could no longer assume under the law that the bishops had been given due time to consider their pleas. The attorney general countered with the argument that the bishops' misdemeanor, being a seditious libel, constituted a breach of the peace and that they could be committed for that reason. Three of the four judges agreed with the attorney general, with Justice Powell dissenting, and the case went forward.[109]

The charge was then read and the bishops were required to plead. Their lawyers made a last-ditch effort at delay, arguing that their clients should have time to consider the charges before pleading and that the case should be delayed until the next law term. They claimed that it had been usual in most cases, until recently, to give the defendant time to plead. The judges asked the clerk of the crown, Sir Samuel Astrey, whether this was indeed the case, but Astrey and his two clerks testified that it had long been the practice of the court to require defendants to plead immediately when they had already been notified of the charge through a warrant of commitment or recognizance. The bishops then presented a written plea asking for time to consider the information. The judges rejected the plea by a vote of three to one, with Powell again dissenting.[110]

After nearly four hours of tactical maneuvering, with the efforts of their counsel stymied at each turn, the bishops finally pled not guilty. The attorney general immediately moved the court to set a trial date of two weeks later, on 29 June. The court allowed the motion, and the bishops' attorneys accepted the date. Arrangements were made for the striking of a jury, and the bishops now agreed to post bail. They left the court shortly past three o'clock, free to go home. The crowds made a path for the prelates to pass through. The bishops moved through the crowd, saying aloud "God Confirm you and bless you," with many of the onlookers kneeling to receive their blessings.[111]

The king had won the first round and had gained the early trial that he desired. But there were ominous signs in the four hours of pretrial argument. Although the judges had ruled against the bishops, all except Allibone had shown a degree of deference to the defendants that was unusual. The lord chief justice referred to the gravity of the case when he said that "the Court will bring in nothing new in any such Case as this." Justice Holloway informed the court that some of the bishops were his "particular Friends" and that he would be "very glad" to "shew respects" to them through his rulings so long as he could do so without violating "the course of Law." Justice Powell consistently sided with the bishops' attorneys in their arguments. Although the king's attorneys had succeeded in winning their point that the commitment of the bishops had been legal, they might find less support from the judges on other questions where settled law was less clear. This was evident in the final skirmish of the day. The king's attorneys proposed that twenty-four jurors should be returned for the coming trial, and the bishops' attorneys proposed that forty-eight jurors should be returned, with each side given the right to challenge twelve jurors. The judges sided with the bishops, for there was no settled rule to follow, and forty-eight seemed "the fairest."[112]

The jury was to be struck at the home of Sir Samuel Astrey, clerk of the crown, on 25 June. Astrey had been in his post for over a decade and had recently pleased the king by giving affirmative answers to the Three Questions regarding the repeal of the penal laws and Tests.[113] The responsibility for striking the jury fell to Astrey because of the nature of the trial: in a trial-at-bar a new jury was struck for each case, and the responsibility for striking it fell to an officer of the court, not, as usual, to the sheriff. In the case of the Court of King's Bench, that officer was the clerk of the crown. As the trial was to be held in Middlesex, and the crime was said to have been committed there, the jury would be composed of residents of Middlesex, with their names taken from the Middlesex freeholders' book. Because the men on trial were peers, at least one of their jurors was required to be a knight.[114]

Astrey was free, at least in theory, to strike a jury of forty-eight Catholics, or forty-eight dissenters, and it was just such an outcome that many feared, although one level-headed observer pointed out that Astrey could not strike a jury of forty-eight Catholics, because there were only five or six Catholic freeholders in Middlesex.[115] The fears of some were heightened when the lord chancellor was observed in the act of taking Astrey to see the king a few days before the jury was to be struck. Moreover, the privy council was said to have been instructed to search for jurymen who would be likely to "yeald to his M[ajesty's] expectations."[116]

The public fears proved to be overwrought as Astrey's picks were largely unexceptionable. They included two baronets, ten knights, and eleven country esquires. Nine were former members of parliament. Although the list included men likely to be partial to the king, such as the royal brewer and auditor, it also included a close ally of the bishops, the former member of parliament Sir Thomas Clarges.[117] Far elevated above the usual pool for a petty jury, this jury was composed of men of property and standing, some of whom might be more likely to favor the king's cause while others might be more likely to favor the bishops.

After Astrey had selected the forty-eight jurors, each side retired for an hour to consider which names to remove. Choosing for the king's side were the recorder of London, Sir Bartholomew Shower; the master of the crown office, Sir Robert Clark; and Astrey himself.[118] Not surprisingly, the king's counselors chose to remove Clarges, the confederate of the bishops. They removed two other former members of parliament: Simon Smith, master of the otter-hounds and muster-master of Middlesex, and Sir John Cutler, who had given an evasive answer to the king's Three Questions. They also removed a London merchant, Sir John Bucknall, and a vintner who was one of the commissioners of the City lieutenancy, Sir Thomas Kinsey.[119]

The bishops were represented by four of their number, the bishops of Ely, St. Asaph, Peterborough, and Bristol, along with two of their attorneys, John Ince and Mr. Grainge.[120] The twelve men they challenged included five knights and three former members of parliament. They struck off an army captain, John Shales; a master of the mint, Sir John Brattle; two deputy lieutenants of Middlesex, Sir Thomas Row and Sir Richard Downton; a brewer and former member of parliament, Sir John Friend; and the banker Charles Duncombe. Friend was a supporter of the court and presumably was removed for that reason.[121] Duncombe was probably considered suspect because of his extensive financial dealings with the government; perhaps the wealthiest banker in London, he had made his fortune as Charles II's financier. The bishops appear to have wasted one of their challenges when they blackballed Ralph Hawtrey, a member for Middlesex in the most recent parliament, who had been ejected from his offices earlier in 1688, presumably for defying the government. Not surprisingly, the bishops also vetoed Sir John Baber, the Presbyterian courtier and former physician to Charles II.[122]

The twenty-four men who remained included a baronet and two knights. Three had been members of parliament. Of the twenty-four, three were from the City, nine from the suburbs or Westminster, and twelve from rural Middlesex. Only a dozen would serve on the final trial jury; the other twelve were alternates who would be called on if any of the first dozen jurors were absent or were challenged by the bishops at the outset of the trial. Of the twelve men who finally served, eleven were Anglicans and one, William Avery, was a Baptist. It is unclear whether the bishops had allowed Avery to slip through because they were unaware he was a Baptist, because they had run out of challenges, or because they hoped for some unknown reason that he would sympathize with their cause.[123]

Some of the jurors, like many wealthy Londoners, had connections at court, but others did not. The overall impression is not of a packed jury but of a jury designed to ensure that the trial would carry the utmost credibility. This was the verdict of Gilbert Burnet, no friend to the king, who wrote, "The jury was fairly returned."[124] The composition of the jury surely influenced the course of the trial, both because the jurors were largely Anglican and also because they were of a higher social standing than a usual petty jury and might be more likely to resist pressure from the judges. The only Catholic who was active in the trial was Justice Allibone, sitting on the bench, and he made it clear that he wished the jury to bring in a verdict of guilty. If the king had instructed Astrey to pack the panel with Presbyterians, Baptists, and Catholics, the outcome of the trial might well have been different.

The Trial of the Seven Bishops

The trial took place in Westminster Hall on Friday, 29 June. This was St. Peter's Day, which might seem to be a propitious day for the bishops, who claimed descent from that original father via apostolic succession. But the conventional wisdom predicted that the day would not bring good fortune to them. The bishop of Carlisle waited impatiently at Rose Castle in Cumberland for the post to arrive, predicting gloomily that "For my own part, I expect no other [news] but that the poor Bishops will be found Guilty, and Fined, right or wrong; otherwise, it would look like a Baffle upon the _____ which must not be." (The omitted word, which the bishop dared not write, was surely "king.") The solicitor general prepared his prosecutorial brief with confidence, satisfied that it was "A good Cause for the King." The archbishop of Canterbury, anticipating a guilty verdict and a crippling fine, was heard to say that he could "live on sixty pieces a year, as I did before."[125]

The confidence of the solicitor general stemmed largely from the highly technical nature of libel law in England at this time. As he recorded in his notes, the jury's assigned role was to determine the question of "whether the Bishops had published the[i]r libellous paper in Middlesex." The jury was responsible only to answer the factual question of whether the petition had been written and delivered to the king on a certain date in a certain place. The judges would determine whether the paper was libelous or not. The four judges of King's Bench were known quantities who had ruled for the king on other politically sensitive cases.[126] Given the current state of law, the outlook for the bishops was grim.

Yet it must have felt otherwise on the morning of 29 June, when the bishops were lifted into Westminster Hall on a sea of popular adulation. The hall was packed; its galleries, full. The audience made their sympathies clear by hissing at the solicitor general.[127] The bishops were readying themselves for a defeat that would be a victory. They would be fined heavily and would lose their lands and goods but would gain the gratitude of their church. Despite the archbishop of Canterbury's dark prognostications about his future income, the bishops knew that they had supporters, especially among the peerage, who would grant them hospitality and patronage if needed. That peerage was arrayed in its splendid ranks to view the trial as it took place. Two marquesses, eighteen earls, two viscounts, and seven barons were in attendance. Of those twenty-nine peers, twenty-six were said to have disapproved of the king's designs to repeal the penal laws and Test Acts.[128] The presence of so many peers surely influenced the judges, who could be called to account for their behavior by the House of Lords when it next sat. At one point in the trial, the earl of Danby, who with the other peers had exercised his privilege to sit on the bench next to the justices, leaned over to Justice Holloway for a brief conversation. Holloway, who noticed that Danby had been taking notes, said that "he hoped his Lordship would beare witness of the favour they [the justices] shewed the Bishops." Danby replied that "as for favour, there was none expected; but their Justice[s] should be examined hereafter in the House of Lords."[129]

Up to this point in his reign, the king had retained firm control of Westminster Hall and its high courts of justice. But that royal control had never been fully tested. The king had interpreted the ruling in *Godden v. Hales*, which found that a Catholic could serve as a military officer by royal dispensation, as referring to a range of different offices, only some of which were military. According to the attorney general, Sir Thomas Powys, a few of the justices had said before the bishops' trial that they had "not yet determined" the "Question of the Kings Power of Dispensation in Juditiall Offices." That power would be tested sooner or later, and, Powys observed, a case pending against Lord Lovelace was sure to call it into question. The court seemed more likely to specify the limits of its previous ruling than to extend it to encompass the uses to which the king had put it.[130]

The bishops had challenged the king's dispensing power in their petition, contending that they could not read the royal *Declaration* because it was "founded upon such a Dispensing Power as has been often declared Illegal in Parliament." But the question of the dispensing power would be discussed during the trial only if the lord chief justice allowed it to be. The defense attorneys might choose to raise the question of the dispensing power; if so, the chief justice could overrule them and prevent them from proceeding. The prosecution, for their part, had no interest in raising the question. They had devised a prosecutorial strategy that focused on the narrow grounds of whether the bishops had in fact signed the petition.[131]

For the first half of the trial, it seemed as though the dispensing power would not be the pivotal issue. The prosecutors had some difficulty at the beginning of the proceedings in demonstrating that the signatures on the petition were in the handwriting of the bishops. They eventually referred, however, to testimony from the clerks of the privy council, who observed that the prelates had confessed their hands in the privy council meeting. The defense retorted that the bishops may have written and signed the petition, but they did so at Lambeth, not in Middlesex, and thus the charge against them was factually incorrect. The prosecution replied that, even if the petition had not been written in Middlesex, it had been delivered to the king at Whitehall, and so it constituted a libel that had been "published" in Middlesex. But the prosecution proved unable to follow through with their rebuttal. They had not anticipated this turn in the trial and had no witness on hand to testify that the accused prelates had delivered a petition to the king at Whitehall. The lord chief justice, seeing an opening to acquit the bishops on a technicality, began to sum up, and Justice Holloway was even heard to say that the "Jury must find them not guilty."[132]

Meanwhile the prosecutors busied themselves in sending an urgent message to the earl of Sunderland, who could testify that he had ushered the bishops in to see the king on the night that they delivered their petition. The lord president arrived in the hall and was able to rescue the prosecution's case by declaring that the bishops had indeed informed him on that evening that they intended to deliver a petition to the king. It was at this point that the defense lawyers, who had heretofore attacked the prosecution's case on merely technical grounds, began to argue a more substantive case. Although the petition had been delivered, they alleged that it could not be considered a libel because there was no word in it "that any way touches the King's Prerogative." The bishops could not be punished for criticizing the dispensing power because that power was itself illegal and not part of the king's rightful prerogative. The defense counsel, in the words of an opposition whig observer, began to "speake such Bold Truths concerning the Dispenceing Power as have not of latter yeares been mentioned in Westminster Hall, or any where else out of Parliament."[133]

This was the pivotal moment in the trial, and the lord chief justice could have ended this line of defense by ruling the new argument out of order. Instead, he permitted it to continue. Williams, the solicitor general, feebly protested: "My Lord, if you will admit every one of the Council to Speech it, before they give their Evidence, when shall we come to an End of this Cause? We shall be here till Midnight." Williams's objection was brushed aside and the trial continued for another four hours, with the defense lawyers speaking against the dispensing power and the solicitor general attempting to defend it. As Williams complained after the trial, the fault lay with the lord chief justice for permitting "the [defense] councell to make speeches upon the dispenseing power."[134]

The trial ended in a muddle. All four justices gave different opinions to the jury. Justice Powell himself attacked the dispensing power in his summation, stating that he did not believe that the king had a power "to Dispense with the Laws concerning Ecclesiastical Affairs" and that, if the king were permitted to assume such a power, it would mean the end of parliament, for "all the Legislature will be in the King." Justice Holloway, while not explicitly attacking the dispensing power, said that the bishops' petition could not be a libel because it was not inspired by a malicious or seditious intent. Justices Allibone and Wright both asserted that the petition was a libel because it had disturbed the government and stirred up the people.[135] But Wright, as chief justice, abdicated his responsibility to clarify these divergent opinions for the jury, who were left to assume that they could decide this point of law for themselves.

This, according to the solicitor general in an angry diatribe written after the trial's close, was a "Grand Miscariadge of the Court." As the solicitor wrote, the court had "put the law upon the Jury"; that is, they had left for the jury to decide whether the petition was "libell or No libell." This point of law was "the proper worke of the Court," not of the jury, who ought to have considered only "the Question of fact of [whether the petition was] published or not published by the Bishops."[136] The court's disarray permitted the jury to determine for itself whether the bishops' petition had been libelous.

The trial ended between six and seven o'clock in the evening, after nine hours of argument.[137] The jurors were sent to deliberate in St. Clement's Vestry. The twelve men included a merchant and a linen draper from London, a baronet from Westminster, seven gentlemen from rural Middlesex, and two former members of parliament who resided in or near Westminster. Of the seven country gentlemen, one was noted for being particularly wealthy, having an income of three thousand pounds a year, and another was a justice of the peace for Middlesex; the rest were obscure. One of the former members of parliament, Michael Arnold, was the king's brewer, and the other, Thomas Done, was the royal auditor. Arnold had substantial financial dealings with the king; one account said that the king owed him £7,000, while another said that he owed the king money in the Exchequer. Three of the twelve jurors were known to be tories, but the politics of the others are not known for certain, though William Avery, the Baptist juror from rural Middlesex, was likely a whig.[138]

The deliberations of the twelve soon became sharp, with witnesses reporting that they heard voices raised. Little is known of the substance of their arguments, but most accounts agree that from the start the bishops' defenders were in the majority, with only a few holdouts refusing to acquit. Among those holdouts were Michael Arnold, the king's brewer, William Avery, the Baptist, and William Withers, the tory linen draper. As was standard practice, the jurors were deprived of food and drink until they came to a consensus. They grew thirsty and, when basins of water were provided for them to wash at four in the morning, drank the water instead. It was said that the holdouts finally gave way after they were confronted by the juror Thomas Austin, who averred: "I am the fattest largest man in the company [but] before I find such a petition a crime, I will stay here, till I be no bigger than a Tobacco pipe."[139]

As a result, the bishops were acquitted, and, in a moment that has been described by many historians, the verdict brought forth a shout of joy from the audience that shook Westminster Hall. When the news reached other areas of the country, it provoked similar bouts of rejoicing.[140] This response has been taken to indicate the unity of the English people in opposing the king's policies.[141] But the composition of the jury suggests a more complicated story. The holdouts in the jury chamber formed a microcosm of the king's supporters in 1688: a tory whose watchword was loyalty, an officeholder eager to please his master, and a dissenter alienated from the Church of England. Later histories have tended to focus on the officeholder, Michael Arnold, with the implication that he held out for financial reasons. Meanwhile, the presence of a Baptist among the holdouts has not been mentioned by any historian of the trial. This lapse does not appear to have been a result of willful oversight, but rather was an echo of the surviving contemporary sources, which tended to celebrate the verdict. Contemporary accounts of the jury's deliberations frequently cited the king's brewer, Arnold, as the representative example of the holdouts. If there had been any support for James's policies, these accounts suggested, it came only from officeholders who were torn between their desire to keep their remunerative posts and their desire to join their fellows in opposing the king.[142]

With the imprisonment and trial of the seven bishops, the Anglican countermovement against repeal gained a potent symbol around which it could rally. A medal was struck in Holland celebrating the seven bishops, and at least one print was distributed in England in the summer of 1688 depicting their likenesses. A poem circulated in manuscript in September of that year, exhorting all "True English men" to "remember the seven / Who supported our cause, / As stout as our Martyrs, and as just as our Laws." The prosecution of the seven bishops was widely held to represent the dangers besetting the Church of England.[143]

The trial also signalled an intensifying concern among the judges and the peers about the uses to which the king had been putting his dispensing power. The law on this question was far from clear, although some legal historians have observed that the medieval precedents in cases concerning the royal prerogative were strongly enough in the monarch's favor that *Godden v. Hales* may well have been decided correctly.[144] But the question also was whether James was truly confining himself to the spirit of the ruling. Before the trial, some of the justices told the king that *Godden* had not sanctioned a suspending power, only a dispensing power; that is, the king could not suspend the operation of laws entirely, only dispense specific individuals from being penalized for breaking them. A few of the justices even suggested that *Godden* might not extend to appointments of judicial officers, such as justices of the peace. These concerns were amplified by the trial itself, when the bishops' counsellors attacked the dispensing power. Their speeches against this branch of the royal prerogative were praised by the marquess of Halifax, who told one of the counsellors, Henry Pollexfen, that "he and the rest of the Gentlemen had in this done like Gentlemen of Learning and Honour; and [he] thank'd them for their breaking the Ice; but told them w[i]thall, that he believ'd when ever a Parliament came, the House of Lords wou'd out pitch them a Barr and an half."[145] A constitutionalist opposition to the king's policies was developing along with a religious one, and the legal objections were not merely a figleaf for religious bigotry.

The shifts in public opinion in 1688 gave the repealers cause for concern. Even before the trial, William Penn had urged the king to call a parliament sooner rather than later, preferably in the spring. He worried that, if elections were not called by April, the enthusiasm of dissenters for the toleration campaign might wane. The king initially promised Penn that the parliament would be held in May. His plans changed, however, when the electoral preparations dragged on and the head of the board of regulators, Robert Brent, asked for a postponement to October. The powerful earl of Sunderland, seconding Brent's request, also urged delay. Taking this advice into consideration, James decided to reissue his *Declaration for Liberty of Conscience* in the spring while simultaneously announcing that the planned parliament would not meet until the autumn. The hope was that the renewed declaration would be enough to satisfy nonconformists for now. All these calculations were thrown awry when the repealer Stephen Lobb successfully persuaded the king to add the supplemental order that the English clergy should read the reissued declaration aloud in church.[146] The result was a political earthquake. The defiance of the bishops shook the royal court, and then the king's control over the judicial system collapsed in spectacular fashion. The king had waited too long to act, and a powerful Protestant countermovement had now mobilized.

7

Dividing a Nation

The Geography of Repeal

Given the debacle of the trial of the seven bishops, some observers wondered whether the king would delay or cancel his planned autumn parliament. But James was determined to press ahead.[1] As a result, two electoral coalitions faced off in the late summer of 1688 in anticipation of the coming battle. One coalition opposed the king's campaign for repeal and drew its support largely from Anglicans and Presbyterians. The other supported repeal and gained the backing of many Baptists, Quakers, Congregationalists, Catholics, and high tories. Both groups included people who were not accustomed to working with each other. Each was unstable in different ways. The electoral alliance of churchmen and Presbyterians might last through the elections, but it could easily break down in parliament as the Presbyterians found that many Anglicans were reluctant to enact comprehension.[2] Meanwhile, the king's coalition included many men who despised each other, with the high tories barely deigning to consort with the more radical nonconformists. It was unclear in September 1688 whether either of these marriages of convenience would hold together through the elections, let alone through the coming parliamentary session.

Neither of the two coalitions was ever fully tested, for the elections to parliament were abandoned in midstream. On 28 September 1688, James issued a proclamation cancelling the elections, only a week after he had announced that they would be held. In his proclamation he cited the impending threat of an invasion from the Netherlands.[3] The parliament of 1688 was a dead letter, but the preparations for it are revealing nonetheless. They show that support for repeal varied from place to place and from region to region. That regional variation helps to explain why the repeal movement succeeded in attracting popular support, and why, despite some early gains, that popular support remained limited.

The Politics of the Cloth Industry

Repealer mobilization developed in a regional pattern with distinct areas of strength and weakness. Support for repeal spread widely but was not distributed evenly. Only 27 parliamentary boroughs sent repealer addresses, despite the fact that 107 such boroughs had been regulated by the king. Those 27 addresses, in turn, were sent by boroughs located in only twenty of the forty English counties.

It is possible to identify three main areas of repealer support in England: one that stretched through East Anglia southward to northern Kent; a second that stretched westward from Berkshire through northern Wiltshire to the River Severn in Gloucestershire; and a third that arced along the shores of Lyme Bay in southwest England, taking in parts of the south coasts of Dorset and Devon. At the same time, other areas of England and Wales showed little or no repealer activity. Those areas included the far southwestern county of Cornwall, the counties along the southeastern coast from Hampshire to south Kent, much of the Midlands and the north of England, and Wales in its entirety. The areas of support for repeal, then, correlate fairly well with the areas of cloth making in England, which included three major zones: East Anglia; the West Country from Berkshire through north Wiltshire and south Gloucester and into Somerset, Devon, and Dorset; and a northern area stretching from south Lancashire into the West Riding of Yorkshire.[4] The first two of these major cloth-producing areas had a high level of repealer activity in 1688. The overlap between the repealer areas and the cloth districts suggests a degree of interconnection between politics, religion, and trade in James II's reign.

The wool-textile industry was England's primary export industry in the medieval and early modern periods, and, although its share was declining by the end of the seventeenth century, it still represented 68 percent of all English exports.[5] In an estimate dating from 1696, Gregory King reckoned that the woolen industry had produced about five million pounds worth of goods in the previous year. He also surmised that about two million pounds worth of woolens had been exported from

England in 1688. These estimates suggest that the cloth industry represented about 7 percent of the English economy as a whole.[6] The cloth
towns held cultural as well as economic power. They had long been on
the leading edge of religious change, with the fourteenth-century Lollards meeting in the cloth towns of East Anglia and the West Country,
and evangelical reformers in the sixteenth century following their trails
to the same places. In the seventeenth century these towns continued
as centers of heterodoxy, from Puritanism early in the century to Presbyterianism later in the century.

The threads of connection between dissent, cloth making, and
repealer ideas were drawn particularly tight in the major entrepôt of
Exeter, which produced about 28 percent of England's cloth exports in
1700.[7] But these connections were also evident in other cloth-producing
areas. The clothiers of Worcester sent an address to James thanking
him for his *Declaration for Liberty of Conscience,* which had given "new
Life to our decayed Trade." The clothiers of Devon and Somerset praised
the king for bringing a "new Life to Trade" and thanked him for bringing
toleration. The serge makers of Taunton thanked the king for freeing
them "from the rapacious hands of those that made a prey of our very
Labour," meaning Anglican persecutors; they hoped that liberty of conscience would cause "the Common Interest, Trade and Safety of the
Nation" to be "advanced and promoted by all."[8]

Despite the optimism of these addresses, manufacturers of English
woolens remained anxious about the future of their trade. This was especially the case in the southern regions of England where the woolen
industry was beginning a process of long-term decline in the face of
competition from calicos imported from India by the East India Company, linens imported from Ireland, and the cottons of south Lancashire
and the West Riding of Yorkshire. Patterns of international competition
favored the northern textile regions in England while hitting the south
hard. Imports of Indian calicos into England peaked in the mid-1680s. In
1686 the East India Company imported over £250,000 worth of textiles
into England, making up over 80 percent of its imports into the country.[9]
An outright embargo on the importation of Indian calicos was not
imposed until 1722, with earlier protectionist measures beginning in
1701.[10] Prices for the heavier and more expensive woolens manufactured
in the southern regions of England fell considerably in the later seventeenth century, while the lighter and cheaper woolens manufactured in

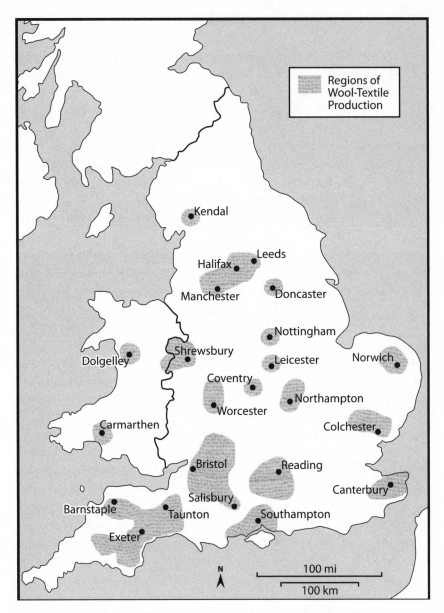

Map 2. Main Regions of Wool-Textile Production in England and Wales, *circa* 1688.

Different regions in England produced different sorts of wool textiles, with Lancashire and the West Riding of Yorkshire tending to produce coarse woolens, the West Country focusing on finer cloths, East Anglia producing worsted cloth, and the East Midlands producing knitted stockings.

Map 3. Repealer Corporations, 1688.

The councils of twenty-seven parliamentary boroughs sent repealer addresses pledging support to James in 1688. Of these, ten were centers of wool-textile production. In addition, the councillors of Bury St Edmunds sent an informal letter of support to the king rather than a formal address, while the councillors of Newbury sent a repealer address even though their town was not a parliamentary borough.

the north tended to gain market share.[11] The result was a steady decline in the cloth-producing regions of East Anglia and the West Country, while the cloth-producing regions of Lancashire and the West Riding held their own. The clothiers of Gloucestershire complained to the king in 1686 about the decay of their trade, as did the clothiers of Suffolk and Essex, but similar complaints were not heard from the north.[12]

King James's response to this situation was to seek to bolster the woolen industry by reducing the price of wool. The cost of wool, which was produced in large quantities by English and Welsh farmers, represented about 38 to 50 percent of the cost of producing a length of cloth, depending on the type of fabric.[13] Reducing the expense of this raw material would make English woolens more competitive against Indian calicos and Irish linens in the domestic market and against Dutch cloth on the international market. In July 1687 James reissued the by-then traditional ban on the export of raw English wool.[14] The king's action prompted grateful addresses from the clothiers, who anticipated that the price of wool would fall as a result.[15]

In addition to reissuing the ban on wool exports, James stepped up its enforcement. In March and April 1688 he dispatched four troops of dragoons to a number of towns in the southeast of England, including Canterbury and Dover, to assist the customs officers and magistrates in "the seizure of wooll or apprehending the persons transporting or assisting the transportacon thereof."[16] The effects of the king's measures can be traced in the diary of Samuel Jeake, a nonconformist wool trader in Rye, a port town in Sussex near the border with Kent. In April, Jeake heard that the king's dragoons had "come to Ashford," a town in Kent about fifteen miles from Rye, "to look after wooll." A few days later the trader recorded the news that the king had issued a new proclamation enjoining strict enforcement of the ban on the export of wool. Jeake's agent in London, Thomas Miller, sent him a letter soon after advising him "to be cautious of med[d]ling with wooll: the King being so much incensed about it." The nonconformist trader, electing not to follow his agent's advice, travelled a month later to New Romney, in Kent "to see if any Wooll could be sold there." His foray proved "ineffectual; the Kings Dragoons being there."[17]

Evasion of the ban on exporting wool became even trickier in June 1688 when the king issued a royal commission to enhance its enforcement. The commission, established at the urging of cloth manufacturers from Devon and Somerset, enabled textile manufacturers to contribute their private funds towards the enforcement of the public ban. This new proclamation delighted the cloth manufacturers of the two counties, who sent an address to the king thanking him for an initiative that they were convinced would revitalize their industry.[18]

King James offered sustained support to the wool-textile industry. His measures came at the expense of the interests of wool traders, wool combers, and sheep farmers, who found their unfinished wares to be increasingly restricted to domestic markets. The royal initiatives can be seen both as a reward to the cloth towns that had supported repeal and as a reminder to those towns to continue to support repeal in the upcoming parliamentary elections. An economic quid would be matched by an electoral quo. Textile manufacturers were in a position to help the king because of their leverage in parliamentary boroughs across England. Many of the new aldermen and common councillors appointed to office by James were weavers and clothiers. The king appointed clothiers to public office in the cities of Gloucester, Canterbury, Norwich, and Salisbury and in the towns of Devizes and Newbury. With the exception of Norwich and Salisbury, all of these centers sent addresses to James after the new officials were appointed, pledging to support the repeal campaign. Similar addresses were sent from the cloth towns of Totnes, Lyme Regis, Reading, and Sudbury after James had appointed new officials to those places.[19]

Not every clothier was a repealer, nor every repealer a clothier. But the priorities of the two groups made for a close fit. The king himself was eager to emphasize the interconnections between his interests and those of clothiers. In June 1687 he received an address from thirty-five leading inhabitants of Leeds thanking him for his *Declaration for Liberty of Conscience*.[20] He told the emissaries of the town that "He expected no Lesse" than this address "from so Rich a Clothing People, whom he would alwayes protect, for in their Riches consisted His Greatness." Noting that Leeds was a "Town that had a greate trade in clothing," he informed them that he aimed "to enrich them" through his policies.[21] The king also met with clothiers from Exeter in February 1688 to hear their concerns about newly imposed French tariffs on English cloth. Perhaps promising more than he could deliver, he had said that he would take up the matter and "would never suffer it [the French tariff]" to prevail.[22]

The clothiers were delighted by the favorable attentions they received from the king. But the wool traders and sheep farmers of England had less reason to cheer. The strict enforcement of the ban on the export of raw wool entailed a transfer of wealth to wool consumers and textile producers from wool producers and traders. It is perhaps unsurprising, then, that the repeal cause found little support among the nonconformists of Rye, the port town where Samuel Jeake based his wool-trading activities. Rye was a hub for smugglers, just a quick sail across the Channel from France. It was also a parliamentary borough and a member of the confederation of Cinque Ports, a military holdover from medieval times. In the parliamentary election of 1685, King James had successfully pressed his traditional right as lord warden of the Cinque Ports to nominate one of the two members of parliament for each of the ports. The lord warden's right of nomination had long been contested, and there was no guarantee that the king would be able to secure that prerogative again in the upcoming elections.

When the regulators sent a letter to Rye asking for nominees to take up offices on the town council, Jeake agreed to serve as town clerk.[23] He and his friends, however, specified that, although they were willing to take office on the council, they would make their own decisions about whom to elect to parliament. They refused "to grant the King the choice of One Member in Parliament." This was unwelcome news to the regulators. The stipulation was "so disagreeable to the then Court relish," Jeake noted with satisfaction, that the regulation did not go through as planned. Later in the year an order of regulation was sent to Rye nominating new councillors, with Jeake conspicuous by his absence among the nominees. The new regulation flopped, as the new town clerk, a man by the name of Samuel Stretton, did not even show up to take his office.[24] As the repeal cause faltered in Rye, Samuel Jeake and his nonconformist friends did not lift a finger to help. When the Revolution came and James was overthrown, Jeake rejoiced that "we were freed from the fears of Popery and Persecution" while the king suffered as "destruction came upon him like a whirlwind."[25] The disgruntled wool smuggler had his revenge.

Regions of Repealer Support

The repeal cause, then, advanced in certain regions while faltering in others. England's capital city was the hub of the movement. Most of the pro-repeal pamphlets were published in London, and many of their authors, including Henry Care, Giles Shute, and Stephen Lobb, lived in the metropolis. Eight of the king's regulators preached at Baptist churches in London or the neighboring boroughs of Westminster and Southwark. But proximity to London was not the leading factor in the spread of repeal. In many cases, the spokes led far away from the hub.

One of the densest concentrations of support for repeal was found on the shores of Lyme Bay, on the southwest coast of England. Of the twenty-seven repealer addresses sent to the king from parliamentary boroughs, five were sent from boroughs in this region. These included the cloth towns of Totnes on the western side of the bay, Lyme Regis on the east, and the great entrepôt of Exeter in the center. Two port towns on the bay were also taken over by repealers: Dartmouth on the western shore and Bridport on the eastern. The regulating campaign had been heading eastward along the shores of the bay when it was brought up short by the sudden recalcitrance of the high court justices in the summer of 1688, after the seven bishops trial had shaken the king's grip on the high courts. The boroughs of Weymouth and Dorchester had been due to have their charters voided by the Court of King's Bench in Westminster, as a preliminary to the issuing of a new charter. Instead of ruling as expected for the king, the court decided abruptly to delay the proceedings until the next term.[26]

The Lyme Bay region had long been marked by dense concentrations of nonconformists and particularly tense relations between the Church and dissent. In the 1670s in the city of Exeter alone, over one thousand dissenters had been prosecuted for their nonconformity. In the early 1680s, the interior fittings of nonconformist chapels at Lyme Regis and Bridport had been destroyed by Anglicans. When James II appointed commissioners in 1687 and 1688 to investigate the levying of fines on nonconformists and Catholics over the previous decade, well-attended hearings were held across south Devon, with nonconformists complaining bitterly of the ill treatment they had received at the hands of conformists.[27]

The repeal cause in south Devon and western Dorset was bolstered by the large number of nonconformists in the region. It benefited also from the activities of several well-placed organizers. One of the ringleaders was John Beare, the former member of parliament for the Devonshire cloth town of Tavistock. Beare had been a persecutor of nonconformists in south Devon in the 1670s and early 1680s. Yet, like some other tories, he followed the king's lead and supported the repeal campaign, giving affirmative answers to the Three Questions and agreeing to vote for repeal if he should be elected to parliament. He was appointed a justice of the peace for Devon and, when a new charter was brought to Totnes in April 1688, the new officeholders swore their oaths of office before him. He himself was appointed an alderman of Totnes under that charter. He served as a local agent of the regulators, who entrusted the supervision of the parliamentary boroughs of Totnes, Honiton, Dartmouth, and Tiverton to his care.[28]

Alongside Beare on the new Totnes council were Sir John Southcote and Richard Burthogge. Southcote was a Catholic who had recently been appointed a justice of the peace in Devon. He was resented by some of his fellow Devonians for the "hot-headed zeal" he showed at this time. His activities took him across the county. He assisted in the regulation of Totnes, interrogated the council of Okehampton, delivered addresses to the king from Ashburton and Kingsbridge, and advised the new mayor of Dartmouth.[29] Both Southcote and Beare were among the Devonshire justices of the peace who ordered that four anti-repeal books, including Halifax's *Letter to a Dissenter,* should be burned publicly by the common hangman.[30] Southcote was eager to nominate himself as a potential member of parliament for Totnes, but the regulators rejected his candidacy on the grounds that it would "not be for your Majesties int[e]rest." As a Catholic, Southcote could not hold a seat in the House of Commons without violating the Test Act of 1678, and the king had no intention of issuing any dispensations from that particular act.[31]

Richard Burthogge joined Southcote and Beare in promoting repeal in Totnes and elswhere in Devon. Burthogge, a Presbyterian, was a physician living in Bowden, about two miles from Totnes. He was also a philosopher, having published in 1678 his *Organum Vetus & Novum.* In 1687 he authored a repealer pamphlet, *Prudential Reasons for Repealing the Penal Laws.* In this work he argued that "Trade is the Interest of England, and Liberty of Conscience the Interest of Trade," noting that the majority of "the Industrious Trading Part of the Nation are either themselves Dissenters, or Favourers of those that are." He praised James II's *Declaration for Liberty of Conscience* for having boosted the trade of England. His pamphlet was controversial enough to provoke a lengthy reply, circulated only in manuscript and now lost, from the pen of the local Anglican minister John Prince. Like many repealers, Burthogge was a nonconformist who was known for associating freely with Catholics. He argued for the toleration of Catholics in his pamphlet, on the grounds that, since the king was a Catholic, one could not think ill of Catholics without thinking ill of the king. One of his less sympathetic readers, the antiquary Anthony Wood, derided the Presbyterian philosopher as a "temporizing Fanatico-Romanus, that is a fanatic in profession and an associate with papists in conversation." The borough of Totnes proved more sympathetic to Burthogge's ideas, proposing to choose him as one of their members in the upcoming parliament.[32]

Eleven parliamentary boroughs in all were located on or near the shores of Lyme Bay in Devon and Dorset. The regulators, in their reports to the king, predicted optimistically that all eleven of these boroughs would vote for repealer candidates in the upcoming elections. The optimism of the regulators presumably stemmed from the large number of nonconformists in the region, the extensiveness of the groundwork laid by sympathetic gentry, and the fact that seven of the eleven boroughs had been regulated by orders of the privy council, with four of the seven also receiving new charters. Each borough would elect two members of parliament. But even if the twenty-two members chosen by this region proved to be repealers, this would represent less than 5 percent of the members of the House of Commons. Lyme Bay by itself was not enough.[33]

The regulators would need to look for success elsewhere as well, and they hoped to find it in other regions such as East Anglia and the Thames estuary. The boroughs in the counties of Cambridgeshire, Essex, Suffolk, and Norfolk together elected thirty-two members of parliament, with another eight members chosen in northern Kent. East Anglia was known for its cloth industry, clustered along the border between Suffolk and Norfolk with a northern outpost centered on the city of Norwich. The region was also known for its gatherings of nonconformists. Ann Docwra, a Quaker in Cambridge, had published a repealer pamphlet in 1687, and Elizabeth Rone, a Familist from the Ely region, published a repealer ballad in 1688.[34]

The repeal cause in East Anglia was organized largely by the Baptist regulators Benjamin Dennis and Richard Adams, in conjunction with a Catholic peer, Lord Dover. Dennis and Adams were not residents of East Anglia; they lived and worked in London where they both led

Baptist congregations. Lord Dover's estate was at Cheveley near Cambridge, but he too spent much of his time in London. Few had risen as quickly as he in James's favor and by 1688 he held multiple positions in the royal administration, serving as a treasury commissioner, privy councillor, lord lieutenant of Cambridgeshire, and colonel of a cavalry regiment. He was active in the regulation of Bury St Edmunds, where he worked hand in glove with Dennis to secure a repealer takeover of the council. The willingness of a Baptist regulator to work in conjunction with a Catholic peer on a political campaign suggests some of the limits of anti-popery in this period. Lord Dover also played a role in the regulations of Orford and Eye in Suffolk and presented the pro-repeal address from Cambridge to the king.[35]

The East Anglian parliamentary boroughs fell one by one to repeal, with the notable exception of Norwich, which held out against the repeal tide. Pro-repeal letters or addresses were sent to James from six boroughs in East Anglia, including Cambridge, and a further two boroughs in Kent. Among these eight repealer boroughs were the cloth centers of Canterbury, Bury St Edmunds, and Sudbury. The bishop of Norwich gloomily predicted that the pro-repeal cause would have considerable success in his home county of Norfolk. As he wrote to the archbishop of Canterbury, "the Corporations in this County, (except Norwich) are so regulated, and terrifyed from above that I doubt, I shall not be able to give your Grace soe good an accompt from [here] as I heartily wish."[36] There were five boroughs in Norfolk, including Norwich, returning ten members of parliament. The bishop had good reason to worry, given that two of those boroughs, Thetford and King's Lynn, had already sent addresses to the king pledging to support his repeal campaign.

Small hiccups in the regulations were quickly suppressed, often by the corporations themselves. The town council of Cambridge received a royal mandate appointing several new members, including a "Samuel Long" as a common councilman. Seeking to obey the royal order, the baffled councillors looked in vain for a man by that name to add to their ranks. Fortunately some of the aldermen had inside knowledge of the regulation, and they assured the corporation that the king had meant to nominate not the mysterious "Samuel Long" but rather the well-known "Ralph Long." Mr. Long was duly added to the corporation. At King's Lynn some of the nominees selected by the king were not freemen, but the town councillors obligingly granted them that necessary honorific before appointing them to office.[37]

The repealers' successes in East Anglia did not necessarily stem from wide popular support. The new mayor of King's Lynn, a local gentleman named John Davy, stirred up substantial local opposition. Davy had been elected as a common councilman in June 1686 and was recommended by James for the mayoralty in June 1688. He took the oaths of allegiance and supremacy upon his elevation, which suggests that he was either a dissenter or an Anglican.[38] When the seven bishops were acquitted on 30 June, he attempted to prevent the townsmen from making celebratory bonfires. His interference aggravated the inhabitants of the town, who built a bonfire in front of his house and threw into it effigies of the devil and the pope. The effigy of the pope burned immediately but that of the devil was made of an incombustible material and thus remained intact within the flames. The devil was carefully positioned with his hand pointing toward the mayor's house as a sign to all who passed of the mayor's villainy. Davy was undeterred by these menaces. On the same day as the bonfire, he had secured an address from the council to the king thanking him for his *Declaration for Liberty of Conscience* and promising to elect members of parliament who "shall make Your Majesty happy, and Your Subjects easie." He delivered the address to the king himself and was voted five guineas by the council for his expenses. A few weeks later, when the common council balked at reelecting him as mayor at the expiration of his term in August, he threatened them with a prosecution for riot if they proceeded to elect any mayor other than him. A mandate soon arrived from the king recommending Davy's continuation in office, and the opposition to his reelection collapsed.[39]

Davy was said to have been assisted by two Baptist "Regulators" of "inferiour rank," presumably Benjamin Dennis and Richard Adams, who attended several meetings of the council, despite the lack of any precedent for outsiders to monitor council business. The regulators hand delivered the royal orders that brought Davy and a mixed group of Catholics, nonconformists, and Anglicans to office in the town. In their report to the king on the state of the borough, they described Davy as "a very right man, and active for Your Majesties service."[40]

Faced with local opposition, repealer corporations in the east of England sought to manipulate the parliamentary electorate in advance of the coming contests. At Cambridge and Canterbury, the electorate was large, consisting of all the freemen, and the new corporations worked assiduously to reshape the electorate by adding new freemen of their own selection. Through this means they might succeed in electing repealer members of parliament, even though the parliamentary franchise was not restricted to the members of the council as it was in many smaller, pocket boroughs.[41] A similar maneuver was made by the king himself, who sent a letter to the councillors of Norwich asking them to admit a group of thirty-eight Quakers to the freedom of that city without requiring them to swear any oath. The king's efforts were foiled when the councillors refused to comply, citing their duty to ensure that all new freemen took the requisite freeman's oath. The city was subsequently issued a new charter in September 1688, with two Quaker clothiers named in it as common councilmen, although the records of the corporation suggest that the new charter was not actually put into force before the parliamentary elections were called off.[42]

Pockets of repealer support were also found scattered across the cloth districts of Berkshire to the immediate west of London and the cloth districts of Wiltshire and Gloucestershire further to the west. Parliamentary boroughs from these three counties sent a total of five repealer addresses to the king, including three from cloth towns. The cloth center of Gloucester, for instance, was firmly in the king's camp. It had, unusually, elected a Catholic as its mayor in 1686, well before the start of the repealer movement, partly through the influence of the soldiers garrisoned there. The city was among the first to be regulated, with a Catholic appointed as its recorder in December 1687. Upon entering his office, the new recorder delivered a pro-repeal speech to the council that was later printed in London. The next day, the corporation agreed unanimously to send an address to the king promising to assist in "the Repeal of the Two Test-Acts, so subject to dangerous interpretations."[43]

The cloth town of Newbury was regulated and sent a pro-repeal address to James even though it did not have the parliamentary franchise. The mayor and aldermen noted with regret that they were "not in a Capacity to elect any Member of Parliament" for the borough, but they hoped nonetheless that God would "dispose the Hearts of Your Great Council in Parliament" to "answer Your Majesties Purposes for the good of Your People." Interestingly, of the nine non-parliamentary‑

boroughs regulated by James across England and Wales, seven were located either in East Anglia, the West Country, or in the area immediately to the west of London. This suggests some of the intensity of support for repeal in these regions: some towns were regulated even when there were no direct electoral gains to be had.[44]

Regions of Repealer Weakness

These regions of repealer strength were more than matched by vast areas of weakness. The entirety of Wales was virtually a lost cause for repeal. The regulators conceded as much when, in a desperate attempt to make some headway, they had writs of *quo warranto* issued to all of the boroughs in Wales, challenging all of their charters at once. These orders alarmed many Welshmen to no real purpose. The writs did not in fact lead to the issuing of new charters, presumably because the regulators lacked the administrative capacity to determine whom to appoint as new officers in the Welsh boroughs. The halting nature of the regulating campaign in Wales is suggested by the fact that no regulators' reports survive for any of the Welsh counties. Without a systematic survey of the boroughs, regulation would not go far. In the end, only two of the Welsh boroughs, Neath and Carmarthen, were regulated by order of the privy council in 1688.[45] Given this record of inattention, the twelve members of parliament elected by Welsh boroughs and the twelve members elected by the Welsh counties seemed likely to be largely opposed to repeal.

Contemporary observers noted the oppositional sentiments of many Welshmen. William Lloyd, bishop of St. Asaph, one of the seven bishops prosecuted by the king in June, led the opposition to repeal in his diocese in North Wales. After the trial Lloyd conducted a visitation of his diocese that became a combination of victory lap and campaign tour. One witness described the visitation as a "progress," with the bishop going from church to church preaching and traveling from the home of one gentleman to the next, gathering groups of gentry together. According to this loyalist observer, the bishop's design was "to incense the People against the King." By September Lloyd had largely succeeded in his goal of uniting the freeholders of his diocese against the royal agenda, as one repealer observed to his dismay. That repealer, the solicitor general Sir William Williams, predicted that the king's program would find limited support in the counties of North Wales, in large part because of "the speeches consults discourses and Advices of the Bishop of St Asaph in his visitation," which had been designed "to frustrate the Kings purposes in having equall Members elected to Parliament in North Wales."[46]

The prospects for the repeal cause in Cornwall were equally bleak. Cornwall was particularly rich in small pocket boroughs, with twenty-one constituencies electing forty-two members of parliament. None of these boroughs had more than two hundred voters, and most had fewer than one hundred. In past elections, these boroughs had frequently elected men from outside the county who came with recommendations from the lord lieutenant of Cornwall or were seen as men of influence. The bishop of Bristol, who was to become one of the seven bishops, conducted a tour in early 1688 of his home county of Cornwall, where he was a powerful landowner in his own right. He wrote that he "was glad to find the Gentry unanimous for the preserving the Test, and our Laws." The gentry of Cornwall were, moreover, determined to prevent the Cornish boroughs from falling into their usual habit of electing men from outside the county in exchange for various favors. The gentry were "resolv'd to appear in their several corporations, and not suffer so many foreigners to be putt upon them."[47] This resolve meant that the regulators would most likely need to find suitable candidates from within the county, not an easy task when most of the gentry opposed repeal. Cornwall was, moreover, a county where relatively few nonconformists resided.

The lord lieutenant of Devon and Cornwall was the tory earl of Bath. In the 1685 elections, he had become known as the "Prince Elector" for his ability to manipulate the tiny Cornish boroughs on the king's behalf. James hoped for a repeat performance and thus allowed the earl a relatively free hand in the county's affairs. The regulators arranged for only a limited number of royal mandates recommending changes to boroughs in Cornwall, and those few that were sent were often resisted. The burgesses of Fowey and Lostwithiel explained in general terms why they could not admit the king's nominees: "they could not with safety to their oaths elect the persons named in the mandate, being contrary to their charters."[48] In other English counties such as Devon and Buckinghamshire, similar refusals had led to burgesses being called to account before the privy council or to borough corporations being dissolved and issued with new charters.[49] But in Cornwall the regulators appear to have showed leniency rather than press the boroughs to submit to the king's demands.

The earl of Bath proved to be a far from reliable partner for the repealers. He used his influence at court and in the countryside to wage a running battle with the regulators, focusing his ire especially on the "irregularities and extravagances" of Edward Nosworthy, the former whig member of parliament for St Ives in Cornwall, who became the local agent of the regulators for that borough.[50] Bath's preference for the *status quo* can be seen in his handling of Okehampton, a borough in central Devon. The councillors of Okehampton had given resolutely negative answers to the Three Questions when interrogated by two Catholic emissaries from Sir John Southcote. A month later Bath himself visited them, to "inspect the Corporation," and pronounced himself "well satisfied" with their "proceedings."[51] Bath's true feelings were revealed even more clearly after William of Orange's invasion, when he plumped for the prince at a crucial moment by conspiring to deliver to him the Plymouth garrison soon after the Dutch landed in Devon in November 1688.[52]

Other areas of the country, while not yet lost causes like Wales or Cornwall, were teetering on the brink. A series of misfires in boroughs across the northwest Midlands and southern Lancashire indicated either a lack of local agents in those areas or a lack of attention from the regulators. The council of Shrewsbury on the Welsh borders was regulated once, partly filled with supporters of repeal, and then abandoned by the regulators. The new members were four votes away from outvoting the old members. In the weeks immediately following the regulation, the inhabitants of Shrewsbury expected that a second regulation would come: "o[u]r affaires here are yet in suspense, though we have past [passed] a slight regulation (of 15 out of 36) . . . but we expect roote and branch in a little time."[53] A second, more exhaustive, "roote and branch" regulation would give the new members control of the council. Months passed and the second regulation never came to the delight of one local observer: "all that were put in were such as they [the regulators] thought fitt to serve a turn and truly I think they [the regulators] were not much mistaken had they [the new members] been more in number but the majoritie being left in they [the new members] have been allways out voted."[54] Rather than find another four men who would "serve a turn" and give the repealers a majority, the regulators sat on their hands. The result was a stymied campaign in Shrewsbury.

A similar set of events took place fifty miles north of Shrewsbury, at Wigan in Lancashire. In March 1688 an order of the privy council removed the mayor, the recorder, the town clerk, four of the eleven aldermen, seven of the eighteen common councillors, and one of the two bailiffs. In their places came a group of Catholics who, according to one local observer, had "noe estate within the said Burrough nor paid any Scott or Lott [scot and lot tax] therein."[55] This regulation had all the hallmarks of the first stage in a two-part regulation in that it removed a substantial part of the council while leaving just over half of the old councillors in place. Had the borough been regulated again, with more Catholic gentry added, the Anglicans would have lost control of the council. But the second regulation never arrived.

What was left in Wigan was a corporation at war with itself. The new Catholic mayor, Thomas Gerrard, lacked the support of the council, which retained a slight majority of old members. The mayor attempted to organize an address to be sent to London, thanking the king for his regulation and promising to support the repeal of the penal laws. The address was never sent, presumably because the council voted against it. When the annual mayoral election was held, the Anglican majority on the common council rallied and elected one of their co-religionists as mayor. In the ensuing celebrations, the populace of Wigan expressed, according to one observer, "the greatest joy that ever was at the election of a mayor in Wigan."[56] Even this spectacle roused no response from the regulators. No report on Wigan survives in the papers of the regulators to reveal their thoughts about this botched regulation, which they could have prevented by sending a second regulation to complete the Catholic takeover. As in Shrewsbury, the regulators had left their work half done.

The regulation of Stafford, fifty miles southeast of Wigan, also bore the marks of an inattentive regulator. Two regulations were sent to the town, but, when the first was implemented only in part and the second not at all, there was no attempt at a third try, even after the council and its new Catholic mayor sent a letter to the regulators asking for their advice. Two months later nothing had been done, and the regulators reported with a seeming lack of urgency that Stafford was "Not yet fully settled, but a good election expected."[57]

Thirty miles northwest of Stafford, at Chester, local nonconformists were offered the opportunity to join the repeal campaign. But these dissenters were, in the main, moderate Presbyterians, and they refused to take political power away from the local Anglicans. The city of Chester received a visit from a "Mr Trinder" in the late summer of 1688. This was possibly Henry Trinder, Robert Brent's co-worker in London, but it is more likely to have been John Trinder, who was on his way from London to Dublin to take up a new position as a revenue commissioner of Ireland. Trinder met with the Presbyterian minister Matthew Henry. According to the minister's later recollections, the king's agent told him that "the King thought the Government of this City needed Reformation, and if I would say who should be put out and who put in their Places it should be done." When the minister refused to cooperate, on the grounds that it was "was none of my Buisness," Trinder met with others in Chester to get the list of names he needed.[58]

A new charter for the city was sealed on 15 September and arrived at Chester a month later. According to Matthew Henry, the charter named to civic office "all the Dissenters of note in the City." The dissenters refused to have anything to do with these nominations, according to Henry, and "unanimously refus'd" to take office under the new charter. In Henry's view, the refusal of the dissenters to take control was a sign of their "Modesty," and "a proof [of] how far they are from an affectation of Power, the key of their Ambition being to live quiet and peaceable Lives."[59] In cities like Chester, where nonconformists were eager to retain the favor of their Anglican neighbors, repeal was a lost cause.

Where regulations did succeed in the northern regions of England, that success could be attributed to the activity of an effective local agent. In Lancaster, the agent was the whig Lord Brandon; in Carlisle, it was the Catholic governor, Francis Howard; in Hull, it was the Catholic governor, Lord Langdale.[60] At Berwick-upon-Tweed, the corporation was under the thumb of the town's Catholic governor, Sir Thomas Haggerston. The council of Berwick ordered that an address be circulated among the burgesses of the town offering to elect anyone whom the king nominated for member of parliament. Any burgess who refused to sign the pledge would be disfranchised. Eight burgesses refused and were removed from the freedom of the town. The councils of Berwick and Carlisle admitted Catholics and others to the freedom in transparent efforts to tip the electorate toward repealer candidates.[61] At Durham, Bishop Crewe demanded that the members of the council sign a paper promising to elect whomever the bishop named to the next parliament. Since Crewe was a known supporter of the king's religious policy, those who made such a pledge would implicitly be committing themselves to cast their votes for repealers. Thirty-three of the thirty-eight councillors signed the paper. One of the aldermen who refused to sign was removed from his office by Crewe, who used his summary powers as bishop under the city charter to dismiss him.[62]

The pattern of support for repeal in the north, then, was different from that in the south. Instead of entire regions organizing in support of repeal, only a few individual towns did so. Those boroughs that moved in the direction of supporting repeal were usually responding to pressure from a powerful individual. The governors of the garrison towns had troops at their disposal, and in Carlisle, Berwick, and Hull many of those troops were Catholics who were committed to repeal. Berwick and Carlisle sent pro-repeal addresses to the king in 1688, and their Catholic governors would probably have been able to control the parliamentary elections held in these boroughs. But there were only a handful of garrison towns in England and not all of them had Catholic governors. These limited pockets of support did relatively little to bolster the wider campaign for repeal.

Testing the Repeal Campaign

Much remains unknown about the preparations of the regulators and the dispositions of the electorates in England and Wales in the waning months of 1688. But a few firm data points do exist, including the results of three parliamentary elections that were conducted before the national campaign was cut short by the imminent Dutch invasion. The elections in these three disparate boroughs provide some inkling of what might have occurred had the national elections gone ahead.

The three boroughs that conducted parliamentary elections in September and October 1688 were Rochester and Queenborough in Kent and Droitwich in Worcestershire.[63] Rochester was a medium-sized borough near the naval shipyard at Chatham with an electorate of about three hundred freemen. The regulators worried that it would be difficult to counter the interest of Sir John Banks, one of the members for

Rochester in the Parliament of 1685, who refused to support repeal. The Catholic lord lieutenant of Kent noted, however, that the king's nominees might hope to gain votes from "the Dissenters, and such as belong to the Dock and Navy, who eat of the Kings bread." The regulators surmised that it was "very probable" that the second member elected would be Sir Phineas Pett, the navy commissioner at Chatham, who was considered more pliable than Banks. But their hopes proved groundless even though the king himself lobbied the town council on behalf of Pett. Sir Phineas went down to defeat, as two opponents of the royal policies, Sir John Banks and Sir Roger Twisden, swept the polls.[64]

At Queenborough, the electorate was smaller, with only about thirty freemen entitled to vote. Daniel Defoe was to describe the place a few years later as "a miserable dirty, decay'd, poor, pitiful, fishing Town." The borough was dominated by the nearby garrison at Sheerness. The king nominated the deputy governor of Sheerness, Robert Crawford, along with Robert Wilford, a naval officer stationed in the area; the regulators predicted that these two would be elected without "dispute." In fact, two men entered the lists to oppose them, James Herbert and Sir William Booth; the first of these was an open opponent of the repeal of the penal laws and Test Acts.[65] Once again the regulators had downplayed the potential opposition to repeal in their report.

The town had been issued a new charter in June, and by that charter Crawford and Wilford, the king's candidates, were made jurats of the town, while Herbert and Booth were not. On the day of the election, twenty-eight men showed up for the poll. Twenty-seven voted for Crawford; the twenty-eighth was Crawford himself, who could not cast a vote for his own candidacy. The second votes were split, with ten going to Wilford, sixteen to Herbert, and two to Booth. The result was that one of the royal nominees, Crawford, won the election, while the other lost. This might appear to suggest some opposition in Queenborough to the king's policies. It is worth noting, however, that there was not a single voter who did not cast a vote for at least one of the royal candidates. The defeat of Wilford, the king's second nominee, may have been in part a result of the local influence of Herbert, who had estates nearby.[66]

The borough of Droitwich was the last to go to the polls; it held its parliamentary election on the first of October, three days after the king had recalled the writs. It was one of the more unusual boroughs in

England, its franchise being held by owners of the local salt works who had been elected as freemen of the borough. About thirty men had achieved this honor, including Sir Thomas Street, one of the justices of the Court of Common Pleas at Westminster, who was a substantial property owner in the town. Street, also the recorder of the borough, had engineered an address from the town in March thanking the king for his *Declaration for Liberty of Conscience*. The address pledged to elect members of parliament who would "answer Your Majesties Expectations." The town's subservience was likely motivated by a lawsuit pending in Westminster Hall challenging the prerogatives of the borough corporation and its control of the salt works. The town subsequently agreed to surrender its charter, and a royal warrant was prepared for a new charter, though for unknown reasons no new charter seems to have been issued.[67]

In October, the borough corporation, presumably anxious about its commercial interests, followed through on its earlier pledge. The earl of Sunderland had sent a letter to the bailiff and burgesses nominating William Bridgeman and Sir John Trevor as members of parliament. Under the close supervision of Justice Street, the burgesses assembled and proceeded to vote for the king's nominees. The election was uncontested. The order electing the royal nominees was signed by the two bailiffs, the recorder, and twenty-three burgesses. The lawsuit about their control of the salt works was still depending before the lord chancellor, and the burgesses surely hoped that their obedience would influence him in their favor.[68]

Neither of the town's newly elected M.P.s had a prior connection to Droitwich, but both had proved devoted to the king's interests. Bridgeman, who was Sunderland's under-secretary of state and a clerk of the privy council, was a key agent in the regulating process, as he drafted and signed most of the privy council orders removing officers from the boroughs. He had sat in the Parliament of 1685, and his willingness to support repeal in the upcoming parliament was not in doubt. Trevor, a high tory, had performed good service for the king as speaker of the House of Commons in 1685. He had served as master of the rolls since 1685 and as a privy councillor since July 1688. He was said to have recommended the policy whereby all the Welsh boroughs were sent writs of *quo warranto* to encourage them to surrender their charters.[69] The king's repeal campaign might have had some chance of succeeding with men such as these in the upcoming parliament, and the Droitwich election had secured their presence, demonstrating that even in the unfavorable climate of October 1688 the king had ways of leaning on certain boroughs for support.

The three elections in Rochester, Queenborough, and Droitwich can be considered as a straw poll for the broader election that was never held. The results appear to indicate that the king might have had more success in smaller boroughs with limited franchises, such as Queenborough and Droitwich, than in the larger freeman boroughs, such as Rochester. It is somewhat surprising that the king did as well as he did in these three boroughs, given that only one of the three, Queenborough, had been regulated or rechartered in advance of the elections, although Droitwich had been threatened with a new charter. Clearly a regulation was not the only way of influencing a corporation, and the king's agents knew how to cajole in more indirect ways. But neither the regulators nor their opponents could take much solace in these results for the elections in these boroughs were exactly split, with royal nominees taking three seats and opposition candidates taking the other three.

Forecasting the Elections

Despite all obstacles, the regulators were confident of success; in their reports from April 1688 they predicted that over one hundred court supporters would be elected in constituencies that had the right to elect 140 members. Their reports from September 1688 were equally sanguine and frequently predicted victory for the king's nominees. This optimism was not always justified. We have already noted two cases where the regulators were excessively confident: in Rochester they predicted that a victory for Sir Phineas Pett was "very probable," when in fact he was defeated, and in Queenborough they stated that Crawford and Wilford would be elected without "dispute," when in fact the election was contested and only Crawford was elected. Such errors were to some degree unavoidable. The regulators were not privy to the designs of their opponents, and they could not be certain that men who espoused the repeal cause on one day would continue to do so on the next.[70]

An accurate forecast is not needed to see that the task facing the repealers was daunting. The House of Lords alone was a formidable obstacle to repeal, though not an insurmountable one. According to estimates drawn up at the time by interested observers, the peerage in 1688 was firmly against repeal, with only about a quarter of the peers supportive of the king's religious policy, a few undecided or undeclared, and the rest in opposition. A repealer House of Lords was, nevertheless, an objective that was within the king's grasp, given that he had the power to create unlimited numbers of peers. James would likely have had to create more than sixty new peers to get his program through the upper chamber. His chief minister, Sunderland, assured doubters that this radical maneuver was a real possibility.[71] Even the threat of such a move might prove to be enough to convince the upper house to comply with the king, if an act of repeal somehow made it through the lower chamber.

A repealer House of Commons was an even more formidable objective. The slim hopes of the repealers rested on the fact that the king was likely to do best in towns with smaller electorates. The small boroughs were so numerous that it was, in theory, possible for a political movement to gain a parliamentary majority in the 1680s while losing every constituency with an electorate of more than two hundred.[72] The medium-sized borough of Rochester, with its electorate of about three hundred, was the kind of constituency that the repealers might have been able to afford to lose.[73] But the results of the addressing campaign should have given the regulators ample cause for concern. While there were over two hundred parliamentary boroughs in England, only twenty-seven sent addresses pledging to support the king's campaign. It is, of course, possible that some other councils favored repeal while deciding, nonetheless, against sending a formal address to that effect. This was the route taken by Bury St Edmunds, which decided to send a more informal letter of support to the king on the grounds that a formal address would be more expensive.[74] Other boroughs were taken over by the king's allies as late as September 1688 and did not have time to send a pro-repeal address before the elections were called off. Hull was one such borough.[75] For these reasons the number of repealer councils was almost certainly larger than the number of councils that sent repealer addresses. Yet several councils are known to have voted against sending such an address, even after the king had restructured their membership.[76] On balance, it is evident that a substantial number of the regulated boroughs did not become repealer boroughs.

A large number of English parliamentary boroughs, moreover, were not regulated at all. James lacked the power in many boroughs to regulate their officials using orders of the privy council. A royal power to remove civic officials had been inserted into the new borough charters passed in the early to mid-1680s during the so-called tory reaction, but not all boroughs had been rechartered during this period. Many of the remaining boroughs could be rechartered if need be, which would enable James to name new officials to their councils. But a considerable number of boroughs were relatively immune even to this more drastic method of regulation. About forty of the parliamentary boroughs were "boroughs by prescription," lacking any chartered corporation or council, and so could not easily be managed by the crown as there was no charter that could be recalled by a writ of *quo warranto.*[77]

The king's powers, then, were limited. Before the campaign began, he held the power to regulate by order of privy council only 113 of the 205 English parliamentary boroughs, and he proceeded to exercise those powers in 94 boroughs. He also regulated London by letters patent and brought 12 other boroughs into his regulatory ambit by recalling their charters and issuing new ones. He thus regulated 107 English boroughs in the key period from November 1687 to September 1688.[78] At the time, this was the most extensive effort of electoral management ever undertaken by the English state. But it was not a complete reshaping of the electorate. The regulated boroughs had the right to elect only 212 members, or about 41 percent of the total membership of the House of Commons, with the remaining members elected by the unregulated boroughs, the Welsh boroughs, the counties, and the universities.

The royal campaign seems unlikely to have been enough to guarantee electoral success. Against the powers of the king and the efforts of the repealers must be weighed the widespread unpopularity of repeal among Anglicans, who made up a majority of the electorate.[79] But to focus exclusively on the potential composition of a parliament that never met would be to miss the wider significance of the repealer movement. The repealers were amassing power, and they could use that power to achieve some of their ends without ever setting foot in the House of Commons. By taking over a significant number of councils, they flexed their muscles. Their maneuvers provoked a series of responses that proved to be as influential as the movement itself.

The responses of the Anglicans to the rise of the repealers took two overlapping forms, both of which had enduring consequences. One set of responses was conciliatory. Many Anglicans were determined to stop the repealers from succeeding and so offered strategic concessions designed to siphon off nonconformist support from the repeal campaign. These strategic concessions eventually bore fruit in the Toleration Act of 1689. The other set of responses was militant. Many Anglicans looked to William of Orange for aid against the repealers. The letter of seven notables to William in June 1688, known as the letter of the "Immortal Seven," cited the possibility of "a packed parliament" in urging him to invade before the elections were held.[80] Both sets of responses derived much of their impetus from the desire of many English Protestants to defeat the king's repeal campaign. The repealers, with their dramatic entry onto the public stage, had caused other actors to shift their positions and rethink their lines. They spurred the growth of a countermovement that in turn helped to create a revolution.

=›•‹=

8

Dancing in a Ditch

Anti-Popery and the Revolution

The Glorious Revolution of 1688–1689 has occasionally been presented as a dynastic coup orchestrated by William of Orange and a few English notables without much reliance on popular support in England. A series of historians ranging from Lucile Pinkham in the 1950s to Jonathan Israel in the 1990s advanced this interpretation, which tended to suggest that the Glorious Revolution was not a genuinely popular revolution.[1] This view, which was never universally accepted, has receded from favor in recent years, with historians now highlighting the popular elements of the Revolution.[2] The case for the Revolution as an elite coup has faltered in large part because it proved to have a considerable defect. William does not appear to have brought enough troops with him to be confident of success without relying on considerable English support. The most authoritative contemporary observers estimated the size of the prince's invading forces at around 15,000 men. Even if the size of the expeditionary forces is raised to a higher estimate of 21,000, as some scholars have sought to do, the prince's army would still have been much smaller than James's army, which fielded about 29,000 to 30,000 men with another 5,000 in reserve.[3] As Sir John Reresby observed at the time, the modest size of the prince's expeditionary force suggested that he expected armed support after he landed: "it being impossible that the Prince durst attack England with an army of under 20,000 men if he expected not very good helpe in England."[4]

The Glorious Revolution was not merely the result of a foreign invasion; local aid was instrumental in its success. That support was provided by popular uprisings in the Midlands and north of England, by groups of armed men who joined the prince after he landed, and by defections from James's army to William's. But even those historians who emphasize these popular uprisings have not denied that the Williamite invasion was critical to the outcome of the Revolution. If the invasion needed the popular uprisings to succeed, the uprisings also needed the invasion. The swelling opposition to James's policies in 1688 might not have gained the force of a revolution without William's army, which provided both a catalyst for action and a rallying point for rebel forces. Preparations for an armed revolt had begun in England before William's arrival, but it was only after the prince landed at Torbay that leading peers such as Delamere and Lovelace took up arms and engaged in open revolt. The invasion and the popular revolution worked like two interlocking gears, each serving to propel the other.[5]

The causes of the Revolution of 1688–1689, then, are found not solely in the forces propelling the English uprisings nor in the impulses driving the invasion but, rather, in the motives underlying both events. This much has been accepted by many historians. But historians have not yet fully examined the interconnections between the forces propelling the uprisings in England and those propelling the Dutch invasion. It is not a coincidence that much of the English population came to support William's descent on England at the same time as much of the Dutch population did. The pattern of conspiratorial thinking known as anti-popery influenced both nations, and this thinking was pivotal to the success of the Revolution. In the absence of anti-popery, William could still have come across the North Sea but without as large a force. Meanwhile the English uprisings might still have happened but without as much popular support. Most historians accept that the anti-popish reaction to James II's policies played a powerful role in fueling the uprisings in England.[6] But historians of the Glorious Revolution have not explored as fully the anti-popery of the Dutch. The interactions of English anti-popery with Scottish anti-popery have been ably charted by Tim Harris; the same sort of analysis has yet to be performed for the interactions between English and Dutch anti-popery in the months before the Revolution.[7] The Revolution proceeded as smoothly as it did because men and women on both sides of the North Sea had come to embrace conspiratorial narratives about the malign intentions of the Catholic King James II.

The King's Concessions

The waning months of James II's reign brought with them conditions ideally suited to the promulgation of arbitrary rule: a foreign invasion coupled with clear evidence of treachery from within the bosom of the state. James's opponents feared an outburst of repression once the king's back was to the wall. Henry Sidney had warned William of Orange in June that, if news of the planned invasion were to leak out more than "a fortnight before it be put in execution," then "all your particular friends will be clapped up, which will terrify others, or at least make them not know what to do, and will, in all probability, ruin the whole design."[8] In Sidney's view, the king was dangerous when threatened.

Yet James chose to defend himself against the Dutch with measures that were more moderate than ruthless. He failed to execute any supporters of the prince of Orange. He refused to declare war on the prince or on the States General of the Netherlands even after William had invaded his country with the support of the Dutch assembly. The most destructive act that he took in the face of the invasion was to have the Great Seal thrown into the Thames upon his first attempt to flee the country, in a futile attempt to prevent William from taking over the government. (A new seal was promptly made.) The king ordered his guards to stand down at two key moments in the crisis, both when his palace was being seized by William's troops and when he was captured during his first attempt to flee England. When the English lord admiral, Lord Darmouth, reported to James that he had been unable to intercept the Dutch navy on its way to England's shores, the king, rather than responding with anger, told him that no one could have done a better job than he had done.[9] When the Catholic Sir Edward Hales, lieutenant of the Tower of London, wanted to train the Tower cannons on London in November 1688 in order to awe the city into submission, James categorically rejected the proposal, noting that such a step "might so farr exasperate the people all over England, as to cause a generall desertion."[10] These were not the sorts of actions that the king's opponents would likely have predicted a few months before.

To reconcile the king's reputation for ruthlessness with his disconcerting turn to mildness, some historians have posited a kind of mental breakdown whereby the king was reduced from his previous arrogance into abject quiescence.[11] Thus, before his supposed breakdown the king was on his way to becoming a full-fledged tyrant, but after it he lost the ability to act according to his true nature. The chief sign of any mental or physical breakdown is the prolonged nosebleed that he suffered on Salisbury Plain in mid-November, which presumably was induced by stress. There were also reports that he was suffering from insomnia around this time and was taking opiates as sleeping pills.[12] Yet a nosebleed and a bout of insomnia hardly add up to a mental breakdown. The king's moderate actions, moreover, began weeks before his visit to Salisbury Plain.

In declining to employ harsh measures against his people, James was rejecting advice given to him by his cousin and fellow monarch, Louis XIV. Louis was baffled by James's hesitant response to the impending crisis. He urged him to act aggressively to intimidate his enemies and embolden his friends. He offered a set of recommendations that together formed a blueprint for martial rule: the English king should declare war against the States General and the prince of Orange, he should confiscate the estates of anyone found to be in league with the prince, and he should award the seized estates to his loyal allies. Anyone who joined the prince's cause should be declared guilty of high treason and face the corresponding penalties. The French ambassador, Paul Barrillon, conveyed this advice to James, and the English king replied that a declaration of war against the States General was not in his interests, because it would disrupt English shipping. He also told Barrillon that a declaration of war against the Dutch, when the Dutch had not officially declared war on him, would lead to him being seen in England "as the aggressor."[13]

To the astonishment of many observers, the king did not attempt to round up and imprison the prince of Orange's known sympathizers. The French ambassador wrote in September 1688 that a decision had been taken to lock up Danby, Shrewsbury, Halifax, Nottingham, and anyone else suspected of conspiring against the king. (Only the first two were active conspirators, having signed the letter of invitation to William in June; the last two had been told of the conspiracy but refused to be involved.) The French ambassador went on to suggest that the jailing of large numbers of suspects, perhaps as many as the four hundred imprisoned in London at the time of Monmouth's Rebellion, would do good service in hampering any treachery.[14] But the plan, which

Barrillon suggested would be implemented as soon as the prince's invasion plans were confirmed, was never put into effect. Among the peers, only Lumley and Lovelace, two whig lords who were actively conspiring with the prince, were ordered imprisoned. Both promptly absconded. Only a small number of English subjects were imprisoned under suspicion of treason, hardly the hundreds that Barrillon anticipated.[15] Observers marvelled at the king's insouciance in the face of peril. Lord Delamere, one of the leading conspirators, later wondered why the king had not clapped up "every Man of Quality or Interest that he suspected." He attributed this fatal error to the king's "fear." Strelley Pegge, no friend of the king's, exulted in the fact that the leading lords were not "secured before" the invasion, a maneuver which could have greatly "prevented" the prince of Orange from succeeding in his campaign.[16] The king, once criticized for his firmness, was now mocked for his mildness.

Even after William had landed in England, James remained reluctant to order the seizure of suspected conspirators. A gentleman of the bedchamber, the earl of Ailesbury, fell on his knees and begged the king to "clap up seven or eight" of the conspirators, naming James's son-in-law Prince George of Denmark, his nephew the duke of Grafton, the duke of Ormond, Lord Churchill, Percy Kirke, and Charles Trelawney. All these were army officers who later deserted *en masse* to the prince, as Ailesbury had feared. But the king took no action. At Salisbury Plain, before the mass desertion had occurred, James considered imprisoning some of the more disgruntled officers but decided, on the advice of the earl of Melfort, that doing so would merely cause other officers to rebel in sympathy.[17] He could not afford to alienate the peerage, the gentry, or his officer corps. Presumably he had learned from his experience with the seven bishops and did not want any other *causes célèbres*. As a result of his lenience, the conspiracy against him grew without hindrance. The conspirators must have marvelled at how easy it all was: overthrowing this king was like pushing at an open door. Strelley Pegge, for one, attributed this inaction to God's providence rather than the king's moderation.[18]

James's moderate measures in the autumn of 1688 were not limited to his reluctance to move against his enemies. In the last months of his reign, he reversed course on some of his most unpopular measures. Even before 23 September, when he became convinced that the Dutch were planning to invade, he had begun making concessions to his English critics. He issued a proclamation on 21 September stating that he would not seek the repeal of that part of the Test Act of 1678 that excluded Catholics from the House of Commons; instead, he would be content to allow his co-religionists to remain excluded from the Commons as long as they could return to the House of Lords. On the twenty-second he ordered the readmission to office of the Anglican justices of the peace and deputy lieutenants who had been deprived of office over the previous two years.[19] After the twenty-third, when the news of the impending invasion reached Whitehall, he moved even more forcefully to repair his relations with his Anglican subjects.[20] He effectively ended the repeal campaign by cancelling the upcoming parliament. He issued a general pardon at the end of September to showcase his clemency.[21] Finally, he reached out to the Anglican bishops to see if he could gain their support through negotiations.

The king held a series of meetings with the bishops, the most consequential of which was on 3 October when nine of the bishops, including the archbishop of Canterbury, presented a list of demands.[22] All Catholics holding government offices would be ejected. Magdalen College would be returned to its Anglican fellows. All Catholic schoolmasters would have their licenses revoked. The boroughs would have their old charters restored. The king would shut down the Ecclesiastical Commission, limit his exercise of the dispensing power, and take religious instruction from the bishops with the aim of reconciling himself to the Church of England. He would call a parliament so that the liberties of his subjects could be secured and provision made "for a due Liberty of Conscience." The adjective "due" in this phrase suggests that the bishops had a limited toleration in mind, which might encompass some nonconformists but not others. This was largely a conservative agenda designed to return the nation to the state it was in at James's accession, with the addition of a limited religious toleration. The bishops refused to be radical even on the question of the dispensing power: instead of calling for its abolition, they suggested that it should be "calmly debated, and argued, and finally settled in parl[i]ament."[23]

James put much of the bishops' program into effect either shortly before or after he met with them. On 2 October he announced the restoration of London's charter; three days later he dissolved the Ecclesiastical Commission. He had already lifted the suspension of the bishop of

London, and he soon ordered the restoration of the Magdalen College fellows.[24] He continued to reinstate Anglicans as justices of the peace and replaced some Catholic lord lieutenants with Protestants. He did not, however, remove the Catholics from the privy council or the armed forces. Instead, he continued to give army commissions to Catholics. He also refused to call an immediate parliament, contending that it was not possible to hold elections in a time of "general Disturbance."[25] Nor is there evidence that he agreed to take any religious instruction from the bishops.

In addition to these concessions to the bishops, the king turned on the repealers. In his destruction of the repealer movement, he went well beyond what the bishops had demanded of him. He called in the regulators and berated them severely, telling them that they had "betray'd his Int[e]rest" by "pr[e]tendinge what great matt[e]rs they would do" but that they had proved "able to do nothing." He then made a public show of washing his hands of them, instructing their natural rivals, the lord lieutenants, to investigate their activities. The earl of Ailesbury, who had always resented the regulators, set to this task with relish, producing a report that outlined the "threatning speeches and high words" employed by certain agents in Bedford and the "imbezel-ling" of public funds by the new mayor of the town.[26] The repealer newspaper, *Publick Occurrences,* was shut down. According to Anthony Wood, the newspaper was "prohibited to please the people"; its thirty-fourth and final issue was printed on 2 October.[27] In a final *coup de grâce* the king conceded a key demand of the bishops and ordered the cancel-ling of most charters of borough corporations granted over the previous decade. He issued a proclamation instructing the former burgesses to take up their civic offices again. The effect of these orders was to reverse most of the regulations of the boroughs that the king had performed over the past year and to throw most of the repealers out of local office. The king's actions were designed to help him regain the trust of Angli-cans like Narcissus Luttrell, who wrote in rhapsodic terms about the concessions provoked by the imminent Dutch invasion: "Oh rare inva-sion, to occasion so many gratious acts in restoring things to their old legall foundation, which hath been the work of some years past to unhinge!"[28]

James was willing to barter the repealer movement for the support of a much larger group of Anglicans. His about-face indicates a certain sensitivity to public opinion: he had been aware of the objections many had to his policies, even if he had chosen up to that point not to heed them. At the same time, he was anxious to preserve his remaining credit with nonconformists, who might still be able to help him in his time of need. In mid-October he met with several Presbyterian, Congregationalist, and Baptist ministers and pledged that he "continued firm to his first Resolutions and Promises of Mainteining Liberty of Conscience." The repealer movement was over, but his *Declaration for Liberty of Conscience* was still in force.[29] James continued to espouse freedom of religion for Protestant groups; it remained a watchword of his political statements.[30] As a result, he had some success, though limited, in retaining nonconformist support. The Baptist regulator John Jones joined one of the king's new regiments in November, along with a few other nonconformists. The Baptist regulator Edward Roberts wrote a plaintive letter to the nonconformist mayor of Nottingham telling him that the king had not truly given up on the repeal cause. Both of these men, Jones and Roberts, later visited James in France, demonstrating their continued loyalty to him even after his overthrow. But their attachment to James was unusual, and their dissenting brethren did not come flooding in to take up arms for the king in the autumn of 1688.[31]

James's greater problem in the weeks before the Dutch invasion was not an erosion in his nonconformist base but rather his inability to regain much Anglican support. His concessions were greeted with understandable skepticism. After investing his own prestige in the repeal campaign, he was in no position to reverse himself suddenly. Even his abandonment of the regulators did not make him appear to be the champion of the Anglicans. His concessions were too easily attributable to the pressure being placed on him by the imminent invasion. The Dutch ambassador reported that the king's concessions did not satisfy the people because they "tell each other, that as soon as the storm has passed the King may retract in every thing." Roger Morrice, the Presbyterian diarist, gave his opinion that the restoration of Magdalen College proceeded "not from Inclination but from necessity." The earl of Oxford, who had been turned out of office for his opposition to repeal, was invited to take up his lord lieutenancy again. He complied but grumbled to one of his former deputies that they had been "ill used" in the past and, once they were no longer needed, would likely "be set aside again." His deputy, sympathizing, noted that "some would thinck one kick of the breech enough for a gentleman."[32] Suspicions of the king's intentions were so widespread by the fall of 1688 that his concessions were simply folded into a larger narrative of royal deceit and misdirection.

The Holy League

The king's program of concessions, though it failed to mollify his critics, did at least change the content of some of their criticisms. It was no longer credible to accuse the king of seeking to pack a parliament in order to impose Catholicism on the nation, since he was no longer engaged in a campaign to remodel the parliamentary constituencies. The king, instead, was deemed to be participating in a covert alliance with France to suppress the Protestant religion, if necessary by inviting a French army to England. Among the king's critics, one conspiratorial narrative was substituted for another. This shift did the king little good, since the new narrative being told about his intentions was even more damaging than the old.

The outlines of the new story were apparent as early as the summer of 1688, when one of the conspirators in the army and a member of the self-named "Treason Club," Lieutenant Colonel Thomas Langston, spread the following story. The colonel contended that the king had "entered into a close League with France to have all the Protestants throats cut in England and Scotland, and that the P[rince] of Or[ange] had given a Valet de Chambre to the K[ing] of France 30000 Pistol[e]s to pick his Pocket of the Original Instrument of Agreement, which he accordingly did and brought it to the P[rince] of Or[ange] and it was all of K[ing] James's own handwriteing." This story of a secret treaty between James II and Louis XIV to extirpate the Protestants of Great Britain was perhaps the most damaging accusation that had ever been levied at the king. It soon spread well beyond the army. William Westby reported from London in late September that "The English feare the French most for every body speaks of a holy League." He later explained that the feared "Holy League" was a treaty between James and Louis "to Extirpate the Protestant Religion." Rumors spread in London in September that French troops were amassing at Boulogne in order to be transported to England. A week later, the report was that the French were amassing at Calais. Their destination, many believed, was the naval base at Portsmouth, which could accommodate their landing and offered quick access to the capital. Lady Bridgeman worried at the beginning of October that her house might be at risk, since it was near the Portsmouth to London road that would presumably be used by the invading Frenchmen.[33]

The rumors of a "holy league" were seen as credible in part because of the widespread knowledge of the secret dealings between Louis XIV and James's elder brother, Charles II, in the 1670s. Those dealings had included Charles receiving payments from the French king in return for promising not to meet parliament. The English king had also agreed to join the French in their assault on the Netherlands in 1672–1673. Much of the contents of these clandestine treaties had become public knowledge over the course of the 1670s, although it was not generally known that Charles had also promised, in the most secret clauses of the secret Treaty of Dover, to convert to Catholicism. Since Charles, who was ostensibly Anglican, had agreed to these treaties with Louis, it only stood to reason, many English Protestants likely thought, that James, a Catholic, would do the same.[34]

The rumors of a "holy league" were also fueled by Louis's efforts to intimidate the Dutch by making it appear that he and James had an undisclosed alliance. The French king, in response to the Dutch military buildup of 1688, ordered his ambassador, the comte d'Avaux, to deliver a message on his behalf to the States General of the Netherlands. The memorial, which was delivered on 29 August, stated that, if the States General invaded England, France would view that as an act of war against itself. As Louis put it, "the bands of Friendship and Alliance" between him and James would "oblige him" to "assist" James were he assaulted by the Dutch.[35] In both England and the Netherlands, the d'Avaux memorial was widely taken as proof of a secret alliance between the French and English monarchs.

James had received money from Louis in the past, and he accepted Louis's offer of £22,000 to assist with his defense in the fall of 1688, but he consistently declined the French king's offers of a formal alliance. He was reluctant to agree to any treaty that might alienate his subjects, especially since a French alliance would not be helpful in promoting the repeal policy that preoccupied him for much of his reign.[36] But James would get no credit for avoiding an alliance with Louis if his subjects came to believe that he had already formed a league with the French king in secret. This presumably was the ultimate point of the d'Avaux memorial. If no one was willing to give James any credit for resisting an alliance with the French, then he might as well go ahead and get the full benefit of it. Louis's goal of reconstructing the Anglo-French alliance of 1672–1673 against the Netherlands would then be achieved.

Yet James continued to resist Louis's embraces. He had his ambassador deliver a memorial to the States General denying that any secret treaty existed between him and the French king. He made personal assurances of the same to the Dutch ambassador in London.[37] To underline this point, he recalled his ambassador from Paris, who had encouraged Louis to send the d'Avaux memorial, and sent him to cool his heels in the Tower of London.[38] He then informed his privy council on 23 September that "while he had a life to lose, a man alive or a ship at sea, he would not suffer a French man to Land on English Ground, though such Reports have been spread abroad falsely of late." A few days later, he pledged that he would rather "lose his Crown" than to allow the French "to Land in England," whatever the "Report about Towne" might say. The king's denials of an alliance could hardly have been more strenuous. In private conversation he noted wearily that the reports of a French expedition to England were simply not credible since the bulk of Louis's troops were then engaged in fighting the Habsburg Empire on the Rhine at Philippsburg.[39]

James's supporters, realizing just how dangerous the rumors of a French alliance could be, attempted to rebut them. Simon Lloyd, a justice of the peace in Merionethshire, wrote in late September that he had heard it reported that "the king will have the French ore [over], to fortifie the strong holds." He described this story as a "malitious fable" designed to "exasperate the people, in order to Alienate their hearts from the king." The rumors were "exorbitant falsities" that played on "the Antipathy between the generality of his subjects and these Forei[g]ners."[40] Lloyd, like the king himself, used the strongest possible language to denounce the rumors. But that did not keep them from spreading.

The evidence, after all, was in the prince of Orange's possession. He surely would reveal it when the time was right. In late October, Roger Morrice repeated a story, similar to Lieutenant Colonel Langston's, about a secret treaty that had been picked out of someone's pocket and sent to the prince of Orange. In Morrice's version of the story, there were at least two copies in circulation, one that had been stolen from the English ambassador to Paris and a second that had been lifted from the earl of Sunderland. Both of these copies had "come to the Prince of Oranges hand [so] that he can prove the League beyond all doubt." The treaty, according to Morrice, included not just James and Louis but also other unnamed "Popish Princes," all of whom had agreed to "make a Catholick war" for the purpose of the "Extirpation" of the Protestant religion "in all Northren Countryes." Meanwhile in late October James had dismissed from office the earl of Sunderland for showing a lack of courage in the face of the coming invasion. This was too juicy a detail not to be folded into the conspiracy theory. Sir John Bramston reported that, in the view of many, the real reason why Sunderland had been dismissed was that he had leaked to William the original copy of the secret treaty.[41]

It was with some surprise, then, that Englishmen read the prince's printed *Declaration of the Reasons Inducing him to Appear in Arms in the Kingdom of England*, which began to circulate at the beginning of November, and found no mention of the long-rumored secret treaty.[42] This was welcome news to those who had remained loyal to the king. One loyalist pamphleteer noted that there had been "strange Stories of ill things whispered, and nothing less than a Secret League between His Majesty of Great Britain, and the French King, to Extirpate all Protestants." It had been widely expected that the secret treaty would be "brought to Light" in the prince's declaration. But, he gloated, there was not "one word of any such Treaty" mentioned in it. Another loyalist pamphleteer pushed the knife in a little deeper. The "first thing" he "looked for" in the prince's declaration, he said, was "the exposing of our Clandestine League with France," but he found "not one word said of France, or any such secret League." This lapse was unexpected, he wrote, since a treaty between James and Louis to destroy Protestants was the "main thing pretended and expected" in England at that time. The secret league, he asserted, was "The Point in which we are most interested." Without evidence of such an alliance, the prince's invasion was, in his view, unjustifiable.[43]

The rumor mills of London quickly went to work remedying this defect in the prince's declaration. By mid-November, it was asserted that the prince had published a new and supplemental declaration that included a copy of the secret treaty. If this phantom declaration ever existed, which is highly unlikely, it is no longer extant.[44] Yet another fake declaration, published in early December without William's authorization, referred to the secret league while not providing full details of it, except that it was designed to extirpate the Protestants. This false declaration, known as the prince's "third" declaration, was accepted as authentic by some at the time, though not by others.[45] A few of the better connected in London also had access to a French-language pamphlet that had come over from the Netherlands in October and claimed to provide extracts from the secret treaty between Louis and James. This pamphlet has not survived and likely did not have a wide circulation.[46] Some pamphleteers loyal to William asserted that the whole point was moot: it was not necessary for the prince to outline the contents of the secret treaty himself because the comte d'Avaux had effectively admitted its existence, they insisted, in his memorial to the States General in August.[47]

William did allude tangentially to the rumors of a foreign alliance in a written appeal to the English fleet that was distributed as an appendix to one edition of his declaration. In this letter, which he had drafted in September, the prince warned the sailors of the English fleet that they were being made use of as "Instruments, to bring both your selves and your Countrey under Popery and Slavery, by the means both of the Irish and the Forreigners who are preparing to compleat your Destruction." Given the widespread rumors about the league between England and France, most English readers would likely have assumed that "Forreigners" meant Frenchmen, especially since in the previous sentence the prince had referred to the "totall ruine" of the Protestant religion that had already been "accomplished in France."[48] This hint was as close as William ever came in an English-language publication to charging James with plotting to bring a French army over to England.

The prince had a difficult balance to strike between his need to appeal to anti-popish Englishmen and his desire to avoid offending his Catholic allies, the Spanish and the Austrians. His publications and declarations in the autumn of 1688 had an audience that stretched far beyond England to Madrid and Vienna. The Austrian emperor, who was already troubled by William's efforts to question the legitimacy of

James's son, the prince of Wales, would not likely have been pleased had the Dutch prince also suggested that French and English Catholics were engaged in a plot to cut the throats of Protestants.[49] The prince of Orange needed to tread carefully and to avoid the appearance of whipping up anti-popery for his own benefit.

Even without the prince's confirmation of the secret league, rumors of an imminent French invasion continued to spread in England. William Westby recorded a report in mid-November that the Dutch navy had intercepted ten French ships loaded with soldiers on their way to England. A newsletter writer relayed a report in early December that forty thousand Frenchmen had landed in Cornwall. The inhabitants of Dover rose up in arms on 8 December after hearing that a French force would soon be landing nearby.[50] These tales all proved to be false, but the credit they gained suggested the extent of English fears. As late as 22 December it was reported that the residents of Cornwall, with their long and unprotected coastline, still feared a French invasion. Whig peers who organized uprisings in the provinces in November and December 1688 referred to the secret league as one of the people's grievances. Lord Lovelace told a crowd in Oxford that the king had plotted to bring over "French and Irish to pull down our Church, take away our Libertys, and Cut our Throats." Lord Delamere informed an audience in Manchester of a plot to massacre the Anglicans by having "the French and Irish" brought "in upon us." Joining the Williamite cause, these insurrectionaries suggested, was the most effective means of countering the plot.[51]

The widespread fears of a French landing help to explain the infamous "Irish fright" that gripped the nation from 13 to 15 December. This *grand peur*, not unlike the later fears that shook France during its revolution a century later, was fueled by tales of invading marauders. Stories of invaders spread across the kingdom, sparked by mysterious letters distributed anonymously through the post, presumably by Williamites who sought to sow chaos and destabilize the king's rule. The invaders were often said in these letters to be over the next hill or in a neighboring town, plundering and pillaging, though they never in fact appeared. Although in most places the marauding forces were said to be disbanded Irish soldiers, at one point early on in the panic, an alarm was raised in London that the Protestants were about to "have their throats cut by the French and by the Papists."[52] The Irish fright can be seen as the culmination of three months of fearmongering about a Catholic invasion. The long-rumored French invasion had put the nation on edge.

The conspiratorial narratives told in the autumn of 1688 about the secret league were not unrelated to the older narratives that had been told about the king and the repealers over the previous two years. The Protestant faith in danger then was the same faith in danger now. The king's behavior in championing repeal had eroded the trust of many Protestants over the previous two years, leaving him vulnerable to claims that he might seek to align himself with a foreign power to destroy English Protestantism. Despite these parallels, the new tales were different in that they predicted a more immediate, existential threat to English Protestants. The French invasion could happen at any time, unlike a packed parliament that would take months to assemble. As the danger was now more urgent, the solution required was more radical. The Anglican movement to counter repeal had aimed to thwart the king's measures through noncompliance, passive resistance, and electoral mobilization. But passive resistance would not stop an onslaught of French dragoons. At a minimum the imminent Catholic invasion required a state of readiness to engage in armed self-defense. Since James could not be trusted to lead the English in their own defense, they would need to gather outside his aegis.

To many, the prince of Orange's arrival seemed heaven-sent. Since the Dutch were largely Protestants, they could be trusted as allies, even though they were of a different nation. The nonconformist Thomas Jolly wrote that "wee must needs wish well to them as protestants." The reason for the prince's coming, in the minds of some, was that he sought to "hinder the French from Landeing" in England. As one doggerel poet put it after the Revolution, William had saved "England from th'Invasion, / Of the black Popish-part of the French Nation, / Which are for killing, burning, devastation."[53]

During the brief interregnum between the king's flight to France on 23 December 1688 and the meeting of the Convention Parliament on 22 January 1689, the English clergyman Dr. William Sherlock published a pamphlet deploring the course that events had taken. He cast doubt on the story of the holy league and lamented the part that the story had played in the events of the previous months. He urged "that the Story of the French League to cut Protestants Throats in England,

may be well examined [in parliament]; for this did more to drive the
King out of the Nation, than the Prince's Army; and if this should prove
a Sham, as some, who pretend to know, say it is, it seems at least to be
half an Argument to invite the King back again."[54] The Revolution,
Sherlock alleged, may have been conducted on false pretenses. There
may never in fact have been a secret league. Given this, it seemed oppor-
tune to ask whether King James might yet be entrusted with the throne.
But the Convention Parliament, when it met, did not heed Sherlock's
advice. Instead of investigating the dubious story of a holy league, the
Convention pressed ahead, first voting that James had left the throne
vacant and then offering the crown jointly to William and Mary. Now
that the invasion had succeeded, most of William's supporters saw little
reason to revisit old stories that could only be substantiated by means of
manufactured evidence.

Doubtless some of the revolutionary leaders had used the French
invasion scare for their own purposes without truly believing in its
immediacy in November and December 1688. The more well informed
of the revolutionaries would surely have known that in the autumn of
1688 the French fleet was in the Mediterranean, engaged in menacing
the papal states, and was in no position to offer aid to James. They
would also have known that the French army was largely engaged in
besieging the fortress of Philippsburg on the Rhine, seeking to wrest it
from the control of the Austrian emperor. But even those Englishmen
who were too well informed to believe in an imminent French invasion
could still believe in a secret alliance between James and Louis, as did
Roger Morrice with his extensive knowledge of European affairs.[55] For
Morrice, the French threat might not be imminent, but it was still dire.

The fears expressed by many English Protestants in the autumn of
1688 do not merely amount to a secular desire to resist France's supposed attempt to establish a "universal monarchy" over other European
nations.[56] The secret league between England and France was generally
described as a plot to extirpate Protestantism, not as a plot to impose
French rule on other European nations. Roger Morrice, as has already
been noted, alleged that the treaty had been concerted not just by James
and Louis but also by other unspecified "Popish Princes." The Irish
Catholics were deemed to be in on the plot as well. The fears of many
English Protestants were captured by Tregonwell Frampton in early
December, who wrote that "the only contest must be between protes-

tant and papist they [the papists] always where ever they had any power made use of it to Exterpate the northerne (as they call it) heresie."[57] Frampton, like many other Protestants, feared a clash of the confessions in which Catholics would attempt to root out the Lutheran heresy once and for all.

The French invasion of 1688 was a non-event. But it was a non-event with great consequences. It inspired English Protestants to fear their king, to dread the Irish, to suspect the English Catholics, and to join with the prince of Orange to rescue their nation from the coming onslaught. After the end of 1688, the rumors of a secret league were rarely mentioned in letters or memoirs. Once James had fled England for France, it no longer made sense to tell stories of a secret alliance. The former king was no longer in a position to usher French troops into England through covert means. He was now clearly a client of France, whatever his previous proclivities had been, and no conspiracy theory was needed to prove that he was in the French king's pocket. Louis had gotten the alliance with James that he wanted, though, to his misfortune, an alliance with England did not come along with it.

Dutch Anti-Popery and the Expedition to England

The story of the secret league told in England was reinforced by a similar narrative of conspiracy told in the Netherlands that had even weightier consequences. The Dutch were more vulnerable than the English to a French invasion since they could be attacked by land as well as by sea. If the English joined in the assault, as in the early 1670s, then the Dutch would be in dire peril. The Netherlands had been saved in the *rampjaar,* or disaster year, of 1672 by the opening of the dikes, which had flooded the low-lying fields and hindered the advance of the French armies. This ploy might not succeed a second time. Many Dutch Protestants worried in 1688, as did many English Protestants, that Louis XIV aimed not just at national aggrandizement but at the extirpation of their religion. The Netherlands, like England, had welcomed thousands of Protestant refugees from France over the previous three years. They had brought with them stories of the sufferings of their co-religionists both before and after Louis's revocation of the Edict of Nantes in 1685.[58] The only thing standing between the Dutch and the dragonnades, many thought, was a thin line of border defenses.

In the Netherlands, as in England, the French memorial communicated by the comte d'Avaux on 29 August fell on fertile ground. Many Dutch Protestants had already come to believe that England was conspiring with France against them. The French pledge to defend England against attack was taken as the final confirmation of their long-held suspicions. An English diplomat posted to the German imperial diet at Ratisbon had written at the end of 1686 that "here as well as in Holland are tricks us'd to make the Protestants believe His Majestie [James II] is of Intelligence with the French King for their Extirpation." The authors of several pamphlets published in the Netherlands in 1688 argued that James had joined an international conspiracy with Louis and the Jesuits to destroy the Protestant faith across northern Europe.[59]

Dutch opinion had been especially agitated by the English king's failure to prevent Algerian corsairs from entering the North Sea via the English Channel in 1687. James had signed a peace treaty with Algiers in the previous year, by which he agreed to allow its ships to "freely pass the Seas" in exchange for similar protections for English shipping in the western Mediterranean.[60] But James also had treaty obligations with the United Provinces that required him to equip twenty ships to assist the Dutch in resisting any foreign naval incursions. The Dutch, believing that the Algerian corsairs represented just such an incursion, demanded in the summer of 1687 that the English king honor his obligations. When James refused, they were understandably upset. In the late spring of that year, an Algerian fleet of fifteen ships had briefly blockaded the mouths of the Texel and the Meuse Rivers, seizing at least four Dutch ships, three of them full of passengers and the fourth laden with a cargo of gunpowder.[61] The grand pensionary of Holland, Gaspar Fagel, alleged that the English king had not only permitted the Algerians to pass through the Channel but also had "lett them have the benefit of his ports." Gilbert Burnet amplified this accusation, contending that James had allowed Algerian ships to sell their captured Dutch booty in England.[62] This story may have arisen from an episode in May 1687 in which an Algerian crew sailing a captured Dutch ship was forced into Falmouth harbor in Cornwall by inclement weather. The welcome they received was not as warm as Fagel and Burnet suspected: the Dutch ship was promptly seized and its contents detained by the port officials.[63] Rumors spread in Holland, nonetheless, that James and Louis had been in contact with the Algerians and had encouraged them to menace the Netherlands. According to a Scottish pamphleteer allied with the prince of Orange, the Algerian corsairs were part of James's larger design to weaken the Dutch so as to render them vulnerable to assault in the war that was sure to come.[64] The corsairs, in the view of many Netherlanders, had, despite their Muslim faith, effectively become part of the popish plot to destroy Dutch Protestantism.

The birth of a prince of Wales in 1688 was yet another incitement to Dutch suspicions. When word reached the Netherlands early in 1688 that James II's wife, Mary of Modena, was pregnant, many Dutchmen dismissed the pregnancy as a fraud. The potential birth of a male heir, who would take precedence over the princess of Orange in the line of succession, was simply too convenient not to be part of a Catholic plot. As early as April 1688, two months before the birth, "satirical caricatures" of the pregnant queen were being printed in the Netherlands. A poem published in English in Amsterdam a few weeks before the birth accused James of seeking to "cheat us with a Brat of base extraction, / T'exclude thine Heir, our greatest consolation." Another work published in French in May in the Netherlands referred to "la pretendüe grossesse de la Reine [the pretended pregnancy of the Queen]."[65] After the birth of the prince of Wales, a celebration organized by the English consul in Amsterdam provoked a riot, with a mob descending on the consul's house, breaking its windows, and doing 220 guilders in damage. The prince of Orange encouraged Dutch skepticism by allowing the infant to be omitted from the customary prayers for the English royal family in his wife's Anglican chapel at The Hague for a few weeks in the summer. William later went even further and openly challenged the legitimacy of the infant prince in his printed declaration of his reasons for invading England.[66]

All these anti-popish fears became fodder for William's war effort. It is unclear whether the prince and his top lieutenant, Hans Willem Bentinck, actually believed in a secret league between James and Louis to attack Protestants, but they certainly exploited the story in rallying support for their campaign against the English king. In July 1688, Bentinck arranged a meeting with Paul Fuchs, a representative of the elector of Brandenburg. The two met incognito at Celle in northern Germany. Bentinck was seeking a loan of troops from the new elector, Frederick III, who was a fervent Calvinist and was thus considered to be sympathetic. At the meeting, Bentinck outlined the existence of an

international conspiracy against Protestantism led by Louis XIV and
James II. The design of the conspirators, he claimed, was first for James
to overturn Protestantism in England and then for him to attack the
Netherlands with Louis's aid. Eventually the joint assault would move
on to Germany, where the Catholic kings would seek to destroy Protestantism in states such as Brandenburg. The Jesuits at the Imperial court
in Vienna were participants in the plot, Bentinck alleged, and had
attempted to win the Austrian emperor to their cause, though they had
not succeeded thus far. The elector of Brandenburg appears to have
been swayed by these arguments, as he eventually agreed to send 5,900
troops to defend the Dutch frontier while William took the bulk of the
Dutch army with him to England.[67]

William shrewdly capitalized on Dutch fears of an Anglo-French
design to destroy Protestantism across northern Europe. In a letter to
the States of Holland that was read by that assembly on 19 September,
the prince made the following allegations: "That it was evident that the
Kings of France and England both were planning to suppress, if possible, the Reformed religion. That in the case of France this cannot be
doubted, as that king had annulled one of the most fundamental laws
of the realm, which had served to end the civil war in France, namely
the Edict of Nantes, and had treated those of the Reformed persuasion
in a manner known by each. That the King of England was no less
zealous for the popish religion, and had tried to supplant it in his
realms." William warned the Dutch assembly that "the religion and the
freedom and well being" of the United Provinces were now "in a perilous constitution."[68] The efforts of the French and English kings to
overthrow Protestantism would eventually reach the Dutch, unless
they acted first. The States of Holland, impressed by the prince's arguments, voted shortly afterward to assist his invasion of England.

The Dutch invasion moved forward on the back of a widespread
belief that the English and French kings were plotting to overthrow the
Protestant religion. In mid-September, the whig exile Thomas Papillon
had reported from Utrecht that the prince of Orange had by secret
means discovered the designs of the French king for "the Ruine of this
State [the Netherlands] in order to the effecting his grand work of
destroyeing the Protestants." By early October, some in the Netherlands
were claiming that the prince's declaration of his reasons for invading
England would include a copy of an agreement between James and

Louis "engageing to suppress the protestant Religion, and destroy these states [the Netherlands] for that end."[69] The States General of the United Provinces cited their fears of such an alliance in justifying their decision to support William's expedition, alleging that the kings of France and Great Britain had formed "a strict and particular Alliance" and that the Dutch had grounds to fear that "both Kings, out of Interest of State, and Hatred and Zeal against the Protestant Religion," would seek to vanquish the United Provinces.[70]

The Dutch were also agitated in 1688 by restrictions that the French king had imposed on their goods and shipping.[71] The Dutch invasion of England in 1688 and the Nine Years' War that followed were not wars undertaken to promulgate a religious creed. But trade alone is not sufficient to explain Dutch support for the war effort. William's expedition to England received the support it did in large part because of widely held fears that Louis XIV and James II were seeking to extirpate the Protestant faith. Though it was not a war undertaken to promote a religion, it was, in the minds of many Englishmen and Netherlanders, a war undertaken in the defense of religion. The secularization of European foreign relations, often heralded in the scholarly literature on the early Enlightenment period, had not yet fully arrived in London and The Hague in the autumn of 1688. Confessionally based fears were crucial in rallying the support of entire populations for the war effort.[72] Many Dutch and English Protestants were of like minds in 1688: they had adopted remarkably congruent anti-popish interpretations of the behavior of James II.

The Fall of James II

Anti-popery was a transnational phenomenon in 1688. Conspiratorial narratives jumped from one country to another via the printing press. As one London resident put it in August of that year, "The Hollanders at this time take care to highthen and aggrevate all things by their Pamphletts which are privately brought over and sold at great prices which hint irreverent refleccons on the Government. . . . Amongst the venemous Insinuacons which they make use of, the Fears and Jealousies of Religion, being of the worst sorte, they press the same the most."[73] Similar "fears and jealousies" were spread by anti-popish tracts from England that were sold in translation in the Netherlands. One scholar has calculated that, of the approximately 126 Dutch-language pamphlets published from January to September 1688, fully 65.1 percent related to events in England, with 68 works commenting on James II's religious policies. Many of the pamphlets were Dutch translations of English-language works critical of James. This flood of publications suggests an intensity of popular interest in English affairs that was unparalleled in recent Dutch history.[74] By the autumn of 1688, many Dutch and English readers had come to share a belief in an international conspiracy against Protestantism that was said to be headed by James II and Louis XIV. They shared this belief in part because they were reading the same things.

Many Protestants on both sides of the North Sea hoped and prayed for William's successful landing in England. Yet despite this widespread support for the prince, his invasion very nearly did not go ahead. It might have been cancelled in late September had Louis moved his troops northward, to threaten the borders of the Netherlands, instead of eastward, to threaten the Holy Roman Empire. But on 18 September the French king besieged the imperial fortress at Philippsburg, a strategically important citadel on the Rhine but one that was over two hundred miles from the Dutch border. D'Avaux wrote that the news of the French attack was greeted at The Hague with delight: "Never had a piece of news pleased the Prince of Orange more, as he apprehended that they [the French] would not come into Flanders or the Cologne region."[75] The States General of the United Provinces could now afford to send a large contingent of troops abroad, safe in the knowledge that the French were engaged elsewhere. The assault on Philippsburg, d'Avaux observed, "rendered the States General very insolent, by the certainty that the King [of France] would not attack them, nor the Spanish Netherlands."[76]

Leading French ministers, meanwhile, seemed unconcerned that the siege of Philippsburg would leave the English exposed to a Dutch assault. The marquis de Chamlay wrote on 1 October that William's prolonged absence from the Netherlands on his planned expedition could have great advantages for France. The French secretary of state, the marquis de Louvois, noted with satisfaction that a revolution in England was sure to be accompanied with "troubles and divisions." Louis XIV's ministers seem to have held out hopes that William's invasion could turn to French advantage, presumably because his forces might remain tied down in England for months or even years. The French king would then have a free hand along the Rhine.[77]

The lack of concern shown by Chamlay and Louvois was not shared by King James, who saw Louis's military strategy as a betrayal. The English king complained to the bishop of Ely that the French had "gone on this expedition [to Philippsburg] on purpose that they might expose him to the Dutch, that the French might force him to close intirely with themselves." The French, in his view, were permitting William to invade England in order to put pressure on him to sign a formal alliance with them. To his naval commander, Lord Dartmouth, the king assailed the French strategy as a "trick" played in order "to force him into a strict league with France if he would not be sacrificed to Holland." But he was determined to defy the French "trick." He was "so far from ent[e]ring into any such League," he averred, that he "vow'd he would one day be revenged upon that King [Louis] for having thus practiced upon him."[78] Joining France's side in a continental war had not been an attractive option for him in the past, and it was not any more so now.

With the French occupied elsewhere in the autumn of 1688, William was free to launch his invasion. Favorable winds enabled him to evade the English fleet and to land on 5 November at Torbay in southwest England. The much-anticipated event had finally arrived. The results were much as the prince and his allies had hoped: within eight weeks of the prince's landing, James's regime had collapsed.

The English king decided to make a stand at Salisbury Plain, midway between London and Torbay. He arrived there on 19 November, two weeks after the prince's initial landing. But his stay at Salisbury was not of long duration. Four days after his arrival, the king, unnerved by the defection of a few of his officers to William's side and urged by his military advisers to avoid an immediate confrontation, ordered a retreat back to London. The abandonment of the West Country signalled to most observers that James was unlikely to defeat the prince of Orange on the battlefield. The king was soon weakened by a more serious round of defections, as many of his leading officers, including his son-in-law Prince George of Denmark, fled to the prince when the retreat from Salisbury began to take effect.[79] Across the country, local risings in favor of the prince multiplied. Nottingham and York had already been seized by the prince's partisans on 21 and 22 November, and the garrison at Hull followed on 3 December.[80] Joining a revolt was

never a risk-free undertaking, but a betting man could easily see that
the odds were turning in William's favor.

The local revolts against the king in late November and early
December 1688 were characterized by anti-popish statements. The published declarations of the men who led these provincial uprisings commonly referred to the need to preserve the nation from "Popery and
Slavery."[81] The "association" signed by the many gentlemen and lords
who joined the prince's side pledged to defend him against any plots by
"Papists, and other Bloody Men" to assassinate him.[82] A printed declaration from the lord lieutenant of Cheshire pledged to preserve the
peace "by taking care to Disarm all Papists, and to secure all Jesuites
and Romish Priests." Lord Delamere rode through the Midlands confis-
cating "all horses belonging to papists" that he came across. Catholics in
Nottingham had their arms and horses seized by the leaders of the rising
there. After the rising at York, some of the rebels "ransacked severall
houses which belonged to papists (or wher[e] they laid) for priests, arms
and horses, and took them wher[e] they found them." The forcible disarming of Catholics only accelerated after 4 December, when the prince's
spurious third declaration appeared in print urging the English authorities to disarm the "Papists." Some who credited the document as authentic
believed that they now had licence from the prince to disarm Catholics;
indeed, this response was presumably what the framer of the false declaration had hoped to achieve.[83]

The wave of forcible disarming of Catholics was accompanied by a
wave of destruction of Catholic chapels and houses across England. Few
were willing to endorse publicly these acts of destruction, which had
not been authorized by the prince, and as a result the crowds that
accomplished them remained largely anonymous. At Hereford on 3
December a group of about four hundred gentlemen from the surrounding shires came into the city to proclaim the prince's declaration.
Immediately afterward a crowd gathered and "defaced" the city's Catholic chapel and "spoyled and stole" its furnishings. Quite possibly the
crowd included many of those who had just declared for the prince; at
the very least, the Williamite uprising became the occasion for the anti-
Catholic violence. At Hull, after the seizing of the citadel by Sir John
Hanmer, "the Mobile forthwith fell upon the Mass-house, and all the
Houses of the Papists in Town, which they ransackt and demolished."[84]
It is unclear whether the Williamite uprising in Hull provided the

personnel for the anti-Catholic violence or merely the occasion for it. Whichever was the case, there is no indication that the Williamites made any serious attempt to stop it.

The anti-popish violence of November and December 1688 was often construed as defensive, aimed at detecting and preventing popish plots. Perhaps because of this defensive rhetoric, the violence did not result in the death of any Catholics, only damage to property.[85] One of the earliest targets in London was the monastery at St John's Clerkenwell, which was attacked by a crowd in mid-November after a report that it contained "gridirons, spits, great cauldrons, etc. to destroy protestants." The rumored objects of cruelty were not found in the monastery, but the crowd succeeded in seizing some goods from the building, which they burned on the street.[86] At Wolverhampton, 1,500 sharp-edged "Instruments of cruelty" were reportedly discovered in a Catholic house, while at Bury St Edmunds, gunpowder was believed to have been laid around the town by Catholics.[87] Rumors of popish plots spurred Protestants across the country to search the homes of their Catholic neighbors for arms, by force if necessary.

But if the anti-popish violence was intended to be aimed at potential plotters, it often missed its mark. At Oxford, a crowd described as two hundred "rabble and boyes" gathered on 4 December armed with clubs and proceeded to smash the windows of the known Catholics in town, including a widow named Harding.[88] The breaking of the windows of a widow's house could hardly have served to halt a popish plot. At Eskdale in Cumberland, the house of a Catholic named Mr. Porter was burned down; again, the violence seemed ill-devised to counter a plot. If Porter had been suspected, he could simply have been taken in for questioning by the authorities. In Cambridge, a Catholic was forced by a Protestant crowd to "dance naked in a Ditch till he promised to change his Religion."[89] Acts such as these might have been seen at the time as rough justice for the perceived injuries done to Protestants by Catholics over the previous three years. But the justice was so carelessly applied that these episodes were clearly marked by religious prejudice.

The targets for reprisals by English Protestants included not only Catholics but also other representatives of James's regime, including some leading repealers. The animosity directed at these repealers suggests a degree of continuity between the anti-repeal movement of early 1688 and the popular risings after the prince's invasion. In mid-December, the bishop of St David's, who had backed the king's religious policies, was discovered by a Protestant crowd near Cambridge. He was forced to mount a horse without a saddle and was led "in a triumphant Manner" to the magistrates of Cambridge with a demand that he be imprisoned in the city's castle.[90] The dean of Chester, Dr. James Arderne, who earlier in the year had been "very free in his discourse, about taking off the Penal Laws, Test, etc.," was seized by a group of Protestants at Nantwich in Cheshire. They debated whether to mount him "on a Wooden Engine" for his supposed flirtations with popery but eventually desisted and let him go free.[91] Thomas Jefford, the repealer and former mayor of Exeter, was caught and jailed in that city on 11 December; he later went on to be suspected of Jacobitism in the 1690s. It was said that the people of Exeter were so "incensed against him" that they would have "Dewitted him," or torn him to pieces like the assassinated Dutch politician Johan de Witt, had they been permitted to.[92] The Baptist regulator Benjamin Dennis was swept up in London on 19 December by a group of soldiers and jailed "for crimes of a high nature." He was presumably later released as he does not appear to have been put on trial.[93] His former master, Robert Brent, the Catholic head of the board of regulators, was also seized; he later skipped bail and fled overseas.[94]

Even the peaceable Society of Friends came in for their share of reprisals. A Quaker meeting house in Sunderland was destroyed in December, presumably because the Quakers were believed by some to be Catholics in disguise. A group of men and boys broke into the building at one in the morning and set it on fire, before moving on to break the windows of several Quakers in the town.[95] The most well-known of all the Quakers, William Penn, was captured by two soldiers in London on 12 December and brought before the lords serving as a governing council in the king's absence. Penn protested that he had committed no crime and had aimed only to promote an "impartiall Liberty of Conscience to be Established by Law." The lords released him on bail and instructed him to appear before the Court of King's Bench at the start of the next term. He was accused repeatedly over the next few years, with considerable justice, of corresponding with the exiled king and offering support to the Jacobite cause.[96]

The anti-popish crowds of November and December 1688 destabilized James's regime and drove some of his most prominent political agents into hiding. But, at the same time, there were many in England, even in December 1688, who did not wish to see their king fall. After James was caught by some fishermen in Faversham on his first attempt at fleeing the country and was compelled to return to London, he was greeted unexpectedly by rejoicing crowds. The citizens cried, "Long live the king," the streets were full, and "the balconies and windows" were "thronged" with people making "loud acclamations."[97] Some of this adulation, no doubt, reflected the loyalism of tories who were now recalling their vaunted record as the supporters of kings. But there was another factor underlying the public relief at the king's safe return. James's loss of power meant that it was easier to see him as a victim and even as a potential martyr. There was a growing fear in December 1688 that the king might be murdered by one of William's allies. The French ambassador wrote on 5 December that if the king were to remain in England he would be in "great hazard of losing his life and the Crown." One anonymous correspondent wrote a desperate letter to the archbishop of Canterbury on 21 December warning that the king was likely to be poisoned and urging him to intervene before it was too late.[98] False reports of James's death spread across the country in mid-December, from London to Derbyshire to Lancashire. One especially misinformed correspondent reported that the king had died only two hours after he had been taken prisoner by the fishermen of Faversham.[99]

The king's death was too neat a solution to the crisis to be over-looked as a potential outcome. If he died, and his young son was declared supposititious by parliament, his daughter Mary, the consort of William of Orange, would regain her position as James's immediate heir and would be crowned as queen of England. This was a resolution that would satisfy almost everyone; only a few Catholics and legitimist tories would contend for the rights of a fatherless infant who was said to have been born under suspicious circumstances. As one Oxford clergyman wrote on 23 December, if the king had died at any point over the previous few months, "the Princess of O[range] would have been certainly proclaimed, and the whole Nation would have owned her Title, and paid their Allegiance to her . . . and so they will do if the Case should happen yet."[100] As a result, the death of the king seemed to many to be the likely conclusion to the crisis provoked by William's invasion.

James could have capitalized on this swelling tide of loyalist sentiment by remaining in the country and presenting himself as a potential martyr prepared to risk all for his country, much as the seven bishops had presented themselves as martyrs to the Church of England when imprisoned in the Tower. He was not forced to leave England. The prince of Orange placed him under house arrest, though in a house conveniently overlooking the River Thames with the garden gate left conspicuously unlocked. It was much in William's interest for the king to flee his kingdom. If James had stayed, he could have been certain that a legitimist party in the upcoming parliament would have championed his interests, even if the negotiations with the Williamites would surely have left him with diminished powers. His political leverage from exile would prove much weaker, as he was to discover over the next thirteen frustrating years until his death in 1701 at Saint-Germain-en-Laye. By leaving the country, he opened up the possibility of a parliament declaring that he had abdicated the throne and that the throne was thereby vacant, which is exactly what the Convention Parliament did early in 1689. From there it was a fairly direct line to the parliamentary offer of the crown jointly to William and Mary on 13 February.[101]

In the end James led one movement too few. By choosing to depart he undercut a loyalist party that had already been rallying to defend him.[102] Without the king to give the lead, or at least to serve as a symbol of fortitude and resolve, his cause in England was grievously wounded. His supporters melted away, only later to re-form as a Jacobite movement in much less promising circumstances. The king left because he believed that he was likely to be killed if he stayed. As he told the earl of Ailesbury shortly before his departure, "If I do not retire, I shall certainly be sent to the Tower, and no King ever went out of that place but to his grave."[103] He hoped that by fleeing when he did, he would live to fight another day. He even imagined that he might be invited to return once his subjects realized the mistake they had made. That was, after all, what had happened to his elder brother, Charles, restored to his throne with full rights in 1660 after a long exile on the Continent. As James told the earl of Ailesbury, "I declare to you that I retire for the security of my person, and I shall always be in a readiness to return, when my subjects eyes may be opened."[104] But he was not to set foot on English soil again.

9

Enacting Toleration

The Repealers and the Enlightenment

This book is an exercise in historical reconstruction. It has started with the premise that much of what is found in the archives is misleading. An archive is not neutral for a historian, in the way that a bed of sediment is for a geologist. Apart from the usual difficulties involved in interpreting ambiguous evidence, the historian faces the additional complication that the archive has been pre-sifted. Only certain documents were preserved by the people who created them, only a subset of these were conserved by their heirs, and only a selection of the remaining documents were collected by archivists. The shape of any archive is marked by the priorities of the groups that established and maintained it. The documents found in any given archival collection tell a story about what people at the time wanted to believe and what later collectors found worthy of preservation. The historian must take these stories into account when using archival sources to reveal the outlines of the past.

England was beset with political disputes in the later Stuart period. But despite this constant drumbeat of conflict, English authors frequently wrote as though they lived in an age of consensus—as though the vast majority of their fellow countrymen were on their side, and anyone who disagreed with them was operating under foreign influences. One of the more common gambits in political debate was to deny that one's opponent had any support in public opinion. These politicized statements should not be used by historians as the basis for our estimates of public opinion. Historians have, nevertheless, frequently cited these statements as fact.

This problem has been accentuated for James II's reign because historians have suggested that one set of statements about public opinion was politicized while another was not. Statements by James's supporters saying that most Englishmen supported the king's policies have been deemed the insincere flattery of sycophantic courtiers. Meanwhile, statements by James's opponents to the effect that most Englishmen opposed the king's policies have been taken at face value. Yet both sets of statements were political rhetoric designed with a polemical purpose and must be subjected to strict scrutiny.

Just as problematic has been historians' use of the opinions of Londoners as a proxy for those of the nation as a whole. London-based observers often had a poor sense of what was going on in the English counties but wrote, nevertheless, about county affairs with a great deal of confidence. Provincial news as reported in the capital tended to be heavily filtered, with intermediaries spinning it to suit their own ideological agendas. Historians who read the letters and diaries of these London-based observers without conducting local research can be led astray. The antidote to this error would seem to be local history. But local historians, for their part, have had surprisingly little influence on the historiography of the Glorious Revolution. The history of the regulation of the boroughs, for instance, has been investigated on both a national and a local level. Studies done on the national level have tended to argue that the regulation of the boroughs was a failure, yet the two most in-depth articles written on the regulation of particular boroughs found both efforts to be successes for the king. Those two studies, of the boroughs of Hull and Bury St Edmunds, had less impact than might have been expected because it was unclear how representative these cases were.[1] One potential solution to this quandary is to do local history on a national scale, by conducting research in provincial archives with national questions in mind, while addressing the problem of representativeness by being as comprehensive as possible.

To capture English diversity, then, requires a history that accommodates a multitude of local perspectives. English opinion was often fractured, and the opinions of Londoners did not always capture that diversity fully. Even in cases where a clear majority in London took a particular stand on an important political question, minority groups, both in London and elsewhere, took divergent positions. When historians write of the "will of the nation," they are using a shorthand in which the views of the majority of politically active adults are deemed to stand for the views of the nation as a whole. But in reality there is no such thing as the national will. A nation does not have opinions or emotions; it cannot hate or love or express an inclination. As a political construct, it lacks these qualities of personhood. What did exist were groups that joined together for particular causes and, in so doing, called upon the supposed will of the nation to justify their actions. These groups sometimes formed political movements whose participants claimed to be working in the interests of the nation as a whole. One such movement in James II's reign was the repealers; another was the countermovement against repeal.

The men and women who rallied against the repealers tended to assume that the English nation was largely opposed to repeal and that anyone who supported it was a foreign interloper or a Jesuit in disguise. As a result, the archives are full of statements that would lead one to believe that the repealer movement did not exist. But the repealers did exist, and most of them were not Jesuits. Archival evidence for their movement is, paradoxically, both ample and scarce at the same time. What is lacking is the kind of evidence a historian dreams of finding—a gripping memoir depicting life inside the movement as it was lived by its participants. Most of the leading repealers did not write memoirs, and the accounts that survive are often evasive and unhelpful. But despite this lacuna, evidence for the movement is abundant. It is found in the lists of names in town minute books, representing the men recommended to public office by King James II. It is found in stray letters that happened to be preserved as part of larger bodies of correspondence. It is found in pamphlets that survived by sheer force of numbers, even though most of the copies of each were discarded. These sources are often bland in character, presumably because the more vivid sources were likely to be suppressed after the Glorious Revolution. As a result each individual source tells us little. Yet collectively they tell us a great deal. Once all these sources are cobbled back together, it seems as though the repealer movement was hiding in plain sight.

The Act of Toleration

As James's government collapsed in the autumn of 1688, so too did the hopes of the repealers. Most of the participants in the movement withdrew from any association with it after William's takeover of the government. Some dissenters even issued public statements disavowing any connection to the repeal campaign. In these actions they were aided and abetted by the new government itself. William came to woo the nonconformists, not to accuse them. His propagandists aimed to suppress the memory of the repealer movement, not to recover it.[2]

Soon after William landed, some repealers began to backtrack. John Baker, a nonconformist in Hull who had presented a pro-repeal address to James, promptly signed a letter praising William for his invasion.[3] He was not alone in his timely tergiversation. If nonconformists wished to gain religious toleration, they needed to pay court to the ruling power. Before he landed in England, William had promised ease for tender consciences, and he secured his promise by pressing parliament to pass an Act of Toleration in May 1689.[4] This act fell short of the repealer ideal, but it went further than it might have gone, offering toleration not just to the moderate nonconformists who had often opposed the repeal campaign, but also to the radical nonconformists who had frequently joined it.

The Act of Toleration underpinned an enduring alliance between William's largely Anglican government and the main Protestant nonconformist groups. The act suspended, though it did not repeal, the penal laws, and it contained specific provisions to accommodate the scruples of Quakers and Baptists who were opposed to oath taking and infant baptism. The act did not permit nonconformists to take public offices or to graduate from the universities, and it specifically excluded from its provisions both Catholics and any nonconformists who denied the doctrine of the Trinity. But in incorporating some of the more radical groups the act was more expansive than might have been expected. After a half-century of conflict, with first the nonconformists in power under Cromwell and then the cavaliers in control under Charles II, each side hitting the other when it had the chance, a new alliance was forged in which the winners in 1689 offered an olive branch to the losers. The English political process shifted into a new phase, as the winner-take-all form of politics of the English Reformation and Civil War gave way to an incorporative form of politics that eventually expanded in the nineteenth century to encompass other marginalized groups, including Catholics and Jews. The alliance of 1689 was ratified in the subsequent historiography, as whig historians chose to overlook the extent to which nonconformists had supported James's toleration campaign.[5]

The incorporative settlement of 1689 did not stem primarily from any growing tolerance among members of the Church of England in the later seventeenth century; it came about because England's geopolitical situation necessitated it. The key transitions were more political than intellectual. The Anglicans had been sharply divided in their approach to nonconformity for nearly a generation. When political parties formed in the late 1670s and early 1680s, they organized themselves in part around the question of toleration, with whigs generally in favor of some relaxation of the penal laws and tories largely opposed. A measure of toleration had nearly been enacted in 1681 at the close of the whig-dominated Second Exclusion Parliament, but the opponents to it decisively regained the initiative after the dissolution of the Oxford Parliament and launched a barrage of persecution during the so-called tory reaction.[6] After this instructive experience with a tory relapse into persecution, many nonconformists demonstrated their willingness to break with Protestant unity by forging a tolerationist coalition with James II and the Catholics. This decisive move brought much of the Anglican leadership to the bargaining table. At the height of the repeal campaign, in the spring of 1688, the archbishop of Canterbury signaled his willingness to demonstrate "due tenderness" for dissenters in the next parliament.[7] In the post-revolutionary crisis, with James rallying troops in France and Ireland, the archbishop's promise could not easily be shrugged off, especially because James was known to be readying his own competing Act of Toleration for passage through the Irish parliament in Dublin. As the whig Sir Henry Capel said in the House of Commons in May 1689 with reference to the nonconformists, "I would not give them occasion to throw themselves out of the Protestant interest."[8]

Some tories found themselves balanced between their dislike of persecution and their dislike of toleration. Persecution had damaged Protestant interests by throwing Anglicans and nonconformists into conflict with each other, but toleration might open the floodgates to blasphemy and irreligion. When the Act of Toleration was debated in parliament, the tory Sir Thomas Clarges proposed a sunset clause whereby the act would expire in seven years, at which point parliament would have to renew it or let it lapse. The goal of this amendment, according to Gilbert Burnet, was to hold the potential loss of toleration over the heads of dissenters as a means of keeping them in check. The amendment was, however, rejected by the Commons.[9] Many tories would, nevertheless, have preferred a more limited toleration than the one enacted in 1689. Sir Henry Goodricke argued in the Commons for the exclusion of Quakers from the toleration on the grounds that they were Catholics in disguise. Another tory, John Evelyn, had proposed in November 1688 that toleration should be granted "to all Sober Dissenters," with the notable exceptions of "Socinians[,] Independents, and Quakers," because Socinians were "scarsly [scarcely] Christian" and the Quakers were "of publiq danger, and unaccountable."[10]

The continued hostility of many tories toward nonconformity was evident in their reaction to King William's speech to parliament on 16 March 1689. The new king urged the two houses to pass a law that, while continuing to exclude Catholics from public office, would "leave Room for the Admission of all Protestants, that are willing and able to serve." William was in effect proposing the abolition of the sacramental Test that had excluded from office anyone who refused to take the sacrament in the Church of England, as required under the Corporation Act of 1661 and the Test Act of 1673. Meanwhile, Catholics could continue to be excluded under the doctrinal Test requiring all officeholders to renounce transubstantiation. The king, who was a Calvinist himself, was happy to employ in the upcoming war effort the Protestant dissenters who had backed his cause. But many tories distrusted the dissenters. On the evening of the king's speech, a large number of tory members of parliament gathered at the Devil Tavern in London to coordinate a response. The number of MPs present was probably more than 150, and the group included five leading tories: Sir Robert Sawyer, Heneage Finch, Sir Thomas Clarges, Sir Christopher Musgrave, and Sir Joseph Tredenham. According to the Presbyterian diarist Roger Morrice, the group decided to oppose the king's proposal and resolved to "Clamour upon the Dissenters as obstinate unreasonable and factious, and so endeavour to raise a new persecution against them."[11]

The Devil Tavern Club, as these men became known, did not in fact raise a new persecution against nonconformists, and they eventually agreed to support, with some misgivings, the Act of Toleration.[12] But they did succeed in forcing the king to back down over the sacramental

Test. They also succeeded in turning back a bill designed to comprehend some of the more moderate nonconformists within the Church of England by relaxing some elements of the canons and liturgy. The bill of comprehension would have enabled the more moderate Presbyterians to rejoin the Church and thereby to regain full privileges of citizenship, including the ability to serve in public office. Such a bill was zealously sought by the moderate Presbyterians and the Latitudinarian whigs and was warmly supported by the king and queen.[13]

It was not clear, at first, whether the Devil Tavern Club would have enough votes to defeat a comprehension bill in parliament. The size of the Devil Tavern Club was variously estimated at the time as being either 160 or about 200 members, which was not enough to command a majority in a full house. In the house as a whole, historians of parliament have estimated, only 232 members voted regularly with the tories, while the other 319 were either whigs or court tories who were usually willing to vote for measures sponsored by the king.[14] These numbers would seem to suggest that William would get his way on Church matters, as he had done in gaining the offer of the crown for himself and his wife. But a series of key votes in late March and early April revealed that some of William's whig and court tory supporters were wary of undermining the supremacy of the Church of England in public life. Contemporary observers noted that the partisans of the Church of England had gained the upper hand in parliament. Lord Yester wrote that the votes taken in parliament showed "how strong the Church party is in both [houses], and that yett too much remains of theire animositye against the dissenters."[15] The tories succeeded in having the comprehension debate postponed from the spring parliament to a convocation of the Church of England that would meet in the autumn. Informed observers realized immediately that this step would doom the measure entirely.[16]

When the elections to convocation were held that autumn, the High Churchmen rallied as expected. According to Gilbert Burnet, "great canvassings were every where, in the elections of convocation men; a thing not known in former times." The lower house of convocation met and selected as its prolocutor a man dedicated to opposing comprehension. The two houses of convocation then spent a week wrangling over the wording of an address of thanks to the king. Members of the lower house took offense at an innocuous phrase thanking the king for his zeal "for the protestant religion in general, and the Church of England in particular," complaining that the reference to the "protestant religion in general" might conceivably include the "Quakers Anabaptists and fifth Monarchy men." The lower house made no move to take up the question of comprehension. Within a month William had taken the temper of convocation and decided to adjourn the body. The comprehension scheme was never again pursued seriously.[17]

It is unclear whether a *quid pro quo* had been explicitly struck in the spring of 1689 whereby the tories in the Devil Tavern Club agreed to support the Act of Toleration in exchange for the postponing of comprehension. The sequence of events, however, suggests that this effectively is what happened.[18] The nature of the resulting settlement was revealing. The enactment of toleration, but not of comprehension, served the interests of Quakers, Baptists, and Congregationalists, who gained freedom of worship while suffering little from the failure of a comprehension bill that would not have applied to them. But the settlement did not satisfy the moderate Presbyterians, who were left outside the Church they had longed to rejoin and were forced to accept second-class status as a tolerated minority without full rights of political participation. This was a bitter pill to swallow for a Presbyterian like Philip Henry, who greeted the Act of Toleration with dissatisfaction: "[un]til the Sacramental Test bee taken off, our Business is not done."[19] That the moderate Presbyterians, who had largely supported the Glorious Revolution, did not get what they wanted suggests that the primary aim of the religious settlement was not to reward loyal nonconformists for their good behavior but, rather, to prevent the more radical nonconformists from straying again.[20]

After 1689, tensions between Anglicans and Protestant nonconformists continued. In the early eighteenth century, tory mobs attacked Presbyterian meetinghouses with alarming frequency. Forty dissenting meetinghouses across the West Midlands and the north of England were sacked in 1715 in the tumult following the Hanoverian succession. Other meetinghouses had been burned after the trial for sedition of the High-Church clergyman Henry Sacheverell in 1710. In some places dissenters found themselves unable to build meeting places at all. Sir John Percival noted that the inhabitants of Newark would "Suffer no Dissenters to live among them, and totherday [the other day] a meeting

house being attempted to be sett up they pulled it down."[21] Among the
High-Church clergy, toleration was no more popular than it was among
the tory laity. Many of the parish clergy denounced toleration as a force
for irreligion. Clergymen suspected that irreligious parishioners were
absenting themselves from church while never quite making their way
to the nonconformist meeting and so were attending no church services
at all on Sundays.[22]

Many Anglicans after the Revolution objected to the practice of
occasional conformity, by which some dissenters qualified themselves
for public office by taking the sacrament in the Church of England once
per year while continuing to worship regularly at dissenting meetinghouses. The practice was not new, but in the early eighteenth century it
attracted the attention of parliament. In 1703 one tory member of parliament expressed his fear that "by the benefit of this Occasional Conformity, the dissenters will come to be the majority of this House." The
Occasional Conformity Act, passed in 1711, penalized the practice with
a fine of forty pounds and ejection from public office. Soon after, a tory
government passed the Schism Act of 1714, which required that all
schoolteachers sign a declaration of conformity and take the sacrament.
Both of these acts were repealed in 1719 by a whig government. Then
came a century or so of relative stasis, with few legislative advances for
Protestant nonconformists. A more complete religious liberty for dissenters came in the early nineteenth century, with Unitarians granted
toleration in 1813 and nonconformists granted access to public office
under the repeal of the Test and Corporation Acts in 1828.[23]

John Locke, William Petty, and the Repealers

The reluctance of many members of parliament to proclaim toleration
as a positive value is indicated by the fact that the act passed in 1689,
commonly known to later ages as the "Act of Toleration," did not, in
fact, include the word "toleration" anywhere in its text. Its full title
suggests its reticence: it was "An Act for Exempting their Majesties Protestant Subjects, Dissenting from the Church of England, from the Penalties of Certain Laws." Yet the act was not unwelcome to tolerationist
thinkers. John Locke noted the limitations of the act while simultaneously celebrating its passage. In a letter to his Dutch friend Philippus

van Limborch, he wrote with a touch of native pride: "No doubt you will have heard before this that Toleration has now at last been established by law in our country. Not perhaps so wide in scope as might be wished for by you and those like you who are true Christians and free from ambition or envy. Still, it is something to have progressed so far. I hope that with these beginnings the foundations have been laid of that liberty and peace in which the church of Christ is one day to be established."[24]

A few weeks earlier, in late April 1689, Locke's *Epistola de Tolerantia*, originally written in 1685, had been published by Limborch at Gouda in the Netherlands. Given the distance between Gouda and London, the date of publication was too late for the tract to have any significant influence on the passage of the Act of Toleration, which was approved by the Commons on 17 May and received royal assent on 24 May.[25] Locke's *Epistola*, with its fulsome espousal of toleration, might seem at first glance to have little in common with the reticent Act of Toleration. But the *Epistola* and the act share certain emphases. Both documents can be seen as compromises struck between principles of liberty and the ideology of anti-popery.

Locke's *Epistola*, famously, equivocated on the question of whether Catholics should be accorded freedom of worship in Protestant domains. The philosopher argued that the theology of Catholics was no grounds to exclude them from toleration but that their politics might be. He wrote, "That Church can have no right to be tolerated by the Magistrate, which is constituted upon such a bottom, that all those who enter into it, do thereby, *ipso facto*, deliver themselves up to the Protection and Service of another Prince." This was a common argument used in England against the toleration of Catholics, on the grounds that they paid allegiance to a foreign prince, the pope in Rome. Locke also contended that no one should be tolerated who did not believe in tolerating others or who held the principles, often associated with Catholicism by Protestants at the time, that "Faith is not to be kept with Hereticks" or that "Kings excommunicated forfeit their Crowns and Kingdoms."[26] Locke's argument did leave open the possibility of toleration for some Catholics. A Catholic who adopted tolerant principles and disavowed any political allegiance to the pope could be tolerated. But many English Protestants believed that Catholics such as this did not exist. The *Epistola de Tolerantia* accommodated itself to the widespread desire of many in England to exclude Catholics from toleration, a desire also reflected in the provisions of the Act of Toleration.[27]

Locke's philosophical acumen did not prevent him from adopting anti-popish ideas and themes. In his unpublished *Essay Concerning Toleration* of 1667–1668, he described papists as "irreconcileable enemys of whose fidelity you can never be secur[e]d, whilst they owe a blinde obedience to an infal[l]ible pope." Because of their political principles, he averred, "I thinke they ought not to enjoy the benefit of toleration." In a treatise written in the early 1680s, Locke excoriated Catholics as the "common Enemy" of Protestants and urged his co-religionists to guard against their schemes: "all Protestants ought now by all ways to be stirred up against them [Catholics] as People that have declared themselves ready by blood, violence, and destruction to ruine our Religion and Government." Even if Catholics were not openly engaging in violence, they might be operating as spies within the body politic: they should be regarded as "either Enemyes in our bowells or spies among us, whilst their General Commanders whom they blindly obey declare Warr, and an unalterable design to destroy us." After the Glorious Revolution, Locke continued to assail what he saw as the malevolent intentions of papists. In a manuscript from 1690, he wrote that the duty of supporting William's government was incumbent on everyone who "would not betray England and expose it to popish rage and revenge."[28]

Given the hostility he expressed toward Catholics, it is not surprising that Locke steered clear of any dealings with James II. This was not for lack of opportunity. Locke had been forced into exile in the Netherlands in 1683, but his friends wrote to him repeatedly during James's reign urging him to return to England and assuring him that he would be treated well if he did so. The earl of Pembroke wrote in 1685 to say that the king had invited Locke to "come over" and had pledged to "never believe any ill reports" of Locke. In May 1687, a month after the *Declaration for Liberty of Conscience* was issued, Locke's friend James Tyrrell urged him to publish a pamphlet in support of the king's toleration campaign: "Your discourse about Liberty of Conscience would not doe amisse now to dispose peoples minds to passe it into a Law whenever the Parliament sits." Locke did not follow Tyrrell's advice. Nor did he accept James's overtures. Indeed, he appears to have dismissed the prospect of accepting a pardon from James, and he objected to the efforts of his friends to procure one for him. Only after the king had fled to France did Locke return to England. He then published his *Two Treatises of Government* with a preface extolling the new King William as "our great restorer."[29]

Locke's views on Catholicism and toleration can be contrasted with those held by another contemporary intellectual, William Petty. A natural philosopher described by Karl Marx as "the father of political economy," Petty had lived in Ireland for much of his life but spent most of James II's reign in London, where he died at the age of sixty-four in December 1687.[30] He was relatively at ease with the prospect of Catholics in power even though he, like Locke, was an Anglican. He argued for religious toleration and did not suggest that Catholics should be excluded from toleration on either political or religious grounds.

Petty's ideas on toleration were expressed in a series of proposals drafted in the early years of James's reign, some of which he composed for the king's benefit. He informed a friend in 1686 that he had been to court and had enjoyed "private and ample Conference" with James. A year later, he attended the king again and showed him a paper he had written. According to the draft proposals that survive, Petty had no objection to Catholics serving in public office. He recommended in 1687 "That there bee an Act for taking away all Tests, Oaths, Penall Laws and Incapacitys depending upon Religion."[31] He proposed that the Test Acts should be replaced by a new test under which "every man shall swear to promote and pr[e]serve the said Liberty of Conscience as the inherent and Indealable Right of Mandkind." The new test would be taken by all members of parliament, by all officers both civil and military, and even by the king himself. This new test was reminiscent of the proposals advanced by some repealer authors in 1687. Petty also expressed a concern, shared by some repealer authors, that an act of parliament was not sufficient to bind all future parliaments. Instead, he proposed a national assembly elected by all men twenty-one years of age or older that would then ratify toleration.[32] The parallels between Petty's arguments and repealer thought may have resulted in part from conversations he is known to have had at the time with William Penn.[33]

To Petty, repeal was not an end in itself; it was part of a larger program of Anglo-Irish integration. Petty was especially alert to the problem of anti-popery, which in his view was tearing Ireland apart and might do the same in England. The end result of his proposals for reform, he hoped, would be to "Take away the hatreds between

English and Irish, Protestant and Papist." In a document from 1685 titled "A Remedy to the fears and Jealousys, which the King of Englands Non:papist subjects, may conceive concerning their being forc't from their Religion," he observed that there were simply too few Catholics in England for them to be a threat to Protestants there. In his *Treatise of Ireland,* dating from 1687, he expressed the hope that his proposals would show "How Fears and Jealousies concerning Religion, and even the Test, may vanish of themselves."[34] William Petty, like many of the repealers, criticized anti-popish rhetoric and believed that anti-popish fears could be effectively countered.

The differences between John Locke's writings on toleration and William Petty's suggest some of the tensions at the heart of early Enlightenment thinking on religious liberty. Locke's thinking accommodated itself to the anti-popish fears prevalent in the Protestant countries that abutted Louis XIV's France. Petty and the repealers, by contrast, pursued a more expansive tolerationist vision that would include Catholics at the expense of wrecking their projects on the shoals of anti-popery. While Petty and the repealers sought to counter anti-popery, Locke did little to challenge anti-popish tropes and narratives, even adopting them at times in his own writing. With his advocacy of a carefully limited toleration and his endorsement of principles that could be used to exclude Catholics from toleration, John Locke chose not to challenge forces that the repealers met head-on.[35]

Anti-Popery and the Reign of James II

From the beginning of his reign, King James refused to allow his policies to be guided by the anti-popish inclinations of many of his people. He dispensed Catholic officers from the Test and allowed them to serve in his army. He issued dispensations protecting Catholics from the penal laws. He urged his subjects not to allow their actions to be guided by "fears and jealousies." He sought to muzzle anti-Catholic preaching. Instead of accommodating anti-popery, he challenged it.

Historians have often wondered why James took these actions. He came to the throne peacefully. His accession was greeted with national rejoicing. He could surely, it is claimed, have arranged a compromise whereby Catholics would be granted an effective toleration so long as he continued to observe the Test Acts and did not insist on a full repeal of the penal laws. Any attempt to do more for Catholics would merely raise trouble for himself.[36] But the problem with sleeping dogs is that they eventually awake, and there was no guarantee that James would always be in as strong a position to deal with them as he was in 1685. This was a year of peace and plenty, marred only by a couple of feeble expeditionary forces under Monmouth and Argyll that were easily parried. The English economy was booming and toryism was cresting. England was not at war with any other power. And the king was fifty-two years old. If he did not try to defeat anti-popery now, to defang it and confine it, when could he? His reign would be permanently threatened by instability if he did not restrain anti-popery, as indeed his brother's had been. It was difficult to predict what crisis might cause another anti-popish panic to emerge. There was no guarantee that England would always be at peace with its neighbors. There was no guarantee that trade would remain buoyant and harvests ample. Moreover, it was unclear how the English might react to the prospect of a popish heir and with it a popish dynasty. Perhaps they were willing to tolerate James on the throne only because he was fifty-two and his two daughters, Mary and Anne, were both Protestants. James's queen, Mary of Modena, was only twenty-six years old upon her husband's accession and could easily bear him a son. If she did, it might provoke a crisis. Indeed, the birth of a royal heir in 1688 did just that.

It is far from clear that James could have avoided this crisis in 1688 had he governed more moderately over the preceding three years. Governing moderately would not have put to rest the anti-popish fear that at some point in the future either James or his successor might cease pursuing moderate counsels and might instead, in the manner of Mary Tudor, lead a ruthless crackdown on Protestant England. Anti-popery was a highly adaptive discourse, and the pursuit of moderate courses would not necessarily have prevented a conspiracy theory from taking hold. Even if James had taken the ultimate conciliatory step and converted to Anglicanism, the problem of anti-popery would not necessarily have been solved, since his brother had been ostensibly Anglican during the Popish Plot crisis of 1678–1681 and his father had been fervently Anglican during the crisis fueled by anti-popery in 1640–1642. A conversion by James could easily have been greeted with suspicion about whether he still harbored some reservoir of attachment to Catholicism. Perhaps the whole thing was a trick, people might say. Furthermore, his own conversion would not have solved the problem that his wife was also Catholic and would presumably have great influence on the upbringing of any male heir.

By the 1680s, England was caught in a cycle in which anti-popish fears brought popular unrest, which in turn caused a conservative reaction, which brought a few years of relative quiet before the next anti-popish panic broke out.[37] The cycle could be adeptly managed, as it was by Charles II, who allowed the panic of the late 1670s to run its course before stepping in to launch a ferocious loyalist countermovement. Or the cycle could be mismanaged, as it was by James II, who heightened anti-popish fears with his many missteps, including his decision to import Catholic troops from Ireland in September 1688 to assist in the defense of England. But adjustments to royal policy could only treat the symptoms of anti-popery, not cure the underlying malady. Anti-popery was such a large-scale, intractable problem that it required a grand solution—a restabilizing of the state on new foundations. It needed to be managed either by being brought fully within the state and becoming a foundational tenet of national politics, or by being repelled and redefined as outside the boundaries of acceptable discourse.

This restabilizing of the state was, in fact, achieved in 1689 when anti-popery was written into the revolution settlement. Under the Bill of Rights of that year, no Catholic would be permitted to sit on the English or Irish throne, nor would any monarch be allowed to marry a Catholic. The revolutionary Convention Parliament had agreed unanimously in January with the resolution that "it hath been found, by Experience, to be inconsistent with the Safety and Welfare of this Protestant Kingdom, to be governed by a Popish Prince."[38] Then in May 1689 King William took England into war with France. With these shifts in England's foreign policy and laws of succession, anti-popery became a less disruptive force, for it was now the popular basis for the government's main initiative, the French wars. Anti-popery proved to be a powerful integrative agent in eighteenth-century Britain and in North America, knitting together Anglicans, Scottish Presbyterians and New England Congregationalists in opposition to French popery.[39] But opposition to anti-popery was also a productive force, and it is possible to imagine an England that might have rallied around a broader toleration that would have reintegrated Catholics into the political system. Such a move would have had profound effects in Ireland, which was never integrated adequately into the anti-popish whig ascendancy of the eighteenth century. Excluding Catholics in 1689 had its costs as well as its benefits, and it was not the only potential resolution to the recurrent crises of the Stuart period. It is no surprise to find that William Petty, always a proponent of Anglo-Irish integration, was also a fierce critic of anti-popery.

Anti-popery is often described in the historical literature as an animus that was directed by English Protestants more against foreign Catholics or imagined threats than against one's own Catholic neighbors. This was not, however, the experience of many English Catholics under the Williamite regime. Although many Protestants were charitable to their Catholic neighbors, others were not. One pamphleteer proposed, shortly after the Revolution, that all male Catholics under the age of fifty with any substantial estates should be forcibly expelled from Great Britain. A group of men petitioned the House of Commons after the Revolution urging the passage of a law requiring all Catholics, "like the Jews at Rome, to wear a mark of distinction on the crowns of their hats visible to all men." Beginning in 1689, a series of parliamentary acts placed new handicaps on Catholics. They were obliged to give up their arms and any horses worth more than five pounds each. Those Catholics not ordinarily resident in the capital were required to leave the City and remain at least ten miles away.[40] These acts were designed to prevent Catholics from mounting a rebellion against William. But the broad brush with which they were applied suggests that many Protestants were anxious about the loyalties of all Catholics, not just the loyalties of a few plotters hiding among the Catholic population.

Even after the immediate revolutionary crisis had passed, the English parliament continued to devise new penalties to impose on Catholics. An act of parliament in 1693 required Catholics subject to the land tax to pay at a double rate. The system of double taxation effectively replaced the earlier system of recusancy fines, which had become more difficult to enforce now that Protestant nonconformists were permitted to absent themselves from church. Catholics were stripped of the parliamentary franchise in 1696. An act of 1700 titled "An Act for the Further Preventing the Growth of Popery," commonly known as the Popery Act, forbade Catholics from purchasing land. Under the provisions of this act, Catholic priests and schoolmasters were liable to "perpetuall Imprisonment." These laws were imperfectly enforced at best, but they did succeed in relegating English Catholics to second-class status. In the early eighteenth century, Catholic priests were rounded up and sent to prison, though not usually for long terms. Eventually the Catholic Relief Act of 1778 lifted a few of the more onerous disabilities. But this act proved so unpopular with many English Protestants that its passage led to the Gordon Riots of 1780, a conflagration that brought the destruction of Catholic chapels and schools in London along with the houses of several leading Catholics. Anti-Catholicism was alive and well in eighteenth-century Britain.[41] It was not laid to rest by the Glorious Revolution but instead was used to legitimize the revolution settlement.

The Repealer Revolution

The repealers failed in their efforts to reorient English policy toward a more encompassing toleration that would include Catholics. The Glorious Revolution, instead, saw a reassertion of anti-popish ideology. Even King William, who would have liked to have done more to help English Catholics in order to appease his Habsburg allies, found himself constrained by what his parliaments would accept. A bill for the toleration of private worship by Catholics was introduced into the House of Lords in December 1689, presumably at William's instigation, but it failed to proceed to a final vote.[42] Neither James nor William had been able to obtain a majority in parliament for measures liberalizing the treatment of Catholics.

The repealers did not, however, fail in all their objectives. It is no coincidence that the Act of Toleration was enacted after eighteen months in which a large group of nonconformists had pressed loudly and insistently for religious toleration. The act might not have included the Baptists and Quakers had the repealers not garnered so much support from those groups. Historians have tended to interpret British political history as a succession of moderate leaders behaving pragmatically and agreeing to undertake needed reforms, with the Glorious Revolution seen as a paradigmatic example. It is often suggested that because England had a moderate revolution in 1688 it avoided a radical one later. It is less often noted that these so-called moderates or pragmatists were generally pushed to act by more radical political movements such as the repealers. The history of British politics is, in fact, the history of popular movements forming and being thwarted but still managing to provoke a certain amount of defensive-minded reform. This is a less celebratory story but a more accurate one.

This interpretation of the Revolution in turn suggests a more complete explanation for the origins of modern constitutionalism. Constitutionalism is often said to have originated in the struggles of nations to limit their rulers; thus popular sovereignty is placed at the center of these accounts, and the Revolution of 1688–1689, among others, is seen as a moment when the will of the people triumphed over an oppressive regime. An account of the repealer movement highlights a different strand in the origins of modern constitutionalism, one in which minorities organized themselves to repel the overbearing demands of majorities. The settlement of 1689 was as much about limiting the oppressive power of the English majority as it was about limiting the oppressive power of the English monarch. The Protestant nonconformists, including the Baptists and Quakers, had some success in carving out a space for freedom for themselves in 1689, even if the Catholics and Socinians were left out of it. The toleration of Protestant nonconformists remained unpopular with large segments of the English population well into the eighteenth century; yet the nonconformist minority had succeeded in circumscribing the capacity of their enemies to act against them.

The repealers sought to achieve a constitutional settlement that would take the most divisive question in early modern English politics, how to deal with religious diversity, off the table. Their proposed settlement provided a permanent toleration that would forever prevent any one religious group from enforcing its will on the others. Their hope was that this settlement would reduce the instability of seventeenth-century England with its movements and countermovements. But the repealers were met by a Protestant countermovement that became a revolution. Their efforts thus created instability rather than reducing it, at least in 1687–1688.

The English public was consumed with the debate between the repealers and their opponents in 1687–1688. In the course of that debate, the attractions of at least part of the repeal agenda became evident. The constitutional settlement of 1689 also sought to take religious diversity off the table, at least with regard to the major Protestant groups, so that English Protestants would no longer feel any need to battle each other over liberty of conscience. Some of the Anglican tories resisted this constitutional settlement in the generation after it was enacted, seeking to limit the benefits it accorded to nonconformists. But gradually even the tories came to accept the presence of long-established nonconformist groups such as the Presbyterians and the Quakers. Over the course of the eighteenth century, their earlier resentments died out, and the animus of tory highflyers shifted to the more novel bugbears of freethinkers, Socinians, and eventually republicans.[43] Political conflict lost some of its destabilizing force in eighteenth-century England once most Protestants had been assured of religious freedom.

If the events of 1688–1689 were indeed "Glorious," it was because leading Anglicans did not use the Revolution to exact vengeance on the nonconformists. Instead, the past was reimagined. King James was presented as an unscrupulous, scheming despot in league with France, while his nonconformist allies were reconceived as a handful of self-seeking turncoats and the vast majority of nonconformists were deemed to be too circumspect to join his schemes.[44] The repealer movement was forgotten. The nonconformists were invited into the eighteenth-century whig state, provided they were willing to forswear any links to the Jacobite cause. This they proved more than willing to do. The new alliance of nonconformists and Anglicans had global implications, helping to knit together the eighteenth-century British Empire, with Congregationalists in Massachusetts, Baptists in Rhode Island, and Quakers in Pennsylvania treated as genuine patriots. This new Protestant alliance was founded on a lapse of memory. The history of the repealers suggests that, at least in a premodern context, reconciliation could best be achieved through forgetting rather than through remembering.

Appendix

A List of Repealer Publications

1. Serials

Publick Occurrences Truly Stated (Feb.–Nov. 1688), eds. Henry Care (nos. 1–24) and Elkanah Settle (nos. 25–34).

The Weekly Test-Paper (May 1688), ed. Charles Nicholets? (nos. 1–4). Bodleian Library, Nichols Newspapers 7, nos. 69, 74, 79, 85.

2. Royal Declarations

James II, *His Majesties Gracious Declaration to all his Loving Subjects for Liberty of Conscience* (1687, J186).

———, *His Majesties Gracious Declaration to all his Loving Subjects for Liberty of Conscience* (1688, J190).

3. Pamphlets and Broadsides

An Address of Thanks, on Behalf of the Church of England, to Mris. [sic] James (1687, A546).

An Address to his Grace the Lord Archbishop of Canterbury, and the Right Reverend the Bishops (1688, A562).

An Address to the Church of England: Evidencing her Obligations both of Interest and Conscience, to Concurr with His Gracious Majestie (n.p., 1688, A564B).

Advice from a Dissenter in the City, to his Friends in the Countrey (1688, A633).

Advice to Freeholders and Other Electors of Members to Serve in Parliament (1687, P1250).

Advice to Protestant Dissenters, Shewing 'tis their Interest to Repeal the Test (1688, A648B).

Advice to the English Youth: Relating to the Present Juncture of Affairs (1688, A655).

Animadversions upon Mijn Heer Fagels Letter Concerning our Penal Laws and Tests (1688, A3204).

An Answer to a Letter from a Clergyman in the City to his Friend in the Country (1688, P3039A).

An Answer by an Anabaptist to the Three Considerations Proposed to Mr William Penn (1688, A3275).

An Answer from the Country, to a Late Letter to a Dissenter (1687, A3278).

An Answer to the City-Conformists Letter, from the Country Clergy-man (1688, A3399A).

An Answer to the Letter to a Dissenter, Detecting the many Unjust Insinuations which Highly Reflect on His Majesty (1687, A3416A).

[Burthogge, Richard], *Prudential Reasons for Repealing the Penal Laws against all Recusants, and for a General Toleration* (1687, B6155).

[Care, Henry], *Animadversions on a Late Paper, Entituled, A Letter to a Dissenter* (1687, C505).

———, *An Answer to a Paper Importing a Petition of the Archbishop of Canterbury, and Six Other Bishops* (1688, C506).

———, *A Discourse for Taking Off the Tests and Penal Laws about Religion* (1687, D1593).

———, *Draconica: Or, An Abstract of all the Penal-Laws Touching Matters of Religion* (1687, C510).

———, *Draconica: Or, An Abstract of all the Penal Laws Touching Matters of Religion*, 2nd edn., enlarged (1688, C511).

———, *The Legality of the Court held by His Majesties Ecclesiastical Commissioners, Defended* (1688, C527).

[Cartwright, Thomas], *A Letter from a Clergy-Man in the Country, to the Clergy-Man in the City* (1688, L1369A).

———, *A Modest Censure of the Immodest Letter to a Dissenter* (1687, N76).

Docwra, Ann, *Spiritual Community, Vindicated amongst People of Different Perswasions in Some Things* (n.p., 1687, D1781).

[Dryden, John], *The Hind and the Panther* (1687, D2281).

[Dyer, William], *The Present Interest of England in Matters of Religion* (1688, D99).

The Examination of the Bishops, upon their Refusal of Reading His Majesty's most Gracious Declaration (1688, E3725).

An Expedient for Peace: Perswading an Agreement amongst Christians (1688, E3872aA).

A Few Short Arguments Proving that 'tis every English-man's Interest as well as Duty, at all Times to Endeavor the Absolute and Effectual Repeal of all the Religious Penal Laws and Tests (1687, F837).

A Friendly Debate upon the Next Elections of Parliament and the Settlement of Liberty of Conscience, no. 1 (n.p., [1688], F2218A).

A Friendly Debate upon the Next Elections of Parliament and the Settlement of Liberty of Conscience, no. 2 (n.p., [1688], F2218C).

[Godden, Thomas], *A Letter in Answer to Two Main Questions of the First Letter to a Dissenter* (1687, G64).

The Good Old Test Reviv'd and Recommended to all Sincere Christians (1687, G1080).

Great and Good News for the Church of England, If they Please to Accept Thereof (n.p., 1688, G1654A).

How the Members of the Church of England Ought to Behave Themselves under a Roman Catholick King, with Reference to the Test and Penal Laws (1687, H2961).

Indulgence to Tender Consciences Shewn to be Most Reasonable and Christian (1687, I157).

Kenrick, Daniel, *A Sermon Preached in the Cathedral-Church of Worcester, at the Lent Assize, April 7th, 1688* (1688, K307).

The King's Dispensing Power Explicated & Asserted ([1688], K592).

A Letter from a Dissenter to the Petitioning Bishops (1688, L1372bA).

A Letter from a Gentleman in the City, to a Clergy-Man in the Country (1688, L1387).

A Letter from a Minister of the Church of England, to the Pretended Baptist, Author of the Three Considerations Directed to Mr Penn (1688, L1417).

[Lobb, Stephen], *A Second Letter to a Dissenter* (1687, L2729A).

Melius Inquirendum: Or, An Impartial Enquiry into the late Proceedings against the Bishops (1688, E43).

The Minister's Reasons for his not Reading the Kings Declaration, Friendly Debated (1688, M2195).

Nahash Revived: Or, The Church of England's Love to Dissenters (1688, N84).

A New Test of the Church of Englands Loyalty (1687, N783).

A New-Years Gift to Dissenters, from a True Friend to the Protestants (1688, N816A).

[Nicholets, Charles], *A Third Dialogue between Simeon and Levi, about Abolishing the Penal Laws and Tests* (1688, T906).

[Northleigh, John], *Parliamentum Pacificum: Or, The Happy Union of King & People in an Healing Parliament* (1688, N1302).

———, *Dr. Burnett's Reflections upon a Book, Entituled, Parliamentum Pacificum: (The First Part) Answered, By the Author* (1688, N1298).

N. N., *Old Popery as Good as New: Or the Unreasonableness of the Church of England in some of her Doctrines and Practices* (n.p., 1688, N47).

Paston, James, *A Discourse of Penal Laws in Matter of Religion* (1688, P665).

Payne, Henry Neville, *An Answer to a Scandalous Pamphlet, Entituled a Letter to a Dissenter* (1687, P887).

[Penn, William], *A Letter form [sic] a Gentleman in the Country, to his Friends in London, upon the Subject of the Penal Laws and Tests* (n.p., 1687, P1318).

———, *A Second Letter from a Gentleman in the Country, to his Friends in London, upon the Subject of the Penal Laws and Tests* (1687, P1361).

———, *A Third Letter from a Gentleman in the Country, to his Friends in London, upon the Subject of the Penal Laws and Tests* (1687, P1381).

———, *Good Advice to the Church of England, Roman Catholick, and Protestant Dissenter* (1687, P1296).

———, *The Great and Popular Objection against the Repeal of the Penal Laws & Tests Briefly Stated and Consider'd* (1688, P1298A).

Plain-Dealing Concerning the Penal Laws and Tests (1688, P2351).

Plant, Thomas, and Benjamin Dennis, *The Mischief of Persecution Exemplified* (1688, P2377A).

The Plea of the Harmless Oppressed, against the Cruel Oppressor ([1688], P2525).

[Popple, William], *Three Letters Tending to Demonstrate how the Security of this Nation against al[l] Future Persecution for Religion, Lys in the Abolishment of the Present Penal Laws and Tests* (1688, P1383).

The Reasonableness of Toleration, and the Unreasonableness of Penal Laws and Tests (1687, P1352).

Reasons for the Repeal of the Tests, in a Letter to a Friend in the Country (1687, R519).

Rone, Elizabeth, *A Reproof to those Church Men or Ministers that Refused to Read the Kings Most Gracious Declaration* (n.p., 1688, R1914A).

Seasonable Advice Humbly Offer'd to the Consideration of the Bishops against their Day of Tryal (1688, S2212).

A Sermon Preached before the People called Quakers, in the Park of Southwark (1688, S2635).

Shute, Giles, *A New Naked Truth, Or the Sandy Foundation of the Sacramental Test Shaken* (1688, S3709).

———, *A New Test in Lieu of the Old One, by way of Supposition* (1688, S3710).

———, *A New Test in Lieu of the Old One, by way of Supposition,* 2nd edn., enlarged (1688, S3711).

A Sober Answer to a Scandalous Paper termed Three Queries (1688, S4406).

Som[e] Free Reflections upon Occasion of the Public Discourse about Liberty of Conscience (1687, P1366).

Some Necessary Disquisitions and Close Expostulations with the Clergy and People of the Church of England (1688, S4528).

Some Reasons to Move Protestant Dissenters to be for the Taking Off Penal Laws, yea and Tests too (1688, S4580).

Stewart, James, *James Steuarts Answer to a Letter Writ by Mijn Heer Fagel* (1688, S5534).

Three Doubts Proposed to the Reverend Bishops (1688, T1087).

Trinder, Charles, *The Speech of Charles Trinder, Esq; Recorder of Gloucester* (1688, T2283).

The True Interest of the Legal English Protestants, Stated in a Letter to a Present Member of the House of Commons (1687, T2714).

A True Representation of His Majesty's Declaration, for Prevention of those Prejudices which are Rais'd against Reading of it (1688, J396).

Two Plain Words to the Clergy: Or, An Admonition to Peace and Concord at this Juncture (1688, T3527).

Vox Cleri pro Rege: Or the Rights of the Imperial Soveraignty of the Crown of England Vindicated (n.p., 1688, V715).

W., C. D., *A Letter from Holland Touching Liberty of Conscience* (n.p., 1688, W3223).

W., T., *Remarkes upon a Pamphlet Stiled, A Letter to a Dissenter* (n.p., 1687, H318).

Abbreviations

Note: Abbreviations and catalogue references for particular manuscript collections may be found in the list of Manuscripts Consulted.

Add. MS	Additional Manuscript
Beinecke	Beinecke Rare Book and Manuscript Library, Yale University, New Haven, Connecticut
BIHR	*Bulletin of the Institute of Historical Research*
BL	British Library, London
Bodl.	Bodleian Library, Oxford
BPL	Boston Public Library
CAC (C)	Cumbria Archive Centre, Carlisle
CAC (K)	Cumbria Archive Centre, Kendal
CJ	*Journals of the House of Commons*
CPA	Archives des Affaires Étrangères, Paris, Correspondance Politique, Angleterre
CSPD	*Calendar of State Papers Domestic*
CTB	*Calendar of Treasury Books*
CUL	Cambridge University Library
EHR	*English Historical Review*
EcHistR	*Economic History Review*
FSL	Folger Shakespeare Library, Washington, D.C.
HEHL	Henry E. Huntington Library, Art Collections, and Botanical Gardens, San Marino, California
HJ	*Historical Journal*

HMC	*Historical Manuscripts Commission*
JBS	*Journal of British Studies*
JEH	*Journal of Ecclesiastical History*
JFHS	*Journal of the Friends Historical Society*
LJ	*Journals of the House of Lords*
LLIU	Lilly Library, Indiana University, Bloomington
LSF	Library of the Religious Society of Friends, London
MS(S)	Manuscript(s)
NAS	National Archives of Scotland, Edinburgh
n.d.	Date unknown
NLS	National Library of Scotland, Edinburgh
NLW	National Library of Wales, Aberystwyth
n.p.	Place of publication unknown
n.s.	New series
NUL	Nottingham University Library
Publick Occurrences	*Publick Occurrences Truly Stated*
RO	Record Office
TNA	The National Archives, Kew
UL	University Library
VCH	*Victoria County History*
WYAS	West Yorkshire Archive Service, Leeds

Notes

Introduction

1. Both of these stories are apocryphal—neither Canute nor Louis XV is likely to have said anything like this—but their hold on the popular imagination suggests the continuing power of hydraulic and thermodynamic metaphors of revolution.

2. See, for instance, *A Letter to a Gentleman at Brussels* (1689, L1658), 15, and John Cordy Jeaffreson, ed., *A Young Squire of the Seventeenth Century: From the Papers (A.D. 1676–1686) of Christopher Jeaffreson*, 2 vols. (London, 1878), ii:212.

3. Alexis de Tocqueville, *The Old Regime and the French Revolution*, trans. Stuart Gilbert (Garden City, N.Y., 1955), 176–177, writing with reference to Louis XVI's reforms in the run-up to the French Revolution. On political opportunities and the sociology of revolutions, see also Charles Tilly and Sidney Tarrow, *Contentious Politics* (Boulder, 2007), 57–59, 75–76, 155–160; Sidney G. Tarrow, *Power in Movement: Social Movements and Contentious Politics*, 3rd edn. (Cambridge, 2011), 26–28, 32–33, 157–174.

4. Charles Tilly, *From Mobilization to Revolution* (Reading, MA, 1978), 55, 100–101.

5. One English courtier noted in February 1688 that Lovelace himself had expected he might be sent to the Tower but that "the present circumstance of things will save him for this time." The peer was charged with a misdemeanor for his offense but his trial was delayed until the autumn of 1688 and was never held due to the Revolution. The king granted permission for him to travel to Germany in September 1688 and then, on 27 September, with the invasion of William imminent, revoked the pass and ordered him to be found and taken into custody for "Abetting the P[rince] of Orange" in his designs. Lovelace remained at large until after William's landing, when he was imprisoned briefly in Gloucester. See NUL, PwA 2148, James Rivers to [Hans Willem Bentinck], 27 Feb. 1688; TNA, PC 2/72, fol. 96v; *Publick Occurrences*, no. 2 (28

Feb. 1688); *The Entring Book of Roger Morrice, 1677–1691,* ed. Mark Goldie, John Spurr, Tim Harris, Stephen Taylor, Mark Knights, and Jason McElligott, 7 vols. (Woodbridge, 2007–9), iv:237, 259–260, 323; BL, Add. MS 34487, fol. 8v, newsletter of 2 July 1688, fols. 9–10, N. Gerrard to Edward Norton, 4 July 1688; BL, Egerton MS 2543, fol. 270v; NLW, Wynnstay MSS, C 25, Sir Thomas Powys to Sir William Williams, *c.* June 1688; BPL, Ms. Am. 1502, vol. 7, no. 38, newsletter dated 19 Sept. 1688; BL, Add. MS 38175, fol. 139, newsletter dated 6 Oct. 1688; TNA, SP 44/338, p. 103.

6. John Dalrymple, *Memoirs of Great Britain and Ireland,* 2nd edn., 2 vols. (London, 1771–73), vol. 2, pt. 1, p. 230.

7. *A Copy of an Address to the King by the Bishop of Oxon* (n.p., 1687, P456 and C6191A); for its circulation, see [Sir Roger L'Estrange], *A Reply to the Reasons of the Oxford-Clergy against Addressing* (1687, L1297), 3; BL, Add. MS 21092, fols. 23r-v; CAC (C), D/Lons/L12/2/15 (memoirs of Sir Daniel Fleming, vol. 2), fols. 233–234; CUL, Dd.3

8. S. Wilton Rix, ed., *The Diary and Autobiography of Edmund Bohun* (Beccles, 1853), 81; *CSPD, James II, 1687–89,* 330–331; *HMC, Seventh Report,* 416; Bodl., MS Tanner 28, fol. 302, Robert Woodward to archbishop Sancroft, 24 Dec. 1688; Bodl., MS Tanner 28, fol. 311, Philip Traheron to archbishop Sancroft, 29 Dec. 1688; Lancashire RO, DDKe/6/37 (notebook of Reverend Walker), p. 11; *Orange Gazette,* no. 1 (31 Dec. 1688); Bodl., MS Add. c.180, pp. 1–5; BL, Add. MS 34487, fol. 54, Robert Cosens to Edward Norton, 25 Dec. 1688; BPL, Ms. Am. 1502, vol. 7, no. 61, newsletter dated 20 Dec. 1688; Bodl., MS Smith 141, fol. 39; NLW, Ottley correspondence no. 1698, notes by Adam Ottley, 10 Dec. 1688.

9. BL, Add. MS 36707, fol. 16v, letter of Thomas Newey, undated (early 1688); FSL, V.a.469 (memoirs of William Westby), fol. 15; J. R. Jones, *The Revolution of 1688 in England* (London, 1972), 135; Lionel K. J. Glassey, *Politics and the Appointment of Justices of the Peace, 1675–1720* (Oxford, 1979), 93–94; Peter Walker, *James II and the Three Questions: Religious Toleration and the Landed Classes, 1687–1688* (Oxford, 2010), 250–251.

10. See Ian K. Steele, *The English Atlantic, 1675–1740: An Exploration of Communication and Community* (New York, 1986), 94–110; Owen Stanwood, *The Empire Reformed: English America in the Age of the Glorious Revolution* (Philadelphia, 2011), 85–112.

11. See especially John Miller, "The Earl of Tyrconnel and James II's Irish Policy, 1685–1688," *HJ,* xx (1977), 816–817; D. W. Hayton, "The Williamite Revolution in Ireland, 1688–91," in Jonathan I. Israel, ed., *The Anglo-Dutch Moment: Essays on the Glorious Revolution and its World Impact* (Cambridge, 1991), 192.

12. Mark Goldie, "The Political Thought of the Anglican Revolution," in Robert Beddard, ed., *The Revolutions of 1688* (Oxford, 1991), 107–108.

13. [John Locke], *A Letter Concerning Toleration* (1689, L2747); E. S. de Beer, ed., *The Correspondence of John Locke,* 8 vols. (Oxford, 1976–89), iii:583–584, 607, 633–634.

14. Owen Stanwood, "The Protestant Moment: Antipopery, the Revolution of 1688–1689, and the Making of an Anglo-American Empire," *JBS*, xlvi (2007), 481–491, 505–508.

15. Jonathan Scott, *England's Troubles: Seventeenth-Century English Political Instability in European Context* (Cambridge, 2000), 26.

16. *London Gazette*, no. 2085 (9–12 Nov. 1685); *CJ*, ix:756–759.

17. Alfred F. Havighurst, "James II and the Twelve Men in Scarlet," *Law Quarterly Review*, lxix (1953), 530–532. The six justices removed were Job Charlton, William Gregory, Thomas Jones, Creswell Levinz, William Montagu, and Edward Nevill.

18. Tim Harris, *Revolution: The Great Crisis of the British Monarchy, 1685–1720* (London, 2006), 149–173.

19. NUL, PwV 53/38, William Blathwayt to Sir Robert Southwell, 8 Jan. 1687.

20. Andrew Clark, ed., *The Life and Times of Anthony Wood*, 5 vols. (Oxford, 1891–1900), iii:172; TNA, PC 2/71, fol. 5; *CSPD, James II, 1686–87*, 71.

21. For the orders of removal, see TNA, PC 2/72, beginning with fol. 54v.

22. Nathaniel Johnston, *The King's Visitatorial Power Asserted* (1688, J879), 115–117; Angus Macintyre, "The College, King James II and the Revolution 1687–1688," in Laurence Brockliss, Gerald Harriss, and Angus Macintyre, eds., *Magdalen College and the Crown* (Oxford, 1988), 63; Harris, *Revolution*, 226–229.

23. Clark, ed., *Life and Times of Anthony Wood*, iii:268; *Depositions taken the 22d of October 1688 before the Privy-Council and Peers of England* ([Edinburgh], [1688], D1081); Dalrymple, *Memoirs of Great Britain*, vol. 2, pt. 1, pp. 228–231; Rachel Weil, *Political Passions: Gender, the Family and Political Argument in England, 1680–1714* (Manchester, 1999), 86–101.

24. Stephen B. Baxter, *William III and the Defense of European Liberty, 1650–1702* (Westport, 1966), 224–225, 231–232; Simon Groenveld, "'J'equippe une flotte tres considerable': The Dutch Side of the Glorious Revolution," in Robert Beddard, ed., *The Revolutions of 1688* (Oxford, 1991), 240; NUL, PwA 341, Hans Willem Bentinck to Everard Danckelmann, 14 July 1688.

25. John Carswell, *The Descent on England: A Study of the English Revolution of 1688 and its European Background* (London, 1969), 169–170; *A True and Exact Relation of the Prince of Orange His Publick Entrance into Exeter* (n.p., [1688], T2458).

26. Clyve Jones, "The Protestant Wind of 1688: Myth and Reality," *European Studies Review*, iii (1973), 201–222; Alan Pearsall, "The Invasion Voyage: Some Nautical Thoughts," in Charles Wilson and David Proctor, eds., *1688: The Seaborne Alliance and Diplomatic Revolution* (Greenwich, 1989), 165–174.

27. Thomas Babington Macaulay, *The History of England from the Accession of James the Second*, ed. C. H. Firth, 6 vols. (London, 1913–15), i:470–472, ii:844–848, iii:1144–1171; George Macaulay Trevelyan, *The English Revolution, 1688–1689* (London, 1938), 45–48, 82–97, 113–122; F. C. Turner, *James II* (London, 1948),

240–243, 303, 330–331, 395, 434; Harris, *Revolution*, 66–67, 268–272, 275–276, 281–296, 308; Steve Pincus, *1688: The First Modern Revolution* (New Haven, 2009), 94–99, 118, 181–186, 196–198, 243–244, 333–338, 348–350.

28. *Entring Book of Roger Morrice*, iv:415.

29. [Samuel Johnson], *A Letter from a Freeholder, to the Rest of the Freeholders of England* ([1688], J834), 8; for the use of this motto by the bishop of London in December 1688, see Edward Berwick, ed., *The Rawdon Papers* (London, 1819), 293; Churchill College Archives Centre, Erle 2/44/2, newsletter dated 20 Dec. 1688. A commonplace of English political rhetoric, the motto dates back to the thirteenth century, when it was used by the barons who confronted King Henry III.

30. Jones, *Revolution of 1688*, 328; J. R. Jones, "The Revolution in Context," in J. R. Jones, ed., *Liberty Secured? Britain before and after 1688* (Stanford, 1992), 11–12, 52; J. R. Western, *Monarchy and Revolution: The English State in the 1680s* (London, 1972), 1–2; David H. Hosford, *Nottingham, Nobles, and the North: Aspects of the Revolution of 1688* (Hamden, CT, 1976), 120–121; John Morrill, "The Sensible Revolution," in Jonathan I. Israel, ed., *The Anglo-Dutch Moment: Essays on the Glorious Revolution and its World Impact* (Cambridge, 1991), 103.

31. Tilly and Tarrow, *Contentious Politics*, 104, 155–160; Tarrow, *Power in Movement*, 210–211. For the view that modern revolutions are typically caused by the conflict between two modernizing programs, see Pincus, *1688*, 8–10, 36, 476.

32. Alec Ryrie, *The Gospel and Henry VIII: Evangelicals in the Early English Reformation* (Cambridge, 2003), 5–9, 237, 248–250; R. W. Hoyle, *The Pilgrimage of Grace and the Politics of the 1530s* (Oxford, 2001), 452–454; Anthony Fletcher and Diarmaid MacCulloch, *Tudor Rebellions*, 5th edn. (Harlow, 2004), 39–47, 59–63.

33. Patrick Collinson, *The Elizabethan Puritan Movement* (Berkeley, 1967), 12–13, 131–133, 286–288, 466–467; Tom Webster, *Godly Clergy in Early Stuart England: The Caroline Puritan Movement, c. 1620–1643* (Cambridge, 1997), 43–44, 67; Hugh Trevor-Roper, *Catholics, Anglicans and Puritans* (Chicago, 1988), 41–51, 76, 103, 110; see also C. John Sommerville, "Interpreting Seventeenth-Century English Religion as Movements," *Church History*, lxix (2000), 751–758.

34. Nicholas Tyacke, "Puritanism, Arminianism and Counter-Revolution," in Conrad Russell, ed., *The Origins of the English Civil War* (London, 1973), 119–129, 143; Nicholas Tyacke, *Anti-Calvinists: The Rise of English Arminianism, c. 1590–1640* (Oxford, 1987), 87, 123, 245–247; Conrad Russell, *The Causes of the English Civil War* (Oxford, 1990), 102–111; Anthony Milton, *Catholic and Reformed: The Roman and Protestant Churches in English Protestant Thought, 1600–1640* (Cambridge, 1995), 8–9, 52, 369–373, 541–546.

35. J. S. Morrill, *Cheshire 1630–1660: County Government and Society during the 'English Revolution'* (Oxford, 1974), 71, 138–140; idem, *Revolt in the Provinces*, 2nd edn. (London, 1999), 69–73; David Underdown, *Pride's Purge: Politics in the Puritan Revolution* (Oxford, 1971), 11–23, 75.

36. Tim Harris, *Politics under the Later Stuarts: Party Conflict in a Divided Society, 1660–1715* (London, 1993), 8, 52–109; Gary S. De Krey, *London and the Restoration, 1659–1683* (Cambridge, 2005), 272–331.

37. Peter Lake and Steve Pincus date the emergence of this public sphere to the reign of Elizabeth I: see Lake and Pincus, "Rethinking the Public Sphere in Early Modern England," *JBS*, xlv (2006), 273–279. On the relationship between partisanship and the print-based public sphere in post-Reformation Britain, see especially Mark Knights, *Representation and Misrepresentation in Later Stuart Britain: Partisanship and Political Culture* (Oxford, 2005), 15–66, 220–271.

38. Alastair Duke, *Dissident Identities in the Early Modern Low Countries,* ed. Judith Pollmann and Andrew Spicer (Farnham, 2009), 137–156; William Beik, *Urban Protest in Seventeenth-Century France: The Culture of Retribution* (Cambridge, 1997), 173–249; H. G. Koenigsberger, "The Organization of Revolutionary Parties in France and the Netherlands during the Sixteenth Century," *Journal of Modern History,* xxvii (1955), 335–351.

39. Tarrow, *Power in Movement,* 37–56; Charles Tilly, "Social Movements and National Politics," in Charles Bright and Susan Harding, eds., *Statemaking and Social Movements* (Ann Arbor, 1984), 301–309.

40. Mark Kishlansky, "The Emergence of Adversary Politics in the Long Parliament," *Journal of Modern History,* xlix (1977), 623, 640; see also Conrad Russell, *Parliaments and English Politics, 1621–1629* (Oxford, 1979), 1–84.

41. Kenneth Fincham and Peter Lake, "The Ecclesiastical Policy of King James I," *JBS,* xxiv (1985), 169–207; W. B. Patterson, *King James VI and I and the Reunion of Christendom* (Cambridge, 1997), 31–74.

42. Jason McElligott, *Royalism, Print and Censorship in Revolutionary England* (Woodbridge, 2007), 13–17, 82–92; Kevin Sharpe, *Image Wars: Promoting Kings and Commonwealths in England, 1603–1660* (New Haven, 2010), 285–303.

43. Charles II, *His Majesties Declaration to all his Loving Subjects, Touching the Causes & Reasons that Moved him to Dissolve the Two Last Parliaments* (1681, C3000).

44. Staffordshire RO, D1778/V/1403, p. 11, James to George Legge, 28 May 1679; *HMC, Dartmouth,* i:34; see also John Miller, *James II: A Study in Kingship* (Hove, 1978), 186; J. S. Clarke, ed., *The Life of James the Second,* 2 vols. (London, 1816), ii:157.

1. Forming a Movement

1. On the king's defiance of public opinion, see, for instance, Thomas Babington Macaulay, *The History of England from the Accession of James the Second,* ed. C. H. Firth, 6 vols. (London, 1913–15), ii:1010, iii:1068–1072; John Miller, *James II: A Study in Kingship* (Hove, 1978), 146–147, 171, 174; W. A. Speck, *James II* (Harlow, 2002), 60–61. On the collaborative nature of the English state, see especially Michael J. Braddick, *State Formation in Early Modern England,*

c. 1550–1700 (Cambridge, 2000), 16–46, 340–341, 425; Patrick Collinson, "The Monarchical Republic of Queen Elizabeth I," *Bulletin of the John Rylands Library*, lxix (1987), 394–424; Mark Goldie, "The Unacknowledged Republic: Office-holding in Early Modern England," in Tim Harris, ed., *The Politics of the Excluded, c. 1500–1850* (Basingstoke, 2001), 153–194.

2. For the view that James could potentially have centralized the English state on an absolutist model, see Steve Pincus, *1688: The First Modern Revolution* (New Haven, 2009), 143–217. For a critique of this book's treatment of James II's reign, see Scott Sowerby, "Pantomime History," *Parliamentary History*, xxx (2011), 236–258.

3. [Marquess of Halifax], *A Letter to a Dissenter* (1687, H311), 2.

4. Henry Hallam, *The Constitutional History of England*, 2 vols. (London, 1827), ii:399–400, 416–417; G. M. Trevelyan, *England under the Stuarts*, rev. edn. (1946), 356; Tim Harris, *Revolution: The Great Crisis of the British Monarchy, 1685–1720* (London, 2006), 166, 171, 179, 196–197, 235–236; Pincus, *1688*, 135–138.

5. Gilbert Burnet, *Bishop Burnet's History of His Own Time*, ed. M. J. Routh, 2nd edn., 6 vols. (Oxford, 1833), ii:27; William Penn, "Fragments of an Apology for Himself," *Memoirs of the Historical Society of Pennsylvania*, vol. 3, part 2 (1836), 241–242; see also H. C. Foxcroft, ed., *A Supplement to Burnet's History of My Own Time* (Oxford, 1902), 52; George Whitehead, *The Christian Progress of that Ancient Servant and Minister of Jesus Christ, George Whitehead* (London, 1725), 622; J. S. Clarke, ed., *The Life of James the Second*, 2 vols. (London, 1816), i:656. For sympathetic accounts of James II's views on toleration see Maurice Ashley, "Is There a Case for James II?" *History Today*, xiii (1963), 347–352; John Miller, "James II and Toleration," in Eveline Cruickshanks, ed., *By Force or By Default? The Revolution of 1688–1689* (Edinburgh, 1989), 14–17; Edward Corp, "James II and Toleration: The Years in Exile at Saint-Germain-en-Laye," *Royal Stuart Papers*, no. 51 (Huntingdon, 1997), 4, 9; Peter Walker, *James II and the Three Questions: Religious Toleration and the Landed Classes, 1687–1688* (Oxford, 2010), 32–35.

6. Robert Barclay to Princess Elizabeth of the Rhine, 12 Sept. 1677, printed in John Barclay, ed., *Diary of Alexander Jaffray* (London, 1833), 412–413; Swarthmore College, Safe 1006, Box 34, MSS 050 (Robert Barclay's "Vindication of his apology"), 6–7; John Pomfret, "Robert Barclay and James II: Barclay's 'Vindication,' 1689," *Bulletin of Friends Historical Association*, xlii (1953), 37–38.

7. *HMC, Buccleuch and Queensberry (Drumlanrig Castle)*, i:215.

8. TNA, PC 2/71, fol. 82B, meeting of 13 Nov. 1685; David S. Katz, "The Jews of England and 1688," in Ole Peter Grell, Jonathan I. Israel, and Nicholas Tyacke, eds., *From Persecution to Toleration: The Glorious Revolution and Religion in England* (Oxford, 1991), 222–224.

9. [Stephen Lobb], *A Second Letter to a Dissenter* (1687, L2729A), 7; [William Penn], *A Third Letter from a Gentleman in the Country* (1687, P1381),

9–10; Whitehead, *Christian Progress,* 577–578; John Miller, *Popery and Politics in England, 1660–1688* (Cambridge, 1973), 203.

10. *CTB,* viii:176; Miller, *Popery and Politics,* 203–205; Harris, *Revolution,* 149–171.

11. Henry Ellis, *Original Letters, Illustrative of English History,* 3 vols. (London, 1824), iii:339; Whitehead, *Christian Progress,* 570–591.

12. Bodl., MS Rawl. d.924, fol. 391; Coventry Archives, BA/L/A/2/3; Burnet, *History,* iii:185–186.

13. *A Proclamation of the Kings Majesties most Gracious and General Pardon* (1685/6, J363); *CSPD, James II, 1686–87,* 71, 138, 303; LSF, Book of Cases, I (1661–1695), pp. 161–180; *HMC, Downshire,* i:139. For the effects of the general pardon on Quakers in prison, see Whitehead, *Christian Progress,* 587–591; *London Gazette,* no. 2245 (23–26 May 1687). For the effects on other denominations, see *The Entring Book of Roger Morrice, 1677–1691,* ed. Mark Goldie, John Spurr, Tim Harris, Stephen Taylor, Mark Knights, and Jason McElligott, 7 vols. (Woodbridge, 2007–9), iii:166; *London Gazette,* no. 2242 (12–16 May 1687), no. 2244 (19–23 May 1687), no. 2263 (25–28 July 1687).

14. Joseph Ivimey, *A History of the English Baptists,* 4 vols. (London, 1811–30), i:464; *Entring Book of Roger Morrice,* iii:194, 325, 344; *CSPD, James II, 1686–87,* 72, 268–272, 323, 388; Andrew Clark, ed., *The Life and Times of Anthony Wood,* 5 vols. (Oxford, 1891–1900), iii:190.

15. NLW, Ottley correspondence no. 1467.

16. BL, Add. MS 52279 (journals of Sir William Trumbull, 1685–1692), fol. 10v. For other statements by James disapproving of Louis's treatment of the Huguenots, see BL, Add. MS 34512, fol. 48, Aernout van Citters to States General, 30 July/9 Aug. 1686; BL, Add. MS 34502, fol. 61, Don Pedro Ronquillo to Francisco Bernardo de Quixos, 5 April 1686, fol. 77v, Ronquillo to King Charles II of Spain, 12 Aug. 1686.

17. NUL, PwV 53/33, William Blathwayt to Sir Robert Southwell, 7 May 1686; TNA, PRO 31/3/166, fol. 5, Barrillon to Louis XIV, 3/13 May 1686.

18. On this question, compare Robin D. Gwynn, "James II in the Light of his Treatment of Huguenot Refugees in England, 1685–1686," *EHR,* xcii (1977), 826–829, with John Miller, "The Immediate Impact of the Revocation in England," in C. E. J. Caldicott, Hugh Gough, and Jean-Paul Pittion, eds., *The Huguenots and Ireland: Anatomy of an Emigration* (Dun Laoghaire, 1987), 162–168.

19. J. R. Western, *Monarchy and Revolution: The English State in the 1680s* (London, 1972), 223; J. P. Kenyon, *Robert Spencer, Earl of Sunderland, 1641–1702* (London, 1958), 188; John Miller, *Cities Divided: Politics and Religion in English Provincial Towns, 1660–1722* (Oxford, 2007), 230; for other statements in this disparaging vein, see Macaulay, *History of England,* ii:872, 883; F. C. Turner, *James II* (London, 1948), 330; Roger Thomas, "The Seven Bishops and their Petition, 18 May 1688," *JEH,* xii (1961), 57–58; George Hilton Jones, *Convergent Forces:*

Immediate Causes of the Revolution of 1688 in England (Ames, IA, 1990), 65. For uses of the term "whig collaborators," see J. R. Jones, "James II's Whig Collaborators," *HJ*, iii (1960), 68–71; J. R. Jones, *The Revolution of 1688 in England* (London, 1972), 41; David H. Hosford, *Nottingham, Nobles, and the North: Aspects of the Revolution of 1688* (Hamden, CT, 1976), 76, 143; Lois G. Schwoerer, *The Declaration of Rights, 1689* (Baltimore, 1981), 41; W. A. Speck, *Reluctant Revolutionaries: Englishmen and the Revolution of 1688* (Oxford, 1988), 66, 169, 175, 184; Robert Beddard, "The Unexpected Whig Revolution of 1688," in Robert Beddard, ed., *The Revolutions of 1688* (Oxford, 1991), 20; Tim Harris, *Politics Under the Later Stuarts: Party Conflict in a Divided Society, 1660–1715* (London, 1993), 126, 214.

20. Basil Duke Henning, ed., *The House of Commons, 1660–1690*, 3 vols. (London, 1983), i:558, 585, 612–613, 616, 619, 633, 670, 676, 704, 709; ii:3, 120, 165–166, 194, 207–208, 247, 263–264, 286, 291–292, 303, 338, 384, 387, 401, 422, 440, 450, 464, 503, 524, 526, 537, 551–2, 577, 582, 612, 616, 655, 674, 697, 712, 718, 731, 738; iii:1, 4, 88, 193, 374, 439, 464, 490, 513, 555, 620, 622, 637, 639, 706, 748, 751, 754, 768, 775, 789, 792.

21. Mark Goldie, "John Locke's Circle and James II," *HJ*, xxxv (1992), 559; Mark Goldie, "James II and the Dissenters' Revenge: The Commission of Enquiry of 1688," *Historical Research*, lxvi (1993), 54–55; see also Eveline Cruickshanks's anticipation of Goldie's skepticism in her "Religion and Royal Succession: The Rage of Party," in Clyve Jones, ed., *Britain in the First Age of Party, 1680–1750* (London, 1987), 23.

22. W. A. Speck, "1688: A Political Revolution," in David Parker, ed., *Revolutions and the Revolutionary Tradition in the West, 1560–1991* (London, 2000), 61.

23. See, for instance, Perry Gauci, *Politics and Society in Great Yarmouth, 1660–1722* (Oxford, 1996), 167, note 44; Paul D. Halliday, *Dismembering the Body Politic: Partisan Politics in England's Towns, 1650–1730* (Cambridge, 1998), 245; Paul Kléber Monod, *The Murder of Mr. Grebell: Madness and Civility in an English Town* (New Haven, 2003), 127. The most recent volumes in the History of Parliament series employ the term "whig collaborator" frequently, sometimes with quotation marks and other times without. See Eveline Cruickshanks, Stuart Handley, and D. W. Hayton, *The House of Commons, 1690–1715*, 5 vols. (London, 2002), ii:465; iii:171, 700, 755, 1008; iv:22, 431, 590; v:532, 628, 717, 731, 956, 961.

24. On the collective identity typically forged by participants in social movements, see Bert Klandermans, *The Social Psychology of Protest* (Oxford, 1997), 17–18, 121, 154, 204–208.

25. The quotation is from William Penn and the slogan appears to have been his invention, although others subsequently adopted it. See [William Penn], *The Great and Popular Objection against the Repeal of the Penal Laws & Tests Briefly Stated and Consider'd* (1688, P1298A), 6, 8, 10, 22; Scott Sowerby, "Of Different Complexions: Religious Diversity and National Identity in James II's Toleration Campaign," *English Historical Review*, cxxiv (2009), 39–43, 48–49.

26. *Publick Occurrences,* no. 21 (10 July 1688), no. 12 (8 May 1688).

27. [Thomas Brown], *Heraclitus Ridens Redivivus* (n.p., [1688], B5059), 4. Brown published his pamphlet at some point between the end of March and the end of June 1688; see the reference in BL, Add. MS 36707, fol. 36v, letter to James Harrington, 21 June 1688. The pamphlet went through two more editions later that year (B5060, B5060A). The 1687 usage of the word "repealer" by the marquess of Halifax was added to the online edition of the *Oxford English Dictionary* in 2009.

28. [Halifax], *Letter to a Dissenter,* 4.

29. [Samuel Johnson], *A Letter from a Freeholder* ([1688], J834), 1. The contents of this tract indicate a publication date of June to September 1688, with the latter date more likely.

30. *HMC, Portland,* iii:406. See also John Tutchin's use of the word "Repealers" on line 175 of his *An Heroick Poem upon the Late Expedition of His Majesty* (1689, T3377), 9.

31. [Brown], *Heraclitus,* 4.

32. This question echoed the second of the "Three Questions" in James II's political survey of the English gentry, which is explored in Chapter 4.

33. [Brown], *Heraclitus,* 4.

34. Statutes 25 Car. II. c. 2; 30 Car. II. stat. 2, c. 1; 1 Eliz. c. 2; 23 Eliz. c. 1; 3 Jac. I. c. 4; 22 Car. II. c. 1. For a summary of the various Tudor and Stuart statutes penalizing nonconformity, see [Henry Care], *Draconica: or, an Abstract of all the Penal-Laws Touching Matters of Religion* (1687, C510).

35. FSL, V.a.469 (memoirs of William Westby), fol. 12, entry for 9 Feb. 1688.

36. Edmund Calamy, *Memoirs of the Life of the Late Rev[eren]d Mr John Howe* (London, 1724), 135; Macaulay, *History of England,* ii:883, 944; William C. Braithwaite, *The Second Period of Quakerism* (London, 1919), 142–145; George Macaulay Trevelyan, *The English Revolution, 1688–1689* (London, 1938), 75; Douglas R. Lacey, *Dissent and Parliamentary Politics in England, 1661–1689* (New Brunswick, N.J., 1969), 182, 203, 215; Pincus, *1688,* 204. See also Gordon J. Schochet, "The Act of Toleration and the Failure of Comprehension: Persecution, Nonconformity, and Religious Indifference," in Dale Hoak and Mordechai Feingold, eds., *The World of William and Mary* (Stanford, 1996), 178–179, where Henry Care is labeled a "pro-Catholic apologist."

37. Macaulay, *History of England,* ii:871–874; Thomas, "Seven Bishops," 57–58, 62; Lacey, *Dissent,* 180–182, 211–212; R. A. Beddard, "Vincent Alsop and the Emancipation of Restoration Dissent," *JEH,* xxiv (1973), 173–181; Speck, *Reluctant Revolutionaries,* 183; Mark Knights, "'Meer Religion' and the 'Church-State' of Restoration England: The Impact and Ideology of James II's Declarations of Indulgence," in Alan Houston and Steve Pincus, eds., *A Nation Transformed: England after the Restoration* (Cambridge, 2001), 54–56; Miller, *Cities Divided,* 229–231; Pincus, *1688,* 199–209.

38. Mark Knights, *Representation and Misrepresentation in Later Stuart Britain: Partisanship and Political Culture* (Oxford, 2005), 114–119. For copies of the addresses, see the *London Gazette* for 1687 and 1688. The originals have not survived and in most cases the number of signatories is not known. The occasional signed drafts and contemporary reports that survive suggest that the number of signatories varied widely, from twenty-nine in one case to over a thousand in another: see E. S. de Beer, ed., *The Diary of John Evelyn*, 6 vols. (Oxford, 1955), iv:553–554; *Entring Book of Roger Morrice*, iv:42, 44; G.D.L., "MSS. Written or Possessed by Ralph Thoresby, F.R.S.," *Publications of the Thoresby Society*, xxviii (1923–7), 442–443; LLIU, Albeville MSS, Robert Yard to marquis d'Albeville, 29 April 1687.

39. This charge was raised in [Halifax], *Letter to a Dissenter*, 3–4, and subsequently elaborated by historians including Lacey, *Dissent*, 180–181, 341; David Norman Marshall, "Protestant Dissent in England in the Reign of James II," (Ph.D. thesis, Univ. of Hull, 1976), 312–325, 339; Miller, *James II*, 172; S. H. Mayor, "James II and the Dissenters," *Baptist Quarterly*, xxxiv (1991), 184–185; B. R. White, "The Twilight of Puritanism in the Years Before and After 1688," in Grell et al., eds., *Persecution to Toleration*, 312; and Harris, *Revolution*, 216, 219–220, 223, 230, 263–264.

40. Address from bishop and clergy of Durham, in *London Gazette*, no. 2243 (16–19 May 1687); from bishop and clergy of Chester, in idem, no. 2246 (26–30 May 1687); from bishop and clergy of Lincoln, in idem, no. 2256 (30 June–4 July 1687); from dean and chapter of Ripon, in idem, no. 2257 (4–7 July 1687); from bishop and clergy of Coventry and Lichfield, in idem, no. 2258 (7–11 July 1687); from bishop and clergy of St David's, in idem, no. 2283 (3–6 Oct. 1687); LLIU, Albeville MSS, Robert Yard to marquis d'Albeville, 29 April 1687, same to same, 20 May 1687; *The Diary of Dr. Thomas Cartwright, Bishop of Chester*, Camden Society, old series, xxii (1843), 47–48, 51; *Entring Book of Roger Morrice*, iv:31–32, 42, 49–50, 62–63, 84–85; *A Copy of an Address to the King by the Bishop of Oxon* (n.p., 1687, C6191A); [Thomas Cartwright], *A Modest Censure of the Immodest Letter to a Dissenter* (1687, N76), 13; Andrew Clark, ed., *The Life and Times of Anthony Wood*, 5 vols. (Oxford, 1891–1900), iii:220; William Durrant Cooper, ed., "Trelawny Papers," in *The Camden Miscellany, Volume the Second*, Camden Society, old series, lv (1853), 17–20; Charles Whiting, ed., *The Autobiographies and Letters of Thomas Comber*, 2 vols. (Durham, 1946–47), i:18.

41. R.B. Wordsworth, ed., *The Cockermouth Congregational Church Book (1651–c.1765)*, Cumberland and Westmorland Antiquarian and Archaeological Society, record series, no. xxi (Kendal, 2012), 93; *London Gazette*, no. 2270 (18–22 Aug. 1687). For a similar case regarding the address presented by the Congregationalists of Great Yarmouth, see Norfolk RO, FC 31/1, Independent Church Book of Yarmouth, 1642–1855, p. 76, entries for 20 May and 6 June 1687.

42. See, for instance, Nottinghamshire Archives, Charles Harvey's

Mayoralty Papers, M8657/1, "An Account of the charges I was at when I went to London with the Address to the King," 1688.

43. Suffolk RO, Bury St Edmunds, E2/41/5, fol. 37r–v, Lord Dover to John Stafford, 22 March 1688. The letter was indeed sent, and the king was reported to have been "much satisfied" with it: see Suffolk RO, Bury St Edmunds, E2/41/5, fol. 48, letter by Lord Dover, 26 June 1688.

44. F. C. Brown, *Elkanah Settle: His Life and Works* (Chicago, 1910), 26; Bodl., MS Eng. lett. c.54, fol. 97, Philip Madoxe to Sir Robert Southwell, 28 Aug. 1688. On Care's religion, see Lois G. Schwoerer, *The Ingenious Mr. Henry Care, Restoration Publicist* (Baltimore, 2001), 23; Tim Harris, *London Crowds in the Reign of Charles II: Propaganda and Politics from the Restoration until the Exclusion Crisis* (Cambridge, 1987), 120; on the networks of correspondents used by Care, see *Publick Occurrences*, no. 7 (3 April 1688).

45. See the contemporary marginal notation inscribed in Bodl., Nichols Newspapers, *Publick Occurrences*, no. 12 (8 May 1688). Care was aware that the length of his editorials tried the patience of some of his readers: see *Publick Occurrences*, no. 4 (13 March 1688), no. 5 (20 March 1688), and no. 8 (10 April 1688). Sir Daniel Fleming subscribed to the paper at the rate of three pence per issue but cancelled his subscription because he met not "with much Newes" in it: see CAC (K), Fleming MSS, WD/Ry HMC no. 3183a, draft letters by Sir Daniel Fleming, 24 March and 12 May 1688.

46. *Publick Occurrences*, no. 11 (1 May 1688); see also no. 6 (27 March 1688) and no. 7 (3 April 1688).

47. *Publick Occurrences*, no. 5 (20 March 1688), no. 22 (17 July 1688).

48. For copies of the *The Weekly Test-Paper*, the first issue of which was called only *The Test-Paper*, see Bodl., Nichols Newspapers 7, nos. 69, 74, 79, 85. The paper was published anonymously, but circumstantial evidence suggests that Nicholets was its author. An advertisement for the serial appeared at the end of Nicholets's pro-repeal tract *A Third Dialogue between Simeon and Levi, About Abolishing the Penal Laws and Tests* (1688, T906), 7. Both *The Weekly Test-Paper* and Nicholets's *Third Dialogue* employed the unusual word "test-monger" to describe those who supported the retention of the Test Acts.

49. This tally does not include James II's own declarations on toleration, nor does it include the two repealer serials, *Publick Occurrences* and *The Weekly Test-Paper*. For all eighty titles, see Appendix.

50. For the political and religious orientations of these publishers, see Henry R. Plomer, *A Dictionary of the Printers and Booksellers who were at Work in England, Scotland and Ireland from 1668 to 1725* (Oxford, 1922), 170, 183–184, 273–274, 287; T. J. Crist, "Francis Smith and the Opposition Press in England, 1660–88" (Ph.D. thesis, Univ. of Cambridge, 1977), ix, xi, 114, 168, 224–228, 270, 314–315, 321, 336–347; Goldie, "John Locke's Circle," 583; Richard Greaves and Robert Zaller, eds., *Biographical Dictionary of British Radicals in the Seventeenth Century*, 3 vols.

(Brighton, 1982–84), s.v. Henry Hills, Francis Smith, Andrew Sowle; Gerard Maria Peerbooms, *Nathaniel Thompson: Tory Printer, Ballad Monger and Propagandist* (Nijmegen, 1983), 42–44, 56, 109; Richard L. Greaves, *British Radicals from the Popish Plot to the Revolution of 1688–1689* (Stanford, 1992), 40–48.

51. For further information on these men, see Chapter 5, page 136.

52. Sir George Duckett, ed., *Penal Laws and Test Act: Questions Touching their Repeal Propounded in 1687–8 by James II*, 2 vols. (London, 1882–83), i:196.

53. John Yonge Akerman, ed., *Moneys Received and Paid for Secret Services of Charles II and James II*, Camden Society, old series, lii (1851), 196–197; NUL, PwA 2162/1, James Rivers to [Hans Willem Bentinck], 23 May 1688. For the prices of pamphlets in 1688, see Stephen Parks, *The Luttrell File: Narcissus Luttrell's Dates On Contemporary Pamphlets 1678–1730* (New Haven, 1999), passim.

54. WYAS, WYL156/48/35, Nathaniel Johnston to Sir John Reresby, 7 April 1687; idem, WYL156/48/25, same to same, 23 June 1687; Nathaniel Johnston, *The Assurance of Abby and other Church-Lands* (1687, J872).

55. Akerman, ed., *Secret Services*, 213; see also Crist, "Francis Smith," 346–348.

56. See [Henry Care], *A Vindication of the Proceedings of His Majesties Ecclesiastical Commissioners* (1688, C536), which was printed by Milbourne and published by Janeway.

57. Brotherton Library, Leeds University MSS, Deposit 1981/2 Clifford Street, Shelf II, No. 2 (Yorkshire Quarterly Meeting Minute Book, 1681–98), fols. 61b, 62v, 63v; LSF, Meeting for Sufferings Minutes, vol. 6, pp. 148, 198; *Vox Cleri pro Rege: Or the Rights of the Imperial Soveraignty of the Crown of England Vindicated* (n.p., 1688, V715); N. N., *Old Popery as Good as New: Or the Unreasonableness of the Church of England* (n.p., 1688, N47); J. S. T. Hetet, "A Literary Underground in Restoration England: Printers and Dissenters in the Context of Constraints 1660–1689" (Ph.D. thesis, Univ. of Cambridge, 1987), 142–143, 151–152.

58. *A Letter from a Clergy-man in the City* (n.p., 1688, H308), 8; *Publick Occurrences*, no. 18 (19 June 1688). For a similar charge against Care, see [Brown], *Heraclitus*, 4.

59. Akerman, ed., *Secret Services*, 199.

60. For details of these translations, see W. P. C. Knuttel, ed., *Catalogus van de Pamfletten-Verzameling Berustende in de Koninklijke Bibliotheek*, 11 vols. (The Hague, 1889–1920). For Dutch versions of repeal pamphlets, see Knuttel nos. 12585, 12913, 12936, 12927, 12887, 12900, 12910, 12932 and 12947 (translations of the repeal pamphlets P1296, P1298A, K592, W3223, N1302, S5534, C510, P3039 and N783). For French versions of repeal pamphlets, see Knuttel nos. 12888, 12899, 12937 and 12948 (translations of the repeal pamphlets N1302, S5534, K592 and N783). For contemporary references to these translations, see BL, Add. MS 38493, fol. 124, Moreau to king of Poland, 5/15 July 1687, fol. 131v, same to same, 26 July/5 Aug. 1687; BL, Add. MS 41815, fol. 237, Daniel Petit to earl of Middleton, 23 April 1688.

61. Keith L. Sprunger, *Trumpets from the Tower: English Puritan Printing in the Netherlands, 1600–1640* (Leiden, 1994), 92; Emma Bergin, "Defending the True Faith: Religious Themes in Dutch Pamphlets on England, 1688–1689," in David Onnekink, ed., *War and Religion after Westphalia, 1648–1713* (Farnham, 2009), 225.

62. William Penn, *England's Present Interest Discover'd* (n.p., 1675, P1280), 39.

63. Ibid., 40–44, 46–47; [William Penn], *The Great Question to be Considered by the King, and this Approaching Parliament* (n.p., 1679, P1300), 6; idem., *A Perswasive to Moderation to Dissenting Christians* (1685, P1337A), 25–26, 30, 33–34. Penn repeated this argument in his *Advice to Freeholders and Other Electors of Members to Serve in Parliament* (1687, P1250), 4–5, and his *Third Letter from a Gentleman in the Country* (1687, P1381), 6.

64. Penn, *England's Present Interest*, 37, 45, 61; idem., *Perswasive to Moderation*, 20–21; idem., *The Great Case of Liberty of Conscience* (n.p., 1670, P1299), 29.

65. [Penn], *Great Question to be Considered*, 8; see also his *Great Case of Liberty*, 21.

66. [William Penn], *Good Advice to the Church of England, Roman Catholick, and Protestant Dissenter* (1687, P1296), 45; idem., *The Great and Popular Objection against the Repeal of the Penal Laws & Tests Briefly Stated and Consider'd* (1688, P1298A), 6, 8, 10, 22. For attribution of these pamphlets to Penn, see FSL, Newdigate newsletters, L.c.1834, 23 July 1687; Mary Maples Dunn and Richard S. Dunn, eds., *The Papers of William Penn*, 5 vols. (Philadelphia, 1981–86), v:347–348, 353–355.

67. Marquis of Lansdowne, ed., *The Petty-Southwell Correspondence, 1676–1687* (London, 1928), 279; John Whiting, *Persecution Expos'd, in some Memoirs Relating to the Sufferings of John Whiting* (London, 1715), 172; Gilbert Cope, "Letter from William Hitchcock to John and Amy Harding, 1687," *JFHS*, iv (1907), 73; John Latimer, *The Annals of Bristol in the Eighteenth Century* (Frome, 1893), 6, 194.

68. Penn also spoke in Bath, Chew Magna, Newbury, Reading, and Windsor. See *HMC, Portland,* iii:403; LSF, A. R. Barclay MSS, no. cxi, Robert Sandilands to John Field, 22 June 1687; Whiting, *Persecution Expos'd,* 172–173; Cope, "William Hitchcock," 73, 75; Longleat House, Thynne MSS, xv, fol. 194, Sir Robert Southwell to Lord Weymouth, 28 July 1687.

69. Shropshire Archives, Leighton MSS, 180/1; *HMC, Westmorland etc.,* 376; Dunn and Dunn, eds., *Papers of William Penn,* iii:163; Liverpool RO, 920 MD 173 (diary of Sir Willoughby Aston), entry for 28 Aug. 1687; CPA, vol. 162, fols. 169v–170, Barrillon to Louis XIV, 10/20 Sept. 1687; LSF, Temp MSS, 285, no. xlii (notebook of Robert Barclay), p. 42; *Diary of Thomas Cartwright,* 74; "The Theatre in Foregate Street, Chester," *Cheshire Sheaf,* III, xliv (1949), 43.

70. Liverpool RO, 920 MD 173 (diary of Sir Willoughby Aston), unpaginated, entry for 27 Aug. 1687. This speech has not previously been cited or

mentioned in any published discussion of James II's reign, with the exception of an article by the current author. For a full account of the speech, see Sowerby, "Of Different Complexions," 29–52.

71. Sir William Temple, *Observations upon the United Provinces of the Netherlands* (1673, T656), 168; John Locke, *A Letter Concerning Toleration* (1689, L2747), 50–51; for other analogies of this sort, see *London Gazette*, no. 2294 (10–14 Nov. 1687); *An Expedient for Peace: Perswading an Agreement amongst Christians* (1688, E3872aA), 9; Daniel Kenrick, *A Sermon Preached in the Cathedral-Church of Worcester* (1688, K307), 11.

72. Isaiah Berlin, *Two Concepts of Liberty* (Oxford, 1958), 6–7.

73. For the eleven recorded uses of this phrase by the king, see Longleat House, Thynne MSS, xv, fol. 199, Sir Robert Southwell to Lord Weymouth, 29 Aug. 1687; Cheshire RO, D/MH/1 (Matthew Henry's Chapel Book, 1687–1923), fol. 7v; WYAS, WYL156/51/50, Leonard Wilson to Sir John Reresby, 7 Jan. 1688; BL, Add. MS 72596, fol. 6, newsletter of Oct. 1687; *Entring Book of Roger Morrice*, iv:185; Matthew Henry, *The Life of the Rev. Philip Henry*, ed. J. B. Williams (London, 1825), 181; Whitehead, *Christian Progress*, 620; M. G. Hall, ed., "The Autobiography of Increase Mather," *Proceedings of the American Antiquarian Society*, lxxi (1961), 325; Burnet, *History of His Own Time*, iii:162, 190; *The Humble Address of the Presbyterians* (n.p., 1687, A2912), 8; FSL, Newdigate newsletters, L.c.1803, 28 April 1687. For the dates of the addresses to which the king was responding in the last two instances, see *London Gazette*, no. 2238 (28 April–2 May 1687), no. 2248 (2–6 June 1687); *Entring Book of Roger Morrice*, iv:39.

74. [William Penn], *A Second Letter from a Gentleman in the Country* (1687, P1361), 18, dated 11 April 1687 on title page; for the attribution to Penn, see Longleat House, Thynne MSS, xv, fol. 180, Sir Robert Southwell to Lord Weymouth, 8 May 1687; Dunn and Dunn, eds., *Papers of William Penn*, v:337.

75. Gerard Croese, *The General History of the Quakers* (1696, C6965), book 2, p. 106. For Penn's presence at court at about this time, see LSF, A. R. Barclay MSS, no. 111, Robert Sandilands to John Field, 22 June 1687; *Entring Book of Roger Morrice*, iv: 73. For the earlier development of Penn's friendship with James, see Penn, "Fragments of an Apology," 241–242.

76. See *London Gazette*, nos. 2288 (20–24 Oct. 1687), 2295 (14–17 Nov. 1687), 2325 (27 Feb.–1 March 1688), 2327 (5–8 March 1688), 2329 (12–15 March 1688), 2351 (28–31 May 1688); BL, Add. MS 70014, fol. 41v, [Robert Harley] to Sir Edward Harley, 26 Sept. 1687. For critiques of Penn's proposal, see *Some Queries Concerning Liberty of Conscience, Directed to William Penn and Henry Care* (n.p., [1688], S4559), 1, 3–4; [Thomas Comber], *Three Considerations Proposed to Mr. William Pen[n], Concerning the Validity and Security of his New Magna Charta for Liberty of Conscience* (n.p., [1688], C5496), 1–2; [Gilbert Burnet], *An Apology for the Church of England* (n.p., [1688], B5762), 8.

77. [Giles Shute], *A New Test in Lieu of the Old One* (1688, S3710), 1, 10; for similar proposals, see [William Penn], *A Letter form [sic] a Gentleman in the*

Country (n.p., 1687, P1318), 11; [anon.], *Som[e] Free Reflections upon Occasion of the Public Discourse about Liberty of Conscience* (1687, P1366), 14; BL, Add. MS 72888, fol. 110v. For complaints about the "new test" as a form of reverse discrimination, see *A Letter to a Dissenter from his Friend at The Hague* (The Hague, 1688, L1633), 3; *Ten Seasonable Queries, Proposed by a Protestant* (n.p., [1688], T674); [Brown], *Heraclitus*, 5; CAC (C), D/Lons/L2/5, Sir John Lowther, "1688 Journal," p. 58.

78. [Henry Care], *Animadversions on a Late Paper, Entituled, A Letter to a Dissenter* (1687, C505), 17, 37; for Care's authorship of this pamphlet, see FSL, Newdigate newsletters, L.c.1862, 27 Sept. 1687. William Penn made a similar argument in his *Third Letter from a Gentleman,* 18–19, as did William Popple in his *Three Letters Tending to Demonstrate* (1688, P1383), 15–16. For Popple's authorship of this last pamphlet, see Caroline Robbins, "Absolute Liberty: The Life and Thought of William Popple, 1638–1708," *William and Mary Quarterly,* III, xxiv (1967), 190 n. 1.

79. Macaulay, *History of England,* ii:664–675, 871–874; Trevelyan, *Revolution,* 56–65, 76–81; Harris, *Revolution,* 187–195, 217, 235–236; Pincus, *1688,* 143–178.

80. Kenyon, *Sunderland,* 146; see also Hallam, *Constitutional History,* ii:396–398; Trevelyan, *Revolution,* 58; David Ogg, *England in the Reigns of James II and William III* (Oxford, 1955), 182; Pincus, *1688,* 172–173.

81. Samuel Weller Singer, ed., *The Correspondence of Henry Hyde, Earl of Clarendon,* 2 vols. (London, 1828), ii:117; Grant Tapsell, "Laurence Hyde and the Politics of Religion in Later Stuart England," *English Historical Review,* cxxv (2010), 1433–1437. James later attempted to excuse these actions while in exile by claiming that he had merely wished to remove the treasureship from one person and put it in the hands of a commission: see Clarke, ed., *Life of James,* ii:101.

82. John Childs, *The Army, James II, and the Glorious Revolution* (Manchester, 1980), 22; Leo Gooch, "Catholic Officers in the Navy of James II," *Recusant History,* xiv (1978), 276–280; Andrew Barclay, "James II's 'Catholic' Court," *1650–1850: Ideas, Aesthetics, and Inquiries in the Early Modern Era,* viii (2003), 163; Miller, *Popery and Politics,* 219.

83. Miller, *Popery and Politics,* 272, 220.

84. Kenyon, *Sunderland,* 146; Miller, *Popery and Politics,* 220–221; Pincus, *1688,* 173.

85. Lancashire RO, DDBL acc. 6121, "Letters, 1672–1693," unfoliated, of which see especially William Blundell to John Warner, 2 May 1687, Blundell to John Gellibrond, 28 May 1687, Blundell to John Warner, 11 Aug. 1687, Blundell to Sir Nicholas Butler, Sept. 1687; Geoff Baker, *Reading and Politics in Early Modern England: The Mental World of a Seventeenth-Century Catholic Gentleman* (Manchester, 2010), 38, 81; BL, Add. MS 47840, fol. 60, A. B. to Francis Radcliffe, 3 Aug. 1688; Charles Dalton, ed., *English Army Lists,* 6 vols. (London, 1892–1904), ii:185.

86. Georgetown University Library, Milton House archives, Belson family papers, box 3, folder 9. The manuscript complaint is located among the papers of John Belson, a Catholic who was active at James's court, but is not in his hand. The complaint refers to the *Pastoral Letter from the Four Catholic Bishops to the Lay-Catholics of England* (1688, P675), which appeared in June 1688, and thus can be dated to the period from June to October of that year. For the dating of the pastoral letter, see BL, Sloane MS 3929, fol. 64, newsletter dated 16 June 1688.

87. *Pastoral Letter from the Four Catholic Bishops*, 7.

88. Lancashire RO, DDBL Acc 6121, "Letters, 1672–1693," unfoliated, William Blundell to John Gellibrond, 9 July 1687; for the use of deputies in the customs administration, see TNA, T1/4, fol. 204, "A sixth proposall for improving [the customs]," 16 Aug. 1689.

89. BL, Add. MS 47840, fol. 60, A. B. to Francis Radcliffe, 3 Aug. 1688.

90. George Agar Ellis, ed., *The Ellis Correspondence*, 2 vols. (London, 1829), i:240; FSL, Newdigate newsletters, L.c.1766, 27 Jan. 1687.

91. Clarke, ed., *Life of James*, ii:641–642; Edward Corp, "James II's Reflections on Kingship 'For my Son, the Prince of Wales,'" *1650–1850: Ideas, Aesthetics, and Inquiries in the Early Modern Era*, viii (2003), 201–210. The commissioners of the treasury were Lord Belasyse, Lord Dover, Lord Godolphin, Sir John Ernle, and Sir Stephen Fox.

92. Bodl., MS Carte 110, fol. 54; Anne Whiteman, ed., *The Compton Census of 1676: A Critical Edition* (London, 1986), lxxxi; Peter Laslett, ed., "17th century MS. Book of Gregory King," in *The Earliest Classics* (Farnborough, 1973), 11; on James II's perceptions of the religious makeup of the English population, see TNA, PRO 31/3/168, fol. 50, Barrillon to Louis XIV, 7/17 March 1687; James Macpherson, *Original Papers; Containing the Secret History of Great Britain*, 2nd edn., 2 vols. (London, 1775–76), i:409. Modern research suggests that the Compton census undercounted nonconformists of all kinds and that the actual proportion of Catholics in England was more like one percent: see Michael R. Watts, *The Dissenters: From the Reformation to the French Revolution* (Oxford, 1978), 270, 491–492, 509; Miller, *Popery and Politics*, 9–12.

93. Clarke, ed., *Life of James*, i:499–500; *CJ*, ix:756; *By the King, A Proclamation* (Edinburgh, 1687, J249).

94. Childs, *Army*, 1–5; *CJ*, ix:756.

95. For exact figures, see C. D. Chandaman, *The English Public Revenue, 1660–1688* (Oxford, 1975), 260, 333, 363; see also the report of Sir Robert Howard in *CJ*, x:55; the accounts for 1685–88 found in HEHL, Ellesmere MS 8583 and in BL, Add. MS 20721, fols. 1v–2r; and the accounts for 1686–87 found in Brotherton Library, University of Leeds, MS 613/8.

96. Chandaman, *English Public Revenue*, 255, 260–261, 338; J. Keith Horsefield, "The 'Stop of the Exchequer' Revisited," *EcHistR*, n.s., xxxv (1982), 515, 517, 523; Statute 12 & 13 Wm. III, c. 12, s. 24; Clayton Roberts, "The Constitu-

tional Significance of the Financial Settlement of 1690," *HJ*, xx (1977), 65; *CTB*, viii:929–930; H. W. Chisholm, ed., Parliamentary Papers, 1868–9, vol. 35, *Public Income and Expenditure*, appendix 1, p. 445; G. E. Aylmer, *The Crown's Servants: Government and Civil Service under Charles II, 1660–1685* (Oxford, 2002), 104–106; R. O. Bucholz, *The Augustan Court: Queen Anne and the Decline of Court Culture* (Stanford, 1993), 22–23, 52.

97. On the Dutch case see Wantje Fritschy, "Taxation in Britain, France and the Netherlands in the Eighteenth Century," *Economic and Social History in the Netherlands*, ii (1990), 64; Wantje Fritschy, Marjolein 't Hart, and Edwin Horlings, "Long-Term Trends in the Fiscal History of the Netherlands, 1515–1913," in Bartolomé Yun-Casalilla and Patrick K. O'Brien, eds., *The Rise of Fiscal States: A Global History, 1500–1914* (Cambridge, 2012), 55. On the English case my figures are similar to Patrick K. O'Brien's: see O'Brien, "The Political Economy of British Taxation, 1660–1815," *EcHistR*, II, xli (1988), 3; idem, "Inseparable Connections: Trade, Economy, Fiscal State, and the Expansion of Empire, 1688–1815," in P. J. Marshall, ed., *The Oxford History of the British Empire*, 5 vols. (Oxford, 1998), ii:64.

98. Frank C. Spooner, *The International Economy and Monetary Movements in France, 1493–1725* (Cambridge, MA, 1972), 315; see also Françoise Bayard, *Le Monde des Financiers au XVIIe Siècle* ([Paris], 1988), 30.

99. Alain Guéry, "Les Finances de la Monarchie Française sous l'Ancien Régime," *Annales*, xxxiii (1978), 237; Philip T. Hoffman, "Taxes and Agrarian Life in Early Modern France: Land Sales, 1550–1730," *Journal of Economic History*, xlvi (1986), 46; Margaret Bonney and Richard Bonney, *Jean-Roland Malet: Premier Historien des Finances de la Monarchie Française* (Paris, 1993), 96; Richard Bonney, "Towards the Comparative Fiscal History of Britain and France during the 'Long' Eighteenth Century," in Leandro Prados de la Escosura, ed., *Exceptionalism and Industrialisation: Britain and Its European Rivals, 1688–1815* (Cambridge, 2004), 192–194; Spooner, *Monetary Movements in France*, 306, 310–315.

100. For the argument that James was seeking to imitate in England the methods of rule employed in France, see Pincus, *1688*, 121–122, 143–162.

101. BL, Add. MS 72866, fols. 19, 53, 134; Lansdowne, ed., *Petty-Southwell Correspondence*, 234.

102. B. R. Mitchell and Phyllis Deane, *Abstract of British Historical Statistics* (Cambridge, 1962), 401; D. W. Jones, *War and Economy in the Age of William III and Marlborough* (Oxford, 1988), 70–1; Clarke, ed., *Life of James*, ii:633; see also Miller, *James II*, 121.

103. CPA, vol. 163, fol. 147v, Usson de Bonrepaus to the marquis de Seignelay, 25 Aug./4 Sept. 1687. The original French reads: "s'y retirer et y estre en seurté en cas de quelque guerre civile dans son Royaume."

104. WYAS, WYL156/48/25, Nathaniel Johnston to Sir John Reresby, 23 June 1687.

2. Writing a New Magna Carta

1. [John Locke], *Epistola de Tolerantia* (Gouda, 1689); idem, *A Letter Concerning Toleration*, [trans. William Popple] (1689, L2747); E. S. de Beer, ed., *The Correspondence of John Locke*, 8 vols. (Oxford, 1976–89), iii:583–584, 607, 633–634, viii:426; Anchitell Grey, *Debates of the House of Commons, from the Year 1667 to the Year 1694*, 10 vols. (London, 1763), ix:258–262; *CJ*, x:151. Locke's earlier *Essay Concerning Toleration* was not published during his lifetime.

2. Histories of toleration and tolerance in England often refer to William Penn, but the other authors who advocated repeal in 1687–1688 are less often discussed. For references to Penn, see John Coffey, *Persecution and Toleration in Protestant England, 1558–1689* (Harlow, 2000), 171, 178, 190; Perez Zagorin, *How the Idea of Religious Toleration Came to the West* (Princeton, 2003), 251; and Alexandra Walsham, *Charitable Hatred: Tolerance and Intolerance in England, 1500–1700* (Manchester, 2006), 233, 246–247.

3. Speech by James II to an assembly of lords and privy councillors, reported in BPL, Ms. Am. 1502, vol. 7, no. 49, newsletter dated 23 Oct. 1688.

4. See Giles Shute, *A New Naked Truth* (1688, S3709), 22, 45; [Giles Shute], *A New Test in Lieu of the Old One* (1688, S3710), 22; [John Northleigh], *Parliamentum Pacificum: Or, the Happy Union of King & People in an Healing Parliament* (1688, N1302), 40; Mark Goldie, "The Hilton Gang and the Purge of London in the 1680s," in Howard Nenner, ed., *Politics and the Political Imagination in Later Stuart Britain* (Rochester, 1997), 43–73. For Shute's authorship of *A New Test*, see the advertisement at the end of his *New Naked Truth*.

5. [Henry Care], *Animadversions on a Late Paper, Entituled, A Letter to a Dissenter* (1687, C505), 14–15; [William Dyer], *The Present Interest of England in Matters of Religion* (1688, D99), 14. For the attribution of these two pamphlets see FSL, Newdigate newsletters, L.c.1862, 27 Sept. 1687; *Publick Occurrences*, no. 21 (10 July 1688).

6. For one maneuver designed to undermine these shelters for nonconformity, see Paul D. Halliday, "'A Clashing of Jurisdictions': Commission of Association in Restoration Corporations," *HJ*, xli (1998), 425–455.

7. [William Penn], *A Letter form [sic] a Gentleman in the Country, to his Friends in London* (n.p., 1687, P1318), 3; see also Peter Borsay, *The English Urban Renaissance: Culture and Society in the Provincial Town, 1660–1770* (Oxford, 1989), 16–28, 145–146; Brian Cowan, *The Social Life of Coffee: The Emergence of the British Coffeehouse* (New Haven, 2005), 101–112, 172–175, 194–211.

8. *Animadversions upon Mijn Heer Fagels Letter* (1688, A3204), 4; [Care], *Animadversions on a Late Paper*, 20.

9. For a full listing of the repealer titles, see Appendix.

10. [William Penn], *Good Advice to the Church of England, Roman Catholick, and Protestant Dissenter* (1687, P1296), 57; see also J. A. W. Gunn, *Politics and the Public Interest in the Seventeenth Century* (London, 1969), 158–189.

11. Northleigh, *Parliamentum Pacificum*, 73; [Care], *Animadversions on a Late Paper*, 38; Bodl., MS Tanner 28, fol. 137v; address of Baptists from Kent in *London Gazette*, no. 2252, 16–20 June 1687; see also James II's speech to the Vice-Chancellor and Doctors of Oxford, related in Bodl., MS Rawl. letters 91, fol. 54, H.S. to Thomas Turner, 8 Sept. 1687.

12. *Publick Occurrences*, no. 28 (28 Aug. 1688).

13. [Care], *Animadversions on a Late Paper*, 38; Shute, *New Naked Truth*, 52–53.

14. *An Address to his Grace the Lord Archbishop of Canterbury* (1688, A562), 5; Shute, *New Naked Truth*, 54; Daniel Kenrick, *A Sermon Preached in the Cathedral-Church of Worcester* (1688, K307), 3.

15. [Elkanah Settle?], *An Expedient for Peace* (1688, E3872aA), 33; [William Popple], *Three Letters Tending to Demonstrate* (1688, P1383), 24.

16. *An Expedient for Peace*, 2.

17. [Care], *Animadversions on a Late Paper*, 15.

18. [Stephen Lobb], *A Second Letter to a Dissenter* (1687, L2729A), 12; for the proverb that Lobb was quoting, see J. A. W. Gunn, "'Interest Will Not Lie': A Seventeenth-Century Political Maxim," *Journal of the History of Ideas*, xxix (1968), 551–564.

19. *An Address to his Grace the Lord Archbishop*, 5.

20. [William Penn], *A Third Letter from a Gentleman in the Country* (1687, P1381), 6; see also *Advice to Freeholders and other Electors* (1687, P1250), 4; *Advice to the English Youth* (1688, A655), 4.

21. C.D.W., *A Letter from Holland Touching Liberty of Conscience* (n.p., 1688, W3223), 3.

22. Shute, *New Naked Truth*, 24.

23. *A Friendly Debate upon the Next Elections*, no. 1 (n.p., [1688], F2218A), 3; *The Reasonableness of Toleration, and the Unreasonableness of Penal Laws and Tests* (1687, P1352 or R463aA), 12, 18–19, 32; *A Letter from a Gentleman in the City, to a Clergy-Man in the Country* (1688, L1387), 21; [Henry Care], *An Answer to a Paper Importing a Petition of the Archbishop of Canterbury, and Six other Bishops* (1688, C506), 4, 18; [Henry Care], *The Legality of the Court held by His Majesties Ecclesiastical Commissioners, Defended* (1688, C527), 32; [Care], *Animadversions on a Late Paper*, 3; James Paston, *A Discourse of Penal Laws in Matter of Religion* (1688, P665), 33; Kenrick, *Sermon*, 32.

24. James II, *His Majesties Gracious Declaration to all his Loving Subjects for Liberty of Conscience* (1687, J186), 2.

25. *A Letter from a Gentleman in the City*, 21; Henry Care, *Draconica: Or, An Abstract of all the Penal Laws*, 2nd edn. (1688, C511), 24.

26. E. A. Wrigley and R. S. Schofield, *The Population History of England, 1541–1871* (Cambridge, 1981), 207–210; Daniel Statt, *Foreigners and Englishmen: The Controversy over Immigration and Population, 1660–1760* (Newark, DE, 1995), 22–23, 48–49, 56–58, 66–96.

27. [Dyer], *Present Interest,* 15; C.D.W., *Letter from Holland,* 4; see also Care, *Draconica,* 27.

28. E. H. Phelps Brown and Sheila V. Hopkins, "Seven Centuries of the Prices of Consumables, Compared with Builder's Wage-rates," *Economica,* n.s., xxiii (1956), 299, 313; Elizabeth Boody Schumpeter, "English Prices and Public Finance, 1660–1822," *The Review of Economics and Statistics,* xx (1938), 26, 34; Phyllis Deane and W. A. Cole, *British Economic Growth 1688–1959: Trend and Structure,* 2nd edn. (Cambridge, 1967), 17.

29. W. J. Smith, ed., *Herbert Correspondence* (Cardiff, 1963), 331; Narcissus Luttrell, *A Brief Historical Relation of State Affairs,* 6 vols. (Oxford, 1857), i:416–417; FSL, Newdigate newsletters, L.c.1869, 13 Oct. 1687; NUL, PwV 61/30, J. Povey to Sir Robert Southwell, 13 Oct. 1687; TNA, PRO 30/53/8/55, William Powle to Lord Herbert of Cherbury, 15 Oct. 1687; BL, Add. MS 72596, fol. 6, newsletter of Oct. 1687; J. R. Jones, *The Revolution of 1688 in England,* (London, 1972), 157; see also BL, Add. MS 34510, fol. 113, Aernout van Citters to States General, 20 April 1688; BPL, Ms. Am. 1502, vol. 7, no. 37, newsletter dated 15 Sept. 1688; BL, Sloane MS 3929, fol. 91, newsletter dated 22 Sept. 1688; *Publick Occurrences,* no. 32 (25 Sept. 1688); Beinecke, OSB MSS 1, box 2, folder 68, Owen Wynne to Edmund Poley, 14 Oct. 1687.

30. William E. Buckley, ed., *Memoirs of Thomas, Earl of Ailesbury, Written by Himself,* 2 vols. (Westminster, 1890), i:103; TNA, PC 2/71, fol. 210, entry for 18 March 1687; *London Gazette,* no. 2226 (17–21 March 1687); compare Steve Pincus, *1688: The First Modern Revolution* (New Haven, 2009), 372–381, which claims incorrectly that James was committed to a zero-sum, land-based vision of property and wealth.

31. James II, *His Majesties Gracious Declaration* (1688, J190), 4; see also Bodl., MS Rawl. a.139b, fol. 105; J. S. Clarke, ed., *The Life of James the Second,* 2 vols. (London, 1816), ii:634.

32. *An Answer from the Country, to a Late Letter to a Dissenter* (1687, A3278), 47.

33. Shute, *New Naked Truth,* 24; *The Examination of the Bishops, upon their Refusal of Reading His Majesty's Most Gracious Declaration* (1688, E3725), 21–22; [John Northleigh], *Dr. Burnett's Reflections upon a Book, Entituled, Parliamentum Pacificum: (The First Part) Answered* (1688, N1298), 99; Sir George Duckett, ed., *Penal Laws and Test Act: Questions Touching their Repeal Propounded in 1687–8 by James II,* 2 vols. (London, 1882–83), i:198; see also John Marshall, *John Locke, Toleration and Early Enlightenment Culture* (Cambridge, 2006), 548.

34. C.D.W., *Letter from Holland,* 4; *A Poem Occasioned by His Majesties most Gracious Resolution* (1687, P2678); see also "The Manifestation of Joy," in W. G. Day, ed., *The Pepys Ballads,* 5 vols. (Cambridge, 1987), ii:247.

35. C.D.W., *Letter from Holland,* 2; [Lobb], *Second Letter,* 13; Shute, *New Naked Truth,* 25; on the episode of the textile-working nonconformists who fled England after Monmouth's Rebellion, see Richard Ashcraft, *Revolutionary Poli-*

tics and Locke's Two Treatises of Government (Princeton, 1986), 508–509; Melinda S. Zook, *Radical Whigs and Conspiratorial Politics in Late Stuart England* (University Park, Penn., 1999), 144 n.

36. [Samuel Johnson], *A Letter from a Freeholder* (n.p., [1688], J834), 4–5.

37. *To the King's Most Excellent Majesty, The Humble Address of the Atheists, or the Sect of the Epicureans* (n.p., 1688, T1503).

38. *An Answer from the Country to a Late Letter to a Dissenter* (1687, A3278), 14.

39. *Animadversions upon Mijn Heer Fagels Letter,* 1.

40. *The Good Old Test Reviv'd and Recommended* (1687, G1080), 3.

41. *Some Necessary Disquisitions and Close Expostulations with the Clergy and People of the Church of England* (1688, S4528), preface, sigs. A2v–A3r. This statement anticipated Voltaire's *Letters Concerning the English Nation* of 1733, which hailed the cosmopolitanism of London's Royal Exchange: "There the Presbyterian confides in the Anabaptist, and the Churchman depends on the Quaker's word." See Peter Gay, ed., *The Enlightenment: A Comprehensive Anthology* (New York, 1973), 151; on the cosmopolitanism of the Exchange, see Margaret C. Jacob, *Strangers Nowhere in the World: The Rise of Cosmopolitanism in Early Modern Europe* (Philadelphia, 2006), 69–77.

42. *An Expedient for Peace,* 34; Liverpool RO, 920 MD 173 (diary of Sir Willoughby Aston), unpaginated, entry for 27 Aug. 1687; see also *Publick Occurrences,* no. 31 (18 Sept. 1688).

43. *Good Old Test Reviv'd,* 4; [Popple], *Three Letters,* 8; *An Address to his Grace the Lord Archbishop,* 5; [Penn], *Third Letter,* 19.

44. *Advice to the English Youth,* 4; see also Kenrick, *Sermon,* 35.

45. *An Expedient for Peace,* 21.

46. *An Expedient for Peace,* 27; *Som[e] Free Reflections upon Occasion of the Public Discourse about Liberty of Conscience* (1687, P1366), 7; *A Friendly Debate,* no. 1, p. 4; Shute, *New Naked Truth,* 39–40; *An Answer from the Country,* 7.

47. Ann Docwra, *Spiritual Community, Vindicated amongst People of Different Perswasions* (n.p., 1687, D1781), 1–3. On Docwra, see Francis Bugg, *The Pilgrim's Progress, from Quakerism to Christianity* (1698, B5382), 59–60; Jacqueline Broad and Karen Green, *A History of Women's Political Thought in Europe, 1400–1700* (Cambridge, 2009), 235–240; Sarah Apetrei, *Women, Feminism and Religion in Early Enlightenment England* (Cambridge, 2010), 160–168.

48. *A Few Short Arguments* (1687, F837), 1; Charles Trinder, *The Speech of Charles Trinder, Esq; Recorder of Gloucester* (1688, T2283), 15–16.

49. *The Minister's Reasons for His Not Reading the Kings Declaration, Friendly Debated* (1688, M2195), 14; see also *An Answer to a Letter from a Clergyman in the City* (1688, P3039A), part 2, p. 10; *Publick Occurrences,* no. 19 (26 June 1688).

50. *The Reasonableness of Toleration,* 4; [Henry Care], *A Discourse for Taking Off the Tests and Penal Laws about Religion* (1687, D1593), sig A4r; see also [Thomas Cartwright], *A Letter from a Clergy-Man in the Country* (1688, L1369A), 14. For the

attribution of *A Discourse* to Care, see FSL, Newdigate newsletters, L.c.1859, 20 Sept. 1687.

51. [Care], *Animadversions on a Late Paper*, 20.

52. T. C. W. Blanning, *Joseph II and Enlightened Despotism* (London, 1970), 64–72, 95–112.

53. Elizabeth Rone, *A Reproof to those Church Men or Ministers that Refused to Read the Kings Most Gracious Declaration* (n.p., 1688, R1914A). The Familists had flourished in the sixteenth century but by the late seventeenth century were largely confined to the Isle of Ely, where they may have numbered as few as sixty members. See Christopher Marsh, *The Family of Love in English Society, 1550–1630* (Cambridge, 1994), 245–247; E. S. de Beer, ed., *The Diary of John Evelyn*, 6 vols. (Oxford, 1955), iv:554; *Elizabeth Rone's Short Answer to Ellinor James's Long Preamble* (1687, R1914B).

54. [Popple], *Three Letters*, 17; see also *Advice from a Dissenter in the City, to his Friends in the Countrey* (1688, A633), 5–6.

55. *A Declaration of His Most Sacred Majesty King James II* (Dublin, 1689, J165), 2.

56. *Som[e] Free Reflections*, 7; Shute, *New Naked Truth*, 54.

57. John Eston to the earl of Peterborough, 6 Dec. 1687, printed in Duckett, ed., *Penal Laws*, ii:61; see also W. M. Wigfield, "Recusancy and Nonconformity in Bedfordshire," *Publications of the Bedfordshire Historical Record Society*, xx (1938), 153, 198–204. Eston's father was an elder in John Bunyan's congregation of nonconformists: see Michael Mullett, "'Deprived of our Former Place': The Internal Politics of Bedford 1660 to 1688," *Publications of the Bedfordshire Historical Record Society*, lix (1980), 26–27; H. G. Tibbutt, ed., *The Minutes of the First Independent Church (now Bunyan Meeting) at Bedford, 1656–1766* (Luton, 1976), 15, 17, 121.

58. *Som[e] Free Reflections*, 7–8; [Shute], *New Test*, 3. Figures provided by Michael R. Watts suggest that the Anglicans likely made up at least 90 percent of the English population in the later Stuart period: see Watts, *The Dissenters: From the Reformation to the French Revolution* (Oxford, 1978), 270, 491–492, 509.

59. [Care], *Animadversions on a Late Paper*, 31; see also [Penn], *Good Advice*, 42; [Shute], *New Test*, 15. Protestant nonconformists had not been excluded by law from sitting in parliament, but the House of Commons had occasionally ordered its members to take the sacrament in the Church of England or face expulsion. The Test Act of 1678 required only that members make a declaration against transubstantiation, which was not a difficulty for Protestant nonconformists. Quakers, however, were effectively excluded by their refusal to take the oath of office. On these points, see Douglas R. Lacey, *Dissent and Parliamentary Politics in England, 1661–1689* (New Brunswick, N.J., 1969), 19; Basil Duke Henning, ed., *The House of Commons, 1660–1690*, 3 vols. (London, 1983), i:11–12; William Braithwaite, *The Second Period of Quakerism*, 2nd edn. (Cambridge, 1961), 413.

60. [Shute], *New Test*, 30; *Animadversions upon Mijn Heer Fagels Letter*, 7.

61. *Som[e] Free Reflections,* 7.

62. Docwra, *Spiritual Community,* 3; on the "common law mind," see J. G. A. Pocock, *The Ancient Constitution and the Feudal Law,* rev. edn. (Cambridge, 1987), 36–37.

63. *Publick Occurrences,* no. 15 (29 May 1688); *The Reasonableness of Tolera-tion,* 13. This pamphlet (*The Reasonableness of Toleration*) has occasionally been attributed to William Penn, but it was not published by Penn's usual printer and some of its contents are not characteristic of a Quaker author. See Joseph Smith, *A Descriptive Catalogue of Friends' Books,* 2 vols. (London, 1867), ii:305; Mary Maples Dunn and Richard S. Dunn, eds., *The Papers of William Penn,* 5 vols. (Philadelphia, 1981–86), v:533–534.

64. [Penn], *Good Advice,* 25–26; Care, *Draconica,* 32.

65. *The Reasonableness of Toleration,* 25.

66. Nabil Matar, *Islam in Britain, 1558–1685* (Cambridge, 1998), 29–31, 106–107; Marshall, *John Locke, Toleration and Early Enlightenment Culture,* 393–395, 549–550; Sir Henry Blount, *A Voyage into the Levant,* 2nd edn. (London, 1636), 110–111; Sir Paul Rycaut, *The Present State of the Greek and Armenian Churches* (1679, R2411), 20–21; idem, *The History of the Present State of the Ottoman Empire,* 5th edn. (1682, R2403), 184–197; Richard Knolles and Sir Paul Rycaut, *The Turkish History, from the Original of that Nation,* 6th edn. (1687, K702), book 1, p. 962.

67. *The Reasonableness of Toleration,* 25–26.

68. For the views of contemporary authors on the expulsion of the Moriscos, see Peter Heylyn, *Cosmographie,* 2nd edn. (1657, H1690), 241; [Antoine de Brunel], *A Journey into Spain* (1670, B5230), 44–45; Knolles and Rycaut, *The Turkish History,* book 1, pp. 899–900. On the Moriscos in exile, see L. P. Harvey, *Muslims in Spain, 1500–1614* (Chicago, 2005), 356–361, 367–368; Már Jónsson, "The Expulsion of the Moriscos from Spain in 1609–1614: The Destruction of an Islamic Periphery," *Journal of Global History,* ii (2007), 206–211.

69. [Shute], *New Test,* 13. Shute was a tobacconist in Limehouse; he had received his B.A. from Oxford in 1672. See *CSPD, James II, 1685,* 241; Joseph Foster, ed., *Alumni Oxonienses: The Members of the University of Oxford, 1500–1714,* 4 vols. (Oxford, 1891–92), iv:1354.

70. On the tolerance of diversity in some early modern composite empires, see C. A. Bayly, "'Archaic' and 'Modern' Globalization in the Eurasian and African Arena, ca. 1750–1850," in A. G. Hopkins, ed., *Globalization in World His-tory* (New York, 2002), 50; idem, *The Birth of the Modern World, 1780–1914* (Malden, MA, 2004), 29, 34–35.

71. For Nicholets's voyage to the Coromandel Coast of India, see his sermon *The Dying Mans Destiny* (1682, N1087), title page. On the trade cards of tobacconists, see Catherine Molineux, "Pleasures of the Smoke: 'Black Virgin-ians' in Georgian London's Tobacco Shops," *William and Mary Quarterly,* III, lxiv (2007), 343–344.

72. *The Reasonableness of Toleration*, 26.

73. Care, *Draconica*, 39, citing Ammanius Marcellinus, *Res Gestae*, 30.9.5.

74. [Shute], *New Test*, 5, 30; idem, *New Naked Truth*, 17; *London Gazette*, no. 2238 (28 April–2 May 1687); see also Cyrus Masroori, "Cyrus II and the Political Utility of Religious Toleration," in John Christian Laursen, ed., *Religious Toleration: "The Variety of Rites" from Cyrus to Defoe* (New York, 1999), 13–36.

75. *Animadversions upon Mijn Heer Fagels Letter*, 7; *How the Members of the Church of England Ought to Behave Themselves under a Roman Catholick King* (1687, H2961), 182–188; [Thomas Cartwright], *A Modest Censure of the Immodest Letter to a Dissenter* (1687, N76), 10–11; Northleigh, *Parliamentum Pacificum*, 68; *The Reasonableness of Toleration*, 26–28.

76. *How the Members of the Church of England Ought to Behave*, 172; see also [Cartwright], *Modest Censure*, 24.

77. Marshall, *John Locke, Toleration, and Early Enlightenment Culture*, 55–58, 69, 79; Peter Lake, "Anti-popery: The Structure of a Prejudice," in Richard Cust and Ann Hughes, eds., *Conflict in Early Stuart England* (Harlow, 1989), 94.

78. On Care's religion, see Lois G. Schwoerer, *The Ingenious Mr. Henry Care, Restoration Publicist* (Baltimore, 2001), 23.

79. Care, *Draconica*, 39; see also the English translation of Damiao de Góis in Joannes Boemus, *The Manners, Lawes, and Customes of All Nations* (London, 1611), 544, 568.

80. For this rhetorical tactic, see James Hankins, "Socrates in the Italian Renaissance," in Sara Ahbel-Rappe and Rachana Kamtekar, eds., *A Companion to Socrates* (Malden, MA, 2006), 340–341.

81. Note, however, that William Penn did refer to the "down-right Toleration in most of his Majesties Plantations abroad" in his earlier tolerationist treatise, *A Perswasive to Moderation* (1685, P1337A), 15.

82. Bodl., MS Clarendon 89, fol. 12, James Harris to Dudley Loftus, 22 Jan. 1686/7; Trinity College, Dublin, T.C.D. MS 1181, p. 6, Christopher Crofts to Sir Robert Southwell, 21 Feb. 1686/7; Longleat House, Thynne MSS, xv, fol. 186v, Sir Robert Southwell to Lord Weymouth, 16 June 1687; Tim Harris, *Revolution: The Great Crisis of the British Monarchy, 1685–1720* (London, 2006), 121–122, 127, 137–140; John Miller, "The Earl of Tyrconnel and James II's Irish Policy, 1685–1688," *HJ*, xx (1977), 815.

83. C. D. Chandaman, *The English Public Revenue 1660–1688* (Oxford, 1975), 259–261, 360–361; Ralph Davis, "English Foreign Trade, 1660–1700," *EcHistR*, n.s., vii (1954), 161; John Hatcher et al., *The History of the British Coal Industry*, 5 vols. (Oxford, 1984–93), i:487–492, 501–502; W. G. Hoskins, "Harvest Fluctuations and English Economic History, 1620–1759," *Agricultural History Review*, xvi (1968), 17–18; Charles Davenant, *The Political and Commercial Works*, ed. Sir Charles Whitworth, 5 vols. (London, 1771), i:148.

84. [Richard Burthogge], *Prudential Reasons for Repealing the Penal Laws* (1687, B6155), 10. For Burthogge's authorship of this pamphlet see Anthony

Wood, *Athenae Oxonienses,* ed. Philip Bliss, 4 vols. (London, 1813–20), vol. 4, cols. 582, 609.

85. [Care], *Answer to a Paper,* 18; see also BL, Add. MS, 41816, fol. 226, marquis d'Albeville to earl of Middleton, 29 Sept./9 Oct. 1688. Several addresses printed in the *London Gazette* echoed this theme: see no. 2243 (16–19 May 1687), no. 2254 (23–27 June 1687), no. 2259 (11–14 July 1687), no. 2263 (25–28 July 1687), no. 2273 (29 Aug.–1 Sept. 1687), no. 2287 (17–20 Oct. 1687), and no. 2315 (23–26 Jan. 1688).

86. Bodl., MS Rawl. a.289, fol. 129v; FSL, V.a.469 (memoirs of William Westby), fol. 15v.

87. *A Friendly Debate,* no. 1, p. 1.

88. *Some Queries Concerning Liberty of Conscience, Directed to William Penn and Henry Care* (n.p., [1688], S4559), 1–2, 4; *Ten Seasonable Queries* (n.p., [1688], T674); Gilbert Burnet, *Six Papers* (n.p., 1687, B5912), 26 (mispaginated in original as p. 22); see also W. A. Speck, *Reluctant Revolutionaries: Englishmen and the Revolution of 1688* (Oxford, 1988), 144–145.

89. Pincus, *1688,* 372–381.

90. On this point, see Mark Goldie, "John Locke's Circle and James II," *HJ,* xxxv (1992), 558–559, 570–576; idem, "James II and the Dissenters' Revenge: The Commission of Enquiry of 1688," *Historical Research,* lxvi (1993), 54–55.

91. *Advice to the English Youth,* 4; *An Answer from the Country,* 47.

92. Evelyn Newton, *Lyme Letters, 1660–1760* (London, 1925), 137; H. Jenkinson, "A Late Surrey Chronicler," *Surrey Archaeological Collections,* xxvii (1914), 11; see also *Publick Occurrences,* no. 8 (10 April 1688); University of Wales Bangor, Mostyn Additional MSS, no. 9070/21, Philip Fowke to Thomas Mostyn, 22 Oct. 1687; BL, Add. MS 69955, fol. 11; *HMC, Lindsey (Supp.),* 272; T. B. Howell, *A Complete Collection of State Trials,* 33 vols. (London, 1809–26), vol. 12, col. 372.

3. Fearing the Unknown

1. C. W. Bingham, ed., *Private Memoirs, (Never Before Published) of John Potenger* (London, 1841), 52–54.

2. J. S. Clarke, ed., *The Life of James the Second,* 2 vols. (London, 1816), i:656.

3. J. P. Kenyon, *Robert Spencer, Earl of Sunderland, 1641–1702* (London, 1958), 112–113; John Miller, *James II: A Study in Kingship* (Hove, 1978), 124; Steve Pincus, *1688: The First Modern Revolution* (New Haven, 2009), 94–104, 118–122.

4. Andrew Clark, ed., *The Life and Times of Anthony Wood,* 5 vols. (Oxford, 1891–1900), iii:134; Scott Sowerby, "Tories in the Whig Corner: Daniel Fleming's Journal of the 1685 Parliament," *Parliamentary History,* xxiv (2005), 175; for similar anxieties expressed soon after the accession, see also Tim Harris, *Revolution: The Great Crisis of the British Monarchy, 1685–1720* (London, 2006), 61–63;

Mark Goldie, "The Political Thought of the Anglican Revolution," in Robert Beddard, ed., *The Revolutions of 1688* (Oxford, 1991), 113; Grant Tapsell, *The Personal Rule of Charles II, 1681–85* (Woodbridge, 2007), 191–193; David Cressy, *Dangerous Talk: Scandalous, Seditious, and Treasonable Speech in Pre-Modern England* (Oxford, 2010), 224–225.

    5. Bodl., MS Rawl. a.289, fol. 129; *The Entring Book of Roger Morrice, 1677–1691*, ed. Mark Goldie, John Spurr, Tim Harris, Stephen Taylor, Mark Knights, and Jason McElligott, 7 vols. (Woodbridge, 2007–9), iv:312; James II, *His Majesties Gracious Declaration to all his Loving Subjects for Liberty of Conscience* (1687, J186), 4.

    6. Bingham, ed., *Memoirs of John Potenger*, 59–61.

    7. John Bramhall, *Bishop Bramhall's Vindication of Himself* (1672, B4237), with preface by Samuel Parker; Andrew Marvell, *The Rehearsal Transpros'd* (1672, M878); Samuel Parker, *A Reproof to the Rehearsal Transprosed* (1673, P473); Andrew Marvell, *The Rehearsall Transpros'd the Second Part* (1673, M882).

    8. For L'Estrange's use of the word "anti-popery," see his pamphlet *The Case Put, Concerning the Succession of his Royal Highness the Duke of York* (1679, L1206), 37. For his use of the phrase "fears and jealousies" to refer to fears of popery, see his *Seasonable Memorial in Some Historical Notes* (1680, L1301), 26; *Remarks on the Growth and Progress of Nonconformity* (1682, L1296), 24, 28–9, 47; and *Brief History of the Times* (1687/8, L1203), part 1, p. 10, part 2, p. 126.

    9. T.D., *Fears and Jealousies Ceas'd: Or, an Impartial Discourse, Tending to Demonstrate, from the Folly and Ill Success of the Romish Politics, that there is No Reason to Apprehend any Danger from Popery* (n.p., [1688], D1884), 8.

    10. *Publick Occurrences*, no. 8 (10 Apr. 1688).

    11. For similarly worded assertions that the Dutch were stirring up "fears and jealousies" in England, see Giles Shute, *A New Naked Truth, or, the Sandy Foundation of the Sacramental Test Shaken* (1688, S3709), 24–26; FSL, V.a.469 (memoirs of William Westby), fol. 34.

    12. [Henry Care], *Animadversions on a Late Paper, Entituled, a Letter to a Dissenter* (1687, C505), 37.

    13. Bodl., MS Rawl. d.850, fol. 38v, d.852, fol. 229r–v.

    14. Denis Granville, "The Cheifest Matters Contained in Sundry Discourses Made to the Clergy of the Archdeaconry of Durham," in *The Resigned & Resolved Christian*, 2nd edn. (Rouen, 1689 and 1691, G1940), part 2, p. 21; idem, "Things which Portend very Fatally to the Government and Church of England," in *The Resigned & Resolved Christian*, part 4, pp. 43–44.

    15. See [Sir Roger L'Estrange], *An Account of the Growth of Knavery* (1678, L1193), 9–10, 18, 21, 23–24; *LJ*, xiii:222, entry for 23 May 1678; Fabian Philipps, *Ursa Major & Minor, or, a Sober and Impartial Enquiry into those Pretended Fears and Jealousies of Popery and Arbitrary Power* (1681, P2019A), 1; Thomas Cartwright, *A Sermon Preached at Holy-Rood House* (Edinburgh, 1682, C704), 18; Granville, "A Discourse Concerning Christian Resignation and Resolution," in *The Resigned & Resolved Christian*, part 1, p. 26.

16. On this group of ultra-loyalists, see Andrew Barclay, "James II's 'Catholic' Court," *1650–1850: Ideas, Aesthetics, and Inquiries in the Early Modern Era*, viii (2003), 161–171; Sowerby, "Tories in the Whig Corner," 160–161, 170–171; *Oxford Dictionary of National Biography*, s.v. "Cavendish, Henry, second duke of Newcastle upon Tyne (1630–1691)" and s.v. "Bruce, Thomas, second earl of Ailesbury (1656–1741)."

17. R. A. Beddard, "Bishop Cartwright's Death-Bed," *Bodleian Library Record*, xi (1984), 220–230; *The Diary of Dr. Thomas Cartwright, Bishop of Chester*, Camden Society, old series, xxii (1843), 9, 44–48, 52, 80–81; BPL, Ms. Am. 1502, vol. 7, no. 65, newsletter dated 3 Jan. 1689; BL, Stowe MS 746, fol. 111, James Bonnell to John Strype, 19 Apr. 1689.

18. [Thomas Cartwright], *An Answer of a Minister of the Church of England* (1687, C696), 23. This pamphlet, though anonymous, is attributed here to Cartwright due to the numerous parallel passages it shares with his *Sermon Preached upon the Anniversary Solemnity of the Happy Inauguration* (1686, C706).

19. [Thomas Cartwright], *A Modest Censure of the Immodest Letter to a Dissenter* (1687, N76), 9; idem, *An Answer*, 24–25, 47; idem, *A Sermon Preached upon the Anniversary*, 22; Nathaniel Johnston, *The King's Visitatorial Power Asserted* (1688, J879), 59; see also *Diary of Thomas Cartwright*, 30. For the attribution of *A Modest Censure* to Cartwright, see WYAS, WYL156/51/16, Nathaniel Johnston to Sir John Reresby, 5 Nov. 1687; *Diary of Thomas Cartwright*, 85; Mark N. Brown, "Bishop Cartwright's Answer to Halifax's 'Letter to a Dissenter' (1687)," *Notes and Queries*, xxi (1974), 104–105.

20. Edmund Ellis [Elys], *An Epistle to the Truly Religious and Loyal Gentry of the Church of England* (1687, E674), 6, 8; idem, *The Second Epistle to the Truly Religious and Loyal Gentry of the Church of England* (1687, E693), 6.

21. *CSPD, James II, 1686–87*, 56–57; Alexander Taylor, ed., *The Works of Symon Patrick*, 9 vols. (Oxford, 1858), ix:505; James II, *To the Most Reverend Fathers in God* (1685/6, J389), 4; see also Clark, ed., *Life and Times of Anthony Wood*, iii:239; Worcestershire RO, Worc. City Ref A14, Box 2 (also catalogued as 496.5, bulk accession 9630), Chamber Order Book, 1669–1721, volume A, fol. 2v, letter from Lord Plymouth to the mayor and aldermen of Worcester, 5 June 1686.

22. John Sharp, *The Works of the Most Reverend Dr. John Sharp*, 7 vols. (London, 1749), vii:123–147; *An Exact Account of the Whole Proceedings Against the Right Reverend Father in God, Henry Lord Bishop of London* (1688, E3591), 7.

23. *Entring Book of Roger Morrice*, iii:281.

24. [Thomas Cartwright], *A Letter from a Clergy-Man in the Country* (1688, C701A or L1369A), 26; idem, *A Modest Censure*, 24.

25. [Cartwright], *A Modest Censure*, 19 (mispaginated in original as p. 23); for Cartwright's earlier opposition to toleration of nonconformists, see Cartwright, *A Sermon Preached July 17, 1676* (1676, C703), 30–36; idem, *A Sermon Preached to the Gentlemen of Yorkshire* (1684, C705), 26–30. On Cartwright's

Erastianism, see Kenneth Fincham and Stephen Taylor, "Episcopalian Conformity and Nonconformity, 1646–60," in David L. Smith and Jason McElligott, eds., *Royalists and Royalism during the Interregnum* (Manchester, 2010), 36–37; Goldie, "Political Thought of the Anglican Revolution," 135–136.

26. Bodl., MS Rawl. d.852, fols. 209–210, speech by Denis Granville, 10 April 1687.

27. Lois Schwoerer, *The Ingenious Mr. Henry Care, Restoration Publicist* (Baltimore, 2001), 23, 44–75, 210–216, 222–223; F. C. Brown, *Elkanah Settle: His Life and Works* (Chicago, 1910), 21–26; Bodl., MS Eng. lett. c.54, fol. 97, Philip Madoxe to Sir Robert Southwell, 28 Aug. 1688; Tim Harris, *London Crowds in the Reign of Charles II: Propaganda and Politics from the Restoration until the Exclusion Crisis* (Cambridge, 1987), 120.

28. *Publick Occurrences*, no. 15 (29 May 1688); Henry Care, *Draconica: or, an Abstract of all the Penal Laws Touching Matters of Religion*, 2nd edn. (1688, C511), 10, 15–17, 21. See also *Publick Occurrences*, no. 8 (10 Apr. 1688), no. 17 (12 June 1688), no. 19 (26 June 1688), no. 23 (24 July 1688); [Care], *Animadversions on a Late Paper*, 5–7, 13–15; FSL, Newdigate newsletters, L.c.1862, 27 Sept. 1687.

29. Elkanah Settle, *A Narrative* (1683, S2700), preface and pp. 24–25. See also *Publick Occurrences*, no. 32 (25 Sept. 1688).

30. Anthony Wood, *Athenae Oxonienses*, ed. Philip Bliss, 4 vols. (London, 1813–20), vol. 2, col. 469; see also *A Letter from a Clergy-Man in the City, to his Friend in the Country, Containing his Reasons for not Reading the Declaration* (1688, H308), 8; Thomas Brown, *Heraclitus Ridens Redivivus* (Oxford, 1688, B5060), 4.

31. *Remarks upon E. Settle's Narrative* (1683, R943), 1, 3–5, 11; *Reflexions upon a Late Pamphlet Intituled, a Narrative* (1683, R716), 3–5; see also Elkanah Settle, *A Supplement to the Narrative* (1683, S2720), 17.

32. Care, *Draconica*, 40.

33. [Henry Care], *A Discourse for Taking Off the Tests and Penal Laws about Religion* (1687, D1593), 29.

34. [Henry Care], *The Legality of the Court Held by His Majesties Ecclesiastical Commissioners, Defended* (1688, C527), 38; [Care], *Animadversions on a Late Paper*, 37; on this point, see also Justin Champion, "Willing to Suffer: Law and Religious Conscience in Seventeenth-Century England," in John McLaren and Harold Coward, eds., *Religious Conscience, the State, and the Law* (Albany, 1999), 19–21.

35. William Shewen, *A Brief Testimony for Religion* (n.p., 1688, S3419), 17; [William Penn], *A Third Letter from a Gentleman in the Country* (1687, P1381), 11; see also George Whitehead, *The Christian Progress of that Ancient Servant and Minister of Jesus Christ, George Whitehead* (London, 1725), 622. For William Penn's frequent belittling of anti-popery, see his *Good Advice to the Church of England* (1687, P1296), 9, 49; his *Second Letter from a Gentleman in the Country* (1687, P1361), 11, 14, 16; his *Third Letter from a Gentleman in the Country*, 8, 14; and NUL, PwA 2129/1, James Rivers to [Hans Willem Bentinck], 13/23 Jan. 1688.

36. [William Popple], *Three Letters Tending to Demonstrate* (1688, P1383),
21. For Popple's friendship with Penn, see William Popple, *A Letter to Mr. Penn,
with his Answer* (n.p., 1688, P2964), 1; Charlwood Lawton, "A Memoir of Part
of the Life of William Penn," *Memoirs of the Historical Society of Pennsylvania*, vol.
3, part 2 (1834–36), 218–220.

37. In addition to the pamphlets cited in the notes above, see also *The Present
State of England in Relation to Popery, Manifesting the Absolute Impossibility of Introducing Popery and Arbitrary Government into this Kingdom* (1685, S2711), reprinted
without a preface as *Salus Britannica: Or, The Safety of the Protestant Religion, Against
all the Present Apprehensions of Popery Fully Discust and Proved* (1685, S511).

38. Thomas Cartwright, *A Sermon Preached upon the Anniversary Solemnity
of the Happy Inauguration* (1686, C706), reprinted three times in 1686 (C706A,
C707, C708); Fabian Philipps, *Ursa Major & Minor* (1681, P2019A), reprinted
once in 1681 (P2019B).

39. *A Dialogue between Two Church of England-Men* (n.p., [1687], D1339A),
8. For another dialogue of this type, where one interlocutor takes the anti-
popish position and the other critiques it, see *A Friendly Debate upon the Next
Elections of Parliament*, no. 1 (n.p., [1688], F2218A).

40. Harris, *London Crowds*, 98–100.

41. John Fitzwilliam, *A Sermon Preach'd at Cotenham* (1683, F1106), 29;
Daniel Kenrick, *A Sermon Preached in the Cathedral-Church of Worcester* (1688,
K307), 21, 25, 34–6; Cartwright, *A Sermon Preached upon the Anniversary*, 22;
Christopher Wyvill, *An Assize-Sermon Preached in the Cathedral-Church of St. Peter
in York* (1686, W3783), 25–26.

42. *London Gazette*, no. 2259 (11–14 July 1687), no. 2270 (18–22 Aug.
1687), no. 2323 (20–23 Feb. 1688), no. 2318 (2–6 Feb. 1688); see also Clarke,
ed., *Life of James*, ii:170.

43. Shute, *New Naked Truth*, 44; *Publick Occurrences*, no. 32 (25 Sept. 1688);
Brown, *Heraclitus Ridens*, 7.

44. On repealers as Jesuits in disguise, see *A Letter, Containing Some Reflections* (n.p., [1688], L1357A), 1; Popple, *A Letter to Mr. Penn*, 2; Mary Maples Dunn
and Richard S. Dunn, eds., *The Papers of William Penn*, 5 vols. (Philadelphia,
1981–86), iii:173; Gilbert Burnet, *Bishop Burnet's History of His Own Time*, ed.
M. J. Routh, 2nd edn., 6 vols. (Oxford, 1833), iii:140.

45. *A Letter to a Dissenter from his Friend at The Hague* (The Hague, 1688,
L1633), 3–4; *Some Queries Concerning Liberty of Conscience, Directed to William Penn
and Henry Care* (n.p., [1688], S4559), 3–4; [Halifax], *A Letter to a Dissenter* (1687,
H311), 6; *A Letter, Containing Some Reflections*, 4–6; TNA, PRO 31/3/168, fol. 49v,
Barrillon to Louis XIV, 7/17 March 1687; CPA, vol. 162, fol. 196, Barrillon to
Louis XIV, 29 Sept./9 Oct. 1687; NUL, PwA 2111, James Johnstone to [Hans
Willem Bentinck], 8 Dec. 1687; *Publick Occurrences*, no. 19 (26 June 1688).

46. [William Penn], *Good Advice to the Church of England* (1687, P1296), 49;
for similar arguments, see also BL, Add. MS 72866, fols. 19v, 35v; BL, Add. MS

72889, fol. 8; [Care], *Animadversions on a Late Paper,* 15; [John Northleigh], *Parliamentum Pacificum* (1688, N1302), 29; [John Northleigh], *Dr. Burnett's Reflections* (1688, N1298), 16. On the modest size of the Catholic population in this period, see John Miller, *Popery and Politics in England, 1660–1688* (Cambridge, 1973), 9–12.

47. *Some Queries Concerning Liberty of Conscience,* 1, 3; [Thomas Comber], *Three Considerations Proposed to Mr. William Pen[n], Concerning the Validity and Security of his New Magna Charta for Liberty of Conscience* (n.p., [1688], C5496), 1–2.

48. Wood, *Athenae Oxonienses,* vol. 4, col. 699; on the similar case of John Bromley, rector of Hadleigh in Essex, see *Oxford Dictionary of National Biography,* s.v. "Bromley, John (*bap.* 1653, *d.* 1718)"; London Metropolitan Archives, DL/A/A/007/MS09531/018, Bishop Compton's register, fol. 77v.

49. *A Letter from a Gentleman in the City, to a Clergy-Man in the Country* (1688, L1387), 25.

50. BL, Add. MS 32096, fol. 331v.

51. Laurence Brockliss, "The 'Intruded' President and Fellows," in Laurence Brockliss, Gerald Harriss, and Angus Macintyre, eds., *Magdalen College and the Crown* (Oxford, 1988), 103–104; Hampshire RO, 44M69/F6/9/83/3, Thomas Hinton to [Thomas Jervoise], 21 Dec. 1687; York Minster Library, Hailstone MS, BB 21, L.P. to bishop of Exeter, 29 Nov. 1687.

52. Bodl., MS Smith 141, fols. 31, 32v.

53. WYAS, WYL156/48/25, Nathaniel Johnston to Sir John Reresby, 23 June 1687; NUL, PwV 53/57, William Blathwayt to Sir Robert Southwell, 12 Nov. 1687.

54. See, for instance, the critique of William Penn's arguments against anti-popery given in *A Letter, Containing Some Reflections,* 1–2, 4.

55. James II, *By the King, A Declaration* (1688, J158).

56. *A Letter Writ by Mijn Heer Fagel* (Amsterdam, 1688, F87), republished twice in 1688, with further editions in Dutch, French, and Latin. At least ten thousand copies of Fagel's letter were printed in English: see NUL, PwA 2126/1, intelligence letter to [Hans Willem Bentinck], 12 Jan. 1688; BL, Add. MS 41815, fol. 127, marquis d'Albeville to earl of Middleton, 3 Feb. 1688; FSL, V.b.287, no. 44, James Fraser to Sir Robert Southwell, 7 Jan. 1688; Longleat House, Thynne MSS, xv, fol. 218, Sir Robert Southwell to Lord Weymouth, 12 Jan. 1688; LLIU, Albeville MSS, John Rowe to marquis d'Albeville, 29 Jan. 1688.

57. *Publick Occurrences,* no. 10 (24 April 1688), no. 21 (10 July 1688); Giles Shute, *A New Naked Truth* (1688, S3709), 27; [Stephen Lobb], *A Second Letter to a Dissenter* (1687, L2729A), 18.

58. NUL, PwA 2148, James Rivers to [Hans Willem Bentinck], 27 Feb. 1688; see also NUL, PwA 2692, anonymous letter of 8 Feb. 1688.

59. *CJ,* x:51; *Entring Book of Roger Morrice,* v:53–54; Henry Horwitz, *Parliament, Policy and Politics in the Reign of William III* (Newark, 1977), 22.

60. [Elkanah Settle?], *An Expedient for Peace* (1688, E3872aA), 33; [Henry Care], *A Discourse for Taking Off the Tests and Penal Laws about Religion* (1687, D1593), sig. A2v; [Popple], *Three Letters*, 24; [Care], *The Legality of the Court*, 38; [Care], *Animadversions on a Late Paper*, 16–17.

61. For a list of repealer authors, see Appendix. Of these authors, John Dryden, Henry Neville Payne, and Thomas Godden were Catholics; Thomas Cartwright, Daniel Kenrick, and James Paston were Anglicans; James Stewart was a Scottish Presbyterian; Henry Care may have been a Presbyterian; Charles Nicholets was either a Presbyterian or a Congregationalist; Stephen Lobb was a Congregationalist; Thomas Plant and Benjamin Dennis were Baptists; Ann Docwra and William Penn were Quakers; and Elizabeth Rone was a member of the Family of Love. On Nicholets, see Alexander Gordon, ed., *Freedom After Ejection: A Review (1690–1692) of Presbyterian and Congregational Nonconformity in England and Wales* (Manchester, 1917), 101.

62. The tories included John Dryden, John Northleigh, and Charles Trinder.

63. *An Answer from the Country, to a Late Letter to a Dissenter* (1687, A3278), 15.

4. Taking Sides

1. Sir George Duckett, ed., *Penal Laws and Test Act: Questions Touching their Repeal Propounded in 1687–8 by James II*, 2 vols. (London, 1882–83), i:29.

2. The Three Questions were also asked of customs officials and the king's councillors at law, although only the replies from the deputy lieutenants and justices of the peace have survived. For the customs officials, see BL, Add. MS 34512, fol. 80, Aernout van Citters to States General, 18/28 May 1688; LLIU, Albeville MSS, Robert Yard to marquis d'Albeville, 15 May 1688; Bodl., MS Tanner 114, fol. 58, letter from Sir Nicholas Butler et al., 15 March 1688; HEHL, STT 882, Sir Nicholas Butler et al. to Noble Waterhouse, 15 March 1688; TNA, T1/3, fol. 99, T1/4, fol. 214r–v; *CTB*, viii:2151. For the lawyers, see Roger North, *The Lives of the Right Hon. Francis North, Baron Guildford, Lord Keeper of the Great Seal*, 3 vols. (London, 1826), iii:180; Duckett, ed., *Penal Laws*, i:378.

3. John Carswell, *The Descent on England: A Study of the English Revolution of 1688 and its European Background* (London, 1969), 238–243; J. R. Jones, *The Revolution of 1688 in England* (London, 1972), 166–168; J. R. Western, *Monarchy and Revolution: The English State in the 1680s* (London, 1972), 212; Tim Harris, *Revolution: The Great Crisis of the British Monarchy, 1685–1720* (London, 2006), 231; Peter Walker, *James II and the Three Questions: Religious Toleration and the Landed Classes, 1687–1688* (Oxford, 2010), 107–112, 249. The returns for Cambridgeshire, Cheshire, Durham, Hertfordshire, Lancashire, Middlesex, Suffolk, Surrey, and Warwickshire are not extant; returns survive for all other English and Welsh counties.

4. John Miller, *James II: A Study in Kingship* (Hove, 1978), 178–179; Harris, *Revolution*, 231.

5. The exceptions were Sir Maurice Berkeley and Sir Robert Kemp, who were removed from office after giving a positive undertaking with a proviso that the Church of England must be secured.

6. CAC (K), Fleming MSS, WD/Ry HMC no. 3149, Sir Daniel Fleming to Sir John Lowther, 2 Dec. 1687. By "closeted," Fleming referred to an interview with the king in which a subject was asked to give his opinion directly. These interviews were often held in the king's study, known as the closet.

7. The two groups are roughly equal in size, with 46.9 percent of all respondents above age fifty and 53.1 percent of all respondents below age fifty.

8. The average age of the ninety-two former members who simply said no was thirty-nine, while the average age of the seventy-seven members who refused to answer the questions until they heard the debates in parliament was forty-one.

9. This figure was arrived at by counting the members of parliament listed in Basil Henning, ed., *The House of Commons, 1660–1690,* 3 vols. (London, 1983) as having been elected from 1660 to 1685, subtracting those who had died before January 1688. The tally includes the elderly and infirm.

10. F. C. Turner, *James II* (London, 1948), 238; Maurice Ashley, *James II* (London, 1977), 266; David H. Hosford, *Nottingham, Nobles, and the North: Aspects of the Revolution of 1688* (Hamden, CT, 1976), 27; Eveline Cruickshanks, "Religion and Royal Succession—The Rage of Party" in Clyve Jones, ed., *Britain in the First Age of Party* (London, 1987), 22; see also [Robert Ferguson], *Representation of the Threatning Dangers, Impending over Protestants* (n.p., [1687], F756A), 32, which made a similar claim that James's "hast[e]" was provoked by his "growing old."

11. James II, *By the King, A Proclamation for Dissolving this Present Parliament* (1687, J332); Scott Sowerby, "Tories in the Whig Corner: Daniel Fleming's Journal of the 1685 Parliament," *Parliamentary History,* xxiv (2005), 167–171.

12. According to the History of Parliament, 468 of the 525 members of parliament in 1685 were tories. See Henning, ed., *House of Commons,* i:47.

13. Benjamin Nightingale, *Lancashire Nonconformity; or, Sketches, Historical & Descriptive,* 6 vols. (Manchester, [1890–93]), i:255; James A. Casada, "The Scottish Representatives in Richard Cromwell's Parliament," *Scottish Historical Review,* li (1972), 138; C. H. Firth, *The Regimental History of Cromwell's Army,* 2 vols. (Oxford, 1940), ii:479; H. V. Koop, *Broughton in Furness: A History* (Bury St Edmunds, 1955; reprint, Beckermet, 1975), 19; W. Lewis, *History of the Congregational Church, Cockermouth* (London, 1870), 68; Margaret F. Thomas, *Tottlebank Baptist Church, 1669–1999* (n.p., 1999), 4; Foster Sunderland, *A Brief History of Tottlebank Baptist Church* (Liverpool, 1965), 6; CSPD, Charles II, July–Sept. 1683, 187.

14. CAC (C), D/Lons/L12/2/15 (memoirs of Sir Daniel Fleming, vol. 2), fol. 170; see also *CSPD, James II, 1687–89*, 102–103.

15. *CSPD, James II, 1687–89*, 47.

16. CAC (K), WD/Ry HMC no. 3147; CAC (C), D/Lons/L12/2/15 (memoirs of Sir Daniel Fleming, vol. 2), fol. 171; see also the more neutral attitudes of the duke of Beaufort, earl of Ailesbury, and lord Petre as described in University of Wales Bangor, Mostyn Additional MSS, no. 9070/25, Sir Roger Mostyn to Thomas Mostyn, 15 Dec. 1687; William E. Buckley, ed., *Memoirs of Thomas, Earl of Ailesbury, Written by Himself*, 2 vols. (Westminster, 1890), 163–164; Lord Braybrooke, ed., *The Autobiography of Sir John Bramston*, Camden Society, old series, xxxii (1845), 307. Lord Craven was depicted by Roger Morrice as putting the questions neutrally in Middlesex, but the tory justice of the peace John Potenger attested that Craven urged him to comply with the king. See *The Entring Book of Roger Morrice, 1677–1691*, ed. Mark Goldie, John Spurr, Tim Harris, Stephen Taylor, Mark Knights, and Jason McElligott, 7 vols. (Woodbridge, 2007–9), iv:169; C. W. Bingham, ed., *Private Memoirs, (Never Before Published) of John Potenger* (London, 1841), 60–61. Lord Jeffreys, predictably, pressed his subordinates to comply with the king; see NLW, Clenennau letters, no. 867, Lord Jeffreys to Sir Robert Owen, 24 March 1688; NLW, Ottley Correspondence no. 1470, Lord Jeffreys to Thomas Ottley, 24 March 1688. Note also the contrary example of the earl of Northampton who, before asking the Three Questions as lord lieutenant of Warwickshire, made a speech opposing the king's religious policy. He was swiftly removed as lord lieutenant: see Hosford, *Nottingham*, 21; *CSPD, James II, 1687–89*, 106; Gilbert Burnet, *Bishop Burnet's History of His Own Time*, ed. M. J. Routh, 2nd edn., 6 vols. (Oxford, 1833), iii:193, note h (note by Lord Dartmouth).

17. CAC (K), WD/Ry HMC no. 3143, Thomas Brathwait[e] to Sir Daniel Fleming, 23 Nov. 1687.

18. Duckett, ed., *Penal Laws*, i:273, 300, ii:53.

19. *VCH Lancashire*, ii:242, viii:234–235; *HMC, Kenyon*, 188; *CSPD, 1690–91*, 22–23.

20. On Preston, see *HMC, Le Fleming*, 162; CAC (K), WD/Ry HMC no. 2900, Peter Brook, Edward Fleetwood, and Lawrence Rawstone to Alexander Rigby, William Fleming, and Thomas Preston, 10 April 1685; *CTB*, x:980.

21. According to the king's orders, the lord lieutenant should set down "what every one Answers, whether he consents, refuseth or is doubtfull": see the instructions to the lord lieutenants in Wiltshire RO, WRO 1300, no. 865; Badminton House Muniments Room, FmC 3/4, fol. 56; and *CSPD, James II, 1687–89*, 87–88.

22. CAC (K), WD/Ry HMC no. 3144, Edward Wilson to Sir Daniel Fleming, 25 Nov. 1687.

23. H. S. Cowper, *Hawkshead* (London, 1899), 121–122; *HMC, Kenyon*, 172; Norman Penney, ed., *Record of the Sufferings of Quakers in Cornwall, 1655–1686* (London, 1928), 144.

24. CAC (K), WD/Ry HMC no. 3143, Thomas Brathwait[e] to Sir Daniel Fleming, 23 Nov. 1687. The sincerity of Roger Kirkby's affirmative answer has been called into question by Irene Cassidy in her biographical entry on Kirkby in Henning, ed., *House of Commons,* ii:689–690. Cassidy contends that Kirkby gave a positive answer because he was hoping for a pardon for having killed a fellow officer in a duel a few days before. This unfortunate interpretation relies on a mistaken reading of the relevant sources. Roger Kirkby was not charged with such a crime, though a Richard Kirkby was. See *HMC, Le Fleming,* 206 and CAC (K), Fleming MSS, WD/Ry HMC no. 3145, Roger Fleming to Sir Daniel Fleming, 25 Nov. 1687.

25. CAC (K), WD/Ry HMC no. 2899, William Kirkby to Sir Daniel Fleming, 9 April 1685.

26. Lancaster District Library, MS 6569, Roger Fleming to Sir Daniel Fleming, 27 Nov. 1687.

27. Lancashire RO, QSC/221.

28. Lancashire RO, QSC/221; *CSPD, James II, 1687–89,* 340; Henning, ed., *House of Commons,* iii:317.

29. CAC (K), WD/Ry HMC no. 3144, Edward Wilson to Sir Daniel Fleming, 25 Nov. 1687; CAC (K), WD/Ry HMC no. 3143, Thomas Brathwait[e] to Sir Daniel Fleming, 23 Nov. 1687. For Wilson's removal from office, see Lancashire RO, QSC/221.

30. Lancaster District Library, MS 6569, Roger Fleming to Sir Daniel Fleming, 27 Nov. 1687.

31. CAC (K), WD/Ry HMC no. 3144, Edward Wilson to Sir Daniel Fleming, 25 Nov. 1687; Lancaster District Library, MS 6569, Roger Fleming to Sir Daniel Fleming, 27 Nov. 1687; CAC (K), WD/Ry HMC no. 3143, Thomas Brathwait[e] to Sir Daniel Fleming, 23 Nov. 1687.

32. CAC (C), D/Lons/L12/2/15 (memoirs of Sir Daniel Fleming, vol. 2), fol. 170r–v.

33. CAC (K), WD/Ry HMC no. 3145, Roger Fleming to Sir Daniel Fleming, 25 Nov. 1687.

34. Lancashire RO, QSC/221; *CSPD, James II, 1687–89,* 122; Duckett, ed., *Penal Laws,* ii:301; CAC (K), WD/Ry HMC no. 3183, Sir Daniel Fleming to Sir Thomas Strickland, 23 March 1688.

35. Lancaster Maritime Museum, Lancaster Corporation MSS, Minute Book B, p. 397; John Brownbill, *A Calendar of Charters and Records Belonging to the Corporation of Lancaster* (Lancaster, 1929), 28–29; Thomas Pape, *The Charters of the City of Lancaster* (Lancaster, 1952), 67; J. D. Marshall, ed., *The Autobiography of William Stout of Lancaster, 1665–1752,* Chetham Society, 3rd ser., vol. 14 (Manchester, 1967), 92, 134; Lancashire RO, DDKe/2/19/11 (notes by Roger Kenyon, n.d.); M. A. Mullett, "Conflict, Politics and Elections in Lancaster, 1660–1688," *Northern History,* xix (1983), 81–82.

36. *CSPD, James II, 1687–89,* 276; Lancashire RO, DDKe/9/61/63, Thomas Preston to Roger Kenyon, 2 Oct. 1688; *HMC, Kenyon,* 196. On Brandon, see *CSPD, James II, 1687–89,* 43, 47; *CTB,* viii:1591, 1677–1678. Preston's letter refers to "Mr Fitton Gerrard" as the Lancaster candidate supported by the Kirkbys; it is unclear why the History of Parliament entry on Lancaster (in Henning, ed., *House of Commons,* i:287) designates Sir Samuel Gerard as Kirkby's partner in the abortive election.

37. *HMC, Kenyon,* 172.

38. CAC (C), D/Lons/L2/5, Sir John Lowther, "1688 Journal," pp. 57–58; John Lowther, Viscount Lonsdale, *Memoir of the Reign of James II* (York, 1808), 18; for similar judgments, see HEHL, HA 10669, Samuel Sanders to earl of Huntingdon, 19 Dec. 1687; HEHL, HA 12974, George Vernon to earl of Huntingdon, 31 Jan. 1688; Andrew Browning, ed., *Memoirs of Sir John Reresby,* rev. Mary K. Geiter and W. A. Speck (London, 1991), 496–497.

39. CAC (C), D/Lons/L12/2/15 (memoirs of Sir Daniel Fleming, vol. 2), fol. 171r–v. Similar joint responses were given in other counties: see Duckett, ed., *Penal Laws,* i:32–42, 61–69, 155–156, 374–378, ii:12–13; Western, *Monarchy and Revolution,* 213–214; Jones, *Revolution of 1688,* 168; Walker, *James II and the Three Questions,* 100, 191, 197.

40. Bodl., MS Tanner 259, fols. 52v–53r, Sir John Holland to [H. Negus], c. Dec. 1687; fol. 53v, same to same, 18 Dec. 1687; fols. 53v–54r, H. Negus to [Sir John Holland], 14 Dec. 1687; Duckett, ed., *Penal Laws,* i:305. On Holland's politics, see John Miller, "A Moderate in the First Age of Party: The Dilemmas of Sir John Holland, 1675–85," *EHR,* cxiv (1999), 844–874.

5. *Seizing Control*

1. Paul D. Halliday, *Dismembering the Body Politic: Partisan Politics in England's Towns, 1650–1730* (Cambridge, 1998), 248. The number of ejections is more precise than the number of additions because all of the orders of removal have survived in the privy council registers, while not all of the mandates of appointment have survived in the minute books of the town corporations. The number of removals was somewhat larger than the number of appointments; James did not always name replacements for the men he removed, although he did so in the great majority of cases.

2. The remaining 301 members were returned by the unregulated English boroughs, the Welsh boroughs, the English and Welsh counties, and the two universities. King James also regulated nine non-parliamentary corporations: Basingstoke, Chard, Doncaster, Great Torrington, Kingston upon Thames, Macclesfield, Newbury, Saffron Walden, and Southwold.

3. John Carswell, *The Descent on England: A Study of the English Revolution of 1688 and its European Background* (London, 1969), 113–114.

4. J. R. Jones, "James II's Whig Collaborators," *HJ*, iii (1960), 66–67; Halliday, *Dismembering*, 227; Basil Duke Henning, ed., *The House of Commons, 1660–1690*, 3 vols. (London, 1983), i:41; John Miller, *Cities Divided: Politics and Religion in English Provincial Towns, 1660–1722* (Oxford, 2007), 220, 229. Note that James in the first two years of his reign had continued Charles's policy of ejecting whigs from corporations through *quo warranto* proceedings and orders of the privy council.

5. For purposes of analysis, the tory ascendancy is deemed here to have lasted from March 1682 to March 1687. For a list of the corporations rechartered under the two campaigns, see Halliday, *Dismembering*, 351–352. For a list of the corporations regulated by privy council order, see the privy council register for 1687–1688 (TNA, PC 2/72). These tallies include London, which lost its charter in 1683, remained under direct royal control until its charter was restored in October 1688, and was regulated in various ways throughout this period. Note that these tallies also include seventeen borough corporations that did not possess the parliamentary franchise (eight in the earlier campaign, one in the later campaign, and an additional eight in both campaigns).

6. R. G. Pickavance, "The English Boroughs and the King's Government: A Study of the Tory Reaction of 1681–85" (D.Phil. thesis, Univ. of Oxford, 1976), 228–235.

7. James in fact removed all 164 members of the corporation in his initial purge, which was designed to disable the corporation completely, but he later reappointed 30 of them in his charter of August 1688. The 2 men removed by Charles whom James restored were William Wright and Robert Pawling; only the former took up the office to which the king appointed him. See TNA, PC 2/72, fol. 126r–v; *CSPD, James II, 1687–89*, 246; M. G. Hobson and H. E. Salter, eds., *Oxford Council Acts*, 5 vols. (Oxford, 1928–62), iii:149–151, 165–166, 181–183, 196–198. Oxford had an unusually large council; most town councils had between twelve and thirty-six members.

8. This is not to say that James never reappointed men who had been removed in earlier purges during the tory reaction. This occurred in Worcester, Leicester, Nottingham, Grantham, Bewdley, Boston, Bridgwater, and Newcastle-under-Lyme: see Todd Michael Galitz, "The Challenge of Stability: Religion, Politics, and Social Order in Worcestershire, 1660 to 1715" (Ph.D. dissertation, Brown Univ., 1997), 199, 206–207; Neil Paterson, "Politics in Leicestershire, c1677 to c1716" (Ph.D. thesis, Univ. of Nottingham, 2007), 226; Zoe Dawn Bliss, "'Threatening and Tempetuous Times': The Impact of and Responses to the Reign of James II from the East Midlands, 1685–1688" (Ph.D. thesis, Nottingham Trent Univ., 2003), 120, 188; John F. Bailey, *Transcription of Minutes of the Corporation of Boston*, 4 vols. (Boston, 1980–85), iv:249, 313–314; Somerset RO, D/B/bw/119, royal mandate to borough of Bridgwater, 6 Dec. 1687; Somerset RO, D/B/bw/2117; Thomas Pape, *The Restoration Government and the Corporation of Newcastle-under-Lyme* (Manchester, 1940), 52. Note, however, that

in each of these cases only some of the new members appointed by James in 1687–1688 had served in the corporation before; the new regulations also introduced inexperienced members as well.

9. John Dalrymple, *Memoirs of Great Britain and Ireland,* 2nd edn., 2 vols. (London, 1771–73), vol. 2, pt. 1, p. 219, cited in J. P. Kenyon, *Robert Spencer, Earl of Sunderland, 1641–1702* (London, 1958), 189.

10. Steve Pincus, *1688: The First Modern Revolution* (New Haven, 2009), 184; Tim Harris, *Revolution: The Great Crisis of the British Monarchy, 1685–1720* (London, 2006), 233; Halliday, *Dismembering,* 247–248; see also Gilbert Burnet, *Bishop Burnet's History of His Own Time,* ed. M. J. Routh, 2nd edn., 6 vols. (Oxford, 1833), iii:192–193.

11. In all, thirty-eight boroughs were regulated only once, thirty were regulated twice, twenty-one were regulated three times, eleven were regulated four times, two were regulated five times, and one borough (Maldon in Essex) was regulated six times. See TNA, PC 2/72, fols. 54v–155. This tally does not include the first regulations of Cambridge, Worcester, and Barnstaple or the second and fifth regulations of Bury St Edmunds, because these orders duplicated names from other orders and were almost certainly redundant orders that were never delivered. The later regulations were in general smaller than the earlier ones. In first and second regulations, an average of twelve members of the corporation was removed in each regulation. In third regulations, an average of seven members was removed. In fourth, fifth, and sixth regulations, an average of five, four, and two members was removed, respectively. These statistics reveal a pattern in which broad initial purges were followed by limited corrections and adjustments, not a pattern of a campaign spinning out of control (compare Halliday, *Dismembering,* 248–249).

12. For historians who have made this understandable inference, see Thomas Babington Macaulay, *The History of England from the Accession of James the Second,* ed. C. H. Firth, 6 vols. (London, 1913–15), ii:984; Kenyon, *Sunderland,* 189–190; Halliday, *Dismembering,* 248–249; Harris, *Revolution,* 233.

13. The following corporations were sampled: from the north, Carlisle and Pontefract; from the Midlands, Leicester, Boston, Nottingham, Coventry, Lichfield, Northampton, Worcester, and Tewkesbury; from East Anglia, Colchester, Maldon, Bedford, Saffron Walden, Bury St Edmunds, Ipswich, Dunwich, Great Yarmouth, and King's Lynn; from the southeast, Canterbury, Maidstone, Chichester, Guildford, Reading, Abingdon, and Newbury; and from the southwest, Bristol, Bath, Salisbury, Devizes, Wilton, Exeter, Totnes, Liskeard, Bridport, and Lyme Regis. The thirty-six corporations surveyed represent over 50 percent of the sixty-seven corporations that were regulated more than once. Of the thirty-one corporations not included in the survey, twenty-eight were excluded because their records upon inspection proved to be too fragmentary or incomplete to permit this kind of analysis, and one corporation (Honiton) was excluded after a search indicated that no relevant records from

the period have survived. The corporations of Oxford and Norwich were also excluded because a different method of regulation was pursued in these two places. Instead of remodeling the corporation through several stages of regulation, the regulators there chose to dissolve the corporation entirely by removing its members in an indiscriminate purge and then securing a new charter from the Crown to reconstitute the corporation and reinstate many of the purged members. On Oxford and Norwich, see TNA, PC 2/72, fol. 126r–v, 152; BL, Add. MS 36707, fol. 32, letter to James Harrington, 12 June 1688; Hobson and Salter, eds., *Oxford Council Acts*, iii:201. For the names of the royal nominees in the thirty-six corporations sampled, see CAC (C), Ca/2/13, fols. 55, 61–62; West Yorkshire Archive Service, Wakefield, WMT/PON/1/1, p. 146; Richard Holmes, *The Book of Entries of the Pontefract Corporation* (Pontefract, 1882), 165–166; Leicestershire RO, BRII/1/3, p. 933; John F. Bailey, *Transcription of Minutes of the Corporation of Boston*, 4 vols. (Boston, 1980–85), iv:313–314; Nottinghamshire Archives, CA 3455, pp. 22, 26; Historical Society of Pennsylvania, Gratz #175, Case 9, Box 25; Coventry Archives, BA/H/Q/A79/48, letter of James II to the corporation of Coventry, 28 Nov. 1687; Coventry Archives, BA/H/Q/A79/49, same to same, 14 Jan. 1688; Coventry Archives, BA/H/C/17/2, fols. 362–364, 374v; Lichfield RO, D77/5/1, fols. 15, 276; Northamptonshire RO, Northampton Borough Records 3/2, pp. 303–309; Worcestershire RO, Worc. City Ref. A14, Box 2 (also catalogued as 496.5, bulk accession 9630), volume A, fols. 5–6, volume B, p. 32; Gloucestershire RO, TBR/A1/5, pp. 167, 185–189; Essex RO, D/B/5/Gb5, fols. 296–297v; Essex RO, D/B/3/1/23, unfoliated (entries for Jan.–June 1688); Bedfordshire and Luton Archives, Bor.B/B2/2, pp. 288–293; Saffron Walden Borough Council, D/B2/BRE1/17–20; Suffolk RO, Bury St Edmunds, D2/5/3; Suffolk RO, Bury St Edmunds, D4/1/2, fols. 218v–220, 223v, 226v; Suffolk RO, Ipswich, C4/3/1/7, pp. 137–139, 143–145; Suffolk RO, Ipswich, EE6/1144/13, fols. 61–62v; Norfolk RO, Y/C19/9, fols. 127v–128v, 145–147v; King's Lynn RO, KL/C7/12, fols. 65–66, 70; William Richards, *The History of Lynn*, 2 vols. (Lynn, 1812), i:842–844; Canterbury Cathedral Archives, A/C/7, fols. 80–81, 86v–87r, 94v–96r; Canterbury Cathedral Archives, Woodruff's List, Bundle 52, nos. 9–15; Centre for Kentish Studies, Md/Acm1/3, fols. 273–275; K. S. Martin, ed., *Records of Maidstone* (Maidstone, 1926), 162–164; West Sussex RO, MF 1145, C/1, pp. 27–29, 34–37; Surrey History Centre, BR/OC/1/3, fols. 26v–27v; Berkshire RO, R/AC1/1/17, pp. 56–63, 72, 78; Berkshire RO, A/AOzc; Bromley Challenor, ed., *Selections from the Municipal Chronicles of the Borough of Abingdon* (Abingdon, 1898), 176–177; Walter Money, *The History of the Ancient Town and Borough of Newbury* (Oxford, 1887), 309–311; Bristol RO, Common Council Proceedings Book of Bristol, 1687–1702, fols. 4v–5v, 9, 18v–19; Bath RO, Council Book of Bath, 1684–1711, 59, 69–71; Wiltshire RO, G23/1/17, unfoliated (entries for 17 Dec. 1687 and 14 March 1688); Wiltshire RO, G20/1/18, unfoliated (entries for 2 Jan., 10 March, 30 March 1688); B. Howard Cunnington, *Some Annals of the Borough of Devizes*, 2 vols. (Devizes,

1925), i:181–182; Wiltshire RO, G25/1/21, pp. 492–495; Devon RO, ECA/B1/13, pp. 77–79; Devon RO, 1579A/9/35, fols. 225–228; Cornwall RO, DD/BK/353, fol. 22; Dorset RO, DC/BTB/H1, pp. 532–533; Dorset RO, DC/LR/B/1/10, pp. 433–436; Dorset RO, DC/LR/B/2/11, pp. 150–151.

14. J. R. Jones, *The Revolution of 1688 in England* (London, 1972), 149 n., citing NUL, PwV 53/62, William Blathwayt to Sir Robert Southwell, 19 Jan. 1688; for critiques of Jones, see Halliday, *Dismembering*, 239, 249, 260–261; Pat E. Murrell, "Bury St. Edmunds and the Campaign to Pack Parliament, 1687–8," *BIHR*, liv (1981), 188.

15. W. Gurney Benham, ed., *The Charters and Letters Patent Granted to the Borough* (Colchester, 1904), 161–162; G. H. Martin, ed., *The Royal Charters of Grantham, 1463–1688* (Leicester, 1963), 223; J. R. Boyle, ed., *Charters and Letters Patent Granted to Kingston upon Hull* (Hull, 1905), 240; see also *CSPD, James II, 1687–89*, 312.

16. W. G. Hoskins, *Industry, Trade and People in Exeter, 1688–1800* (Manchester, 1935), 30, 53, 123; W. G. Hoskins, "The Population of Exeter," *Devon and Cornwall Notes and Queries*, xviii (1938–39), 246–247; Ransom Pickard, *The Population and Epidemics of Exeter in Pre-Census Times* (Exeter, 1947), 18; Allan Brockett, *Nonconformity in Exeter, 1650–1875* (Manchester, 1962), 71–72; Peter William Jackson, "Nonconformists and Society in Devon, 1660–1689" (Ph.D. thesis, Univ. of Exeter, 1986), 321–322.

17. W. B. Stephens, *Seventeenth-Century Exeter: A Study of Industrial and Commercial Development, 1625–1688* (Exeter, 1958), 85, 100; Richard Izacke, *Remarkable Antiquities of the City of Exeter* (London, 1723), 186; BL, Add. MS 41804, fol. 109b, letter of Exeter magistrates to earl of Middleton, *c.* July 1686; Devon RO, ECA/B1/13, pp. 39, 79; TNA, PC 2/72, fols. 58, 68.

18. *CSPD, James II, 1687–89*, 160; Izacke, *Remarkable Antiquities*, 183–184; Devon RO, ECA/B1/13, pp. 77, 79–80, 84; Brockett, *Nonconformity in Exeter*, 40–41, 44, 50, 57, 71–72; Stephens, *Seventeenth-Century Exeter*, 179; Jackson, "Nonconformists and Society," 321–322. On Crispin, see also Joyce Youings, *Tuckers Hall Exeter: The History of a Provincial City Company through Five Centuries* (Exeter, 1968), 124–125, 138, 231, plate 9; Beatrix F. Cresswell, *A Short History of the Worshipful Company of Weavers, Fullers and Shearmen of the City and County of Exeter* (Exeter, 1930), 89–90. The ten Presbyterians were Humphrey Bawdon, Thomas Crispin, Andrew Jeffery, John Starr, and Edmond Starr, aldermen; and John Boyland, Jerome King, Anthony Mapowder, John Pym, and Robert Tristram, common councillors. Also added as common councillors were Hugh Bidwell and Tobias Allen, who had previously been fined for nonconformity and may have been Presbyterians.

19. Robert Newton, *Eighteenth Century Exeter* (Exeter, 1984), 11; George Trosse, *The Life of the Rev. Mr. George Trosse* (Exeter, 1714), 93.

20. Cornwall RO, Carlyon of Tregehan MSS, DD/CN, no. 3480, James Salter to Charles Trewbody, 30 July 1688; Devon RO, ECA/B1/13, pp. 77–79,

86. Although Thomas Jefford was probably not himself a Presbyterian, he was said to have attended nonconformist services in 1688 with some of the aldermen: see *The Entring Book of Roger Morrice, 1677–1691*, ed. Mark Goldie, John Spurr, Tim Harris, Stephen Taylor, Mark Knights, and Jason McElligott, 7 vols. (Woodbridge, 2007–9), iv:218.

21. *CSPD, James II, 1687–89*, 305; BL, Add. MS 41805, fol. 118, earl of Bath to earl of Middleton, 5 Nov. 1688; Mark Goldie, "James II and the Dissenters' Revenge: The Commission of Enquiry of 1688," *Historical Research*, lxvi (1993), 75–76.

22. *CSPD, James II, 1687–89*, 150, 157–158; *London Gazette*, no. 2332 (22–26 March 1688).

23. *Publick Occurrences*, no. 7 (3 April 1688); M. E. Curtis, *Some Disputes between the City and the Cathedral Authorities of Exeter* (Manchester, 1932), 41; *CSPD, James II, 1687–89*, 160–161, 305; M. C. S. Cruwys, "The Diary of John Cruwys of Cruwys Morchard (1682–8)," *Devon and Cornwall Notes and Queries*, xviii (1934–35), 263. For Cruwys's antipathy to Catholics and to the dissenting "sects," see ibid., 261.

24. Jonathan Barry, "Exeter in 1688: The Trial of the Seven Bishops," in Todd Gray, ed., *Devon Documents* (Tiverton, 1996), 9–11; Devon RO, ECA/C1/66, fols. 198–199v.

25. *A New Ballad, To the Tune of, Good People Give Ear* (n.p., [1688], N576). Exeter had a mayor, eight aldermen, ten common councilmen, four bailiffs, a sheriff, a chamberlain, a recorder, a deputy recorder, a sheriff, a coroner, and three minor officials.

26. *London Gazette*, no. 2315 (23–26 Jan. 1688); original draft of address in possession of the author; Brockett, *Nonconformity in Exeter*, 54.

27. BL, Add. MS 41805, fol. 118, earl of Bath to earl of Middleton, 5 Nov. 1688; *London Gazette*, no. 2360 (28 June–2 July 1688); Devon RO, ECA/B1/13, pp. 79–80.

28. Margery M. Rowe and Andrew M. Jackson, eds., *Exeter Freemen, 1266–1967* (Exeter, 1973), xxvii, 177–180. The 226 freemen added from February to September 1688 represent just over 40 percent of the total number of freemen added during the entire decade of the 1680s. The size of the Exeter electorate was fairly large, at about 550 voters in 1689: see Henning, ed., *House of Commons*, i:197.

29. Sir George Duckett, ed., *Penal Laws and Test Act: Questions Touching their Repeal Propounded in 1687–8 by James II*, 2 vols. (London, 1882–83), ii:231; Henning, ed., *House of Commons*, i:200. Shower had been knighted after presenting the Middlesex grand jury's address of thanks for the *Declaration for Liberty of Conscience*: see *London Gazette*, no. 2242 (12–16 May 1687).

30. Catherine Glover and Philip Riden, eds., *William Wooley's History of Derbyshire* (Derby, 1981), 41.

31. Anton Rippon, *The Book of Derby: From Settlement to City* (Buckingham,

1980), 95; Glover and Riden, eds., *William Wooley's History,* 23–24; A. W. Davison, *Derby: Its Rise and Progress* (London, 1906), 240–243; Daniel Defoe, *A Tour Thro' the Whole Island of Great Britain,* ed. G. D. H. Cole, 2 vols. (London, 1927), ii:564.

32. HEHL, HA 12981, George Vernon to earl of Huntingdon, 19 Aug. 1688; see also Robert Simpson, *A Collection of Fragments Illustrative of the History and Antiquities of Derby,* 2 vols. (Derby, 1826), i:428–429, ii:745; Glover and Riden, eds., *William Wooley's History,* 33.

33. For one Presbyterian minister's abandonment of this tradition at about this time, see *An Account of the Life and Death of Mr. Philip Henry, Minister of the Gospel near Whitchurch in Shropshire* (1698, B1100A), 169, 171.

34. HEHL, HA 12979, George Vernon to earl of Huntingdon, 1 July 1688; HA 12981, George Vernon to earl of Huntingdon, 19 Aug. 1688. On the fissure within Presbyterianism, see Roger Thomas, "Parties in Nonconformity," in C. G. Bolam et al., eds., *The English Presbyterians: From Elizabethan Puritanism to Modern Unitarianism* (Boston, 1968), 98, 100–101; idem, "Comprehension and Indulgence," in Geoffrey Nuttall and Owen Chadwick, eds., *From Uniformity to Unity, 1662–1962* (London, 1962), 208–211, 236–237; R. A. Beddard, "Vincent Alsop and the Emancipation of Restoration Dissent," *JEH,* xxiv (1973), 166, 176; Mark Goldie, *Roger Morrice and the Puritan Whigs* (Woodbridge, 2007), 227–230, 237.

35. HEHL, HA 12978, George Vernon to earl of Huntingdon, 8 June 1688.

36. HEHL, HA 12981, George Vernon to earl of Huntingdon, 19 Aug. 1688; HA 10668, Samuel Sanders to earl of Huntingdon, 19 Oct. 1687; HA 370, John Bagnold to earl of Huntingdon, 26 March 1688; HA 372, same to same, 25 April 1688; HA 12978, George Vernon to earl of Huntingdon, 8 June 1688; HA 12983, same to same, *c.* Sept. 1688.

37. Duckett, ed., *Penal Laws,* i:167; Eveline Cruickshanks, Stuart Handley, and D. W. Hayton, eds., *The House of Commons, 1690–1715,* 5 vols. (Cambridge, 2002), v:886–887.

38. Andrew Browning, ed., *Memoirs of Sir John Reresby,* rev. Mary K. Geiter and W. A. Speck (London, 1991), 398; Henning, ed., *House of Commons,* ii:100–101.

39. TNA, PC 2/72, fol. 71; BL, Add. MS 6669, fol. 232, royal mandate to town of Derby, 2 Jan. 1688; HEHL, HA 12980, George Vernon to earl of Huntingdon, 6 Aug. 1688.

40. HEHL, HA 12980, George Vernon to earl of Huntingdon, 6 Aug. 1688; HA 12979, same to same, 1 July 1688.

41. Derbyshire RO, D258/17/31/58, John Gisborne Jr. to Sir John Gell, 4 Aug. 1688.

42. While it is possible that the new alderman of Derby was John Gisbourne Sr., who was still alive at the time, this seems unlikely. John Gisbourne Jr. was a forty-four-year-old man in 1688; his father, Gisbourne Sr., was eighty-six years of age, possibly in poor health (he died a year later), and

unlikely to be able to return to the council on which he had once served as mayor in 1659. See Simpson, *Collection of Fragments*, i:419, 421, ii:745; BL, Add. MS 6669, fol. 232, royal mandate to town of Derby, 2 Jan. 1688.

43. HEHL, HA 12974, George Vernon to earl of Huntingdon, 31 Jan. 1688; HA 12980, same to same, 6 Aug. 1688.

44. Stephen Crisp declined the offer of a magistrate's position in Colchester in 1688 and William Mead refused to be an alderman in London in 1687: see William Sewel, *The History of the Rise, Increase, and Progress of the Christian People called Quakers* (London, 1722), 610; BL, Mic M/636, reel 42, Claydon House letters, Henry Paman to Sir Ralph Verney, 17 Aug. 1687.

45. See HEHL, HA 6949, Sir Henry Hunloke to earl of Huntingdon, 14 July 1688; William E. Buckley, ed., *Memoirs of Thomas, Earl of Ailesbury, Written by Himself*, 2 vols. (Westminster, 1890), i:152; John Miller, *Popery and Politics in England, 1660–1688* (Cambridge, 1973), 224.

46. On Catholic responses to the Three Questions, see John Miller, *James II: A Study in Kingship* (Hove, 1978), 178. The split among English Catholics between moderates and zealots, or a more cautious group affiliated with the pope and a more militant one affiliated with the French and the Jesuits, has been a running theme in the historiography of the Glorious Revolution since the nineteenth century: see Macaulay, *History of England*, ii:704–718, 980–982; George Macaulay Trevelyan, *The English Revolution, 1688–1689* (London, 1938), 59–60; F. C. Turner, *James II* (London, 1948), 325, 351–352; David Ogg, *England in the Reigns of James II and William III* (Oxford, 1955), 164–165; Kenyon, *Sunderland*, 122, 125, 145–146, 195; Jones, *Revolution of 1688*, 33–34; Miller, *Popery and Politics*, 223–225; Pincus, *1688*, 138–142. A degree of caution must be used in discussing these divisions. Although a factional divide was evident among many Catholics at court during James's reign, there is less evidence to indicate whether Catholics outside the court identified with either of the two factions.

47. For letters by Catholics to Protestants urging them to support repeal, see Bodl., MS Tanner 259, fol. 54v, Henry Bedingfield to Sir John Holland, 3 Jan. 1688; CAC (K), WD/Ry HMC no. 3180, Sir Thomas Strickland to Sir Daniel Fleming, 17 March 1688; North Yorkshire RO, ZQH, Microfilm 948, 9/5/46, Edward Burdett to Sir William Chaytor, 3 Jan. 1688. For repealer pamphlets written by Catholics, see [John Dryden], *The Hind and the Panther* (1687, D2281), and Henry Neville Payne, *An Answer to a Scandalous Pamphlet* (1687, P887). See also the support for James's policies expressed in *A Speech Spoken by Mr. Hayles, A Student of University-Colledge of Oxford* (1687, H1209). The Catholic Justice Sir Richard Allibone's pro-repeal charge to the assizes at Croydon circulated in manuscript in 1688: see Bodl., MS Tanner 28, fols. 137–138v.

48. *Publick Occurrences*, no. 31 (18 Sept. 1688).

49. [Elkanah Settle?], *An Expedient for Peace: Perswading an Agreement amongst Christians* (1688, E3872aA), 30–31, 14. For parallel phrases found in

the *Expedient for Peace* and in Settle's writings for *Publick Occurrences,* compare the *Expedient,* 13, with *Occurrences,* no. 31. Both the *Expedient* and the *Occurrences* were printed by George Larkin.

50. *Expedient for Peace,* 16, 14, 17.

51. *Publick Occurrences,* no. 32 (25 Sept. 1688); *Som[e] Free Reflections upon Occasion of the Public Discourse about Liberty of Conscience* (1687, P1366), 17; see also *Expedient for Peace,* 33–34, which also described the use of denominational labels as a "malignity."

52. N. N., *Old Popery as Good as New* (n.p., 1688, N47), 3.

53. *Expedient for Peace,* 14; N. N., *Old Popery,* 3.

54. *Indulgence to Tender Consciences Shewn to be Most Reasonable and Christian* (1687, I157), 6.

55. Daniel Kenrick, *A Sermon Preached in the Cathedral-Church of Worcester* (1688, K307), 29, 26; on the relationship between soteriology and toleration in the early modern period, see Stuart B. Schwartz, *All Can Be Saved: Religious Tolerance and Salvation in the Iberian Atlantic World* (New Haven, 2008).

56. *Som[e] Free Reflections,* 13.

57. W. M. Spellman, *The Latitudinarians and the Church of England, 1660–1700* (Athens, GA, 1993), 51–52; Roger Thomas, "The Seven Bishops and their Petition, 18 May 1688," *JEH,* xii (1961), 60–63. On Burnet's opposition to the repealers, see especially Gilbert Burnet, *Six Papers* (n.p., 1687, B5912), 1–7, 21–30; [Burnet], *An Apology for the Church of England* (n.p., [1688], B5762), 2, 7–8; [Burnet], *The Ill Effects of Animosities among Protestants in England Detected* (n.p., 1688, B5802), 9, 14. For Henry Care's critique of the Latitudinarian opposition to repeal, see his *Animadversions on a Late Paper, Entituled, A Letter to a Dissenter* (1687, C505), 6–7.

58. Bodl., MS Ballard 12, fol. 38, George Hickes to Arthur Charlett, 30 July 1688; Worcestershire RO, Ref. 899:209, bulk accession 1834, bishop of Worcester to George Hickes, 7 April 1688; Kenrick, *Sermon,* 32; *CSPD, James II, 1687–89,* 343.

59. *The Grove; or, a Collection of Original Poems* (London, 1721), iv; P. J. Wallis and R. V. Wallis, *Eighteenth Century Medics,* 2nd edn. (Newcastle, 1988), 340; Bodl., MS Eng. Misc. e.4 (life of George Hickes), fols. 23v–24; *Oxford Dictionary of National Biography,* s.v. "Kenrick, Daniel (*b.* 1649/50)"; *CSPD, James II, 1687–89,* 343.

60. Jones, "Whig Collaborators," 68, 71–72; Jones, *Revolution of 1688,* 144; Henning, ed., *House of Commons,* i:41; Halliday, *Dismembering,* 244.

61. Murdina MacDonald was the first to note that some of the regulators (four, by her count) had been Baptist ministers, but the findings of her Oxford D.Phil. thesis of 1982, "London Calvinistic Baptists 1689–1727: Tensions within a Dissenting Community under Toleration," 15–17, were overlooked in the subsequent literature. See also Gary S. De Krey, "Reformation and 'Arbitrary Government': London Dissenters and James II's Polity of Toleration, 1687–1688,"

in Jason McElligott, ed., *Fear, Exclusion and Revolution: Roger Morrice and Britain in the 1680s* (Aldershot, 2006), 25–26; Miller, *Cities Divided*, 229; *Entring Book of Roger Morrice*, iv:226, 230.

62. For attendance figures, see FSL, Newdigate newsletters, L.c.1782, 8 March 1687; W. T. Whitley, *The Baptists of London, 1612–1928* (London, [1928]), 112; James M. Renihan, "The Practical Ecclesiology of the English Particular Baptists, 1675–1705" (Ph.D. dissertation, Trinity Evangelical Divinity School, 1997), 62–63; TNA, SP29/419, no. 55, analyzed in W. T. Whitley, "London Churches in 1682," *Baptist Quarterly,* i (1922–23), 82–87. All figures except those for Plant are from 1682, at a time when attendance was depressed due to religious persecution. Of the nine ministers, Cox, Collins, Dennis, and James Jones were Particular Baptists, Marner was a General Baptist, John Jones was a seventh-day Baptist, Thomas Plant steered clear of an affiliation with either the Particulars or the Generals, and Richard Adams was a Calvinist in his personal beliefs but ministered at a General Baptist Church. The ninth pastor, Elias Bowyer, was a General Baptist minister in Nottinghamshire. On the backgrounds, occupations, and prior political activities of the regulators, see Scott Sowerby, "Forgetting the Repealers: Religious Toleration and Historical Amnesia in Later Stuart England," *Past and Present*, no. 215 (May 2012), 92–95. On the history of the Particular Baptists and their division from the General Baptists, see Stephen Wright, *The Early English Baptists, 1603–1649* (Woodbridge, 2006), 5–12, 75, 114, 138–142; B. R. White, *The English Baptists of the Seventeenth Century,* 2nd edn. (Didcot, 1996), 9.

63. Each regulator received ten pounds to purchase a horse and one pound per day for travel expenses. On payments to the regulators, see NUL, PwA 2160, James Rivers to [Hans Willem Bentinck], 4 Apr. 1688; John Yonge Akerman, ed., *Moneys Received and Paid for Secret Services of Charles II and James II,* Camden Society, old series, lii (1851), 196–197, 205; *London Courant,* no. 4 (18–22 Dec. 1688).

64. Thomas Plant and Benjamin Dennis, *The Mischief of Persecution Exemplified* (1688, P2377A), 45–46, dated 7 May 1688 on the title page.

65. Duckett, ed., *Penal Laws,* i:195–198; Bodl., MS Rawl. a.139b, fol. 105r–v; *Memorandums for those that Go into the Country to Dispose the Corporations to a Good Election* (n.p., [1688], M1680), 2, 4.

66. On Trinder, who may have been a Roman Catholic, see Anchitell Grey, *Debates of the House of Commons, from the Year 1667 to the Year 1694,* 10 vols. (London, 1763), ix:340; *Entring Book of Roger Morrice,* iv:226–227; *CSPD, James II, 1687–89,* 275; Lambeth Palace Library, MS 3898, no. 6, Henry Paman to bishop of Norwich, 18 Aug. 1687; Longleat House, Thynne MSS, xxiv, fol. 77, Sir Thomas Clarges to marquess of Halifax, 6 Nov. 1689. On the privy council subcommittee, see TNA, PC 2/72; *LJ,* xiv:388; Narcissus Luttrell, *A Brief Historical Relation of State Affairs,* 6 vols. (Oxford, 1857), i:420–421; NUL, PwA 2146, James Rivers to [Hans Willem Bentinck], 21 Feb. 1688.

67. These patents were an expedient that had been rendered superfluous when James proclaimed his *Declaration for Liberty of Conscience* in April 1687. For Brent's role in issuing them, see Joseph Ivimey, *A History of the English Baptists,* 4 vols. (London, 1811–30), i:464; *Entring Book of Roger Morrice,* iii:194, 325, 344; *CSPD, James II, 1686–87,* 66, 71–2, 268, 323, 358, 388; BL, Add. MS 41813, fol. 171, Bevil Skelton to earl of Middleton, 29 June/9 July 1686. On Brent's background and influence, see *HMC, Ormonde,* n.s., v:32; *CTB,* v:910; S. C. Ratcliff, H. C. Johnson and N. J. Williams, eds., *Warwick County Records,* 8 vols. (Warwick, 1935–64), vol. viii, pp. xxviii–xxix; Duckett, ed., *Penal Laws,* i:240; *Entring Book of Roger Morrice,* iii:377; *The Pension Book of Gray's Inn,* ed. Reginald J. Fletcher, 2 vols. (London, 1901–10), ii:92; BL, Add. MS 75366, Robert Brent to Lord Melfort, 17 Nov. 1688.

68. Badminton House Muniments Room, FmE2/4/25, letter to Mr. Burgis of Malmesbury, *c.* Jan. 1688. This letter was signed by Roberts, Marner, Bowyer, Cox, Plant, Collins, Dennis, and James Jones.

69. *LJ,* xiv:388; *Entring Book of Roger Morrice,* iv:226–227, 230–231.

70. T.P., *Multum in Parvo* (1688, P115), title page; George Withers, *The Grateful Acknowledgment of a Late Trimming Regulator* (1688, W3161), 3–4; *London Mercury,* no. 4 (22–24 Dec. 1688); on the French dragoons as "booted apostles," see [James Welwood], *An Answer to the Late King James's Declaration* (1689, W1298), 28; *The Twelfth and Last Collection of Papers* (1689, T3392), ii; Pierre Bayle, *A Philosophical Commentary on these Words of the Gospel,* 2 vols. (London, 1708), ii:381 (original French edition published in 1686).

71. *CSPD, James II, 1687–89,* 138, 305.

72. William E. Buckley, ed., *Memoirs of Thomas, Earl of Ailesbury, Written by Himself,* 2 vols. (Westminster, 1890), i:175–176.

73. The twelve counties visited were Cambridgeshire, Norfolk, Suffolk, and Essex in the east; Hampshire and Sussex in the south; Devon, Dorset, Somerset, and Wiltshire in the southwest; and Lincolnshire and Yorkshire in the northeast. See Duckett, ed., *Penal Laws,* ii:218, 221, 233–234. Rutland also was untouched, as it did not have any parliamentary boroughs. Durham, as a county palatine, was regulated by order of the bishop of Durham, not by privy council order. Of the Welsh boroughs, only one was regulated in this period: Neath in Glamorgan. In London, the livery companies were heavily regulated in this period: see Mark Knights, "A City Revolution: The Remodelling of the London Livery Companies in the 1680s," *EHR,* cxii (1997), 1158–1163.

74. Duckett, ed., *Penal Laws,* ii:234–253. The newly visited counties were Surrey, Kent, and Buckinghamshire in the home counties and Worcestershire, Shropshire, Staffordshire, Derbyshire, and Nottinghamshire in the Midlands. Other new counties may have been visited by regulators in the second round, but, if so, the reports do not survive.

75. Mary Maples Dunn and Richard S. Dunn, eds., *The Papers of William Penn,* 5 vols. (Philadelphia, 1981–86), iii:176.

76. Grey, *Debates,* ix:340. The advantage of entrusting delivery to local correspondents was that these correspondents could time the delivery of the orders to achieve maximum tactical advantage, or even choose not to deliver them if they seemed unnecessary. For examples of such practices, see Norfolk RO, Y/C19/9, fols. 145–146; Duckett, ed., *Penal Laws,* i:315; Perry Gauci, *Politics and Society in Great Yarmouth, 1660–1722* (Oxford, 1996), 167–168; *CSPD, James II, 1687–89,* 174; Bristol RO, Common Council Proceedings Book of Bristol, 1687–1702, fol. 4v. For payments to the royal messengers, see Huntingdonshire Archives, Corporation MSS, box 6, bundle 4; W. M. Wigfield, "Recusancy and Nonconformity in Bedfordshire," *Publications of the Bedfordshire Historical Record Society,* xx (1938), 203; Herefordshire RO, Leominster Borough MSS, S67/4/2/100; Beverley RO, BC/II/5/1, fol. 19; Hobson and Salter, eds., *Oxford Council Acts,* iii:198.

77. Dunn and Dunn, eds., *Papers of William Penn,* iii:175–177; TNA, PC 2/72, fols. 94, 126v, 154v; Besse, *A Collection of the Sufferings,* i:261–264, 268.

78. Duckett, ed., *Penal Laws,* i:263, 269, ii:202, 207; Henning, ed., *House of Commons,* ii:326, iii:3; Pape, *Newcastle-under-Lyme,* 50; Molly McClain, *Beaufort: The Duke and his Duchess, 1657–1715* (New Haven, 2001), 183–184; TNA, PC 2/72, fols. 62v, 65.

79. *CSPD, James II, 1687–89,* 305; Lord Braybrooke, ed., *The Autobiography of Sir John Bramston,* Camden Society, old series, xxxii (1845), 304.

80. See, for example, the asking of the Three Questions in Carlisle by the Catholic governor of the town's garrison, Francis Howard, described in CAC (K), Fleming MSS, WD/Ry HMC no. 3152, Sir Christopher Musgrave to Sir Daniel Fleming, 8 Dec. 1687; idem, no. 3154, letter to Richard Lowry, 23 Dec. 1687; Luttrell, *Brief Historical Relation,* i:419. Various local councils were also interrogated by the Catholic governor of Hull, lord Langdale; the Catholic governor of Berwick, Sir Thomas Haggerston; Bishop Crewe of Durham; the Catholic earl of Peterborough in Northampton; and the Catholic justices of the peace Sir Walter Vavasour and John Middleton in Leeds. Note that these interrogations did not always include the asking of the Three Questions in their precise wording. See Hull City Archives, BRL 2759a, fol. 38; Hull City Archives, DMX/134.1, p. 161; Berwick-upon-Tweed RO, B1/13, fols. 138, 146; Duckett, ed., *Penal Laws,* i:115; Durham County RO, Du 1/4/5, fol. 26; Durham County RO, Du 1/35/1, p. 40; Margaret Child, "Prelude to Revolution: The Structure of Politics in County Durham, 1678–1688" (Ph.D. dissertation, Univ. of Maryland, 1972), 131–134; Northamptonshire RO, Fermor Hesketh Baker MS 712, fols. 54v–55v; Northamptonshire RO, Northampton Borough Records 3/2, pp. 303–7, 309; Thomas Brooke, ed., "Extracts from the Journal of Castilion Morris," *Yorkshire Archaeological and Topographical Journal,* x (1889), 161; Duckett, ed., *Penal Laws,* i:86–87; Michael Eric Watts Maddison, "The Justices of the Peace and the Administration of Local Government in the East and West Ridings of Yorkshire between 1680 and 1750" (Ph.D. thesis, Univ. of Leeds, 1986), 76.

81. *CSPD, James II, 1687–89,* 102–103.

82. See, for example, *CSPD, James II, 1687–89,* 138.

83. Hull City Archives, BRL 2759a, fol. 40v, letter of 27 April 1688.

84. Nottinghamshire Archives, M8657/1, "An Account of the charges I was at when I went to London with the Address to the King"; *London Gazette,* no. 2328 (8–12 March 1688). Harvey also paid a bill of two pounds and five shillings for a dinner at a tavern with Brent and twelve others. On Harvey, who had served as groom of the bedchamber to Oliver Cromwell, see Nottinghamshire Archives, CA 1659, M8650, M8651; C. H. Firth, ed., *The Clarke Papers,* 4 vols. (London, 1891–1901), iii:47; W. C. Abbott, ed., *The Writings and Speeches of Oliver Cromwell,* 4 vols. (Cambridge, MA, 1937–47), iv:871; Violet W. Walker, "The Confiscation of Firearms in Nottingham in Charles Harvey's Mayoralty, 1689–1690," in J. H. Hodson, P. A. Kennedy, and Violet W. Walker, eds., *A Nottinghamshire Miscellany,* Thoroton Society Record Series, xxi (Nottingham, 1962), 21, 24–25.

85. Devon RO, ECA/B1/13, pp. 79–80; Dorset RO, DC/LR/G/9/36; Dorset RO, DC/LR/G/1/3, p. 103; *London Gazette,* no. 2345 (7–10 May 1688).

86. Pape, *Newcastle-under-Lyme,* 52; Nottinghamshire Archives, CA 3455, p. 49; Nottinghamshire Archives, CA 4692 c/5, letter of George Langford et al. to unknown, 26 June 1688; see also Challenor, ed., *Selections from Chronicles of Abingdon,* 178. At least two of the three local men who arranged for the regulation of Newcastle-under-Lyme were nonconformists: see J. H. Y. Briggs, "The Burning of the Meeting House, July 1715: Dissent and Faction in Late Stuart Newcastle," *North Staffordshire Journal of Field Studies,* xiv (1974), 65.

87. Coventry Archives, BA/H/C/17/2, fols. 374v–375.

88. The local agents included Richard Jobson (or perhaps another local Quaker) in Huntingdon, John Scanfield in Preston, Francis Howard in Carlisle, Lord Langdale in Hull, Sir Thomas Haggerston in Berwick, Caleb Wilkinson and Timothy Tomlinson in Nottingham, John Oneby in Leicester, Lord Brandon in Lancaster, Henry Ravening in Barnstaple, Michael Cadman in Rye, and Sir John Reresby in York. On Scanfield, see Anthony Hewitson, ed., *Diary of Thomas Bellingham* (Preston, 1908), 16; "The Defection of John Scanfield," *JFHS,* v (1908), 177–187. On Oneby, see HEHL, HA 9778, John Onebye to earl of Huntingdon, 23 Jan. 1688; HA 9779, same to same, 7 Sept. 1688; HA 13677, Sir Nathan Wright to earl of Huntingdon, 21 April 1688; *Entring Book of Roger Morrice,* iv:70–71. On Brandon, see *HMC, Kenyon,* 213, 233–234. On Ravening, see J. R. Chanter and Thomas Wainwright, eds., *Reprint of the Barnstaple Records,* 2 vols. (Barnstaple, 1900), i:76–77; North Devon RO, B/1/3984, pp. 48, 69–70, 77–78; North Devon RO, B/1/615. On Cadman, who appears to have been an Anglican or a partial conformist though he was friendly with the nonconformists of the town of Rye, see William Andrews Clark Memorial Library, MS.1959.005, pp. 41, 44, 76–77; Michael Hunter and Annabel Gregory, eds., *An Astrological Diary of the Seventeenth Century: Samuel Jeake of Rye, 1652–1699*

(Oxford, 1988), 146, 158, 163, 173–174, 192, 208; East Sussex RO, RYE 1/17, pp. 120, 141. On Reresby, see *Memoirs of Sir John Reresby*, 508–510.

89. Murrell, "Bury St. Edmunds," 205–206. Benjamin Dennis, one of the Baptist regulators, was active in the regulation of Bury St Edmunds, which brought in a Catholic mayor.

90. On the informants, Caleb Wilkinson and Timothy Tomlinson, see Charles Deering, *Nottinghamia Vetus et Nova* (Nottingham, 1751), 105; Patricia Ann Lloyd, "Politics, Religion and the Personnel of Politics in Nottingham, 1642–1688" (M.Phil. thesis, Univ. of Nottingham, 1983), 309; NUL, CU S/1, p. 1, accounts for building of the Congregational meetinghouse in 1689; Walker, "Confiscation of Firearms," 23.

91. Dunn and Dunn, eds., *Papers of William Penn*, iii:176.

92. For Joseph Wright, the new mayor of Maidstone, who was a Baptist minister and a physician, see Ivimey, *English Baptists*, ii:237–238; Centre for Kentish Studies, Md/Acm1/3, fols. 273, 282; Hunter and Gregory, eds., *Astrological Diary*, 238 n. For Nathaniel Bayly, the Baptist mayor of Marlborough, see *CSPD, James II, 1687–89*, 262; Wiltshire RO, G22/1/318, affidavit of John Furnell, 11 Oct. 1688. For the other Baptist appointees, see Wiltshire RO, G25/1/21, p. 495; Arthur Tucker, "Porton Baptist Church, 1655–85," *Transactions of the Baptist Historical Society*, i (1908–1909), 60; Hobson and Salter, eds., *Oxford Council Acts*, iii:197; *HMC, Portland*, iii:405; Berkshire RO, A/AOzc, James II to corporation of Abingdon, 28 Nov. 1687; Bromley Challenor, ed., *Selections from the Municipal Chronicles of the Borough of Abingdon* (Abingdon, 1898), 176–177; Arthur E. Preston, *The Church and Parish of St. Nicholas, Abingdon* (Oxford, 1935), 138, 140, 142 n.; *CSPD, James II, 1686–87*, 181–182.

93. Although at least thirty-six Quakers were appointed to office, in most cases the surviving evidence is not adequate to show whether or not they actually served. Six of them, however, can be definitively shown to have taken up their offices: Edward Gilbert as capital burgess of Devizes, Caleb Wood Sr. as alderman of Guildford, Thomas Penford as common councilman of Leicester, John Bowers as alderman of Banbury, Thomas Buckingham as common councilman of King's Lynn, and Edward Deekes as alderman of Bury St Edmunds. See Wiltshire RO, G20/1/18, unfoliated (entries for 2 Jan., 10 March, and 30 March 1688); Wiltshire RO, G20/1/19, fol. 1; Surrey History Centre, BR/OC/1/3, fol. 27v; Surrey History Centre, BR/OC/1/9, unpaginated (entries for 28 April, 7 May, 28 May, 18 June 1688); Leicestershire RO, BRII/18/36, nos. 87, 88; Oxfordshire RO, B.B.XVII/i, fol. 166; J. S. W. Gibson and E. R. C. Brinkworth, eds., *Banbury Corporation Records: Tudor and Stuart* (Banbury, 1977), 287, 302; King's Lynn RO, KL/C7/12, fols. 66, 71; Henry J. Hillen, *History of the Borough of King's Lynn*, 2 vols. (Norwich, 1907), i:444, ii:470–471; Suffolk RO, Bury St Edmunds, D4/1/2, fols. 208, 210, 220, 222, 223v, 224v; Murrell, "Bury St. Edmunds," 193–194, 205. On the other Quaker appointees who may or may not have served, see Scott Sowerby, "James II's Revolution: The Politics of Reli-

gious Toleration in England, 1685–1689" (Ph.D. dissertation, Harvard Univ., 2006), 121–125. In addition to these thirty-six Quakers, two members of a separatist Quaker meeting were appointed in Newbury but subsequently refused to take the oath of office: see Berkshire RO, Aca1, fol. 92; Berkshire RO, D/F/2/B/2/6, unfoliated (entry for 3 Sept. 1690); Money, *History of Newbury*, 310. The Quaker Charles Lloyd of Dolobran served as a justice of the peace in Montgomeryshire: see J. R. S. Phillips, ed., *The Justices of the Peace in Wales and Monmouthshire, 1541–1689* (Cardiff, 1975), 154; Duckett, ed., *Penal Laws*, i:262, 285, 447.

94. Richard L. Greaves, *Glimpses of Glory: John Bunyan and English Dissent* (Stanford, 2002), 570–572; M. J. Short, "The Corporation of Hull and the Government of James II, 1687–8," *Historical Research*, lxxi (1998), 194; Lloyd, "Personnel of Politics in Nottingham," 310; Basil Short, *A Respectable Society: Bridport, 1593–1835* (Bradford-on-Avon, 1976), 24, 26; Norfolk RO, Y/C19/9, fols. 128r–v, 145v–146; B. Cozens-Hardy and A. Stuart Brown, "Old Meeting House, Norwich, and Great Yarmouth Independent Church," *Publications of the Norfolk Record Society*, xxiii (1951), 9–10, 13–15, 17–26, 28, 32–33, 35–36, 39; J. E. Clowes, *Chronicles of the Old Congregational Church at Great Yarmouth* (Great Yarmouth, 1912), 49; Gauci, *Great Yarmouth*, 169; M. A. Mullett, "Conflict, Politics and Elections in Lancaster, 1660–1688," *Northern History*, xix (1983), 81; BL, Add. MS 34152, fol. 17, Anthony Heyford to [William Blathwayt], 14 April 1688.

95. J. A. Hilton, "The Catholic Ascendancy in the North 1685–1688," *North West Catholic History*, no. 5 (1978), 4–5; idem, "The Catholic Ascendancy in the Midlands 1685–1688," *Staffordshire Catholic History*, no. 18 (1978), 15–18; idem, "The Catholic Ascendancy in the South West 1685–1688," *London Recusant*, vii (1977), 71–72; idem, "The Catholic Ascendancy in the Eastern Counties, 1685–88," *Essex Recusant*, xx (1978), 16; Galitz, "Challenge of Stability," 199; Michael John Short, "The Political Relationship between Central Government and the Local Administration in Yorkshire, 1678–90" (Ph.D. thesis, Univ. of Leeds, 1999), 355, 361, 370.

96. Duckett, ed., *Penal Laws*, ii:227, 231; Michael R. Watts, *The Dissenters: From the Reformation to the French Revolution* (Oxford, 1978), 270, 509.

97. West Sussex RO, MF 1145, C/1, p. 28.

98. Murrell, "Bury St. Edmunds," 204–205; Suffolk RO, Bury St Edmunds, D4/1/2, fols. 207–210, 220–224v. The Quakers called the town Edmundsbury, an abbreviation of the variant name for the town, St Edmundsbury: see Joseph Besse, *A Collection of the Sufferings of the People called Quakers*, 2 vols. (London, 1753), i:671, 676.

99. Several historians have suggested that the Quakers largely withdrew from politics after the Restoration: see Leopold von Ranke, *A History of England, Principally in the Seventeenth Century*, 6 vols. (Oxford, 1875), iii:580–581; N. H. Keeble, *The Literary Culture of Nonconformity in Later Seventeenth-Century England*

(Leicester, 1987), 19–26, 192–193; Douglas R. Lacey, *Dissent and Parliamentary Politics in England, 1661–1689* (New Brunswick, N.J., 1969), 11–12; Christopher Hill, *The Experience of Defeat: Milton and Some Contemporaries* (1984), 136; idem, "Quakers and the English Revolution," in Michael Mullett, ed., *New Light on George Fox* (York, 1993), 31–34. For historians who have argued for the continued involvement of Quakers in politics after the Restoration, see Richard L. Greaves, "Shattered Expectations? George Fox, the Quakers, and the Restoration State, 1660–1685," *Albion*, xxiv (1992), 237–259, and George Southcombe, "The Responses of Nonconformists to the Restoration in England," (D.Phil. thesis, Univ. of Oxford, 2005), 3–6, 101–103, 125–126, 262. No Quakers are known to have served on English town councils from 1669 to 1687, but this lack of office-holding was almost certainly due to their conscientious objection to swearing an oath of office: see Mary Geiter, "Affirmation, Assassination, and Association: The Quakers, Parliament and the Court in 1696," *Parliamentary History*, xvi (1997), 281–282; Nicholas Morgan, "The Social and Political Relations of the Lancaster Quaker Community, 1688–1740," in Michael Mullett, ed., *Early Lancaster Friends* (Centre for North-West Regional Studies, Univ. of Lancaster, Occasional Paper no. 5, 1978), 22.

100. LSF, Yearly Meeting Minutes, vol. 1 (1668–93), pp. 200–201; Brotherton Library, Leeds University MS Deposit 1981/2 (Clifford Street), Shelf II, No. 2, fol. 68r–v. The voting guide itself has not survived.

101. NUL, PwV 61/23, J. Povey to Sir Robert Southwell, 13 Aug. 1687; CUL, Microfilm MS 9528 (repertories of the court of aldermen of London), repertory 92, pp. 525–526; LLIU, Albeville MSS, Robert Yard to marquis d'Albeville, 14 Sept. 1688; William Orme, ed., *Remarkable Passages in the Life of William Kiffin* (London, 1823), 84–88. The council of Maidstone, led by its Baptist mayor, passed an order permitting office-holders to serve without wearing formal gowns: see Centre for Kentish Studies, Md/Acm1/3, fol. 277, entry for 3 April 1688.

102. Badminton House Muniments Room, FmE2/4/25, "Returne of the Burrough of Malmesbury to his Majesties Letter of Mandam[us]," *c*. Jan. 1688. The speaker was Thomas Eastmell/Eastmeade; for Eastmeade, see J. H. Chandler, ed., *Wiltshire Dissenters' Meeting House Certificates and Registrations 1689–1852* (Devizes, 1985), 9, 12. On the Baptist community in Malmesbury, see J. M. Moffatt, *The History of the Town of Malmesbury* (Tetbury, 1805), 159; George Lyon Turner, ed. *Original Records of Early Nonconformity*, 3 vols. (London, 1911–14), i:558, 560.

103. Walker, "Confiscation of Firearms," 23; NUL, PwA 2146, James Rivers to [Hans Willem Bentinck], 21 Feb. 1688. The borough minutes give the name of the newly appointed mayor of Tewkesbury (Thomas Hitchman, gent.) but provide no evidence that would lead one to believe that he was Jewish: see Gloucestershire RO, TBR A1/5 (Chamber Book of Tewkesbury, 1686–1704), fols. 53, 67. On the small size and limited scope of the heterodox group the

Family of Love, see Christopher Marsh, *The Family of Love in English Society, 1550–1630* (Cambridge, 1994), 245–247.

104. Bodl., MS Ballard 23, fol. 26, [John Laughton] to Arthur Charlett, 6 Aug. 1688.

105. *A New Ballad, To the Tune of, Good People Give Ear* (n.p., [1688], N576).

106. NUL, PwA 2146, James Rivers to [Hans Willem Bentinck], 21 Feb. 1688. Twenty-four members of the council were removed by an order of the privy council dated 23 Dec. 1687; see TNA, PC 2/72, fol. 68; Tyne and Wear Archives Service, MD/NC/1/3, fol. 185v. For the names of some of their replacements, see J. C. Hodgson, ed., "Mark Browell's Diary," Surtees Society, cxxiv (1915), 181–182.

107. Richard Welford, "A Sketch of Newcastle during the Reign of James II," *Northern Catholic History,* no. 41 (2000), 28–29; C.S., ed., *The Life of Ambrose Barnes, Sometime Alderman of Newcastle* (Newcastle, 1828), 24 n.; see also C. H. Hunter Blair, *The Mayors and Lord Mayors of Newcastle upon Tyne,* Archaeologia Aeliana, IV, xviii, (Newcastle, 1940), 79.

108. Hodgson, ed., "Browell's Diary," 184; WYAS, WYL156/54/7, Henry Goodricke to Sir John Reresby, 2 March 1688. This alteration appears to have been made by the councillors themselves, rather than by order from the king, as there was no new order of the privy council sent to them.

109. W. H. D. Longstaffe, ed., *Memoirs of the Life of Mr. Ambrose Barnes, Late Merchant and Sometime Alderman of Newcastle upon Tyne,* Surtees Society, vol. 50 (1867), 176 n., 178–179; Child, "Prelude to Revolution," 211–212.

110. Bodl., MS Rawl. a.139b, fol. 106; Longstaffe, ed., *Memoirs of Barnes,* 176 n.

111. HEHL, HA 1703, Joseph Cradock to earl of Huntingdon, 28 May 1688; Leicestershire RO, BRII/18/36, no. 89.

112. West Sussex RO, MF 1145, C/1, p. 33.

113. John Latimer, *The Annals of Bristol in the Seventeenth Century* (Bristol, 1900), 448.

114. The two councillors whose votes are unclear in the records are Samuel Clarke and Holier Houd/House. See Bristol RO, Common Council Proceedings Book of Bristol, 1687–1702, fols. 10–11.

115. Beinecke, OSB MSS 1, box 2, folder 78, newsletter from Whitehall dated 20 April 1688; a map of the twenty-seven boroughs is provided in Chapter 7.

116. John Childs, *The Army, James II, and the Glorious Revolution* (Manchester, 1980), 108, 110; Bodl., MS Ballard 12, fol. 33v, George Hickes to Arthur Charlett, 28 May 1688.

117. The mayor was Ammiell Hartt. A copy of this address with a list of the forty-seven signatories, headed by Hartt, survives in the corporation records: see Dorset RO, DC/LR/D/2/1.

118. The mayor, John Mendham, was in his second consecutive term and received a royal mandate in Sept. 1688 appointing him to a third consecutive term, which the council refused to authorize. Mayors generally served for one term only. See Thetford Town Hall, T/C2/6, pp. 61, 73, 75; *CSPD, James II, 1687–89*, 33.

119. The mayor was John Kingsford Sr.: see Canterbury Cathedral Archives, A/C/7 (Canterbury Burghmote Minutes, 1684–1695), fols. 81, 96v.

120. The mayor was William Mannowry. See Devon RO, DD.63634, DD.63637.

121. The mayor was Thomas Aslaby. See *A New Song of a New Wonder in the North* (1688, N764); BL, Mic M/636, reel 43, Claydon House letters, Anne Nicholas to John Verney, 11 Sept. 1688; BL, Add. MS 34512, fol. 96, Aernout van Citters to States General, 14/24 Sept. 1688.

122. *London Gazette*, no. 2349 (21–24 May 1688), no. 2360 (28 June–2 July 1688), no. 2348 (17–21 May 1688).

123. CAC (C), Ca/2/21, fol. 55; TNA, PC 2/72, fol. 134. The ejected men were George Lankake/Sankald, Francis Atkinson, and John Carnaby. For a similar example in Bury St Edmunds, see Suffolk RO, Bury St Edmunds, E2/41/5, fol. 44, Lord Dover to John Stafford, 31 May 1688; ibid., fol. 45, same to same, 9 June 1688.

124. *Entring Book of Roger Morrice*, iv:70.

125. [Marquess of Halifax], *A Letter to a Dissenter* (1687, H311), 3; on the popular demand for copies of this pamphlet, see Mark N. Brown, ed., *The Works of George Savile, Marquis of Halifax*, 3 vols. (Oxford, 1989), i:81–82. For Halifax's account of his dismissal from office in Oct. 1685, see *Letters of Philip, Second Earl of Chesterfield, to Several Celebrated Individuals* (London, 1829), 295–301.

126. [Care], *Animadversions*, 21, 24–5. See also *A Letter to a Friend, in Answer to a Letter to a Dissenter* (1687, L1646), 2.

127. [Halifax], *Letter to a Dissenter*, 4.

128. HEHL, HA 12980, George Vernon to earl of Huntingdon, 6 Aug. 1688; NUL, PwA 2148, James Rivers to [Hans Willem Bentinck], 27 Feb. 1688, PwA 2100, same to same, 17 Nov. 1687, PwA 2185, anonymous letter to [Bentinck], undated.

6. Countering a Movement

1. Bert Klandermans, *The Social Psychology of Protest* (Oxford, 1997), 156; David S. Meyer and Suzanne Staggenborg, "Movements, Countermovements, and the Structure of Political Opportunity," *American Journal of Sociology*, ci (1996), 1630–1632.

2. Gilbert Burnet, *Bishop Burnet's History of His Own Time*, ed. M. J. Routh, 2nd edn., 6 vols. (Oxford, 1833), iii:186.

3. NUL, PwA 2142, James Rivers to [Hans Willem Bentinck], 5/15 Feb.

1688; for a written paper defending the penal laws that seems to date from this period, see Beinecke, OSB MSS 2, box 3, folder 54. For critiques of nonconformity and toleration published before 1687, see [William Assheton], *A Seasonable Discourse Against Toleration* (1685, A4041), 7–9, 17, 85; *The Danger and Unreasonableness of a Toleration* (1685, D177), 1–4; *Sober and Serious Considerations* (1685, A26), 35, 40–41.

4. Anthony Wood, *Athenae Oxonienses,* ed. Philip Bliss, 4 vols. (London, 1813–20), vol. 4, col. 608–609; John Prince, *A Sermon Preached at Exon* (1674, P3478), 12–13, 32–33, 40–41.

5. See, for instance, Benjamin Laney, bishop of Lincoln, *A Sermon Preached before His Majesty* (1665, L348), 3–4, 7, 12–18; on this point, see also Mark Goldie, "The Theory of Religious Intolerance in Restoration England," in Ole Peter Grell, Jonathan I. Israel, and Nicholas Tyacke, eds., *From Persecution to Toleration: The Glorious Revolution and Religion in England* (Oxford, 1991), 346–358.

6. [Henry Care], *Animadversions on a Late Paper, Entituled, A Letter to a Dissenter* (1687, C505), 32–33; *Publick Occurrences,* no. 6 (27 March 1688), no. 7 (3 April 1688), no. 10 (24 April 1688), no. 11 (1 May 1688), no. 15 (29 May 1688), no. 27 (21 Aug. 1688); [Stephen Lobb], *A Second Letter to a Dissenter* (1687, L2729A), 10, 18.

7. James II, *His Majesties Gracious Declaration to all his Loving Subjects for Liberty of Conscience* (1688, J190); for the order requiring the *Declaration* to be read from the pulpits of churches, see *London Gazette,* no. 2344 (3–7 May 1688).

8. For this and all other details of Simpson's deliberations, see Bodl., MS Rawl. letters 94, fol. 169, Simpson to bishop of Ely, 22 June 1688.

9. Simpson wrote that the order had been "delivered to me at the visitation"; on the delivery of the order, see also *The Entring Book of Roger Morrice, 1677–1691,* ed. Mark Goldie, John Spurr, Tim Harris, Stephen Taylor, Mark Knights, and Jason McElligott, 7 vols. (Woodbridge, 2007–9), iv:264–265. On previous such orders, see Burnet, *History of His Own Time,* iii:223; A. Tindal Hart, *William Lloyd, 1627–1717* (London, 1952), 93–94.

10. Alexander Taylor, ed., *The Works of Symon Patrick,* 9 vols. (Oxford, 1858), ix:510; *Entring Book of Roger Morrice,* iv:260–267.

11. William Robinson, *The History and Antiquities of the Parish of Stoke Newington* (London, 1842), 2.

12. Roger Thomas, "The Seven Bishops and their Petition, 18 May 1688," *JEH,* xii (1961), 62–65. For contemporary copies of this document, see Lancashire RO, DDKe/6/28; *Entring Book of Roger Morrice,* iv:266; *Publick Occurrences,* no. 14 (22 May 1688).

13. *A Collection of Papers Relating to the Present Juncture of Affairs* (1688, C5169A), 1.

14. *Entring Book of Roger Morrice,* iv:260–261.

15. *VCH, Middlesex,* viii:195, 206.

16. For instances in which various church officials absented themselves or pretended to have mislaid their copy, see Samuel Weller Singer, ed., *The Correspondence of Henry Hyde, Earl of Clarendon*, 2 vols. (London, 1828), ii:173; BL, Add. MS 32096, fol. 334v; BL, Add. MS 34512, fol. 82, Aernout van Citters to States General, 22 May/1 June 1688.

17. For references to other ministers who changed their minds in a similar fashion, see FSL, V.a.469 (memoirs of William Westby), fol. 22v; BL, Add. MS 36707, fol. 29, [George Smalridge] to James Harrington, n.d. [May or June 1688].

18. Contemporary estimates of the number of readers varied from one or two to seven. If we add up the City churches where the *Declaration* was reported to have been read, the number comes to six. See Singer, ed., *Clarendon Correspondence*, ii:172–173; Richard Lapthorne, *The Portledge Papers*, ed. Russell Kerr and Ida Coffin Duncan (London, 1928), 33; John Lowther, Viscount Lonsdale, *Memoir of the Reign of James II* (York, 1808), 29; Campana de Cavelli, *Les Derniers Stuarts à Saint-Germain en Laye*, 2 vols. (Paris, 1871), ii:198; BL, Add. MS 36707, fol. 27, [Arthur Maynwaring] to James Harrington, n.d.; NUL, PwA 2162/3, James Rivers to [Hans Willem Bentinck], 23 May 1688; Hampshire RO, 9M73/G247/6, letter to Edward Clarke, May 1688; Charles Whiting, ed., *The Autobiographies and Letters of Thomas Comber*, 2 vols. (Durham, 1946–47), ii:158; Burnet, *History of His Own Time*, iii:229. On the number of parishes in London, see Roger Finlay, *Population and Metropolis: The Demography of London, 1580–1650* (Cambridge, 1981), 168–171.

19. *Entring Book of Roger Morrice*, iv:268–269; Lancashire RO, DDKe/6/28; BL, Add. MS 34512, fol. 82, Aernout van Citters to States General, 22 May/1 June 1688; Narcissus Luttrell, *A Brief Historical Relation of State Affairs*, 6 vols. (Oxford, 1857), i:440; NLW, Ottley correspondence no. 1467; LLIU, Albeville MSS, Robert Yard to marquis d'Albeville, 25 May 1688; LLIU, Albeville MSS, same to same, 29 May 1688. The Rolls Chapel was under the influence of Sir John Trevor, master of the rolls, a tory courtier. The quotation is from FSL, V.a.469 (memoirs of William Westby), fol. 22v.

20. Taylor, ed., *Works of Symon Patrick*, ix:512; *Entring Book of Roger Morrice*, iv:268–269; E. S. de Beer, ed., *The Diary of John Evelyn*, 6 vols. (Oxford, 1955), iv:584; CAC (K), WD/Ry HMC no. 3203, bishop of Carlisle to Sir Daniel Fleming, 2 June 1688; LLIU, Albeville MSS, Robert Yard to marquis d'Albeville, 22 May 1688.

21. Francis Thompson inscribed this account on the inside cover of his copy of Herbert Croft, bishop of Hereford, *A Short Discourse Concerning the Reading of His Majesties Late Declaration* (1688, C6976), now held at the Folger Shakespeare Library, catalog number C6976. I would like to thank Owen Stanwood for this reference. On Thompson, the minister of St Matthew Friday Street, see Joseph Foster, ed., *Alumni Oxonienses*, 4 vols. (Oxford, 1891–92), ii:1476, and John Venn and J. A. Venn, eds., *Alumni Cantabrigienses*, 4 vols. (Cambridge,

1922–27), iv:223. Meriton appears to have reconsidered his support for the *Declaration* after his conversation with Simpson in the coffeehouse, as his name does not appear in the contemporary lists of those who read it.

22. NUL, PwA 2164, James Rivers to [Hans Willem Bentinck], 27 May 1688; Singer, ed., *Clarendon Correspondence*, ii:177; *Entring Book of Roger Morrice*, iv:260.

23. Croft, *Short Discourse*, 7–9; Bodl., MS Tanner 28, fol. 167, bishop of Hereford to archbishop of Canterbury, Aug. 1688.

24. Thomas, "Seven Bishops," 59–63.

25. NUL, PwA 2162/3, James Rivers to [Hans Willem Bentinck], 23 May 1688; TNA, PRO 30/53/8/61, Andrew Newport to Lord Herbert of Cherbury, 22 May 1688.

26. *A True Copy of a Paper Presented to His Majesty* (n.p., 1688, T2628); *The Proceedings and Tryal in the Case of the Most Reverend Father in God William Lord Archbishop of Canterbury* (1689, S564), 90; see also Longleat House, Thynne MSS, xv, fol. 235, Sir Robert Southwell to Lord Weymouth, 21 May 1688; Thomas, "Seven Bishops," 67; Bevill Higgons, *A Short View of English History* (London, 1734), 333. Higgons's account, which gives the time of publication of the petition as Friday 18 May at midnight, may not be reliable, as his account is retrospective and contains several inaccuracies.

27. *Publick Occurrences*, no. 15 (29 May 1688); Beinecke, OSB MSS 1, box 2, folder 80, newsletter sent from Whitehall to Edmund Poley, 1 June 1688.

28. CPA, vol. 165, fol. 316, Barrillon to Louis XIV, 21/31 May 1688. The original French reads: "jusqu'a present il n'a point esté donné de copies."

29. Burnet, *History of His Own Time*, iii:231–232; Bodl., MS Tanner 28, fols. 34–36. The bishop of St. Asaph later asserted that because of the limited number of copies, the king could have suppressed the petition had he chosen to: see Gloucestershire RO, Lloyd papers, D3549/2/2/1, no. 101; Bodl., MS Tanner 28, fol. 102.

30. NLW, Coedymaen papers, Group I, no. 42.

31. BL, Add. MS 34512, fol. 81v, Aernout van Citters to States General, 22 May/1 June 1688; CPA, vol. 165, fol. 329, Barrillon to Louis XIV, 24 May/3 June 1688. Other manuscript copies of the petition are found in Lancashire RO, DDKe/6/28; *Entring Book of Roger Morrice*, iv:267–268; CAC (C), D/Lons/ L12/2/15 (memoirs of Sir Daniel Fleming, vol. 2), fols. 175v–176; Royal Institution of Cornwall, Enys 1206; BL, Add. MS 37682, fol. 134.

32. [Henry Care], *An Answer to a Paper Importing a Petition* (1688, C506 and C507); see also *HMC, Seventh Report*, 349.

33. Seven of these bishops signed the petition after it was delivered, thereby indicating their support of it. The bishop of Carlisle gave his support in a letter to the archbishop. See Bodl., MS Tanner 28, fols. 35–36, 39, 44, 50.

34. FSL, V.b.287, no. 67, James Fraser to Sir Robert Southwell, 2 June 1688.

35. Under pressure from his dean, the bishop reversed himself and subsequently instructed his clergy not to read the *Declaration*, but the clergy did not receive this new instruction until after the date of the first reading of the *Declaration* had passed. See Edmund Elys, *A Clergy-man of the Church of England his Vindication of Himself for Reading His Majesties Late Declaration* (1688, E665), 1; Bodl., MS Tanner 28, fol. 158, bishop of Bristol to archbishop of Canterbury, 16 Aug. 1688.

36. Bodl., MS Tanner 29, fol. 80, bishop of St. Asaph to archbishop of Canterbury, 9 Oct. 1687; University of Wales Bangor, MS 1549, no. 1, bishop of Bangor to Lord Jeffreys, 15 Jan. 1687; Wood, *Athenae Oxonienses*, vol. 4, col. 873.

37. Five of the seven bishops had been appointed to their first see in the period from 1683 to 1685. The exceptions were archbishop Sancroft, who was appointed to his first see, the archbishopric, in 1678, and William Lloyd, appointed bishop of St. Asaph in 1680. On the shift from Erastianism to clericalism in the late 1670s and early 1680s, see Goldie, "Religious Intolerance," 334.

38. These were Jonathan Trelawny of Bristol, Thomas White of Peterborough, and John Lake, promoted from Bristol to Chichester.

39. *HMC, Buccleuch and Queensberry (Montagu House)*, vol. 2, part 1, p. 32.

40. On the distribution in the City of London and its vicinity, see *Entring Book of Roger Morrice*, iv:264–265. The *Declaration* was distributed in the diocese of Gloucester during the bishop's absence, against his wishes: see T. Simpson Evans, ed., *The Life of Robert Frampton, Bishop of Gloucester* (London, 1876), 151.

41. Whiting, ed., *Autobiographies of Thomas Comber*, i:20. On the political opinions of the precentor and dean of York, see also Sir George Duckett, ed., *Penal Laws and Test Act: Questions Touching their Repeal Propounded in 1687–8 by James II*, 2 vols. (London, 1882–83), i:72–73.

42. The author of this work was identified, probably erroneously, as the marquess of Halifax in *The Life of the Reverend Humphrey Prideaux* (London, 1748), 41. Tim Harris identified the author, more reasonably, as William Sherlock, the High Church clergyman: see Tim Harris, *Revolution: The Great Crisis of the British Monarchy, 1685–1720* (London, 2006), 561, note 60.

43. CAC (C), D/Lons/L12/2/15 (memoirs of Sir Daniel Fleming, vol. 2), fol. 176; *A Letter from a Clergy-man in the City, to his Friend in the Country* (1688, H308), 8. A second edition also appeared (1688, S3294C). For critical replies to the *Letter*, see *An Answer to the City-Conformists Letter* (1688, A3399A); *The Countrey-Minister's Reflections, on the City-Ministers Letter* (1688, C6561); [Thomas Cartwright], *A Letter from a Clergy-Man in the Country* (1688, C701A or L1369A); *The Minister's Reasons for his Not Reading the Kings Declaration, Friendly Debated* (1688, M2195); *An Answer to a Letter from a Clergyman in the City* (1688, P3039A); *A Reply to an Answer to the City-Minister's Letter* (1688, R1058). For a publication written in support of the original *Letter*, see *An Answer to the City Ministers Letter from his Country Friend* (n.p., 1688, A3400).

44. *Life of Prideaux,* 41–44; HEHL, HA 1040, Theophilus Brookes to earl of Huntingdon, 2 June 1688; Bodl., MS Ballard 12, fol. 33, George Hickes to Arthur Charlett, 28 May 1688.

45. *A Letter from a Clergy-man,* 5–6, 8; for a similar condemnation of the king's *Declaration* as an "unlimited Toleration," see Edward Stillingfleet, "Case of Reading King James's Declaration in 1688," in *Miscellaneous Discourses on Several Occasions by the Right Reverend Edward Stillingfleet* (London, 1735), 371.

46. *The Countrey-Minister's Reflections,* 8; *An Answer to a Letter from a Clergyman in the City,* 19.

47. *Life of Prideaux,* 41; Bodl., MS Tanner 28, fol. 50r–v, bishop of Carlisle to archbishop of Canterbury, 3 June 1688.

48. Andrew Clark, ed., *The Life and Times of Anthony Wood,* 5 vols. (Oxford, 1891–1900), iii:267; BL, Add. MSS, 36707, fol. 28, Thomas Newey to James Harrington, 30 May 1688; Whiting, ed., *Autobiographies of Thomas Comber,* ii:160.

49. Evans, ed., *Life of Frampton,* 151; Whiting, ed., *Autobiographies of Thomas Comber,* i:20, ii:160; BL, Add. MS 34510, fol. 128v, Aernout van Citters to States General, 12/22 June 1688; *London Gazette,* no. 2374 (16–20 Aug. 1688).

50. Bodl., MS Ballard 12, fol. 38, George Hickes to Arthur Charlett, 30 July 1688; TNA, PRO 30/53/8/63, Andrew Newport to Lord Herbert of Cherbury, 9 June 1688; J. C. Hodgson, ed., "Mark Browell's Diary," Surtees Society, cxxiv (Durham, 1915), 186; NLW, Plasgwyn Papers and Documents (1924 Deposit), no. 78, letter to Rev. John Jones, *c.* July 1688.

51. *CSPD, James II, 1687–89,* 210; George Ornsby, ed., *The Remains of Denis Granville,* Surtees Society, xxxvii (Durham, 1860), 98 n.; George Ornsby, ed., *The Remains of Denis Granville,* Surtees Society, xlvii (Durham, 1865), 147; Bodl., MS Rawl. d.850, fol. 73; Margaret Child, "Prelude to Revolution: The Structure of Politics in County Durham, 1678–1688" (Ph.D. dissertation, Univ. of Maryland, 1972), 195.

52. Bodl., MS Carte 130, fol. 317, Robert Price to duke of Beaufort, 30 June 1688; see also *Ten Modest Queries, Humbly Offer'd* (n.p., [1688], T672B), 3–4.

53. Anthony Wood's estimate that only four hundred clergy across England read the *Declaration* seems plausible. See Clark, ed., *Life and Times of Anthony Wood,* iii:267. One anonymous letter writer provided a lower estimate of eighty readers across England: see NLW, Plasgwyn Papers and Documents (1924 Deposit), no. 78, letter to Rev. John Jones, *c.* July 1688.

54. *London Gazette,* no. 2374 (16–20 Aug. 1688); CUL, Ee.6.43, fol. 213a, letter of the bishop of Lincoln, 29 May 1688; John Stoughton, *History of Religion in England,* rev. edn., 6 vols. (London, 1881), iv:147; see also Bodl., MS Tanner 114, fol. 56, petition of Abiel Borset, 18 June 1688.

55. Daniel Kenrick, *A Sermon Preached in the Cathedral-Church of Worcester* (1688, K307), 9, 28, 31–32; *CSPD, James II, 1687–89,* 343. For another, similar,

case, see the pro-repeal pamphlet by the rector of Little-Livermere in Suffolk, James Paston, *A Discourse of Penal Laws in Matter of Religion* (1688, P665), 30–31, 36–37. Paston was chaplain to the chief justice of King's Bench, Sir Robert Wright.

56. NLW, Ottley correspondence no. 1725, bishop of Hereford to James II, 6 June 1688; BL, Add. MS 70113, unfoliated, bishop of Hereford to James II, [6 June 1688]; NLW, Ottley correspondence no. 1723, bishop of Hereford to Adam Ottley, 8 Aug. 1688.

57. Croft, *Short Discourse,* 8–9, 5–6.

58. Bodl., MS Rawl. a.179, fol. 61, John Loton to Samuel Pepys, 4 June 1688.

59. BL, Mic M/636, reel 42, Claydon House letters, William Butterfield to Sir Ralph Verney, 13 May 1688; see also Frances Parthenope Verney and Margaret M. Verney, eds., *Memoirs of the Verney Family,* 4 vols. (London, 1892–99), iv:411, which demonstrates that Butterfield, the minister of Middle Claydon in Buckinghamshire, later advocated comprehension for at least some dissenters.

60. *Entring Book of Roger Morrice,* iv:262. On Dr. Edward Fowler, vicar of St Giles Cripplegate, who made this statement, see Thomas, "Seven Bishops," 61.

61. Bodl., MS Firth c.13, fol. 9, George Hickes to Edmund Bohun, 18 Aug. 1687; Matthew Jason Storey, ed., *Two East Anglian Diaries, 1641–1729* (Woodbridge, 1994), 173.

62. NUL, PwA 2126/1, unknown to [Hans Willem Bentinck], 12 Jan. 1688; the original letter reads, in French, "Mais vous savez que dans l'Eglise Anglicane comme dans toutes les Eglises du monde, il y a une espece de Bigots, qui . . . sont incapables de raison."

63. NUL, PwA 2119, James Rivers to [Hans Willem Bentinck], 16 Dec. 1687.

64. James II, *His Majesties Gracious Declaration to all his Loving Subjects for Liberty of Conscience* (1688, J190), 2.

65. *An Answer to the City Ministers Letter from his Country Friend* (1688, A3400), 3; *Some Queries Concerning Liberty of Conscience* (n.p., 1688, S4559), 1.

66. John Gutch, ed., *Collectanea Curiosa,* 2 vols. (Oxford, 1781), i:378; *The Proceedings and Tryal,* 106.

67. J. C. Davis, *Fear, Myth and History: The Ranters and the Historians* (Cambridge, 1986), 21–75.

68. *The Fourth (and Last) Collection of Poems, Satyrs, Songs* (1689, F1684), 25.

69. BL, Sloane MS 3929, fol. 69v, newsletter for 7 July 1688.

70. On Baxter, see Thomas, "Seven Bishops," 58; NUL, PwA 2162/2, James Rivers to [Hans Willem Bentinck], 23 May 1688. On Lobb, see H.A. Beecham, "Samuel Wesley Senior: New Biographical Evidence," *Renaissance and Modern Studies,* vii (1963), 106.

71. On persecution during the "tory reaction," see Burnet, *History of His Own Time,* ii:442; Peter William Jackson, "Nonconformists and Society in

Devon, 1660–1689" (Ph.D. thesis, Univ. of Exeter, 1986), 138–146; David Scott, "Politics, Dissent and Quakerism in York, 1640–1700," (D.Phil. thesis, Univ. of York, 1990), 196–197; Bodl., MS Tanner 35, fol. 67, bishop of Bristol to [archbishop of Canterbury], 12 Aug. 1682.

72. NUL, PwA 2148, James Rivers to [Hans Willem Bentinck], 27 Feb. 1688.

73. Lambeth Palace Library, MS 2932, fol. 31; BL, Add. MS 34487, fol. 11, unknown to countess of Suffolk, 12 July 1688; Longleat House, Thynne MSS, xv, fol. 256v, Sir Robert Southwell to Lord Weymouth, 24 July 1688; Robert Beddard, "Observations of a London Clergyman on the Revolution of 1688–9: Being an Excerpt from the Autobiography of Dr. William Wake," *Guildhall Miscellany,* ii (1960–68), 409–410, 414; *The Bishop of Lincoln's and Bishop of Norwich's Speeches in the House of Lords* (London, 1710), 3–4; George Every, *The High Church Party, 1688–1718* (London, 1956), 23–24.

74. Bodl., MS Tanner 28, fol. 171v, bishop of Ely to archbishop of Canterbury, 3 Sept. 1688; George Agar Ellis, ed., *The Ellis Correspondence,* 2 vols. (London, 1829), ii:63; Henry Fishwick, ed., *The Notebook of the Rev. Thomas Jolly,* Chetham Society, n.s., xxxiii (Manchester, 1894–95), 90; James Mackintosh, *History of the Revolution in England in 1688* (London, 1834), 286.

75. John E. Southall, ed., *Leaves from the History of Welsh Nonconformity* (Newport, 1899), 147; Gloucestershire RO, D3549/2/2/3, William Lloyd to John Edward, 17 July 1683.

76. *A Seasonable Discourse Shewing the Necessity of Union amongst Protestants in Opposition to Popery* (1688, S2228), title page and p. 13; [Gilbert Burnet], *An Apology for the Church of England, with Relation to the Spirit of Persecution: For which she is Accused* (n.p., [1688], B5762), 3, 5; *A Plain Account of the Persecution, Now Laid to the Charge of the Church of England* (n.p., [1688], P2339), 2; G. C. Moore Smith, ed., "Extracts from the Papers of Thomas Woodcock (Ob. 1695)," Camden Society, III, xiii (1907), 77.

77. [Lobb], *Second Letter to a Dissenter,* 7.

78. BL, Add. MS 41816, fol. 169, marquis d'Albeville to earl of Middleton, 28 Aug./7 Sept. 1688; [Burnet], *Apology for the Church of England; The Articles Recommended by the Arch-Bishop of Canterbury to all the Bishops* (n.p., [1688], S550), 4.

79. Andrew Browning, ed., *Memoirs of Sir John Reresby,* rev. Mary K. Geiter and W. A. Speck (London, 1991), 500.

80. NUL, PwA 2135, James Rivers to [Hans Willem Bentinck], 13/23 Jan. 1688; NUL, PwA 2148, same to same, 27 Feb. 1688; NUL, PwA 2168/4, same to same, 13 June 1688.

81. *Nahash Revived: Or, the Church of England's Love to Dissenters* (1688, N84), 2; *Publick Occurrences,* no. 14 (22 May 1688); see also *A Paraphrase on the Clergies Address to the King* (n.p., 1688, P341), 1; *A Dialogue between the Arch-B[ishop] of C[anterbury] and the Bishop of Heref[ord] Containing the True Reasons Why the Bishops*

Could not Read the Declaration (1688, D1326), 2; *A Letter from a Dissenter to the Petitioning Bishops* (1688, L1372bA), 2.

82. *Nahash Revived*, 7.

83. For the refusal of many clergy to send addresses, see BL, Add. MS 34487, fol. 5, N. Gerrard to Edward Norton, 4 May 1687; BL, Mic M/636, reel 42, Claydon House letters, Henry Paman to Sir Ralph Verney, 4 May 1687; Lambeth Palace Library, MS 3898, no. 6, Henry Paman to bishop of Norwich, 18 Aug. 1687; Bodl., MS Ballard 12, fol. 25, George Hickes to Arthur Charlett, 4 May 1687.

84. TNA, PRO 30/53/8/64, letter to Lord Herbert of Cherbury, 16 June 1688; *An Answer to the City Ministers Letter*, 2. Some contemporaries named William Penn or Edward Petre as the originator of the proposal, but both men were said to have denied this: see BL, Add. MS 34512, fol. 82, Aernout van Citters to States General, 22 May/1 June 1688, fol. 87, same to same, 25 May/4 June 1688; NUL, PwA 2162/2, James Rivers to [Hans Willem Bentinck], 23 May 1688. On Sir Nicholas Butler's conversion to Catholicism and his influence at court, see *HMC, Downshire*, i:237; NUL, PwV 53/55, William Blathwayt to Sir Robert Southwell, 20 Oct. 1687.

85. NLW, Ottley correspondence no. 1467; R. W. Blencowe, ed., *Diary of the Times of Charles the Second by the Honourable Henry Sidney*, 2 vols. (London, 1843), ii:375.

86. BL, Add. MS 34512, fol. 82, Aernout van Citters to States General, 22 May/1 June 1688; Campana de Cavelli, *Les Derniers Stuarts*, ii:206.

87. NUL, PwA 2176, p. 2, James Rivers to [Hans Willem Bentinck], 2 July 1688; Taylor, ed., *Works of Symon Patrick*, ix:511–512; *Entring Book of Roger Morrice*, iv:269.

88. CPA, vol. 165, fol. 332v, Barrillon to Louis XIV, 24 May/3 June 1688; Mackintosh, *History of the Revolution*, 255.

89. BL, Add. MS 34510, fol. 123, Aernout van Citters to States General, 11 June 1688; Burnet, *History of His Own Time*, iii:229; CPA, vol. 165, fols. 329v–330, Barrillon to Louis XIV, 24 May/3 June 1688; Martin Haile, *Queen Mary of Modena* (London, 1905), 183; NUL, PwA 2164, James Rivers to [Hans Willem Bentinck], 27 May 1688.

90. Charlwood Lawton, "A Memoir of Part of the Life of William Penn," *Memoirs of the Historical Society of Pennsylvania*, vol. 3, part 2 (1836), 230–231; Campana de Cavelli, *Les Derniers Stuarts*, ii:236; NUL, PwA 2168/3, James Rivers to [Hans Willem Bentinck], 13 June 1688.

91. CPA, vol. 165, fol. 351, Barrillon to Louis XIV, 31 May/10 June 1688.

92. CPA, vol. 165, fol. 365, Barrillon to Louis XIV, 7/17 June 1688, fol. 379, same to same, 11/21 June 1688; NLW, Coedymaen papers, Group I, no. 48. Although many of his former whig allies regarded Sir William Williams as a turncoat, there was some continuity in his anticlerical behavior in that there had never been any love lost between him and high ecclesiastics. See Cheshire

RO, ZCR63/2/691/39, fol. 49, [Sir Willoughby Aston] to [Sir John Crewe], 23 Feb. 1688; NLW, Plasgwyn Papers and Documents (1924 Deposit), no. 84, Humphrey Humphreys to Rev. John Jones, n.d. (*c*. 1688–89).

93. BL, Add. MS 36707, fol. 28v, Thomas Newey to James Harrington, 30 May 1688; BL, Add. MS 34510, fols. 123–124, Aernout van Citters to States General, 11 June 1688.

94. Statute 16 Car. I, c. 10; see also NUL, PwA 2176, p. 8, James Rivers to [Hans Willem Bentinck], 2 July 1688.

95. NLW, Ottley correspondence no. 1467; Singer, ed., *Clarendon Correspondence*, ii:172; Longleat House, Thynne MSS, vol. 19, fol. 53, letter to Lord Weymouth, n.d. Note that two weeks later, when the lord chancellor asked the twelve high court justices the same question, three of the them were said to have joined Allibone in countenancing a praemunire: these were Sir Robert Wright, Sir Thomas Jenner, and Sir Christopher Milton, younger brother of the poet. On this point, see CAC (C), D/Lons/L12/2/15 (memoirs of Sir Daniel Fleming, vol. 2), fol. 176.

96. de Beer, ed., *Diary of John Evelyn*, iv:585; CAC (C), D/Lons/L12/2/15 (memoirs of Sir Daniel Fleming, vol. 2), fol. 176.

97. NLW, Ottley correspondence no. 1467.

98. Singer, ed., *Clarendon Correspondence*, ii:177, 179.

99. Gutch, ed., *Collectanea Curiosa*, i:341; CPA, vol. 165, fols. 373v–374v, Barrillon to Louis XIV, 11/21 June 1688; *The Proceedings and Tryal*, 29; for the date of Michaelmas term, see Luttrell, *Brief Historical Relation*, i:470.

100. Bodl., MS Ballard 33, fol. 8r–v, [Dr. Sykes?] to Arthur Charlett, [9 June 1688]; *Entring Book of Roger Morrice*, iv:279–280; *The Proceedings and Tryal*, 13, 33–34; Beinecke, OSB MSS 1, box 2, folder 81, Owen Wynne to Edmund Poley, 15 June 1688.

101. Bodl., MS Tanner 28, fol. 58.

102. George D'Oyly, *The Life of William Sancroft*, 2nd edn. (London, 1840), 172–173; Bodl., MS Tanner 28, fol. 62v; *Entring Book of Roger Morrice*, iv:277.

103. *Entring Book of Roger Morrice*, iv:279–280; for a copy of the warrant, see Bodl., MS Tanner 28, fol. 67.

104. *Entring Book of Roger Morrice*, iv:277; de Beer, ed., *Diary of John Evelyn*, iv:586; *HMC, Portland*, iii:410; *A True and Exact Account of the Manner of Committing the Bishops to the Tower* (1688, T2429), 2.

105. *Memoirs of Sir John Reresby*, 499.

106. FSL, V.b.287, no. 71, James Fraser to Sir Robert Southwell, 12 June 1688; CPA, vol. 165, fol. 373, Barrillon to Louis XIV, 11/21 June 1688; Singer, ed., *Clarendon Correspondence*, ii:175–176; Luttrell, *Brief Historical Relation*, i:444; Bodl., MS Smith 52, fol. 193, Lord North and Grey to [Dr. Thomas Smith], 15 June 1688; Gutch, ed., *Collectanea Curiosa*, i:360.

107. NLW, Plas-yn-Cefn papers, no. 2939, bishop of St. Asaph to [Dr. Dodwell], 9 June 1688; *Entring Book of Roger Morrice*, iv:278; University of Wales

Bangor, Mostyn Additional MSS, no. 9094/29, newsletter to Thomas Mostyn, 12 June 1688; FSL, V.a.469 (memoirs of William Westby), fol. 24v; NUL, PwA 2172, James Rivers to [Hans Willem Bentinck], 18 June 1688; Beinecke, OSB MSS 1, box 2, folder 81, newsletter from Whitehall sent to Edmund Poley, 15 June 1688.

108. *An Account of the Proceedings at the Kings-Bench Bar* (1688, A359), 1; Singer, ed., *Clarendon Correspondence*, ii:177; *The Proceedings and Tryal*, preface, p. 1; *Entring Book of Roger Morrice*, iv:283–285; LLIU, Albeville MSS, Robert Yard to marquis d'Albeville, 15 June 1688.

109. *The Proceedings and Tryal*, 4, 14, 17–9; Lord Braybrooke, ed., *The Autobiography of Sir John Bramston*, Camden Society, old series, xxxii (1845), 308; *Entring Book of Roger Morrice*, iv:281–285.

110. *The Proceedings and Tryal*, 31, 34, 37–39, 43, 46–47; LLIU, Albeville MSS, Robert Yard to marquis d'Albeville, 15 June 1688; Longleat House, Thynne MSS, xv, fol. 247v, Sir Robert Southwell to Lord Weymouth, 26 June 1688.

111. *Entring Book of Roger Morrice*, iv:283; *The Proceedings and Tryal*, 43–44; *An Account of the Proceedings at the Kings-Bench*, 2; de Beer, ed., *Diary of John Evelyn*, iv:587–588.

112. *The Proceedings and Tryal*, 27, 43–44.

113. George W. Marshall, ed., *Le Neve's Pedigrees* (London, 1873), 382; *The Proceedings and Tryal*, 31; Duckett, ed., *Penal Laws*, i:268. Astrey was later nominated as a court candidate for Gloucestershire in the parliamentary elections planned for the autumn: see Bodl., MS Carte 130, fol. 24.

114. Giles Jacob and T. E. Tomlins, *The Law-dictionary*, 2 vols. (London, 1797), s.v. "Jury" and "King's Bench"; Bodl., MS Smith 52, fol. 191.

115. FSL, V.b.287, no. 74, James Fraser to Sir Robert Southwell, 21 June 1688.

116. Singer, ed., *Clarendon Correspondence*, ii:178; BL, Add. MS 34510, fol. 130v, Aernout van Citters to States General, 22 June 1688.

117. For a full list of the forty-eight, including the twelve excluded by the king and the twelve excluded by the bishops, see *Entring Book of Roger Morrice*, iv:288–289; *Oprechte Haerlemse Dingsdaegse Courant*, no. 28 (13 July 1688). For Clarges's friendship with the bishops at this time, see Bodl., MS Tanner 28, fol. 78v, Sir Thomas Clarges to bishop of Norwich, 14 June 1688.

118. *Entring Book of Roger Morrice*, iv:254, 289; Singer, ed., *Clarendon Correspondence*, ii:178; FSL, V.a.469 (memoirs of William Westby), fol. 27v.

119. Basil Duke Henning, ed., *The House of Commons, 1660–1690*, 3 vols. (London, 1983), ii:74–81, 183–184, iii:443–444; Duckett, ed., *Penal Laws*, i:358; William Arthur Shaw, *The Knights of England*, 2 vols. (London, 1906), ii:261; Marshall, ed., *Le Neve's Pedigrees*, 401; J. R. Woodhead, *The Rulers of London, 1660–1689* (London, 1965), 102. Little is known about the seven other men removed by the king, with the exception of John Byfield of Hackney, who is

noticed in Foster, ed., *Alumni Oxonienses,* i:226, and in John Cordy Jeaffreson, ed., *Middlesex County Records,* 4 vols. (London, 1886–92), iv:277.

120. FSL, V.a.469 (memoirs of William Westby), fol. 27v.

121. Shaw, *Knights of England,* ii:233, 257; Foster, ed., *Alumni Oxonienses,* i:51; Henning, ed., *House of Commons,* ii:242–243, 369–370; *CSPD, James II, 1687–89,* 62, 101, 136, 271; Charles Dalton, ed., *English Army Lists,* 6 vols. (London, 1892–1904), ii:28, 46, 89, 137, 178. John Friend was executed in 1696 for Jacobite plotting. The bishops were wise to exclude John Shales, the commissary-general of the army, who later subscribed an abhorrence of their petition as foreman of the Middlesex grand jury in July 1688: see BL, Add. MS 34487, fol. 11, letter to countess of Suffolk, 12 July 1688.

122. CPA, vol. 166, fols. 331v–332, Barrillon to Louis XIV, 11/21 Oct. 1688; Christopher Clay, *Public Finance and Private Wealth: The Career of Sir Stephen Fox, 1627–1716* (Oxford, 1978), 81–82, 196; Peter Duncombe, *Great Goldsmith: A Life of Sir Charles Duncombe* (Chippendale, New South Wales, 2001), 86–115; Eveline Cruickshanks, Stuart Handley, and D. W. Hayton, eds., *The House of Commons, 1690–1715,* 5 vols. (Cambridge, 2002), iv:303. For Baber, see David Norman Marshall, "Protestant Dissent in England in the Reign of James II," (Ph.D. thesis, Univ. of Hull, 1976), 263–264, 313, 329; R. A. Beddard, "Vincent Alsop and the Emancipation of Restoration Dissent," *JEH,* xxiv (1973), 175; Archives Nationales, Paris, K1351, no. 4, fol. 54v. The bishops also removed four men who were not as prominent as some of the others: Josiah Golliard, who had served on a Middlesex jury in 1678; Andrew Lawrence, who was a justice of the peace for Middlesex in 1687; Thomas Eresby; and Humphrey Bradshaw. On Golliard and Lawrence, see Jeaffreson, ed., *Middlesex County Records,* iv:277, 314.

123. William E. Buckley, ed., *Memoirs of Thomas, Earl of Ailesbury, Written by Himself,* 2 vols. (Westminster, 1890), i:171; BL, Add. MS 34510, fol. 137, Aernout van Citters to States General, 6 July 1688; Ellis, ed., *Ellis Correspondence,* ii:3; *Publick Occurrences,* no. 20 (3 July 1688); *Oprechte Haerlemse Saturdaegse Courant,* no. 28 (10 July 1688); Edward Berwick, ed., *The Rawdon Papers* (London, 1819), 290. On the jurors's religious affiliations, see LLIU, Albeville MSS, Robert Yard to marquis d'Albeville, 3 July 1688; BL, Mic M/636, reel 42, Claydon House letters, John Verney to Sir Ralph Verney, 28 June 1688.

124. Burnet, *History of His Own Time,* iii:236.

125. CAC (K), WD/Ry HMC no. 3217, bishop of Carlisle to Sir Daniel Fleming, 2 July 1688; NLW, Coedymaen papers, Group I, no. 49; CPA, vol. 166, fol. 24, Barrillon to Louis XIV, 28 June/8 July 1688. The original French in the quotation from Barrillon reads: "vivre de soixante pieces par an, comme je faisois auparavant."

126. NLW, Coedymaen papers, Group I, no. 49; on the judges, see Alfred F. Havighurst, "James II and the Twelve Men in Scarlet," *Law Quarterly Review,* lxix (1953), 530–532; idem, "The Judiciary and Politics in the Reign of Charles II," *Law Quarterly Review,* lxvi (1950), 246–249; TNA, C/193/9, pp. 123–127.

127. *HMC, Portland*, iii:412–413.

128. Compare *The Proceedings and Tryal*, preface, with the two lists of peers in K. H. D. Haley, "A List of the English Peers, *c.* May, 1687," *EHR*, lxix (1954), 304–306, and David Hosford, "The Peerage and the Test Act: A List, *c.* November 1687," *BIHR*, xlii (1969), 116–120. The two lists are not in complete agreement and it is possible that the earl of Rivers, the earl of Clarendon, the earl of Sussex, and Lord Chandos, who were all present at the trial, were merely neutral on the question of repeal rather than being firmly opposed to it.

129. NLW, Plasgwyn Papers and Documents (1924 Deposit), no. 78, letter to Rev. John Jones, *c.* July 1688.

130. NLW, Wynnstay MSS, C25, Sir Thomas Powys to Sir William Williams, June 1688; Sir Edward Herbert, *A Short Account of the Authorities in Law, upon which Judgement was Given in Sir Edw. Hales his Case* (1688, H1496), 7, 22–24; Braybrooke, ed., *Autobiography of Sir John Bramston*, 339. On the Lovelace case, which was occasioned by a peer telling a constable not to obey a Roman Catholic justice of the peace, see *Entring Book of Roger Morrice*, iv:237, 259–260.

131. For Sir William Williams's notes outlining this strategy, see NLW, Coedymaen papers, Group I, no. 46.

132. *The Proceedings and Tryal*, 52–77, 82, 87–93 (quote at 87); Beinecke, OSB MSS 1, box 2, folder 83, newsletter from Whitehall sent to Edmund Poley, 29 June 1688.

133. *The Proceedings and Tryal*, 94–97 (quote at 97); Hampshire RO, 9M73/ G239/6, [Edward Clarke] to Thomas Stringer, 30 June 1688.

134. *The Proceedings and Tryal*, 107; NLW, Coedymaen papers, Group I, no. 49; see also NUL, PwA 2176, pp. 4–5, James Rivers to [Hans Willem Bentinck], 2 July 1688; *Entring Book of Roger Morrice*, iv:291.

135. *The Proceedings and Tryal*, 137–139; LLIU, Albeville MSS, Robert Yard to marquis d'Albeville, 29 June 1688; NUL, PwV 53/70, William Blathwayt to Sir Robert Southwell, 30 June 1688; NLW, Plasgwyn Papers and Documents (1924 Deposit), no. 78, letter to Rev. John Jones, *c.* July 1688.

136. NLW, Coedymaen papers, Group I, no. 49; see also G. V. Bennett, "The Seven Bishops: A Reconsideration," in Derek Baker, ed., *Religious Motivation* (Oxford, 1978), 284.

137. Luttrell, *Brief Historical Relation*, i:448; Singer, ed., *Clarendon Correspondence*, ii:179; Bodl., MS Carte 130, fol. 317, Robert Price to duke of Beaufort, 30 June 1688.

138. Bodl., MS Tanner 28, fols. 95–96; *The London Directory of 1677* (London, 1878), unpaginated, s.v. "Jeff. Nightingall"; Woodhead, *Rulers of London*, 179; George Edward Cokayne, *Complete Baronetage*, 6 vols. (Exeter, 1900–1909), ii:88; BL, Add. MS 34487, fol. 15, newsletter to countess of Suffolk, 17 July 1688; Henning, ed., *House of Commons*, i:547, ii:220–221.

139. Braybrooke, ed., *Autobiography of Sir John Bramston*, 310; FSL, V.b.287, no. 76, James Fraser to Sir Robert Southwell, 3 July 1688; CPA, vol. 166, fol. 33,

Barrillon to Louis XIV, 2/12 July 1688; *Entring Book of Roger Morrice,* iv:293; Bodl., MS Tanner 28, fol. 104, John Ince to archbishop Sancroft, 30 June 1688; FSL, F.c.32, Thomas Booth to John Booth, 30 June 1688; Lancashire RO, DDKe/9/61/40, George Allanson to Roger Kenyon, 30 June 1688; for Thomas Austin's quote, see NUL, PwA 2176, p. 6, James Rivers to [Hans Willem Bentinck], 2 July 1688.

140. *The Proceedings and Tryal,* 140; Singer, ed., *Clarendon Correspondence,* ii:179; Luttrell, *Brief Historical Relation,* i:448; TNA, PRO 30/53/8/65, letter to Lord Herbert of Cherbury, 30 June 1688; Essex RO, Dawtrey MSS, D/Dfa/F22, H. Hall to Justice Dawtrey, 2 July 1688; BL, Add. MS 71692, fol. 13v, Sir William Boothby to Dr. Horneck, 15 July 1688; Longleat House, Thynne MSS, vol. 15, fol. 251, Sir Robert Southwell to Viscount Weymouth, 21 July 1688.

141. Thomas Babington Macaulay, *The History of England from the Accession of James the Second,* ed. C. H. Firth, 6 vols. (London, 1913–15), ii:1030–1039; J. P. Kenyon, *Robert Spencer, Earl of Sunderland, 1641–1702* (London, 1958), 200; Steve Pincus, *1688: The First Modern Revolution* (New Haven, 2009), 196–197.

142. BL, Add. MS 29563, fol. 207, newsletter sent to Viscountess Hatton, 30 June 1688; York Minster Library, Hailstone collection, BB 22, R.W. to Edward Trotter, 30 June 1688; NUL, PwA 2176, p. 8, James Rivers to [Hans Willem Bentinck], 2 July 1688; Longleat House, Thynne MSS, xv, fol. 249v, Sir Robert Southwell to Lord Weymouth, July 1688; *Entring Book of Roger Morrice,* iv:293; Herbert Mortimer Luckock, *The Bishops in the Tower* (London, 1887), 159–160; Harris, *Revolution,* 267; William Gibson, *James II and the Trial of the Seven Bishops* (Basingstoke, 2009), 132.

143. *Memoirs of Sir John Reresby,* 501; FSL, V.a.469 (memoirs of William Westby), fol. 33; BL, Add. MS 36707, fol. 39, [Arthur Maynwaring] to James Harrington, 9 Aug. 1688; Edward Hawkins, *Medallic Illustrations of the History of Great Britain and Ireland,* 2 vols. (London, 1885), i:621–622; Lincolnshire Archives, Monson 7/12/60, newsletter to Lady Newton, *c.* Oct. 1688; Freeman O'Donoghue and Henry Hake, *Catalogue of Engraved British Portraits Preserved in the Department of Prints and Drawings in the British Museum,* 6 vols. (London, 1908–25), v:75–76; for the poem celebrating the bishops, see Bodl., MS Rawl. letters 75, fol. 45v, Simon Priest to Joshua Barnes, 13 Sept. 1688.

144. W. S. Holdsworth, *A History of English Law,* 3rd edn., 9 vols. (London, 1922–26), vi:223–225; Paul Birdsall, "'Non-Obstante'—A Study of the Dispensing Power of English Kings," in Carl Wittke, ed., *Essays in History and Political Theory* (Cambridge, MA, 1936), 68–75; Howard Nenner, *By Colour of Law: Legal Culture and Constitutional Politics in England, 1660–1689* (Chicago, 1977), 92–101.

145. York Minster Library, Hailstone collection, BB 22, R.W. to Edward Trotter, 30 June 1688.

146. Kenyon, *Sunderland,* 191–192; NUL, PwA 2120/1, James Rivers to [Hans Willem Bentinck], 21 Dec. 1687, PwA 2129/1, same to same, 13/23 Jan. 1688; WYAS, WYL156/51/53, Nathaniel Johnston to Sir John Reresby, 24 Jan.

1688; *Publick Occurrences,* no. 17 (12 June 1688); TNA, PRO 30/53/8/58, letter to Lord Herbert of Cherbury, 14 Feb. 1688.

7. Dividing a Nation

1. LLIU, Albeville MSS, Robert Yard to marquis d'Albeville, 17 July 1688, same to same, 20 July 1688; Longleat House, Thynne MSS, xv, fol. 263, Sir Robert Southwell to Lord Weymouth, 10 Aug. 1688; FSL, V.a.469 (memoirs of William Westby), fol. 34; Lord Braybrooke, ed., *The Autobiography of Sir John Bramston,* Camden Society, old series, xxxii (1845), 312.

2. E. S. de Beer, ed., *The Diary of John Evelyn,* 6 vols. (Oxford, 1955), iv:590; NUL, PwA 2143/3, James Rivers to [Hans Willem Bentinck], 14 Feb. 1688; Lambeth Palace Library, MS 3286, fols. 33–36, Sir George Wheler to William Beveridge, 15 March 1701.

3. James II, *By the King, a Proclamation* (1688, J260); idem, *By the King, a Declaration* (1688, J158).

4. On the geographic distribution of the English cloth industry, see Peter J. Bowden, *The Wool Trade in Tudor and Stuart England* (London, 1962), 45–56.

5. Ralph Davis, "English Foreign Trade, 1700–1774," *EcHistR,* n.s., xv (1962), 292. This figure, which does not include re-exports of foreign goods, refers to woolen exports only and does not include exports of other textiles, including silks, cottons, and linen.

6. George E. Barnett, ed., *Two Tracts by Gregory King* (Baltimore, 1936), 46, 67; Phyllis Deane, "The Output of the British Woolen Industry in the Eighteenth Century," *Journal of Economic History,* xvii (1957), 209; see also Ralph Davis, "English Foreign Trade, 1660–1700," *EcHistR,* n.s., vii (1954), 164–165, which gives a figure of £3,045,000 per annum in exports of woolens during the years 1699–1701.

7. W. G. Hoskins, *Industry, Trade and People in Exeter, 1688–1800* (Manchester, 1935), 66–74.

8. Address from the clothiers of Worcester, *London Gazette,* no. 2273 (29 Aug.–1 Sept. 1687); address from the clothiers of Devon and Somerset, *London Gazette,* no. 2365 (16–19 July 1688); address from the weavers and combers of Taunton, *London Gazette,* no. 2284 (7–10 Oct. 1687); see also the address from the dissenters of Cirencester, the address of the Company of Clothworkers in London and the address of the Company of Weavers in London, in *London Gazette,* nos. 2282 (29 Sept.–3 Oct. 1687), 2290 (27–31 Oct. 1687) and 2297 (21–24 Nov. 1687).

9. John Cary, *An Essay on the State of England, in Relation to its Trade* (Bristol, 1695, C730), 51–53; Nuala Zahedieh, "Overseas Expansion and Trade in the Seventeenth Century," in Nicholas Canny, ed., *The Origins of Empire: British Overseas Enterprise to the Close of the Seventeenth Century* (Oxford, 1998), 401, 412–414; James A. Mann, *The Cotton Trade of Great Britain* (London, 1860), 5–6;

Alfred P. Wadsworth and Julia de Lacy Mann, *The Cotton Trade and Industrial Lancashire, 1600–1780* (Manchester, 1931), 42–53, 75–89; Julia de Lacy Mann, *The Cloth Industry in the West of England from 1640 to 1880* (Oxford, 1971), 7–36; K. N. Chaudhuri, *The Trading World of Asia and the English East India Company, 1660–1760* (Cambridge, 1978), 547; Patrick O'Brien, Trevor Griffiths, and Philip Hunt, "Political Components of the Industrial Revolution: Parliament and the English Cotton Textile Industry, 1660–1774," *EcHistR*, n.s., xliv (1991), 399–400.

10. Beverley Lemire, *Fashion's Favourite: The Cotton Trade and the Consumer in Britain, 1660–1800* (Oxford, 1991), 12–42; O'Brien, Griffiths, and Hunt, "Political Components," 404–409.

11. Carole Shammas, "The Decline of Textile Prices in England and British America Prior to Industrialization," *EcHistR*, n.s., xlvii (1994), 483–485, 488–502.

12. *CSPD, James II, 1686–87*, 87, 126.

13. Shammas, "Decline of Textile Prices," 494.

14. James II, *By the King, A Proclamation* (1687, J254); see also FSL, Newdigate newsletters, L.c. 1832, 16 July 1687; Bowden, *Wool Trade in Tudor and Stuart England*, 184–217.

15. Address from the clothiers of Worcester, *London Gazette*, no. 2273 (29 Aug.–1 Sept. 1687); address from the Stroudwater clothiers, *London Gazette*, no. 2276 (8–12 Sept. 1687); address from the dissenters of Cirencester, *London Gazette*, no. 2282 (29 Sept.–3 Oct. 1687).

16. Canterbury Cathedral Archives, Woodruff's List, bundle 52, number 12, James II to Lord Cornbury, colonel of the royal regiment of dragoons, 20 March 1688; TNA, WO 5/3, p. 102, marching order of 1 April 1688; see also BL, Add. MS 34152, fol. 17, Anthony Heyford to Lord Feversham, 14 April 1688; TNA, WO 4/1, p. 81, William Blathwayt to Anthony Heyford, 7 June 1688; TNA, PC 2/72, fols. 117v, 119v.

17. William Andrews Clark Memorial Library, MS.1959.005, pp. 74, 78, 83; James II, *By the King, A Proclamation* (1688, J356).

18. *CSPD, James II, 1687–89*, 220; James II, *By the King, A Proclamation* (1688, J259); TNA, PC 2/72, fol. 96; address from the clothiers of Devon and Somerset, *London Gazette*, no. 2365 (16–19 July 1688).

19. Gloucestershire RO, GBR B3/6, fols. 170, 175; Peter Ripley and John Jurica, eds., *A Calendar of the Registers of the Freemen of the City of Gloucester, 1641–1838* (Gloucester, 1991), 40; *London Gazette*, no. 2313 (16–19 Jan. 1688); Canterbury Cathedral Archives, A/C/7, fol. 87; Canterbury Cathedral Archives, Woodruff's List, bundle 52, number 10, royal mandate to city of Canterbury, 17 Dec. 1687; Joseph Meadows Cowper, *The Roll of the Freemen of the City of Canterbury* (Canterbury, 1903), cols. 169, 229, 278; *London Gazette*, no. 2349, 21–24 May 1688; Wiltshire RO, G/20/1/18, unfoliated (entries for 2 Jan., 10 March, and 30 March 1688); *CSPD, Charles II, 1683–84*, 83; E. K., "Draper Guild, Devizes,"

Wiltshire Notes and Queries, viii (1915), 551; *London Gazette,* no. 2351 (28–31 May 1688); Edmund Nevill and Reginald Boucher, "Marriage Licenses of Salisbury," *The Genealogist,* n.s., xxxiv (1918), 165; idem, "Marriage Licenses of Salisbury," *The Genealogist,* n.s., xxxvii (1921), 51; idem, "Marriage Licenses of Salisbury," *The Genealogist,* n.s., xxxviii (1922), 53; Wiltshire RO, G23/1/17, entry for 17 Dec. 1687; Walter Money, *The History of the Ancient Town and Borough of Newbury* (Oxford, 1887), 300, 310; *London Gazette,* no. 2343 (30 April–3 May 1688); Norfolk RO, NCR 16C/7, fol. 39v, entry for 30 March 1688; Bodl., MS Tanner 396, fol. 38v; C. H. Evelyn White, "Friends as Weavers," *JFHS,* iv (1907), 83–84; Arthur Eddington, *The First Fifty Years of Quakerism in Norwich* (London, 1932), 149; *CSPD, James II, 1687–89,* 270.

20. *London Gazette,* no. 2254 (23–27 June 1687); G.D.L., "MSS. Written or Possessed by Ralph Thoresby, F.R.S.," *Publications of the Thoresby Society,* xxviii, (1923–27), 442–443.

21. Yorkshire Archaeological Society, Thoresby papers, MS4/142, Robert Ross to Elkanah Hickson, 28 June 1687, MS3/77, letter from Nathaniel Johnston, 24 June 1687.

22. NUL, PwA 2142, [James Rivers] to [Hans Willem Bentinck], 5/15 Feb. 1688; see also Bodl., MS Don. c.169, fol. 60, Henry Ashurst to Conrado Calkbarner, 25 Oct. 1687; TNA, PC 2/72, fols. 75v, 118v; Charles Woolsey Cole, *French Mercantilism, 1683–1700* (New York, 1943), 12–13, 296.

23. William Andrews Clark Memorial Library, MS.1959.005, pp. 41, 44, 76–77, 81; Michael Hunter and Annabel Gregory, eds., *An Astrological Diary of the Seventeenth Century: Samuel Jeake of Rye, 1652–1699* (Oxford, 1988), 192.

24. Hunter and Gregory, eds., *Astrological Diary,* 187; East Sussex RO, RYE 1/17, p. 141; TNA, PC 2/72, fol. 154.

25. William Andrews Clark Memorial Library, MS.1959.005, pp. 4, 124. On this episode, see also Paul Kléber Monod, *The Murder of Mr. Grebell: Madness and Civility in an English Town* (New Haven, 2003), 127–129, which curiously does not mention the economic reasons for the estrangement between James's administration and the wool traders of Rye.

26. *The Entring Book of Roger Morrice, 1677–1691,* ed. Mark Goldie, John Spurr, Tim Harris, Stephen Taylor, Mark Knights, and Jason McElligott, 7 vols. (Woodbridge, 2007–9), iv:293–294; Beinecke, OSB MSS 1, box 2, folder 85, newsletter from Whitehall sent to Edmund Poley, 6 July 1688.

27. Robert Newton, *Eighteenth Century Exeter* (Exeter, 1984), 11; *CSPD, Charles II, July-Sept. 1683,* 60; Mark Goldie, "James II and the Dissenters' Revenge: The Commission of Enquiry of 1688," *Historical Research,* lxvi (1993), 68–76.

28. Basil Duke Henning, ed., *The House of Commons, 1660–1690,* 3 vols. (London, 1983), i:612–613; Sir George Duckett, ed., *Penal Laws and Test Act: Questions Touching their Repeal Propounded in 1687–8 by James II,* 2 vols. (London, 1882–83), i:373, ii:240–242, 264, 299; *CSPD, James II, 1687–89,* 183; Bodl., MS Tanner 28, fol. 158v, bishop of Bristol to archbishop of Canterbury, 16 Aug.

1688; Devon RO, QS 1/13, fol. 126; Peter William Jackson, "Nonconformists and Society in Devon, 1660–1689" (Ph.D. thesis, Univ. of Exeter, 1986), 264, 273, 279–286; [John Hickes], *A True and Faithful Narrative, of the Unjust and Illegal Sufferings, and Oppressions of Many Christians* (n.p., 1671, H1881), 7–19.

29. Plymouth and West Devon RO, MS 373/2, entry for Sir Edward Seymour; Edward Windeatt, "The Dismissal of Sir Edward Seymour from the Recordership of Totnes by James II, 1687," *Report and Transactions of the Devonshire Association for the Advancement of Science, Literature, and Art,* viii (1876), 360–369; Devon RO, 1579A/9/35, fols. 225–226, 229, 234; Devon RO, 3248A/9/1, entry for 6 Jan. 1688; Devon RO, 3248A/3/12, fol. 72; *London Gazette,* no. 2256 (30 June–4 July 1687), no. 2260 (14–18 July 1687); *CSPD, James II, 1687–89,* 150, 183, 199, 223; Devon RO, Calendar of Deeds and Documents in Exeter City Library, Dartmouth Corporation, DD.63634.

30. *Publick Occurrences,* no. 14 (22 May 1688); Devon RO, QS/1/13, fol. 108. The four books ordered to be burnt were Halifax, *Letter to a Dissenter*; [Gilbert Burnet], *An Enquiry into the Reasons for Abrogating the Test* (n.p., n.d., B5813); *Reflexions on Monsieur Fagel's Letter* (n.p., 1688, R700); and *A Copy of an Address to the King by the Bishop of Oxon, to be Subscribed by the Clergy of his Diocess; with . . . the Reasons Against it* (n.p., 1687, P456).

31. Duckett, ed., *Penal Laws,* ii:231; on James's policy of not allowing Catholics to stand for seats to the House of Commons, see CAC (C), D/Lons/W2/1/22/31, Thomas Tickell to Sir John Lowther, 12 July 1687; CAC (C), D/Lons/W2/1/22/34, Sir John Lowther to Thomas Tickell, 19 July 1687; *The King's Dispensing Power Explicated & Asserted* (London, [1688], K592), 6–7; James II, *By the King, A Declaration* (1688, J158).

32. Mark Goldie, "John Locke's Circle and James II," *HJ,* xxxv (1992), 579–581; Richard Burthogge, *Organum Vetus & Novum: Or, A Discourse* (1678, B6154); [Richard Burthogge], *Prudential Reasons for Repealing the Penal Laws* (1687, B6155), 9–10; Anthony Wood, *Athenae Oxonienses,* ed. Philip Bliss, 4 vols. (London, 1813–20), vol. 4, cols. 582, 609; Duckett, ed., *Penal Laws,* ii:231.

33. Duckett, ed., *Penal Laws,* ii:231–233, 240–242.

34. Duckett, ed., *Penal Laws,* i:361–365, 410, ii:227–228, 246–248; Ann Docwra, *Spiritual Community, Vindicated amongst People of Different Perswasions* (n.p., 1687, D1781); Elizabeth Rone, *A Reproof to those Church Men or Ministers that Refused to Read the Kings Most Gracious Declaration* (n.p., 1688, R1914A).

35. Suffolk RO, Bury St Edmunds, E2/41/5, fol. 41, Lord Dover to John Stafford, 12 May 1688, unfoliated, same to same, 23 Aug. 1688; Pat E. Murrell, "Bury St. Edmunds and the Campaign to Pack Parliament, 1687–8," *BIHR,* liv (1981), 189–191, 193; Duckett, ed., *Penal Laws,* ii:227–228.

36. John T. Evans, *Seventeenth-Century Norwich* (Oxford, 1979), 314–315; BL, Add. MS 34487, fol. 25, newsletter to countess of Suffolk, 22 Aug. 1688; Bodl., MS Tanner 28, fol. 183, bishop of Norwich to archbishop of Canterbury, 26 Sept. 1688.

37. Cambridgeshire County RO, Shelf C/9, p. 107; King's Lynn RO, KL/C7/12, fol. 66.

38. Davy was included in a list of Roman Catholics to be disarmed in December 1688, but it is unclear how accurate this list was, as the dragnet also caught up a common councilman of King's Lynn, William Thompson, who was most likely an Anglican. A local chronicler who carefully marked out the Catholics and dissenters among the new councillors of King's Lynn in June 1688 did not specify the religion of Davy and Thompson, which suggests that both men were believed to be Anglicans at the time. Davy was not mentioned in the return of notable Catholics from Norfolk sent to parliament in 1680. See B. Cozens-Hardy, ed., "Norfolk Lieutenancy Journal, 1676–1701," *Norfolk Record Society,* xxx (1961), 95–96; Norfolk RO, BL/AQ 2/13, fol. 58v; King's Lynn RO, KL/C7/12, fol. 66; *A Calendar of the Freemen of Lynn, 1292–1836* (Norwich, 1913), 194; House of Lords Record Office, Main Papers, MS 321, fols. 111–113.

39. BL, Add. MS 71573, fol. 51v, Oliver Le Neve to Peter Le Neve, 11 July 1688; *London Gazette,* no. 2371 (6–9 Aug. 1688); Norfolk RO, BL/AQ 2/13, fols. 57v–61; King's Lynn RO, KL/C7/12, fols. 66, 68v, 72.

40. Norfolk RO, BL/AQ 2/13, fols. 58v, 60v; Duckett, ed., *Penal Laws,* i:315. Three of the new common councilmen, Peter Busby, Francis Kirby, and William Thompson, were Catholics, as was the new town clerk, Matthew Oufande. One of the new councilmen, the mariner Thomas Buckingham, was a Quaker. Two of the new aldermen and three of the new common councilmen were dissenters of unknown type. See B. Cozens-Hardy, ed., "Norfolk Lieutenancy Journal," 95–96; Henry J. Hillen, *History of the Borough of King's Lynn* (Norwich, 1907), 444, 470–471; *A Calendar of the Freemen of Lynn, 1292–1836* (Norwich, 1913), 178, 189, 193, 197, 199, 201; King's Lynn RO, KL/C7/12, fols. 66, 72; Norfolk RO, BL/AQ 2/13, fol. 60v.

41. Cambridgeshire County RO, Shelf C/9, pp. 115–116, 118, 120, 122, 124; Canterbury Cathedral Archives, A/C/7, fols. 104–105v; Bodl., MS Ballard 23, fol. 26, [John Laughton] to Arthur Charlett, 6 Aug. 1688.

42. Norfolk RO, NCR 16C/7, Assembly Book of Norwich, 1683–1714, fols. 43–45v; White, "Friends as Weavers," 83–84; Eddington, *Quakerism in Norwich,* 149; *CSPD, James II, 1687–89,* 270; see also Norfolk RO, 13C/4, John Danson to Henry Lombe, 22 Sept. 1688. For a similar effort to add Quakers to the freedom in Bristol in 1688, see Bristol RO, Common Council Proceedings Book of Bristol, 1687–1702, fol. 21; Russell Mortimer, "Bristol Quakers and the Oaths," *JFHS,* xliii (1951), 75.

43. *Entring Book of Roger Morrice,* iii:271; Gloucestershire RO, GBR B3/6, fols. 170, 174, 175v, 182; *The Speech of Charles Trinder, Esq; Recorder of Gloucester* (1688, T2283), 15; *London Gazette,* no. 2313 (16–19 Jan. 1688).

44. *London Gazette,* no. 2343 (30 April–3 May 1688). The nine non-parliamentary corporations regulated by James included two in East Anglia (Saffron Walden and Southwold); five in a band stretching from just west of

London through to Devon (Kingston upon Thames, Basingstoke, Newbury, Chard, and Great Torrington); and two in the north (Macclesfield and Doncaster).

45. University of Wales Bangor, Mostyn Additional MSS, no. 9070/29, letter to Thomas Mostyn, 2 Feb. 1688; Paul D. Halliday, *Dismembering the Body Politic: Partisan Politics in England's Towns, 1650–1730* (Cambridge, 1998), 251; TNA, PC 2/72, fols. 105, 149v; Carmarthenshire Archive Service, Mus 156, fol. 123. For scattered evidence of activity by the regulators in Wales, see Duckett, ed., *Penal Laws*, i:249–250; NLW, Wynnstay MSS, C 26, Lord Brandon to Sir William Williams, *c.* Aug. 1688.

46. BL, Lansdowne MS 828, fol. 10v; NLW, MS 11020E, no. 17, Sir William Williams to [Lord Jeffreys], 16 Sept. 1688.

47. Bodl., MS Tanner 28, fol. 139, bishop of Bristol to archbishop of Canterbury, n.d.; M. G. Smith, *'Fighting Joshua': A Study of the Career of Sir Jonathan Trelawny* (Redruth, 1985), 54; Duckett, ed., *Penal Laws*, i:379–380.

48. *CSPD, James II, 1687–89*, 304.

49. The travails of the burgesses of Buckingham and Barnstaple can be followed in BL, Mic M/636, reel 42, Claydon House letters, Sir Ralph Verney to Sir Richard Temple, 24 March 1688, same to same, 15 March 1688, William Grosvenor to William Coleman, 4 April 1688; Centre for Buckinghamshire Studies, B/Buc 3/1, fols. 29–30; TNA, PC 2/72, fols. 91v, 101v, 113v; Narcissus Luttrell, *A Brief Historical Relation of State Affairs*, 6 vols. (Oxford, 1857), i:441; J. R. Chanter and Thomas Wainwright, *Reprint of the Barnstaple Records*, 2 vols. (Barnstaple, 1900), i:76–77; *Publick Occurrences*, no. 10 (24 April 1688); BL, Sloane MS 3929, fol. 48, newsletter for 21 April 1688; North Devon RO, B/1/3984, pp. 55, 57, 69–70; TNA, PC 2/72, fols. 65, 81v, 121v; *CSPD, James II, 1687–89*, 221, 275.

50. See *CSPD, James II, 1687–89*, 267, 286–287, 294, 304–305, 315 (quote at 304); Duckett, ed., *Penal Laws*, ii:217, 232, 241; TNA, T1/2, fol. 185, letter of the earl of Bath, 23 Oct. 1688; BL, Add. MS 41805, fol. 119, earl of Bath to earl of Middleton, 5 Nov. 1688.

51. Devon RO, 3248A/3/12, p. 72; Devon RO, 3248A/9/1, unfoliated, entry for 6 Jan. 1687/8; on the earl of Bath's handling of electoral politics in 1688, see also Peter Walker, *James II and the Three Questions: Religious Toleration and the Landed Classes, 1687–1688* (Oxford, 2010), 235.

52. *CSPD, James II, 1687–89*, 357, 364–365; John Childs, *The Army, James II, and the Glorious Revolution* (Manchester, 1980), 191.

53. University of Wales Bangor, Mostyn Additional MSS, no. 9070/3, Philip Fowke to Thomas Mostyn, 22 Jan. 1687/8. The actual number removed was sixteen, including the recorder: see TNA, PC 2/72, fol. 71.

54. Centre for Buckinghamshire Studies, D135/B1/4/24, Edward Kynaston to [Lord Jeffreys], 20 Oct. 1688. Kynaston, an Anglican, was one of the men removed from the town council of Shrewsbury by order of the privy council in January 1688.

55. TNA, PC 2/72, fol. 95v; Wigan Archives Service, Court Leet rolls, bundle 61, fol. 4; Lancashire RO, DDKe/9/73/36, J. Keeling to Roger Kenyon, 9 March 1688.

56. *HMC, Kenyon*, 189, 196 (quote at 196); Wigan Archives Service, Book of Common Council of Wigan, 1685–1688, fol. 22; idem, Charter Translations Book of Wigan, pp. 43–77; Henry Foley, *Records of the English Province of the Society of Jesus*, 7 vols. (London, 1877–83), v:319; Bodl., MS Ballard 1, fol. 80, letter of Mr. Richmond, 6 April 1688. The *London Gazette* published no address from Wigan in 1688.

57. *CSPD, James II, 1687–89*, 312; Staffordshire RO, D1323 A/1/1, p. 350; Josiah C. Wedgwood, *Staffordshire Parliamentary History from the Earliest Times to the Present Day*, 2 vols. (London, 1919–22), vol. 2, pt. 1, p. 155; House of Lords RO, Main Papers, MS 321, fols. 125–127; Duckett, ed., *Penal Laws*, ii:251.

58. *CTB*, viii:2019, 2062; Cheshire RO, D/MH/1, fol. 7v.

59. Cheshire RO, D/MH/1, fol. 7v. For a similar case in Ipswich, see Ebenezer Turell, *The Life and Character of the Reverend Benjamin Colman* (Boston, 1749), 29.

60. For Brandon, see Lancashire RO, DDKe/2/19/11 and Lancashire RO DDKe/4/9; for Howard, see CAC (K), WD/Ry HMC no. 3152, Sir Christopher Musgrave to Sir Daniel Fleming, 8 Dec. 1687; CAC (K), WD/Ry HMC no. 3154, letter to Richard Lowry, 23 Dec. 1687; and Luttrell, *Brief Historical Relation*, i:419; for Langdale, see Hull City Archives, BRL 2759a, fol. 38; Hull City Archives, DMX.134.1, pp. 161–162; and M. J. Short, "The Corporation of Hull and the Government of James II, 1687–8," *Historical Research*, lxxi (1998), 178–182.

61. Berwick-upon-Tweed RO, B1/13, fols. 125v–127, 135–136v, 138r–v, 146–147, 149, 151r–v, 153; Childs, *Army*, 108; CAC (C), Ca/2/2, p. 16; CAC (C), Ca/2/21, fol. 61; for an even more drastic purge of the freemen in Oxford, see BL, Mic M/636, reel 42, Claydon House letters, Sir Ralph Verney to Edmund Verney, 11 June 1688.

62. Duckett, ed., *Penal Laws*, i:115; Durham County RO, Du 1/4/5, fol. 26; idem, Du 1/35/1, p. 40; Margaret Child, "Prelude to Revolution: The Structure of Politics in County Durham, 1678–1688" (Ph.D. thesis, Univ. of Maryland, 1972), 131–134.

63. Henning, ed., *House of Commons*, i:418, claims mistakenly that a parliamentary election was held in 1688 in Arundel, Sussex. The claim is based on an oral tradition first written down in the nineteenth century. According to this tradition, Lord Jeffreys came to Arundel in 1688 in an attempt to get the king's candidates elected but was rebuffed, and the king's candidates were defeated. Further research reveals that this event could not have taken place in 1688 but likely took place in 1685 instead. There is no reference to an election in 1688 in the Arundel corporation minute book. Moreover, according to Lord Clarendon's diary, Jeffreys was in London from 22 September to 2 October

1688, the period of time when an election could possibly have been held in Arundel. A 1685 date is more plausible. William Bridgeman wrote on 30 March 1685 that he and Jeffreys were planning to travel to Sussex that day, which was two days before Arundel held its election. Arundel elected a whig and a trimmer in the 1685 election, which also fits the story. See Thomas Astle and Francis Grose, eds., *The Antiquarian Repertory*, 4 vols. (London, 1807–09), i:185–186; James Dallaway, *A History of the Western Division of the County of Sussex*, 2 vols. in 3 (London, 1815–32), vol. 2, part 1, p. 179; Samuel Weller Singer, ed., *The Correspondence of Henry Hyde, Earl of Clarendon*, 2 vols. (London, 1828), ii:188–192; BL, Add. MS 41803, fol. 205, William Bridgeman to earl of Middleton, [30 March 1685]; West Sussex RO, MP 1926, pp. 146–148.

64. Henning, ed., *House of Commons*, i:280–282; Duckett, ed., *Penal Laws*, i:353, 362–363, 365; Lord Braybrooke, ed., *Memoirs of Samuel Pepys*, 2 vols. (London, 1825), ii:96, 98; John Smith, ed., *The Life, Journals, and Correspondence of Samuel Pepys*, 2 vols. (London, 1841), ii:146–149; Medway Archives, Rochester City Council 1227/1974/RCA/A1/02, fol. 260.

65. Daniel Defoe, *A Tour thro' the Whole Island of Great Britain*, ed. G. D. H. Cole, 2 vols. (London, 1927), i:110; *CSPD, James II, 1687–89*, 274; Duckett, ed., *Penal Laws*, i:339, 360–361, 363–365.

66. Henning, ed., *House of Commons*, i:279–280; *CSPD, James II, 1687–89*, 220; Centre for Kentish Studies, Qb/RPp. W. A. Speck, in an uncharacteristic lapse, stated incorrectly that the royal nominees were Wilford and Booth, thereby transforming the result into a dead loss for the king. See W. A. Speck, *Reluctant Revolutionaries: Englishmen and the Revolution of 1688* (Oxford, 1988), 132–133.

67. Henning, ed., *House of Commons*, i:464–465; *London Gazette*, no. 2264 (28 July–1 Aug. 1687), no. 2343 (30 April–3 May 1688); Bodl., MS Ballard 12, fol. 33v, George Hickes to Arthur Charlett, 28 May 1688; London Metropolitan Archives, CLC/B/050/D/011/MS14187, Sir Walter Blount to Lord Jeffreys, 4 July 1688; *CSPD, James II, 1687–89*, 177, 186, 209, 215–216, 244, 248; TNA, PC 2/72, fol. 147r–v. Although a warrant for a new charter was issued, the proposed charter does not appear to have been enrolled under the Great Seal: see TNA, SP 44/338, pp. 54–56; TNA, C233/8, fols. 128–133; Halliday, *Dismembering*, 352. Street's property holdings in Droitwich are documented by deeds and leases in Worcestershire RO, Ref. 899:749, Acc. 8782, parcels 59–61.

68. *CSPD, James II, 1687–89*, 279; Worcestershire RO, Ref. 6497, Acc. 8445, parcel 1, fol. 28v; Bodl., MS Carte 130, fol. 307, letter of Robert Price, 22 Nov. 1688. The entry on Droitwich in Henning, ed., *House of Commons*, i:464–465, does not mention the election of 1 Oct. 1688; the entry appears to have been drafted without reference to the minute book of Droitwich, which records the election.

69. Henning, ed., *House of Commons*, i:718–719, iii:604–607; University of Wales Bangor, Mostyn Additional MSS, no. 9070/29, Robert Hookes to Thomas Mostyn, 2 Feb. 1687/8.

70. Duckett, ed., *Penal Laws,* i:365, ii:220–221; see also John Miller, *James II: A Study in Kingship* (Hove, 1978), 197.

71. K. H. D. Haley, "A List of the English Peers, *c.* May, 1687," *EHR*, lxix (1954), 302–306; David Hosford, "The Peerage and the Test Act: A List, *c.* November 1687," *BIHR*, xlii (1969), 116–120; TNA, PRO 31/3/174, p. 9, Usson de Bonrepaus to the marquis de Seignelay, 24 Nov./4 Dec. 1687; NUL, PwA 2148, James Rivers to [Hans Willem Bentinck], 27 Feb. 1688; Bodl., MS Ballard 21, fol. 18, [Dr. Sykes?] to Arthur Charlett, 14 May 1688; CPA, vol. 166, fol. 203r–v, Barrillon to Louis XIV, 8/18 Sept. 1688; Gilbert Burnet, *Bishop Burnet's History of His Own Time,* ed. M. J. Routh, 2nd edn., 6 vols. (Oxford, 1833), iii:262 n.; BL, Add. MS 51511, fol. 46.

72. This figure has been arrived at through a composite analysis of the sizes of the electorate in each constituency as given in Henning, ed., *House of Commons,* i:125–522.

73. Henning, ed., *House of Commons,* i:280.

74. Suffolk Record Office, Bury St Edmunds, E2/41/5, fols. 37r–38v, Lord Dover to John Stafford, 22 March 1688, fol. 48, letter of Lord Dover, 26 June 1688; Murrell, "Bury St. Edmunds," 191–197. The letter from Bury St Edmunds, not being a formal address, was not published in the *London Gazette.* The lack of publication of informal letters makes it difficult to know whether Bury St Edmunds's letter was unique or whether similar letters were sent to the king by other councils.

75. Short, "Corporation of Hull," 186–190.

76. Bristol, Newcastle-upon-Tyne, Leicester, and Chichester voted against sending an address. See Bristol RO, Common Council Proceedings Book of Bristol, 1687–1702, fols. 10–11; W. H. D. Longstaffe, ed., *Memoirs of the Life of Mr. Ambrose Barnes, Late Merchant and Sometime Alderman of Newcastle upon Tyne,* Surtees Society, vol. 50 (Durham, 1867), 176 n.; Leicestershire RO, BRII/18/36, no. 89; West Sussex RO, MF 1145, C/1, p. 33.

77. This tally is based on a reading of the constituency histories in Henning, ed., *House of Commons,* i:125–522. See also J. R. Jones, *The Revolution of 1688 in England* (London, 1972), 157; BL, Add. MS 34510, fol. 143r–v, Aernout van Citters to States General, 17 Sept. 1688. Although royal charters had been issued to several boroughs by prescription in the early and middle years of the 1680s, James and the regulators did not attempt to revive such practices in 1687–1688: see Henning, ed., *House of Commons,* i:158–159, 207–208, 438; Cornwall RO, DD/R.5508, "The humble Answeare of the Towne and Burrough of Fow[e]y to his Majesties Quo warranto," 17 Aug. 1684; Charles Henderson, *Essays in Cornish History* (Oxford, 1935), 38–41.

78. Note that some of the 107 boroughs (23 in all) were both regulated and rechartered. For the corporations regulated by order of the privy council, see the privy council register for 1687–1688 (TNA, PC 2/72). For a list of the corporations rechartered, see Halliday, *Dismembering,* 352. For the regulation of

London, see BL, Add. MS 17748, fols. 14–16v; CUL, Microfilm MS 9528, repertory 92, pp. 342, 362–364, repertory 93, fols. 76, 188. Non-parliamentary corporations have been excluded from these tallies.

79. Historians have differed on this matter. J. R. Jones argued that the king might have succeeded in "packing" the parliament had William not intervened. His argument was countered by Paul Halliday. See Jones, *Revolution of 1688*, 17, 138, 164–172; Halliday, *Dismembering*, 239, 249, 260–261. On this point, see also Speck, *Reluctant Revolutionaries*, 131–135.

80. John Dalrymple, *Memoirs of Great Britain and Ireland*, 2nd edn., 2 vols. (London, 1771–73), vol. ii, pt. i, p. 230.

8. Dancing in a Ditch

1. Lucile Pinkham, *William III and the Respectable Revolution* (Cambridge, MA, 1954), 158–162; J. P. Kenyon, *The Nobility in the Revolution of 1688* (Hull, 1963), 4–5, 12–13, 19; William L. Sachse, "The Mob and the Revolution of 1688," *JBS*, iv (1964), 23, 39–40; Jonathan I. Israel, "The Dutch Role in the Glorious Revolution," in Jonathan I. Israel, ed., *The Anglo-Dutch Moment: Essays on the Glorious Revolution and its World Impact* (Cambridge, 1991), 120–128; Dale Hoak, "The Anglo-Dutch Revolution of 1688–89," in Dale Hoak and Mordechai Feingold, eds., *The World of William and Mary: Anglo-Dutch Perspectives on the Revolution of 1688–89* (Stanford, 1996), 16–19, 24–26; see also Eveline Cruickshanks, *The Glorious Revolution* (Basingstoke, 2000), 25–26, 30.

2. See Tim Harris, *Revolution: The Great Crisis of the British Monarchy, 1685–1720* (London, 2006), 11–15, 275–276; Steve Pincus, *1688: The First Modern Revolution* (New Haven, 2009), 223–224. For earlier treatments of the Revolution as a popular revolt, see Thomas Babington Macaulay, *The History of England from the Accession of James the Second*, ed. C. H. Firth, 6 vols. (London, 1913–15), iii:1042–1047, 1155–1158, 1178–1180; George Macaulay Trevelyan, *The English Revolution, 1688–1689* (London, 1938), 94–95, 103, 113.

3. The estimate of 15,000 is based on two reliable contemporary sources: the eyewitness testimony of John Whittle, who came over with William and recorded that "The number of all his Forces and Souldiers [was] about fifteen thousand four hundred and odd Men," and the published account in the *London Gazette*, which gave a total of 14,352 men. For these sources, see [Whittle], *An Exact Diary of the Late Expedition* (1689, W2044), 40; *London Gazette*, no. 2397 (5–8 Nov. 1688). Other contemporary sources that also indicate a figure of around 15,000 are discussed in John Carswell, *The Descent on England: A Study of the English Revolution of 1688 and its European Background* (London, 1969), 169–170, and Arjen van der Kuijl, *De Glorieuze Overtocht: De Expeditie van Willem III naar Engeland in 1688* (Amsterdam, 1988), 41; see also the lower estimate of "about 13,000 men" given in *Memoirs of Isaac Dumont de Bostaquet*, ed. and trans. Dianne E. Ressinger (London, 2005), 191. In arguing for a higher figure of 21,000 men,

Jonathan Israel and Geoffrey Parker wrote that "James II's ambassador in The Hague was close to the truth when he put the total strength of William's invasion army at 21,000, including some 5,000 volunteers": see Jonathan I. Israel and Geoffrey Parker, "Of Providence and Protestant Winds: The Spanish Armada of 1588 and the Dutch Armada of 1688," in Israel, ed., *Anglo-Dutch Moment,* 337. This appears to be a misreading of the original source. What the English ambassador wrote in the letter cited by Israel and Parker was that "The prince has not above 20000 fighting men." Thus the ambassador provided a slightly lower number, which he presented not as a definite figure but as an upper bound for his estimate: see BL, Add. MS 41816, fol. 266v, marquis d'Albeville to earl of Middleton, 20/30 Oct. 1688. An even lower estimate of 11,212 has been cited occasionally, as in J. R. Western, *Monarchy and Revolution: The English State in the 1680s* (London, 1972), 259. This estimate is based on a misreading of a column of figures in an article in the *Journal of the Society for Army Historical Research.* Adding up the figures in the column reveals that the total of 11,212 refers only to the foot soldiers, and that an additional 4,057 cavalrymen came with William, thereby yielding a total estimate of 15,269, which is close to the figure from Whittle. For this article, see Marquess of Cambridge, "The March of William of Orange from Torbay to London—1688," *Journal of the Society for Army Historical Research,* xliv (1966), 152–153. For other historians who accept an estimate in the neighborhood of 15,000, see Harris, *Revolution,* 274; Stephen Saunders Webb, *Lord Churchill's Coup: The Anglo-American Empire and the Glorious Revolution Reconsidered* (New York, 1995), 141; and W. A. Speck, *James II* (London, 2002), 76. For the size of James's army, which is mercifully uncontested, see John Childs, *The Army, James II, and the Glorious Revolution* (Manchester, 1980), 4.

4. Andrew Browning, ed., *Memoirs of Sir John Reresby,* rev. Mary K. Geiter and W. A. Speck (London, 1991), 525.

5. W. A. Speck, "The Orangist Conspiracy against James II," *HJ,* xxx (1987), 461–462; Robert Beddard, "The Unexpected Whig Revolution of 1688," in Robert Beddard, ed., *The Revolutions of 1688* (Oxford, 1991), 11–12; Jonathan Scott, *England's Troubles: Seventeenth-Century English Political Instability in European Context* (Cambridge, 2000), 206; Harris, *Revolution,* 276, 283–285.

6. For an exception to this view, see Pincus, *1688,* 92–94, 122, 210–211, 339.

7. Harris, *Revolution,* 31–34, 171, 184–185.

8. John Dalrymple, *Memoirs of Great Britain and Ireland,* 2nd edn., 2 vols. (London, 1771–73), vol. 2, pt. 1, p. 231.

9. Sir Hilary Jenkinson, "What happened to the Great Seal of James II?," *Antiquaries Journal,* xxiii (1943), 1–2; E. S. de Beer, "The Great Seal of James II: A Reply to Sir Hilary Jenkinson," *Antiquaries Journal,* xlii (1962), 85; *The Entring Book of Roger Morrice, 1677–1691,* ed. Mark Goldie, John Spurr, Tim Harris, Stephen Taylor, Mark Knights, and Jason McElligott, 7 vols. (Woodbridge, 2007–9), iv:382; *The Works of John Sheffield, Earl of Mulgrave,* 2 vols. ([The Hague],

1726), ii:78; William Denton, "Historical Fragment: James II at Faversham," *Notes and Queries,* III, v (14 May 1868), 391; Staffordshire RO, Dartmouth papers, D1778/V/1403, p. 122, James II to Lord Dartmouth, 9 Nov. 1688; see also William E. Buckley, ed., *Memoirs of Thomas, Earl of Ailesbury, Written by Himself,* 2 vols. (Westminster, 1890), i:185–186.

10. BL, Add. MS 63780, fol. 114, earl of Middleton to Lord Preston, 22 Nov. 1688; see also *HMC, Seventh Report,* 349; BL, Add. MS 34510, fols. 191v–192, Aernout van Citters to States General, 27 Nov./7 Dec. 1688; *HMC, Second Report,* 11.

11. Stephen B. Baxter, *William III and the Defense of European Liberty, 1650–1702* (Westport, 1966), 240; W. A. Speck, *Reluctant Revolutionaries: Englishmen and the Revolution of 1688* (Oxford, 1988), 71–72, 87, 118–121, 138; W. A. Speck, *James II* (London, 2002), 76.

12. *HMC, Seventh Report,* 417; CPA, vol. 167, fol. 157v, Barrillon to Louis XIV, 29 Nov./9 Dec. 1688; Bodl., MS Don. c. 39, fol. 17, newsletter dated 27 Nov. 1688; BL, Add. MS 36707, fol. 50, Thomas Newey to James Harrington, 4 Dec. 1688; Cheshire RO, DSS/1/2/6, Mary Thelwall to Lady Shakerley, [17 Dec. 1688]; Charles T. Gatty, ed., "Mr. Francis Gwyn's Journal," *Fortnightly Review,* n.s., xl (1886), 362–364.

13. CPA, vol. 166, fols. 368–369v, 370v, Louis XIV to Barrillon, 22 Oct./1 Nov. 1688; CPA, vol. 167, fols. 62v-63, Barrillon to Louis XIV, 5/15 Nov. 1688; see also Berkshire RO, D/ED/C32, J. Hill to Sir William Trumbull, 20 Oct. 1688; BPL, Ms. Am. 1502, vol. 7, no. 51, newsletter dated 1 Nov. 1688. The quoted phrase in the original French reads "Comme l'aggresseur."

14. CPA, vol. 166, fol. 193r–v, Barrillon to Louis XIV, 8/18 Sept. 1688, fol. 221, same to same, 13/23 Sept. 1688, fol. 230, same to same, 17/27 Sept. 1688; John Dalrymple, *Memoirs of Great Britain and Ireland,* 2nd edn., 2 vols. (London, 1771–73), vol. 2, pt. 1, pp. 235–237; Gilbert Burnet, *Bishop Burnet's History of His Own Time,* ed. M. J. Routh, 2nd edn., 6 vols. (Oxford, 1833), iii:278–279.

15. *CSPD, James II, 1687–89,* 285–286, 303, 316, 326, 329, 331, 335, 340; *Memoirs of Sir John Reresby,* 524; *HMC, Dartmouth,* i:170; Narcissus Luttrell, *A Brief Historical Relation of State Affairs,* 6 vols. (Oxford, 1857), i:468, 472.

16. *The Works of the Right Honourable Henry Late L[ord] Delamer* (1694, D873), 56; Rosamond Meredith, "Beauchief Abbey and the Pegges," *The Derbyshire Archaeological Journal,* lxxxvii (1968 for 1967), 104; see also *Entring Book of Roger Morrice,* iv:335.

17. Buckley, ed., *Memoirs of Ailesbury,* 184; CPA, vol. 167, fols. 132v, 135, Barrillon to Louis XIV, 21 Nov./1 Dec. 1688; see also R. W. Blencowe, ed., *Diary of the Times of Charles the Second by the Honourable Henry Sidney,* 2 vols. (London, 1843), ii:377; BL, Add. MS 34510, fol. 167r–v, Aernout van Citters to States General, 6/16 Nov. 1688; Childs, *Army,* 141–142.

18. Meredith, "Beauchief Abbey and the Pegges," 104.

19. James II, *By the King, A Declaration* (1688, J158); *London Gazette,* no. 2385 (24–27 Sept. 1688); *CSPD, James II, 1687–89,* 280, 286; *HMC, Seventh Report,*

263; TNA, PRO 30/53/8/71, James II to marquess of Powis, 22 Sept. 1688. The proposal to retain that part of the Test Act of 1678 barring Catholics from the House of Commons had been mooted well in advance by the king, though it was not announced publicly until 21 September. On this proposal, sometimes described as "the expedient," see NUL, PwA 2100, James Rivers to [Hans Willem Bentinck], 17 Nov. 1687; NUL, PwA 2129/1, same to same, 9/19 Jan. 1688; NUL, PwA 2135/3, same to same, 13/23 Jan. 1688; NUL, PwA 2142, same to same, 5/15 Feb. 1688; *Entring Book of Roger Morrice*, iv:232; Mark N. Brown, ed., *The Works of George Savile, Marquis of Halifax*, 3 vols. (Oxford, 1989), i:92–93; [Henry Care], *Animadversions on a Late Paper, Entituled, A Letter to a Dissenter* (1687, C505), 37.

20. BL, Add. MS 41816, fol. 205r-v, marquis d'Albeville to earl of Middleton, 20/30 Sept. 1688; CPA, vol. 166, fol. 258r-v, Barrillon to Louis XIV, 23 Sept./3 Oct. 1688; BL, Add. MS 34512, fol. 103v, Aernout van Citters to States General, 25 Sept./5 Oct. 1688; Samuel Weller Singer, ed., *The Correspondence of Henry Hyde, Earl of Clarendon*, 2 vols. (London, 1828), ii:189.

21. James II, *By the King, a Proclamation* (1688, J260); James II, *His Majesties Most Gracious and General Pardon* (1688, J213).

22. Singer, ed., *Clarendon Correspondence*, ii:190–193; *Entring Book of Roger Morrice*, iv:322. The meeting on 3 Oct. included the seven bishops put on trial in June 1688 with the exception of the bishop of Bristol, plus the bishops of London, Winchester, and Rochester.

23. Bodl., MS Tanner 28, fols. 187–188; N. N., *An Account of the Late Proposals of the Archbishop of Canterbury, with some other Bishops, to His Majesty* (1688, N25), 1–4; Lord Braybrooke, ed., *The Autobiography of Sir John Bramston*, Camden Society, old series, xxxii (1845), 322–324.

24. *CSPD, James II, 1687–89*, 296, 309, 329; TNA, PC 2/72, fol. 160; *London Gazette*, no. 2386 (27 Sept.–1 Oct. 1688); Luttrell, *Brief Historical Relation*, i:464–466, 468; *Entring Book of Roger Morrice*, iv:315–316, 320–323.

25. *CSPD, James II, 1687–89*, 293, 297, 302, 319–320, 322, 337; Luttrell, *Brief Historical Relation*, i:464, 469; *London Gazette*, no. 2391 (15–18 Oct. 1688).

26. CAC (K), WD/Ry HMC no. 3263a, newsletter of 27 Sept. 1688; *London Gazette*, no. 2389 (8–11 Oct. 1688); *CSPD, James II, 1687–89*, 306, 311, 315, 323; HEHL, HA 7165, James II to earl of Huntingdon, 9 Oct. 1688; Wiltshire RO, WRO 1300, no. 856, unfoliated, earl of Ailesbury to James II, 17 Oct. 1688. See also Cornwall RO, B/TRU/102/1, p. 18; NLW, Penrice and Margam MSS, L202, duke of Beaufort to Sir Edward Mansell, 12 Oct. 1688; NLW, Brogyntyn PQN3/1/33, newsletter to Sir Robert Owen, 20 Oct. 1688.

27. Anthony Wood, *Athenae Oxonienses*, ed. Philip Bliss, 4 vols. (London, 1813–20), vol. 4, col. 689; see also BPL, Ms. Am. 1502, vol. 7, no. 47, newsletter dated 6 Oct. 1688; Bodl., MS Don. c.38, fol. 299, newsletter dated 9 Oct. 1688.

28. *London Gazette*, no. 2391 (15–18 Oct. 1688); James II, *By the King, A Proclamation for Restoring Corporations to their Ancient Charters* (1688, J344); Lut-

trell, *Brief Historical Relation,* i:468; see also FSL, X.d.436 (37), John Sydenham to William Blathwayt, 22 Oct. 1688.

29. BL, Sloane MS 3929, fol. 99v, newsletter dated 20 Oct. 1688; *HMC, Le Fleming,* 216; BL, Add. MS 34512, fol. 118r-v, Aernout van Citters to States General, 19/29 Oct. 1688; *CSPD, James II, 1687–89,* 329.

30. Northamptonshire RO, IC 1426, newsletter of 23 Oct. 1688; *His Majesties Reasons for With-drawing Himself from Rochester* (n.p., 1688, J376); James II, *A Declaration of His Most Sacred Majesty* (Dublin, 1689, J165); *HMC, Ormonde,* n.s., viii:391.

31. *Entring Book of Roger Morrice,* iv:345; Charles Deering, *Nottinghamia Vetus et Nova* (Nottingham, 1751), 257–258; Joseph MacCormick, ed., *State-Papers and Letters, Addressed to William Carstares* (Edinburgh, 1774), 149; *HMC, Stuart Papers,* vi:56; Paul Antony Hopkins, "Aspects of Jacobite Conspiracy in England in the Reign of William III" (Ph.D. thesis, Univ. of Cambridge, 1981), 128–129; on the nonconformity of the mayor of Nottingham, see Patricia Ann Lloyd, "Politics, Religion and the Personnel of Politics in Nottingham, 1642–1688" (M.Phil. thesis, Univ. of Nottingham, 1983), 312.

32. BL, Add. MS 34510, fol. 152, Aernout van Citters to States General, 9/19 Oct. 1688; *Entring Book of Roger Morrice,* iv:323; Braybrooke, ed., *Autobiography of Sir John Bramston,* 326; see also E. S. de Beer, ed., *The Diary of John Evelyn,* 6 vols. (Oxford, 1955), 599–600; BL, Add. MS 32096, fol. 332v; Martin Haile, *Queen Mary of Modena* (London, 1905), 199, 204.

33. Bodl., MS Rawl. d.148, fol. 3v; FSL, V.a.469 (memoirs of William Westby), fols. 37, 48; CPA, vol. 166, fols. 235v–236, Barrillon to Louis XIV, 17/27 Sept. 1688; BL, Mic M/636, reel 43, Claydon House letters, Lady Bridgeman to Ralph Verney, 3 Oct. 1688; see also *Entring Book of Roger Morrice,* iv:303; Lincolnshire Archives, Monson 7/12/60, newsletter to Lady Newton, *c.* Oct. 1688; *An Alarm to England: Or, a Warning-Piece to all True Protestants* (London, 1688, A827A), 1–2.

34. *A Memorial from the English Protestants, for their Highnesses the Prince and Princess of Orange* (n.p., [1688], M1686), 6–8.

35. *Memorials lately Presented by the French and English Ambassadors to the States General of the United Provinces* (n.p., [1688], A4270A); see also LLIU, Albeville MSS, Robert Yard to marquis d'Albeville, 4 Sept. 1688.

36. John Miller, *James II: A Study in Kingship* (Hove, 1978), 194–195; Jeremy Black, "The Revolution and the Development of English Foreign Policy," in Eveline Cruickshanks, ed., *By Force or by Default? The Revolution of 1688–1689* (Edinburgh, 1989), 140–142; CPA, vol. 166, fol. 303r-v, Louis XIV to Barrillon, 7/17 Oct. 1688, fol. 367v, same to same, 22 Oct./1 Nov. 1688.

37. BL, Add. MS 41823, fols. 71v–72, earl of Middleton to marquis d'Albeville, 11 Sept. 1688; BL, Add. MS 41816, fols. 212v–213, marquis d'Albeville to earl of Middleton, 24 Sept./4 Oct. 1688, fol. 216r–v, same to same, 26 Sept./6 Oct. 1688; *Entring Book of Roger Morrice,* iv:315; BL, Add. MS 34512,

fols. 93v–94, Aernout van Citters to States General, 11/21 Sept. 1688; Edme Mallet, ed., *Négociations de Monsieur le Comte d'Avaux en Hollande, depuis 1679, jusqu'en 1688*, 6 vols. (Paris, 1752–53), vi:260–261.

38. *Entring Book of Roger Morrice,* iv:308; LLIU, Albeville MSS, Robert Yard to marquis d'Albeville, 14 Sept. 1688; CPA, vol. 166, fol. 168, Louis XIV to Barrillon, 6/16 Sept. 1688; London Metropolitan Archives, CLC/B/050/D/014/MS14190, Bevil Skelton to Lord Jeffreys, 19 Sept. 1688.

39. Bodl., MS Don. c.38, fol. 295, newsletter dated 25 Sept. 1688; BL, Sloane MS 3929, fol. 93v, newsletter dated 29 Sept. 1688; BL, Add. MS 32096, fol. 332v.

40. NLW, Wynnstay MSS, C 27, Simon Lloyd to Sir William Williams, 24 Sept. 1688; on Lloyd, see Leicester RO, DG7, Box 4967, Law 15.

41. *Entring Book of Roger Morrice,* iv:326; Braybrooke, ed., *Autobiography of Sir John Bramston*, 327; J. P. Kenyon, *Robert Spencer, Earl of Sunderland, 1641–1702* (London, 1958), 220–223. Sunderland actually did suffer the type of mental collapse often attributed to James.

42. On the circulation of the prince's declaration, see *Entring Book of Roger Morrice,* iv:328; BL, Add. MS 41816, fol. 237, Daniel Petit to earl of Middleton, 5/15 Oct. 1688.

43. *The Prince of Orange his Declaration: Shewing the Reasons Why he Invades England* (1688, W2331), 3, 14; *Some Reflections upon his Highness the Prince of Oranges Declaration* (1688, S4589), 1.

44. *Entring Book of Roger Morrice,* iv:347; Bodl., MS Carte 130, fol. 307, [Robert Price] to duke of Beaufort, 22 November 1688.

45. [Hugh Speke?], *The Prince of Orange his Third Declaration* (n.p., 1688, S4914D), 3; credited as authentic in *HMC, Le Fleming*, 226; *HMC, Eliot Hodgkin*, 75; Bodl., MS Don. c.39, fol. 46v, newsletter dated 8 Dec. 1688; Beinecke, OSB MS File 9295, Sir John Lowther of Whitehaven to Sir John Lowther of Lowther, 8 Dec. 1688; but seen as inauthentic in *London Courant,* no. 2 (12–15 Dec. 1688); Luttrell, *Brief Historical Relation,* i:485.

46. BL, Add. MS 45731, fol. 24v, Owen Wynne to Edmund Poley, 19 Oct. 1688; BL, Add. MS 41816, fol. 215r–v, Daniel Petit to earl of Middleton, 25 Sept./5 Oct. 1688.

47. *An Answer to a Paper, Intitled, Reflections on the Prince of Orange's Declaration* (n.p., [1688], A3331), 1; *A Review of the Reflections on the Prince of Orange's Declaration* (n.p., 1688, R1199), 1.

48. *The Declaration of His Highnes[s] William Henry, by the Grace of God Prince of Orange* (The Hague, 1688, W2328C), 15; an earlier draft of this letter is in NUL, PwA 1664, prince of Orange to the English fleet, 19/29 Sept. 1688.

49. Israel, "Dutch Role," 136–138; Lois G. Schwoerer, "Propaganda in the Revolution of 1688–89," *American Historical Review,* lxxxii (1977), 854; H. Manners Sutton, ed., *The Lexington Papers* (London, 1851), 327, 331–334, 354–355.

50. FSL, V.a.469 (memoirs of William Westby), fol. 45; Bodl., MS Don.

c.39, fol. 35, newsletter dated 1 Dec. 1688; BL, Add. MS 63780, fol. 169, William Stokes to Lord Preston, 9 Dec. 1688; see also Luttrell, *Brief Historical Relation,* i:481; Bodl., MS Don. c.39, fol. 40, newsletter dated 4 Dec. 1688.

51. FSL, Newdigate newsletters, L.c.1951, newsletter dated 22 Dec. 1688; Bodl., MS Eng. hist. c.6, fol. 123, letter from Oxford dated 7 Dec. 1688; Bodl., MS Don. c.39, fol. 3, William Fleming to Roger Fleming, 24 Nov. 1688.

52. *Entring Book of Roger Morrice,* iv:384; George Hilton Jones, "The Irish Fright of 1688: Real Violence and Imagined Massacre," *BIHR,* lv (1982), 148–153.

53. Henry Fishwick, ed., *The Notebook of the Rev. Thomas Jolly,* Chetham Society, n.s., xxxiii (Manchester, 1894–95), 91; FSL, V.a.469 (memoirs of William Westby), fol. 37; Thomas Plunket, *The Character of a Good Commander* (1689, P2629), 6.

54. [William Sherlock], *A Letter to a Member of the Convention* (n.p., [1689], S3298), 4.

55. *Entring Book of Roger Morrice,* iv:326, 347, 384. On Morrice's intelligence gathering from the continent, see Stephen Taylor, "An English Dissenter and the Crisis of European Protestantism: Roger Morrice's Perception of European Politics in the 1680s," in David Onnekink, ed., *War and Religion after Westphalia, 1648–1713* (Farnham, 2009), 177–195.

56. For this argument, see Steven Pincus, "The English Debate over Universal Monarchy," in John Robertson, ed., *A Union for Empire: Political Thought and the British Union of 1707* (Cambridge, 1995), 52–62; idem, "Nationalism, Universal Monarchy, and the Glorious Revolution," in George Steinmetz, ed., *State/Culture: State-Formation after the Cultural Turn* (Ithaca, 1999), 195–198, 203–204; Pincus, *1688,* 313–314, 336–337, 363–365.

57. *Entring Book of Roger Morrice,* iv:326; Churchill College Archives Centre, Erle 2/25/1, Tregonwell Frampton to [Thomas Erle], 6 Dec. 1688.

58. G. C. Gibbs, "The Reception of the Huguenots in England and the Dutch Republic, 1680–1690," in Ole Peter Grell, Jonathan I. Israel, and Nicholas Tyacke, eds., *From Persecution to Toleration: The Glorious Revolution and Religion in England* (Oxford, 1991), 296–297, 303–304.

59. Houghton Library, Harvard Theatre Collection, fMS Thr. 11, p. 57, Sir George Etherege to earl of Rochester, 30 Dec./9 Jan. 1686/7; Emma Bergin, "Defending the True Faith: Religious Themes in Dutch Pamphlets on England, 1688–1689," in David Onnekink, ed., *War and Religion after Westphalia, 1648–1713* (Farnham, 2009), 230, 235–240.

60. *Articles of Peace and Commerce between the most Serene and Mighty Prince James II . . . and . . . the most Illustrious Lords, the Douletli Basha, Aga & Governours of the Famous City and Kingdom of Algiers* (1687, J153), 5.

61. BL, Add. MS 41814, fol. 268, marquis d'Albeville to earl of Middleton, 24 June/4 July 1687; TNA, PRO 31/3/171, fol. 48v, Barrillon to Louis XIV, 7/17 July 1687, fols. 77v–78, same to same, 18/28 July 1688, fol. 140, same to same,

20/30 Aug. 1687; *Entring Book of Roger Morrice*, iv:92–93, 96. For the 1678 Anglo-Dutch defensive treaty that was being invoked by the Dutch, see the *Actes et Memoires des Negotiations de la Paix de Nimegue*, 2 vols. (Amsterdam, 1679), ii:297–298.

62. BL, Add. MS 41816, fol. 175, marquis d'Albeville to earl of Middleton, 4/14 Sept. 1688; [Gilbert Burnet], *The Ill Effects of Animosities among Protestants in England Detected* (n.p., 1688, B5802), 23.

63. *Entring Book of Roger Morrice*, iv:96; TNA, PC 2/72, fols. 33, 57v.

64. Warwickshire County RO, CR2017, C7, no. 17, intelligence letter, *c.* April–July 1687; BL, Add. MS 41814, fol. 250v, marquis d'Albeville to earl of Middleton, 3/13 June 1687; [Robert Ferguson], *Representation of the Threatning Dangers, Impending over Protestants* (n.p., [1687], F756A), 35.

65. LLIU, Albeville MSS, John Rowe to marquis d'Albeville, 29 Jan. 1688; Haile, *Mary of Modena*, 180; BL, Add. MS 41816, fol. 40, marquis d'Albeville to earl of Middleton, 18/28 May 1688, fols. 47–49v, Daniel Petit to earl of Middleton, 25 May/4 June 1688; *Le Triomphe de la Liberté, ou l'Irrevocabilité du Test* (n.p., [1688]), 123; see also BL, Add. MS 41815, fol. 240, marquis d'Albeville to earl of Middleton, 14/24 April 1688; BL, Add. MS 41816, fol. 106v, same to same, 10/20 July 1688; LLIU, Albeville MSS, Philippe La Grice to marquis d'Albeville, 15 Aug. 1688; *Consultation de l'Oracle par les Puissance de la Terre, pour Savoir si le Prince des Galles Dieu-donné, est Supposé ou Legitime* (n.p., 1688), 18; A. Th. van Deursen, "Propaganda: The Battle for Public Opinion," in J. D. North and P. W. Klein, eds., *Science and Culture under William and Mary* (Amsterdam, 1992), 26–29; Bergin, "Defending the True Faith," 237–239; F. G. Stephens et. al., eds., *Catalogue of Prints and Drawings in the British Museum, Division I: Political and Personal Satires*, 12 vols. (London, 1870–1954), i:711–716.

66. BL, Add. MS 41821, fol. 213, invoice from Daniel Petit; BL, Add. MS 41816, fol. 133, marquis d'Albeville to earl of Middleton, 20/30 July 1688, fol. 146, same to same, 3/13 Aug. 1688; *HMC, Portland*, iii:416; Burnet, *History of His Own Time*, iii:260; *The Declaration of His Highnes[s] William Henry*, 7–8.

67. Marion E. Grew, *William Bentinck and William III* (London, 1924), 113–114; David Onnekink, *The Anglo-Dutch Favourite: The Career of Hans Willem Bentinck, 1st Earl of Portland* (Aldershot, 2007), 50–51; Israel, "Dutch Role," 106–107.

68. *Secreete Resolutien van de Ed. Groot Mog. Heeren Staaten van Hollandt en West-Vrieslandt*, 18 vols. (The Hague, 1791), v:230. The Dutch original reads as follows: "soo ten opsichte van de Religie als de Vryheyt en het welvaaren van den Staat, die beyde bevondt in een seer periculeuse constitutie. Dat het evident was, dat de Koningen van Vranckryck en Engelandt beyde toelegh maackten, om de Gereformeerde Religie, was het mogelijck, te dempen. Dat men in het reguarde van Vranckryck daar aan niet behoefden te twyffelen, dewyle die Majesteyt, een van de alderfondamenteelste Wetten van het Rijck, gedient hebbende, om den civilen oorlogh in Vranckryck te doen verseeren, te

weeten het Edict van Nantes hadde te niet gedaan, en de Gereformeerden gehandelt op een soodanigen maniere als yeder bekent was. Dat den Koningh van Engelandt met geen minder zele was aangedaan voor de selve Paapsche Religie, en getracht hadde, die in sijn Rijcken, soo veel mogelijck, te supplanteeren." The English translation used in the text is from David Onnekink, "The Last War of Religion? The Dutch and the Nine Years War," in David Onnekink, ed., *War and Religion after Westphalia, 1648–1713* (Farnham, 2009), 86.

69. Centre for Kentish Studies, U1015, C28, p. 11, letter from Thomas Papillon, 15/25 Sept. 1688; BL, Add. MS 41816, fol. 238v, marquis d'Albeville to earl of Middleton, 5/15 Oct. 1688.

70. *Extract of the States General their Resolution* (n.p., 1688, N482); BL, Add. MS 41821, fol. 272r–v; see also J. F. Gebhard, *Het Leven van Mr. Nicolaas Cornelisz Witsen*, 2 vols. (Utrecht, 1882), ii:169, 173.

71. Israel, "Dutch Role," 111–119; Israel, "The Dutch Republic and the 'Glorious Revolution' of 1688/89 in England," in Charles Wilson and David Proctor, eds., *1688: The Seaborne Alliance and Diplomatic Revolution* (Greenwich, 1989), 36–38; Mallet, ed., *Négociations d'Avaux*, vi:175–176, 190, 321.

72. On the religious causes of the Nine Years' War, see Onnekink, "Last War," 69–88; Tony Claydon, *Europe and the Making of England, 1660–1760* (Cambridge, 2007), 160–172; Benjamin J. Kaplan, *Divided by Faith: Religious Conflict and the Practice of Toleration in Early Modern Europe* (Cambridge, MA, 2007), 340–341; for the contrary view, see the emphasis on the secular origins of the Nine Years' War in Steven Pincus, "'To Protect English Liberties': The English Nationalist Revolution of 1688–1689," in Tony Claydon and Ian McBride, eds., *Protestantism and National Identity: Britain and Ireland, c.1650–c.1850* (Cambridge, 1998), 95–104; Pincus, "Nationalism," 195–199; Pincus, *1688*, 339–350, 363–365.

73. FSL, V.a.469 (memoirs of William Westby), fol. 34; on the importation of pamphlets from the Netherlands into England, see also BL, Add. MS 34487, fol. 17v, newsletter to countess of Suffolk, 25 July 1688; Giles Shute, *A New Naked Truth* (1688, S3709), 24–26.

74. Emma Theresa Bergin, "The Revolution of 1688 in Dutch Pamphlet Literature: A Study in the Dutch Public Sphere in the Late Seventeenth Century," (Ph.D. thesis, Univ. of Hull, 2006), 10, 97–101, 110–112, 133–134, 214–215.

75. Mallet, ed., *Négociations d'Avaux*, vi:267–268; see also *Entring Book of Roger Morrice*, iv:324. The original French reads: "Jamais nouvelle n'a plus réjoüi le Prince d'Orange, car il appréhendoit qu'on ne vînt en Flandres ou du côté de Cologne."

76. Mallet, ed., *Négociations d'Avaux*, vi:273. The original French reads: "rendit les Etats Généraux fort insolens, par la certitude que le Roi ne les attaqueroit pas, ni les Pays-bas Espagnols."

77. Camille Rousset, *Histoire de Louvois*, 4 vols. (Paris, 1862–63), iv:152–153; Duc de Villars, *Mémoires du Maréchal de Villars*, 6 vols. (Paris, 1884–1904), i:101;

see also *Recueil des Instructions Données aux Ambassadeurs et Ministres de France*, 31 vols. (Paris, 1884–1998), xxi:395 n.

78. BL, Add. MS 32096, fol. 332v; see also James's complaint to Barrillon about Louis's troop movements, recorded in CPA, vol. 166, fol. 280v, Barrillon to Louis XIV, 27 Sept./7 Oct. 1688.

79. Luttrell, *Brief Historical Relation*, i:476, 479; J. S. Clarke, ed., *The Life of James the Second*, 2 vols. (London, 1816), ii:223–224; CPA, vol. 167, fols. 140v–142, Barrillon to Louis XIV, 23 Nov./3 Dec. 1688; Childs, *Army*, 188–190.

80. David H. Hosford, *Nottingham, Nobles, and the North: Aspects of the Revolution of 1688* (Hamden, CT, 1976), 92, 95; *Memoirs of Sir John Reresby*, 528–531; *English Currant*, no. 1 (12 Dec. 1688); Andrew Browning, *Thomas Osborne, Earl of Danby and Duke of Leeds, 1632–1712*, 3 vols. (Glasgow, 1944–51), ii:142–143, 147–148.

81. For references to securing the nation from "Popery and Slavery," see *The Declaration of the Nobility, Gentry, and Commonalty at the Rendezvous at Nottingham* (n.p., [1688], D717); *Lord Del—r's Speech* (n.p., [1688], D880); *The Declaration of the Lord Lieutenant . . . of Chester* (n.p., 1688, D703A); see also *Memoirs of Sir John Reresby*, 529; Braybrooke, ed., *Autobiography of Sir John Bramston*, 338.

82. *The General Association of the Gentlemen of Devon* (Exeter, 1688, G488B); *The Association* (n.p., [1688], A4057); for the signing of the association, see Luttrell, *Brief Historical Relation*, i:479, 483; *Entring Book of Roger Morrice*, iv:371, 409–410, 417, 421, 426; Robert Beddard, *A Kingdom Without a King: The Journal of the Provisional Government in the Revolution of 1688* (Oxford, 1988), 151; *CJ*, x:7.

83. *The Declaration of the Lord Lieutenant . . . of Chester* (n.p., 1688, D703A); Andrew Clark, ed., *The Life and Times of Anthony Wood*, 5 vols. (Oxford, 1891–1900), iii:284; *Entring Book of Roger Morrice*, iv:356, 364; *Memoirs of Sir John Reresby*, 531; [Hugh Speke?], *The Prince of Orange his Third Declaration*, 3; Beddard, *Kingdom Without a King*, 29–31.

84. Bodl., MS Tanner 28, fol. 283, Samuel Sanders to archbishop of Canterbury, 10 Dec. 1688; *English Currant*, no. 1 (12 Dec. 1688).

85. Charles Jackson, ed., *The Diary of Abraham de la Pryme*, Surtees Society, liv (Durham, 1870), 16; FSL, V.a.469 (memoirs of William Westby), fol. 52.

86. Luttrell, *Brief Historical Relation*, i:474; FSL, V.a.469 (memoirs of William Westby), fol. 45r–v; *Entring Book of Roger Morrice*, iv:337–338.

87. *Entring Book of Roger Morrice*, iv:363; *A Copy of a Letter out of the Country* (n.p., 1688, C6131A); Bodl., MS Ballard 45, fol. 20r–v, Mr. Jones to Arthur Charlett, 8 Dec. 1688.

88. Clark, ed., *Life and Times of Anthony Wood*, iii:286; Bodl., MS Eng. hist. c.6, fol. 123, letter from Oxford dated 7 Dec. 1688.

89. *HMC, Le Fleming*, 226, 231–232; Bodl., MS Don. c.39, fol. 40, newsletter of 4 Dec. 1688.

90. *Universal Intelligence,* no. 5 (22–26 Dec. 1688); *London Courant,* no. 4 (18–22 Dec. 1688); *Entring Book of Roger Morrice,* iv:431.

91. Bodl., MS Eng. hist. c.711, fols. 90v, 91v; *Orange Gazette,* no. 1 (31 Dec. 1688); Clark, ed., *Life and Times of Anthony Wood,* iii:291; *Universal Intelligence,* no. 6 (26–29 Dec. 1688).

92. *English Currant,* no. 3 (14–19 Dec. 1688); *Entring Book of Roger Morrice,* iv:379; *Universal Intelligence,* no. 4 (18–22 Dec. 1688); *HMC, Finch,* ii:294, iii:378. Jefford had been removed as mayor of Exeter on 4 Nov. 1688 by order of the privy council: see BL, Add. MS 41805, fol. 118, earl of Bath to earl of Middleton, 5 Nov. 1688.

93. *London Courant,* no. 4 (18–22 Dec. 1688); *Entring Book of Roger Morrice,* iv:397; *CSPD, James II, 1687–89,* 382.

94. BL, Sloane MS 3929, fol. 129v, newsletter of 19 Jan. 1688/9; *Orange Gazette,* no. 5 (10–17 Jan. 1689); *CJ,* x:19, 110.

95. Joseph Besse, *A Collection of the Sufferings of the People Called Quakers,* 2 vols. (London, 1753), i:189–190.

96. *Entring Book of Roger Morrice,* iv:384–385; *London Mercury,* no. 1 (15 Dec. 1688); *English Currant,* no. 2 (12–14 Dec. 1688); Beddard, *Kingdom Without a King,* 77; on Penn's Jacobitism, see Paul Kléber Monod, *Jacobitism and the English People, 1688–1788* (Cambridge, 1989), 155; Mary K. Geiter, "William Penn and Jacobitism: A Smoking Gun?" *Historical Research,* lxxiii (2000), 213–218. On the phenomenon of whig Jacobitism, which can be seen as an offshoot of the repealer movement, see Paul Monod, "Jacobitism and Country Principles in the Reign of William III," *HJ,* xxx (1987), 297–301; Tim Harris, *Politics Under the Later Stuarts: Party Conflict in a Divided Society, 1660–1715* (London, 1993), 214–215; Mark Goldie and Clare Jackson, "Williamite Tyranny and the Whig Jacobites," in Esther Mijers and David Onnekink, eds., *Redefining William III: The Impact of the King-Stadholder in International Context* (Aldershot, 2007), 177–199.

97. Duke of Berwick, *Mémoires du Maréchal de Berwick, Écrits par Lui-Même,* 2 vols. (Paris, 1778), ii:37; Buckley, ed., *Memoirs of Ailesbury,* 214–215; *London Mercury,* no. 2 (15–18 Dec. 1688); Harris, *Revolution,* 303–305.

98. CPA, vol. 167, fol. 187, Barrillon to Louis XIV, 5/15 Dec. 1688; Bodl., MS Tanner 28, fol. 296, letter to archbishop of Canterbury, 21 Dec. 1688; see also *Works of John Sheffield,* ii:76; NLW, Kemeys-Tynte MSS, C136, John Romsey to Sir Charles Kemeys, 25 Nov. 1688. The original French in the letter from Barrillon reads "grand hazard de perdre la vie et la Couronne."

99. BL, Add. MS 34487, fol. 50v, Robert Cosens to Edward Norton, 16 Dec. 1688; BL, Add. MS 29563, fol. 377, William Longueville to Viscount Hatton, 15 Dec. 1688; BL, Add. MS 71692, fol. 61, Sir William Boothby to Dr. Horneck, 19 Dec. 1688; Bodl., MS Don. c.39, fol. 69, William Fleming to Sir Daniel Fleming, 18 Dec. 1688; Anthony Hewitson, ed., *Diary of Thomas Bellingham, An Officer under William III* (Preston, 1908), 37; Edward Maunde Thompson, ed., *Correspondence of the Family of Hatton,* 2 vols. (Westminster, 1878), ii:125.

100. Lancashire RO, DDKe/6/37 (notebook of Reverend Walker), p. 13.

101. *CJ*, x:14, 29; BL, Add. MS 75366, rough notes by the marquess of Halifax on the debates of the assembly of the lords, n.d. [17 Dec. 1688]; Eveline Cruickshanks, David Hayton, and Clyve Jones, "Divisions in the House of Lords on the Transfer of the Crown and Other Issues, 1689–94: Ten New Lists," *BIHR*, liii (1980), 57–65.

102. Singer, ed., *Clarendon Correspondence*, ii:231; *Entring Book of Roger Morrice*, iv:432–433; H. C. Foxcroft, ed., *A Supplement to Burnet's History of My Own Time* (Oxford, 1902), 535–536; Buckley, ed., *Memoirs of Ailesbury*, i:193–196; Robert Beddard, "The Guildhall Declaration of 11 December 1688 and the Counter-Revolution of the Loyalists," *HJ*, xi (1968), 403–420.

103. Buckley, ed., *Memoirs of Ailesbury*, i:224; see also Denton, "Historical Fragment," 393; *Entring Book of Roger Morrice*, iv:396.

104. Buckley, ed., *Memoirs of Ailesbury*, i:224.

9. Enacting Toleration

1. M. J. Short, "The Corporation of Hull and the Government of James II, 1687–8," *Historical Research*, lxxi (1998), 175, 189, 192; Pat E. Murrell, "Bury St. Edmunds and the Campaign to Pack Parliament, 1687–8," *BIHR*, liv (1981), 188–189, 201.

2. On these points, see Scott Sowerby, "Forgetting the Repealers: Religious Toleration and Historical Amnesia in Later Stuart England," *Past and Present*, no. 215 (May 2012), 107–114.

3. Hull City Archives, DMX/132, p. 175; *London Gazette*, no. 2288 (20–24 Oct. 1687); University of Hull, Brynmor Jones Library, DDHO/13/2b, James Bradshaw et al. to Sir John Hotham, 15 Dec. 1688; Short, "Corporation of Hull," 189.

4. *The Declaration of His Highnes[s] William Henry, by the Grace of God Prince of Orange* (The Hague, 1688, W2328C), 8; *London Courant*, no. 5 (22–25 Dec. 1688); G. V. Bennett, "King William III and the Episcopate," in G. V. Bennett and J. D. Walsh, eds., *Essays in Modern English Church History* (New York, 1966), 112–113, 115–116; Jonathan I. Israel, "William III and Toleration," in Ole Peter Grell, Jonathan I. Israel, and Nicholas Tyacke, eds., *From Persecution to Toleration: The Glorious Revolution and Religion in England* (Oxford, 1991), 151–155.

5. Sowerby, "Forgetting the Repealers," 115–116.

6. H. Horwitz, "Protestant Reconciliation in the Exclusion Crisis," *Journal of Ecclesiastical History*, xv (1964), 209–214; Grant Tapsell, *The Personal Rule of Charles II, 1681–85* (Woodbridge, 2007), 64–91. On the lack of any broad shift toward greater tolerance in this period, see Alexandra Walsham, *Charitable Hatred: Tolerance and Intolerance in England, 1500–1700* (Manchester, 2006), 8–10, 39–49, 300; Benjamin J. Kaplan, *Divided by Faith: Religious Conflict and the Practice of Toleration in Early Modern Europe* (Cambridge, MA, 2007), 5–6, 353–357.

7. *A Collection of Papers Relating to the Present Juncture of Affairs* (n.p., 1688,

C5169A), 1; George Every, *The High Church Party, 1688–1718* (London, 1956), 20–25.

8. Anchitell Grey, *Debates of the House of Commons, from the Year 1667 to the Year 1694*, 10 vols. (London, 1763), ix:261; James II, *By the King, A Proclamation* (Dublin, 1689, J269), 2; *The Entring Book of Roger Morrice, 1677–1691*, ed. Mark Goldie, John Spurr, Tim Harris, Stephen Taylor, Mark Knights, and Jason McElligott, 7 vols. (Woodbridge, 2007–9), v:117; *HMC, Ormonde,* n.s., viii:391–392; Gilbert Burnet, *Bishop Burnet's History of His Own Time,* ed. M. J. Routh, 2nd edn., 6 vols. (Oxford, 1833), iv:21. For contemporary concerns about a potential alliance between the Quakers and the exiled King James, see BL, Add. MS 70014, fol. 219, [Robert Harley] to Sir Edward Harley, 19 Apr. 1689; LSF, Portfolio 15.104, Isaac Sadly to Joseph Knight, 2 July 1689.

9. Grey, *Debates,* ix:260–262; Burnet, *History of His Own Time,* iv:16–17; David L. Wykes, "Friends, Parliament and the Toleration Act," *JEH,* xlv (1994), 47–48.

10. Grey, *Debates,* ix:258–9; BL, Add. MS 78299, fol. 53, letter of John Evelyn, November 1688; see also the set of arguments against the proposed Act of Toleration written in an unknown hand and preserved in the Finch manuscripts at the Leicestershire Record Office (DG7, Box 4958, P.P. 85).

11. *CJ,* x:51; Henry Horwitz, *Parliament, Policy and Politics in the Reign of William III* (Newark, DE, 1977), 22; *Entring Book of Roger Morrice,* v:53–54.

12. *Entring Book of Roger Morrice,* v:118.

13. Every, *High Church Party,* 32–33, 36; Roger Thomas, "Comprehension and Indulgence," in Geoffrey F. Nuttall and Owen Chadwick, eds., *From Uniformity to Unity, 1662–1962* (London, 1962), 245–253; Bennett, "King William III and the Episcopate," 112–120; John Spurr, "The Church of England, Comprehension and the Toleration Act of 1689," *EHR,* civ (1989), 938–939; Horwitz, *Parliament, Policy and Politics,* 23–25; NLS, MS 14404, fol. 26, Lord Yester to earl of Tweeddale, 14 March 1689; CUL, Buxton 59/138, [John Herne] to Sarah Herne, 11 March 1689; CUL, Buxton 59/139, John Herne to [Robert Herne], 18 March 1689; Henry Ollion and T.J. de Boer, *Lettres Inédites de John Locke à ses Amis Nicolas Thoynard, Philippe van Limborch et Edward Clarke* (The Hague, 1912), 184 n.; *Entring Book of Roger Morrice,* v:137–138.

14. Bodl., MS Ballard 30, fol. 26, Abel Campion to Arthur Charlett, 2 April 1689; Bodl., MS Ballard 45, fol. 35, [Robert Woodward?] to [Arthur Charlett?], 8 April 1689; Basil Duke Henning, ed., *The House of Commons, 1660–1690*, 3 vols. (London, 1983), i:42, 47.

15. NLS, MS 14404, fol. 29v, Lord Yester to earl of Tweeddale, 21 March 1689, fol. 32v, same to same, 26 March 1689; BL, Add. MS 36707, fol. 62, [Arthur Maynwaring] to James Harrington, 21 March 1689; Bodl., MS Ballard 22, fol. 48, James Newton to Arthur Charlett, 28 March 1689; *HMC, Portland,* iii:435–436; Henry Horwitz, *Revolution Politicks: The Career of Daniel Finch, Second Earl of Nottingham* (Cambridge, 1968), 91; Horwitz, *Parliament, Policy and Politics,* 22.

16. Andrew Browning, ed., *Memoirs of Sir John Reresby,* rev. Mary K. Geiter and W. A. Speck (London, 1991), 572; see also Durham UL, Add. MS 1106, earl of Clarendon to Dr. Thomas Tenison, 8 April 1689.

17. Burnet, *History of His Own Time,* iv:57–58; Edward Cardwell, *A History of Conferences,* 3rd edn. (Oxford, 1849), 444–445; BL, Add. MS 29573, fol. 351, [Charles Hatton] to [Viscount Hatton], 21 Nov. 1689, fol. 362v, same to same, 5 Dec. 1689, fol. 364, same to same, 10 Dec. 1689, fol. 366, same to same, 14 Dec. 1689; see also BL, Egerton MS 3337, fol. 2, letter to Charles Bertie, 10 April 1689; BL, Add. MS 71692, fol. 112, William Boothby to Dr. Horneck, 3 Sept. 1689; Cheshire RO, DAR/G/42, newsletter from London dated 26 Nov. 1689; BL, Add. MS 72516, fols. 94v-95, Sir Charles Cottrell to Sir William Trumbull, 14 Dec. 1689; Thomas Lathbury, *A History of the Convocation of the Church of England,* 2nd edn. (London, 1853), 325–332; G. V. Bennett, "Loyalist Oxford and the Revolution," in L. S. Sutherland and L. G. Mitchell, eds., *The History of the University of Oxford: The Eighteenth Century* (Oxford, 1986), 26–28; Every, *High Church Party,* 57–58.

18. Horwitz, *Parliament, Policy and Politics,* 25; Horwitz, *Revolution Politicks,* 93.

19. Matthew Henry Lee, ed., *Diaries and Letters of Philip Henry* (London, 1882), 362, 364.

20. For the view that the Act of Toleration was a reward to nonconformists for their good behavior, see Sir William Holdsworth, *A History of English Law,* 7th edn., ed. A. L. Goodhart and H. G. Hanbury, 16 vols. (London, 1956–66), vi:200, viii:410.

21. Geoffrey Holmes, "The Sacheverell Riots: The Crowd and the Church in Early Eighteenth-Century London," *Past and Present,* no. 72 (Aug. 1976), 64–66; Geoffrey Holmes, *The Trial of Doctor Sacheverell* (London, 1973), 161–174, 234–235; Nicholas Rogers, "Riot and Popular Jacobitism in Early Hanoverian England," in Eveline Cruickshanks, ed., *Ideology and Conspiracy: Aspects of Jacobitism, 1689–1759* (Edinburgh, 1982), 76–78; Paul Kléber Monod, *Jacobitism and the English People, 1688–1788* (Cambridge, 1989), 173–174, 182–194; *CJ,* xviii:227; Jan Maria Albers, "Seeds of Contention: Society, Politics and the Church of England in Lancashire, 1689–1790," (Ph.D. dissertation, Yale Univ., 1988), 405–413; Mark R. Wenger, ed., *The English Travels of Sir John Percival and William Byrd II: The Percival Diary of 1701* (Columbia, 1989), 99.

22. John Spurr, *The Restoration Church of England, 1646–1689* (New Haven, 1991), 377–378; Edward Carpenter, "Toleration and Establishment: Studies in a Relationship," in Geoffrey F. Nuttall and Owen Chadwick, eds., *From Uniformity to Unity, 1662–1962* (London, 1962), 293–297; David L. Wykes, "'So Bitterly Censur'd and Revil'd': Religious Dissent and Relations with the Church of England after the Toleration Act," in Richard Bonney and D. J. B. Trim, eds., *Persecution and Pluralism: Calvinists and Religious Minorities in Early Modern Europe, 1550–1700* (Oxford, 2006), 304–305.

23. William Cobbett, *Cobbett's Parliamentary History of England*, 36 vols. (London, 1806–20), vol. 6, col. 155; Carpenter, "Toleration and Establishment," 296, 314–316.

24. E. S. de Beer, ed., *The Correspondence of John Locke*, 8 vols. (Oxford, 1976–89), iii:633.

25. de Beer, ed., *Correspondence of Locke*, iii:607, 633; Mario Montuori, *John Locke on Toleration and the Unity of God* (Amsterdam, 1983), xv, xx; Grey, *Debates*, ix:258-262; *CJ*, x:151.

26. John Locke, *A Letter Concerning Toleration and Other Writings*, ed. Mark Goldie (Indianapolis, 2010), 44, 50–52.

27. On Locke's position on the toleration of Catholics, see especially Mark Goldie, "John Locke and Anglican Royalism," *Political Studies*, xxxi (1983), 84; Richard Ashcraft, *Revolutionary Politics & Locke's Two Treatises of Government* (Princeton, 1986), 502–504; Jonathan I. Israel, "Spinoza, Locke and the Enlightenment Battle for Toleration," in Ole Peter Grell and Roy Porter, eds., *Toleration in Enlightenment Europe* (Cambridge, 2000), 103–104; Jeremy Waldron, *God, Locke, and Equality: Christian Foundations of John Locke's Political Thought* (Cambridge, 2002), 218–223; John Marshall, *John Locke, Toleration and Early Enlightenment Culture* (Cambridge, 2006), 37–41, 686–692.

28. John Locke, *An Essay Concerning Toleration*, ed. J. R. Milton and Philip Milton (Oxford, 2006), 291; John Marshall, *John Locke: Resistance, Religion and Responsibility* (Cambridge, 1994), 110; idem, *John Locke, Toleration and Early Enlightenment Culture*, 37; James Farr and Clayton Roberts, "John Locke on the Glorious Revolution: A Rediscovered Document," *HJ*, xxviii (1985), 395; see also de Beer, ed., *Correspondence of Locke*, i:111.

29. de Beer, ed., *Correspondence of Locke*, ii:729, iii:191, 384, 406–407, 450, 455; Maurice Cranston, *John Locke* (London, 1957), 298, 301–302; Mark Goldie, "John Locke's Circle and James II," *HJ*, xxxv (1992), 568–569; John Locke, *Two Treatises of Government and a Letter Concerning Toleration*, ed. Ian Shapiro (New Haven, 2003), 3.

30. Karl Marx, *Capital: A Critique of Political Economy*, trans. Ernest Untermann, 3 vols. (Chicago, 1909–13), i:299; see also Tony Aspromourgos, *On the Origins of Classical Economics: Distribution and Value from William Petty to Adam Smith* (London, 1996), 9–72; Ted McCormick, *William Petty and the Ambitions of Political Arithmetic* (Oxford, 2009), 1–3, 40–66, 216–230.

31. Marquis of Lansdowne, ed., *The Petty-Southwell Correspondence, 1676–1687* (London, 1928), 234, 282–283; BL, Add. MS 72888, fol. 68.

32. BL, Add. MS 72888, fol. 110v; Bodl., MS Rawl. a.171, fol. 275; see also [Giles Shute], *A New Test in Lieu of the Old One* (1688, S3710), 10; *Som[e] Free Reflections upon Occasion of the Public Discourse about Liberty of Conscience* (1687, P1366), 14.

33. Lansdowne, ed., *Petty-Southwell Correspondence*, 155, 166, 279; Marquis of Lansdowne, ed., *The Petty Papers*, 2 vols. (London, 1927), ii:96–97, 121.

34. BL, Add. MS 72889, fol. 87; BL, Add. MS 72888, fols. 92–93v; Charles Henry Hull, ed., *The Economic Writings of Sir William Petty*, 2 vols. (Cambridge, 1899), ii:550, 591–592; McCormick, *William Petty*, 253.

35. For a comparison of Locke's thought on toleration with the more expansive tolerations proposed by some other Enlightenment philosophers, including Spinoza and Pierre Bayle, see Jonathan I. Israel, *Radical Enlightenment: Philosophy and the Making of Modernity, 1650–1750* (Oxford, 2001), 265–270; idem, *Enlightenment Contested: Philosophy, Modernity, and the Emancipation of Man, 1670–1752* (Oxford, 2006), 137–161.

36. See Thomas Babington Macaulay, *The History of England from the Accession of James the Second*, ed. C. H. Firth, 6 vols. (London, 1913–15), ii:670–672, 704–706; George Macaulay Trevelyan, *The English Revolution, 1688–1689* (London, 1938), 59–60; F. C. Turner, *James II* (London, 1948), 238.

37. Jonathan Scott, *England's Troubles: Seventeenth-Century English Political Instability in European Context* (Cambridge, 2000), 24–27, 164–166, 208–211.

38. *CJ*, x:15; *LJ*, xiv:110.

39. Linda Colley, *Britons: Forging the Nation 1707–1837* (New Haven, 1992), 53–54; Owen Stanwood, *The Empire Reformed: English America in the Age of the Glorious Revolution* (Philadelphia, 2011), 4–5, 177–206.

40. *A Short and Sure Method Proposed for the Extirpation of Popery* (n.p., [1689], S3553), 5; *HMC, Portland*, viii:22; 1 Gul. & M., sess. 1, cap. 9; 1 Gul. & M., sess. 1, cap. 15.

41. 4 Gul. & M., cap. 1, section XXXIV; 7 & 8 Gul. III, cap. 27; 11 Gul. III, cap. 4; J. Anthony Williams, *Catholic Recusancy in Wiltshire, 1660–1791* (Newport, 1968), 45–46, 50–51; Hugh Aveling, "The Catholic Recusants of the West Riding of Yorkshire, 1558–1790," *Proceedings of the Leeds Philosophical and Literary Society, Literary and Historical Section*, vol. 10, part 6 (1963), 257–258; Colin Haydon, *Anti-Catholicism in Eighteenth-Century England, c. 1714–80* (Manchester, 1993), 204–215.

42. Campana de Cavelli, *Les Derniers Stuarts à Saint-Germain en Laye*, 2 vols. (Paris, 1871), ii:295; Nicholas Tyacke, "The 'Rise of Puritanism' and the Legalizing of Dissent, 1571–1719," in Grell et al., eds., *From Persecution to Toleration*, 42; *HMC, Manuscripts of the House of Lords, 1689–1690*, 385–388; see also Jonathan I. Israel, "William III and Toleration," in Grell et al., eds., *From Persecution to Toleration*, 154–157.

43. Stephen Taylor, "Plus ça Change . . . ? New Perspectives on the Revolution of 1688," *HJ*, xxxvii (1994), 465; Pasi Ihalainen, *Protestant Nations Redefined: Changing Perceptions of National Identity in the Rhetoric of the English, Dutch and Swedish Public Churches, 1685–1772* (Leiden, 2005), 501–503.

44. *A Memorial of God's Last Twenty Nine Years Wonders in England* (1689, M1691), 112, 126; [Daniel Defoe], *The Advantages of the Present Settlement* (1689, A601), 6–8; [Edmund Bohun], *The History of the Desertion* (1689, B3456), 2, 134.

Manuscripts Consulted

Algemeen Rijksarchief, The Hague

A.R.A. 1.10.29: Fagel family archive
A.R.A. 3.01.19: Heinsius archive

American Philosophical Society, Philadelphia

974.8 P365, vol. 1: William Penn memoirs, often called the "Fragments of an Apology for Himself"

Archives du Ministère des Affaires Etrangères, Paris

Correspondance Politique, Angleterre, vols. 155–167: Correspondence of Barrillon and Bonrepaus with Louis XIV and the marquis de Seignelay, 1685–1688

Archives Nationales, Paris

K1351, no. 4: Correspondence and memoir of Bonrepaus, Sept. 1688

Badminton House Muniments Room, Badminton

FmC3/4: Letters and papers of the duke of Beaufort
FmE2/4/25: Letters and papers regarding Malmesbury borough, 1688
FmE3/8: Political papers, *c.* 1688
FmE4/3/1: Letter of Sir Robert Southwell to the duke of Beaufort, 14 Dec. 1688

Bath and North East Somerset Record Office, Bath

Council book of Bath, 1684–1711
Transcripts of mayor's accounts of Bath

Bedfordshire and Luton Archives and Record Service, Bedford

Bor.B/B2/2: Bedford corporation minute book, 1664–1688
Bor.B/B2/3: Bedford corporation minute book, 1688–1718
D.D.FN. 1246–1266: Francklin transcripts regarding address to James II
HW: How manuscripts

Beinecke Rare Book and Manuscript Library, Yale University, New Haven, Connecticut

OSB MSS 1, Box 2: Poley correspondence
OSB MSS 2: Blathwayt papers
OSB MSS 6: Danby papers
OSB MSS 41: Southwell papers
Osborn Shelves b.209: Edward Rawstorne commonplace book
Osborn Shelves fb.190, vols. 3–4: Dartmouth papers
Osborn Shelves fb.210: Hamon newsletters, 1688–1689
Osborn MS File 767: Letter from the bishop of Lincoln to Thomas Miles, 27 Oct. 1688
Osborn MS File 8998: Letter of Sir Roger L'Estrange, 23 Aug. 1677
Osborn MS File 9252: Papers from Westmorland, Dec. 1688
Osborn MS File 9295: Letters from Sir John Lowther of Whitehaven to Sir John Lowther of Lowther, 1687–1688

Berkshire Record Office, Reading

A/AOzc: Letter of James II to the corporation of Abingdon, 28 Nov. 1687
Aca1: Newbury corporation minute book, 1676–1742
D/ED/C32–33: Letters from J. Hill to Sir William Trumbull, 1685–1718
D/EHR/B2: Letterbook of Henry Hunter, 1683–1698
D/F/2/B/2/6: Newbury Meeting-House minute book, 1682–1720
R/AC1/1/17: Reading corporation diary, 1685–1688
W/A/Aca2: Wallingford "Statute Book," 1648–1766
WI/AC1/1/1: Windsor minute book, 1653–1725

Berwick-upon-Tweed Record Office, Berwick-upon-Tweed

B1/13: Berwick-upon-Tweed guild minute book, 1681–1697
B6/3: "Third Book of Enrolments" of Berwick-upon-Tweed, 1677–1729
H2/17: Annual account book of Berwick-upon-Tweed, 1688
ZHG: Papers of Sir Thomas Haggerston

Beverley Record Office, Beverley

BC/II/5/1: "Great Order Book" of Beverley, 1584–1821
BC/II/7/5: Beverley minute book, 1659–1707

DDHE/5/1: Minute book of Quarter Sessions and of Court Leet of Hedon, 1657–1745

Bodleian Library, Oxford

MS Add.c.180: Wagstaffe manuscripts relating to the Revolution, 1688
MS Add.c.217: Correspondence of Bishop William Nicolson, 1686–1716
MS Ashmole 1136: Diary of Elias Ashmole
MSS Ballard: Arthur Charlett correspondence
MSS Carte: Ormonde, Beaufort, Huntingdon and Wharton papers collected by Thomas Carte
MSS Clarendon: Clarendon state papers
MSS Don.c.38–39: Fleming newsletters, 1688–1689
MSS Don.c.169: Correspondence of Henry Ashurst, 1679–1701
MS D.D. Weld c/13.8: Orders to constables in Stafford, 1685–1689
MS Douce 357: English political poems, chiefly satirical
MS Eng.hist.b.209: Writings of Sir Richard Cocks, 1682–1701
MS Eng.hist.c.6: Oxford newsletters, 1687–1689
MS Eng.hist.c.237: Guard-book of letters and papers, 16th–19th century
MS Eng.hist.c.711: Roger Whitley's diary, 1684–1697
MS Eng.hist.d.1: Papers chiefly relating to the nonjurors, 1689–1741
MS Eng.hist.d.150: Guard-book of letters and papers, 17th–20th century
MS Eng.lett.c.29: Letters to Henry Dodwell, 1675–1710
MS Eng.lett.c.53–4: Letters to Sir Robert Southwell from Philip Madoxe, 1683–1690
MS Eng.lett.e.29: Correspondence of the Henry family, 1652–1713
MS Eng.misc.e.4: Life of George Hickes, dean of Worcester
MS Firth c.13: Miscellaneous 17th and 18th century letters and papers
MS Firth c.15, p. 228: Poem on Sir William Williams, 1687
MS Gough Somerset 2: James Stewart's History of Bristol
MS Rawl. a.139b: Tyrconnell manuscripts
MSS Rawl. a.171, a.179, a.189: Pepys manuscripts
MS Rawl. a.289: Miscellaneous papers
MS Rawl. c.732: Response to Henry Care's *Animadversions, c.* 1687
MS Rawl. c.983: Letters to Bishop Henry Compton, 1676–1710
MS Rawl. d.148: Account of the revolution in the army, 1688, by Ambrose Norton
MS Rawl. d.372: Depositions to the commission of inquiry into recusancy fines in Devon, 1687–1688
MSS Rawl. d.849–852: Papers of Denis Granville
MS Rawl. d.864: Papers of Elias Ashmole
MS Rawl. d.924: Miscellaneous papers
MS Rawl. letters 40: Letters to Joshua Barnes, 1679–1711
MS Rawl. letters 48: Correspondence of Sir Edmond Warcupp, 1682–1690

MS Rawl. letters 75: Correspondence of Joshua Barnes, 1668–1710
MS Rawl. letters 91: Letters to Dr. Thomas Turner, 1671–1699
MS Rawl. letters 94: Letters to Francis Turner, bishop of Ely, 1684–1690
MS Rawl. letters 107: Miscellaneous letters, 1507–1752
MSS Smith 47–54: Correspondence of Dr. Thomas Smith
MS Smith 141: Diary of Dr. Thomas Smith, 1668–1708
MS Talbot b.1: Letters and papers of the Talbot family, 1438–1728
MSS Tanner: Papers of Archbishop Sancroft and other bishops
MS Top. Oxon.c.325: Papers regarding Oxford
MS Wood d.7 (5): List by Anthony Wood of the mayors and bailiffs of Oxford
Nichols Newspapers

Boston Public Library, Rare Books and Manuscripts Department, Boston, Mass.

Ms. Am. 1502, vol. 7: Mather papers, including newsletters to Colonel Bishop from London (1688–1689)

Bristol Record Office, Bristol

Common Council proceedings of Bristol, 1687–1702

British Library, London

Additional Manuscripts:
4164: Birch transcripts
4194: Ellis newsletters
4236: Birch collection, John Tillotson letters, 1680–1691
4224: Birch collection, biographical anecdotes
4274: Thoresby papers, letters of bishops and archbishops, 1551–1721
4276: Thoresby papers, letters of English divines, 1584–1722
4478B: Birch miscellanea, letters of the English royal family, 1686–1688
4292: Birch collection, letters of John Tillotson and others
5015*: Letters of James II to Lady Waldegrave and other papers
6488: Proceedings of the Parliament of 1685
6669: Derbyshire collections
9712: Correspondence of Sir Robert and Edward Southwell, 1664–1711
9735: Letters of Sir John Reresby to William Blathwayt
10118: Notes on James II by Ralph Benet Weldon
11364: Annals of Coventry to 1703
15551: Proceedings of the Parliament of 1685
15949: Correspondence of the Evelyn family, 1681–1824
15897: Clarendon papers relating to pensions and establishments
17677 UUU: Netherlands transcripts, secret correspondence, 1684–1688

17748: Dockets of patents, commissions, pardons, and proclamations passed in the Clerk of the Crown's office, 1679–1689

20721: Accounts of the public revenues, 1685–1699

21092: Miscellaneous papers, 1554–1834

22910: Letters to Dr. John Covel, 1655–1699

23138: Lauderdale correspondence, 1676–1678

25335: William Batley's collections for a history of Ipswich

26774: Mayor's accounts of Romsey, co. Hampshire, 1668–1690 (transcripts)

27447: Paston correspondence, 1520–1680

27448: Paston correspondence, 1681–1701

27989: "Adversaria Miscelanea" of Sir John Perceval

28037: Proceedings of the Common Council of Dover, 1674–1768

28053–4: Danby correspondence, 1661–1711

28087: Correspondence of Viscount Latimer, 1678–1688

28226: Caryll correspondence, 1648–1711

28227: Caryll family correspondence, 1672–1718

28252: Caryll manuscripts, political and religious tracts

28569: Savile and Finch family correspondence, 1626–1720

29562–4: Hatton family correspondence, 1687–1690

29573: Hatton family correspondence, 1687–1691

29584: Letters from English and Irish prelates to Hatton family, 1636–1704

29910: Letters to John Swynfen, 1646–1694

32010: Biography of Robert Frampton, bishop of Gloucester

32095: Malet papers, 1677–1695

32096: Memoirs of Francis Turner, bishop of Ely, 1688 (extracts)

32523: Political papers of Roger North

33286: Papers concerning the birth of the prince of Wales in 1688

33512: Letters and papers of Sandwich, co. Kent, 1570–1729

33923: Diary of Sir John Knatchbull

34079, no. 26: Letter of the earl of Peterborough to William Blathwayt, 13 Sept. 1688

34152: Letters and papers relating to co. Kent, 1553–1734

34727: West papers, 1532–1734

34487: Mackintosh collection of newsletters, 1687–1688

34502: Mackintosh collection of letters from Cardinal Ferdinando d'Adda and Don Pedro Ronquillo (copies and translations), 1685–1689

34510: Aernout van Citters correspondence, 1687–1688 (translations)

34512: Aernout van Citters correspondence, 1686–1688 (translations)

34526: Mackintosh collections

34729: West papers

36707: Harrington correspondence, 1669–1693

36988: Paston correspondence, 1551–1699

37682: Taylor family papers, 1655–1820

38175: Correspondence and papers of Sir Sackville Crow, 1671–1744

38493–5: Letterbooks of Antony Moreau, Polish ambassador to The Hague, 1686–1689

38695: Blathwayt correspondence, 1688–1691

38848: Hodgkins military and naval papers, 1601–1786

40160: Commonplace book of William Lloyd, bishop of St. Asaph

40175: Quarter Sessions order book of Denbighshire, 1685–1688

40621: Harley papers

41057: Chronicle of Salisbury, co. Wilts, 1327–1703

41803–5: Middleton letters and papers, 1660–1688

41813–6: Middleton letters, 1685–1688

41821: Middleton enclosures, 1688

41823: Middleton letters, 1684–1688

42849: Henry family papers, 1661–1805

45731: Letters to Edmund Poley, 1688–1689

47840: Radcliffe family papers, 1530–1688

51511: Devonshire House notebook, transcript by C. J. Fox

52279: Journals of Sir William Trumbull, 1685–1692

61126: Sunderland papers, 1679–1717

61486: Sunderland papers, 1671–1688

61989: Harley papers

63465: Lovelace correspondence and papers, 1671–1693

63754: Preston papers, royal letters, 1629–1689

63773: Preston papers, parliamentary and colonial, 1672–1691

63780: Preston letters and papers, 1688–1689

69953: Coke papers and account books, *c.* 1684–1689

69955: Coke papers, *c.* 1685–1690

70013: Harley papers, 1679–1686

70014: Harley papers, 1687–1690

70233: Letters of Sir Edward Harley, 1680–1691

70518: Portland papers, miscellaneous, 1540–1706

71446: Miscellaneous documents on politics and religion, 1629–1719

71573: Letters from Oliver Le Neve to Peter Le Neve, 1682–1697

71692: William Boothby letterbook, vol. 4, 1688–1689

72450: Trumbull papers, 1672–1688

72481: Trumbull correspondence from Dolben family, 1668–1708

72513: Letters to Sir William Trumbull from Charles Trumbull, 1677–1716

72516: Letters to Trumbull family from Sir Charles Cottrell, 1685–1692

72517: Letters to Trumbull family from Cottrell family, 1685–1741

72526: Correspondence of Sir William Trumbull, 1687–1688

72595–6: Sir William Trumbull newsletters, 1683–1689

72866, 72888–9: Sir William Petty papers

75359–61, 75363, 75365–6: Correspondence and papers of the marquess of Halifax, 1661–1694

75376: Notebook containing letters to the marquess of Halifax, 1664–1699

78299: Letters from John Evelyn, 1679–1698

78301: Letters to John Evelyn, 1665–1705

78318: Correspondence of John Evelyn, 1680–1699

Egerton Manuscripts:

1628: Diary of Edward Southwell, 1659–1699

2543, no. 35, fols. 268–273: Papers relating to the trial of the seven bishops, June 1688

2621: Correspondence and papers of Admiral Arthur Herbert, 1680–1690

2717: Correspondence of the Gawdy family, vol. 5, 1650–1689

3335–7: Danby correspondence, 1688–1689

Surrogates:

Mic M/636: Verney Papers from Claydon House, co. Buckinghamshire (on microfilm)

Harleian Manuscripts:

6798: Gilbert Burnet letter, 1688

6845, fols. 251–82: Nathaniel Wade's confession regarding the Monmouth Rebellion

7187: Proceedings of the Parliament of 1685

Lansdowne Manuscripts:

253: Proceedings of the Parliament of 1685

507: Proceedings of the Parliament of 1685

828: Collections of Capt. John Stevens

937: Diary of White Kennett, 1680–1688

1013: Correspondence of White Kennett with Rev. Samuel Blackwell, 1687–1720

1152B: Papers of William Bridgeman

1236: Royal letters

Sloane Manuscripts:

836: Collections of Sir Edward Sherburne

3929: Henry Muddiman's newsletters, 1687–1689

Stowe Manuscripts:

119, no. 12: Papers relating to the Convocation of 1689

241, no. 30: Bevil Skelton to the earl of Sunderland, 16/26 June 1688

746: Miscellaneous original letters, 1678–1690

Brotherton Library, University of Leeds, Leeds

MS 8: Notebook of Joseph Bufton, 1677–1708

MS 10: Commonplace book of Joseph Bufton, 1680–1716

MS 613/8: Account of crown revenues for 1687
Leeds University MS Deposit 1981/2 (Clifford Street), Shelf II, No. 2: York-
    shire Quarterly Meeting minute book (Quaker), 1681–1698
WH/Wooley Hall MSS, box 20, no. 123: Answer to the Three
    Questions, *c.* 1688
WH/Wooley Hall MSS, box 56, no. 56: Answer to the Three Questions,
    24 Dec. 1687

Cambridgeshire County Record Office, Cambridge

R59/25/1/5: Cambridge Quarterly Meeting minutes (Quaker), 1670–1756
Shelf C/9: "Common Day Book" of Cambridge corporation, 1681–1722

Cambridge University Library, Cambridge

Buxton 59: Buxton correspondence
Dd.3.64, no. 59, fols. 132–133: Reasons against subscribing the Oxford
    address, 1687
Dd.3.88, no. 12: Address to Mary of Modena, 1688
Ee.6.43, fol. 213a: Letter of the bishop of Lincoln, 29 May 1688
Ll.1.19: Letterbook of John Warner
Microfilm MS 9528: The repertories of the Court of Aldermen of London,
    1685–1689
Mm.I.51: The bishop of Norwich's journal of proceedings in the House of
    Lords, 19–23 May 1685
Mm.VI.49: Correspondence of Rev. John Strype, 1679–1721
MS Add. 1: Correspondence of Rev. John Strype, 1649–1699
MS Add. 5: Correspondence of Rev. John Strype, 1647–1729
MS Add. 4403: Correspondence of Edmund Bohun

Canterbury Cathedral Archives, Canterbury

A/C/7: Canterbury Burghmote minutes, 1684–1695
Woodruff's List, Bundle 52, nos. 7–15: Official correspondence of Canterbury,
    1687–1688

Carmarthenshire Archive Service, Carmarthen

Mus 156: Order book of the borough of Carmarthen, 1582–1752

Centre for Buckinghamshire Studies, Aylesbury

B/Buc/1/12: Translation of Buckingham charter of 1684
B/Buc/3/1: Buckingham corporation memoranda and register book,
    1567–1835

B/Buc/3/4: Order of Privy Council to Buckingham corporation, 8 April 1688
D135/B/1: Papers of Lord Jeffreys
D135/B/2/1: Correspondence of Lord Jeffreys

Centre for Kentish Studies, Maidstone

Fa/AC4: Minutes of Faversham, 1633–1740
Md/Acm1/3: Burghmote minutes of Maidstone, 1644–1694
Qb/Jbs2: Queenborough court book, 1673–1735
Qb/RPp: Poll books for Queenborough
U269/C98/17: Letter from corporation of East Grinstead
U1015: Papillon papers

Cheshire Record Office, Chester

AB/2–3: Assembly minute books of Chester, 1624–1724
DAR: Arderne collection
D/Basten/8: Diary of Sarah Savage, 1686–1687
DCH/K/3/8: Cholmondeley estate correspondence, 1688–1690
DDX 384/2: Diary of Sir Thomas Mainwaring, vol. 2, 1674–1688
DLT/B55: Account books of Thomas Jackson, Tabley estate steward
D/MH/1: "Chapel Church Book" of Matthew Henry, 1687–1923
DSS/1/2–3: Shakerley correspondence
LBM/1/1: Assembly minutes of Macclesfield, 1619–1744 (viewed on
    MF122/1)
MA/B/VI/13: Privy Council order and royal mandate to the corporation of
    Macclesfield, 22 and 23 July 1688 (viewed on MF122/1)
ML/4: Chester mayor's letters, 1674–1715
ZCR63/2/691: Earwaker collection: correspondence of Sir John Crewe
Z/P/Cowper: Historical collections concerning Chester, compiled by William
    Cowper

Chippenham Museum, Chippenham

"Bayliffs Book of Accounts" of Chippenham, 1685–1789
Register of Chippenham, 1684–1774

Christchurch Borough Council, Christchurch

Council minute book or "Boke of Record" of Christchurch, 1562–1857

Churchill College Archives Centre, Cambridge

Erle-Drax papers

Codrington Library, All Souls College, Oxford

MS 273: Papers of Owen Wynne

Coventry Archives, Coventry

2/5: Coventry annals, 1003–1703
BA/A/A/26/3: Book of the chamberlains of Coventry
BA/H/C/17/2: Council minute book of Coventry, 1635–1696
BA/H/C/22/2: Bailiff's accounts of Coventry, 21 Dec. 1687
BA/H/Q/A79: Coventry official correspondence
BA/L: Mr. Ford's Collection

Cornwall Record Office, Truro

AR22/46: Appoinment of Sir John Arundell as deputy lieutenant of Cornwall, 1688
AR25: Arundell correspondence
AR33: Bellings correspondence
B/BOD/288: Bodmin mayor's accounts, 1684–1691
B/TRU/102/1: Truro corporation order book, 1685–1707
DD/BK/353: Constitution book of Liskeard, 1588–1725
DD/CN, no. 3480: Letter of James Salter to Charles Trewbody, 30 July 1688
DD/J.1933: Order of Privy Council to borough of Grampound, 21 Jan. 1687
DD/R.5508: "The humble Answeare of the Towne and Burrough of Fow[e]y to his Maiesties Quo warranto," 17 Aug. 1684
LOS/275/2: Maritime Water of Fowey court book, 1631–1708
PB8/1: Letter book of Humphrey Prideaux, 1677–1690
SF/31: Liskeard Monthly Meeting minutes (Quaker), 1679–1702
SF/202: Falmouth Monthly Meeting minutes (Quaker), 1671–1693
SF/203: Marazion Monthly Meeting minutes (Quaker), 1679–1713
WH/5192: Volume containing parliamentary poll sheets of Mitchell, 1672–1714
X1277: Trelawny family papers (the "Collectanea Trelawniana")

Cumbria Archive Centre, Carlisle

Ca/2/2: Carlisle common council order book, 1689–1705
Ca/2/13: Carlisle assembly rough orders, 1666–1781
Ca/2/21: Carlisle common council memoranda
Ca/2/27: Register of admission of Carlisle freemen, 1612–1741
D/Lons/L1: Lowther correspondence
D/Lons/L2/5: Sir John Lowther of Lowther, "1688 Journal"
D/Lons/L12/2/15: Sir Daniel Fleming, "Memoirs of the family of the Flemmings," vol. 2

D/Lons/W2/1/22: Correspondence of Sir John Lowther of Whitehaven and Thomas Tickell, 1687–1688

Cumbria Archive Centre, Kendal

WD/Ry: Correspondence and papers of Sir Daniel Fleming
WSMB/K, box 1, no. 2: Book of proceedings in Kendal Court of Record, 1684–1700
WSMB/K, box 27: Accounts of the chamberlains of Kendal

Cumbria Archive Centre, Whitehaven

D/Cu: Curwen family papers

Denbighshire Record Office, Ruthin

BD/A/1: Minutes of Court of Convocation of Denbigh borough, 1597–1740
BD/A/2: Draft minutes of Court of Convocation of Denbigh borough, 1648–1738
DD/WY/6635: Letters of Sir William Williams to Ellis Lloyd, 1683–1686

Derby Central Library, Derby

Parcel 200: Minute book of Derby Mercers Company, 1674–1740

Derbyshire Record Office, Matlock

D258: Chandos-Pole-Gell manuscripts

Devon Record Office, Exeter

1579A/9/35: Totnes court book, 1672–1772
3248A/3/7: Okehampton minute book, 1674–1741
3248A/3/12: Proceedings of the Okehampton corporation, 1623–1693
3248A/9/1: Rattenbury diary
DD.63634: Audit of William Mannowry's accounts, *c.* 1690
DD.63637: Mayoral accounts of William Mannowry of Dartmouth, 1688
ECA/B1/13: Act book of the Exeter Chamber, 1684–1730
ECA/C1/66, Minute book of the Sessions of the Peace of Exeter, 1682–1688
QS/1/13: Devon Quarter Sessions order book, 1685–1693
R4/1/C/301: Papers relating to elections in Tiverton, 1688–1719

Doncaster Archives Department, Doncaster

AB2/1/3: Doncaster courtier book, 1625–1754

Dorset Record Office, Dorchester

D/BLX/F56: Trenchard letters, 1680–1693
DC/BTB/H1: Bridport minute book ("Red Book called Domesday"),
    1444–1817
DC/LR/B/1/10: Lyme Regis court book, 1672–1692
DC/LR/B/2/11: Calendar of Lyme Regis court book, 1672–1692
DC/LR/B/3/9: Lyme Regis draft court book, 1684–1698
DC/LR/D/1/3a: Lyme Regis orders of common council, 1594–1789
DC/LR/D/2/1: Correspondence of mayor and town clerk of Lyme Regis,
    1570–1696
DC/LR/G/1/3: Lyme Regis mayor's accounts, 1662–1699
DC/LR/G/9/36: Bills and receipts of Lyme Regis corporation, 1687–1688
DC/PL/B/1/1/1: Poole record book, 1566–1701
DC/SYB: Shaftesbury minute book, 1664–1719
D/FSI: Papers of Sir Stephen Fox

Dublin City Archives, Dublin

MSS MR/18: Minutes of the Dublin Aldermen ("Monday Booke"), 1658–1712

Durham County Record Office, Durham

Du 1/4/5: Durham corporation minutes, 1688–1689
Du 1/35/1: Durham corporation election book, 1686–1746

Durham Dean and Chapter Library, Durham

MSS Hunter, folio 7: Letters
MSS Hunter, folio 10: Letters of Dr. Basire
MSS Hunter, folio 36: Letters of Denis Granville

Durham University Library, Durham

Surtees Raine MS 21: Diary of Jacob Bee, 1681–1707
Additional MS 1106: Letter of the earl of Clarendon to Dr. Thomas Tenison,
    1689

Dr Williams's Library, London

Morrice MSS: Roger Morrice's "Entring Book"
MS 24.67 Letters relating to Daniel Williams, 1688
MS 38.81 General Baptist church book, Canterbury, 1665–1695
MS 90.6 Transcript of letters from Matthew Henry to Philip Henry,
    1685–1686
MS 533.B.1 Seventh Day Baptist church book of Mill Yard, 1673–1850

East Kent Archives Centre, Dover

H/1211a: Hythe Assembly minute book, 1683–1783
NR/AC2: New Romney Common Assembly minute book, 1622–1701
NR/Aep/55: Letters seeking election at New Romney, Oct. 1688–Jan. 1689
Sa/AC/8: "Year Book E and F" of Sandwich, 1642–1730
Sa/ZB2/184: Journal of events in Sandwich, 8–14 Dec. 1688

East Sussex Record Office, Lewes

RYE/1/17: "Corporation Hundred Book" of Rye, 1673–1727
Winchelsea 58: Winchelsea court book, 1628–1691

Essex Record Office, Chelmsford

D/B/3/1/3: Customal or "White Book" of Maldon
D/B/3/1/23: Book of sessions and assemblies and other courts of Maldon,
    1678–1696
D/B/5/Gb5: Assembly book of Colchester
D/Dfa/F22: Dawtrey family correspondence, 1665–1700

Flintshire Record Office, Hawarden

D/DM/86: Manuscript sermons of Philip Henry and Matthew Henry,
    1677–1695
D/HE: Rhual manuscripts

Folger Shakespeare Library, Washington, D.C.

C6976: Herbert Croft's *A Short Discourse,* with MS notes by Francis
    Thompson
C.c.1 (3): Letter of Francis Atterbury to Jacob Tonson, 1687
F.c.17–34: Letters of Thomas Booth to John Booth, 1683–1689
L.c.1–3950: Newdigate newsletters, 1675–1714
MS Add. 865: Letters of James, duke of York, to the countess of Lichfield,
    1681
V.a.216: Life of John, Lord Belasyse, by his secretary Joshua Moone, *c.* 1688
V.a.343: Letters and speeches of Sir John Cotton, 1677–1695
V.a.469: William Westby, "A Continuation of my Memoiers [sic] or
    Memorand[a] Booke from January 1688 to January 1689"
V.b.150: Sir Robert Southwell's collections on the Revolution, 1688–1691
V.b.253: Extracts from records of cases in Common Bench, 1685–1702, by Sir
    Richard Heath
V.b.287: Letters of James Fraser to Sir Robert Southwell, 1685–1688
X.d.436 (1–62): William Blathwayt papers, 1664–1748

Georgetown University Library, Washington, D.C.

Milton House Archives: Belson family papers

Gloucestershire Record Office, Gloucester

D1799: William Blathwayt papers
D1844: Sir John Newton papers
D3549: Bishop William Lloyd papers
D4944/2/1: Tewkesbury Baptist church book, 1655–1843
GBR B3/6: Gloucester minute book, 1681–1690
TBR A1/5: Chamber book of Tewkesbury, 1686–1704
TBR B1/5: Application for new charter for Tewkesbury, Nov. 1688

Hampshire Record Office, Winchester

9M73: Malmesbury papers
27M74A/DBC/2: Lymington town book, 1616–1715
37M85/4/AC/14: Accounts of Andover
44M69/F6/9: Jervoise correspondence
148M71/1/3/3: Basingstoke town council proceedings, 1687–1716
W/B1/7: Seventh book of ordinances of Winchester, 1684–1706
W/B2/4: First proposal book of Winchester, 1663–1704

Henry E. Huntington Library, Art Collections, and Botanical Gardens, San Marino, Calif.

Ellesmere MS 8583: "Abstract of the Expences of the late King James the 2d," 1685–1688
HA Parliament Box 4, Folder 28: Votes in parliament, 6 Feb. 1689
HA Religion Box 2, Folder 4: Case of the Nottinghamshire and Leicestershire Quakers, 1685
HA Religion Box 2, Folder 5: Ecclesiastical Commission proceedings, 1686–1688
HA: Hastings correspondence
STT: Temple Stowe manuscripts

Herefordshire Record Office, Hereford

S67/4/2/100: Accounts of the chamberlain of Leominster, 1688
S67/5/3/3: Letter of James II to burgesses of Leominster, 12 May 1688
S67/5/3/4: Letter of James II to burgesses of Leominster, 18 April 1688

Hertfordshire Archives and Local Studies, Hertford

D/ELw/F28: Wittewronge correspondence, 1688–1690
D/ELw/F29: Wittewronge correspondence, 1665–1691

D/EP/F83: Cowper copies of broadsheets and satirical verse
Bound vol. 20: Book of proceedings of the Months Court of Hertford, 1683–1711

Historical Society of Pennsylvania, Philadelphia

Gratz #175, Case 9, Box 25: Letter of James II to the corporation of Nottingham, 5 March 1688
Penn-Forbes Collection: Letters to William Penn

Houghton Library, Harvard University, Cambridge, Massachusetts

fMS Thr. 11 and fMS Thr. 11.1: Letterbooks of Sir George Etherege, 1685–1689
MS Eng 218.2: Orrery papers
MS Eng 586: Commonplace book of John Digby

House of Lords Record Office: The Parliamentary Archives, London

Main Papers, MS 321: Lists of Roman Catholics, classified by county, 1680

Hull City Archives, Hull

DMX/132: Abraham de la Pryme's "History of Hull" (copy)
DMX/134.1: Abraham de la Pryme's "History of Hull" (copy)
BR/B6: Hull corporation bench book, 1682–1741
BRL/1111–1115: Hull letters
BRL/1499–1509: Hull letters
BRL/2759a: Hull corporation letter book, 1685–1688 and 1707–1713

Huntingdonshire Archives

Corporation MSS, box 6, bundle 4: Accounts of Henry Angell, chamberlain of Huntingdon, 1688

Inner Temple Library, London

Petyt Collection, MS 538, vol. 17: Letters, including two by Thomas Barlow, bishop of Lincoln

Isle of Wight County Record Office

GW10/49: Letters of Sir Robert Holmes, 1688–1689
JER/BAR/3/9/10: Assembly book for the borough of Newtown, 1670–1696
NBC45/2: "Old Leidger" book of Newport, 1460–1717

John Rylands University Library, Manchester

English MSS 213: Correspondence of the Dalton family relating to Roman
   Catholicism, 16th-18th century
Legh of Lyme papers

Kingston Museum and Heritage Service, Kingston upon Thames

KB1/1: Court of Assembly book of Kingston, 1680–1725
KB12/1/26a: Mayoral election minute, 24 Sept. 1688

King's Lynn Record Office, King's Lynn

KL/C7/12: King's Lynn Hall book 10, 1684–1731

Lambeth Palace Library, London

MS 674: Miscellaneous correspondence
MS 1834: Compton manuscripts, miscellaneous letters and papers, 1572–1802
MS 2932: Autobiographies of William Wake (copies)
MS 3286: Papers of Sir George Wheler, 1681–1703
MS 3898: Papers of William Lloyd as bishop of Norwich, 1637–1688

Lancashire Record Office, Preston

CNP3/1/1: The "White Book" of Preston, 1608–1782
Diary of Lawrence Rawstorne, 1687–1689 (typed transcript)
DDBl, Acc. 6121: "Great Hodge Podge" of the Blundell family, 1560–1698
   (viewed on MF 1/62)
DDBl, Acc. 6121: William Blundell's letter book, 1672–1693
DDFr/7/2: Letter of Sir Thomas Clarges to Roger Kenyon, 24 Oct. 1674
DDKe: Roger Kenyon correspondence and papers
DDSt, box 15, no. 17: Commission of Sir Nicholas Shirburne as deputy lieu-
   tenant of Northumberland, 28 June 1688
DDX 1637/7/5: Miscellaneous documents regarding Clitheroe borough
FRL/1/1/1/1: Minute book of the Lancaster Quarterly Meeting (Quaker),
   1669–1711
FRL/1/1/22/1–6: Quaker correspondence, 1667–1699
FRL/2/1/1/1: Minute book of the Lancaster Monthly Meeting (Quaker), 1675–1704
QSC/221: Notes by Roger Kenyon regarding the commissions of the peace,
   1686–1688

Lancaster District Library, Lancaster

MS 6568: Letter of Edward Wilson to Sir Daniel Fleming, 22 June 1688
MS 6569: Letter of Roger Fleming to Sir Daniel Fleming, 27 Nov. 1687

Lancaster Maritime Museum, Lancaster

Minute book B of Lancaster corporation

Leicestershire, Leicester and Rutland Record Office, Wigston Magna

12D39/1: Minute book of the Leicester Quarterly Meeting (Quaker),
     1671–1724
14D32/493–4: Miscellaneous correspondence of Nov. 1688
BRII/1/3: Hall book of Leicester, 1587–1707
BRII/18/36: Hall papers of Leicester, 1685–1690
DG7: Finch family manuscripts

Library of Congress, Washington, D.C.

MS 18,124, vol. 9: London newsletters, Jan. 1684–Dec. 1685

Library of the Religious Society of Friends, London

A. R. Barclay MSS
Epistles received by London Yearly Meeting, vol. 1, 1685–1706
Friends MSS, Book of Cases, I (1661–1695)
Meeting for Sufferings minutes, vol. 6
Microfilm 84: Lisburn Men's Meeting minutes, 1675–1735
Microfilm 239: Wales Yearly Meeting minutes, 1682–1797
Microfilm 863: Kingston Men's Meeting minutes
Morning Meeting minutes, vol. 1
MS Box 5.20 (4): Address of Scottish Quakers to James II and VII, 1687
MS Vol. 101, no. 51: Declaration of James II, 2 Aug. 1689
Portfolio 1.44: Letter of Barbara Blaugdon to James II, 11 Sept. [1685]
Portfolio 3.105: Warrant for discharging Quakers, 1686
Portfolio 3.106: Address of London Quakers to James II
Portfolio 6.147: Letter from Charles Lloyd, 1688
Portfolio 15.104: Letter of Isaac Sadly to Joseph Knight, 2 July 1689
Portfolio 16.25: Letter from Irish Quakers, 1687
Registers of Births, Marriages, and Deaths
Representatives to London Yearly Meeting (typescript catalogue)
Reynolds MSS, MS Box I 3/4: Report of the Yearly Meeting in Wales, 1688
Temp MSS, 210, 1/17–43: Lloyd family manuscripts
Temp MSS, 285, no. 42: Notebook of Robert Barclay
Wiltshire East Monthly Meeting minute book, vol. 1, 1677–1706 (transcript)
Yearly Meeting minutes, vol. 1, 1668–1693

Lichfield Record Office, Lichfield

B/A/19: Correspondence of Richard Raynes
D77/5/1: Hall book of Lichfield, 1679–1732

Lilly Library, Indiana University, Bloomington

Albeville MSS: Letters to Ignatius White, marquis d'Albeville

Lincolnshire Archives, Lincoln

Grantham Borough 5/1: Minute book of Grantham, 1633–1704
L/1/1/1/6: Entries of Common Council of Lincoln, 1655–1710
Monson 7/12: Sir John Newton correspondence

Liverpool Record Office, Liverpool

920 MD 173: Diary of Sir Willoughby Aston, vol. 2, 1684–1690
920 MOO: Moore family papers
Liverpool town book, vol. 4, 1671–1703

London Metropolitan Archives, London

Acc/0262/44: Stowe Hall records in the Wood family papers
CLC/179/MS20228/001A: Devonshire Square church minute book (Baptist), 1664–1727
CLC/179/MS20228/001B: Petty France church minute book (Baptist), 1675–1727
CLC/186/MS00592/001: Minutes of White's Alley Baptist meeting, 1681–1700
CLC/509/MS05099: Letter from Lord Jeffreys, 5 Oct. 1688
CLC/521/MS12017: Autobiography of Sir John Fryer
CLC/B/050/A/034/MS24586: Petition of Francis Price, vicar of Blackburn, 1687
CLC/B/050/D/011/MS14187: Letter of Sir Walter Blount to Lord Jeffreys, 4 July 1688
CLC/B/050/D/014/MS14190: Letter of Bevil Skelton to Lord Jeffreys, 19 Sept. 1688
DL/A/A/007/MS09531/018: Bishop Compton's register
MJ/SB: Middlesex Quarter Sessions minute books
MJ/SP: Middlesex Quarter Sessions papers

Longleat House, Warminster

Muddiman MSS: Journal of events in England by Henry Muddiman, 1667–1689
Thynne MSS (viewed on microfilm)

Magdalen College Archives, Oxford

MS 249: Papers of Sir Charles Hedges
MS 311: Notebook of Alexander Pudsey
MS 418: Papers of Nathaniel Johnston regarding the visitation of Magdalen College
MS 421: Correspondence and papers of Henry Holden, 1687–1688
MS 422: Account of the proceedings of the Lords Commissioners against Dr. Hough
MS 426: Account of the proceedings against Magdalen College
MS 428: Thomas Bateman's account of the proceedings against Magdalen College
MS 429: Diary of Thomas Jenner
MS 430: Account of the king's meeting with the Magdalen fellows, 1687

Magdalene College, Pepys Library, Cambridge

MS 2482: Debates of the House of Commons, 1685
MS 2527: List of royal pardons, 1663–1688
MS 2861: Admiralty letters, vol. 14, Jan.–Sept. 1688
MS 2879: Miscellany of matters historical, political, and naval, vol. 11

Malmesbury Borough Council, Malmesbury

Malmesbury Corporation MSS, no. 5: General proceedings in the borough court, 1660–1721

Medway Archives and Local Studies Centre, Rochester

Rochester City Council 1227/1974/RCA/A1/02: Minute book of Rochester corporation, 1653–1698

National Archives, Kew

C 110/80: Satirical verses, temp. James II
C 115/109: Scudamore papers
C 193/9: Entry book of officers sworn by the Clerk of the Crown, 1639–1703
C 219/67–70: Parliamentary election writs, 1685
C 231/8: Crown Office, docket book, 1678–1699
C 233/8: Docket book of warrants for the Great Seal, 1675–1699
FO 95/554: D'Avaux transcripts
PC 2/71: Privy Council register, Feb. 1685–March 1687
PC 2/72: Privy Council register, April 1687–Dec. 1688
PRO 28/39–40: Barrillon correspondence with Louis XIV from 1685 and 1688 (on microfilm)

PRO 30/53/8: Powis Castle manuscripts and general correspondence, 1681–1772

PRO 31/3/161–175: Correspondence of Barrillon and Bonrepaus with Louis XIV and the marquis de Seignelay, 1685–1688 (Baschet transcripts)

PSO 5/14: Privy Seal Office, docket book, 1685–1690

SO 1/12: Signet Office, Irish letters, 1685–1693

SO 3/19: Signet Office, dockets of warrants under sign manual

SO 7/91: Signet Office, king's bills, Jan 1688–April 1688

SO 8/20: Signet Office, warrants for king's bills, series 1, 1687–1688

SP 8: King William's chest

SP 29: State papers, temp. Charles II

SP 31: State papers, temp. James II

SP 44/50: Warrants, Henry Coventry, Sir Leoline Jenkins, and earl of Middleton, 1677–1688

SP 44/56: Secretary's letters, earl of Sunderland, 1679–1688

SP 44/66: Warrants, Sir Leoline Jenkins, Sept. 1681–March 1684

SP 44/70: Warrants, Sir Leoline Jenkins, Sidney Godolphin, earl of Middleton, and Viscount Preston, March 1684–Nov. 1688

SP 44/71: Petitions, earl of Sunderland, August 1684–April 1688

SP 44/335: Warrants and passes, earl of Sunderland, 1683–1685

SP 44/337: Warrants and passes, earl of Sunderland, 1686–1688

SP 44/338: Warrants and passes, earls of Sunderland, Middleton, and Shrewsbury, 1688–1689

SP 105/82: Miscellaneous diplomatic correspondence and papers of George Stepney

T 1/2–4: Treasury papers, 1685–1689

WO 4/1–2: War Office, general letters, 1683–1704

WO 5/3: War Office, marching and militia orders, 1687–1688

WO 26/6: War Office, miscellany book, 1683–1698

National Archives of Scotland, Edinburgh

GD18/2090: Journal of John Clerk of Penicuik

GD406: Hamilton papers

National Art Library, Victoria and Albert Museum, London

Forster MSS (viewed on microfilm)

National Library of Ireland, Dublin

MSS 2367–2441: Ormonde letters and papers

National Library of Scotland, Edinburgh

Dep. 313–314: Sutherland papers
MS 1384: Letters of Aeneas Macpherson, 1685–1690
MSS 7011, 7026, 7102–3, 14403–4, 14414: Tweeddale papers

National Library of Wales, Aberystwyth

Bodewryd manuscripts
Brogyntyn PQN3: London newsletters, 1676–1710
Canon Trevor Owen manuscripts
Clenennau letters and papers (read on microfilm)
Coedymaen papers, group I: Papers of Sir William Williams
Kemeys-Tynte manuscripts
Ottley correspondence
Penrice and Margam manuscripts
Plas-yn-Cefn papers
Plasgwyn papers and documents, 1924 deposit
Wynnstay manuscripts
MS 8472E: Sir Robert Clayton manuscripts
MS 11020E: Sir Robert Clayton letters and papers

Newberry Library, Chicago

Case MS E5.C 5434: Letters from the earl of Clarendon to the earl of
   Abingdon, 1687–1699

Norfolk Record Office, Norwich

BL/AQ2/13: Bradfer-Lawrence antiquarian papers of King's Lynn: "A Cata-
   logue of the Mayors of Lynn . . . with some Annual Occurrences,"
   1204–1693
BL/Y/2/120: Letter to Lord Paston, 27 Jan. 1688
13C/4: Returns of dissenters and Quakers
NCR 16C/7: Assembly book of Norwich, 1683–1714
FC 31/1: Independent church book of Yarmouth, 1642–1855
Y/C19/9: Assembly book of Great Yarmouth, 1680–1701

North Devon Record Office, Barnstaple

2558M/5/1: Receivers' accounts, Great Torrington, 1685–1767
2258M/6/1: Borough Quarter Sessions book, Great Torrington, 1686–1745
B/1/3984: Sessions Court book of Barnstaple, vol. 14, 1684–1716
B/1/615: Minute of resolution concerning a *quo warranto* against the charter of
   Barnstaple, 1684

North East Lincolnshire Archives, Grimsby

1/102/9/1: Grimsby Mayor's Court book, 1657–1689
1/600/59: Accounts of the chamberlain of Grimsby, 1687–1688

North Yorkshire County Record Office, Northallerton

DC/RIC II 1/1/3, MIC 892: Minutes of Ripon corporation, 1667–1743
DC/RMB 2/1/1, MIC 620: Richmond borough coucher book, 1589–1833
DC/RMB Finance 2/1, MIC 3386: Accounts of the chamberlain of Richmond, 1688
DC/SCB, MIC 1320/1844: Scarborough miscellaneous papers
ZBO, MIC 2063: Powlett family papers
ZCG, MIC 2554/1–127: Letter book of Nathaniel Cholmley, 1682–1691
ZCG, MIC 2554/128–201: Letter book of John Cholmley, 1664–1695
ZDV: Accounts of Arthur Palmer, steward of Lord Fauconberg, 1685–1708
ZON 13/1/1–335, MIC 593: Correspondence and papers of Thomas Worsley
ZQG, MIC 2051: Tunstall family papers
ZQH, MIC 948: Papers of Sir William Chaytor of Croft
ZS, MIC 1261: Papers of Sir Abstrupas Danby
ZS, MIC 1274: Correspondence of Sir Abstrupas Danby

Northampton Public Library, Northampton

Local Collection, 5606, 198.732: Letters of John Conant, *c.* 1646–1693

Northamptonshire Record Office, Northampton

Br. 14–18: Charters of James II to Brackley
Fermor Hesketh Baker MS 712: Chronicle of events in Northampton, 1435–1694
IC: Isham letters
Misc Ledger 106: First assembly book of Daventry, 1586–1783
Northampton Borough Records 3/2: Second assembly book of Northampton, 1628–1744

Northumberland Record Office, Newcastle-upon-Tyne

NRO 322, box 5: Swinburne family letters
QSO/1–2: Quarter Sessions order books of Northumberland, 1680–1697
ZRI/30/1: Letters of William Beveridge to Elizabeth Neale, 1681–1698
ZSW 27/4: Letter of Nicholas Thornton to Sir Thomas Swinburne, 10 Nov. 1688

Nottinghamshire Archives, Nottingham

CA 1659: Accounts of the chamberlains of Nottingham, 1688
CA 3455: Hall book of Nottingham, 1687–1688

CA 4692: Nottingham letters, 1688–1689
CA 4744–61: Letters of George Langford, 1688
DD/P: Portland manuscripts
DD/SR: Savile collection
M8646–8657: Charles Harvey's mayoralty papers

Nottingham University Library

CU M/1/1: Castle Gate church book
CU S/1: Castle Gate church scrapbook
Hi 2 M/1: High Pavement Chapel birth and death register, 1691–*c.* 1720
Hi R/1: High Pavement Chapel baptism register, 1691–1724
MS 140: Autobiography of William Bilby
Portland Manuscripts:
Pw1: Correspondence of Henry Cavendish, second duke of Newcastle
PwA 341: Letter of Hans Willem Bentinck to Everard Danckelmann, 14 July 1688
PwA 1613–1666: Letters of William of Orange to Hans Willem Bentinck,
    1685–1688
PwA 1858–1868: Letters of Hans Willem Bentinck to his wife, Oct.–Nov. 1688
PwA 2086: Manuscript pamphlet about the birth of the prince of Wales
PwA 2087–2178: Intelligence letters from England, 1687–1688
PwA 2692: Anonymous letter, 8 Feb. 1688
PwV 53: Letters of William Blathwayt to Sir Robert Southwell, 1685–1688
PwV 60–1: Letters of J. Povey to Sir Robert Southwell, 1684–1705

Oxfordshire Record Office, Oxford

B.B.XVII/i: Banbury town book, 1562–1741
B.76 (1)/2: Acts of the Woodstock council, 1679–1699

Pembrokeshire Record Office, Haverfordwest

HAM/SE/1/1: Haverfordwest minute book, 1675–1734
Haverfordwest corporation MSS 414–5: Letters of William Wogan, 1688
Haverfordwest corporation MS 2128: Letter of William Barlow, 9 May 1688
PEM/6: Order book of Pembroke corporation, 1678–1763

Portsmouth Museums and Records Service, Portsmouth

CE1/10: Election and session book of Portsmouth, 1684–1700

Plymouth and West Devon Record Office, Plymouth

1176/5: Devon and Cornwall Quarterly Meeting minutes (Quaker), 1676–1717
W48: "White Book" or "The Book of Constitutions" of Plymouth, 1560–1754

W51: Sessions book of Plymouth, 1675–1694
W133: Plymouth receivers' books
W267: Plymouth survey book, 1666–1694
MS 373/2: Manuscript of second part of "Worthies of Devon," by John Prince

Powys County Archives Office, Llandrindod Wells

B/BR/100/1: Minute book of Brecon, 1667–1807

Religious Society of Friends Historical Library, Dublin

1/2 YM A1: Minutes of the Half-Yearly National Meeting, 1671–1688
QMIA1: Minutes of Leinster Province Meeting, 1670–1706
Sharp manuscripts

Royal Institution of Cornwall, Truro

(Note: the Enys papers were sold at auction in 2004)
Enys 495: Letter of Edward Fowler to George Hickes, 8 Sept. 1687
Enys 1206: Petition of the seven bishops (copy)
Enys 1392: Letter of the earl of Tyrconnell, 15 Feb. 1688
HH/13/1/5: Surrender of Grampound charter, 25 Sept. 1684
MEN/79/B: Address of Cornish gentry to William of Orange, 3 Dec. 1688
T/1: Trelawny documents

Saffron Walden Borough Council, Saffron Walden

D/B2/BRE1/17–20: Royal mandates and orders of Privy Council to Saffron
    Walden, 1688
D/B2/BRE5/1: Saffron Walden mayor's book and accounts, 1587–1792
D/B2/BRE7/1: Saffron Walden Court of Record book, 1685–1715

Scottish Catholic Archives, Edinburgh

BL/1/1–187: Blairs letters, 1627–1694
KJ/1–5: Dicconson MSS, memoirs of James II

Shakespeare Birthplace Trust Records Office, Stratford-upon-Avon

BRU2/4: Stratford council minute book, 1657–1695
BRU5/2: Stratford chamberlain's bill, 1688

Sheffield Archives, Sheffield

60502: Letters to John Spencer of Cannon Hall, 1658–1718
WWM: Sir John Bright papers

Shropshire Records and Research Centre, Shrewsbury

DA1/100/1: Bishop's Castle council minutes, 1612–1713
LB/2/1/3: Ludlow minute book, 1648–1690
Leighton MSS, 180/1: "Old Book of Remarkeable Occurences of Bailiffs Mayor and Sheriffs of the Town and County of Salop"
Shrewsbury borough records, box II, no. 68: Assembly book no. 2 of Shrewsbury, 1546–1863

Somerset Record Office, Taunton

D/B/bw/107: Order of Privy Council to Bridgwater corporation, 4 Dec. 1687
D/B/bw/119: Royal mandate to Bridgwater corporation, 6 Dec. 1687
D/B/bw/2117: Depositions regarding surrender of Bridgwater charter in 1683
D/B/ch/1/2/1: Chard corporation manuscripts
D/B/ta/1/2/6: Translation of the 1677 charter of Taunton
D/B/wls/35/8: Accounts of the overseers of the poor of Wells, 1685–1698
DD/GC/99: Commission of Sir Francis Warre as deputy lieutenant of Somerset, 1688
DD/PH: Phelips family papers
DD/SFR/10/1: Epistles to the Quarterly Meeting of Somerset (Quaker), 1662–1737
DD/SFR/10/2: Epistles and papers of early Quakers, 1658–1746
DD/SFR/8/2: Somerset sufferings book (Quaker), 1659–1695
DD/WY/Box 1685: Diary of John Wyndham, 1687

Staffordshire County Record Office, Stafford

D1323 A/1/1: Order book of Stafford, 1648–1691
D1778/V/1403: Letters from James II to Lord Dartmouth, 1679–1688
D593, D868: Leveson-Gower papers
D1721: Sir Walter Bagot papers

Suffolk Record Office, Bury St Edmunds

E2/41/5: Letters of Lord Dover to John Stafford, 1688, from the Cullum papers
D2/5/3: Letter of James II to the corporation of Bury St Edmunds, 5 March 1688
D4/1/2: Bury St Edmunds corporation book, 1652–1691
EE501/6/169: Town clerk's formulary and precedent book of Sudbury, 1688

Suffolk Record Office, Ipswich

C4/3/1/7: Assembly book of Ipswich, 1680–1724
C6/1/7: Assembly book of Ipswich, 1680–1726

EE1/E1/2: Order book of Aldeburgh, 1643–1746
EE2/I/2: Assembly book of Eye, 1670–1690
EE5/2/3: Corporation act book of Orford, 1663–1701
EE6/1144/13–14: Assembly books of Dunwich, 1676–1790

Suffolk Record Office, Lowestoft

491/3A/1: "Dole and Common Book" of Southwold
491/3E/4: Sessions rolls and papers of Southwold, 1684–1701

Surrey History Centre, Woking

BR/OC/1/3: Court book of Guildford, 1676–1777
BR/OC/1/9: Court book of Guildford, 1683–1703
G124/1/1: Guildford and Godalming Men's Monthly Meeting minute book
    (Quaker), 1668–1729
1248: Midleton papers

Swarthmore College, Friends Historical Library, Swarthmore, Penn.

Safe 1006, box 34, mss 050: Robert Barclay's "Vindication of His Apology"

Tamworth Castle, Tamworth

Wood XII.1: Minute book of Common Hall of Tamworth, 1664–1758

Thetford Town Hall, Thetford

T/C2/6: Thetford minute book, 1682–1718

Trinity College, Dublin

T.C.D. MS 1181: Papers of Sir Robert Southwell, 1683–1711
T.C.D. MSS 1995–2008: Correspondence of William King, 1679–1728

Tyne and Wear Archives Service, Newcastle-upon-Tyne

MD/NC/1/3: Newcastle common council orders, 1656–1722

University of Essex, Albert Sloman Library, Colchester

Correspondence of Stephen Crisp, 1657–1692

University of Hull, Brynmor Jones Library, Hull

DDBM/32: Bosville correspondence
DDCV/15/282: Legal opinion regarding charter of Beverley, 15 Sept. 1688

DDEV/55/67: Appointment of Sir Philip Constable as deputy lieutenant of the
East Riding of Yorkshire, 5 July 1688
DDEV/67–8: Constable manuscripts relating to Roman Catholic affairs
DDHA/18/39: Appointment of earl of Langdale as deputy lieutenant of the
East Riding of Yorkshire, 5 July 1688
DDHO/13/2b–c: Letters regarding Hull affairs in 1688
DDHO/20/10: List of commissioners of the customs, 1671–1761
DQR/11/7: Scarborough Monthly Meeting minute book (Quaker), 1669–1699

University of Wales, Bangor

Bangor MS 1549, no. 1: Letter of the bishop of Bangor to Lord Jeffreys,
15 Jan. 1686
Baron Hill Additional MS 6737: Letter of Humphrey Humphreys, 11 Jan.
1689
Baron Hill Additional MS 6740: Account of the Revolution of 1688
Mostyn Additional MSS, no. 9070: Mostyn correspondence, 1687–1688
Mostyn Additional MSS, no. 9094: London newsletters, 1688–1689

Warwickshire County Record Office, Warwick

C7: Denbigh papers, miscellaneous letters, 1624–c. 1700
CR136: Newdigate papers
CR1618: Warwick corporation order book, 1664–1690
CR1998: Throckmorton manuscripts
CR2017: Everard van Dijkvelt correspondence and papers, 1672–1702

Wells City Record Office, Wells

Act book of Wells corporation, 1687–1709

Westminster Diocesan Archives, London

A35: Chapter archives, 1687–1688
B6: Capt. William Barker's manuscripts
Old Brotherhood MSS, vol. III: Sir Edward Hales's papers
Old Brotherhood MSS, vol. IV, no. 137: Relation of a conference before the
king and the earl of Rochester, 30 Nov. 1686

West Sussex Record Office, Chichester

Gordon family correspondence
MF 1145, C/1: Minute book of the Common Council of Chichester, 1685–1737
MP 1926: Arundel corporation minute book, 1539–1835
Shillinglee manuscripts

West Yorkshire Archive Service, Bradford

Spencer-Stanhope manuscripts

West Yorkshire Archive Service, Leeds

WYL100: Temple Newsam correspondence, 1651–1689
WYL109/1: Letter book of Lady Elizabeth Lowther, 1682–1689
WYL156: Sir John Reresby correspondence

West Yorkshire Archive Service, Wakefield

WMT/PON/1/1: The "Booke of Entries" or minute book of Pontefract corporation, vol. 1, 1653–1726

Wigan Archives Service, Leigh

Book of the Common Council of Wigan, 1685–1688
Charter translations book of Wigan
Wigan Court Leet rolls, bundle 61, 1688

William Andrews Clark Memorial Library, Los Angeles

C5577Z: Chronological listing of events in the history of Bristol, 1216–1746
L793L: Letter of Thomas Lloyd to Sir Charles Kemeys, Feb. 1685
MS.1959.005: Samuel Jeake, "Astrological Experiments Exemplified"
P314L: Letter of Simon Patrick to James Graham, 11 Sept. 1688

Wiltshire and Swindon Record Office, Trowbridge

1699/38: Wiltshire Quarterly Meeting minute book (Quaker), 1678–1708
G18/1/1: Guild steward's book of Calne, 1561–1814
G20/1/18: Entry book of Devizes, 1660–1688
G20/1/19: Entry book of Devizes, 1688–1749
G22/1/24: General entry book of Marlborough, 1684–1696
G22/1/318: Marlborough corporation letters, 1672–1688
G23/1/4: "Ledger D" of Salisbury
G23/1/17: Corporation minutes of Salisbury, 1683–1705
G25/1/21: General entry book of Wilton, 1454–1705
WRO 1300, no. 856: Ailesbury manuscripts, 1681–1693
WRO 2667: Arundell of Wardour accounts and household papers

William Salt Library, Stafford

Aston of Tixall papers, 45/57, folders 3 and 7
Salt MS 478/7/6: Letter to William Garraway, 8 Dec. 1685 (19th cent. copy)

Worcestershire Record Office, Worcester

Ref. 498, bulk accession 8681, bundle 1: Bewdley transcripts
Ref. 899:209, bulk accession 1834: Letter of the bishop of Worcester to George Hickes, 7 April 1688
Ref. 899:749, bulk accession 8782: Worcester City Library deposit
Ref. 6497, bulk accession 8445, parcel 1: Minute book of Droitwich, 1676–1883
Ref. b261.5: Minute book of Evesham, 1684–1758
Ref. 496.5, bulk accession 9630 (also catalogued as Worc. City Ref. A14, Box 2): Chamber order book of Worcester, 1669–1721

York City Archives, York

Acc. 104, Ant/3: Thomas Hammond's chronicle of York, 1273–1727
B.38: York corporation house book, 1663–1688
E40: Correspondence of York corporation
M: York corporation draft minute book, 1685–1692

York Minster Library, York

Hailstone collection
Memoir of Brian Fairfax (copy)

Yorkshire Archaeological Society, Leeds

MSS 1–28: Correspondence of Ralph Thoresby
DD5/28: Royal grant of restitution of the charter of Chester, 27 Oct. 1688
DD38: Copley manuscripts

Acknowledgments

The research for this book began in earnest when I got the keys to my brother's car. I had been living for a year in Cambridge, England, conducting research at the Cambridge University Library and taking the train or the bus to various local archives. The distance that I could travel in a day trip was dictated by the train and bus schedules. I remember a particularly meandering three-hour bus ride from Cambridge to Northampton. With a car, my research agenda expanded immediately. I want to thank first my brother Craig Sowerby for agreeing to sell me his vehicle at a discount when he left England to work in Spain. I am also grateful to my father, Ronald Sowerby, who generously provided the funds to enable me to purchase the car from my brother. The gift paid great dividends. Over the next three years I logged twenty thousand miles and visited libraries in every English county except Rutland, which is the only county without its own record office.

I would like to thank by name the archivists in each of the 136 manuscript repositories I visited, but I fear that I would try the patience of my readers in doing so, and I regret that I have forgotten many of their names. But I cannot fail to mention the intelligence and good cheer of the staffs at the Lancashire Record Office, the Carlisle and Kendal branches of the Cumbria Archive Centre, and Duke Humfrey's Library at the Bodleian. I would especially like to recognize Tabitha Driver, Josef Keith, and the late Malcolm Thomas at Friends House Library in London, surely the happiest little archive in England. The warm welcome of all these librarians more than made up for the nightmare of trying to find parking in English city centres. I remember with particular fondness the archivist in Grimsby who helped me to move a rubbish bin so that I could squeeze my car into a narrow spot. I would also like to thank the friends who provided so much kindness and hospitality as I was conducting my research in England, including Peter Wilson, Gwenda Barlow, the late Alan Barlow, and especially Adrian Barlow. I could not have done this without them.

My thanks are due to the Social Sciences and Humanities Research Council of Canada for awarding me a fellowship and to Harvard University for awarding me the Packard and the John Clive Fellowships. I was able to use this funding to conduct four years of research in England, and I am grateful for the opportunities this support afforded. During my years at Harvard, I was fortunate to find not one, but two houses to shelter me: Dudley House in Harvard Yard, where I met Susan Zawalich, Todd Squires, and Nancy Elam Squires; and Currier House in the Quad, where I met Joe Badaracco, Pat O'Brien, and Patricia Gnazzo Pepper. My life is far richer for having these friends in it. I would especially like to thank Susan Zawalich for her eagle-eyed editing.

A portion of Chapter 1 is reprinted from my article "Of Different Complexions: Religious Diversity and National Identity in James II's Toleration Campaign," *English Historical Review,* vol. 124, no. 506 (Feb. 2009). Portions of Chapters 3 and 9 include sections of my article "Opposition to Anti-Popery in Restoration England," *Journal of British Studies,* vol. 51, no. 1 (Jan. 2012). Chapters 1, 5, 7, and 9 incorporate passages from my article "Forgetting the Repealers: Religious Toleration and Historical Amnesia in Later Stuart England," *Past and Present,* no. 215 (May 2012). I would like to thank the editors and publishers of all three journals for permission to reprint these passages. I would also like to thank Don Pirius for his assistance with the maps.

I spent three happy years teaching in the History and Literature program at Harvard, where my fellow teachers Stephanie Lin Carlson, Nenita Elphick, Jeanne Follansbee, and Michele Martinez offered comradeship, wise counsel, and good humor. I would also like to thank Tim Breen, Deborah Cohen, Dyan Elliott, Peter Hayes, Joel Mokyr, Ed Muir, and all of my colleagues in the Department of History at Northwestern University for their friendship and advice. My greatest intellectual debt is to Mark Kishlansky, who has been an unfailing source of encouragement. I have been fortunate to have found such a perceptive and generous mentor and friend.

This book has benefited from conversations and communications with many scholars, including Alex Barber, Andrew Barclay, Ann Blair, Bill Bulman, Tom Cogswell, John Craig, Rowan Dorin, Rebecca Goetz, Paul Halliday, Eleanor Hubbard, Clyve Jones, Natalie Mears, Steven Ozment, David Smith, Ruth Smith, Andrew Starkie, Grant Tapsell, and David Wykes. John Morrill offered more tea, sympathy, and letters of reference than any young scholar could legitimately ask for. Brian Cowan and Stephen Taylor read drafts of the book; their thoughts and suggestions have been invaluable. Tim Harris read portions of the manuscript and offered helpful comments. Patrice Higonnet lent support to the project at a crucial stage. Owen Stanwood and Evan Haefeli reached out across the Atlantic divide to bring a broader perspective to my work; without their contributions this book would be much less than it is. I would especially like to thank Noah McCormack for his intellectual companionship and friendship. It has been a privilege to share with him the experience of living half one's life in the seventeenth century. His insights, his careful readings of drafts of the book, and his willingness to provide many useful references have improved this work immensely.

My deepest gratitude goes to two individuals. I would like to thank my mother, Lynne Sowerby, the first reader of my work and still the best. My love of history comes from her. And I would like to thank Wayne Huang for his encouragement and inspiration. Every day he shows me how to be a better person. This book is for both of them.

Index